WHAT OTHERS SAY

Carl Llewellyn Weschcke has mentored and given hundreds an opportunity to become published author's and indeed he is often called "Father of the New Age" as a result of his management and establishment of "Llewellyn Publications" the largest distributor in the world of esoteric material.

He has not produced just a book, or a magnum opus, rather he has produced a treasure trove of books amounting to an Encyclopedia of the occult, esoteric and alternative world he so carefully spent a life time studying and nurturing.

I am one of the author's he introduced to publishing and I am ever grateful to him and salute the cornucopia of arcane knowledge he has made available in the last few years."

—Dr Jonn Mumford (Swami Anandakapila Saraswati)
Author of *A Chakra & Kundalini Workbook, Death: Beginning or End?*
Ecstasy through Tantra, and *Yoga Nidra Meditation audio CD*

If you are looking for a comprehensive compendium on every aspect of extra-sensory vision, *Clairvoyance for Psychic Empowerment* is for you. Authors Carl Weschcke and Joe Slate have examined all forms of "clear seeing" that extend beyond the limits of physical sight. From ecstatic visions of prehistoric shamans to the modern practice of remote viewing that was developed under the Pentagon's cold-war Star Gate program, the full scope of this fascinating subject is laid bare.

Using the tattvas—ancient but simple visual symbols that represent the five occult elements—a complete course of practical exercises are designed to guide the reader in the development of his own innate faculty of clairvoyance. The goal is psychic empowerment, to awaken the sleeping abilities of the mind for personal fulfillment in life.

—Donald Tyson
Author of *1-2-3 Tarot, The 13 Gates of the Necronomicon, Alhazred, The Demonology of King James I, The Dream World of H. P. Lovecraft, The Fourth Book of Occult Philosophy, Grimoire of the Necronomicon, The Necronomicon, The Necronomicon Tarot, Portable Magic, The Power of the Word, Runic Astrology, Scrying for Beginners, Serpent of Wisdom, Soul Flight, Three Books of Occult Philosophy*

"This groundbreaking book presents a more comprehensive examination of spirit communication and its many applications than has ever before been offered. With information on shamanism, ecstatic trance, E.S.P., mediumship, and more, *Communicating with Spirit* empowers the reader with the insight, tools, and techniques to truly unlock the full potential of the human psyche and start communicating and working with Gods, Goddesses, Spirits of the deceased, Guardian Angels, and more. A must-have for any seeker on a path to greater enlightenment, deeper, more personal spirituality, and increased psychic *power*."

—Melanie Marquis
Author of *A Witch's World of Magick* (Llewellyn, 2014)
and *The Witch's Bag of Tricks* (Llewellyn, 2011)

"*Communicating With Spirit* is the book everyone has been waiting for. An entire library in a single book, this comprehensive volume brings together thousands of years of spiritual wisdom and practices from various cultures and presents this information from a personal and unique perspective. Rather than simply interpreting the rich history of various spiritual traditions, authors Dr. Joe Slate and Carl Weschcke demonstrate the practical methods by which individuals can use this knowledge to enrich and transform their own lives. Much more than a compendium of spiritual traditions, *Communicating With Spirit* is a guidebook showing readers how to apply this wisdom and spiritual energy to their own lives, thus manifesting their highest potential. This phenomenal book affirms the power of the individual to tap into the energy of the universe and use it to attain personal and spiritual transformation. As Dr. Slate said in his book *Psychic Empowerment for Everyone,* "You have the power, learn how to use it."

—Dr. Penne J. Laubenthal

Dr. Penne J. Laubenthal is Professor Emerita of English and former chair
of the English Department at Athens State University. Dr. Laubenthal
is a freelance writer who lives and works on Elk River near Athens, Alabama.

"Finally, two diverse historically-minded authors have addressed the phenomenon of paranormal experiences with compassion, comprehension, and precise candor. Whether you are a novice, or a professional, a new age student preparing for the transition of a loved one, or just wanting to understand the nature of spiritual human consciousness and its place in the universe, you will be inspired and uplift by this book as you learn and evolve with a fresh temporal view. This groundbreaking anecdotal and scientific research leaves no doubt as to the compelling relationships between human civilization's greatest mysteries in *Communicating with Spirit* and our intrinsic need to understand the unseen."

—LaMont Hamilton

Internationally recognized Clairvoyant/Psychic & blogger (WorldPsychic.org)
and coordinator of The Paranormal Study center, Huntsville, Alabama.

COMMUNICATING
WITH
SPIRIT

CARL LLEWELLYN WESCHCKE is Chairman of Llewellyn Worldwide, Ltd., one of the oldest and largest publishers of New Age, Metaphysical, Self-Help, and Spirituality books in the world. He has a Bachelor of Science degree in Business Administration (Babson), studied Law (LaSalle Extension University), advanced academic work toward a doctorate in Philosophy (University of Minnesota), has a certificate in clinical hypnosis, and honorary recognitions in divinity and magical philosophy.

In addition to book publishing he has worked in the pharmaceutical industry, furniture manufacturing, and real estate management. With Llewellyn, he has worked in all aspects of the business: advertising, editing, production, writing, astrological calculation, design and layout, typesetting, cover design, direct selling, bookstore management, trade sales, designing systems and procedures, printing and purchasing, warehouse and shipping, and mopping floors.

He is a lifelong student of a broad range of metaphysical, spiritual, and psychological subjects, and variously studied with the Rosicrucian Order and the Society of the Inner Light. After corresponding with Gerald Gardner and several of his associates in the late 1950s and early 1960s, he became known for holding the "Weschcke Documents," including a carbon copy of Gardner's own Book of Shadows.

He is a former Wiccan High Priest, and played a leading role in the rise of Wicca and Neo-Paganism during the 1960s and 1970s. Author Donald Michael Kraig has referred to him as "the Father of the New Age" because of his early and aggressive public sponsorship of new understanding of old occult subjects. In the fall of 1973, Weschcke helped organize the Council of American Witches and became its chairperson. Weschcke rightfully prides himself on having drafted "The Thirteen Principles of Belief" Statement, one of the cornerstones of modern Wicca. This document went on to be incorporated into the US Army's handbook for chaplains.

While no longer active in the Craft, he retains ties to the Wiccan and Neo-Pagan communities through Llewellyn. He is seventh Past Grandmaster of Aurum Solis, an international magical order founded in Great Britain in 1897. He withdrew from the order in 1991, and is not actively affiliated with any group at the present time.

Still actively associated with Llewellyn, he is devoting more time to studies and practical research in parapsychology, quantum theory, Kabbalah, self-hypnosis, psychology, Tantra, Taoism, Tarot, Astrology, Shamanism, Wicca, Magick, and World Spirituality. He is also actively writing, and has coauthored four books with Dr. Joe Slate (*Psychic Empowerment for Everyone, Self-Empowerment through Self-Hypnosis, Self-Empowerment & Your Subconscious Mind* and *Llewellyn's Complete Book of Psychic Empowerment*) and a new edition with commentary of *The Compete Magick Curriculum of the Secret Order G∴B∴G∴*, originally authored by Louis Culling in 1969. He is currently planning several books based on tantra and the Western Old Religion as systems of self-empowerment. He and Dr. Slate are planning several more projects.

JOE H. SLATE holds a Ph.D. from the University of Alabama, with post-doctoral studies at the University of California. Dr. Slate was appointed Professor Emeritus in 1992, after having served as Professor of Psychology, Head of the Division of Behavioral Sciences, and Director of Institutional Effectiveness at Athens State University in Alabama. He is an Honorary Professor at Montevallo University and former Adjunct Professor at Forest Institute of Professional Psychology. Dr. Slate is a licensed psychologist and member of the American Psychological Association. He is listed in the National Register of Health Service Providers in Psychology and the Prescribing Psychologist's Register.

Warren H. McLemore

As head of Athens State University Psychology Department and Director of Institutional Effectiveness, he established the University's parapsychology research laboratory and introduced experimental parapsychology, biofeedback, hypnosis, and self-hypnosis into the instructional and research programs. His research includes projects for the US Army Missile Research and Development Command, the Parapsychology Foundation of New York, and numerous private sources. He is founder of the Parapsychology Research Institute and Foundation (PRIF) (over 500 memers) which has endowed scholarship programs in perpetuity at both Athens State University and the University of Alabama as well as undertaking research projects in dream work and mind/body health.

His official research topics have included: Rejuvenation, health and fitness, the human aura, psychotherapy, reincarnation, precognition, retrocognition, telepathy, clairvoyance, psychokinesis, objectology, numerology, astral projection, sand reading, crystal gazing, dowsing, dreams, the wrinkled sheet, table tipping, discarnate interactions, psychic vampires, hypnosis, self-hypnosis, age regression, past-life regression, the afterlife, preexistence, the peak experience, natural resources, learning, problem solving, and the subconscious, to list but a few.

He established the Dr. Joe H. and Rachel Slate Scholarship at the University of Alabama (Tuscaloosa), and the Dr. Joe H. and Rachel Slate Scholarship for the Arts at Athens State University. Each scholarship exists in perpetuity and is awarded annually to students who need financial assistance.

Dr. Slate has appeared on several radio and television shows, including *Strange Universe,* the *History Channel,* and *Sightings.*

TO WRITE TO THE AUTHORS

If you wish to contact the authors or would like more information about this book, please write to the authors in care of Llewellyn Worldwide Ltd. and we will forward your request. The authors and publisher appreciate hearing from you and learning of your enjoyment of this book and how it has helped you. Llewellyn Worldwide Ltd. cannot guarantee that every letter written to the authors can be answered, but all will be forwarded. Please write to:

Carl Llewellyn Weschcke and Joe H. Slate, Ph.D.
% Llewellyn Worldwide
2143 Wooddale Drive
Woodbury, MN 55125-2989

Please enclose a self-addressed stamped envelope for reply,
or $1.00 to cover costs. If outside U.S.A., enclose
international postal reply coupon.

Many of Llewellyn's authors have websites with additional information and
resources. For more information, please visit our website at
http://www.llewellyn.com.

FREE CATALOG & SERVICE FROM LLEWELLYN

For more than one hundred and ten years Llewellyn has brought its readers knowledge in the fields of metaphysics and esoteric philosophy, astrology and divination, lunar gardening and "green" living, psychic empowerment and the paranormal, spiritual growth and self-empowerment, natural herbal and energy healing, Tarot books and decks, magick and the Kabbalah, Pagan and Wiccan practices, hypnosis, self-hypnosis, meditation and visualization techniques, tantra and yoga, and much more. Learn about the newest techniques of personal growth and genuine spirituality; use Llewellyn audio CDs to facilitate your psychic development and empowerment; secure inexpensive professional astrological guidance. Enjoy book reviews, New Age articles, a calendar of events, and access to Llewellyn's on-line Paranormal, Magickal and Occult Encyclopedia and the Llewellyn Journal.

You can order directly from Llewellyn or know the new titles to look and ask for at your favorite bookstore. To get your free copy of Llewellyn's New Worlds, send your name and address to:

Llewellyn's New Worlds of Mind and Spirit
2143 Wooddale Drive
Woodbury, MN 55125-2989, U.S.A.

COMMUNICATING
WITH
SPIRIT

Here's How You Can Communicate with (and Benefit from)
Spirits of the Departed, Spirit Guides & Helpers, Gods & Goddesses,
Your Higher Self and Your Holy Guardian Angel

CARL LLEWELLYN WESCHCKE
JOE H. SLATE, PH.D.

Llewellyn Publications
Woodbury, Minnesota

FIRST EDITION
Second Printing, 2021

Cover art © iStockphoto.com/30983756/©selensergen
Cover design by Lisa Novak
Editing by Jennifer Ackman
Illustrations on pages 9, 11, 12, 132, 162, 177, 199, 201, 202, 243, 246, 247, 275, 305, 311, 319, 349, 360, 362, 429, 435, 442, 479 © Mickie Mueller
All other interior illustrations by the Llewellyn Art Department

Llewellyn is a registered trademark of Llewellyn Worldwide Ltd.

Library of Congress Cataloging-in-Publication Data
Weschcke, Carl Llewellyn, 1930–
 Communicating with spirit : long suppressed in western culture and religions here's how you can communicate with (and benefit from) spirits of the departed, spirit guides & helpers, gods & goddesses, your higher self and your holy guardian angel / Carl Llewellyn Weschcke, Joe H. Slate, Ph.D.
  pages cm
 At head of title: A personal empowerment book
 "Includes Verifiable Techniques drawn from World Religions, East & West / New Age. Spirituality: Yoga, Tantric Sexuality, Taoist Martial Arts, the Pagan Revival, Theosophy and Empowering Meditations / Quantum Science & Paranormal Research / Esoteric & Psychological Studies / New Psychic Developmental Practices - Ageless Shamanism, Ecstatic Consciousness & Out-of-Body Journeys / Modern Intuitive Shamanism, Power Animals, Sensual Magic & Sub-Space / Pre-Hindu Shamanic Tantra & Deific Possession / Spiritualist Mediums & Channelers / Magic, Evocation & Invocation / Spiritual Communication between Mind & Psyche / The Ways of Attainment: the Astral Room, Magick Circle, Qabalistic Cross, Evocation of Guardian Powers, American Middle Pillar & Auric Energizer, Invoking Your Holy Guardian Angel, Opening the Third Eye, and Meditation to Raise Consciousness to the Highest Human Potential."
 Includes bibliographical references and index.
 ISBN 978-0-7387-4468-1 (alk. paper)
 1. Spiritualism. I. Title. II. Title: A personal empowerment book.
 BF1261.2.W47 2015
 133.9—dc23
                    2015011599

Llewellyn Worldwide Ltd. does not participate in, endorse, or have any authority or responsibility concerning private business transactions between our authors and the public.
 All mail addressed to the author is forwarded, but the publisher cannot, unless specifically instructed by the author, give out an address or phone number.
 Any Internet references contained in this work are current at publication time, but the publisher cannot guarantee that a specific location will continue to be maintained. Please refer to the publisher's website for links to authors' websites and other sources.

Llewellyn Publications
A Division of Llewellyn Worldwide Ltd.
2143 Wooddale Drive
Woodbury, MN 55125-2989
www.llewellyn.com

Printed in the United States of America

Other Books
by Joe H. Slate, Ph.D.

Astral Projection & Psychic Empowerment +
Aura Energy for Health, Healing and Balance –
Aura Energy for Better Health & Happiness –
Beyond Reincarnation +
Connecting to the Power of Nature – *one day*
Energy Psiquica – ?
Handbuch der Aura-Energie – ?
Kirlian Connection – ?
Los Vampires Psiquicos – ?
Mas Alla de la Reencarnacion – ?
Psychic Vampires –
Psychic Empowerment +
Psychic Empowerment for Health & Fitness +
Psychic Phenomena: New Principles, Techniques & Applications – ?
Rejuvenation ⎤ – ?
Rejuvenezca ⎦
Self-Empowerment: Strategies for Success ✗

by Carl Llewellyn Weschcke
and Joe H. Slate, Ph.D.

All About Auras (Llewellyn e-book)
All About Tea Leaf Reading (Llewellyn e-book)
Astral Projection for Psychic Empowerment CD Companion
Astral Projection for Psychic Empowerment
Clairvoyance for Psychic Empowerment
Doors to Past Lives & Future Lives
The Llewellyn Complete Book of Psychic Empowerment
Moving Objects with Your Mind (Llewellyn e-book)
Psychic Empowerment for Everyone
Remembering Past Lives (Llewellyn e-book)
Self-Empowerment and Your Subconscious Mind
Self-Empowerment through Self-Hypnosis
Self-Empowerment through Self-Hypnosis Meditation CD Companion
Self-Hypnosis for Success in Life (Llewellyn e-book)
Vibratory Astral Projection & Clairvoyance CD Companion

By Carl Llewellyn Weschcke

The Complete Magick Curriculum of the Secret Order G∴B∴G∴
(An expansion of the original book by Louis T. Culling
as authorized by his daughter)

Dream ESP
(Based on the original research and writing of Louis T. Culling)

Forthcoming
By Carl Llewellyn Weschcke
and Joe H. Slate, Ph.D.

The New Book of Dream Power
Changing the Future: Making Things Happen
Self-empowerment: Techniques for Personal Growth

Dedication

This book is gratefully dedicated to Dr. Carl Jung in recognition of his enormous influence on contemporary psychology and spirituality.

For Jung, the rigid dogma of organized religion stifled the human psyche's ability to create a living, personal myth necessary to the modern creative individual separated from the "herd" of previous times. Jung considered the spontaneous images of dreams as a spiritual call for the active imagination to instigate the transformative process of dream or fantasy to provide a meaningful myth to live by. Here was a method for the personal unconscious to access the ageless wisdom of the Collective Unconscious to provide guidance to meet the immediate needs of the individual.

Jung described dreams as the "Voice of God" giving the individual his or her own religious process. The images provided in dreams, visions, and fantasies become a means of dialogue between the conscious and subconscious to give structure to a person's purposeful activities.

For Jung, psychology was religion for the New Age.

Acknowledgements

We also want to give special recognition to Melanie Marquis for her helpful critique and suggestions in regards to our chapters on Shamanism as the forerunner of spiritual practices in many world religions, and especially to those techniques of trance-inducing ecstatic states of consciousness common to most indigenous Spiritist practices and the Sensual Magick of modern Intuitive Shamanism and Pagan Revivalism; the many restraints on Spirit in the Old Time male-dominated and monotheistic Abrahamic Religions of Middle Eastern origin; and the action involvement of Spirit in the New Age Religions and the non-religious forms of New Age Spirituality.

Melanie is author of *The Witch's Bag of Tricks* (Llewellyn 2011) and *A Witch's World of Magick* (Llewellyn 2014)

ABOUT LLEWELLYN'S "PSYCHIC EMPOWERMENT" SERIES

We all, to some extent, suffer from the illusion of *powerlessness*. Many of us live from day to day feeling that "something" is missing, or that we are victims of circumstances that beyond our control, that happiness and success are improbable. We may envy other their apparent happier lives, and then blame others, or the system, or one thing or another for our own unhappier ones. We may feel "left behind" as the train pulls out with other, luckier people aboard.

From childhood on, we experience situations beyond our control. We may learn from our parents that "we just can't do anything about it." In schools taught to prepare for the "future". If we go on to higher education we anticipate a bright and rewarding career. Religions teach that there is a "greater power," but we find it to be of no help in our personal affairs. As young adults we look for love and romance, shared understanding and sensual enjoyment. We go to parties and play games, go to concerts and sports events, and anticipate that happiness is just around the corner. For some of us, college and advanced studies may bring mental stimlulus and excitement, and the promise of good things to come. As adults, we may find meaning through independent studies or in our first "real jobs," in travel and foreign adventure, and then on into marriage and family, in advancing in our work.

But slowly things begin to dim, our sex life is merely repetitius; home, marriage adn family bring chores, debt, adn unexpected challenges; aging includes illness and decline; we find that our employment is unable to meet all our needs and dreams; and our government is limited in providing all the things we ask of it, and the world becomes more threatening.

We no longer even dream of a "better tomorrow." But the "outer world" is only part of the story.

Let's instead look at "personal power" from another angle, and refer to it as "success." We all want to be successful in social and athletic endeavors, in education and training, employment and career, in marriage and parenting and having the home we desire, participating in our community, attaining financial security, enjoying health and long life, and—ultimately—in feelings of personal accomplishment, personal worth, and spiritual wholeness.

Success is really what life is all about. It's how we may be measured after we depart mortal life, going onward and *upward* to still greater opportunities in "life after death."

Success happens from the inside out! Real success is what you can take with you.

The secret to success is really no secret at all. Just ask any successful person. The "secret" is really a universal truth that belongs to each and every human being on the planet. That truth is: Success begins in the mind and the greatest barrier to success is the illusion of helplessness and powerlessness. It is the illusion that you have no choices in life. *But, you do!*

The good news is that you have the power—inside yourself now—to sweep illusions from your mind and use your mind for what it was intended: *to lift human consciousness to a higher level and make this world a better place for you and your children. You have the power!*

Success is your destiny. When you are self-empowered, you become the sole architect of your life. Why wait? *Seize your power, now!*

How Is This Accomplished?

That's where Llewellyn's *Psychic Empowerment* books come in. Techniques and tools are available to activate your inner resources and create exciting new potentials in your life. Some techniques specifically involve psychic empowerment because your innate psychic powers must be developed into psychic skills that are integrated into your Conscious Wholeness.

We are not "finished products!" Physical Adulthood is not even half the story. Psychic Empowerment techniques and tools directly engage your innate but mostly undeveloped and ignored Un*conscious* powers and bring them into the Conscious Mind for ready application in making a better life, a life of greater Success and Happiness. With expanding conscious awareness of your inner powers and abilities, you advance into the development of your Super-Conscious Mind.

Starting with simple meditations and affirmation procedures, we move onward with more complex and specific empowering procedures to meet your needs and your challenges, to make your life all it can be. With each step forward more opportunities become available to you. With each advancement the Greater Cosmos opens before you.

Each technique of Personal Empowerment embodies a firm regard for the divine spark of greatness existing in everyone. With their development, you *grow towards greater Self-fulfillment.* Success and Happiness are achieved through your own efforts and not from external factors or through other people. You are the source of your own greatness, but all the parts of self must be awakened and empowered, and then centered in your own Higher Self.

You are more than a physical being, more than an emotional being, more than a mental being—all these can be incorporated into your spiritual being. You are all these and spirit as well—but as you center your consciousness in Spirit, you can communicate from Spirit to Spirit. Communicating at spiritual levels through the techniques presented in this book, the knowledge and wisdom of beings throughout the Cosmos are accessible to you.

Spirit is everywhere and in everything. Communicating with Spirit you have access to all there is, to all the knowledge and wisdom there is, to other spiritual beings, and to Universal Consciousness. The Greater Cosmos welcomes your every advancement.

WHAT THIS BOOK IS ALL ABOUT
The Table of Contents

Why so much detail?

Why so much detail? While many of the concepts presented in this book are historically familiar, others are actually revolutionary and challenging to many familiar ideas and historic myths. On a chapter-by-chapter basis, readers may easily embrace what we've provided in one chapter, question what is in another chapter, and not recognize the challenge in a third. Yet, we do believe that what the whole book provides will find not only acceptance but also support—perhaps even enthusiastic endorsement.

Each chapter stands alone, and yet is integral to the whole system of New Age Spiritual Communication that reflects what we call "New Age" and "Aquarian thought and action." We support the transition from "old age" Piscean ways to New Age/Aquarian (and Information Age) ways with sufficient detail and commentary to show the evolutionary movement of human culture through historic cycles.

We believe that these chapter summaries pointing to the transitional challenges from the 5,000 years of the repressive political and social domination of male-dominant monotheism to the New Spirituality will help the reader focus on the real psychic, psychological, and spiritual factors involved in *Communicating with Spirit* in contrast to the historic and mythic claims and common assumptions about Spirit and Spirituality.

The Human Person is a complex multi-dimensional entity with conflicting drives and needs that are resolvable as the Spiritual Dimension is engaged. Each chapter is a progression towards that goal.

We encourage you to read the entire Table of Contents before moving on to Forewords and onward through the book as a whole, including Appendices, Glossary, and even familiarize yourself with the Index as a working tool.

In one sense, we are following the well-travelled teachers' road.

1. Here's what we're going to tell you (the table of contents);
2. Here's what we are telling you (the chapter text and ending meditation); and
3. Here's what we've told you (the glossary and in-depth index).

The glossary presents the special words and phrases as they were used in the book. The definitions provided summarize ideas from the book as a whole while pointing to the parts with suggestions for further study and development.

Every book is a Shared Endeavor between Reader(s) and Author(s)

Every book is shared endeavor between authors and readers. We, the co-authors, put a lot of work into the book—*always with the reader in mind*. We try to clearly <u>communicate</u> ideas, recognize those that may be challenging to the reader, and provide a series of charts and tables, programs, exercises, rituals, and meditations to work with the reader in our shared endeavor. At the end of most chapters we suggest a simple meditation—not as a formal and structured program or ritual, but simply an idea to think about in a particular way.

Meditation on an idea

The Procedure is simple: We suggest having a journal (preferably a loose-leaf binder so you easily go back to expand an idea) for your work with this book, and starting off by writing down the idea for the first meditation. Sit back and relax, with pen or pencil in hand, or with a tablet computer at the ready (if that will be your journal).

Passively *ruminate* (literally to "chew the cud") and thoughtfully go over the idea, and let it "talk to you." Don't make an effort, just relax; don't get out the dictionary or look up anything in an encyclopedia or on-line, just relax; if you want, just relax and close your eyes. Whenever it seems right, just write down whatever seems right. End the session.

Before you start the meditation on a second idea, read over what you wrote about the first to establish a passive continuity between them, and then proceed as with the first.

Thank you, and Good Wishes from your partners, Joe Slate and Carl Weschcke *xix*

INTRODUCTION—THE WORLD OF SPIRIT.............................. 17

Survival after Physical Death. Belief vs. Faith, and Personal Responsibility for your own growth and empowerment. *Psychic Empowerment & Self-Knowledge:* Knowing your own body, mind & spirit is the foundation for this journey of a life-time to *become more than you are! The True Answers come from within*—not from teachers, religionists or sacred literature. They may help, but you are your own best teacher and the answers live within you. Never accept answers on faith alone.

Contents include: What, and Who is Spirit? It is the "surviving personality," a unique manifestation of the Soul, but not the Soul itself. "Spirits" are everywhere: spirit guides & teachers, guardian angels & invisible helpers; nature spirits & elementals, fairies, gnomes, elves, sprites, and more; angels and ruling spirits of places & forces; higher intelligences and archangels; ascended masters, inner plane adepti, astral travelers (living persons projecting out-of-body); consciously and un-consciously created thought-forms, mythic and deific images empowered by ritual and prayer; religious entities & powers, gods and goddesses, etc. with the surviving personalities of so-called "Dead People."

Spiritual Communication is real, and you will learn it. Mind under Will functions *downward* through the Astral to manifest in the Physical World. You can learn to communicate *upward* to invoke the powers of your Higher Self and higher bodies and energies to manifest a good life. Surviving Personality of a deceased person in transition to another dimension (This is discussed in considerable detail, along with what happens when the personality moves "upward"). While incarnate in the physical vehicle, the personality also functions in the astral, mental, and causal vehicles operating together but with the physical predominant. After physical death, the personality is focused in the astral vehicle still united with the mental and causal, all to be successively cast off. With each level, the opportunities of experience and learning change.

You don't have to die to consciously focus, experience, and work in and through the astral, mental and causal vehicles. It is this expansion of consciousness and extension of focused awareness that we call "psychic empowerment" which comes as you *become more than you are* and *all you can be.* Spiritual Communication follows certain "rules" involving prayer, magick, shamanic and other extensions of consciousness, invocation and "worship" "bringing within" all the attributes, symbolism, and energies focused into a specific deific image that is alive on the astral level of universal consciousness. All interaction with the astral and higher worlds is consciousness-expanding and empowering. We *grow* not only through learning material facts and rational thinking but through Mind-extending experiences and Psychic Development, Training, and Empowerment enabling our function at higher levels of consciousness.

Communicating with your Higher Self is the goal of most magical and spiritual training, and leads to what psychologists call "integration" of the elements of the psyche.

CHAPTER ONE—THE NATURE OF THE SPIRIT REALM AND THE NATURE OF SPIRIT COMMUNICATIONS 35

Contents include: The Reality of the Spirit World, and its distinction from, and inclusion, of the physical and astral planes. The six dimensions of Space, Time, Thought, Love, Intuition, and Divine Union. The Nature of the Spirit World: Sprit is the universal "Divinity" that is everywhere and in everything and everyone, and can be experienced as "person" or "force." There are many levels and forms of spirit entities, but the way most people today experience them is determined by their religious *faith* rather than actuality. All perception can become a matter of personal choice. Most religions substitute spiritual experience with "faith" and deny personal communication. True Spiritual Communication is not a passive but an active relationship with a spiritual entity. Spirits are forms of consciousness, as are we. New Age replaces hierarchy with equality, restores man and woman as partners, values knowledge over authority, and disclaims sexuality from being sinful and evil to being a source of joy and union with the Divine in all there is. Three kinds of Spirits. The 59 varieties of male Monotheism; the many variations of female Polytheism. Other kinds of spirits, hauntings, poltergeists, and psychic residue. ***Magick is communication with Spirits, and is the oldest and truest form of religion!*** The nature of spirituality and the process of "Becoming." In your communication, ask questions and test and verify the answers by age-proven "correspondences." Psychic Empowerment comes through Involvement in life, not Avoidance. The three methods of communication.

"Meditation: The Nature of the Spirit World" 51

CHAPTER TWO—INTERACTIONS BETWEEN THE SPIRITUAL AND PHYSICAL 53

Contents include: Spirit and Consciousness are everywhere. There is no place where there is absence of consciousness and spirit. They are not the same, nor are they opposites. There are no firm barriers separating this from that—only beliefs do that. To open ourselves to the "whole" view, we have to free ourselves of inhibiting beliefs. Spiritual and Physical are not opposites. Duality, as a perspective, is a fact of *physical* life, and life is in all things including so-called "in-animate" matter. Matter *and* Energy are convertible, one into the other, although not simultaneously. All energy manifests as positive *and* negative, universally but not simultaneously. Movement from Duality to Trinity always requires Action. *To merge Consciousness with Spirituality requires a unity of action charged with energy and purpose* involving forms of meditation, ritual, magical evocation and invocation, and ecstatic practices to bridge the gap.

Every Man and Every Woman is a Star. We move forward through the empowering technologies and transcending communications derived both from ancient shamanism and the new science of the paranormal. We raise our levels of consciousness through the use of rituals, self-hypnosis, meditation, mantras, sex magick, astral projection, chakra work, visualization, dance and gestures reflecting purpose, desire, and aspiration. **The Cosmic Directive is for growth and development,** but Spirit responds best to our initiative, to our conscious action, and to our expressed needs.

Ask, and Ye shall Receive!

CHAPTER THREE—THE NATURE OF MIND, BODY, AND SPIRIT INTERACTIONS 63

Spirituality defines who and what we are. Spirituality is the guiding force that empowers us to become "all that we can be." It gives us strength in daily life to meet life's challenges.

Science and Spirituality, acting together, unleash our potentials for solving the most challenging world problems as well as improving the quality of life—health, longevity, career, and more. Overcoming Self-imposed Limitations. Scientific research into the paranormal teaches us that every problem is capable of solution and that every secret is capable of being unveiled, and applied.

Scientific Research into the paranormal: understanding both physical and spiritual realities, advancements in psychology, relevance of past-life experiences to present-level development, spirituality and longevity, medicine and psychotherapy, empowering effect of Near Death Experiences, evidenced of spirit guides, astral projection and other realities.

Overcoming Self-imposed Limitations, your subconscious mind can become a channel through which you can draw upon universal resources to balance and empower your total being—mentally, physically, and spiritually.

Programs in this chapter:

14-Step Spiritual Equilibrium is Power in Action Program to balance mind, body, and spirit, merging energies with the Etheric Double to facilitate interaction with higher dimensions, planes, and guiding spirits as sources of knowledge and power. **68**

The program has four major applications:

Program Application: Spiritual Equilibrium for Psychotherapy and Self-empowerment for managing stress, reducing pain, overcoming depression, extinguishing phobias, and instantly generating an empowered state of well-being and security. **71**

Program Application: Spiritual Equilibrium for Psychotherapy and Self-empowerment Health & Fitness for weight loss, slowing aging, activating rejuvenating energies. **73**

Program Application: Spiritual Equilibrium for Psychotherapy and Self-empowerment Resolving Conflict. Through holistic balancing of the mind, body, and spirit, you become empowered to resolve conflict, regardless of its nature. **73**

Program Application: Spiritual Equilibrium for Psychotherapy and Self-empowerment Diversity, Clairvoyance and Creativity. Expanded awareness leads to insights related to stress, past-life images, social situations and spirit presences. **73**

"Meditation: What does 'Interaction with Spirit' mean to you, now? 75

CHAPTER FOUR—BI-DIRECTIONAL ENDLESSNESS OF SPIRIT 77

You are Mind, Body, and Spirit. Spirit is the energizing force that identifies and sustains your personal existence in each lifetime and in-between. Within that endless scope, spirit gives identity and meaning to your evolving being uniquely different from that of all others.

Spirit is the Essence that empowers you to learn, grow, and succeed, overcoming all obstacles. The doors to opportunity, growth, and abundance is never closed when mind, body, and spirit work together in harmony.

Motivation, and the Zeigarnik Effect: Nothing ends as long as we can begin again—returning again and again to complete the tasks we've set for ourselves.

Spirituality is the essential core of our existence: Our research from controlled laboratory studies to surveys and subjective reports shows the bi-directional endlessness of our personal existence, increasing our understanding of spirituality as the essential core of our existence. We have uncovered evidence of higher spiritual planes and developed ways of engaging their specialized powers. At a deeply personal level our research expands our awareness of protective spirit guides, personal growth facilitators, and even rejuvenation and longevity resources.

Motivation in the Afterlife, and again in the Next Life is consistently multi-purposeful and growth oriented. In addition to completing unfinished tasks each lifetime was motivated by a variety of needs to correct and compensate for past-life mistakes and failures, to set new goals and fulfill specific growth needs and achieve higher levels of personal growth by assimilating past experiences, to gain new experiences that will become growth resources in the afterlife, and even for unforeseen rewards in a new lifetime on Earth.

Setting Life Goals brings Quality and Long-Term Meaning. The driving force underling the choice to reincarnate is the need to maximize growth potentials and raise them to new levels of possibilities.

Preservation of Peak Growth: existence is a continuous, never-ending growth process. Past growth experiences, whether in each lifetime or the discarnate realm, are never lost, because of the continuously cumulative and persistent nature of our personal growth. At our transition to the sprit realm, preservation of peak growth is instantly activated.

The decision is yours. While often facilitated by benevolent spirit guides and growth specialists, the decision to experience a lifetime is never forced upon the individual, and the responsibility for each lifetime is yours alone.

Spiritual Alignment is the *supreme force* that energizes your growth and gives quality to your existence from your endless pre-existence to present moment and beyond. Once you are spiritually aligned, you become empowered to engage the spiritual realm as a source of both power and enlightenment, to more fully develop you extrasensory powers and to activate them as needed, to increase awareness of your relevant past and past-life experiences that hold special significance to the present, to engage precognitive awareness of future personal and global events, to experience clairvoyant awareness, often in imagery form, to include distant situations and events related to your present life situation.

Programs in this chapter:

Two Spirituality in Action Programs designed to generate a state of both inner and outer spiritual alignment.

8-Step Spiritual Alignment through Automatic Writing Program engages a conscious-subconscious interaction empowering you to reach beyond the commonly perceived limits of your existence. It recognizes the subconscious as not only a wealth of past experience but a powerhouse of insight and potential as well. **82**

6-Step Synchronicity in Action Program. Each lifetime offers particular potentials that may require accessing resources buried in the subconscious while engaging other dimensions of power, including the spirit realm. This program promotes your total growth and empowers you to engage new sources of power and apply them to achieve specifically stated goals. **87**

"Meditation: What is your main goal in this life, and how will it affect your next life?" 89

Becoming Open to Spirit. *Once you are receptive to the spirit realm, nothing is beyond your reach.* Its limitless wealth of empowering resources becomes readily available to you.

Spirit is always positive, always purposeful, and always ready to intervene. Spontaneous spirit manifestations and interventions are consistently purposeful and empowerment driven, providing new sources of information and power to meet life-threatening circumstances and avoid adversity, cope with misfortune, solve pressing problems, and even shape future events.

No Evil in the Spirit World. Contrary to myth and religious mis-representation, we find no evidence of any negative destructive spiritual force. But there may be subconscious *negative mental projections* of oneself upon external influences, correctable through self-understanding and personal growth.

The Boomerang Effect. The spirit dimension is a positive repository of power to enrich your existence, accelerate your progress and achievement. Negativity and malevolence in any form cannot co-exist with that power. Any attempt to engage spiritual power and negatively target it will return upon the sender with disempowering forcefulness.

Meeting Worldly Challenges is our problem. Evil does exist in *the physical world*, but to attribute that force to the spirit realm shifts responsibility away from ourselves as beyond our control and our capacity to correct it on both personal and global levels. By assuming responsibility and taking corrective action we can we make the world a better place for all.

No Evil Possession. Our research into cases of alleged evil possession consistently showed them as subconscious defense against "unwanted" thoughts, emotions, or actions following a painfully traumatic experience or the repression of "unacceptable" thoughts or behaviors denied conscious awareness or expression. Claims of evil possession thus become a defense mechanism that allows the free expression of otherwise unacceptable drives or impulses justified by attributed to an evil force beyond the control of the individual. Simply identifying the source and "ventilating" the stress associated with the condition are often sufficient to fully "expiate" the perceived possession.

Dreams are Spiritual Gateways to interaction with spirit guides, connecting us to higher planes, providing insight for important decisions, sources of creativity, activating subconscious resources, enriching social interaction, generating clairvoyant insights, uncovering past life experiences, and facilitating Out-of-Body travel for knowledge and power.

Dreams can be used as Spiritual Therapy to relieve past life trauma through insight into the source of fear and pain, often located in a past-life experience.

Lucid Dreams and Out-of-Body Travel during Sleep facilitate creativity and Astral Plane Interactions for healing, viewing Akashic records, interacting with your spirit guide, experiencing insight and illumination, and gaining needed personal information and accelerated growth.

Spontaneous Intervention in Emergency Situations. Spontaneous intervention, by benevolent spirit guides, can warn of danger and in some instances, actually intervene to prevent injury or other adverse consequences.

Animals as Intervention Specialists. As spirit messengers, animals can connect us to the spirit realm in ways that enrich and empower our lives. Among the familiar examples are animal companions that often appear to sense danger and then act purposefully to warn of risks.

The Spirituality of Nature. Inspiration, success, enlightenment, enrichment, and an unlimited range of spontaneous spirit manifestations and interventions are all available through mindfully connecting to the power of nature.

CHAPTER SIX—DELIBERATE AND INDUCED INTERACTIONS

Simple Techniques for Your Personal Experience. Nothing is more convincing of the power of spirituality than personal experience, and it is your controlled personal experience that will open the doors to purposeful interaction. Numerous strategies are available to facilitate personal spiritual interactions, among which meditation, self-hypnosis, automatic writing, the pendulum, crystal gazing, table tipping, and séance work are all relatively low key in terms of time and money invested and yet extremely productive of real knowledge, verifiable information, and measurable results.

Each of the interactive programs presented here show spirituality as an interactive experience that defines the quintessential nature of personal existence.

9-Step Program for Spiritual Empowerment through Interactive Meditation is a research based program that focuses on the capacity of mental, physical, and spiritual functions to interact in ways that unleash new power and enlightenment from both within the self and beyond. Spiritual enlightenment, enriched personal relationships, accelerated learning, academic and career success, better health and fitness, and even financial achievement are all possible through the application of this approach. **106**

Spiritual Empowerment through Table Tipping commonly involves four participants seated around a light-weight 4-legged "card" table, their hands relaxed and resting lightly

CHAPTER SEVEN—SCIENCE AND THE SPIRIT

CHAPTER EIGHT– SHAMANISM & SPIRIT.....................129

To go Beyond the Ego without losing consciousness. That's where Spirit comes into the picture. Spirit is the *substance* of consciousness, and it is *consciousness* and energy that move the Universe. Spirit, and Spirits, are everywhere and Spirituality is Universal. Spirit is the primal substance fundamental to all existence, to all life, to all there is. Spirit is the "beginning," and the *matrix* for what follows. Spirit is not something "high," and *beyond* ordinary life. *It is Life.* Spirit is not "non-sexual," because sexuality is just as spiritual as chastity and self-denial. *Shamans are Spirit Talkers* and are the "direct experiencers" of ecstatic union with "Spirit" and the entities active in the inner world also influencing the outer world. Shamans were the witches and "wise women," the medicine men and women, herbal and spiritual healers, the midwives facilitating women giving birth, the travelers to and messengers from the Spirit World, and the visionaries able to describe the non-physical inner worlds in understandable mythic language and poetry. The primary mode of Shamanic Transcendence is that of Ecstasy, leading to the trance induced journey during which the spirit body leaves the physical body *to enter the non-physical Spirit World to gain knowledge and solicit the help of spirit entities for their people. Shamanism is not a religion, it has no dogma, no theology, no "priesthood."*

The Forgotten Inner World:—Shamans were forgotten about in our modern materialist age. Spirit was ignored by modern science and spirits were relegated to superstition and horror fiction, and religionists twisted spiritualty as they sought control over their human "sheep." Spirit was placed in fictional "heaven" outside of physical reality and beyond human reach. Altered States of Consciousness can go *beyond* ecstasy to "trance with a purpose." *Training, Mind Control, Discipline, and Intuitive Shamanism* enable the shaman to continue the journey, and to follow new directions as they may appear. It was the *shaman's ability to ask questions of spiritual entities and receive answers that led to the beginnings of the spiritual technologies* that were then further developed into the *sciences* of astrology, alchemy, magick, Tantra, yoga, and other ways to understand and apply knowledge of "how things work" from the non-physical to the physical dimensions.

The New Age of Shamanism contrasts with the Old Age of organized Religion and Institutionalized Values! Shamans are individuals who look beyond the ordinary and thus become extraordinary through their own personal study and actions. They are not limited to how they learn, so learn anyway they want and study whatever interests them, they turn within and learn from "spirits" and from the World Around. You *can* learn shamanism from books, from lectures, workshops, teachers, and whatever you want, *and from your own direct experience.* Today's shamans study the psychology of altered states of consciousness, the construction of the human brain and central nervous system, chakras and the subtle energy systems, the body's sexual system and the trigger points and psychic switches leading to ecstatic experience and those particular states "beyond orgasm," and what is known as "sub-space" in relation to Power Animals, forms of spirit and god possession, and states of consciousness shared between the inspired Lover and the Beloved.

The oldest, and most fundamental of these, are shamanic practices that raise consciousness to induce trance and ecstatic states to take us from outer to inner worlds. These and other trance inducing techniques include: Meditation and Visualization (*the extended focus of attention on a perceived and then visualized image*), Trance Dancing (*repetitive whirly and swaying sensory actions leading to fatigue)* and Sensory Overload *(drumming at 200-220 beats per minute, flashing lights, and repetitive chanting),* Restrained Movement with *light bondage while dancing, walking)* and Sensory Deprivation *(sleep or meditation mask),* Tantric Sex *(extended arousal through stimulation of many of the physical "trigger points" to the edge of orgasm, and then "holding back" until starting again and again to finally "explode" in a long and sometime multiple orgasms,* and Orgasmic Denial *(continued arousal and denial leading to prolonged mystical or "sub-space" trance),* Drugs *(natural hallucinogens and psychedelics)* and Wine *(never to the point of inebriation),* Rites with a Purpose *(rituals of invocation of specific deities to gain their qualities)* and Initiation *(rituals to impress the group's egregore upon a new member by multiple visualization or to bind the member to priest or priestess, usually by sexual union),* S/M (Sensual Magic of *heightened body awareness through sensual dress and adornment)* and Fantasy Role-playing *(in which committed consensual partners unite in a power-exchanging relationship in which one enters into prolonged trance or "Sub-Space" for a guided journey).* All Spirit Communication requires energy, and the "higher you go, the more you need." *Sexual Energy and Sexual Fantasy (a particular aspect of the Imagination) are extremely powerful "tools for Consciousness Work.* **Repeat:** Sexuality is not contra to Spirituality but intrinsic to all life.

The Bicameral Mind & the Triune Brain. Until about 3,000 years ago, we were essentially "asleep" and many people are still "mostly asleep" even today. We lacked full, alert "conscious awareness" and were mostly reacting automatically just like animals. We accepted words from "authorities" (religious, political, governmental, teachers, counselors) as *commands from gods,* and most still seek such guidance in preference to rational analysis and assuming responsibility for our own thoughts and acts. Thus, *the "secret knowledge" of raising and altering consciousness, inducing trance and ecstatic vision* was violently suppressed over the past several thousand years by the male dominated monotheistic religions. Our modern world is too large, too complex, and too integrated for any sectarian religious theology or political ideology to dominate and repress human consciousness as espoused by militant and repressive religion. We must move forward, not backward for world peace and human survival are at stake.

Pre-Hindu Shamanic Tantra from before the Aryan Invasion of the Indus Valley has survived and contributed to our knowledge and aptitude to work with both the physical and the metaphysical (more subtle) forces and substances of shamanic Tantra in which *there are no real boundaries between the worlds. Shamanism is Empowering and Transformative and shamans* can cross the barrier between human and animal in a variation of *Animism.* One variation of this is found in Voodoo where a god *(loa)* possesses a human and is said to "ride the human as if a horse." That, however is an inadvertent possession, while others have deliberately sought to be a horse, or wolf, tiger or other "were" creatures. Such "possession" is not *demonic* as claimed by the Church but *a means of experiential knowledge of alternate realities* that are part of the greater cosmic reality.

Partnering with Power Animals, Allies, and Totem Animals. Each species of animal has unique characteristics, and *the spirit of the Power Animal represents the species as a whole. One variation of this "Intuitive Shamanism and involves the three companion animals— horse, dog and cat. The domestic cat may be used as a "Fetch," or the "Witch's Familiar" serving as a magical envoy into the spirit world.* Another other comes during a shamanic journey in which the traveler discovers and meets his/her Power Animal which then serves as a Guide. "Some people identify with their spirit animal to the point where they feel themselves to be that animal and their actions, responses, and perceptions reflect the energy of the animal guide." In addition, there is the transformative assumption of the Power Animal encountered in B/d induced role-playing "subspace"* during which one *temporarily becomes the animal spirit.* A Growing numbers of psychotherapists use guided visualization techniques to evoke images of 'power animals' or 'spirit guides' and then encourage clients to interact with and learn from them. Guide Fantasy is "visualization," and *visualization* is intrinsic to "the Magickal Imagination" that connects us directly to the subconscious mind and to levels of the "spirit world." The subconscious mind is our personal door into the Collective Unconscious, which is, in turn, part of Universal Consciousness. Humans, spirit animals, and real companion animals share consciousness at the lower astral level and can communicate with one another through human controlled fantasy.

Sexuality that is conscious has the power of transformation, and the greater the sexual energy the greater the potentials for self-transformation and spiritual development. Sex is a powerful shamanic and magical tool that stimulates creativity and enables particular forms of communication beyond normal human limitations. And, Sex is a powerful means to the blending of two unique persons in a complementary partnership.

One of the newly encountered Altered States of Consciousness that S/M couples are experiencing in their sexual practice is known as "Sub-space," in which the submissive person (most often the female, less often a male) totally submits to the dominant's control for her (the "sub's") pleasure, and then into other aspects of their consensual dance. She let's go of objective awareness to turn within—sometimes to pure nothingness as in deep meditation, other times to a wealth of fantasies, and—then—under his guidance or her own intention, she awakens feminine archetypes in her subconscious to communicate directly her needs and questions. These may take the form of goddesses and spirits in communication with her at high spiritual levels or just a flow of mostly unconscious awareness. Such sexual role play or the extended shamanic experience that can be developed in a carefully scripted "ritual drama" that is open-ended so that new psychological and spiritual experience can occur for both partners whether as shaman and assistant or as sexual partners and role players.

Every Man is a god, but with a goddess companion; every Woman is a goddess, with a god companion. And it is the ultimate goal of every human to become Deity. In our partnership, we develop the inner divinity in every way, whether in sexual play or in what we say, and all we do day after day. The constant interplay of consciousness and energy is physical and spiritual, emotional and mental, and—above all—magical, mystical, and alchemically transformative. When we live in *Awareness,* we are awake and alive in every sense.

Where Spirit is No Longer Found! We're devoting three major chapters to the discussion of Spirit and Religion because religion is where most people expect to find "Spirit," and where—unfortunately—it's no longer to be found. Rather than Spiritual *Communication* with a loving and accessible power, the religions that now dominate half the world's populations demand *worship* of a distant deity through institutional intermediaries. These old Abrahamic religions (all Middle Eastern in origin) are organized around "stale-dated" theologies and laws.

Human Bondage through male-dominant "religion." Islam, and fundamentalist Christianity seek to impose antiquarian theology and religious "law" on everyone by dominating education, laws regulating public and private behavior, politics and government, the economy and military while denigrating all independent thought and any behavior contrary to their dated codes.

Theocratic and Monopolistic. These religions are theocratic and monopolistic by intent with no place for democracy nor modernization, and seek to eliminate all competition, forbidding spiritual communication other than prescribed rote prayer and public ritual, proclaiming procreation women's only justification, that any sexual pleasure proves her sinful origin, and that scientific knowledge is a waste. *Why should any religion worship Death in preference to Life? How can any religion promise eternal life in exchange for taking life from others? Transcendence* does not demand sacrifice, denial, chastity, or repression, nor does it call for the blood sacrifice of "unbelievers."

Shamanism and Religion. As we've seen, Shamanism is not religion but the origin of religion itself. It is a collection of verifiable spiritual technologies and practices leading to individual transformation and transcendence, ecstatic states of consciousness and shamanic journeying producing a heritage of spiritual knowledge, multi-body healing wisdom, extensive botanical knowledge, life-based relationship counseling, and life-supporting information. As a living tradition and practice, shamanism is both ancient and perpetually new.

The Astral ("Spirit") World is Real. *Know-How brings power and access.* By imaging thought into form, you create a "search engine" to access universal consciousness. An astral thought form can become a vehicle for personal communication with a chosen spiritual entity. ***Never doubt the capacity of the Human Mind!*** The whole purpose of spiritual practice and study is to ***become more than we are*** and ***all we can be***—which is potentially ***all there is***. And since consciousness is everywhere and in everything and every being, the best thing we can do is to understand and train our own consciousness to go everywhere and enter into anything, to communicate with any being as we perceive need and value. The better our mind is trained, the more disciplined we are emotionally, the better and more broadly we are educated, the greater will be our ability to gain knowledge and know-how, to innovate to meet new challenges and opportunities, and to transform experience into wisdom.

All Religions are "man-made," but Spirit is real, constantly manifesting within all things. From natural perception came the "worship" of the Feminine as mother of all life and of the Earth as the Great Mother of all Nature. Spirituality identified with the inner feeling of the Feminine as the Source of All, and sexuality as the direct experience of the invisible spirit moving within woman's and man's bodies. From sexual pleasure men and women discovered love, and with understanding of their shared involvement in reproduction arose the joy of family and the fundamental partnership of man and woman in committed relationship that started the long road through Family, Community, and Culture to what we now call "Civilization."

Religions evolve from myths that were attempts to understand the world in story-form. Most myths remain as part of the descriptive qualities of each of the many deific forms in polytheistic religions. But those that adopted a monotheism around a single Father God proclaimed their myth to be real history even when the various elements are readily seen as derived from older myths and contradicted by verifiable fact and common sense.

We study the three types of religion, and the presence or absence of Spirit in each. In the dominant patriarchal religions, there is no place for the human Spirit for the intent is control through emotional manipulation and threat. Religions of "faith," are emotional, irrational and undemocratic. We review the functional factors of all religions, the geo-cultural classifications, the theistic categories, and the styles of worship in preparation for our analysis of the Old Time Religions in chapter ten and the New Spirituality in chapter eleven.

Serving the "Plan." The dominant Abrahamic religions have been used to assert political and "spiritual" control over the various populations of Europe and the Middle East. Originating in the Middle East, Judaism, Christianity, and Islam are all *monotheistic* and *male-dominated*. The emphasis is on humans serving an undisclosed "PLAN" of a distant masculine *One God* as interpreted, and *enforced by* His male-dominant hierarchical institutions whose fundamentalist goals are intellectual and sexual repression, restraint on scientific, social and economic advancement, and suppression of women.

Refuse to be Limited! Today, people who are free to choose a religion or spiritual practice want more than an antique myth, other than a stale-dated morality defying common sense while seeking to impose irrational and anti-scientific claims on their lives. People today expect more than mind control, more than denial of Spirit within, other than worship of death rather than life and to joyfully kill others and sacrifice their own lives to impose one religion on all people. They lose respect for a religion that tells them how to dress, who to talk with, that practices terror and murder in place of personal growth, that honors corruption, theft, piracy, and ransom over work, enterprise, and skill. "Don't think, just Believe" that Nature can be abused and Science ignored in the expectation that "The Lord will provide." That *Religion*, except as implemented through terror, fails in today's world of educated people with developed minds; people who can determine for themselves what to wear and who to talk to and when and if to conceive children; people who wish to improve their own lives and that of their children; people unwilling to merely "follow the leader" when they can see he (never a "she") will lead them over a cliff towards an ideological disaster.

Mind and Spirit, and Evolution. Perhaps the most mis-understood and the most important concept in any study of Spirit and Consciousness is the Process of Becoming, or "Evolution." Evolution began at the "Beginning," and continues as confirmed by Science generally and most Esoteric teaching. Evolution is not limited to Cosmology and Biology, but everything continues to change and evolve. Even our psychic and psychological nature and or human institutions evolve, and so it is with the Human Spirit. Spirit manifests in "structures" that change and evolve, enabling individuals to evolve, grow, and become.

That Old Time Religions tried to "hold back Time" with their frozen myths and theologies from the past. The Church persecuted free thinkers, the wise women known as Witches, the healers known both as wizards, the heathen honoring the Natural world and its cycles, the astronomers who said the Earth rotated around the Sun, and tried to confine education (limited mostly to reading and writing) only to its priests. Even into the mid-twentieth century the Church prohibited its members from reading books that offended its censors. Today we see the Feminine "returning" and taking on new roles—not merely in equality with the Masculine but—as we will later discuss—transformative in both outer institutions and in the re-balancing of the inner dimensions of Man and Woman.

As the first kind of religion, the matrilineal, was based on Love, so the second kind, the patrilineal, is based on Law. *Where is Spirit in these two forms of religion?* In the first, Spirit was seen everywhere, in the second it is seen nowhere. Spirit that first appeared to the lone prophet next appeared to the priest behind closed curtains. What had been open to all was now closed to all but the few. In the third, as we will later see, Spirit can be seen and invoked by all. The Church's formula for control of its people was adopted in the 20th century by both German National Socialism (Nazi fascism) and the Soviet Union's World Communism to intrude another particular worldview and belief system on an entire people, surrounding them with a unifying symbol, stirring music and public drama to inspire acts of devotion, and to enforce adherence through rewards and punishments to establish the superiority of the "faithful" over all *Outsiders* who were therefore to be defeated, converted, or enslaved and eliminated.

Why should we be taught to fear God? The God of Abraham is a jealous God demanding obeisance to Him alone; obeisance which is tested as when God orders Abraham to murder his own son as proof of his faith, as when Lot's wife looked back and was turned into a pillar of salt, and "those who don't obey the gospel of our Lord Jesus: They will be punished with eternal destruction." And in Islam: "Anyone who disobeys God and His messenger will abide in the fire of hell forever . . ." We are told we must fear punishment because we are all "born in sin." While Christianity promises that Jesus' death on the cross redeemed all humanity, today's preachers still thunder that we must fear God, and obey His message. *But what of Love? What of Mercy, What of Justice and Goodness?* No—in essence we must beg for favors from His interpreters. And to follow orders from our those who are the managers on Earth for God's Will.

The real issue is what any religious or spiritual set of practices can do for its followers. We need no longer merely stay in a religion because we were "born" into it. Instead of being dominated by it, we can choose what we want, what we believe in, what we feel will help us, etc. Instead of being "bound" to the "state religion" we make choices, we move about, look for alternatives, and determine what best serves our spiritual, emotional and social needs.

The chapter reviews the essential details of each of the three monotheistic religions and their related sects, and of the challenges and problems each presents to the modern world. These include Baha'i, Druze, Rastafari, and Samaritanism. The chapter includes a discussion of the Dominant Characteristics of Monotheism and concludes with a discussion of What Went Wrong? and the necessary lesson we must extract. We must take back control! You can't give control over your life to a theocratic institution nor to a distant master. You cannot abandon your own person-hood, nor can you give up responsibility for your own decisions. You need to control your own powers by not giving others control over yourself—not physically, not emotionally, not mentally, not of your will, and not of you spirit. All power must flow through your Body and Personality—under Management of your Higher Self—the incarnate representative for your discarnate Soul. Your Immortal Soul grows through your life journey—life after life and lives between lives.

Ultimately, Self-Control, Self-Initiative, and Self-Responsibility are the foundation to your Self-Empowerment–without which, you would be nothing! And we conclude with instructions on how to invoke your Higher Self.

The chapter concludes with a "Ritual To Invoke Your Higher Self" *268*

"Meditation: What does it mean to you that your Spirit or Soul is continuing to evolve, and that Humanity, as a whole, is also continuing to evolve?" 268

CHAPTER ELEVEN—THE NEW AGE RELIGIONS, SPIRITUAL BUT NOT RELIGIOUS! 271

Those Old Time Religions that Lost their Spirit. A review of the 10 characteristics: 1) They are all monotheistic; 2) Their "One God" is male; 3) They have a common Middle Eastern origin from Abraham born 1812 BCE; 4) The share a common mythology of messengers, commandments, miracles, and relationships; 5) All practice wars of aggression, territorial expansion, conversion, and "justified" acts of terror against internal unbelievers and external enemies. 6) All claim a religious law superior to human law; 7) All seek to impose their theology and religious laws on all people; 8) All forbid Spiritual Communication; 9) They had no place for the Human Spirit; 10) Intellect is subordinate to required "faith" manipulated by clergy as Spiritual Leader, Father, Mentor, Confessor, Administrator of Punishments, and Absolver of "sins."

The Beginning of the New Age, and of New Age Spirituality began even before 1809 when mystic artist and poet William Blake described the coming New Age of spiritual and artistic advancement, the new energies were reflected in changes from the repressive, faith-bound, anti-intellectualism of Pisces (symbolized by two fish swimming in opposite directions) into the Aquarian expectation that rationality and science would bring an age of technological progress and economic plenty. While called a "Western" movement, it is really global.

From Spiritualism to Quantum Physics. In the 1848 it got a physical grounding and a metaphysical boost with the birth of Spiritualism and Blavatsky's *The Secret Doctrine* in 1888. From metaphysics the New Age spread to science and then to socialism and politics in 1894 and the arts in 1908 and finally into quantum physics. In the 1960s it took on shamanic twist with the psychedelic culture that quickly spread into a widespread and transformative cultural movement. Already the "new world" is vastly different and the new times have barely begun.

Born Again Witchcraft. In the 1970s, both the New Age and the Age of Aquarius became synonymous with the rebirth of Witchcraft, Paganism, and "born again" astrology, chakras, magick, meditation, mysticism, and yoga. Today the New Age is so pervasive that subjects like Tantra, Taoism, Kabbalah, Tarot, Theosophy, Alchemy, etc. are no longer specifically identified as New Age any more than is parapsychology, Jungian psychology, or the quest for peace.

Ages of Enlightenment and Reason. On the one hand, the New Age is essentially an occult movement, while on the other hand it is the direct opposite of the old meaning of that word as *secret* and *hidden.* New Age beliefs and practices are blatantly public, open-minded, participatory and invitational. Rather than antiquarian, it in the forefront of science, environmentalism, women's rights, life extension, democratic principles, high-tech, and all that contributes toward the modern open society.

The Aquarian Age is here, and here to stay for more than 2,000 years, while the New Age will be even more enduring but under new names. Both are transformative of our culture from economics to politics and to science. It is reflected in the new technologies of the Internet, communications, 3-D printing, small particles, space travel, higher consciousness and more—all rapidly accelerating and demanding social changes that are both rational and spiritual, causing reactions from the "Old Guard" politicians, religionists, and elitists who prefer the old ways.

New Age Spiritual Movements. The bulk of this chapter is taken up with short comparative descriptions of 47 major spiritual and religious movements commonly identified with the New Age, along with an analysis of their distinctive meaningful factors and mention of various associated movements.

CHAPTER TWELVE– THE SPIRIT, THE MEDIUM, THE CHANNEL, AND YOU 379

We are all Spirit Communicators—unconsciously broadcasting and unconsciously receiving at the deepest levels of our etheric and astral bodies. Each living person incarnates Mind and Spirit, Feeling, Will and Purpose within a single multi-level physical and non-physical vehicle we see as a physical body and experience as personality or psyche.

You are—potentially—a Power House. *But* most people are barely "awake" at the physical and subtle levels of conscious awareness, and have little control over the non-physical levels of feeling, thought and will. Our bodies are alive at the deepest levels where we are constantly *broadcasting* messages from and between body cells and organs, and radiating it all from *inner* selves to all selves everywhere.

Reacting without Thought. Mostly we react without thought or awareness to physical events. Our attention is drawn to stories of crime and disaster and exciting events of no real meaning, all tending to produce unintentional emotional reactions which are energetically broadcast to the Universe. We *react* unconsciously rather than acting consciously and intentionally, and don't even know the difference. We are "asleep at the switch" like a hot race car, all gassed up, engine roaring, and no driver, no map, no guidance, no flag to drop.

Know, and Take Charge. The potential for greatness is here, but without willful purpose the only direction to go is nowhere. You have to understand who you are and what you are, wake up and take charge of your own life. Don't let others, not their institutions, nor their automated systems rob you of purpose and your precious assets and life energies for their self-serving benefit.

It's Small Thing that Control Big Things. The modern world is a *Brave New World in a New Age of Challenge and Response.* It's the awakening of a bigger New World, but Quantum Physics shows that *small* things control bigger things in a fundamental dimension of Particles or Waves, Matter or Energy, responding to human attention and intention introducing change at fundamental levels of Reality. All Big things are built from small things as points of leverage which can influence and change Big things to bring about corrections in those big institutions out of harmony with the natural world and the fundamental cosmic purpose of individual growth and evolutionary development. In Spirit you have the Power.

We have to find our own Answers. It's as we become conscious and intentional communicators that our actions become transformative. Spirit Communication should be more than just exchanging pleasantries between human and spirit, and needs sufficient psychic empowerment of the human to make *interaction* meaningful and reliable. Just passively listening to a spiritual entity claiming to be your guide, an ascended master, or an angel speaking of wonderful futures or advising radical changes of lifestyle is as useless as coercive guidance from an old time religionist in the confessional booth. Ask and question the answer, analyze and examine, *test and verify.*

Conscious and Deliberate Spiritual Communication. This chapter describes the types and mechanics of spiritualist trances and séance phenomena, and the types of and methods of channeling. At one level, there is little difference between the medium, the channel, and the shaman.

Connection to Spirit. There's *connection* to Spirit but with a difference: for the Medium and the Channel, the connection is to an external spiritual entity—whether a surviving personality of a deceased person or to a spirit guide or higher entity—or for the shaman the connection starts with the astral body traveling to other realms to observe, learn, and inter-communicate.

Vibration is Identity. The shaman and the channel alters her consciousness to release the subtle body and become harmonious with the targeted level or being. It's only as levels of consciousness are synchronous that real intercommunication is possible.

The Structuring of Consciousness. While discussed in chapter eight, shamanism is mentioned here to better distinguish the methodology of the medium and the channel. In all cases, even though rarely mentioned, it is the intentional imposition of "structure" on the consciousness of the actor in a manner similar to that of ritual magic (to be discussed in chapter thirteen) that intentional goals become realized.

Spirituality is not passive. It is important to realize that *spirituality* is not a passive "wishy-washy" out-of-this-world state. While it can be defined as an attitude or as a state of-mind, it is a matter of study and discipline to *become more than you, and all you can be.*

Chapter Thirteen—Magick, Evocation & Invocation

Wake up, and Live! Most people are barely "awake," going through life more unconscious and reactive than conscious and "in charge." The brain does not **think** by itself, it only operates automatically and reflexively, reacting to stimuli received from the physical body, the physical world, or through non-physical psychic perceptions. The untrained and un-disciplined and *wasted* through lack of understanding of its nature and potential, and its domination by emotions of fear, hate, worry, fantasy, and the insatiable desire to be en-tertained. Magickal Power is a Skill to be learned, like any other, through study, practice, and experience, self-analysis and development, and applied to daily life to make every day better in every way. The Great Secret: *Magick is a Way of Conscious Living.*

Magick is an Art, a Science, a Philosophy, a set of Psychological Principles, a collection of Consciousness-changing Technologies and their many applications in both what we call "high" and "low" forms, and spiritual development. Magick is Applied Mind Power by means of techniques of focused intention and visualization involving a systematic orga-nization and movement of symbols and their accompany psychological forces to accom-plish specific psychic and material benefits. At the foundation of the symbol system are 'correspondences' based primarily on the Kabbalistic Tree of Life and other practices, many derived from Tantra and Taoism. The common element is energy as power and consciousness focused on a specific goal.

Spiritual Communication is between the middle self (Conscious Mind), the lower self (Subconscious Mind), and the higher self (Super Conscious Mind). As directed by the Conscious Mind we communicate with spiritual entities either through the Subconscious Mind or the Super Conscious Mind. The more we understand each of these "worlds" occupied by the three selves, the more power each gains, the more integration of the three we create, and the more effectively magical Mind Power can be applied to magical living and our evolutionary goal to make Magick conscious and to fully integrate Inner with Outer, Subjective with Objective, and Cosmos with Psyche.

Before time began, when the devolution of spirit into incarnation was incomplete, there was interaction between spiritual entities and forces with humans. Here we had the appearances of Gods and Goddesses, elementals, angels and other forces. Here, too, was the beginnings of Magick, the foundation of spirituality and religion, with the develop-ment of symbols and accessories, and of "correspondences" for magical control and veri-fication. We have the functions of Worship as Invocation, Meditation as Evocation and the Conscious Interaction between Inner and Outer, Lower and Higher, and of Humans with Deities to bring Spirit Power down into the Mental & Astral to bring about effects on the Etheric/Physical. And, as Spiritual Beings we reach up to the Spiritual to access not only the powers within but the limitless powers beyond.

Invocation and Evocation. Moving from the generally ineffective *external* religious forms to the *interior* "scientific" forms of spirituality and magick, worship takes on a different role than rote prayer and the *unconscious* groveling and posturing before "graven images." Instead, *Conscious* "Worship" becomes an active method of *assumptive* meditation and visualization we call Invocation, and a method of active and intentional prayer and focused meditation we call Evocation. Both are forms of communication with "spiritual entities" of all types ranging from *functional aspects* of the Universe to *human-created* "Thought Forms" both deliberately and spontaneously imagined.

Integrating Visions from East and West. In this particular magickal program, we deal with two major visions—East and West—of Tantra and Kabbalah in their non-religious "science" aspect. We further recognize the influence of ancient Egyptian Magick, Chinese Taoism, the Greek and Roman pantheons, the Celtic-Druidic, and other traditions from around the world as all contributing to our integrated worldview. Nevertheless, while particularly recommending the Tantric and Egyptian deities along with Kabbalist tools for a your later magickal studies, because of the relatively wide range of deities and the richness of symbol and detail for each, we want to keep our examples simple and familiar to make the principles of practice easier. We will work with the Roman goddess **Libertas** so familiar to us in the Statute of Liberty located at the Gateway into America, and with the Greek **Athena,** goddess of wisdom, law and justice, courage, inspiration, crafts and skills, and patron of education, her statute seen in the reconstructed Parthenon in the city of Nashville, TN, home of Vanderbilt University.

Are Gods, Goddesses, and other spiritual entities real? Yes and No. Magick (or Religion, or any other system) may not seem fully valid for you, but change your procedural perspective and see individual aspects as tools and you can learn to apply them to accomplish your specific goals. We've become conditioned to think of gods and goddesses as spiritual entities to be "worshipped" from afar, but that's the error of religion. And it's a serious error on the part of historians, scholars and theologians to see all deities as functional only within a "religion" and even worse to classify all these systems that have deities as "religions" within the same definition of what are essentially political and business institutions as we've seen in the previous chapters.

Ancient Ways and Modern Magick. All deities are ancient, and all were man-made in a time when the creation of such deific thought forms was natural and spontaneous. Early humans saw things that they didn't understand, things to which they responded emotionally, and slowly they created stories that "humanized" these things to give them a human perspective. Deities live! And become complex compounds of energy and meaning. Over time, these stories became more complex and the Gods and Goddesses gained stature and power and each came to "rule" various functions of nature and psyche. Deity as a "magickal formula of psychic procedures in humanized form." Each major deity became and remains a compound of psychic energy, emotional (astral) images and powers that can be organized into a collection of knowledge and "facts" related to their assigned "rulerships" that we can access, study, and employ in carefully choreographed programs to accomplish appropriately related goals. It works because The human person in all its dimensions has the "circuitry," the "structures," the "spaces," the "zones," the "cells," the "energies," and the awakened and unawakened "correspondences" to all there is known through the Hermetic principle *As Above, So Below.* And equally as imaged in the Kabbalistic *Tree of Life* which provides the organizing principle worksheet for all magickians.

The chapter provides complete guidance to the Invocation or Evocation of the Goddesses of Liberty and Wisdom in formulas that can be adapted for any deity, and the reasons for either procedure, and the ways for their specific application to your particular goals.

CHAPTER FOURTEEN—BECOMING MORE THAN YOU ARE, EVOLVING TO ALL YOU CAN BE 459

You're not Finished! "Becoming more than you are" is not simply a *motivational* phrase, nor is "Evolving to all you can be" only a statement of possibility—it's all about what you can do to accelerate your own multi-dimensional evolution. *And what you should do!*

A Complex Multi-Dimensional Being: The first step is the fundamental need to recognize, and *remember,* that the human person is a far more complex being than commonly perceived as just the physical body, brain, and the familiar personality. You are more than you think you are—a multi-level being of subtle energy bodies beyond the physical—but your degrees of unawareness limits your abilities to function at greater levels. Mostly, you are *asleep at the switch,* and have little or no idea of what being even a little more awake would be like. *Reactive Emotionality, or Developed, Balanced, and Reliable:* The more we develop our "lower" vehicles (Astral/Emotional and Mental) and perfect natural Psychic powers into reliable skills and dependable abilities, the more accessible become the powers of the "higher" vehicles to develop the Intuitive Mind and other faculties of the Super-consciousness. *A Life of Purpose:* Instead of passive acceptance and response to "whatever comes your way," you can act with understanding of your needs and true desires and plan ahead to live a life of purpose, with growth and development to become all you can be.

Real Human Growth is through Intentional Self-Improvement: The next step is the recognition that *real* human growth and development is *intentional and purposefully transformative.* It marks a shift from simple biological "passive" evolution that happens within a *mass* (or species) *context* to that of a willful and "active" drive for *self-improvement* in an individual and personal context. We need to understand that evolution, growth and development is not only physical but non-physical as well, that it is Cosmic in extent but also specific to humanity, that for the human it is singular and multiphasic, and not uniform in all vehicles, sub-vehicles, levels, states of awareness, etc. Some growth is spontaneous, driven by cumulative effects of past actions, while other growth is developmental.

Bigger Steps. Throughout history, in many cultures, there have been more fully awakened individuals who have left us guidelines and examples by their teachings and in the lives they lived. The awakened states of consciousness have many names: *Ascension. Buddhahood, Cosmic Consciousness, Enlightenment, God Consciousness, Liberation, Rising on the Planes, Salvation, Samadhi, Self-Realization, Super-Consciousness, Union, Way of Return,* and others. The methods and techniques themselves vary and the best known mostly reflect the historic achievement of one person but no one way is universal, and all religious institutions denying personal spiritual fail in this manner.

Different Strokes for Different Folks. There is little uniformity among the transformative systems other than the belief that the human person is something more than a physical entity and that what is in the non-physical is of considerable transforming power and glory such that the one transformed becomes a "Super Person" able to perform miracles of a paranormal nature. Yet, within the mainstream of Western religion there is no encouragement to the individual person to *become more than they are,* and of the many teachers of non-religious transformative systems most will caution their students that the development of paranormal powers is a diversion from the true path of Attainment. **Others disagree.** All intrinsic powers (psychic, mental, spiritual) should be developed and become reliable skills, *fulfilling the potential for all you can be* provided for in the plan for both personal and species-wide human attainment. That personal plan is the matrix around which each of the individual's bodies is formed as a basic structure of its potentials based on genetic programming and the carry-forward karmic memories from past lives as planned prior to conception. The structure is formed for each body from causal down through mental, astral, etheric and physical, and then developed within each body as the current life progresses through the natural cycles of growth, maturity, and decline.

The Ways of Growth are Developmental through the Higher Dimensions by means of consciousness functioning in the coincidental vehicles. All transformative techniques are systematic programs involving the etheric, the astral, and the mental vehicles in their several levels—sometimes specifically, sometimes progressively, and sometimes collectively. With further development, we move on into the causal level where all becomes one. Beyond that there is no need for physical incarnation. **Your Assignment—that You must not refuse—**is the "wholeness" of your being that will be brought to the point of transition between the lower and middle worlds, still below what is called the "Abyss" that eventually must be crossed into the higher world. But first we have to leave behind the "garbage" otherwise known as *karma* that clutters the astral and mental bodies together called the "Spirit" to then center consciousness in the causal body which when united is called the "Soul"—although not yet the ultimate individuality also known as the *SOUL.* Your goal for now is to transform and perfect the essential natures of the lower bodies including that of *Intuitive Intelligence* so that you become "master of your own destiny," no longer dependent on others for the knowledge that empowers the Self in daily life. **You do "take it all**

with you!" It is the "whole self," in which the Lower Self has been "alchemically" purified and transformed into the Higher Self.

Where do we go from here? To become an "integrated whole" you have to purify and transform the lower complex of physical and etheric bodies as well as the middle complex of astral, mental and lower causal bodies, and then unify them into the higher causal body. This is your purpose and your assignment that must be completed before you are ready to call your Holy Guardian Angel, and hold conversation with that entity to prepare to cross the Abyss. All the knowledge and information you need is available to you in print and online, in classes and lectures, and through question-and-answer courses. But, not only must you seek out that information and knowledge, but you must learn to qualify and judge its importance and direct value to you. The responsibility is on you to ask the right questions and seek out the right answers. Your growing Intuitive Mind must recognize "right from wrong." Move onward to a higher dimension of Spirit and your Higher Consciousness, communicate with your Higher Self, Listen to your Intuitive Mind, and discover your True Will. These are not empty phrases, but real challenges to overcome the Past and welcome the Future. Of course there is great value in techniques and programs from those great, mostly nameless pioneers whose practices and systems were at the source of pre-religious esoteric wisdom. Our need is to simplify those old ways back to their pure essence for effective spiritual experience. We have mostly adapted from models based on the Kabbalah and Tantra—the core wisdom of East and West. Most will be familiar to students of both, and it is that key familiarity of terms and systems, symbols and images that opens the doors to the perennial wisdom that is both ancient and still living. In the techniques that follow, we have attempted to do that, but it is up to you not to merely follow the formula but to directly experience each step of the way *under your own authority. That's what we are trying to accomplish in this work of Becoming More than You Are.*

THE WAY OF ATTAINMENT: ***Your True Will, Your True Path, Your True Love.*** *Here we offer several progressive procedures to initiate the programs that ultimately will become your own Intuitive Way to Attainment.* Included are specific adaptations of:

CHAPTER FIFTEEN—EXCELLENCE AS CONTINUOUS GROWTH 505

Spiritual Excellence is a dynamic, endless process of Personal Development and Self-Improvement. Through the belief in excellence for continuous growth, all barriers to our personal development and fulfillment can be dismantled and replaced with new resources that accelerate growth and generate personal empowerment.

There's an old saying: *Seeing is Believing*, but a more meaningful saying could be: *Unless you believe, you cannot see!* Embracing the concept of Excellence opens the doors of perception to the universe that is in contrast to that of limited expectation. Expectation is like a cause, and for every cause there is an effect. We grow, the universe grows, and we expect more, and more becomes new reality. Once embraced, the dynamic of Spiritual Excellence can actively banish negativity, insecurity, feeling of inferiority, and all self-imposed limitations. It can build a powerful expectancy effect that is essential to self-empowerment and the successful achievement of personal goals.

Program: 9-Steps for Building Excellence through Spiritual Interaction   509

Expectation, like Intention, is Causal and expands your world of opportunities. Set your goals both realistically and expansively. Your universe of opportunities expands as your imagination soars.

Program: 8-Steps for Experiencing Your Spiritual Element   512

Our review of case reports showed repeatedly that personally experiencing the unique spiritual element through this program can activate your inner growth potentials while connecting you to the highest resource of the spirit realm. Once situated within the energy orb as your unique spiritual element, you can stimulate the spiritual growth process and focus it on personal goals. You can activate dormant inner potentials while accessing the outer sources of spiritual enlightenment and power. You can generate a state of spiritual balance and attunement that is essential to your success.

"Meditation: What does 'endless process of Personal Development and Self-Improvement' mean to you?"   515

CHAPTER SIXTEEN—REWARDS OF
SPIRIT INTERACTIONS 517

Communication, Interaction, Growth, Integration. Spirit interactions are essential to our spiritual growth. Without them, spirituality becomes merely a concept with little relevance to our existence as spirit beings. The spirit dimension is rich with empowering resources and rewards and is constantly receptive to our interactions. Through spirit interactions and their accompanying energy and information flow we discover the true nature of spirituality and the immense rewards of spirit interactions. The primary goal of sprit interactions is spiritual growth. *We are here to learn and grow, but* our spiritual growth, whether in each lifetime or between lifetimes, is *endless yet uneven.* Periods of growth are followed by stagnation during which we review lives' lessons and gain new insights and resolve growth barriers. We grow through the evolutionary process of challenge, insight, and response.

Through the exercises given here, we make spiritual connections that activate potentials and gain awareness of spirit guides, and become empowered to meet new challenges.

APPENDIX A—HOW TO MAKE AND USE A MAGICK MIRROR
FOR SELF-EMPOWERMENT, SELF-DISCOVERY, MAGICKAL
OPERATIONS, EVOCATION, AND DIVINATION 529

Properly used for Self-Discovery, a Magick Mirror, can reveal important information to the "Seeker." And, *properly used,* the Magick Mirror (also known as a *Black Mirror*) is a power tool not only for *Self-Discovery,* but more commonly for Divination (also known as *skrying),* as well as the more esoteric operations of *Self-Empowerment, Self-Improvement, Evocation, and in Magickal Operations.*

The nature and value of the Magical Black Mirror as a doorway into the astral dimension is described, and the multiple uses discussed in ways to encourage the reader engage in the practice. The important function of active imagination and the necessity of its conscious management is fully developed. Several applications not previously well-known are described for the benefit of students of Tarot, Astrology, Kabbalah, and with applications for health and healing, divination, dream-working, evocation of spirits and other entities, as well as magickal operations. Detailed instruction on making and using the mirror are given.

APPENDIX B—TRAVELING IN SPIRIT 543

Astral projection was long ago known as "Traveling in Spirit" and may have been a more common experience before modern times when we all became more focused on physical reality as the cultures changed and our physical needs became more demanding. This was further reinforced as the Church claimed dominion over all things spiritual and philosophy and science more and more focused on the mysteries of the physical universe. *In recent years, Astral Projection is again practiced with the aid of especially prepared audio CDs.*

Vibrational Astral Projection is especially attractive and accessible to nearly anyone in the product described here.

The research projects discussed in this book include instruction research activities as well as controlled laboratory studies.

The detailed research reports to these projects are available in the Library Archives at Athens State University in Athens, Alabama.

Note: The primary intention of a Glossary is specific to words and concepts as used within this book's text. As such, it is not a comprehensive dictionary or encyclopedia and doesn't include words believed to be generally familiar to the reader unless the usage here varies considerably from "standard" definitions for reasons that will be generally obvious. For further reference, please refer to the Llewellyn Encyclopedia at www.llewellyn.com.

For most words, reference to the extensive Index will provide all the definition and details needed. However, in this glossary we have included more detail for certain words and concepts than is usual for a Glossary when we consider them important developmental steps in expanding your awareness and background knowledge in relation to the subject of this book. We want to make this book as complete as possible by providing all the tools you need for actual practice rather than only "reading about," although we believe you will find it a "good read" and an interest intellectual journey.

The occasional reference (See Index & text) directs you to the Index because the subject is considered so important that we prefer that you review what has been written rather than any alternative.

In addition, please remember that to a limited extent, this glossary performs the third function mentioned in the Detailed Table of Contents: "This is what we're going to tell you, this is what we are telling you, and this is what we told you." This "Three-Fold Learning Experience" has been used over many years in various forms in many situations. Remember too that the numbers Three and Seven are recognized as powerful factors in psychological and magickal operations.

This Index is more extensive and detailed that are most. Our reason for this is the belief that our readers will find value in returning to previous discussions and expositions of certain words and concepts, and then even a initial "casual" mention will later add to further studies on the same subject.

Shumanism

Everyone and everything have a past but it all depend on how we look at it!

* *Important factor is how we look at the evidence "*

A New Beginning

Everything has a "PAST"

Any "Beginning" is *new*, and anything "New" is a *beginning—so what are we talking about?*

Everything we do builds on "the Past"—but there are vast differences in what that means and how you look at it. Each person has a "past," every *community* of interest has a "past," as does every *subject* of interest. The study and practice of any subject involves the past of the person, of the community, and the subject—but the most (important factor is how you look at "the evidence.")

It can get really complicated, but we'll soon get to the point.

Don't Let the Past limit your own
SELF Discovery and Development

You see, the Past can be a *limitation* to your own discovery and development. What others have said and written can inhibit fresh thinking; the opinions and *statements* of others—especially those recognized in any manner as "authorities" either directly (or even indirectly) related to the subject can act like a *stop sign* to your independent investigation, and if backed by the seeming "moral authority" of a religious leader or famous scientist may lead you to "recant" your own beliefs.

This is a book on "Communicating with Spirit" and you, the reader, comes to this point with a "past" that may be very minimal or pretty complex; it may include your participation in a community sharing an interest and experiences in various forms of communication with a variety of non-physical entities; and you may have previously researched the subject and read extensively about its history, its evolution into and then from shamanism and religion into new practices and technologies of spirituality, and you yourself may have contributed to such research.

Nevertheless, this moment and each coming moment is a "new beginning" for the simple reason that everything you now do is a "Next Step" that may affirm or overthrow your previous beliefs and lay the foundation for new perceptions and new understanding.

A "Fresh Start"

"What's past is prologue" wrote William Shakespeare, but it is essential that we do not allow the past to *write the future!*

In other words, whatever your past interest and study has been, "that was then and this is now." Now is a new beginning and we want you to see it as a "fresh start." Everything that you know includes the past, and is always with you even if not in your immediate conscious awareness, but an "open mind" means that you don't let the past, and most especially the opinions and biased statements of others prejudice your new study of this subject.

We are reminded of the history of St. Joan of Arc who was burned at the stake by the so-called "*Holy* Inquisition" because she would not recant her claim that angels spoke to her. Catholic doctrine said that only its priests (male only) could do that and that all others should believe that any listening "to voices" of non-physical entities was to expose their souls to the unholy work of the mythical "the devil himself."

In this book, we want to provide more than just a review of this subject's history and encourage you see your own history of study and your own experiences no matter their depth of nature with a fresh new look. We hope to encourage you to "participate" in study and research, to use the programs and procedures we provide for your own direct experiences, and then to record and analyze your experiences, to relate them to your entire study and communal involvement, and—perhaps—contribute your findings and conclusions to the scientific community and to others as well. Share your successes, admit your failures, and be open to new sources and help.

Yes, there is a History, but there's a "New Age" too!

The story of spirit communication is as ancient as is humanity itself, and encompasses much more than "talking with the dead." As you will see here in chapter and text, shamans and priests (male and female), and many "ordinary" people have communicated with ancestral and other spiritual entities through spontaneous or induced trances and altered states of consciousness, and through dreams, omens, and divination as recorded in sacred and mundane writing, in myth and folklore, and as evidenced by ancient artifacts and in pre-historic cave drawings.

Access to Information and Knowledge

In this New Age there is nearly universal access to Information and Knowledge once available only through long apprenticeship, required adherence to theological indoctrination combined with training in specified rituals, controlled initiation into secret teachings involving specific gestures and incantations, and other elitist restraints intended to produce a hierarchical class of trained income-earning professionals.

Today's "Information Age" is replacing Hierarchy with Equality

We've all heard that *Knowledge is Power!* And it is the wide availability of knowledge through physical, psychic, mental and spiritual technologies that enables *self-empowerment* without restrictions of class or affiliation. Books and the Internet have replaced the old controlled access to restricted Church libraries; lectures and classes have replaced the old limited access of secret orders; conferences and digital up-dates keep us in touch with new developments; and even the news and entertainment media by-pass the censorship of church and state still rampant into the late 20th century.

But, with this new way comes new responsibilities: you have to do the work, provide your own self-discipline to study and practice, and to determine the quality and value of the resources. In the old way, you were either "locked in" or "locked out" of a particular resource that had become more of a "belief system" than genuine sources of knowledge and information.

This New Age is a two-way street! What you learn through study, experiment, and practice is shared with others. There are no *real* "secrets." Knowledge thrives in democracy, and leads to innovation. And, open knowledge, innovation, and democracy require responsible and ethically rational behavior. But Liberty requires constant vigilance against the continuing attempts by elitist special interests to control progress for their own financial and political self-interests, and each caring person in a democratic society must remain alert against their attempts.

Spirituality is Dynamic

Spirituality **is** *reality* in its highest form. Rather than a fixed dimension, it is a dynamic force that is constantly present and forever evolving. At a personal level, it is the essential essence of our existence as evolving souls. At a more comprehensive level, it is the energizing force that sustains all that exists, both seen and unseen, and moves us ever forward, ever upward.

While much of our growth as spiritual beings can be spontaneous and thus effortless on our part, it is only through our purposeful and deliberate interactions with the spirit realm that we attain our peak levels of personal evolvement. Aside from that, the discovery of our past personal history and destiny may well rest upon our interactions with the spiritual realm as the ultimate source of knowledge. On a much broader scale, spiritual enlightenment could result in greater understanding of the universe/multiverse and the powers that sustains them.

Our greatest spiritual challenge as evolving souls is to discover knowledge and use it for the higher good. Through our spiritual interactions, we can become empowered to achieve that important goal. Fortunately, the spiritual dimension with its wealth of growth resources constantly beckons us, but it is up to each of us to respond and access its powers. A major goal of this book is to facilitate that important effort.

"Ye are Gods in the Making."

As the great American seer, Edgar Cayce, repeated many times in his reading, "Ye are gods in the making," for that is the obvious purpose of our existence—to evolve and fulfill our highest potential, to become all that we can be, and thus to realize the unity of human and the universe:

As Above, So Below

MEDITATION

What does "Communicating with Spirit" mean to you?

PREFACE

AFTER DEATH: WHAT? WHERE?
*As Channeled from A Ghost named George**

The Importance of the Question before the Answer

In this dictation, my job is to answer a set of questions about "what" and "where" after physical death thus to describe the "spirit process" from an *inside perspective.*

I must explain that I am not a writer, but a dictator. No! That's not right, is it? I don't use words or images, just ideas that I push out to the channel. It's not like a TV channel that anyone can tune into but a human personality with whom I have a sympathetic relationship. That makes it easier for ideas to become impressions and then silently transferred words. But, remember that these words are not *definitive* in the same way that "normal" human conversation appears.

And most importantly, note: *the "question" comes first.* Without a question, there can be no answer, and the way the "question" is framed is of the utmost importance to the quality and definitive power of the answer. I cannot go about "spouting off" on my own, you know. And, that's another point: my ideas and words come through interactions with my channel's mind.

The Physical Body is a "temporary vehicle."

Look at yourself: "You" are not a body. The physical body is a temporary but necessary *vehicle* for "you" to occupy during physical life. The real "you" is an aspect of your *consciousness* we know as a "person" and identify as that "personality."

Throughout your physical life, your body grows and changes and ages, and then dies. Throughout your physical life, your personality likewise grows and changes, and "ages" but does so differently and doesn't die with your physical body.

At the same time, there is more than just the physical body and the personality through which you function and experience incarnate life. There is a composite vehicle composed of etheric, astral, mental and causal substances and energies that along with the physical body enable the personality to function and experience at the energy, emotional, mental, and multiple spiritual levels. This can be perceived clairvoyantly as the aura.

After Death Survival

After physical death, your personality survives in that composite vehicle, moving out of the physical body, dropping the etheric-energy body to decompose a few days later, and simply moving on to primarily function in the astral-emotional *vehicle* commonly called a "spirit" and while often presumed to be the "soul," it is only an aspect of that which we will discuss later. This "surviving personality" sometimes returns to communicate in dreams, sometimes it manifests in paranormal activity as in a "haunting," and sometimes as a "spirit" as in a *séance*. But, sooner or later, it must move on.

The Spirit Body is also a "temporary vehicle."

Just as the physical body or vehicle was inclusive of that multiple composite, so does that astral vehicle include the composite of mental, causal and higher spiritual levels. That "after death" vehicle is also temporary just as was the physical body, and the surviving personality continues to learn and grow just as it did in the physical world but with a new mission and set of *experiential* opportunities specific to its new "home." That temporary vehicle is made of *astral* substance and continues for as long as the personality "lives" in the astral world. The astral world is a much larger non-physical and non-spatial dimension than the physical world. You won't find it on any map, but you do see it indicated on many drawings illustrating the various dimensions of the *Cosmos*: Physical, Astral, Mental, Causal, and others variously named but more often simply grouped together as *spiritual*.

This, of course, can be confusing since "spirit" and "spiritual" are words used both in relation to the astral world and to that group above the causal level. However, neither the astral nor the spiritual dimensions are a permanent "retirement home" or the "heaven" of religious promise. That heaven (or "paradise") is an illusion of false expectations created in the "faithful" by their religious leaders as a reward for following "commandments" and theocratic laws and the "orders" of church leaders.

The Nature of Karma

While that giant astral illusion lives on, the personal illusion eventually—like other artificial *thought forms*—soon passes away. The reality, for most of us, is that we will return to live another life planned to exhaust the negative "karma" created during life by thoughtless action. "Following orders" is no excuse for the killing, rape, and other crimes executed under direction of power driven leaders. The emotion of "guilt"—whether acknowledged or suppressed—becomes karma that will later be recalled and acknowledged in an emotional release.

mental now?

"You" are not your Soul

The "You" you know is a manifestation of "Soul," but your personality is not the *whole* soul but one of many aspects of it incarnating life after life and occupying a series of temporary vehicles each composed of the substance of one dimension after the other. Then the essence of each of life's lessons is abstracted and further refined until the soul is ready to progress on into still higher spiritual dimensions. The soul continues on its journey through the Cosmos, learning and/or "working" on behalf of the *Great Plan* set in motion by the "Creator Source" of all that is—which is better realized as *Unity* when not given a defining and hence *limiting* name.

What we forget, and What we remember

The "surviving" personality we knew during physical life and may encounter during its continuing astral life is constantly "growing and learning," and moving on, level after level, life after life. Growth, Learning, Development, Becoming more than we were—that's what all our lives are about. *Growth after life!*

But, just as there are "stages" in physical life so there are many more stages in astral life. The "senior citizen" stage of physical life has forgotten most of its infant stage as the personality grew and learned while moving on through its physical life cycle. The same is true of its astral life cycle, although the astral, and then the mental and causal cycles, are usually much longer. The Personality forgets because it doesn't need those infant memories, and the same 'censorship' applies in all stage of our many lives in different vehicles. *as we learn and grow we forget!*

However, those forgotten memories are "recorded" first in the Subconscious Mind and then in different detail in the *Akashic Records*. What we may need to remember can be recalled through the psychic technology we know as "Past Lives Regression" *???*

using self-hypnosis or deep meditation. Regression can bring together many skills and past knowledge that can be of practical benefit in one's current life.

Know what you need, *and it will be given onto you!*

Decaying Remnants

After a time the "spirit" encountered in a *séance* loses connection with the surviving personality as it moves on, leaving behind a decaying remnant—not of the astral vehicle but of the "thought form" automatically created during that period in response to the active communication between the surviving personality and the "earthy" communicators.

A Ghost

Astral substance is very sensitive and reactive to thought and emotion, and it is this fact that accounts for much paranormal, magickal, and religious "supernatural" phenomena.

This is a challenging concept to try to explain even for a "ghost" as Carl fondly calls me. A *real* "ghost" is rarely the astral vehicle of the surviving personality but is rather an "impression" initially created out of the lowest level of astral substance through *poltergeist-like actions* involving mostly human emotions—fear, love, remembrances, excitement in relation to mystery, hope, and more—and then sometimes, but not always, reinforced by identification with a known person and memories associated with that person.

As long as the ghostly impressions continue in the memories of new generations of descendants or of tourists in famous haunted castles, etc., the phenomena will continue, and even change character in reflection of new stories. When there is no continued reinforcement, the ghost eventually "dies."

Why Spirits of Famous People get Dumb with age

While the surviving personality occupies a "living" astral vehicle, active communications between the physically living and the astral living creates a thought form impression of the astral vehicle. When the "spirit" moves on—as it must—it leaves behind that thought form which has *recorded* conversations and memories so that further communications seem, for a while, to be as "real" as they were previously but in actuality they come from a decaying astral remnant. The decaying astral remnants of the "spirits" of famous historical figures will last longer than others but a time will come when those decaying remnants will no longer reflect the brilliant and loving personality you may have known during the physical life and early astral phase. It is then that séance spectators will wonder at the seeming naiveté or even "dumbness" of the decaying remnant of even the most vivid of famous historical personalities. The answer is that those Spirits have moved on.

Where is the Land of Oz?

I refer to the fictional "Land of Oz, located somewhere over the rainbow" for a reason. Fantasy and Fiction—like Myth—are stories created in and with *the aid of the imagination*. The imagination is the "key" to the Inner Worlds, and these Inner Worlds are where we enter the Astral World and the other Cosmic dimensions.

"It's all in your imagination" is more meaningful that usually credited. <u>Beings</u>, <u>Spirits, Forms, and Places have a real and continuing *essential* life in the astral</u>, but there are also temporary *experiential* "creations" and "impressions" of astral substance that are experienced as just as real to the astral traveler but can be "blown away" by an act of will, or that otherwise will "fade away" <u>without energy</u> input.

[handwritten margin note: astral substance fade w/o energy inpo]

And, more important, that which is created on the astral and properly "energized" can manifest in the physical world. Sometimes this is more or less seemingly miraculous or magickal, and in other ways can be seen as a simple process in the nature of an idea on the astral being converted to a blue print from which a physical creation is composed. Even though not "miraculous" it did originate on the astral.

[handwritten margin note: manifestation from astral world can easily exist in physical]

There is a real and a subtle connection between the essential astral dimension and the astral world of our experience. Dorothy, in the fictional *Wizard of Oz*, traveled to the "astral" land over the rainbow via a physical *whirling tornado*, but she returned to "physical" Kansas by closing her eyes and clicking her heels three times. Here we are presented with a seemingly real (the essential) land over the rainbow, but it is an act of imagination to return from the essential astral dimension and the experiential one by means of an act of imagination.

What's "real?"

Both the essential and the experiential astral worlds are "real," but we have to shift our concept of "what's real" away from the outer world to the inner world. We are conditioned to think that the outer world is the only reality but we fail to realize that everything we physically sense in the outer world is just a set of vibrations, and that these are transmitted via nerves to sections of the brain where they are "translated" into the sight, sound, taste, taste, and touch that define the outer world for us. "Reality" is what we "perceive" or make out of those vibrations.

The Shamanic "tornado"

A long time ago, a little known American occultist named Ophiel told Carl that the author of the OZ books was a brilliant occultist. What he didn't say was that what Dorothy Gale experienced in the whirling tornado carrying her out of physical Kansas to inner world Oz represented a typical shamanic method of inducing trance by which one can access the inner worlds. The dizzying dance of the Whirling Dervish leads to a mystical state of consciousness that opens the door to astral travel.

The three clicks of Dorothy's heels signal the return to ordinary consciousness. "Everything happens in three's" means that the episode comes to an end.

To understand spiritual realities, we have to reverse our normal concepts of "the outer world," thinking spatially of *heavens above,* and instead turn *inward* to find spirit, the astral, heaven, and Creative Source. The physical universe spreads out before us in infinite Outer Space; while the Cosmos spreads deeply within infinite Inner Space. Realize that it is only the physical universe that occupies physical "space."

The "boundary" between inner and outer is the Wizard's domain

We use psychic science and technologies to explore inner space, and physical science and technologies to explore outer space. "We" are the boundary between inner and outer and it is with our Wizard's techniques of hypnosis/self-hypnosis, meditation, magick, divination, shamanism, mediumship and channeling that we probe inner space and bring back *experiential knowledge* into our conscious realization.

You have the potential

Each of us has both the potential and the obligation to become "wizards" able to function between the worlds and bring back the knowledge and know-how of the gods to empower each person to become more than she/he is and all he/she can be.

> *Life is a fascinating, rich and rewarding journey that we all make. Each of us can make that journey also magickal and miraculous and transform ourselves and the world we live in.*
> —George

Who is George?

*Who is "George?" I frankly don't know, but I know that he is not a traditional "ghost "haunting just a particular location.

I first encountered George when I purchased an old and very large stone mansion on our city's prestigious main residential avenue. The house had been built in the late 1800s by a lumber baron, and later occupied by a succession of wealthy families until one of them donated it to become an art school and gallery from whom I purchased it when they moved to a larger and more modern facility in the main downtown area.

I had attended evening art classes there, and heard stories about George as that "strange gentleman in evening clothes wandering the halls," but I never encountered him. When I was buying the house I was warned of several ghostly manifestations over the years, including George seen dressed formally in evening clothes and "Martha" who could be heard banging pots and pans in the kitchen when no one was there.

In "real life" there had been two deaths associated with the old house. The first was an unfortunate immigrant *servant girl* who had gotten pregnant (so she said) by the chauffer who then wanted nothing to do with her. Depressed and alone, she hanged herself in the stairwell between second and third floors. This supposedly was Martha. The second had been an associate of the art school who (it was said) had been falsely accused of theft, and likewise committed suicide. This supposedly was George. I was told that neither name was "real," but somehow was inspired and had stuck through the years.

After purchasing the old place, at first I came there at night to start renovation before moving in. My first work was to sand the floors badly scared from moving art displays and furniture about, getting rid of false walls in front of the seven fire places and parts of the seven bathrooms, and dividing several of the bedrooms. There were no floor plans left, and I needed to draw my own to know what I had to work with.

Working there at night I heard plenty of noises—sounds of someone walking about, doors slamming shut behind me, windows being opened (which I then had to close and lock), along with the squeaks and groans of an old and still empty house. I got into the habit of calling out "George, it's just me" more in fun than anything else. But it seemed to have the effect of calming things down.

Once I knew what I wanted to do, I hired two excellent "all-around workmen" to install wood paneling, build library book shelves, restore plumbing, add new lighting, tile the kitchen, pantry, and the old ice room, add storm windows and screens, refinish wood, change over from oil to gas heat, and repair the immense north facing skylight over the third floor studio (the original 'ball room'). Then I moved myself in, while continuing renovation of the living areas, and moved the then small business of Llewellyn Publications into the old kitchen and ice-room, and large parts of the basement and the garage space in the carriage house on the alley behind the house. The house and the carriage house in back totaled 32,000 square feet of space. I rented out two apartments in the carriage house that had been "servants' quarters" to help pay the heating costs.

Now, most of the "ghostly manifestations" had ceased and I thought fondly of George and sorry for Martha. Still, occasionally, I saw odd lights and swirling energies, and the cat would stare at empty spaces. None of this was attributed to George.

Living alone in a big house, empty except for me at night often working until midnight and later, I got into the habit of talking out loud—essentially voicing problems and questions to George, and often getting answers—not as spoken words but as thoughts and feelings that made sense. I never debated as to whether *this* George was the *old* George, whether he was a spirit or just an "imaginary friend," or even my Guardian Angel or Spirit Guide, or if I was creating a "splinter" personality. George was a convenient "foil" and I enjoyed having a companion other than the cat.

Llewellyn soon grew to the point where I had to purchase a building in downtown Minneapolis where I also created the *Gnostica Bookstore* and the *Gnostic School for Self-Development*. We also sponsored the *Gnosticons* bringing lecturers from around the world, many of whom were or became Llewellyn authors. We also developed and published *Gnostica Magazine* which later reincarnated as *New World of Mind & Spirit*.

After Sandra and I married, and son Gabriel (Gabe) came along we decided it would be better to raise our son in the country. We bought a beautiful home on a lake outside of nearby Woodbury. And, to my surprise and pleasure, George moved with us. Later, we moved again because Woodbury's population suddenly exploded and became a city, and we moved again, to our present home on a bluff overlooking the Mighty Mississippi River just ten minutes from the new Llewellyn "campus" we'd built in Woodbury to accommodate the company's continued expansion.

With each move, George came along. I mention all of this simply because by any definition George is some form of consciousness that is a recognizable spiritual entity. Today Llewellyn is well managed by Sandra, Gabe, and a capable and experienced staff. With advanced age I've become handicapped with severe arthritis and work primarily at home. I am today a researcher and a writer. I still sometimes talk out loud (perhaps not politely) and voice questions I'm thinking about, and sometimes I address specific questions to George. When I do, I usually get ideas and impressions in response. I don't hear him answer with words nor does he move my fingers on the keyboard. When I write in response to these ideas it is with a writer's voice different than my own. Many writers have this experience when using pseudonyms: the "pretend" person does take on a personality of her own and soon seems to possess knowledge outside that of her creator. George, however, is more than a pseudonym, and regardless of his "true nature"—whether as part of my consciousness or a spirit, or guide, a "living thought form" on the astral, or anything else, he is a friend too. I still call him a "Ghost named George" because that's now his name, not a definition nor a pseudonym.

Now, for one point: As will be further explained elsewhere and in Chapter 14 in particular, in such *subjective* conversations with a seeming external entity, it is important that you *objectify* the entity as if external to yourself even if you believe (know) it is part of your own consciousness. *Why?* Read the book! Well, really, it reduces the hazard of obsession and ego-inflation which is potential in all psychological and spiritual work.

—*Carl*

MEDITATION
"You are not the Physical Body"

INTRODUCTION

Spirit, and The World of Spirit

Survival After Physical Death

Most people do not really believe in a "world" or dimension of Spirit. While many do believe in something called "Soul" (or Spirit) that survives the death of the physical body and that may go on to a place called "heaven" or, alternatively, to other dimensions that culminates in rebirth (reincarnation), they give little thought to either *Soul* or the *Next World, until—perhaps—when their confrontation with death is imminent.*

Rather than think about it now, at most they leave it all to Fate or Faith with the same blind acceptance of things as they are rather than showing any concern towards acting now to make a Better World for tomorrow and generations to come, or even to assume some responsibility of their own health and well-being.

If you place all responsibility for your life on someone else—whether doctor, lawyer, fireman or chief, or politicians, preachers, guardian angels, or God/Goddess/Creator, etc.—nothing really changes for your soul while your physical body merely gets older.

Of course, *it doesn't have to be that way!*

You can take charge of your own life to the degree that you are willing to learn, and then to act with knowledge and acceptance of responsibility for your actions. You *can* learn more about yourself than any doctor or other person, and you *can* work in active partnership with such a trained person if they are willing to work *with* you rather than as the single authority of "doctor knows best."

Psychic Empowerment & Self-Knowledge

Ultimately we are talking about *Psychic Empowerment*—the very real 'potential' <u>you</u> have to better know you own *body, mind, and spirit* than anyone else no matter what their training or credentials may be. But, it is only 'potential' until you do activate the power and skills involved in *becoming more than you are!* That's what this book and the others in this series of "Personal Empowerment Books" intends to do. We are *not* suggesting that you NOT seek medical (or other professional) advice or help, but we ARE encouraging you to gain self-knowledge and better understand your own self and needs to act intelligently so that you may avoid a future medical (or other) crisis and able to give your care provider (or other advisor) better information to better work with you.

You do have the psychic awareness to know these things, but you have to acknowledge it and learn to use it! And, it is indeed worth it because you then *become more than you* on the road to becoming *all you can be!*

These words and thoughts may seem strange here in a discussion of "Spirit," but we have to try and understand what or who is *Spirit.* If there is a *World of Spirit* then where and what is it? Is "Spirit" the same as "Soul?" Is the "World of Spirit" the same as "Heaven," or is the "After World" something else?"

Let's clarify something right now, here at the beginning of this book on *Communicating with Spirit* and *Psychic Empowerment.* You are not going to get any real answers by merely turning to quotations from the Bible or any other "sacred literature" or the writings of spiritualists, shamen, occultists, religionists, psychologists or parapsychologists, agnostics or atheists, anthropologists or archaeologists, philosophers or historians, or even your present authors—*unless* you relate their words to your self-understanding and integrate their meaning to you with your self-knowledge and purpose in this life.

The Answers come from within

All these resources *can* be helpful, but *real* answers are those in response to your own questions, and that you work hard to understand in relation to your own experience and self-determined interest and research 'filtered' through your mind. You are reading this book because you want to learn and know certain things, find particular answers, and then to do something based on your new knowledge. *Action makes the difference!*

The first thing you must do is to state to yourself what you are seeking. In that regard, we earnestly recommend that you start a journal or notebook that you will use throughout this particular journey, really an adventure. And start by writing down what it is you want to know regarding Spirit and Spirit Communications and what you hope to accomplish.

What, and Who is Spirit?

We do, however, need to define for ourselves the terms we use within a meaningful and unambiguous foundation for our discussion and exploration of Spirit Communication. Of course, we can and should tap into respected and genuinely <u>secular</u> resources to *refine* these definitions in the context of our usage. And, to make this specific and useful, we will add them to the Glossary for this book so that we can constantly reaffirm their meanings as specific to our discussion.

For most people the answer is that a "Spirit" is the person formerly living in a physical body and now living in a non-physical body or "vehicle" in "the Next World" also called the Spirit World. But for Metaphysical* Researchers and an increasing number of psychologists and paranormal scientists, the entity called a "spirit**" in séance and other Spiritualist phenomena is better understood as the "surviving personality" of a deceased person in transition to another dimension, temporarily occupying a vehicle composed of the substance of the currently occupied dimension.

> * The words Metaphysics, Metaphysicians, etc. are increasingly used as alternatives to Occultists, Esotericists, "Seekers," and Spiritualists to avoid typical negative confusions with the prejudicial usage by theologians, preachers, and even scientists who really know little about the subject matter. In addition, Metaphysical has become a common trade term in the book industry for the full range of subjects from alchemy through yoga that all in various ways involve the concepts of Spirit and Spirituality. At this point, we see no need to define "Metaphysics" as your dictionary or the Internet does a good enough job.

It may all seem a bit convoluted and confusing at the moment, but clarity will come with understanding as we further progress in this discussion.

> ** As always, we face a problem of word definitions in non-fiction writing because English, the world's dominant language, often uses and abuses the same word for a range of different meanings. "Spirit" is one of those that has been used both as the vehicle for personality in the so-called "next world" and also as an alternative for personality and soul, and for the inner nature of various things, ideals, and beliefs—often leading to further confusion as, for example, when we speak of "the Spirit of Liberty" we can mean either the ideal of Liberty or an actual deity (Goddess) called Liberty, or we may be referring to our belief in Liberty as a political necessity for advancing human civilization or that our goal is to achieve Liberty from political or sectarian religious domination.

The Surviving Personality and its Astral Vehicle

In other words, we are saying that it is not a "spirit" who manifests through a physical vehicle during what we call life, and it is not a "spirit" who manifests through a "spirit vehicle" but what we will first call a "surviving personality" and then later arrive at an understanding of a higher entity we call "soul" that partially incarnates as a new personality (with memories of its previous personalities) successively occupying new physical-etheric,*** astral-emotional, and mental-causal vehicles before moving on to further advance in non-physical "life," or to reincarnate in the form of a new personality manifesting successively—again—through new physical, astral, mental, and causal vehicles that provide further growth opportunities.

> *** We've compounded (hyphenated) the initial reference to the physical-etheric and other vehicles in the last paragraph because that will be helpful in understanding their primary manner of manifestation. In each of those groupings there are seven "sub-levels" of which each relates to particular energies and substances that uniquely characterize the denizens and functions potential to those levels as active <u>consciousness</u> as specifically focused at those levels to benefit from their unique opportunities and limitations. Reference to the tables in the Glossary will help clarify these concepts.

During what we call "life," the personality functions through all these vehicles (physical-etheric-astral-mental-casual-spiritual) simultaneously but with different levels of awareness and purpose. In this life, the primary focus of consciousness is through the physical *(biological)* vehicle. After death there is movement into the energy aspect of the physical known as the "Etheric Double" from which it quickly moves on to focus through progressive levels of the astral vehicle with degrees of *emotional* awareness, and then to the mental & causal vehicles. It is an astral-mental-causal unity primarily focused through the astral vehicle commonly called "spirit" in the séance and other forms of spirit communication.

We can see now that *Spirit* is used with little specific definition. Our interest is in the surviving personality and two important clarifications are made here:

1. The personality is not the Soul of the person. It is *descended* from the Soul, and eventually returns to the Soul and contributes its *life lessons* to the 'wholeness' that the Soul is becoming.
2. The non-physical body that *ascends* from its former 'home' in the physical body before death and continues on as a 'vehicle' occupied by the personality after death is better known as the "astral vehicle."

In the same sense, the former physical body likewise served as a "vehicle" (or some esoterics prefer the term "envelope"), and the personality will eventually transition from the astral into a mental vehicle, and then into a causal vehicle.

It must be noted that not all Spiritualists and other readers interested in the subject and practice of "Spirit Communication" believe in reincarnation, nor is that belief necessary within the context of this book. While, perhaps a majority of our readers are either "believers" or are open-minded in regard to the general subject of previous lives, it is not the dominant theme of this book and mentions will only be occasional.

Reincarnation & Life's Lessons

It is in the causal vehicle that the experiences of the incarnating personality are abstracted and absorbed as "life's lessons" into the Soul, and joined with lessons from previous lives. That personality we experienced as "Self" dissolves just as the physical body did. Particular memories from previous lives can be recalled through Past Life Regression techniques but with increasing abstraction as time passes and memories fully become lessons. The Soul's knowledge derived from lives' lessons becomes further abstracted to lay the foundations for coming lives' plans.

Even so, the causal vehicle is <u>not</u> itself the soul, but rather a kind of final vehicle.

Spirit Guides, Guardian Angels, Nature Spirits & Elementals, and more

Along with spirits (surviving personalities) of so-called "Dead People," there is a long tradition and history of other entities manifesting through this same non-physical world: spirit guides & teachers, guardian angels & invisible helpers, and special classes of nature spirits & elementals including fairies, gnomes, elves, sprites, and more; angels and ruling spirits of places & forces; higher intelligences variously called archangels, ascended masters, inner plane adepti, and many other names and forms from different cultures and times. There are also astral travelers (living persons projecting out-of-body), consciously and un-consciously created thought-forms, mythic and deific images empowered by ritual and prayer, and a great many more forms and beings including religious entities & powers, gods, goddesses, etc. that we will discuss in due course.

Before going into great detail, we want to step back and firmly establish that the human personality we identify with is neither a product of the physical brain nor a mere biological product of the physical body. Of course physical life has an effect on personality but is always important to distinguish effect from cause. What we call Spirit is just the same personality occupying another body that happens to be non-physical rather than physical. And to avoid confusion *we prefer the word "vehicle" to that of "body" for the obvious reason that we readily perceive a* vehicle *as a temporary conveyance.* The spirit vehicle is itself not the personality of a formerly living person inhabiting a physical vehicle, and the vehicle itself—just as with the previously inhabited physical body—will return to its "native substance" once the occupying personality moves on to its next vehicle in a yet "higher" world. More about that later.

But there is another point to establish as we relate this personality to the body or "vehicle" in which it manifests: *The personality itself is not limited to or defined by the vehicle.* As previously mentioned, the personality has other vehicles to use as it progresses through its "Cosmic Life" following a plan of developmental evolution (not the Darwinian biological evolution but a *continual progressing evolutionary development* of cosmic nature). Within each of its temporary conveyances, it focuses its conscious awareness to the then primary vehicle while there is also a mostly unconscious awareness of its next successive vehicle as well as one derived from ALL its previous vehicles of Past Lives.

Each of these vehicles progresses in *substance* from physical to astral, mental, and causal, and each of these <u>primarily</u> manifests in a world or plane (dimension) made of the same substance as that of the vehicle, and each such world has its own particular laws, rules, and *energy* determining the functionality of the occupied vehicle.

The most important of these rules as they affect the transiting personality and its *work* is that actual *manifestation proceeds from higher to lower.* We can sum it up most simply as *Thought* moves downward from the mental vehicle and world into *Feeling (Emotion)* in the Astral (so-called 'Spirit') vehicle and world, and thence downward into the physical vehicle and world of Action.

From Mind/Thought to Emotion/Feeling to Action/Reaction

Equally important is the realization that while incarnate in the physical vehicle, the personality *also* functions in the astral, mental, and causal vehicles operating together but with the physical predominant. After physical death, the personality becomes primarily focused in the astral vehicle, but is still united with the mental and causal. And, later, it casts off the astral to center in the mental, and finally in the causal. With each level, the opportunities of experience and learning change.

An even greater realization is that you don't have to die to consciously focus, experience, and work in and through the astral, mental and causal vehicles. It is this expansion of consciousness and extension of focused awareness that we call "psychic empowerment." Psychic empowerment comes as you successively *become more than you are* and *all you can be.*

What, and Where, is the World of Spirit?

What some call the "Afterworld" is better understood as the astral world, and it is important to understand that the astral (also referred to as a "plane" or "dimension") is much larger than both the physical/etheric and the mental levels. In using this word "level" we generally mean both the *vehicle* and the *world* of its manifestation. Each level (both as vehicle and world) is unique in substance and energy, and the "laws" of their manifestation. Just as there are physical laws so there are astral, mental and causal laws describing the way things function at those levels.

Within that understanding, most of what we call "spirits" and the "spirit world" occupy only a narrow range of the sub-divisions of the astral world. Because "spirits" are the familiar term for the astral manifestations of the surviving personality of the deceased person, we will continue to use that terminology for the major portion of this book, and carefully distinguish from those discussions involving communication and interaction with other non-physical and specifically astral entities and phenomenon.

Rules of Spirit Communication

Spirit Communication follows certain "rules" and has distinguishing and characteristic phenomenon that differs from clairvoyant vision of nature spirits, elementals, and other more-or-less permanent denizens of the astral world. And there are also differences in forms of communication and interaction with angels, archangels, mythic and religious deities, with Great Teachers and Ascended Masters,* and perhaps yet other greater beings.

> * This word, "master" should not be confused with "ruler." This Master is used in the sense of one who has mastered a subject, skill, or level of being. A Master of Botany is one who has become expert in the subject and now can teach it. An Ascended Master is expert in Life Science to the level of being a teacher or guide.

Of all the other of these entities, perhaps the most important and "useful" to us are those very specific "powers" and "intelligences" contacted through prayer, magick, shamanic and other extensions of consciousness, and that form of invocation also known as "worship" in mostly non-monotheistic religious and spiritual practices. Such "worship" is not posturing before a *graven image* or praying (or begging for help) to a far distant heavenly deity, but a "bringing within" of all the attributes, symbolism, and energies focused into a specific deific image that is alive on the astral level of universal consciousness.

Spirit Communication is more than just conversation with "dead people" who eventually "move on," and definitely more than just interesting psychic phenomena. All interaction with the astral world and with higher worlds is consciousness-expanding and empowering experience. We *grow* not only through learning material facts and rational thinking but through Mind-extending experiences and what we call Psychic Development, Training, and Empowerment. Growth is always a matter of "attainment." We become able to function at higher and greater levels of consciousness, and every "spiritual" and "psychic" experience and skill brings us ever closer to becoming **more than we are** and more **of the whole person** that is our destiny.

The "Spirit World" is real, but *Spirits of the Dead* move on to continue to live in this and higher levels, constantly experiencing and growing. Communications with a particular *surviving personality* change in character over time. The person you knew if life slowly "loses it" and no longer gives you the wise advice you once expected. That surviving personality has moved on leaving behind an astral *shell* that slowly decays in the same way as the physical shell and then etheric shell decays once the living personality moves on.

Communicating with Spirit

We do need to make a distinction between "Spirit Communication" and "Communicating with Spirit." In the first we are communicating with various spiritual entities by various means often involving intermediaries of mediums, guides, channels, and such tools as spirit boards, writing instruments, pendulums, etc. In the second, we are communicating by means of Spirit, that quality or power innate to every person.

Spirit Communication is not just conversation with "dead people" but can *ascend* into communication with "higher" beings known variously as Guides, Teachers, Guardian Angels, Ascended Masters, Inner Plane Adepti, and—perhaps a strange thought at first—your own Higher Self. With each higher level we move from Spirit Communication toward and ultimately only to Communicating with Spirit, i.e. Spirit to Spirit by Spirit.

The "Inner Worlds" are far greater in "size" (an inappropriate measure) than even the whole physical universe. Just as you are learning that you are much more than the "surface" personality you think of as your own self, so can you also learn to communicate with these various selves that make up the whole of your Personality (the Lower Sub-Conscious Self, the Conscious Self and the Higher Superconscious Self).

And, just as you can communicate—for a time—with the spirits of dead people, so can you learn to communicate with these Guides, Teachers, and other Higher Beings.

Humans have been *communicating with spirits* of all kinds for many eons through recorded history and before as known to us through lore and myth.

The communications 'technology' is essentially the same but with minor variations indicated by the nomenclature. Mediumship, Channeling, Astral Travel, Clairvoyance, forms of Meditation, Mysticism, Shamanism, Visions, Invocation, Worship, and others are all forms of Trance and Altered States of Consciousness that we will be discussing in the following chapters of this book.

We do "talk to ourselves" and sometimes hear ourselves talk in sleep or various altered states. Sometimes you may find this "scary," but you can learn to direct the conversation and then benefit from those memories retained in the subconscious mind, and the wisdom and intuition of the superconscious mind, all related interactively with the knowledge and purpose of the conscious mind.

And this is a major point: <u>interaction</u> means a "two-way conversation" in contrast to rote prayers prescribed in most sectarian religions. Spirit Communication is not a religious practice and is, in fact, condemned by much of Christianity and Islam. But Spirit Communication is not wrong, and those that condemn it are only trying to "protect their turf" in asserting a monopoly in which the designated clergy are the only officials "authorized" to communicate with the spiritual world. Unfortunately, they threaten others with irrational superstitions and even dire threats intended to keep their flocks of sheep under control and paying their dues.

You, readers of this book, are free people, not enslaved in spirit any more than the many once enslaved as property. You are free to learn, and in taking this opportunity of learning you are also taking responsibility to learn to communicate well and to protect yourselves from psychic residues left by such malicious intentions and from the psychic residues left by decaying shells in the same way you need to protect yourself from the bacteria of decaying physical forms.

Psychic Self-Defense is simple to learn and practice and most people do it automatically as simply as washing hands. Simply visualizing your protective aura will provide inner strength and a spiritual barrier against these things. A simple form of this is a common practice in most spiritual procedures, and it is included in the following chapters.

Some Answers to Questions

Why is "Spirit" important?

Spirit is itself a dimension of consciousness that we all possess, just as there is physical consciousness, emotional consciousness, mental consciousness, so is there spiritual consciousness.

Physical level consciousness is defined by the perceptions of the five physical senses that can and should trained, further developed, and experienced not only at the physical dimension but at each of the higher dimensions which are perceived as enrichments of the "basic five."

With each higher dimension, other senses become available, including those of movement through time and space, and beyond the apparent limitations of time and space, and of "*Self*" through consciousness itself.

We evolve through the perception of "Self" through all dimensions.

What is the significance of spirit communication today—what's new?

With the Changing of the Ages—from three "animal" signs of Taurus the Bull, (4700 BCE to 2500 BCE), Aries the Ram (2500 BCE to 300 BCE), and Pisces the Fishes (300 BCE to 1900 CE) into the Human sign of Aquarius (1900 CE to 2100 CE)—we are transitioning into a major shift in the nature and experience of consciousness itself.

The Animal period was characterized by objective wars (butting heads) for control of territory and subjective wars (swimming in opposite directions) for control of belief.

The Human period is characterized by extended awareness at both objective and subjective levels (conscious and subconscious) of consciousness.

What does it do for us? What will this book do for the reader?

The Animal period was ruled by Emotion, the Human period is increasingly ruled by the Mind. Instead of feeling, we move to thinking, from irrationality we move to rationality, from religions of mass violence and domination we move toward personal spirituality and psychic development.

With the shift in consciousness toward mentality we move away from the "bigness" of corporate domination, mass production, and the politics of greed and party control toward that "smallness" of high-technology, family proprietorships and personal production, and the politics of responsibility and citizen democracy.

This book returns Spirit to the person, opens the doors to communication at the spiritual levels, and extends perception from the material limitations towards the inclusiveness of higher dimensional awareness.

How does the New Age of Aquarius change Communication?

It's a New Age that is personal and active. Communication of all sorts is direct, concise, and interactive. Communication is inclusive and aware of higher dimensions of consciousness. Our understanding of "Spirits" is no longer limited to "spirits of the dead" but recognizes a vast field of spirit entities and the Human Spirit (not soul) that is part of the subject matter of "Communicating with Spirit." Spirit, and spirits, are everywhere, in all beings and all things.

Spiritual Communication is no longer only a passive state of waiting to hear the spirits speak through a medium or channel, but increasingly an active state of conscious and direct communication with specific spirits and spiritual entities.

Spiritual Communication today, in all its dimensions, is unlike mediumship and so-called prophecy of the past 7,500 years. While intermediaries (mediums and channels) are still used, more and more we move toward direct "Spirit to Spirit" communication involving the *raising of one's level of consciousness to harmonize with that of another entity.*

Communicating with Spirit is a "do it yourself" movement, personal and individual, no longer dependent on groups and institutions for power or authority.

Some Things to Think About Throughout the Book

The following suggestive thoughts and questions and are intended to encourage the development of some degree of overall perspective in your own frames of reference.

TABLE
FIFTEEN TYPES OF "SPIRITS"

1. "Surviving Personality:" That part of consciousness now primarily resident in the astral body after death of the physical body and the disintegration of the etheric double.

2. "Historic Persons:" Entities in the astral world responding to "calls" to the deceased that may be an "astral incarnation/thought form of memories" resident in Universal Consciousness? This might be especially the case of famous people like William James or Abraham Lincoln.

3. "Guides:" Higher evolved souls returning to the astral plane to function as "guides" connecting persons living on the physical plane to the surviving personalities on the astral plane?

4. "Helpers:" Higher evolved souls manifesting as "helpers" in the astral world? What distinguishes a "guide" from a "helper"?

5. Animal Spirits:" Survivals of pets? Of Wild Animals? What about Shamanic "Power Animals" and God and Goddess of the species, Lord and Lady of the herd?

6. "Spirits of Place:" Astral forms of varying complexity and power existing naturally around springs, lakes, rivers, mountains, etc., and that may be further developed by human recognition and worship.

7. "Nature Spirits:" Elementals and other Astral entities that live on the astral plane, that influence non-human life on the physical plane, and that may appear to humans as gnomes, sprites, salamanders, etc.

8. "Angels & Archangels:" Mental and Spiritual entities that originate at higher levels but manifest at the astral level to communicate with physical entities primarily through their astral bodies. Some are attributed as "powers" and "rulers" of cosmic forces and magical functions.

9. "Deities of Place:" Thought forms constructed of astral and mental forces to "rule" a city, state, or nation, and embodying the character and ideals of the inhabitants. They may be purely non-physical as expressed in the "Spirit of America," or they may develop around a physical symbol such as the "Statute of Liberty." Every place—particularly when given form by a structure (such as a church building)—has a "deity" formed out of the collective intention of the designers and builders, the and attention of its users.

10. "Group Mind:" Every human grouping (and even of animals as in herds) of two or more forms a collective intelligence that embodies the team work of the group. It attracts intelligence from spirit above and allows the group to function as one. The Group Mind can be formalized by giving it a name (the ABC Corporation, the ABC Board of Directors, etc.), representing it with a symbol or logo, and energized it by establishing a group "mantra" used to open and close meetings, etc.

11. "Inner Plane Adepti," Ascended Masters," etc. Ascending humans taking on responsibilities to guide ideal human interests from "behind the scenes"—

such as a nation, perhaps the United Nations, perhaps an institution like the Catholic Church, etc. It may not mean that these adepts are themselves guided by the highest ideals rather by their own ideology.

12. "Deities:" Gods & Goddesses, and other deific entities. Are they created and nurtured Mental or Causal level "thought forms" carefully constructed to embody very specific natural forces, human aspirations and needs, spirits of places, etc.?

13. "Higher Self:" The highest level of self-hood corresponding to the Causal Vehicle, and sometimes identified as one's "Holy Guardian Angel."

14. "Soul:" The highest level of individuality that itself does not incarnate, but "send" fragments of itself into incarnation via the Causal Vehicle.

15. "God:" We don't know if there is a "real single creative power" external to the Cosmos or one that is internal and collective of all Life, or none at all—but we can see that the same process involved in creating a Group Mind and a Deity of Place would result in a monotheistic Jehovah or Mother Goddess or Father God of human creation regardless of cosmic reality. It is obvious that the "God" of Biblical scripture and major mythologies is of human origin with human characteristics of jealousy, love, hate, greed, etc. Such a God may be built around a once living person or a mythic person, and given a specific personality by a religion's founders and administrators for the purpose of controlling a people. Once formed, the God becomes greater than its creators.

TABLE

FOUR DEFINITIONS OF "THE SPIRIT REALM"

Other names for the Subtle World that otherwise we consider either as just the Astral Plane, or the Astral, Mental, Causal Planes together—sometimes with others that are "permanent." Each plane is accessible to the human psyche during life and afterlife, but awareness on any level is dependent on maturity, particular technologies, unusual circumstances, etc."

- Where God lives.
- Where we go after death: "Heaven," "Hell," "Purgatory," Paradise," etc. the location of Summerland, etc. (Most esoterics place it in the lower astral world.)
- Where Souls come from.

• Different sub-planes for different levels of entities, different levels of astral substance, and different levels for energy and functions?

TABLE

FOURTEEN BASIC CONSIDERATIONS IN RELATION TO COMMUNICATION WITH SPIRIT (CONSCIOUSNESS)

1. Consciousness is universal—in all things.

2. In some sense, Consciousness and Spirit are the same thing, and both may also be Divinity.

3. Since Consciousness is all things, people, "spiritual entities" "Divinities," etc., how do we communicate with them? Perhaps *Spirit to Spirit?*

4. Each "unit of consciousness" has a unique set of characteristics centered about a core "vibratory state" that—for simplicity—we identify with a NAME, or a WORD for groups of similar entities, units, or things.

5. While all "units" are distinguished by sets of characteristic, those of "higher" entities become more and more complex and require additional efforts to distinguish units of a similar "class" from one another in addition to their NAME. However, those in a "class" share similar characteristics and through these "correspondences" we can find cultural twins.

6. We can "observe" (and study) a "lower" entity by lowering our own vibratory state, or bridging from higher to lower by means of a "tool." That tool, unfortunately, may be very limiting in regard to all the connections that unit has with others in a surrounding "territory."

7. We can "communicate" with a "higher" entity by raising our own vibratory state, or bridging from lower to higher by means of a "tool," but that tool will also be limiting and communications may be distorted or actually "off target."

8. Thus, "tools" may be helpful but sometimes will prove inadequate in transmitting or receiving the desired message consisting of Question and Answer. As a result we may prefer direct communications between the human "seeker" and the higher "source."

9. Changes in the Seeker's vibratory rates have been accomplished by many traditional means:

   a. Shamanic, mostly involving techniques of sensory overload or sensory deprivation all resulting in altered states of consciousness mostly described as "ecstatic." They involve extended and energetic dancing, chanting, singing, or the use of drugs, fasting, sleep deprivation, physical exhaustion, induced body pain through uncomfortable bondage positions, flagellation, cutting, branding, spatial distortions through swinging, partial burial, lost in a wilderness, induced fear though dramatic performances involving mythic places, monsters and devils, etc.

b. Magickal, mostly involving rituals that may be long and hypnotically repetitive, sometimes just being sophisticated adaptations of shamanic techniques.

c. Religion, similar to (b) above but in specific accordance with the particular religion's mythic story, theology, and organizational goals.

Note: in all the above, the missing ingredient not listed is specific focus on the target Source unit, and the question being asked.

10. Involvement of a "professional" facilitating entity such as an entranced "Medium" or non-entranced "Channel" (also known as a priest or guide) between Seeker and Source. But, the Medium may be as limiting and distorting (lacking in pertinent knowledge) and the Channel likewise (having a private agenda or fixed perspective) as any other tool. An alternative form of "medium" is the entranced shaman who herself becomes an alternative consciousness or "changeling"—the revered power animal such as a bear, horse, wolf, eagle, serpent, etc.

Sometimes the "changeling" returns to human form with the desired messages, other times a human translator interprets the changeling's animal noises into intelligible messages. In most cases, that interpreter is either the shaman's mate or a director of operations.

An interesting variant of this is that in the "New Sexuality," where role-players (mostly women) adopt many of the shamanic techniques of ecstatic trance induction while dressing and acting as horses or ponies, dogs or puppies, birds, etc., and becoming the spirit or even a deity of the animal.

11. Direct communication between Seeker and Source without traditional methods of consciousness change or trance. For convenience we are adopting the term "Conscious Channel" for this. How does the Seeker raise her consciousness to the level either matching or in harmony with that of the Source?

a. Meditation (often including yogic postures), generally involving established use of names, symbols and images identifying the targeted Source. The meditation procedure sometimes includes visualized movement (as in Kabbalistic path-working). It is often accompanied by—

b. Mantras, i.e. established sound patterns associated with the Source, or the related level of consciousness. Mantras can be used by themselves or combined with other methods, and may be directly uttered by a solitary person or a group, or used in a recording.

c. Prayer, generally combining elements of both (a) and (b) above.

d. Ritual *evocation* of the Source by which the Seeker brings the Source into her conscious presence.

e. Ritual *invocation* of the Source in which the Seeker brings the Source temporarily within her personal consciousness.

Note: The missing ingredient is active focus on the question being asked.

12. Hypnosis and Self-Hypnosis as programs and procedures combining some elements from the lists in (11) above, but always including the question or a limited related series of questions asked of the targeted Source.

a. The obvious advantage of Self-Hypnosis is the simplicity and "purity" of the method, and the heightened ability to focus consciousness on both the Source and the Question. At the same time, it can, and probably should be combined with several of the listed elements above to "secure" the target Source without ambiguity.

13. The "Granddaddy" question: *If all is Consciousness, then are units of consciousness all within the "Universal Consciousness" and perhaps all efforts at communication with specific units or entities only reach those "memories" of the individuals stored within the Universal Consciousness?* Perhaps there never is contact with the "spirit" (surviving personality) of President Abraham Lincoln but only with "Akashic Record" of *Lincoln, President Abraham.*

14. If No. 13 is true, then perhaps we need to refine our methods of communication to focus at that "Akashic" level? We want to make CONTACT with the higher levels, however they may exist.

Our main purpose in listing these "matters for discussion throughout the book" is to encourage active *inner discussion* as you read. Think and Ask, Ask and Think. Probe the Answers. No matter the facts involved the real need is for you to make the thoughts your own. The "facts of the case" are only the starting points of discussion and discovery. We don't learn through *memorization* but by our usage, interpretation, development, and exploration.

We are discussing "Communication" and all communication involves two entities. As a reader, a student, a user, you are both entities—a researcher seeking answers to put to use and experiment. Every experiment lays the foundation for more research and further experiment. That's how we learn.

MEDITATION
"What, and Who, is Spirit?"

1

THE NATURE OF THE
SPIRIT REALM & THE NATURE OF
SPIRITUAL COMMUNICATIONS

The Reality of the Spirit World

We inhabit a Physical Universe* that our five physical senses experience as a solid measured by three dimensions of space plus a fourth of time. And, yes, there is a fifth dimension, and some physicists are of the belief that there may be a total of eleven dimensions as well as parallel universes to our own. We, the residents of planet Earth (also called *Gaia*), are not alone! Spirit, Life, Intelligence is everywhere, and *we can communicate with other beings at spiritual levels beyond the confines of physical space.*

> * In this usage, we are also referring to the esoteric concept of the physical or material "plane," also called a "world" or "level." Most esoteric writers chart a Cosmos of eight dimensions within seven planes of manifestation, plus three more planes beyond manifestation that guide the process, and three more above and outside of manifestation from which it is sourced. A pretty complex system, but we don't need to get into that except to make it clear that **the Cosmos is far more complex and infinitely larger than what we ordinarily see and think.** This is important to our discussion of Communications with all Spiritual Entities, to all forms of Psychic Development, to all aspects of Spiritual Growth and Attainment. Realize that the entire Cosmos opens to you—you don't need to go through any intermediary of teacher, priest, bishop or secret chief, but you should do the developmental work for yourself. That's how you grow and become more than you are towards the fulfillment of each lifetime's purpose. See tables in the Glossary.

The physical universe is characterized by *physical* Space, in which experience Matter and Energy through the *motion (vibration)* of the sub-atomic particles of our physical environment and of our physical bodies while we are *alive.* We also know that physical objects, including our own bodies, are mostly empty space despite the appearance and feel of solidity. "Superficial" appearances are often deceptive relative to the purpose and nature of our observation.

The truth may be that such "emptiness" is Spirit itself, and offers the opportunity to focus consciousness to induce healing and magickal changes in the physical manifestations.

Time—the 4th Dimension

Unlike those physical spatial dimensions you can see and feel, in which you can move from a current position up or down, forward or backward, to one side or another, you can't *touch* or *see* time, and you can only measure it's movement as a seeming forever forward passage from past through present to the future. You experience the past only through memory (personal or recorded, as in books), and you can only *think* (or imagine) the future and maybe mark an anticipated future moment on your calendar.

And that something is unique: you can plan the future, hence to varying degrees you help shape the future. But there is also the possibility that the Future helps shape us. Think about the for a moment: if you have a plan of action for the future and then act upon, each step forward in that plan already exists and takes on solidity as the plan each step is completed.

Humans Shape Reality

Just as we shape (and thus change) the Future (Time) through our plans and acts, so do we shape the three dimensions of Space. We construct buildings and the cities with which we work, live and play. We construct roads and highway, and canals and ports to connect our cities. We re-construct the land from forest and prairie into farms and ranches to feed our populations. We change the environment through deforestation, adding chemicals to the soil and the aquifers beneath and the rivers running through the land. And we affect the air with pollutants. But not only did we affect Space, but the changes we made *externally* affect us *internally* not just physically but in the Body but also in Mind and Spirit. There is constant <u>interaction</u> between Time and Space, and Human Spirit.

The Astral World

The fourth dimension of time is a function of the non-physical Astral World which is characterized by time and *emotional substance* and *energies.** We refer to time as a dimension separate from the physical, but we also *feel* and *recognize* the passage of time as a measure of physical phenomena. In other words: separate dimensions but with <u>interaction </u>between the two worlds or planes.

* Do make note of the repeated occurrence of Trinities—in the movements within each dimension, and the characteristics of each plane or world. Trinities (the recurrence of groups of three) and Septets (groups of seven) are so prevalent in descriptions of the Cosmos that you should look for their occurrence. See the two tables appended to the Introduction of our book Clairvoyance for Psychic Empowerment, Slate & Weschcke, 2013 for a detailed understanding of this complex structure.

The Mental World, and the Power of Interaction

How do we know that? We "think," *therefor it is*. The fifth dimension of thought is a function of the non-physical Mental Realm characterized by thought and *mental substance* and *energies*. Again, we have separate dimensions that we—through conscious and unconscious awareness—experience in their interactions between all three levels.

The sixth dimension is experienced as unlimited love; a seventh dimension is experienced through intuition and the eighth as union with the Divine beyond which individuality ceases. All these higher dimensions interact with the lower ones, and as we grow in knowledge and power that *action becomes conscious, causal,* and *transformative.*

Do observe that in all these dimensions (or worlds) human action occurs, and as we grow in maturity that action becomes more and more "consciously" experienced, and undertaken. The human function is to be interactive in all levels of the Cosmos.

What, then, is the Nature of the Spirit World?

One answer is that it is "not this, not that" meaning that it is not a place but is everywhere and that Spirit is the universal "Divinity" that is everywhere and in everything and everyone, and can be experienced both or either as "personal"* or as a "force." In other words: we are saying that the non-physical/spiritual reality—lying behind physical reality with the potential to re-shape physical phenomena—can be experienced in various ways as *determined by choices we make and actions* (interactions) we take.

* "Personal" deities are anthropomorphic because they are "formed in man's image." It's the nature of human consciousness to anthropomorphize to one degree or another most of our experiences of a psychological or psychic nature. In pre-history, most deities were feminine—in the form of the Great Mother Goddess and many other goddesses. At approximately 5000 BCE, goddesses were beginning to be replaced by gods as the solar-based hunter-herder-warrior cultures supplanted the earlier lunar-based agricultural cultures. With that change, the personal and community based magickal relationship with Spirit and Deity became replaced by the institutional and hierarchical male dominated myths and religions. The older personal contact and communication with Spirit and Deity was supplanted by the new role of male priests as the only "lawful" communicants with deity.

As already discussed, there are many levels and forms of spirit entities, but at the ultimate level of religious experience, we may perceive Spirit either as a single person-deity or as multiple person*-deities, or characterize the ultimate source of all reality only through impersonal abstract symbolism.

> * We are trying to make distinctions on how deities are "seen." Mostly we think of the creative sources of reality in a human-like form rather than as a pure force described symbolically or mathematically. To appreciate these distinctions, recall your lessons in mythology where most deities appear as gods and goddesses, named and costumed in certain ways to symbolize their nature as gods of thunder, the sea, war, wisdom, lust, or as goddesses of love, crafts, agriculture, child-birth, healing, and so on. In some cultures, the goddesses in particular manifest in hundreds of carefully crafted forms distinctly varied by color of skin and of costumes, ornaments and the jewels, metals and shapes of their construction and where they are worn on the body, postures and gestures, names, associated mantras, powers, locales, their companions, and more. Both gods and goddesses are sometimes given other attributes drawn from the non-human 'kingdoms' of animals' heads, horns and hooves; birds' heads, wings, feathers and claws; fish tails; and even insect shapes. All these distinctions are meaningful and are related in worship and meditation, or used in prayer or magical acts to manifest the particularized powers to meet human needs and desires.
>
> In addition, some cultures do not humanize the creative powers, but see them only as abstract symbols such as the most familiar Yin and Yang, but also in particular symbols directly associated with a single deity, such as the Christian Cross, the Jewish Star of David, the Egyptian Ankh, the Radiant Sun, the Crescent Moon, Thor's Hammer, and others. Even mathematical formulae have taken on a near or actual religious-like significance as in the case of Einstein's famous $E=mc^2$ symbolizing our entry into the "Atomic Age."

Conscious Choices

The choices you make in this regard are powerful determinants of how you live your life. We can't influence your decision in this regard, but suggest you give it the careful thought (making a conscious choice) that is not usually given in our parental and cultural environment where religion is commonly a "given."

In addition, along with conscious choice there are differences in how you can relate to and experience, and *communicate*, with all Spirits and Deities.

The most important realization is that *all perception can become a matter of personal choice*, and our experience of reality is either unconscious and passive or conscious and active. With personal development and empowerment individuals can increasingly shape their relationship to the environment, and when enough individuals awaken to this realization, the sphere of control enlarges.

With Power Comes Responsibility

With power comes responsibility to restore and then live in harmony with the natural environment in all levels, or to accept the current corruptive domination and abuse of Nature and Her resources for short-term profit and engineered deceit concerning the long-term destruction of the soil, the water, the air, currents of energy, and the spirit of the planet.

As we become empowered at the level of Spirit, we will see more clearly instead of through a "glass darkly" as has been the result of the last several thousand years of <u>man</u> dominated politicalized and institutionalized religions controlling thought and feeling. From the level of Spirit—as we raise our consciousness—we will perceive more clearly, communicate at a higher level, and with greater effect. The future is not hopeless, and with the coming of the New Age characterized by the message of Aquarius, the poles of thought will shift and we will undo the damage wrought by "Man's dominion over the fish of the sea, over the birds of the air, and over every living thing that moves on the earth . . ." and of Man's false rule over Woman.

The New Age *replaces hierarchy with equality,* restores man and woman as partners, values knowledge over authority, and disclaims sexuality from being sinful and evil to being a source of joy and union with the Divine in all there is.

The Nature of Spiritual Communication

That's the subject of this book, and we will only touch on it for a moment, and then come back to it in a few paragraphs. Note: we wrote that "the non-physical/spiritual reality—lying behind physical reality with the potential to re-shape physical phenomena—can be <u>experienced</u> in various ways." And then "there are many levels and forms of spirit entities, but at the ultimate level of religious experience, we may perceive Spirit either as a single person-deity or as multiple person-deities, or characterize the ultimate source of all reality through abstract symbolism."

And we followed that with "The choices you make in this regard are powerful determinants of how you live your life."

That word, "experienced," is <u>passive</u>. It can be made active in the sense that one can *seek* out experiences—like going on a safari into the Amazonian jungle or taking a ride on a roller coaster—but even though every experience offers opportunities for some kind of action (from slapping mosquitoes to climbing down off a stalled roller car) one essentially just wants to enjoy the overall experience. If you buy a ticket on an expensive cruise ship, you don't expect to have to row a boat to shore.

Real Communication is Action-based between Two Entities

"Spiritual Communication" calls for an <u>active</u> relationship with a spiritual entity, not a passive experience. To make the choice on how you are going to relate to non-physical reality, please take note of what this means. In essence, in the modern world, the non-physical is often seen as a *religious choice*. For most people, religion defines their experience of non-physical reality and whether it is a passive or an active relationship with Spirit.

Before discussing the nature or those religious choices, we are going to make a definitive, un-provable, statement that may be controversial and disturbing: ***"Magick is communication with Spirits, and is the oldest and truest form of religion!"*** Elsewhere, we will write that **Shamanism is the source of all religions**. A seeming contradiction that is resolved only as we discuss "attitude" in religions. Magick is the active creation of spiritual experience to influence physical reality; **Shamanism is the active seeking of Spiritual Knowledge** that may include influence of physical reality.

Earlier, we wrote that "Spirit is the universal Divinity in everything and everyone, and can be experienced both or either as "person" or "force." We also remarked that physical objects, including our own bodies, are mostly empty space, and "maybe that such "emptiness" offers the opportunity to focus consciousness for healing and magickal changes." *Spirit is in everything and everyone, including—or especially—in that empty space.*

We also wrote: "there are many levels and forms of spirit entities, but at the ultimate level of religious experience, we may perceive Spirit either in the form of a single person-deity or as forms of multiple person-deities, or characterize the ultimate source of all reality through abstract symbolism."

All of this rather abstract discussion provides the background for a more down-to-earth discussion of Spirits in relation to human action.

Spirits are Consciousness, just as We are

"Nature abhors a vacuum" is an old adage. A modification would be that "Empty Space invites <u>active</u> Consciousness. " *Thought and Feeling, guided by Will, create Forms and Energizes them.* Whether these forms are created consciously or unconsciously, they exist, and the more attention, and <u>intention,</u> is focused on them, the more Life and Power they have.

There are, then, perhaps, three kinds of *Spirits:*

1. Bodies of consciousness created by the Soul to progressively incarnate into a series of vehicles, such as now occupied by you and me, and all living people. And then at death, these include the traditional spirits of the surviving personalities of people and—in a different fashion—animals.

2. Units of consciousness created as functioning parts of the Cosmos out of the substance and energies of each cosmic plane, such as the Sun, Moon, and Planets for the physical plane; such as Elementals and Nature Spirits and others for the astral plane; such as Thought Forms and Magickal Constructs for the mental plane; and Angels and Archangels for the Causal Plane. But, notice—contrary to materialist beliefs—we are stating the stars, their satellites, and the planets all are active forms of consciousness, and are all spiritual entities.

3. Forms of consciousness created through the human imagination, drawing substance and energies from all four of the lower planes, in varying degrees dependent on unconscious to conscious to intentional responses to initial stimulus and opportunity.

   a. In this third category we include unconscious projections via the imagination of thought forms created in response to natural stimulus—such as the energies surrounding a natural spring inhabited by water sprites and other elementals. The human response might picture a feminine deity (water being a feminine element) who then acts to further draw energies to herself to protect the spring from harm, and to create an atmosphere of love and nurture beneficial to all who come to the spring.

   b. A second form as humans respond to natural forces and earth currents (ley lines) that instinctively trigger thoughts and images of snakes and dragons. With repetition, and recognition of their importance as guides to planting and other activities, the images take on life and consciousness, and become objects of worship or magickal interaction.

   c. A third form of unconscious projection comes in response to strong and repeated emotions such as love, lust, hate, fear which take on person-like images of goddesses and gods. Here we have not only the opportunity for worship but for magick—defense again objects and causes of hate and fear, invocation for the goddesses of love and lust. With more conscious attention focused on these deities, they become multiple and specific, and are presented in detailed symbolism to represent all the variation of their manifestation.

d. A fourth form comes with conscious projection developed from knowledge of magickal principles where abstract symbols become charged with energies of attraction and repulsion. Gods and Goddesses of the household, of the city and the nation, sometimes projected on to the memories of heroes and great leaders. Many of the Christian and Buddhist saints are so charged with energies that they too function as spirits. Sometimes, animals are the matrix for projection of consciousness and psychic energies—in particular the horse, the cow, the goat, the dolphin, the cat and the dog—because of their special role between Man and Nature.

Estimated Number of Planets: 1,000,000,000,000,000,000,000,000.

Ultimately, there are a lot of spirits wherever we look, for Spirit is in all things and in all places. Start with the current estimate as to the number of stars in the physical universe: 1 septillion! That's "1" followed by seven sets of three zeros each, or 1,000,000,000,000,000,000,000,000. Now add the estimate of the number of planets 1,000,000,000,000,000,000,000,000. And think how each is itself a spiritual being and home to other spiritual beings. Don't think that we are alone in the universe! And doubt very much that our planet Earth is totally unique within a totally unique Solar System just dedicated to human beings. And certainly you should question any notion that *our* God is only concerned with earth humans, and most especially any notion that only "true believers" in this one god can go to "heaven." *How many "one Gods" are there?* Consider the following:

Monotheism, the belief in a single and almost universally *male* God represented in 59 different religions (plus an unknown number of sects)—is the choice of more than half the world's population today. Each claims "one God" but with 59 or more variations and differing identifications of angels, saints, and also "devils."

When the choice is among the polytheistic religions of Hinduism, Sikhism, African Spiritist, various Pagan revivals, Buddhism, Jainism, Taoism, Shinto, Voudoun, Santeria, Candomble, Genism, Asatru, Wicca, and many more—including, by some definitions, both Mormonism and Catholicism (worshiping Father, Son and Holy Spirit) each with of plurality person-deities, there remains a further distinction of religious acceptance of multiple deities (or place or natural forces) or the "magickal" use of deities, mostly feminine, who are dressed, colored, adorned, and named to represent distinctive and very specific natural forces in <u>interaction</u> with the individual person down to the physical level. Magick, in this respect, is a very advanced technology involving the four lower planes with primary emphasis on the Astral. Even in the three major monotheistic religions in their dominant sects you will find most of these same person-deities represented as guides, saints, elementals, nature spirits, angels, archangels, and many others to whom you can speak, pray, worship through evocation or invocation, "call down" in magickal operations, and other forms of communication.

Other Kinds of "Spirits"

For thousands of years up through modern times and modern psychic researchers, there has been all sorts of phenomena attributed to "spirits" that mostly fall outside of the classifications above and mostly outside our interest in communication. They include haunting that are probably not really "surviving personalities" of the deceased but rather some kind of psychic residue and typical poltergeist phenomena that seems associated with loose psychic energies projecting from young people going through puberty and the extreme emotionality of adolescence.

Others probably include the sounds of footsteps, the slamming of doors, the creak of floors, animal sounds where there are no animals, occasional spoken words and names, sights out of the corners of eyes, even kisses and other caresses sometimes experienced during the state between waking and sleep, haphazard noises from empty rooms—(especially from basements and attics), and other anonymous events.

It is unlikely these are associated with real spirit entities, but they probably do emanate from the lower astral plane that is included in the "Spiritual Realm." They are best ignored, and any efforts to communicate with them, exorcise or otherwise treat them seriously—even if they seem a "bother" or even a "danger"- will often tend to "feed" them. If they are too extensive, the best course of action is to build your own psychic shield against them. (See resources at end of chapter for books on psychic defense.)

All these entities exist in the "Spirit Realm" which is also understood as specific sub-planes of the Astral. And, we should look at this complex spiritual world mindful of the words of that great occultist, Dion Fortune: "All gods are one god, and all goddesses are one goddess, and there is one initiator," and perceive an utter simplicity in the direct relationship between person and Spirit. (*The Sea Priestess*, 1957, Aquarian Press, London)

The Nature of Spirituality

While we talk of Spirit as a thing, and describe some people as more Spiritual than others; and we talk of the "Spirit of" Liberty, and of America or of some other ideal to which we aspire, we basically mean that spirit is the "essence" of a person, of life itself, as the highest emotion and thought we can conceive of.

In the most common sense of the words, Spirit and Spirituality, we are speaking of the "inner essence" of the thing, the person, the force, the ideal, the power, and all the ways we interpret and relate to the worlds (plural) about us. To see and relate to that inner essence, we have to do so from our own inner essence. And when the communicant is of a higher nature, we have to raise our own "vibes" to match or at least *harmonize* with the higher source.

While not a direct comparison, realize that if you want to *communicate* with the President of the United States (not just with a one-sided post card or a yelled hello in a crowd), you have to raise your own position—not spiritually in this example but politically.

In some sense or another, you have reach a point of approximate equality. (In the example of the Presidency, even as a citizen who *votes*, everyone knows that a single vote can be decisive, hence you are in a position of equality.)

Spirituality represents the "process" of Becoming

Yes, in this book, our initial reference to "spirit" has been to that inner essence of a person that survives death of the physical body, i.e. the surviving personality. In that same context, we refer to the Astral Plane as the Spirit World in which the surviving personality occupies an astral vehicle in place of the previous physical body. We have also indicated that the surviving personality eventually moves on from the astral vehicle just as it did the physical one. Before again incarnating in a physical body, the surviving essence of the person once occupying a physical body moves to a Mental Vehicle and then one most commonly called the Causal Vehicle where it unites with the Soul. It is the Soul that again sends part of the essence into a new incarnation, descending through each of the described worlds to form in succession a new causal vehicle, a new mental, a new astral, and a new etheric matrix which forms a new physical body.

Do note, that in these lower planes, from Causal down to Physical, that spiritual essence always needs a vehicle to function, and then is primarily but not entirely limited by the nature (substance, energy, and laws) of that level of manifestation. You become effective at the particular level involved by mastering your vehicle and learning the technologies developed in relation to the "scientific laws" of that plane. In familiar terms, we all need to learn the "three R's" of *Reading, 'Riting,* and *'Rithmetic*;" to speak one or more dominant languages; master resources of information; the functions of the physical body; etc. As you later learn to "Rise on the Planes" similar mastery of the laws of each is part of your agenda.

The "incarnating personality" appears in a series of egg-like forms surrounding the eventual physical body. It is these egg shapes that are the "aura" seen in clairvoyant vision.

The "new" incarnating personality is not the Soul itself but a "vehicle of potentials," like a new "file folder" on your computer to which you will add the files containing the many experience of the new lifetime. At the same, the main file folder does include certain essential memories of previous lives and it is these memories that call for new lessons to fulfill the potential of the whole person each of us is destined to become.

1. The Lower Unconscious
   (or the Subconscious)

2. The Middle Unconscious

3. The Higher Unconscious
   (or the Superconscious)

4. The Field of Consciousness

5. The Conscious Self, or "I"

6. The Higher Self (or the Soul)

7. The Collective Unconscious

8. The Etheric Double

9. The Astral,
   or Emotional, Body

10. The Mental Body

11. The Casual Body

12. Other non-physical bodies

13. Field of Universal
    Consciousness

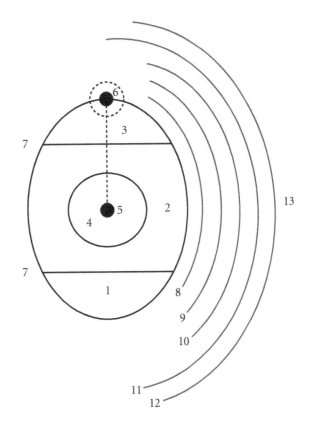

Spirituality is not avoidance but is <u>Developmental</u>

In learning the laws of each plane of manifestation, it is important to understand that—contrary to some misguided puritanical religious ranting—Spirituality is not the avoidance of life or love or sex or hard work; rather, it is their fulfillment through personal growth and responsible action of adding spirit to all we do. It is a *developmental process* we also call the evolution of the individual person and hence of all of humanity. It is not the Darwinian evolution described as "survival of the fittest," but is growth in fulfillment of the potential outlined in the individual matrix or plan that the Soul has prescribed for this incarnation.

What we call "psychic empowerment" comes from *involvement,* and that is largely based on "communication" with other spiritual beings, *and* learning to communicate with your own Higher Self to draw upon past life memories and the core experiences and essential wisdom in your subconscious mind and the Universal Consciousness, or it may involve communication with surviving personalities in service to their growth or as a help to your own, or it may involve communication with Angelic beings, spirit guides, and even with those beings identified as gods, goddesses, nature spirits and others.

True Communication always involves <u>Two Parties</u>

Communication always should involve an intelligent and purposeful choice of communicants and only rarely a general call to anyone who is listening. Think of it as similar to using a search engine on the World Wide Web: the more specific your call is the higher quality will be the response.

While it is common for "beginners" to use a simple method, like *Table Tipping,* and ask "Is anyone there?" you want to get beyond that quickly and develop your communication skills. You don't want an "open mic" or old-fashioned "party line" country telephone where anyone could and would listen in to your conversations as a form of entertainment before there was radio or television. Likewise, you don't want anyone or everyone to access your e-mail or your identity. Privacy is important to affirm its specificity and meaningfulness for you and the credibility of your communicant.

At the same time, true communication involves two-way traffic whether you may be communicating with the "spirit" of a recently deceased relative or with your "guardian angel." To assure understanding, ask questions, clarify the message, rephrase both question and answer. In communication "between two worlds," **trust but verify.** Know who you are speaking with. Primarily we do this by "directing our call" through a choice of known "correspondences" developed over thousands of years, and recorded in various compatible systems of which the most comprehensive and specific are those of the Kabbalah, Tantra, and Taoism, along with any that may be more specific to your own culture, such as Santeria, Wicca, or the catalog of Catholic Saints as described on their "Holy Cards."

Methodologies:

In future chapters, we will give guidance to interaction with Spirits through unconscious paranormal phenomena as with poltergeists, hauntings, rappings, etc.; the practices of mediumship and channeling; communication with saints, guides, teachers; the magickal practices of invocation and evocation; touch on the various shamanic techniques; meditation and prayer; clairvoyance and astral projection, intuition; ecstatic union; and other forms of interaction.

These methods break down into three models:

1. The use of a "tool" as an intermediary between the "caller" on this side and the "recipient" on the other side. Like a telephone, an Ouija Board, or a crystal ball, pendulum, or even e-mail on your computer or tablet, is essentially "blind" and the recipient on the other side might not be the entity you are calling, and could even be your own higher or lower self.

2. The use of a human intermediary, such as a medium or channel to call the recipient on other side or to receive calls initiated by entities from the other side. These entities range from surviving personalities to guides, teachers, or advanced intelligences. You can test the identity of the surviving personality with questions, and you may be able to test those entities claimed to be higher intelligences, but you may have "to take their word for it."

3. Direct contact by means of astral projection or clairvoyance or similar means where you are essentially raising your consciousness (your rate of vibration) to match or harmonize with that of the other entity. You can't really communicate unless you are on the same "wavelength." Many of these techniques originated in ancient shamanism as astral travel and in pre-religious Tantra as worship and invocation of the Goddess.

No matter the methodology of communication we use, it is important to remember that spirituality is not in the facilitating tool or intermediary but within us and in everything. It's a matter of perspective: *Look and ye will see!* All limitations are in the viewer, once you begin to open the doors of your own perception your understanding (a function of consciousness) will expand to see the spiritual nature alongside the material view.

The Power and Wisdom of Spirituality

Spirituality is more than theory—it is the combination of power and wisdom as a collective, creative force that energizes and sustains all that exists, from the lowliest forms of life to the most advance. The illimitable force of spirituality energizes even the material manifestations of creative power, from a grain of sand to the immeasurable multiverse. (See *Connecting to the Power of Nature* by Joe H. Slate, 2009, Llewellyn).

Understanding the power and wisdom of spirituality must begin with a consideration of the nature of physical reality, but it cannot stop there. It must include the nature of human existence to include its cognitive, emotional, sensory, and behavioral components. At a more comprehensive level, understanding spirituality must include a consideration of the complex factors that energize and sustain both physical and non-physical realities. Within that broad scope, spirituality becomes a dynamic force rather than a fixed set of concepts, observations, and theories. It emerges as a force that functions independently of time, space, and any other imposed constriction.

At a personal level, spirituality is the essence of our existence as evolving beings. It sustains our personal identity we call our *spiritual genotype*. With its countless components, spirituality functions as a source of both enlightenment and power. Like our personal existence, it is infinite and bi-directional in nature—it has neither beginning nor end, a concept we call *bi-directional endlessness*. Whether experienced directly or indirectly, collectively or singularly, spirituality is the triangulating force that defines and gives substance to the totality of our existence as mind, body, and spirit.

Destiny for Greatness

If devoid of spirituality, our existence would become merely "a vapor that appeareth for a little while and then vanisheth away." But given the power and the wisdom of spirituality, we become evolving beings whose destiny is greatness. Spirituality, however, calls for action. Passive acceptance is not decision making. We cannot succeed at something we are unwilling to attempt. The best predictor of success at any task is a willingness to try, and if necessary, to try again and again. A decisive commitment to change thus becomes the centerpiece of spirituality as a source of personal power and wisdom.

Spirituality as a power and wisdom force is persistently positive in nature. It can assert itself both volitionally and spontaneously for the attainment of some positive end. It can open totally new doorways to accelerated growth and increased understanding. It can reveal new sources of knowledge from both within the self and other dimensions. It can blend personal commitment with success. Through spirituality, vast realms of advanced knowledge and growth potential become within the reach of everyone.

Spirituality as power and wisdom exists in many forms. As a multi-purposeful, energizing phenomenon, it is the central core of our personal being without which we would not exist in the first place. It is the essence of all life. Beyond that, it is the power that sustains physical reality, including both substance and motion. It exists in perpetuity and extends to infinity.

Spirituality as Cosmic Power and Wisdom

The power and wisdom of spirituality can be seen clearly through the prism of cosmic structure and action. Rather than merely a component of the cosmos, spirituality is the essential, energizing force that underlies and sustains it. The design and functions of the multiverse from its smallest particle to its endless spatial reaches are clear manifestations of the power and wisdom of spirituality.

Spirituality as cosmic wisdom and power is infinite in its scope and functions. It sustains not only the multiverse, but our personal existence as endless beings. At a practical level, spirituality as cosmic power can banish all existing growth limitation and replace them new possibilities. Through spirituality as cosmic power, we can expand our awareness by reaching into our distant past and retrieving knowledge relevant to present life situations. We can uncover past achievements and use them to facilitate our present growth. We can probe the future, and discover knowledge relevant to present strivings. We thus become empowered with a more comprehensive picture that embraces the totality of our existence—past, present, and future.

Aside from its relevance to our personal empowerment, spirituality as cosmic power and wisdom can equip us with the knowledge and resources required to bring forth important global change. Hunger, disease, social injustice, and environmental pollution, to list but a few, are all receptive to the power and wisdom of spirituality at a global scale. *Among our greatest challenges is to promote positive global change through a firm commitment and responsible application of the wisdom and power of spirituality.*

Higher Dimensions of Power

Through the power and wisdom of spirituality, the higher realms and planes of power are readily available as sources of enlightenment, inspiration, and success. At last, you can now master ways of accessing those dimensions and using their resources. Here are a few examples of the empowering possibilities now available to through personally interacting with higher dimensions of spirituality:

1. You can discover spiritual growth specialists and personal guides with power to guide your growth and promote success in achieving your personal goals.

2. You can interact with spiritual planes of power and apply their resources to activate your dormant growth potentials and in some instances, introduce totally new growth possibilities.

3. You can extinguish growth blockages, awaken dormant potentials, and accelerate success in achieving your highest goals.

4. You can build self-confidence, increase security feelings, break disempowering habits, and resolve conflicts that slow our growth.

5. You can view your personal archival records and apply them to promote your growth and achieve your personal goals.

6. Rejuvenation, longevity, health and fitness are all within the scope of interacting within the power of higher dimensions of spirituality.

7. From a global perspective, you can bring forth important global change and help make the world a better place for all.

We are all on the same journey, and as more people awaken to their own spirituality the more will spiritual vision be the primary determinant of personal and collective action. And with that comes recognition of the unity of all with all and the divisions that separate one from another, of humanity from nature, of physical from spiritual, and of planet Earth from multiverse will pass as the restrictive vision of the Piscean Age is replaced by higher open vision of the New Age symbolized in Aquarius.

Some Things to Think About

As we did at the end of the Introduction, we'd like to leave you with things to think about as you read this book. In this case, we are borrowing the following from Fred Alan Wolf, former profess of physics at San Diego State University and author of award-winning books including *Taking the Quantum Leap* and *Star Wave*, which is the source of these paraphrased points:

- The Future is more important than the past in deciding the present.
- The past already exists while the Future is continually being created.
- Time, as we presently understand it, is an illusion
- Evolution is a consequence of the Future and not of the past.
- Quantum physics provides a basis for a new religion, and an understanding of the human spirit.

MEDITATION
"The Nature of the Spirit World"

Sources for this chapter:

Fortune, D.: *The Sea Priestess*, 1957, Aquarian Press, London

Stead, W.T.: *The Blue Island—Experiences of a New Arrival Beyond the Veil, recorded by Estelle Stead & Pardoe Woodman*, 1922, Hutchinson & Co., London

Resources—Books on Psychic Defense:

Denning & Phillips: *Practical Guide to Psychic Self-Defense—Strengthen Your Aura*, 2002, Llewellyn

Penczak, C.: *A Witch's Shield, Protection Magick and Psychic Self-Defense*, 2004, Llewellyn

Slate, J.H.: *Connecting to the Power of Nature*, 2009, Llewellyn

Slate, J.H.: *Psychic Vampires—Protection from Energy Predators and Parasites*, 2002, Llewellyn

Webster, R.: *Psychic Protection for Beginners—Creating a Safe Haven for Home and Family*, 2010, Llewellyn

Resources—Books on Quantum Physics

Wolf, Fred Alan: *Star Wave—Mind, Consciousness and Quantum Physics*, 1984, Macmillan

2

INTERACTIONS BETWEEN
THE SPIRITUAL & THE PHYSICAL

Spirit & Consciousness are everywhere

There is no thing, no place, no person, animal, bird or fish where there is absence of consciousness and spirit. They are like two sides of the same coin, two ends of the same stick, and two points of view—but *they are not opposites,* and where one is present and dominant the other is present but in a different manner. At the same time, they are as different as night and day, negative and positive, and male and female but each is always inclusive of the other just as day slumbers through the night and night through the day.

In our now regressive materialist-dominant culture, everything has been seen in mostly "either/or" terms of opposites: black or white, good or evil, us or them, rich or poor, smart or dumb, honest or dishonest, Republican or Democrat, one political ideology against another, this religion against that, war or peace, and on and on to "physical or spiritual" and perhaps worst of all, such thinking has pitted Man against Nature.

In truth, there are no real opposites, no firm barriers separating this from that—only beliefs do that, and the labels those belief systems try to paste on everything in sight as either approved or disapproved.

Spiritual and Physical are not opposites

Words can be misleading. Some people confuse "dominance" with totality. Things are not "either/or" nor is dominance the same things as "domination." Dominance means simply "more of" one thing than another relative to some other perspective. The physical world simply has more physicality than it has astral or mental, or "spiritual," characteristics—but all are present even when not accounted for.

Duality, as a perspective, is a fact of *physical* life, and life is in all things including so-called "in-animate" matter. Yet, every duality leads to a trinity that begins a new duality. Matter *and* Energy are convertible, one into the other, although not simultaneously. All energy manifests as positive *and* negative, universally but not simultaneously, yet unites in motion. Living Matter decomposes and releases energy that generates new life; apparent lifeless matter burns and releases energy that generates power; waves crash against the shore and release energy, winds blow and their energy can be captured, and radio-active matter can also release nuclear energy or transform it in an nuclear explosion. At the same time, in radiation an electron and a positron come together as energy converts to matter.

In physical life, gender is always present, and its duality permeates the entire culture and is present in everything we do and see. When the masculine is dominant, the feminine is present and "active" but not to the extent or in the same manner that the masculine is. When the feminine is dominant, the masculine is present and "active" but not to the extent or in the manner of the feminine. Still, masculine and feminine, man and woman, unite in humanity. Duality always merges into unity through trinity to become part of a new duality.

In animal life, the masculine animal almost always plays a dominant role in the social life of the herd and in sexual interplay—but, note, it is generally the seasonal release of female hormones that instigates the male response so in another perspective the feminine is dominant. Yet, in their sexual interplay the female is almost always *appears to be submissive to the male in getting what she wants*—except in defense of her young. But there are many variants and apparent (superficial) exceptions as Nature loves variety and seems to experiment even to the extent that in some species the male serves to perform little else than fertilization and then is eaten by the female to nourish her young.

In human life, the masculine has been socially and sexually dominant in most cultures for the last five thousand or more years, and particularly so through the now passing Piscean Age dominated by male-oriented monotheism. Nevertheless, modern science now has a more comprehensive and less biased understanding of female physiology, psychology, and sexuality while at the same time political, religious, and economic repression (and overt oppression) of the feminine is being replaced by a new equality of relationship in which feminine sexuality, creativity, and expression is given higher credence than the masculine in these and other areas. In politics and government, in business and education, in science and medicine, and in areas other than in the major religions, women are increasingly recognized as equal and in certain areas as qualifiedly superior.

In the physical world, *Reproduction is always a favored activity regardless of social structure.* In human life, "Sex," may just be a single act for the male, but it is a fundamental "fact of life" and expression for the female and not limited to reproduction of the species but is inclusive of home and family life, and the design and production of new creations.

In the area of reproductive rights, women are still often repressed and their rights denied under laws passed by male legislators under the influence of male religious figures and male-expressive doctrine. Their theology still sees women as weak, less worthy and their sexuality as evil and dangerous, requiring laws and regulations and domination and control by men.

Denials of the true natures of men and women in their physical life has repercussions in their spiritual life and in the ability to communicate with spirit.

"Male and Female created "He" them"

That's a phrase from male dominated sacred books of the last several millennia. It suggests equality, but is followed by the claim that the first woman ate the fruit of the Tree of *Knowledge* against her Lord's commandment. Since the apple was offered to her by the "penis symbolizing" Serpent, her sexuality was called evil and she was further instructed to find bliss in ignorance and to fully submit to male domination in all things—including her mind, body, and sexuality.

This abuse only started to change in the last few hundred years as the New Age/ Aquarian worldview is slowly replacing that of Pisces. The Aquarian view shows a human offering knowledge and wealth to all the world, while the Piscean image is of two fish swimming in opposite directions, thereby accomplishing *nothing other than ignorance and conflict!* War has dominated the history of the last two thousand years.

To clarify, in modern life, dominance is not balanced by submission but with partnership and the respective acceptance of responsibilities. Adult Men and Women can live and grow as they participate in the many roles and opportunities that life today offers. Sexuality offers joy in adult interplay, and transcendence when understood in its full magnificence, and in its energy into alchemical transformation and spiritual empowerment.

Every Man and Every Woman is a Star

Despite the cultural bias of the last two thousand years, women played an equal role in shamanic practices worldwide. In Europe, this was called Witchcraft and condemned out of hate and ignorance by the Church as evil and an *estimated* seven million (record-keeping by the "Holy" Inquisition was not very meticulous) of Wise Women, Healers, and Herbalists were publically burned at the stake along with dissenters like St. Joan of Arc who claimed to speak with angels when the pope said only priests had that authority, and scientists who disputed the Church view that the Earth was the center of the universe.

Psychology now recognizes that every woman has a bit of a man in her psyche—called the "animus," and every man has a bit of a woman in his psyche—called the "anima." In other words, "Male and Female He created them" means that every human in their wholeness is psychologically, mentally and spiritually inclusive of both genders. Sexual organs are not the "end all" but the "beginning." Women and Men are equal in the eyes of creation and in the eyes of the law. It's time that all Men see likewise

As Aleister Crowley said: *"Every Man and Every Woman is a Star."*

Sexuality, Kundalini, and Transcendence

Why so much discussion of gender and sexuality in a book about Spiritual Communication? Sexuality is fundamental to our physical nature and functions through the biological force (called *Kundalini* in Sanskrit) that itself empowers life even while "sleeping" at the base of the spine. When "awakened" Kundalini transforms consciousness as it spirals upward through the body's centers to bring union with the Divinity within each of us, and unity with Spirit and Universal Consciousness. Other actions besides sex—meditation, magick, prayer, ritual, shamanic practices, etc.—can activate the same process. All of these are denigrated by the religious institutions since they by-pass their hierarchical structures and endanger their huge investments in physical assets, showy cathedrals and vestments, and political lobbying.

Sex and feminine sexuality, along with mediumship and communicating with spirits, are called evil and sinful by many religionists. They are *not!* Nor are they "dirty" and non-spiritual, nor are any other psychic and transformative practices. *It is the fulfillment of your spiritual destiny to become psychically and spiritually empowered by whatever means not harmful to others.*

Communication requires Interaction

"Communication" is a *sharing* by a variety of means. As we will discover, within *Sexual Union* we have the perfect *"down home" formula for Spiritual Communication and Attainment.*

Within the Taoist conception, the "opposites of Yin & Yang are united in all there is. If we go back to the image of a stick where one end is Spirit and the other end is Consciousness, we have represented duality but also their unity in the center at the point of balance. Go one step further, bend the stick into a circle uniting the two ends and you have a representation of Male and Female, consciously uniting in their physical centers, reaching orgasmic ecstasy and union with the Devine at the point where biological (physical) energy merges with Spirit to find wisdom. Herein is the formula of Spirit Communication: When two communicants come together in the third point known as Trinity, we have the potential for greater knowledge and understanding found through partnership and intentional sharing.

Movement from Duality to Trinity always requires Action. To merge Consciousness with Spirituality requires a unity of action charged with energy and directed purpose. The culmination is Divine Union facilitated by Intention and Vision, but always requires that additional focus of energy.

From Duality to Trinity

And Baby makes three? No! Sex isn't only for reproduction. But Sexual <u>Interaction</u> between Man and Woman that culminates beyond ordinary climax in *Orgasmic Ecstasy <u>and</u> Divine Union* illustrates fully the formula of *Communication between the planes brought to its highest level.*

Communication is always between two entities, sometimes facilitated by mechanical or other means—a cell phone, the Internet, a crystal ball, etc.—and sometimes by a third entity—a medium or channel, a spirit guide or an angel, etc. Direct communication between entities located on different planes involves some transition in consciousness between their levels of substance by means of energizing actions. It is the "Raising of Consciousness" through forms of meditation, ritual, magical evocation and invocation, and ecstatic practices to bridge the gap.

Interaction between the planes

In the previous chapter we pointed to the dimensional interaction between the planes, and also to intentional interactions. But there are many others.

Contrary to common misperception and deliberate false teachings intended to deny the opportunities of transcendence to those outside institutional religious hierarchies, there are no *barriers* between the planes—and specifically not between the physical and spiritual (astral, mental and causal) worlds—that can be bridged only by religious actions or complex and difficult techniques available only to high initiates, and top officials of churches and secret orders.

In the course of their denials, many of those believing they have the secret knowledge and know-how have lost their way. That which they deny to others they have lost to themselves. Their methodology is so lost within their antique and politicalized theology that it no longer works in the real world and only functions within the illusions of their closed systems.

It is time to open those restrictive institutional doors and let the Light shine in. There <u>are</u> simple but powerful actions—like prayer, meaningful evocative meditation, and real (not necessarily "religious") worship involving magickal invocation—that have been robbed of their effectiveness by teachings that turn them into emotionless rote repetitions of words and movement without beneficial pertinence to those reciting and gesturing now meaningless formulae.

The keys to effective interactions between physical and spiritual are found through an understanding, primarily, of the nature of the physical and astral energies, and also those of the mental and causal levels. These energies are increased and focused, images and symbols are explored through meditation, and deities are invoked to receive their power so that men and women can grow and transcend past restraints and today's institutionally imposed and biased limitations.

We move forward through the empowering technologies and transcending communications derived from ancient shamanism and the new science of the paranormal. We raise our levels of consciousness through the use of simple but real rituals, self-hypnosis, meditations that combine visualization of symbols and chanting of related mantras, sex magick, astral projection, chakra work, directed and controlled imagination, dance and gestures, and many other techniques leading to the awakening and movement of the biological/etheric energy called Kundalini—all of which reflect purpose, desire, and aspiration. None of these techniques are difficult or complex, but do require knowledge and understanding—and that's the intention of all our books and audio products.

Simply speaking, *Consciousness follows intention*. Many years ago, Napoleon Hill wrote a classic best-selling book titled "Think and Grow Rich;" we can follow that formula and "Think and Grow in Spirit;" "Think and Become More than you are;" and "Think and Become all you can be."

Take Control of the Communication

Communication with Spirit and with spiritual entities guides us into personal understanding in response to our questions and needs, and actions suited to our skills and knowledge. We build upon our past and present to synergize with our already existing future potentials and the evolutionary goals for all humanity and those determined for ourselves.

Yes, we learn from others through contemporary books and teachings, but as we learn to communicate directly with spiritual entities matching their wisdom with our needs and abilities, and with aspects of our own consciousness and Higher Self, we are effectively guided at levels of our greatest benefit where we can ask questions of the most immediate importance to us.

"Ask, and ye shall receive," but also learn to "Test, and Verify."

Verification comes through demonstration of benefit. Don't be misled or *befuddled* by "high-sounding" words and phrases in imitation of Biblical prophets or Eastern masters. Ask and speak in clear words and phrases that say exactly what you mean, and demand answers that are just as clear and meaningful. Don't play games with spiritual intelligences, and don't let them play games with you.

It's all up to you!

In a very real sense, the Cosmos exists for you to grow and develop. It's not for you to do "God's Work" as channeled through institutions of church and state, but for you to reach inward and upward yourself to fulfill the opportunity and promise to *become more than you are, and all that you can be.*

That, too, is the message and promise of this New Age, and it's for all, not the few. As we reach upward from the physical to the spiritual, those of spirit reach downward to welcome each of us in our aspirations for knowledge and expanding consciousness.

Ask, and ye shall receive

The unspoken Cosmic Directive is for growth and development, but Spirit responds best to our initiative, to our conscious action, and to our expressed needs. All Humanity grows through the conscious efforts and intentions of individuals and not in response to the empty promises and shouted prayers of the sheep herders spiritually blinded by their greed for money, power and self-aggrandizement.

The following is not intended to imitate a religious text but it's framed that way as a reminder of the need for thought and common sense when we talk of spirituality. Too often, when spirituality is involved, mind is "turned off." We are whole beings: Body, Mind, Spirit *and* Emotion (Feeling), and it is in your wholeness that development is *wholesome* and balanced, enabling you to become more than you are!

Turn Away, Deny, and Turn Within

Turn away from men who claim they alone have authority to speak with God and for God;

Turn away from men who demand hate in place of love, war in place of peace, and acts of terror in place of justice;

Turn away from men who practice greed in place of honesty and laugh at your trust as naïve;

Deny gods demanding dominion over all earth in exchange for promises of paradise in another life;

Deny those who teach that women are inferior, sinful and evil, that women must remain ignorant and uneducated, that women must submit to men in all things and have no life of their own;

Sing not hymns to gods demanding obedience and threatening pain and suffering;

Kneel not to men demanding confessions of sin in their eyes;

Beware of men dressed in cloth of gold and carrying jeweled ornaments;

Beware of faulty connections offered by intermediaries where none are needed;

Turn within, and reach upward to your own spiritual self and connection with Universal Spirit.

The truth is, you don't need a gatekeeper or intermediary between you and Spirit, and many times their connections can be faulty, their interpretations biased and manipulative, and fail to meet your needs. And your growth depends on your own development and communication skills.

Practical programs and techniques that work!

In the chapters to come, we provide specific techniques and programs that work, along with theory, practices, cases showing their applications, and touches of history to give foundations to their methodology and overall interest to our subject of *Spirit Communication and Psychic Development.*

The greatest value of Spirit Communication is in your Psychic Development but is also gives you immediate and practical benefit based on the needs you express and the questions you ask. As has been said in all traditions:

Ask, and Ye shall Receive!

<u>MEDITATION</u>
"How are Consciousness and Spirit everywhere and in everything?"

Sources & Suggested Reading:

Alexander, S.: *Sex Magic for Beginners—The Easy & Fun Way to Tap into the Law of Attraction*, 2011, Llewellyn

Michaels, M. S. & Johnson, P.: *Tantra for Erotic Empowerment—the Key to Enriching your Sexual Life*, 2008, Llewellyn

Mumford, J.: *Ecstasy through Tantra*, 1987, Llewellyn

Yudelove, E. S.: *The Tao & The Tree of Life—Alchemical & Sexual Mysteries of East & West*, 1995, Llewellyn

3

THE NATURE OF MIND & BODY
AND SPIRIT INTERACTION

*"The man who has no more problems to solve
is out of the game." —Elbert Hubbard*

Spirituality Defines Who and What We Are

Spirituality as a powerful integrative force provides the most advanced evidence of the evolving nature of our being—mentally physically, and spiritually. It defines who and what we are at the moment while encompassing the bi-directional endlessness of our existence. It is the guiding force that energizes the endless scope of our existence—past, present, and future. When we view our existence by looking backward through the prism of spirituality, we see no beginning; when we look forward, we see no ending. Spirituality is an ever-present force that seeks balance and attunement among the many interactive functions of mind, body, and spirit. In that spiritually balanced and attuned state, we become energized with the power required to achieve our highest personal goals and reach levels of growth otherwise unattainable. Simply put, *spirituality empowers us to become "all that we can be."*

As an advanced integrative phenomenon, spirituality can become a balancing force that can add significance and meaning to your daily life. It can accelerate your growth by equipping you with the resources and skills required to effectively overcome growth blockages, achieve career goals, and cope with difficult life situations such as the breakup of a relationship, financial reversal, and the loss of a loved one, to list but a few. It can Empower you to resolve deep-seated conflicts, including those related to your past-life experiences as well as present-life demands. Through the balancing and attuning power of spirituality, you can become increasingly receptive to the supportive presence and intervention of spirit guides, particularly at times of danger or unforeseen reversal. In that spiritually balanced, attuned state, you will become progressively more empowered to develop our psychical powers and use them to achieve your personal goals. Aside from these, spirituality on a much broader scale can become the defining, universal force that accelerates humanitarian progress and brings forth world peace. The need for spirituality in the world today has never been greater!

Science and Spirituality Together

In this age of scientific advancement and digital-driven technology, spirituality still rules. It remains the supremely sustaining force underlying all that exists. It is the fundamental, energizing essence that sustains not only our personal existence, but the infinite multiverse as well. While both science and spirituality are essential to the discovery and application of knowledge, spirituality is the validating force that underlies knowledge in its purest form.

Admittedly, when looking at science and spirituality we often see a peculiar rift between them, especially when viewed from afar. But the closer we look, the more any disjunction seems to disappear. Dormant knowledge, once uncovered, becomes an active force of spiritual origin that can work hand-in-hand with science to open totally new gateways to both personal growth and global advancement. The results include not only the uncovering of potentials but the activation of them, often through step-by-step procedures developed in the scientific research setting. By embracing the hidden powers of the mind, body, and spirit, spirituality and science together can become an interactive force that accelerates the achievement of stated goals and the full actualization of both personal and global potentials.

Scientific research into the paranormal over the years has taught us that every problem is capable of solution. It has also taught us that every secret is capable of being unveiled, and not only unveiled, but applied. A key question arises, however, when the results of paranormal research appear either to lie outside the accepted scientific map or to be in discord with the quantitative methods of conventional science. That dilemma can best be resolved when we consider ways in which science and spirituality affect humanity. Among the major challenges we face today is not only discovering knowledge, but applying it in ways that promote the common good. That, in fact, is the ultimate challenge of both science and spirituality.

Science & Spirituality together are Interactive, and Relevant

When viewed in proper perspective, science and spirituality become increasingly relevant and interactive. *Scientific research into spirituality together with spirituality research into science* has shown relevance, not only to quality of life but to cultural progress as well. Here are a few examples:

- Controlled studies related to the existence of the spirit realm and the relevance of spiritual knowledge to our understanding of both physical and spiritual reality.
- Controlled lab studies on the nature of spirituality that led to major advancements in psychology.
- Studies related to past lives that uncovered the relevance of past-life experiences to present-life development.
- Studies on longevity that revealed the impact of spirituality on both longevity and quality of life.
- Controlled lab studies on the nature of human consciousness and its relevance to both medicine and psychotherapy.
- Case studies that revealed the empowering effects of the near-death experience.
- Controlled studies that uncovered powerful evidence of the existence of ministering spirit guides and their empowering functions to include support, guidance, and protective interventions particularly in life and death situations.
- Case studies on astral projection as a source of increased knowledge and awareness of other realities—both physical and spiritual.

When we add to these the emerging studies concerning the nature of the universe and its place among other universes, the complementary functions of science and spirituality become even more evident.

The relevance of paranormal research as a source of spiritual enlightenment is probably best expressed by Descartes in *Discourse on Method*: "There is nothing so far removed from us as to lie beyond our reach, or so hidden that we cannot discover it, provided only we abstain from accepting the false for the true and always preserve in our thoughts the order necessary for the deduction of one truth from another." Spirituality does not decry reason based on science; it instead exalts reason to a higher plane. It is limitless in its capacity to lift us to the heights of both personal and global progress.

Spiritual enlightenment goes far beyond awareness as simply a sensory or cognitive experience. At its peak, it becomes a state of mental, physical, and spiritual empowerment. It transcends the ups and downs of life in which progress at one stage is too often followed by decline at another. It is a continuous "onward and upward" process that empowers you to reach for things greater than you are at the moment. It adds both success and meaning to your life.

Authentic Spirituality and the Personal Self, and Beyond

Authentic spirituality begins with awareness of the nature of your personal existence as an endless being of dignity and incomparable worth, but it does not end there. Authentic spirituality reaches beyond the self to embrace the wellbeing of others regardless of differences in culture, status, intelligence, orientation, or any other defining characteristic. Aside from that, authentic spirituality is committed to bringing forth important humanitarian change. *Contributing to the greater good* is what keeps spirituality alive on both a personal and global scale. The major error of humanity over the ages is the tendency to limit its capacity to reach out and help others in times of need. Correcting that error requires courage, compassion, commitment, and persistence.

All too often we put humanitarian causes on the chopping block. We fail to recognize global needs and ways of meeting them. We fail to acknowledge global injustices and take responsible action to correct them. Human trafficking, child labor, world hunger, and poverty, to list but few, cry out to us but we too often fail to hear them. Adding to these is our frequent failure to recognize the value and rights of animal beings, from the lowliest to the most highly evolved. The history of civilization has taught us that the best single measure of how far we have advanced as a culture is the quality of our treatment of others, including persons and animals alike.

Another defining characteristic of authentic spirituality is its focus on our treatment of the Earth itself. At this point in our spiritual evolution, we have no backup plan in place should the Earth become an unfriendly, uninhabitable place. Today as never before, our planet is at risk, largely because of our reckless depletion of natural resources, environmental pollution, and climate change. When we add to these the widespread acceleration of cultural turmoil and abuse of human rights along with the increasing threats of war, the future of the planet becomes even more tenuous. Authentic spirituality demands constructive action. We must do what we can now to save the planet, not only for ourselves but for future generations as well.

Overcoming Self-imposed Limitations

Spirituality is at its finest and most powerful when free of self-imposed limitations. The only limits to your spiritual progress are the ones you place upon yourself. In the words of Jessie B. Rittenhouse (1869–1948),

> "I bargained with Life for a penny,
> And Life would pay no more,
> However I begged at evening
> When I counted my scanty store;
>
> For Life is just an employer,
> He gives you what you ask,
> But once you have set the wages,
> Why, you must bear the task.
>
> I worked for a menial's hire,
> Only to learn, dismayed,
> That any wage I had asked of Life,
> Life would have paid."

The Underdeveloped Potential of the Subconscious Mind

You have the power to aim high. Complementing that power is the vast wealth of resources and underdeveloped potential existing in your subconscious mind. Once activated, your subconscious mind can become a channel through which you can draw upon universal resources to balance and empower your total being—mentally, physically, and spiritually.

Spiritual equilibrium is power in action. Through a step-by-step strategy called **Equilibrium in Action** developed in our labs at Athens State University (Alabama), you can generate a state of equilibrium in which your mind, body, and spirit are balanced and attuned. The program is based on the premise that spirituality is at its peak when the mind, body, and spirit are balanced, attuned, and energized to inter-act in harmony. Through this program, you will become empowered to access the vast wealth of resources existing both within yourself and beyond. You will become empowered to achieve both personal and humanitarian goals. Through this strategy, you can activate dormant inner potentials including those related to your personal growth and quality of life.

Spiritual Equilibrium is Power in Action & The Etheric Double

Our lab studies showed Equilibrium in Action to be especially effective in its capacity to merge etheric energies with the Etheric Double. It is specifically structured to facilitate interaction with higher dimensions, planes, and guiding spirit entities as sources of knowledge and power. Once you have achieved a state of spiritual equilibrium, you will become empowered to dissolve all barriers to your growth and success. You will discover that *by simply visualizing your goals, momentarily holding them in your mind, and believing in your ability to achieve them, you will succeed.* Better health and fitness, rejuvenation, longevity, enlightenment, and happiness along with career and financial advancement are all within the scope of this program. On a much broader scale, Equilibrium in Action when applied globally can promote humanitarian progress and global peace.

Through this program, *spirituality becomes clothed in reality.* This is the basic theme of spirituality not obscured in any elaboration of doubt and trepidation. Once clothed in reality, spirituality becomes the decisive force that empowers you with the essentials required for your complete success. Through this step-by-step program, you will become empowered to reach beyond all prevailing limitations. You will discover new sources of both inner and outer power and how to connect to them. This program challenges you to add power and quality to your life by renouncing failure and embracing success. Here's the program:

14-Step Spiritual Equilibrium is Power in Action Program

Step 1. Preliminaries. Allow approximately one hour for the program which is conducted in a quiet, comfortable place with soft, indirect lighting. To facilitate relaxation, loose fitting clothing with shoes removed is recommended. State in your own words your goal of achieving a state spiritual equilibrium and balance. Upon stating that goal, you can specify other goals, limiting them to no more them three. Visualize each goal as an existing reality awaiting unfoldment, and affirm your complete success in achieving them through this program.

Step 2. Progressive Relaxation. While resting comfortably in a prone or semi-prone position with your legs uncrossed, close your eyes and take in a few deep breaths, taking a little longer to exhale. Clear your mind of active thought and allow a passive mental state to slowly unfold. Develop a slow, rhythmic breathing pattern as relaxation flows throughout your body, beginning at your forehead and slowly spreading downward, and right through the tips of your toes. Take plenty of time for relaxation to spread deeply and permeate every joint, muscle, and tendon of your body.

Step 3. Progressive Serenity. As you breathe deeply and rhythmically, sense peaceful bright energy centered deep within your body and gently flowing outward. Let that bright energy permeate your body and then fully envelop it with a glow of serenity and power. Take plenty of time to allow bright energy centered within to flow gently outward and fully envelop your physical body. Note the serenity that accompanies this process. Affirm in your own words the empowering effects of this experience as bright energy continues to infuse and envelop your physical body with a comforting glow.

Step 4. Cupped Hand Grip. Cup your hands and bring them together to form a tight grip but with a space between your palms. Hold the cupped hand-grip position as you feel the tightness building in your hands. Allow the hand-grip to continue building until it seems to have reached its peak.

Step 5. Energy Infusion. Slowly relax the hand grip as you sense bright energy building in the enclosed space between your cupped hands. Note the warmth in your palms, a sensation typically accompanying this step.

Step 6. Palm Energy Orb. As energy continues to build in the enclosed space between your cupped hands, further relax your hands to form an orb of bright energy between your palms.

Step 7. Spherical Visualization. Slowly open your hands and with your palms turned upward, sense the warm orb of bright energy gently resting in your palms. Visualize the orb glowing with empowering energy. (Should you decide to do so, you can momentarily open your eyes briefly to view the bright energy orb resting above your palms.)

Step 8. Cosmic Energy Orb. As your eyes remain closed, visualize a distant cosmic orb glowing with powerful energy. Take a few moments for a clear image of that distant sphere of pulsating energy to emerge.

Step 9. Spherical Infusion. Focus your awareness again upon the orb of warm energy resting in your palms as you visualize bright streams of energy from the distant sphere infusing the orb in your hands with new energy.

Step 10. Full Energy Infusion. As energy from the distant sphere continues to infuse the orb of energy in your hands, sense the infusion of energy in your hands gently spreading throughout your body, first into your arms and shoulders, and from there throughout your full body.

Step 11. Energy Balance and Attunement. Once your full body is infused with powerful energy, turn you attention again to the orb of energy resting in your hands. Visualize as before bright rays of energy connecting the orb in your hands to the distant sphere of limitless power. Sense again the merging of energies and the bright infusion of energy throughout your total being. Now fully infused with powerful energy, sense the attuning and balancing effects of the experience.

Step 12. Empowering Affirmation. Affirm: *I am now fully energized and empowered mentally, physically, and spiritually. I have access to all the power I need to achieve my highest goals.* Again visualize your goals as specified in Step 1 and affirm in your own words your complete success in achieving them.

Step 13. Post-procedure Cue. Bring your hands together to form the cupped hand grip as you affirm: **I can at any moment activate a state of mental, physical, and spiritual equilibrium and empowerment by simply bringing my hands into the cupped hand-grip position.**

Step 14. Conclusion. Relax your hands and reflect on the empowering effects of the experience. Be receptive to spontaneous insight that often unfolds at this final stage of the program. Conclude with the affirmation:

I am now empowered with complete success.

As with all Development and Improvement programs, we must "Live It" every day to make it part of who we are and what we do. That doesn't mean repeating the 14 steps day after day, but thinking it and repeating that culminating affirmation as you step forward in its application. One old adage coming from the early days of Self-Programing is:

Think it, Speak it, Apply it

It's a continuous process of structuring and restructuring both neural and subtle circuitry, of merging *outer* and *inner*, of making *effort* into <u>conscious</u> *habit* so that each day's accomplishment remains a solid building block for tomorrow's additions.

I am now empowered with complete success. Profound awareness of personal guides and growth facilitators will often emerge during this procedure, particularly at Step 9 with the infusion of energy from the distant sphere. It's also at that step that solutions to complex problem situations and insight of both clairvoyant and precognitive significance will unfold.

I am now empowered with complete success. Equilibrium in Action is an excellent preparatory procedure when practiced prior to an important event, such as an interview, public presentation, or performance. The balancing effect of the procedure builds self-confidence, stimulates intellectual efficiency, and elevates the quality of a wide range of skills. Improvements in persuasive and other interpersonal skills are particularly receptive to this program.

I am now empowered with complete success. College students who regularly practiced this program showed marked improvements in such skills as comprehension, problem-solving, rate of learning, and retention. Having practiced the full program, they found that periodic use of post-procedure hand-grip cue greatly increased the effectiveness of the program. The cue requires only seconds to implement and can be used in a wide range of situations. Students who participated in our development of the procedure reported success in using the cue immediately before and during course examinations to reduce test anxiety and dramatically improve their test performance. Along another line, students majoring in creative writing reported that regular use of the cue greatly improved the quality of their writings by generating highly creative ideas. Doctoral students found the procedure to be especially effective in accelerating their mastery of another language as required for their degree.

The following discussion explores four major applications of the 14-step Spiritual Equilibrium in Action Program:

1. Spiritual Equilibrium for Psychotherapy and Self-empowerment in Action

Equilibrium in Action has shown remarkable potential when used for therapeutic purposes, such as more effectively managing stress, reducing pain, overcoming depression, and extinguishing phobias. The evidence is clear: This program when appropriately applied can put you in touch with the best of all therapists—the one existing within yourself. Following practice of the full procedure, the simple hand-grip cue can be used in any stressful situations to instantly generate an empowered state of well-being and security. It can be used before and during public presentations, such as speeches and debates, to eliminate negative stress and facilitate clear thinking. College students reported that the cue, when practiced during job interviews, tended to reduce stress, build security feelings, increase clear thinking, and generate positive expectations. In social situations, the cue can be used to promote positive social interactions and rewarding relationships. As a pain management technique, the hand-grip cue can be used to reduce pain by promoting relaxation and facilitating healing through its balancing and attuning effects.

When used prior to past-life regression through hypnosis, Equilibrium in Action as a preparatory procedure tended to set the stage for hypnosis and generate a state of readiness to experience the unexpected, including painful past-life trauma which is often shown to be the source of present-life phobias, compulsions, and other anxieties. Not unexpectedly, simply uncovering the past-life source of an irrational fear is typically sufficient to give rationality to the fear, and as a result, to extinguish the fear altogether. Following hypnosis, the hand-grip cue can be used to promote positive integration of the experience and to extinguish any residual stress related to it. Replacing self-defeating fear with self-empowering insight is among the most important goals of psychotherapy. Equilibrium in Action when appropriately applied effectively achieves that important goal.

Equilibrium in Action has shown unusual promise when used as a self-improvement strategy, including building feelings of self-worth, coping with stress, and overcoming blockages related to sexual behavior, including but not limited to impaired desire, arousal, and orgasm. Male erectile disorders, including the ability to obtain an erection and maintain it as well as premature ejaculation, are especially receptive to this program. Following application of the full procedure, which can be done jointly by both partners if preferred, the post-procedure cue can be used immediately prior to (and possibly during) the sexual experience. The results are typically a dramatic increase in the quality and satisfaction of the experience as well as increased feelings of security and worth. Our studies also found that the technique can also be effective when used by couples to promote sexual fertility.

2. Spiritual Equilibrium for Health & Fitness in Action

Among the many practical applications of Equilibrium in Action is its use as a health and fitness strategy. It can be used for such wide ranging goals as losing weight, breaking unwanted habits, slowing aging, and even reversing the visible effects of aging. Through their introduction of rejuvenation goals in Step 1 of the program, several middle-aged and older subjects who participated in our development of the procedure became convinced that it generated rejuvenating energies that slowed the aging process while extinguishing its visible signs. Our research, which included the use of biofeedback and electrophotography, appeared to validate that claim. When used following practice of the full procedure, the simple hand-grip cue tended to generate a glow of youth that enveloped the full body. The long-ranging results reflected an apparent reversal of the physical signs of aging. In the words of an 82-year-old participant in our research program, "The hand-grip cue is a rejuvenation gem!"

3. Spiritual Equilibrium for Resolving Conflict in Action.

Conflicts are a fact of life, and resolving them can be a very difficult needle to thread. Through the holistic balancing of the mind, body, and spirit, you can become empowered to resolve conflict, regardless of its nature. Whether in choosing between options, Equilibrium in Action can not only generate the insight required for your complete success. The program can identify the preferred options through precognitive imagery that advances relevant awareness into the future. It can also generate clairvoyant awareness of unseen but highly critical factors related to responsible choosing.

4. Spiritual Equilibrium for Diversity, Clairvoyance and Creativity in Action

Accompanying the attuning and balancing effects of this program, a diversity of responses can accompany the merging of energies generated by the program. Among the common responses are insight related to stressful situations, images of past-life relevance, innovative solutions to pressing problems, insight related to social relationships, and awareness of a spirit presence. The merging of energies through this program and the resultant enlightenment can be peak experiences with profound empowerment results. Here are a few examples illustrating the diverse nature of the experiences:

- A student experienced the sudden awareness of a ministering guide who guided her through a complicated relationship she described as a "tangled web."

- A businessman experienced a precognitive image that detailed a highly successful business expansion plan.

- An architect experienced during the early planning stage a detailed view of a municipal building his firm had been contracted to design.

- A counseling psychologist's experienced a detailed clairvoyant image of the university where she would later head a psychology program.

- A student being tutored in a foreign language required for her doctorate in psychology spoke the language fluently upon the merging of the energies. She used the post-procedure cue to rapidly accelerate her mastery of the language. She mastered the language in record time and successfully passed the language exam.

- A fashion designer experienced detailed images of garments that were to receive the praise of critics as "fusion design at its best."

Repeated practice of Equilibrium in Action can make spirituality an increasingly powerful force in your life. It can add significance to your existence as an endless being whose destiny is growth and greatness.

Conclusion

We cannot follow the evolvement of our existence through the ages without realizing that the purpose of life is to forever move forward. Experience teaches us that the future is in our hands. By embracing and working with spirituality, you will discover that nothing is beyond your reach. It is a limitless force—a reserve of power—that readily responds to your call. It is a power without limit. It asks only that you call upon it. It is the power that inspires progress and generates optimistic expectations. It is the power to be whatever you decide to be, to accomplish whatever you set out to do. The challenge is to get acquainted with that power, embrace it, and discover how to use it.

<u>MEDITATION</u>
"What does 'Interaction with Spirit' mean to you, now?"

Suggested Reading List:

Slate, J. H. & Weschcke, C. L.: *Self-Empowerment and Your Subconscious Mind—Your Unlimited Resource for Health, Success, Long Life & Spiritual Attainment,* 2010, Llewellyn

Slate, J. H. & Weschcke, C. L.: *Self-Empowerment through Self-Hypnosis—Harness the Enormous Potential of the Mind,* 2010, Llewellyn

4

THE BI-DIRECTIONAL
ENDLESSNESS OF SPIRIT

"Nothing ends so long as we can begin again."
—Anonymous

You are Mind, Body, and Spirit

Have you ever questioned the limits to your personal existence? *Is your existence limited to mind and body, or does it include spirit? Is it limited to your present lifetime, or does it include your past lifetimes as well as your life between them? Did you exist before your first lifetime, and will you exist beyond your last? How long did you exist before your first lifetime, and how long will you exist beyond your last?*

The evidence is powerful and clear: You are not only mind and body, you are also spirit. But spirit is more than simply a part of you—it is the *essential you*, the very essence of your total being. Without the spirit, you would not exist at all. It is the energizing force that identifies and sustains your personal existence in each lifetime as well as between lifetimes. Beyond that, it is the life force that characterizes your individual existence before your first lifetime and beyond your last. Within that endless scope, the spirit is the *force* that gives identity and meaning to your existence as an evolving being. It is characterized by a *spiritual genotype* that remains forever fixed and gives identity to your existence as uniquely different from that of all others. It is the spiritual genotype that endows you with unlimited potential for endless growth.

Spirit is the Essence that Empowers You

Spirit as the essence of your being empowers you to learn and grow. Because you are spirit, you can dream lofty dreams and achieve them. You can overcome obstacles, redeem lost opportunities, and reverse even the most hopeless of situations. The door to opportunity, growth, and abundance is never closed when the mind, body, and spirit work together in harmony. As Archimedes put, "Give me a base of support, and with a lever I will move the world." When the base of support is spiritual and the mind and body are the levers, you are mentally, physically, and spiritually empowered to succeed, whether a player on the soccer field or a CEO in the board room. A team of empowered soccer players, not unlike the CEO, stands a good chance of winning the game, whatever it is!

Motivation, and the Zeigarnik Effect

Personal experience teaches us that *nothing ends so long as we can begin again.* The bi-directional endlessness of spirit provides the opportunity to begin again and to complete old tasks while taking on new ones, whether in a given lifetime or the afterlife. Motivational studies conducted in the controlled setting show that unfinished tasks tend to linger in our memory, a condition called the **Zeigarnik Effect** that motivates us to return to complete the task. The intrusive thoughts of tasks not yet completed tend to occur until the task is finally finished. Consistent with that concept, past-life case studies repeatedly show that incomplete tasks or unachieved goals of a past lifetime tend to linger in afterlife as past-life residues that await our action and motivate us to fulfill them, either in the afterlife realm or in another lifetime.

Spirituality is the essential core of our existence

While personal experience provides perhaps the most convincing evidence of the spiritual nature of our existence, the findings of research can add to our understanding of the power of spirituality. Our research ranging from rigidly controlled laboratory studies to surveys and subjective reports, showed convincing evidence of the bi-directional endlessness of our personal existence. Through research, we have increased our understanding of spirituality as the essential core of our existence. We have uncovered evidence related to higher spiritual planes and developed ways of engaging their specialized powers. At a deeply personal level, the results of research can help expand our awareness of protective spirit guides, personal growth facilitators, and even rejuvenation and longevity resources.

Motivation in the Afterlife, and again in the Next Life

Our case studies revealed that motivation in afterlife to become embodied in another lifetime was consistently multi-purposeful and growth oriented. In addition to completing unfinished tasks, each lifetime was motivated by a variety of needs including but not limited to the following:

- To initiate entirely new goals.
- To correct past-life mistakes.
- To compensate for past-life misdeeds and failures.
- To fulfill specific growth needs.
- To achieve higher levels of personal growth through assimilating past experiences.
- To gain totally new experiences that would become growth resources in the afterlife.
- To experience the unforeseen rewards of a new lifetime on Earth.

Setting Life Goals brings Quality and Long-Term Meaning

Aside from these needs, such altruistic goals as helping those in need and contributing to a better world emerged as increasingly important. Almost without exception, a driving force underlying the choice to reincarnate was the need to maximize existing growth potentials and raise them to new levels of possibilities. In our studies, it became increasingly clear that setting important life goals, regardless of chronological age, not only gives quality to life in the present, it adds long-term meaning to afterlife. Among the participants in our studies, the persistent need to reach higher levels of growth was the motivating factor that gave purpose and meaning to each lifetime and to the afterlife that followed it. That intrinsic cycle offers convincing credence of the bi-directional endlessness of our existence as forever evolving spiritual beings.

Preservation of Peak Growth: Existence as a never-ending growth process

The participants of our studies became convinced that past growth experiences, whether in each lifetime or the discarnate realm, are never lost, a concept we call *the preservation of peak growth*. That concept recognizes both the continuously cumulative and persistent nature of our personal growth. Our research related to this concept showed that, at our transition to the sprit realm, preservation of peak growth is instantly activated. All impairments in mental or physical functions are instantly erased and replaced by the full activation of our past peaks of growth. Through the power of the transition event, death itself becomes a peak growth experience, yet another finding that personal existence is a continuous, never-ending growth process.

The Decision is Yours

Our studies consistently showed that the decision in afterlife to experience another lifetime was that of the individual alone. While often facilitated by benevolent spirit guides and growth specialists, the decision to experience a lifetime was free of any manipulation or demand. Since embodiment in another lifetime was never forced upon the individual, it clearly follows that the responsibility for each lifetime rests with the individual and the individual alone. For each lifetime, *we do indeed choose to be born!*

Our research over the years revealed absolutely no evidence of negative forces or evil beings in afterlife. The existence of evil or disempowering influences in the spirit realm is contradictory to the very nature of spirituality as comprehensive, bi-directional, and endless.

Spiritual Alignment

Spirituality is the positive, infinite force that sustains your existence as both endless and bi-directional. It not only sustains your past and future, it gives meaning to the moment we call "the now." Beyond that, spirituality is the motivating force that inspires us to press onward and upward toward greater heights of growth and power.

A major purpose of each lifetime and life between lifetimes within the endless span of our existence is to experience first-hand the infinite power of spirituality. Spiritual alignment is an *enlightened state of being* that empowers you to achieve that important goal. Through spiritual alignment, you will discover that spirituality is more than a thought or emotion—it is the *supreme force* that energizes your growth and gives quality to your existence from your endless pre-existence to present moment and beyond. In that aligned state of attunement and balance, you will experience the relevance of spirituality to your total existence—past, present, and future.

Once spiritually aligned, you will discover your power to set your highest goals and more importantly, how to succeed in fulfilling them. You will experience the thrill of opening totally new gateways to your future growth. You will discover effective ways of overcoming blockages to your growth, solving difficult problems, and healing emotional scars. Even more importantly, you will experience greater understanding of yourself as an endless being of incomparable worth. You will discover the power of love for yourself and others alike. On a much larger scale, you will discover that inner peace as well as world peace must flow, not from power of destruction, but from the positive power of spirituality.

Through spiritual alignment, you can experience first-hand an overview of the bi-directional endlessness of your existence. You will become empowered to engage new sources of enlightenment and power from within as well as from external sources. Once you are spiritually aligned, you become empowered to engage the spiritual realm as a source of both power and enlightenment. You become empowered to more fully develop you extrasensory powers and to effectively activate them as needed. You become empowered to engage retrocognition to increase awareness of your relevant past, including past-life experiences that hold special significance to the present. You become empowered to engage precognitive awareness of future personal and global events. You will become empowered to experience clairvoyant awareness, often in imagery form, to include distant situations and events related to your present life situation.

Spirituality in Action Programs

Two spiritual alignment programs, each developed in the controlled laboratory setting at Athens State University (Alabama), are designed to generate a state of both inner and outer spiritual alignment. Each program focuses on the empowering potential of spiritual alignment. In the aligned state, you will experience expanded awareness in which you actually view the infinite multiverse and the bi-directional endlessness of your personal existence within it. You will experience your personal alignment to the spiritual parallel of the multiverse as the unifying force that holds it all together. Finally through the resultant attunement and balancing effects of spiritual alignment, you will experience the unlimited possibilities available to you at the moment.

Spiritual Alignment through Automatic Writing Program

Spiritual Alignment through Automatic Writing is a procedure based on the simple premise that *you are the center of your existence* in the complex equation of life. From that central point, you have the potential to view the totality of your existence—past, present and future.

The step-by-step approach focuses on using automatic writing, or "psychography," to engage a conscious-subconscious interaction that empowers you to reach beyond the commonly perceived limits of your existence. It recognizes the subconscious as not only a wealth of past experience but a powerhouse of insight and potential as well. By expanding your awareness through automatic writing, you can get an overview of the bi-directional endless nature of your existence while remaining at the center point of your life at the moment.

Countering the often implied simplicity of automatic writing is its capacity to engage higher dimensions of power and interact with them. While typically focusing on the subconscious as a storehouse of insight, automatic writing is receptive to the intervention of other realms of enlightenment and power. Extra-dimensional sources, including advanced spirit guides, are believed frequently to intervene when needed during automatic writing as messengers of important information related to current situations and needs. In that state of heightened awareness, you alone retain the power to intervene into the experience and focus it on specific goals. Here's the procedure:

8-Step Spiritual Alignment through Automatic Writing Program

Preliminaries. The only materials required for this procedure are a writing pen (or pencil) and a blank sheet of paper. In a comfortable, quiet setting conducive to writing, with writing materials at hand, begin the procedure by settling back, taking in a few deep breaths, and clearing your mind of active thought.

> **Step 1. Goal Statement.** Formulate your primary goal of exploring the bi-directional nature of your existence. Formulate other goals, should you decide to do so, including interactions with the spirit realm as sources as enlightenment and power. You may wish to specify goals related to your present life situation, including interpersonal relationships, problem situations, past-life experiences, and future happenings.

> **Step 2. Visualization.** With the writing pen in hand, draw a circle at the center of the page. Rest your pen point at the center of the circle and with your eyes closed, visualize the paper, the circle, and the pen in hand resting at the center of the circle.

> **Step 3. Affirmation 1.** With eyes remaining closed, affirm in your own words:

>> *The circle at the center of this page represents my present lifetime with the center of the circle representing my existence at this moment. I am*

now ready to explore the time limits of my past by allowing the pen to draw a line to the left through the circle and beyond. The line beyond the circle will represent my life before this present lifetime. The length of the line will depict the time limits of my past. The left edge of the paper represents infinity and the endlessness of my past existence.

Allow the pen to draw the time line representing your past. Once the line is drawn, open your eyes and bring the pen back to the center of the circle.

Step 4. Affirmation 2. With pen point resting again at the center of the circle, close your eyes and visualize the scene as before. With eyes remaining closed, affirm:

I am now ready to explore the time limits of my future by allowing the pen to draw a line to the right, extending through the circle and beyond. The line beyond the circle will represent my life beyond this present lifetime. The length of the line will depict the time limits of my future. The right edge of the paper represents infinity and the endlessness of future existence.

Allow the pen to draw the time line representing your future. Once the line is drawn, open your eyes as before and bring the pen back to the center of the circle.

Step 5. Bi-directional Visualization: Close your eyes and visualize the scene to include the lines representing your past and future. Take a few moments to reflect on the significance of the lines drawn, to include their relevance to your personal existence at the moment.

Step 6. Free Flowing Automatic Writing. With writing pen still in hand, place the point elsewhere on the page and with your eyes closed, allow the pen to write automatically. Take plenty of time for meaningful writing to occur. Although apparently meaningless scribble may first occur, important messages of subconscious origin as well as interactions with spirit guides are common at this stage.

Step 7. Interpretation. View the results of free-flowing automatic writing, and take plenty of time to reflect on the significance of the written messages, to include direct messages, metaphors, and communications in symbolic form. Although each symbol can have various interpretations, a triangle or pyramid usually symbolizes mental, physical, and spiritual balance; whereas a square often symbolizes constriction or feelings of isolation. A wavy line usually symbolizes uncertainty or indecisiveness. A circle anywhere on the page typically represents a peaceful state of mind or completeness.

Step 8. Conclusion. Place the writing materials aside, settle back and reflect on the experience. Note any impression of a spirit presence, and let yourself become receptive to messages of spiritual origin. Note your state of compete attunement and oneness with the spirit realm.

Where's the Evidence?

A group of 64 undergraduate students enrolled in Experimental Parapsychology at Athens State University was administered the program in our effort to evaluate its efficacy as a spiritual alignment procedure. Here are a few of the results.

- All participants drew lines reaching beyond the circle at the center of the page to both the right and left edges of the paper, a pattern indicating the bi-directional endlessness of their existence as spiritually infinite.

- Their lines to both the left and right of the circle at the center of the page often extended beyond the edges of the page, a pattern that appeared to emphasize the importance of recognizing the endless nature of our spiritual existence along with the infinity of the spirit realm.

- All participants experienced during the procedure a powerful sense of spiritual alignment and oneness, both within themselves and with the spirit realm.

- Several participants experienced fleeting views of their past lives as they automatically drew the line to the left of the circle. In some instances, the writing was spontaneously arrested as awareness of an important past-life experience emerged.

- Subconscious insight related to past-life experiences was common. A pre-med student drew an image of a primitive surgical instrument that he concluded connected him to a past life as a surgeon, an experience that solidified his decision to become a surgeon.

- In drawing the line to the right side of the circle, impressions of a spiritual presence were common. Familiar spirit guides in some instances seemed to literally guide the writing.

- Awareness of higher sources of power, often in the form of bright orbs or colorful planes, likewise emerged. The empowering effects of these experiences were often described as unforgettable and profound.

- Automatic writing, along with drawings in the upper and lower sections of the page, was seen as sources of not only enlightenment but power as well. The drawings often related to current life situations and concerns. Examples included insight related to pressing life demands, including in one instance, the recovery of a lost animal companion.

- The participants in this exercise concluded that endlessness in future is possible only when balanced with endlessness in the past. In their words, "You can't have one without the other."

Benefits of the Program

Our case studies of students who regularly used this program consistently reported marked improvements in the quality of their daily lives. While automatic writing often provided specific information on a "need-to-know basis," it also became a source of power in its capacity to engage dormant inner resources.

The results included a progressively empowered state in which mind, body, and spirit became aligned both within the self and with the spiritual realm. Through their repeated practice of this program, spirituality became a continuously interactive function of daily life. For them, practice of the program generated an integrated effect that gave new meaning and significance to their lives.

These are only a few examples of the empowering effects of this program. With practice, the program becomes increasingly effective as a multifunctional alignment program. It yields both enlightenment and empowerment while providing insight as needed at the moment. Nothing it seems is beyond the reach of this powerful program.

Synchronicity in Action

A major purpose of each lifetime is to fulfill the growth potentials offered by that lifetime. Achieving that goal may require accessing resources buried in the subconscious while engaging other dimensions of power, including the spirit realm. Within the endless scope of our existence, it is important to keep in mind the straightforward fact: *We are here at this place in this moment to learn and grow.* Through a program called *Synchronicity in Action* which was developed in the controlled lab setting at Athens State University, you can become empowered to achieve even your loftiest of goals. It is especially effective in increasing awareness of the endlessness of your existence within a reality that is both physical and spiritual. The procedure is designed to bring forth synchronicity and oneness with that reality while focusing on a specifically stated goal.

Complexity seeks simplicity

Synchronicity in Action illustrates the familiar concept: *Complexity seeks simplicity.* It is among the simplest of self-empowerment procedures, yet it is one of the most effective. It can be applied to a seemingly unlimited range of goals. Although typically used as an individually self-administered program, it can be adapted for use as a group strategy. It has been used in the classroom setting to increase student motivation and awareness of the infinite nature of personal existence within a physical Multiversal reality that is also infinite. It has been used in business settings for such goals as promoting professional growth and improving the quality of services. It has been used in the educational setting for goals ranging from increasing instructional effectiveness to expanding campus facilities. Along a highly practical line, it has been used by college students for such goals as quitting smoking, losing weight, improving grade point average, and even finding true love.

Synchronicity in Action is designed to promote your total growth while empowering you to engage new sources of power and apply that power to achieve specifically stated goals. Through this program, you can tap into the powers within yourself while reaching beyond to engage other sources. It is based on the premise that the realities we perceive are but mere particles of all that exists. Through this approach, you can reach beyond the limits of sensory perception and conventional concepts of reality...You can engage spiritual realities and their energizing powers. You can expand your awareness of spirituality as the underlying infinite force that sustains all that exists, both seen and unseen. More importantly, you can experience an empowered state of synchronicity and oneness with both spiritual and physical realities.

The program does not require complex tactics or altered states of consciousness. It does, however, require practice. You will find that practicing the approach, especially before falling asleep, improves its effectiveness by facilitating imagery and firm commitment.

The program begins with a clearing and balancing process that focuses awareness on the bi-directional endlessness our spirituality. *It focuses present* awareness at the center point of that polarity system. It holds the view that your past is forever in back you and your future is forever in front of you—they are both forever yours. Here's the program which requires approximately thirty minutes in a comfortable, quiet setting free of distractions.

6-Step Synchronicity in Action Program

Step 1. Clearing and Balancing. Settle back, clear your mind of active thought, and take in a few deep breaths, exhaling slowly while focusing only on your breathing. With your eyes closed, let free-flowing images come and go as you experience peaceful relaxation throughout your body. In that tranquil, relaxed state, let yourself flow with the images as your awareness expands to embrace the totality of your existence, from your endless past to your endless future. Think of your existence at the moment as at the center of that bi-directional endlessness. Allow plenty of time for a balanced state of attuned awareness to emerge.

Step 2. Goal Statement. As you remain in that balanced state, formulate a single goal. Specifically state your goal in positive terms, and slowly repeat it at least once. Take time for your stated goal to become an integral part of your being.

Step 3. Commitment. Having stated your goal, embrace it as a part of yourself. Firmly commit yourself to achieving it. You can energize your commitment by simply completing the open-ended sentence: *"This goal is important to me because..."*

As you enumerate each reason the goal is important to you, relate it to your present life situations along with the totality of your existence. Remind yourself that through the power of personal commitment, you are now succeeding in your effort to achieve your goal. Let the synchronicity and commitment related to your goal slowly unfold as an energizing force that ensures your complete success.

Step 4. Visualization. Clearly visualize your stated goal as an existing reality. Think of that reality as *your personal reality*. Embrace it and let it become a part of you. Note your feelings of success as the goal becomes a reality in your life.

Step 5. Relevance. Embrace the spiritual essence of your being as forever evolving, and sense your connection to spiritual realm with its abundant resources, including those related to your goal. You can, at this state, give yourself permission to interact with higher sources of specialized power. The comforting presence of spirit guides is not unusual at this stage.

Step 6. Conclusion. Again, note the comforting relaxation and balancing effects of this program. Conclude with the simple affirmation:

I am now empowered

In our research related to this program, we found that a panoramic view of the endless past and endless future alike almost always emerged in Step 1 during the clearing and balancing process. Participants typically experience a flow of vivid images of their previous lifetimes as they scanned their endless past. Upon reaching their first incarnation, their impressions of their past did not end. Instead, they almost always viewed a stream of energy that extended into the past as far as the spiritual eye could conceive. Likewise, in scanning their future, they experienced flowing images of what seemed to be future lives along with a stream of energy that extended into the endless future. Their experience of the endlessness of their past and future added meaning to their present existence and resulted in powerful feeling of self-worth. It likewise built self-confidence and powerful expectations of success in fulfilling their present life goals. As one participant put it: "I felt in an instant that nothing was beyond my reach. I knew that I would succeed at whatever I set out to do."

At Step 5 of the program, feelings of a powerful connection to the spirit dimension almost always emerged. That connection was typically accompanied by strong impressions of a spirit guide, or as one participant put it, "a loving presence." Interestingly, impressions of that presence often lingered long after completing the program. According to a pre-law major who participated in our development of this program, "Through this program, I discovered a life-long friend, or perhaps better said, an *endless* friend."

Synchronicity in Action as a goal-centered, self-empowerment approach may seem overly optimistic to some, but optimism builds success while pessimism either prevents or destroys it. *Affirm the power, accept it, and success is yours.*

Conclusion

Within the endless span of our existence, a major challenge is *to become all that we can be! That challenge, rather than a finished product, is an endless journey of discovery and growth.* The more we discover and the greater our growth, the more we realize what is yet to be achieved. Now is the time to set your life goals and become firmly committed to achieving them. You are a person of both **endless existence** and **endless worth**. Through the techniques presented in this chapter, you can add a third critical factor to your existence: **endless self-empowerment!**

<u>MEDITATION</u>
"What is your main goal in this life, and how will it affect your next life?"

Suggested Reading:

McCoy, E.: *How to do Automatic Writing*, 1994, Llewellyn

Slate, J.H. & Weschcke, C.L.: *Clairvoyance for Psychic Empowerment—The Art & Science of "Clear Seeing" Past the Illusions of Space & Time & Self-Deception— Includes Developing Psychic Clarity & True Vision*, 2013, A Personal Empowerment Book, Llewellyn

Slate, J.H. & Weschcke, C.L.: *The Llewellyn Complete Book of Psychic Empowerment—A Compendium of Tools & Techniques for Growth & Transformation*, 2011, Llewellyn—includes material on automatic writing.

5

SPONTANEOUS SPIRIT MANIFESTATIONS & INTERVENTIONS

Becoming Open to Spirit

Once you are receptive to the spirit realm, nothing is beyond your reach. Its limitless wealth of empowering resources becomes readily available to you. Protection, comfort, support, healing, enlightenment, and joy—all of these are possible through spontaneous spirit manifestations and interventions.

Always ready to intervene

Spontaneous spirit manifestations and interventions are consistently purposeful and empowerment driven. By transcending the limits of time and space, they become totally new sources of the knowledge and power required to achieve otherwise unattainable goals. They can intervene and empower in situations ranging from routine daily activities to emergency, life-threatening circumstances. They can provide the insight and power required to avoid adversity, cope with misfortune, solve pressing problems, and even shape future events. They can provide relevant information regarding your past, present, and future, yet they are never designed to control your actions or make decisions for you. They recognize your autonomy as an evolving spirit entity.

Spirit is always positive, always purposeful

The spontaneous manifestations and interventions of guides, angels, and guardians offer convincing evidence of the positive nature of the spirit dimension. They recognize your incomparable worth as an individual with power to determine your personal destiny. They recognize the bi-directional endless nature of your existence along with your power to choose to experience multiple lifetimes within that endless life span.

Our studies of the spirit dimension and its spontaneous expressions consistently showed that our existence in each lifetime is by personal choice—a lifetime is never forced upon anyone. Clearly, to be spiritually "sentenced" to a given embodiment would defeat the very purpose of your personal existence. Your past, present, and future are forever yours, not through predestination or fate, but through your power to set personal goals and shape your own future. You are forever evolving, and you alone are the architect of your existence.

The Boomerang Effect

The spirit dimension as a positive repository of spiritual power can enrich your existence and accelerate your progress in achieving your destiny for greatness. Negativity and malevolence in any form cannot co-exist with that power. Our studies clearly showed that any attempt to engage spiritual power and negatively target it will return upon the sender with disempowering forcefulness, a phenomenon we call the *boomerang effect*. Conversely, our studies consistently showed that the positive, altruistic targeting of spirituality is empowering, not only to the sender and receiver, but to the outside observer as well. The results include enrichment, success, rejuvenation, and better quality of life.

No Evil in the Spirit World

Although beliefs that evil exists in afterlife are common, our research over the years at Athens State University found no clear evidence to support the survival of evil or any other negative, destructive force in the spirit world. A wide range of carefully controlled studies including the séance, table tipping, channeling, hypnosis, and dream analysis along with numerous reports of near-death experiences repeatedly showed that all forms of evil are contradictory to the very nature of spirituality as a positive, empowering force. The evil characteristics all too often attributed to the spirit realm were found to be either a misrepresentation or the result of *mental projection* in which negative perceptions of oneself are subconsciously projected upon external influences, including other persons or conditions including the spirit realm.

Meeting Worldly Challenges is <u>our</u> problem

Admittedly, evil as a destructive, disempowering force clearly exists in the physical world as we know it—but to attribute the origin of that force to the spirit realm is to shift responsibility for it away from ourselves and to rationalize it as beyond our control. Such a shift impairs our ability to cope with negativity on both a personal and global scale. As a result of that shift, we tend to rationalize evil as beyond our control and thus minimize our capacity to correct it. Assuming responsibility and taking corrective action for adverse global conditions, from global hunger to climate change, are among the major challenges we face in the world today. By meeting these challenges, we can we make the world a better place for all.

The Preservation of Peak Growth

Our studies of the afterlife showed that our transition at death to the spirit realm is consistently positive and empowering. Through the transition experience, all negativity is instantly extinguished, all past growth is restored, and the potential for continued growth remains intact. Simply put, your spiritual achievements as well as your spiritual identity is forever yours. Although it may seem that you lose certain growth achievements within a given lifetime because of injury, illness, or age-related cognitive decline, your past development and accomplishments are an enduring part of your endless life history as documented in your cosmic growth records. More importantly, they become integrated into you spiritual genotype as resources for your continued growth in afterlife as well as any future lifetimes.

The preservation of our past growth experiences does not eliminate our need in afterlife to fulfill our unachieved past-life goals and to resolve any residual past-life karma that could inhibit our future growth. While all the resources of the afterlife realm are available to facilitate our spiritual evolvement, the progressive realization of our growth potentials may require other lifetimes. Because our spiritual growth is endless, multiple lifetimes become increasingly relevant, not only to promote our personal evolvement but to contribute to the evolvement of others as well. When we add to that the importance of contributing to global progress, the relevance of reincarnation becomes even greater. We are here in each lifetime to learn and grow while contributing to the greater good. Now is the time to take responsibility not only for our personal development but for global progress as well.

It is reassuring to know that our spiritual existence—whether before our first lifetime, within each lifetime, between lifetimes, or beyond our last lifetime—is by its inherent nature not only endless but forever forward.

No Evil Possession

Let's face it: Evil clearly exists in the world today. Claims of possession by evil spirits, however, raise the critical question: *Can evil function as a destructive inner sprit force beyond all personal control.* Although reports of possession by evil spirits or entities are not uncommon, our studies showed no clear evidence of personal possession by evil spirits, whether in a given lifetime or in the afterlife. Furthermore, our controlled studies found absolutely no evidence of the survival of evil in any form in the afterlife realm. Evil in any form simply fails the test of our transition at death to the spirit realm. Additional studies showed likewise that the concept of a separate spirit realm inhabited only by evil spirits or beings is contradictory to the very nature of spirituality as a positive, empowering force that underlies our very existence.

Our analysis of cases of alleged evil possession consistently showed that personal claims of being possessed by an invading evil force are typically a subconscious defense against unwanted thoughts, emotions, or actions. Claims of evil possession often begin with either a painfully traumatic experience or the systematic repression of unacceptable thoughts or behaviors that, once denied conscious awareness or expression, find outlets through uncontrolled manifestations of so-called "evil possession." Claims of evil possession thus become a defense mechanism that allows the free expression of otherwise unacceptable drives or impulses. The unacceptable behavior is consequently justified since it can be attributed to the possession of an evil force beyond the control of the individual.

The psychotherapeutic view of purported evil possession focuses on the obsessive-compulsive nature of the condition. Aside from examining the behavioral and thought patterns associated with the condition, the therapeutic view considers the potential relevance of such factors as psychological trauma and various forms of indoctrination and behavioral programming by authority figures and self-styled "enlightened leaders." A variety of de-programming and re-orientation methods, including hypnotherapy and cognitive-behavioral therapy, have been developed to promote enlightenment and self-empowerment. Once the diagnosis is accurately determined and the dynamics of the condition are identified, the prognosis for recovery through appropriate therapeutic intervention is positive. Simply identifying the source and "ventilating" the stress associated with the condition are often sufficient to fully "expiate" the perceived possession and replace it with enlightenment and self-empowerment.

Our case studies showed that personal experiences of so-called evil possession are typically sporadic in nature. Unfortunately, the residual effects including guilt, insecurity, and recurrent impressions of possession tend to linger.

Dreams are Spiritual Gateways

Our studies of dream journals showed that dreams are among the most familiar channels for spontaneous spiritual interaction. Dreams of spiritual origin can open totally new gateways of opportunity and personal empowerment. Here are a few examples of the empowerment potential of dreams as spontaneous spiritual gateways:

- They can be channels for interaction with personal spirit guides as sources of enlightenment and power.
- They can connect us to higher planes and dimensions of specialized power.
- They can provide the insight required to make important decisions and solve complex problems.
- They can be therapeutic in their capacity to alleviate stress, build self-confidence, and generate feeling of security and wellbeing.
- They can be important sources of creativity.
- They can activate the dormant subconscious resources required to accelerate learning and improve memory,
- They can enrich social interactions and promote the development of social skills.
- They can generate clairvoyant and precognitive insight related to personal and career goals.
- They can be sources of rejuvenating and healing energies.
- They can uncover relevant past life experiences.
- They can facilitate out-of-body travel to higher spiritual planes of both knowledge and power.
- On a global scale, they can provide the enlightenment and inspiration required to promote progress and achieve world peace.

These are only a few of the many possibilities of dreams as sources of spiritual empowerment.

The dream experience as an empowerment gateway often unfolds as a series of dreams related to complex life situations, including problems solving and decision making. That capacity of the serial dream was dramatically illustrated by a college student whose indecisiveness regarding her future career had increasingly become a source of anxiety. As the weight of career uncertainty increased, she experienced, by her own report, a series of dreams in which she was actively engaged as a counselor in a health service setting. Each dream was accompanied by the powerful presence of a spirit guide and a sense of personal fulfillment. As a result of the interactive dream experiences, she successfully clarified her career goals and is today a counseling psychologist whose professional practice includes the analysis of dreams as spiritual gateways.

In an unrelated example of the serial dream as a spiritual gateway, a veterinarian experienced through a series dream the progressive unfolding of a plan for the recovery and care of abandoned animals. Each dream in the series included interactions with a specialized spirit guide who designated the planned program as the *Animal Empowerment Project*. The series of dreams unveiled images of an advanced animal empowerment center along with concepts related to the care and recovery of injured or abused animals. Adding to the relevance of the veterinarian's experience was the inclusion of animals as spirit beings in the dream. In her dreams, she experienced what seemed to be astral travel to the spirit world during which she interacted with familiar deceased animals that had been patients in her clinic. In her own words, "The presence of animals in the spirit realm and our future reunion with them not only add to the importance of our caring for animals as beings of spiritual worth, it greatly increases the appeal of the spirit realm as a heavenly place for our continued growth in afterlife. How could it be heavenly without the presence of animals?"

Dreams as Spiritual Therapy

There's a growing body of evidence that dreams of spiritual origin are often therapeutic in their capacity to dissolve growth blockages that impede our progress and constrict our lives. Examples include blockages often related to phobias and feelings of inferiority. That possibility was illustrated by a college student whose inferiority feelings were accompanied by intense fear of enclosed places severely constricted her daily activities. Having struggled with the dual condition that seemed to worsen over the years, she experienced a vivid dream in which she entered a narrow corridor that led to an enclosure with a gold throne situated inside. As she walked through the narrow corridor, she felt her fear of enclosed places slowly dissolving away. Finally, upon entering the small enclosure at the end of the corridor and becoming comfortably seated upon the gold throne, she experienced a powerful sense of personal worth and security as all feelings of inferiority vanished. The results of the experience were both permanent and profound. The dream experience effectively activated the subconscious sources of spiritual power and unleashed the resources required to enrich and empower her life.

Traumatic experiences, including those of past-life origin, are likewise receptive to spiritual intervention through dreams that identify the painful experience and disarm its disempowering effects. That role of dreams as spiritual instruments of power was dramatically illustrated by a graduate student whose fear of touching or being touched (aphephobia) not only restricted her interactions with others, it was a source of persistent anxiety. She avoided any social situation in which physical contact, such as shaking hands, might be expected. The fear became so intense that she became increasing isolated from others, including family members. Even when wearing gloves, she avoided touching items such as door knobs, phones, and writing pens that may have been recently touched by others. Likewise, when shopping, she avoided purchasing items that may have been in physical contact with others.

Finally, through a spontaneous dream experience which she believed to be of spiritual origin, she experienced insight into the source of the fear and a full liberation from its disempowering effects. The dream occurred soon after of her graduation with a Master's Degree in Economics which she had accepted in absentia because of the phobia. In the dream, which she described as "in full color," she was accompanied by a gentle spirit presence into a shadowy street setting where countless men, women, and children were suffering from what appeared to be a devastating pandemic. Some were weeping and others seemed to be unconscious and near death. Suddenly, she recognized herself among them.

Still accompanied by the spirit presence, she was then guided gently above the distressing scene where she viewed it as it slowly faded away. It was then that she experienced a gentle fading and full liberation from the fear of touching or being touched. By her report, the spontaneous spirit intervention not only gave rationality to the fear, it fully extinguished it. Now the owner of a thriving retail business, she attributes her career success largely to the dream experience that became a channel for spirit intervention and full liberation from a severely constrictive fear.

Lucid Dreams and Out-of-body Travel during Sleep
Have you ever personally visited the spirit realm and interacted with its vast wealth of empowering resources? The possibility of such visitations finds support not only

in the controlled lab setting but in numerous reports of spontaneous out-of-body travel during sleep that seems to engage the spirit realm. From that perspective, sleep is seen as a state in which the astral body disengages the physical and, while typically remaining suspended over it throughout sleep, often spontaneously travels to distant destinations, including the spirit world. In that projected state of awareness, which is sometimes described as lucid dreaming, the astral body becomes liberated to interact with higher planes of power as well as advanced spirit guides and growth specialists. Through that spontaneous interaction, enlightenment as well as specialized power related to current life situations often emerges. The results can include spiritual insight and a host of specific mental and physical benefits such as facilitating problem solving, resolving conflicts, alleviating depression, and promoting health, fitness, and rejuvenation.

Aside from these benefits, increasing creativity is among the most frequently reported results of the spontaneous out-of-body travel during sleep. A fashion designer known for his extraordinarily creative fashions reports that spontaneous OBES emerging during lucid dreaming often depicts in minute detail his outstanding designs. The innovative designs, by his report, are typically the products of a familiar spirit guide he calls his "creative partner." Along another line, an artist widely known for his impressionistic paintings reports frequent spontaneous out-of-body interactions during sleep in which he observes the merging of color with figurative designs that generate a unique energy force. "The goal of my art," he noted, "is to convey that energy force."

OBEs during sleep offer the opportunity to deliberately intervene into the spontaneous state in order to purposefully direct travel to certain destinations for specifically chosen purposes. Travel can include both spontaneous and personally driven astral interactions with physical as well as spiritual destinations related to your personal goals which may be formulated either before spontaneous travel or during the travel experience. Here are a few examples of travel possibilities during the spontaneous out-of-body state:

- **Astral Plane Interactions.** You can travel to specific astral planes of color related to your particular goals. For instance, you can direct travel to astral planes of indigo for goals related to spiritual enlightenment, whereas for goals related to social enrichment, self-confidence, and career success you can target travel to planes of bright blue. You can travel to bright gold planes and draw from them the power to accelerate learning, including the mastery of languages and various technical skills. You can travel to iridescent emerald planes to access healing energy, promote rejuvenation, and literally reverse the visible signs of aging. You can engage planes of very light blue know for their capacity to promote serenity and emotional balance.

- **Empowerment Forum Interactions.** You can direct travel to the so-called *Empowerment Forum* where you can interact with enlightened growth and healing specialists.

- **Cosmic Fountain Interactions.** You can bathe in the comforting spray of so-called *Cosmic Fountains of Peace and Power* which are found among the majestic gardens located throughout the astral realm.

- **Viewing Archival Akashic Records.** You can view your personal archival records as sources enlightenment and power.

- **Spirit Guide Interactions.** You can interact one-on-one with your familiar spirit guides and specialized growth specialists to experience renewal, inspiration, and enlightenment. You may discover other totally new ministering guides who are relevant to your present life strivings.

- **Comfort and Renewal.** You can experience comfort and resolution of grief through your interactions with the departed, including persons and animals alike.

- **Accelerating Growth.** You can accelerate development of your highest mental powers through your interactions with orbs and other forms of concentrated energy found throughout the spirit realm. You can embrace the energy forms, and in some instances, you can literally enter them to experience their innermost centers of specialized power.

- **Expanding Insight.** Through your exploration of the spirit dimension with its myriad of empowering resources, you can expand your perception and understanding of the afterlife and the infinite nature of your personal existence.

- **Cosmic Illumination.** Through your out-of-body probes of the distant reaches of the spirit realm, you can experience *cosmic illumination* that expands your awareness and understanding of the universe as well as the infinite nature of multiverse.

- **Spiritual Oneness**. You can experience an attuned state of spiritual oneness with the highest sources of energy, knowledge, and power.

Spontaneous out-of-body travel during sleep, once embraced, can become a powerful learning experience that promotes your total growth, including your mastery of out-of-body skills. Given the spontaneous experience, you can develop your ability to exercise your out-of-body powers and deliberately induce travel to destinations, both tangible and intangible, that are relevant to your personal goals.

Spontaneous Intervention in Emergency Situations

Our case studies showed that both protection and prevention are possible through spiritual intervention in situations of urgency or impending danger. Spontaneous intervention, including those of benevolent spirit guides, can warn of danger and in some instances, actually intervene to prevent injury or other adverse consequences. They can offer protection that becomes a shield against tragedy even when the danger is unknown to us. Only in retrospect do we become aware of the potential tragedy and the shield that protected us against it. That possibility was dramatically illustrated by a high-school math teacher who had misplaced her prescribed medication while out-of-town on a two-week vacation. Upon her return, she checked with her physician and was advised to immediately discontinue the medication because of potentially serious reactions. She is convinced that her misplaced medication was due to the protective intervention of a personal spirit guide. In another instance of possible spirit intervention, a student's lost concert ticket may have prevented her injury in a serious auto accident. The accident occurred when the group of students she would have accompanied to the concert were involved in a serious auto accident. The lost ticked which prevented her attendance was, in her opinion, due to the prompt intervention of a personal spirit guide.

In another remarkable instance of possible spirit manifestation involving urgency, a group of five students who became lost while exploring a cave reported a small orb of bright light that led them to safety. They remain convinced that the orb was a purposeful manifestation of a benevolent spirit guide.

Animals as Intervention Specialists

The behavior of animals, from the migratory behavior of geese in perfect formation to the lowly lizard's unscripted motions, offers convincing evidence of both the complexity and orderliness of spirituality. Through their interventions as spirit messengers, animals can connect us to the spirit realm in ways that enrich and empower our lives. Among the familiar examples are animal companions that often appear to sense danger and then act purposefully to warn of risks. That possibility was illustrated when a hiker's dog companion appeared to sense danger and then acted to block the hiker from crossing a ravine on a cable bridge that was later found to be damaged and about to collapse.

The Spirituality of Nature

Perhaps nothing is more convincing of the power of spirituality than the magnificent manifestations seen throughout nature. By simply viewing the unparalleled beauty of nature, you can experience its creative and sustaining power. Through your up-close interactions with nature, you will experience an unlimited range of spontaneous spirit manifestations and interventions. Inspiration, success, enlightenment, and enrichment are all available through mindfully connecting to the power of nature. (*See Connecting to the Power of Nature* by Joe H. Slate 2009, Llewellyn.)

Conclusion

Through the many spontaneous spirit manifestations and interventions now available to you, you will experience the spiritual essence of your existence. You will discover not only your uniqueness but the endless nature of your existence as a spirit being. Your will discover the empowering nature of the spirit realm with its abundant growth resources that are available to you at any moment. You will experience your capacity to interact with the spontaneous spirit manifestations of power and focus them on your personal goals. You will discover that your past growth experiences are never lost—they become forever entwined into your existence as both endless and forever forward.

As mentioned previously, your Dreams not only are often spontaneous manifestations of Spirit, but whatever has been experienced spontaneously can become a program inviting interaction with the Spirit Realm. Here is such a program taken from our book, *Self-Empowerment & Your Subconscious Mind.* Page 120–122

Dream Works Program: Interactions with the Spirit Realm

Since the spirit realm is the overarching, energizing force that sustains our existence as evolving souls, it is not surprising to find that dreams often tap into that dimension as an ever-present reality rather than a distant, impersonal dimension. It's a dimension that invites our awareness and interaction, not only during dreaming, but at any moment. The interventions of that dimension into our lives are consistently empowering and probably far more common than most of us realize. They can range from simply the comforting awareness of a caring spirit guide to the powerful intervention of a protective force at a time of great personal danger.

The Dream Works Program recognizes our existence as essentially spiritual and characterized by on-going interactions with the spirit dimension. You are constantly connected to that dimension through the **Center of Spiritual Power** existing in your subconscious mind as discussed earlier in this book. By actively interacting with that center of power, you have instant and direct access to all the resources of the spirit realm, including spirit guides and growth specialists who are constantly poised to enrich and empower you life. What better way to become intimately connected to the spirit realm and its abundant resources than through the center of spiritual power existing within yourself?

The Dream Works Program is designed to provide direct access to the powers within yourself and, by extension, to the spirit realm at large. Through this program, you can get to know your personal spirit guides and other growth specialists who are constantly poised to enrich your life. You can actively interact with higher spiritual planes to empower your life mentally, physically, and spiritually. Through your inter-actions with the spirit realm, you can reach your highest pinnacle of growth and ful-fillment. Nothing is beyond your reach when you become intimately connected and attuned to the spirit dimension. Here's the program.

1. **Goal Statement.** Although this program requires no goal statement other than to experience the spiritual essence of your existence, you may wish to state in your own words specific outcomes, such as spiritual enlightenment, healing, rejuvenation, happiness, and abundance. Document your goals by recording them in your dream journal. Documentation builds commitment to achieve your goals and positive expectations of success, both of which work together to promote your personal empowerment.

2. **Empowering Imagery.** Upon becoming comfortable and relaxed before falling asleep, visualize the bright Center of Spiritual Power deep within the core of your being. Let yourself experience that center not simply as a part of yourself but as the very essence of your existence as an evolving soul. Note the bril-liance of that center radiating throughout your subconscious to energize and illuminate your total being. Visualize distant dimensions of spiritual power, and sense your connection to them. Let yourself become fully enveloped in the glowing energy that typically accompanies spiritual enlightenment. Allow impressions of worth, serenity, and well-being spring forth to accompany that

glow. If you goal is to achieve a more highly specific goal, let relevant images emerge to become a part of your intended destiny for success.

3. **Spiritual Interactions.** At this stage, awareness of a personal spirit guide will often emerge. In the presence of that personal guide, you may experience a profound astral state in which you travel out-of-body to distant astral planes to experience their multiple powers. At this stage, you may also experience interactions with discarnate beings who have crossed over to the spirit realm. It is important, however, to allow these interactions to emerge spontaneously rather than deliberately calling forth a spirit guide or discarnate entity. The key to spiritual empowerment using this program is to maintain a state of spiritual receptivity to the resources available to you from the spiritual realm. Conclude this step by allowing relevant impressions of both present and future relevance to unfold.

4. **Empowering Affirmation.** Upon awakening, affirm in your own words your attunement to the Center of Power within as your connection to the spirit realm beyond. Record the empowering effects of the experience upon awakening in your dream journal.

Summary of Purpose & Benefits

With practice, you will master your skill in using this approach to increase your awareness of the spirit realm and build rewarding relationships with your spiritual helpers and guides. Aside from that, you will develop your ability to tap into your subconscious powers, to include those related to healing, rejuvenation, intelligence, learning, memory, and self-development. You will soon discover that all the resources you need are available to you. Through this program, you can now reach out, embrace them, and use them to empower your life.

MEDITATION
"How to become 'Open' to Spirit?"

Suggested Reading:

Clement, Stephanie & Rosen, Terry Lee: *Dreams Working Interactive*, 2000, Llewellyn

McElroy, Mark: *Lucid Dreaming for Beginners—Simple Techniques for Creating Interactive Dreams*, 2007, Llewellyn

Webster, Richard: *Spirit & Dream Animals—Decipher their Messages, Discover Your Totem,* 2011, Llewellyn

Books that discuss Nature and Animals:

Slate, Joe H.: *Connecting to the Power of Nature* (2009), Llewellyn

Books that discuss Akashic Records:

McCoy, Edain: *Astral Projection for Beginners—I Techniques for Traveling to Other Realms,* 1999, Llewellyn

Goldberg, Bruce: *Astral Voyages—Mastering the Art of Interdimensional Travel,* 1998, Llewellyn

Ambrose, Kala: *The Awakened Aura—Experiencing the Evolution of Your Energy Body,* 2011, Llewellyn

Webster, Richard: *The Practical Guide to Past Life Memories—Twelve Proven Methods,* 2001, Llewellyn

Slate, Joe H. & Weschcke, Carl Llewellyn: *Astral Projection for Psychic Empowerment—the Out-of-Body Experience, Astral Powers & Their Practical Application,* 2010, Llewellyn

6

DELIBERATE & INDUCED
INTERACTIONS

Simple Techniques for Your Personal Experience

Nothing is more convincing of the power of spirituality than personal experience, and it is your own controlled personal experience that will open the doors to purposeful interaction.

Interaction with the Spirit Realm

Fortunately, numerous strategies, some developed in the highly controlled laboratory setting, are now available to facilitate personal spiritual interactions. Among them are meditation, self-hypnosis, automatic writing, the pendulum, crystal gazing, table tipping, and the séance, to mention but a few. The results can range from simple impressions of a spirit presence to profound spiritual interactions that open totally new gateways to personal growth and power.

Each of the interactive programs presented in this chapter is based on the concept that spirituality, rather than a possession, is an interactive phenomenon that defines the quintessential nature of personal existence. Each program focuses on your uniqueness as an endless life-force being and your capacity to overcome all barriers to your growth. Finally, each program recognizes the existence of a higher spiritual realm and your capacity at any moment to experience its limitless powers through you interactions with it.

Interactive Meditation

Spiritual Empowerment through Interactive Meditation is a research based program that focuses on the capacity of mental, physical, and spiritual functions to interact in ways that unleash new power and enlightenment from both within and beyond the self. It is based on the capacity of mental, physical, and spiritual processes to induce an integrated, balanced state of full harmony. It is in that spiritually empowered state that the highest sources of power become activated to promote success in achieving otherwise unattainable personal goals. Spiritual enlightenment, enriched personal relationships, accelerated learning, academic and career success, better health and fitness, and even financial achievement are all possible through the application of this approach.

9-Step Program for Spiritual Empowerment through Interactive Meditation

In our development of this 9-step meditation program, we made sure that proper research supported the procedure. In the controlled experimental setting, each step was carefully implemented and in post-procedure interviews, successful achievement of specific goals was carefully monitored. Our controlled studies showed the approach to be among the best known for achieving an integrative state of personal empowerment. Here's the program:

> **Step 1. Preliminaries.** Allow approximately one hour for the procedure which is conducted in a quiet, safe setting during which there are no interruptions. In your own words, specify your goal of becoming spiritually empowered through the application of this program.

> **Step 2. Relaxation.** To begin the procedure, settle back into comfortable, relaxed position with your hands resting in your lap or at your sides. With your eyes closed, take in a few deep breaths and slow your breathing, taking a little longer to exhale. As you breathe slowly and rhythmically, clear your mind of active thought as your cares and concerns slowly fade away. Note the relaxation and serenity permeating your total being.

> **Step 3. Finger-tip Engagement.** While in that relaxed, peaceful state, bring the tips of your fingers together and affirm in your own words your inner state of balance and security. Take a few moments for peaceful serenity to infuse your total being.

> **Step 4. Energy Infusion.** Disengage your fingertips and with your cupped palms turned upward, think of your hands as your body's spiritual antennae. Visualize bright streams of energy from the highest realms of spiritual power interacting with the energy in your palms and from there, permeating your total being. As the infusion of energy from higher realms interacts with your own

energy system, you may experience pleasurable tingling sensations, first in your hands, and then throughout your full body. Allow plenty of time for the dynamic interactive process to reach its highest peak.

Step 5. Balance. To balance the powerful interactive flow of energy throughout your being, first bring your hands together in a "praying hands" position and then affirm in your own words the energizing and balancing effects of the interaction. It's at this step that awareness of benevolent ministering guides and spiritual growth specialists often emerges, to include not only vivid images of a spirit presence but clear messages related to present life situations.

Step 6. Empowering Imagery. As you remain balanced and attuned to the infusion of spiritual energy, allow empowering imagery of spiritual origin to unfold, often in detailed, colorful form. Sense the empowering significance of the imagery, to include its relevance to your present and future alike. Allow plenty of time for the imagery process to fully unfold.

Step 7. Cosmic Power Mode. Enveloped in energy and fully energized, relish the *cosmic power mode* in which abundant power in its finest form infuses and envelopes your total being.

Step 8. Empowering Affirmation. While remaining in the cosmic power mode, take a few moments to reflect on the empowering effects this interactive program. You can affirm your power to achieve certain specific goals of special relevance, to include those related to spiritual evolvement, interpersonal relationships, health and fitness, and career success, to mention but a few.

Step 9. Conclusion. Conclude this program by simply affirming: I am now empowered mentally, physically, and spiritually.

Perhaps not unexpectedly, the effectiveness of this program dramatically improves with practice. Whether used for spiritual enlightenment, personal enrichment, or success in achieving wide ranging goals, Interactive Meditation when repeatedly practiced can accelerate your spiritual growth by adding both meaning and power to your daily life.

Often occurring in Step 6 (Empowering Imagery) of the program are various clear energy forms, typically in vivid color. Common examples include bright orbs, distant planes, and other figurative designs including pyramids, pulsating threads, and wavy horizontal lines that beckon interaction related to specific life situations, including important decision making and health concerns. Likewise often unfolding at this step are highly positive images of the departed and other spirit beings, including familiar spirit guides. Almost always accompanying these interactions are feelings of security and wellbeing. Our research of this program found no valid manifestations of so-called malevolent or evil influences.

Interactive Table Tipping

Table tipping (also called *table tapping, table tilting,* or simply *tabling*) with a long and interesting history continues to rank prominently among the more effective approaches known for promoting productive spiritual interactions. The history of this approach dates to the 19th century séance setting in which the table often spontaneously tilted, and while in that suspended position, tapped out upon the floor answers to yes-or-no questions posed by members of the group as their hands rested upon the table. Typically, a single tap of the table upon the floor signified a "yes" response to questions posed by the group while two taps signified a "no" response.

Spiritual Empowerment through Table Tipping

Still practiced in both Europe and the U. S., this so-called *physical mediumship approach* as practiced today typically requires four to six active participants seated comfortably at a light table such as a folding card table in a quiet setting free of distractions. Participants at the table can either designate a leader or they can simply allow the procedure to spontaneously unfold. While an observing audience seems neither to facilitate nor impede the procedure, the messages conveyed by the table can be directed toward not only participants at the table but members of the audience as well.

Table tipping is typically initiated by the formulation of objectives by participants at the table followed by the joining of hands as a gesture of group cohesiveness. Hands are then placed palm sides down upon the table as the body is relaxed and the mind is cleared of active thought, a process often called "letting go." With hands relaxed and resting lightly upon the table, the group remains responsive throughout the session to emerging energy manifestations in the table. A slight pulsation or mild vibration in the table can signal an energy presence that often precedes tilting.

Once tilting occurs, participants mentally acknowledge the energy presence as an information source and affirm their commitment to engage in spiritual interaction with that presence. An "interactive communication code" is then designated—typically one tap of the table upon the floor for "yes" and two taps for "no" to questions posed by participants at the table. A receptive state that focuses on working *with* the table rather than *against* it for the duration of the session is essential to successful table tipping.

In table tipping, information is conveyed through a wide range of table movements, a phenomenon we call *table kinetics*. Aside from the standard *yes* or *no* responses, table kinetics include such variations as hesitation, repeated or sequential tapping, light or heavy tapping, and vibrations, to list but a few. Once interaction has been established, a hesitation response suggests incertitude while a rapid tap of the table in response to a question signifies decisiveness. A forceful tap of the table suggests authority while a gentle tapping communicates caring and understanding. A repetitive tapping of the table to a single question suggests the possible intervention of more than one information source. A strong vibrational pattern in the table is associated with an assertive, forceful source while a less intense pulsating pattern is associated with a more reserved source.

In rare instances, the table has been known either to pivot on one leg or to fully levitate with all legs clearing the floor as participants hands continued to rest palm sides down upon the table. Pivoting on one leg typically suggests the convergence of energies and the possible consolidation of energies prior to meaningful tapping. Full table levitation is generally considered to be related to dire situations or impending life-changing events. The good news is that upon return to the tilted position, the table often provides through tapping highly relevant information of corrective or preventative relevance.

Table tipping is usually concluded with expressions of appreciation by the group as their hands remain upon the table in the "at rest" position. Upon conclusion of the exercise, group discussions can complement the knowledge gained by exploring its relevance and finding ways it can be applied.

In developing your table tipping skills, repeated group practice is essential. Practice can enrich the interaction and provide greater insight into the nature of the spirit realm. More specifically, practice can provide solutions to personal and global problems and at a deeply personal level, expand awareness of spiritual specialists, including personal spirit guides and growth specialists. It can offer solutions to both personal and global problems and provide information concerning important future events. These benefits of practice become even greater when we add to them the sheer pleasure of working with an enlightened table-tipping group and experiencing together the rich discovery of new knowledge and power.

Table tipping as an interpersonal experience involves personal interactions with participants at the table as well as spirit beings including teachers, personal guides, and growth specialists in the spirit realm. Because the most effective interpersonal interactions are positive in nature, an arrogant or disparaging approach to table tipping is typically counterproductive. Such authoritative directives by the group as: *We demand answers to our question; Show yourself to us; Prove to us that you are here;* and *Are you trustworthy?* are inappropriate and counterproductive. They can extinguish any positive on-going interaction while preventing further communication. Recognizing the potential benefits of table tipping as an interpersonal experience while maintaining a positive state of mind is consequently critical to the success of the procedure.

Here are a few examples of the diverse empowering effects of table tipping:

- A college student experienced through table tipping a deeply meaningful interaction that confirmed the wisdom of her decision to pursue a career in cultural anthropology. Now a professor of cultural anthropology at a leading university, she concludes, "The table tipping experience introduced me to an advanced specialist who was to become a valuable guide throughout my career."

- The owner of a faltering women's fashion firm experienced through table tipping the unfolding of an expansion plan that included the addition of children's clothing. Motivated by the experience, she initiated the plan which resulted in unprecedented growth for the firm. She remains convinced that the advice gained through table tipping not only prevented failure of the firm, it gave a new life to it.

- A couple who jointly participated in a table tipping session discovered an intervening energy they described as a *couple's specialist*. The specialist, by their report, connected them in a way that opened new doors for growth in their relationship. By their report the experience was multifunctional—it answered specific "yes or no" questions through tapping while connecting them both mentally and emotionally; it clarified certain blockages in their relationship and identified ways of overcoming them; it identified specific concerns, including financial and revealed strategies that would resolve them. By their report, table tipping was for them a "perfect couple's therapist."

- An unemployed social worker discovered through table tipping several career options, to include existing job vacancies as well as employment opportunities in related fields. He then used table tipping to narrow the information down into an exact plan of action that he described as the "optimal career development." In his own words, "Unemployment combined with table tipping became a formula for my career success."

Spiritual interactions through table tipping are consistently empowerment oriented. Table tipping can explore spiritual mysteries while at a highly practical level, provide information. It can identify sources of phobias, anxiety, and depression while the providing the therapeutic insight to resolve them. Table tipping can connect you to the best of therapists—the one existing within yourself along with those specialists existing in the spirit realm. Given these resources, therapeutic self-empowerment is available at any moment for everyone. Even the past-life sources of disempowering distress are subject to the therapeutic intervention of table tipping. That may seem unrealistically optimistic to some, but spiritual manifestations and interactions through table tipping remain among our best and most convincing teachers as well as among our most advanced growth experts.

Interactive Pendulum Swinging

The pendulum—typically a small weight suspended on a chain or string—is a simple device for gathering highly objective information often unavailable from other sources. A variety of movements of the pendulum when suspended from one's hand can convey a variety of responses to questions posed by the individual holding the pendulum as well as, with permission, from objective observers. Typically, a two-and-fro movement of the pendulum signifies a "yes" response, a side-to-side movement signifies a "no" response, and a circular movement signifies a neutral or "cannot say" response to questions posed.

Spiritual Empowerment through Pendulum Swinging

Several views have emerged in efforts to explain the pendulum as a communication or interactive device. One popular view holds that the pendulum can function as sensitive antennae with the capacity to respond directly to meaningful energy stimuli, including that of subconscious origin, when suspended over the subject's hand. That view emphasizes the potential of the pendulum as not only an information retrieval tool but a therapeutic technique with both diagnostic and treatment implications. Such conditions as phobias, obsessions, and compulsions, including those of past-life origin, are particularly receptive to this application of the pendulum. Once the sources of the symptoms are identified through the pendulum, the disorder is often resolved and the disempowering symptoms disappear.

Yet another view of the pendulum as an information retrieval device holds that the pendulum, when suspended over a tangible object, can respond to the energies of the individual as well as the events associated with that object. That view is especially relevant to the forensic application of the pendulum as an investigative tool. Examples include identifying the location of a missing person by suspending the pendulum over an article of clothing belonging to that person; identifying the location of suspects as well as crime related objects, including weapons, by suspending the pendulum over a map; and determining the relevance of tangible evidence by suspending the pendulum over the object. Aside from these, the pendulum as an investigative tool has been used to locate lost animals, recover stolen works of art, and retrieve hidden caches of stolen money.

The pendulum as a self-empowerment tool focuses on its capacity to induce a receptive state of attentiveness that connects conscious awareness to the spiritual sources of power and enlightenment, including ministering guides and spiritual planes. Through its movements when held over one's own hand, it can initiate an interaction with multiple functions, clears the mind and activates the inner resources required for successful mental and physical performance. As a preparatory activity, it can function to improve psychomotor performance and enhance mental functioning. It can function as an integrative tool that improves concentration and generates more effective motor coordination. It can unleash dormant skills, improve memory, and expand awareness of other realities, including the spirit dimension with its abundant growth resources.

Pendulum Rejuvenation Program

A program developed by the Parapsychology Research Institute and Foundation (PRIF) shows promising evidence of the pendulum's capacity to inhibit aging. The program, called simply *Pendulum Rejuvenation*, uses a pendulum consisting of an appropriately programmed quartz crystal suspended on a chain. Effective programming of the crystal requires simply allowing warm, not hot, water to flow gently over the crystal, and while stroking it, inviting the crystal to become a channel for rejuvenating energy. Upon air drying, the crystal pendant is then suspended over the palm of either hand and allowed to move spontaneously. Typically within seconds, mild vibrating energy sensations are noted, first in the hands and then throughout the full body. The pendulum is then placed aside and, with eyes closed and palms turned upward, radiant images of color are allowed to spontaneously emerge. As the colorful forms of energy unfold, special attention is focused on iridescent green images, to include planes, spheres, and various other forms. At this stage, mild vibratory energy is usually noted, first in the hands and from there, spreading throughout the full body. The experience is concluded by simply bringing the hands together and affirming the rejuvenating effects of the experience. With practice of this program, the energies of rejuvenation become more and more evident as the physical signs of aging are progressively reversed.

Interactive Crystal Gazing

Crystal gazing using a crystal ball is among the oldest techniques known for engendering both spiritual enlightenment and personal empowerment. Under appropriately controlled conditions, it can unleash hidden potential and open new levels of personal awareness. In the psychotherapy setting, it can facilitate relaxation of the frontalis muscle in the brow that rapidly progresses downward through the total body, an application that is particularly useful in the treatment of a variety of anxiety related disorders.

Spiritual Empowerment through Crystal Gazing

Crystal gazing has shown unusual effectiveness as a meditation approach that promotes empowering interaction with not only the subconscious sources of power but higher spiritual sources as well. That two-fold function of crystal gazing can be effectively generated through the so-called peripheral glow *technique* that begins by focusing attention on the center of crystal ball. Peripheral vision is then gradually expanded to its limits, after which a whitish glow ensues and perception of physical surroundings fades. They eyes are then closed and the physical body is relaxed as enlightenment of both subconscious and spiritual origin unfolds. At this stage, the expanded awareness of inner sources of power as well as spiritual teachers and guides frequently emerge. Meaningful interactions with personal guides that result in solutions to existing problems along with clear perceptions of future realities are likewise common.

Group Involvement

Aside from its usefulness in individual viewing, the crystal ball is particularly adaptable for use by groups. When the ball is situated at the center of the group, crystal viewing as a group technique can generate positive group interactions that facilitate spiritual enlightenment as well as cooperation and success in achieving both group and individual goal. It is an excellent technique that facilitates the formulation objectives and strategies for achieving them. Our studies showed that crystal gazing in groups resulted in a synergistic effect in which personal experiences, when shared with the group, resulted in a cumulative group effect far greater than simply the sum of the experiences. The integration of group experiences often became a peak experience for individual members of the group with an effect that was profoundly enlightening and personally empowering.

Conclusion

Spiritual empowerment is at last available to everyone. Whether through tangible or intangible means, you can probe the depths of spirituality and discover new meaning to your existence as an evolving spirit being. You can activate a spiritual interaction that fully engages the sources of spiritual power from both within yourself and beyond. When spiritually empowered, nothing is beyond your reach.

MEDITATION

"How can simple exercises empower you spiritually?"

Suggested Reading:

Andrews, Ted: *Crystal Balls & Crystal Bowls—Tools for Ancient Scrying & Modern Seer ship*, 2002, Llewellyn

Chauran, Alexandra: *Crystal Ball Reading for Beginners—Easy Divination & Interpretation*, 2011, Llewellyn

Lo Scarabeo Pendulums: Nearly 30 especially designed and constructed pendulum available from www.Llewellyn.com and metaphysical stores.

Cunningham, Scott: *Divination for Beginners—Reading the Past, Present & Future*, 2003, Llewellyn

Gadini, Roberto: *Pendulum Power Magic Kit*, 2004, Lo Scarabeo/Llewellyn

Slate, Joe H., & Weschcke, Carl Llewellyn: *The Llewellyn Completer Book of Psychic Empowerment*, 2011, Llewellyn

Webster, Richard: *Pendulum Magic for Beginners*, 2012, Llewellyn

7

SCIENCE & THE SPIRIT

Quantum Physics and the New Paranormal

The Merging of Science and Spirit

Authentic spirituality is a progressively empowering energy force that actively embraces the scientific search for new knowledge. As a result, modern spirituality and science together become progressively committed to the application of science in ways that promote both personal and global progress. As EO Wilson noted, "The human condition is the most important frontier of the natural sciences." (Wilson, EO, 1998. *Consilience: The unity of knowledge.* New York: Alfred A. Knopf. p. 334). Although we are "conditioned" to view reality in familiar physical terms, science, including modern physics and quantum theory, offers a meeting point for a better understanding of the non-physical as an extension of a greater reality. The result is a collective merging of science and spirit that generates a totally new body of knowledge with potential to enrich and empower our present and future existence.

It is, however, important to note that a better understanding of greater reality through the merging of science and the spirit does not imply infallibility. Empirical in nature, scientific theory is always open to uncertainty, revision, and even reversal. As the philosopher Karl Popper noted, scientific knowledge consists in the search for *truth rather than the search for certainty.* He further notes that *all human knowledge is fallible and therefore uncertain.* (Popper, Karl, 1996. In Search of a Better World. New York: Rutledge, New York).

The Merging of Paranormal and Esotericism

Notwithstanding the potential fallibility of conventional science, we can discover new knowledge by drawing from paranormal-related studies conducted in the experimental laboratory setting as well as from traditional esoteric sources. These sources, when combined with pertinent elements of modern physical and quantum theory, become reasonable extensions of a greater reality inclusive of both the physical and supra-physical. As a result, such experiences as that of near-death, out-of-body, lucid dreaming, past-life memories, life-between-lifetimes recall, and the bi-directional endlessness of personal existence assume critical relevance to our understanding of the interrelatedness of science and spirit.

THE NEAR-DEATH EXPERIENCE (NDE)

The Personal Experience of Spirit

While the most convincing evidence of the power of spirituality is personal experience, authentic spirituality often seeks objective validation. Arguably at least, possibly no human experience, aside from death itself, could more convincingly validate the power of spirituality than the near-death experience (NDE). Our efforts to investigate that possibility included numerous case reports along with personal interviews with NDE subjects conducted in a controlled setting.

Not Dead, but More Alive

Diversity in both personal background and age characterized the participants in our studies. The youngest of our subjects was age 18 and the oldest was age 92. Regardless of age, they each described their personal near-death experience as both unforgettable and empowering. None of them reported a sense of being dead; they experienced instead a sense of being more fully alive. Rather than viewing their personal near-death experience as negative or in any way disempowering, they consistently viewed it as adding meaning and purpose to their existence by "re-introducing" them to the "other side" and equipping them with the resources required for more successfully continuing their life on "this side."

Life-Changing Perspectives

Our research, which included post-NDE interviews, showed the near-death experience was often a peak event with life-changing effects. It was frequently a critical "meeting point" for the physical and non-physical worlds that expanded understanding of both. Beyond that, it often became an extension of a "greater reality" that was inclusive of both the physical and the supra-physical. At an intensely personal level, it often initiated empowering interactions with spirit guides, growth specialists, and in many instances, the departed. For many of the subjects, time seemed to stand still throughout the experience. As reported by one subject, "The sense of timelessness gave comfort, peace, and feelings of wellbeing throughout the experience and beyond." Feelings of being separate from the physical body as well as separate from the world were common. Viewing the body as if outside and above it often occurred at the beginning and ending phase of the experience.

Perceiving the Greater Reality

The beginning stage of the NDE was often accompanied by a sense of effortlessly moving upward and away from the body within a glowing tunnel of light. Vivid perceptions of being enveloped in bright light that extended "as far as the eye could see" were prevalent. Interactions with beings of light, including familiar spirit guides, often added meaning to the experience.

Overview of Past and Present, and the Life Between

The NDE can include a vivid overview of the present lifetime as well as past lifetimes and life between them. In scanning the past, it can uncover experiences of current relevance. It can increase awareness of important past accomplishments as well as unfinished tasks and unattained goals. As a result, it can become a powerful motivational force that includes clear images of relevant past-life experiences as well as unfinished present-life works in progress. Glimpses of the bidirectional endlessness of personal existence were also common. In some instances, the NDE revealed in clear detail future events of important personal relevance.

With Awakening, there is Renewal

Changes in perspectives related to distressful life situations frequently followed the near-death experience. Problem situations became new growth opportunities and hopelessness situations become success possibilities. It often increased self-confidence and built strong expectations of success. As a result, the experience not only increased motivation, it provided the skills required for the achievement of difficult goals. It often generated positive changes in the perception of distressful life situations and activated the inner therapeutic resources required to resolve conflict, cope with stress, and overcome growth blockages.

With Awakening, there is Healing

Some the most striking accounts of NDEs among our subjects included a wide range of healing benefits. Their interactions with so-called "healing specialists" as well as a variety of bright forms of light, including radiant orbs and planes that were seen as infusions of healing energy. They explained their often accelerated recovery from serious injury or illness following the experience to their near-death interactions with the advanced healing powers of the spirit dimension.

With Awakening, there is Reunion

For many, the NDE included re-unions with significant others who had crossed over, including relatives, associates, and friends. Also included in the near-death accounts were frequent interactions with beloved animal companions, including animals that had been treasured companions over many years. In one instance, a college instructor who experienced a near-death auto accident was reunited with a beloved black cat named Midnight that had arrived at his home on the day of his birth and remained with him as a treasured companion during his early childhood years. His relationship with Midnight, however, did not end with the death of the beloved animal. Over the years, his memories of Midnight combined with frequent impressions of the cat's presence became important growth resources that increased his appreciation of animals as beings of dignity and worth. Inspired by the near-death reunion with Midnight, he became an active supporter of animal rights that included the protection of endangered species.

With Awakening, there is Spiritual Connection

Among the subjects of our studies, the NDE often ended by voluntarily deciding to return to the physical body and reengage the present lifetime. In many instances, the ending of the experience, whether voluntary or spontaneous, was accompanied by a familiar spirit presence who became a guide for the safe return and re-engagement of the physical body. The familiar guide typically remained present as needed following the NDE as a comforting, healing presence.

Renewal and Rejuvenation

Although the NDE is typically brief in duration, the benefits of the experience can be enduring. The subjects of our studies consistently viewed the NDE as an experience that in the long-term added quality and meaning to their lives. Changes in values, beliefs, and perceptions were common. The experience often promoted a deeper understanding of themselves and others alike. It inspired them to "live in the moment" and motivated them to fulfill their highest potentials for growth and fulfillment. Equally as important, it inspired them to contribute to the greater good, including the well-being of others. These altruistic effects of NDEs could help explain the rejuvenating, renewal effects of the experience. As an 83-year-old retired professor reported, "The near-death experience gave me a totally new outlook on life that alleviated all fear of death." For her, the multi-functional experience activated the rejuvenating effects of altruism and fully eradicated the aging effects of fear. She is steadfast in his belief that altruism, to include the altruistic treatment of persons and animals alike, is the best single measure of personal and cultural advancement. Supportive of that belief are the repeated findings of controlled research that altruism as a personal trait is the key to rejuvenation, longevity, and quality of life (Slate, J. 2001. *Rejuvenation: Living Younger, Longer, and Better.* Llewellyn).

New Meaning of Life, and of Death and Afterlife

Taken together, the results of our studies found that the near-death experience can be a critical learning event in which awareness of the essential meaning of life, death, and the afterlife emerges, often in striking detail.

THE OUT-OF-BODY EXPERIENCE (OBE)

Astral Projection and the Spirit World

Since experiences of being outside the physical body were often characteristic of reported NDEs, our research on spirituality included the investigation of the out-of-body experience (OBE) as a phenomenon that can occur independently of near-death. The OBE, also called astral projection and soul travel, typically includes sensations of being outside the physical body and in some instances, traveling to distant destinations, to include the spirit world. While conventional science often considers OBEs as simply hallucinations, there is a wealth of research showing evidence that the spirit, or so-called astral or subtle body, is empowered not only to temporarily detach itself from the physical body, but also to travel either spontaneously or deliberately to distant destinations, including both temporal and spiritual realities.

New Sources of Energy and Knowledge

Although reports of spontaneous OBEs are common, explaining the dynamics of the experience to include its empowering functions remains a very difficult needle to thread. Our controlled studies designed to explore the dynamics of the phenomenon found that the out-of-body experience is typically multifunctional. Whether spontaneous or intentionally induced, it can expand awareness and access sources of power otherwise unavailable to us. It can activate out-of-body travel to both physical and spiritual realities, to include the higher spirit realm. It can promote empowering communications with spirit guides, teachers, and growth specialists. It can engage spiritual planes and dimensions as powerful sources of energy and knowledge. At a highly practical level, it can result in an infusion of power required for the achievement of wide-ranging personal goals. Accelerating learning, increasing creativity, facilitating problem solving, reducing stress, and promoting better health and fitness are all within the scope of its functions. It is also used to achieve such goals as breaking unwanted habits, extinguishing phobias, promoting rejuvenation, and even reversing the signs of aging.

The Sleep Travel Technique

Among the most effective applications of OBEs are programs specifically designed to accelerate personal achievement of designated goals that can range from self-enlightenment to out-of-body interactions with distant realities. The *Sleep Travel Technique* is a program developed in our sleep labs and designed to achieve specifically designated goals, including travel to chosen destinations, both tangible and intangible. The procedure perceives that sleep is an out-of-body state during which the astral body spontaneously disengages the physical body and typically rests above it for the duration sleep. That concept was supported in our lab by electro-photographic recordings of the corona discharge patterns surrounding the right index finger pad during sleep. The results showed the "broken-corona" effect, a pattern characterizing the OBE state, emerging as sleep ensued and continuing for the duration of sleep. (For more information on the "broken-corona effect," see Weschcke, C. and Slate, J. *Astral Projection and Psychic Empowerment,* Llewellyn, 2012.).

The Finger Spread Method*

The Sleep Travel Technique uses the so-called *finger spread method* in which the fingers of either hand are held in a spread position during the drowsy stage as the intent to travel out of body is formulated. Specific goals, which can include both directed and spontaneous OBE travel, are then shaped as drowsiness deepens. Finally, the fingers are relaxed to free the astral body to disengage the physical body and in that disengaged state, to experience realities related to the specified goals.

* The Sleep Travel Technique with the Finger Spread Method, along with other methods of Astral Projection, is described in detail in our book, Astral Projection for Psychic Empowerment. See Sources Listing at the end of this chapter.

The travel and interactive experience can continue spontaneously for the duration of sleep or it can be intentionally ended by simply deciding to return to the so called "at rest" position above the physical body. Complete astral re-engagement of the physical body will occur spontaneously upon awakening from sleep. The empowering results of sleep travel can be dramatically increased by taking a few moments to reflect on the experience upon awakening and affirming in your own words the positive effects of the experience.

As always, we recommend that the reader/student record experiences in a journal, and periodically review those entries spontaneously attracting attention and further record additional insights. Record Experience, Observation, Analysis, Experimentation, Practice, further Observation, and more Analysis turns the casual seeker into a New Age Scientist of the Paranormal—really of the "Super-normal" and Science of Spiritual Attainment.

Making Astral Awareness an Every Night Opportunity

With repeated use of the *finger spread method*, you will discover that astral disengagement can be rapidly induced during the drowsy state preceding sleep though intent alone. It is important, however, to clearly formulate specific out-of-body travel goals before sleep ensues.

Sleep Travel as Therapy

The Sleep Travel Technique can be used to achieve a wide range of personal empowerment goals. The results can range from the activation of dormant inner potentials to the discovery of totally new sources of power. As a psychotherapy technique, it can initiate so-called "sleep therapy" that unleashes important insight of therapeutic relevance. It can uncover the sources of phobias, anxieties, feelings of inferiority, and other growth blockages while providing the power to fully resolve them. For instance, discovering through sleep travel the past-life sources of a present life phobia can instantly extinguish it. As a learning technique, it can initiate so-called "sleep learning," an advanced process that facilitates the mastery of new skills. Becoming fluent in a new language, unleashing creative potentials, and accelerating the developing a host of performance skills are all within the scope of this technique.

Sleep Therapy and Spirit Guides

The Sleep Travel Technique has been used for out-of-body travel not only to distant physical realities, but to the highest spirit realm as well. Almost immediately upon engaging the spirit realm, profound interactions to include those related to previously stated goals typically unfold. Included are interactions with personal spirit guides as well as spiritual planes and other dimensions of power.

Astral Therapy and Color Infusion

The sheer emergence of the spirit dimension with its so-called "celestial planes" and other structures is usually sufficient to initiate empowering interactions. Typically, the color of plane can provide a key to its empowering potential, with the brightness of the plane signifying its present relevance. For instance, bright planes of iridescent green are associated with healing and rejuvenation. Out-of-body interactions with that plane and bathing in its energy can infuse the physical body with healthful vigor. Out-of-body Interactions with planes of glowing yellow are associated with improved intellectual functioning. Bathing out-of-body in their energies can accelerate the development of a wide range of cognitive skills. College students who regularly interacted with planes of yellow experienced a dramatic improvement in their academic performance. A mechanical engineer who practiced the technique regular as a college student attributes his extraordinary academic success to out-of-body sleep learning in which he interacted with a certain yellow plane. As a mechanical engineer, he continues to regularly practice the technique.

Astral Therapy and Stress Management

Interactions with planes of blue are typically associated with effective stress management along with increased feelings of personal worth. As a self-empowerment technique, it can build feelings security and self-confidence. It can increase the ability to cope with stress, overcome adversity, and solve difficult problems. In the words of a psychology graduate student, "My out-of-body interactions with planes of blue generated powerful expectations of success and gave me the resources I needed to overcome all barriers to my academic success. I plan to use the technique with my patients in my clinical practice."

Astral Therapy and Energy Structures

Aside from its planes of color, the spirit realm includes a myriad of energy structures and designs that invite out-of-body interactions. Among them are pyramids, orbs, and gardens of power. Out-of-body embracement of an orb of power can generate the power to achieve such difficult life goals as breaking unwanted habits, slowing aging, activating creative thinking, enriching social relationships, and generating solutions to difficult problems. Typically, the brightness of the orb indicates its relevance to your present life situation. Similar to astral planes, orbs of glowing green are associated with health, fitness, and rejuvenation; radiant orbs of gold are associated with intellectual prowess, including the acceleration of learning; and orbs of blue are associated with security feelings and effective stress management. Following an interaction with a particular cosmic plane or orb, the aura typically takes on the coloration of that interaction, often as a layer of enveloping color.

The Celestial Gardens of Power

OBEs with the spirit realm can include rewarding interactions with the so-called Celestial Gardens of Powers. Colorful and diverse in both design and function, each garden is unique in its empowering potentials. They can be sources of power through your personal interactions with such specific features as winding trails, colorful plants, and flowing streams. Situated in the central region of the realm is the so-called *Celestial Fountain* which has gained recognition as the *Fountain of Unlimited Power*. Bathing in the fountain's shimmering spray of energy can in an instant invigorate and rejuvenate. As the ultimate fountain of youth, it generates a continuous spray that can slow the aging process and literally dissolve the physical signs of aging. Taking time to bathe in the cosmic fountain's spray can fully rid you of any excess baggage that accelerates aging and impedes your progress. It can reverse age-related cognitive decline and replace it with enriched mental functions. It can equip you with the resources required for your complete success regardless of the nature of your goals. All barriers to your personal progress can be "washed away" and replaced with the radiant glow of self-empowerment. The results include an instant acceleration of personal growth accompanied by increased awareness of your unlimited potential.

OBE Stimulation for the Inner Body

Our studies found that the Sleep Travel Technique, aside from its out-of-body travel applications, can be equally effective when used to probe the inner self, a method called *Inner Body Travel*. By focusing awareness on the inner self, you can awaken dormant inner powers and direct them toward specific self-empowerment goals. You can uncover past-life achievements as sources of power and apply them toward the achievement of present-life goals, a phenomenon called *OBE Stimulation*. For instance, you can awaken your past-life development of musical abilities and apply them toward the achievement of your present musical goals. That possibility was illustrated by a music composer who used the Sleep Travel Technique to travel inward in his effort to improve his composing skills. Through the inner travel experience, he discovered a past life in which he was an accomplished composer. Through out-of-body retrieval of that experience, he supplemented his present composing skills and markedly improved the quality of his work.

OBE Stimulation of Past-Life Skills

Among other possibilities of OBE stimulation are the inner awakenings of past-life achievements in language, art, and science, to mention only a few. Although present-life manifestations of exceptional past-life accomplishments can be repressed and denied further development, they can fortunately be re-awakened and effectively applied. Through its capacity not only to identify dormant past-life achievements but also to awaken and apply them, OBE Stimulation has become one of the most powerful learning techniques known.

OBE Stimulation to resolve Growth Barriers

Aside from increasing awareness of past-life achievements, OBE Stimulation can be used to identify and resolve a wide range of subconscious growth barriers. Examples include phobias, obsessions, and conflicts that thwart our growth and deplete our adjustment resources. Through OBE stimulation, the sources of growth barriers are identified and the disempowering stress related to them released. The results include not only the discovery of new potential but the rapid acceleration of new growth related to them as well.

OBE Probes of the Subconscious Mind

The discovery and application of both inner and outer growth resources through out-of-body programs illustrate with impressive clarity the powerful connection between science and spirit. Our controlled studies revealed the out-of-body nature of sleep along with detailed characteristics of the spirit realm's abundant sources of power. The celestial planes of power and other structural designs of the spirit realm along with its spirit guides and growth specialist await our probes and invite our interactions. Equally as important, our studies revealed the empowering effects of out-of-body probes of the subconscious in which dormant skills and potentials are activated. We discover that nothing is beyond our reach when science and spirit merge.

CONCLUSION

Spiritual Empowerment

Through their contributions to each other, science and spirit have joined hands to become the most powerful interactive force known for probing the empowering nature of spirituality. By working together, they have identified new sources of growth and identified barriers that can thwart the growth process. They have reached beyond the perceived limits of enlightenment and developed new ways of accessing knowledge.

Spiritual Embrace

By each contributing to the other, science and spirit have developed a self-empowerment approach that has become among the most powerful known. Spirituality when combined with scientific research consistently reveals not only the power of spirituality, but also ways of effectively applying it. As a result, research-based programs have been developed to access new sources of power, to include those existing from within the self to the far reaches of the spirit realm. Uncovering and actualizing hidden potentials, achieving career goals, enriching personal relationships, probing the past and future, activating creativity, accelerating learning, slowing aging, and even scanning the universe and multiverse—all are within the scope of possibilities when science and spirit unite.

Spiritual Exploration

When objectively viewed, the results of both spiritual exploration and scientific research consistently reveal empowering nature of the spirituality. The objective scientific analysis of both guided and spontaneous experiences indicated no form of negativity relative to authentic spirituality. All apprehension related to exploring the spirit dimension was erased in an instant upon engaging the inspiring beauty and power of that realm.

Spiritual Enlightenment

Beginning now, you can push back the borders and discover new sources of growth and power both within yourself and the spirit realm. The beauty and power of spirituality merge at the moment to invite your interaction. Spiritual enlightenment and the sheer pleasure of discovering new growth possibilities are among the many rewards.

The following program is a further development and application of the Out-of-Body Experience to the development and application of intentional astral consciousness.

Program: The Astral Sweep Procedure

Introduction. This Out-of-Body procedure does not require, but can include, astral travel to distant destinations. Here is the seven-step procedure:

Step 1. Statement of Goals. For the focused form of the procedure, formulate your goals around a particular target situation or condition. You may, for instance, focus on a particular individual, a specific geographical setting, a certain event, or a given situation. For the open-ended form of the procedure, formulate your goals in general terms, thus allowing your clairvoyant faculty to select its own target situation and access any information related to it.

Step 2. Out-of-Body Induction. For this procedure, the recommended Out-of-Body induction strategy is called *upward scan*. While in a relaxed, reclining position, envision yourself surrounded and protected by the glow of empowering cosmic energy. Picture relaxation as a fog spreading slowly over your physical body from your feet upward until your body is fully enveloped. Envision the fog then slowly lifting from your body, with your consciousness rising gently with it. Once your consciousness is suspended, view your body resting comfortably below. Affirm:

> *I am fully empowered and protected mentally, physically, and spiritually by the highest powers of the cosmos. I can return to my body at will by simply deciding to do so.*

Step 3. Activating Out-of-Body Clairvoyance. Once the Out-of-Body state has been achieved, the metaphor of mountain climbing is introduced to activate clairvoyance. Envision yourself as a psychic explorer, slowly ascending an astral mountain from its base to its peak. Each step upward expands the scope of your clairvoyant powers. Allow yourself plenty of time to scale the mountain and experience the progressive release of your psychic potentials. When you finally reach the summit, your psychic scanning powers are at their peak.

Step 4. Clairvoyant Sweeping. As already noted, clairvoyant sweeping can be either open-ended or focused. For open-ended sweeping, survey the surrounding reality from your astral observation point at the mountain's peak. With your clairvoyant powers now fully activated and free of constrictions, you can probe the most distant realities and access the highest sources of knowledge. Allow your clairvoyant powers to gather relevant information from any source, zooming in for a closer look whenever necessary. For focused clairvoyant sweeping, center your scanning efforts on certain designated targets, and scan their surroundings for additional information as desired. Continue scanning until you gather the information you need.

Step 5. Astral Travel (Optional). Astral travel to distant destinations during scanning can be useful in gathering additional, highly detailed information, or in accessing higher astral planes. Travel can be initiated following either open-ended or focused sweeping by first centering your attention on the desired destination and then intentionally engaging it as a present reality. In the Out-of-Body state, intent alone is usually sufficient to engage even the most distant reality.

Step 6. The Return. Reuniting with your physical body is initiated by the simple intent to reunite with your body, then envisioning your body in its familiar surroundings, and giving yourself permission to re-engage it. The simple affiliation: *I will now re-unite with my body,* facilitates an easy re-entry. The return is concluded by focusing on various physical sensations and affirming: *I am now at oneness with my body and the universe.*

Step 7. Resolution and Reflection. Review the Out-of-Body experience, paying particular attention to the clairvoyant information derived from it. Reflecting on the experience, if only briefly, dramatically increases its empowering effects.

Summary of Purpose & Benefits: *Cosmic survey, Locate lost animals & personal items, Survey criminal scenes.*

Although Astral Sweep can be used to survey cosmic planes and initiate empowering interactions with them, it has many highly practical, down-to-earth applications. It is particularly useful in locating lost animals and personal items. A student trained in Astral Sweep decided to use the technique to locate a horse that had wandered into the countryside. Through astral surveying of the surrounding wilderness, he located the horse grazing peacefully with other horses in a remote wasteland. Another student, also trained in astral sweep, used the technique to recover a lost bracelet. Through astral sweep, she discovered the bracelet near a park bench where she had joined a friend for lunch the previous day.

Astral Sweep is also useful as a criminal investigative procedure for surveying crime scenes and gathering relevant information. In one case, a psychic consultant used the procedure to locate a kidnap victim being held for ransom. Using a combination of open-ended sweeping and focusing, the psychic located the mountain cabin where the victim was being held, and then zoomed in to gather critical information that led to a successful rescue.

Although clairvoyant scanning can occur using other less-specialized OBEs procedures, Astral Sweep is often preferred because of its functional design and high degree of accuracy. Given even moderate practice, almost everyone will discover the practical benefits of this useful procedure.

This and additional procedures may be found in complete detail in *Astral Projection for Psychic Empowerment—The Out-of-Body Experience, Astral Powers, and their Practical Application*, 2012, Llewellyn, by Joe H. Slate, Ph.D. & Carl Llewellyn Weschcke.

MEDITATION
"How are we 'conditioned' to overlook the spiritual aspects of Reality?"

Sources and Suggested Reading:

Popper, Karl, 1996. *In Search of a Better World*. New York: Rutledge, New York.

Slate, J. 2001. *Rejuvenation: Living Younger, Longer, and Better*. Llewellyn.

Slate, Joe H. & Weschcke, Carl Llewellyn: *Astral Projection and Psychic Empowerment—the Out-of-Body Experience, Astral Powers, and their Practical Application*, 2012, Llewellyn

Wilson, EO, 1998. *Consilience: The unity of knowledge*. New York: Alfred A. Knopf. p. 334

SHAMANISM & SPIRIT

"Each being contains within itself
the whole intelligible world.
Therefore, ALL is everywhere . . . .
Man as he is now ceased to be the All.
But when he ceases to be a mere ego,
he raises himself again
and penetrates the whole world."
–Plotinus

To go Beyond the Ego without losing consciousness

The above quotation from the 2nd century CE Greek neoplatonic philosopher sums up the Shamanic concept that all is knowable through *transitions in consciousness* that take the human beyond the ego. *It's up to us to figure out how to go beyond the ego without losing consciousness.*

That's where Spirit comes into the picture. Spirit is the *substance* of consciousness just as matter is the *substance* of energy. Consciousness and Energy move the Universe.

Spirit, and Spirits, are everywhere—and Spirituality is Universal

Spirit is fundamental to all existence, even at the most basic physical level.

Spirits are fundamental to all life, even at the most basic botanical, biological, and *elemental* levels.

Spirituality is fundamental to all levels of consciousness.

Words easily said, *but what do we really mean?* First of all, words mean what we say they mean when we say them—hence no word in any language has a time-enduring definition no matter the language and no matter what their users may claim. From day to day we see things differently, but for one moment in time these words mean what we want them to mean in the context of what we are saying. *Don't look for absolutes until you transcend this universe!*

Spirit is the Primal Substance

"Spirit" derives from the Latin *spiritus,* meaning "breath." In Hindu and other mythically expressed cosmologies, the Cosmos comes into manifestation on the "outbreath" of the Creative Force, and is withdrawn on an eventual "in-breath" at the end of all time (until, maybe, the *next* time!). Spirit is the primal *substance. Spirit is the "beginning," and the matrix for what follows.* The Cosmos, and ultimately the physical universe, evolves, layer after layer, upon this primal immortal spirit *substance. It is the Holy Spirit* that is fundamental to, and the Hidden Reality behind, all existence even as it is also the idealist pattern for all intentional activity, the goal and culmination of all action, and the completion of our reason to be. We exist to fulfill the purpose of existence.*

> * This "Holy Spirit" is not that identified with that of the Trinity of the Roman Catholic Church. It may have been intended that way, but—if so—the original concept was lost in the theological struggle to keep everything masculine and non-Pagan.

Nothing can be without Spirit

Spirit is in all things, and in all we do. That's why we can speak of the "Spirit of" whatever. There's Spirit in Love, and in Lust and Ecstasy and there's Spirit in Action and in Non-action. Spirit is not something "high," and beyond ordinary life. It is Life. Spirit is not opposite something called "sin," it is not something "non-sexual," because it is sexual and sexuality is just as spiritual as chastity and self-denial.*

> * Sex as sinful and contrasted to spirituality is discussed further in Chapters Nine, Ten, and Eleven. The absurdity of calling sexuality sinful is largely confined to the West and Muslim Middle East and Northern Africa as founded in the Abrahamic religions of Christianity and Islam. While some repression of women and hence of feminine sexuality followed the Aryan invasion into the Indus Valley, showing up in some sects of Hinduism, Buddhism and many minor religions, sexual "puritanism" is a relatively modern (the last 2,000 years) Western phenomenon.
>
> As quoted from the Tantric scholar, Dr. Jonn Mumford (Swami Anandakapila Saraswati): "Chinese Taoist texts and the Hindu *Kama Sutra,* amongst others, shows that they (Eastern Spiritual masters) did not have a Puritanical Western Abrahamic viewpoint—although often patriarchal in the sense they viewed women as sources of energy and repletion to prolong their (male) lives."

"Spirits" are the primal manifestations in individual life-forms that breathe—including botanical (plants do *breathe*) as well as biological entities. As long as there is life, there is breath; as long as there is breath, there is life—but the form may change. And the animate spirit survives beyond one form to animate another form. "Spirits" are Beings.

Spirituality is a State of Awareness enabling the perception of Spirit

"Spirituality" is a particular state of awareness enabling a human person to perceive Spirit within and without his/her own self and in doing so become able to communicate across the limitations of form and substance.

Thus, "Spirit Communication" is the ability to communicate with other spiritual beings by moving from one level of consciousness to another. For convenience, we call them all "spirits" whether they are Nature Spirits, Elemental Spirits, Spirits as Surviving Personalities, Spirits functioning as gods and goddesses, Spirits that are units of consciousness imbued with character and intent by human observers, or Spirits that are humanly created Thought Forms empowered to carry out particular assignments.

Spiritual Communication is the ability to "communicate" between one conscious being and another via the animating spirit level of consciousness.

Shamans are Spirit Talkers

Today, we mostly refer to those people who long ago talked with spirits, and who still do, as *Shamans.* And, despite the "man" portion of that word, the earliest *archeologically* recognized shamans—40,000 years ago—were just as often women as men were. (An interesting side note is that the male shaman often dressed as a woman, a practice continued by Catholic priests today)

Shamans were the first explorers of Spirit, the first Cosmic Travelers, the first discovers of Spiritual Technologies, the first practitioners of Spiritual Therapies of Healing and Transcendence, the first teachers of Spiritual Knowledge. Shamans were the first observers and experimenters of Altered States of Consciousness.

Shamans were and are the "direct experiencers" of ecstatic union with "Spirit" and the "Gods and Goddesses" and other entities both active in the inner world and influencing the outer world.

These shamans were and are the witches and "wise women," the medicine men and women, herbal and spiritual healers, the mid-wives facilitating women giving birth, the travelers to and messengers from the Spirit World, and the visionaries able to describe the non-physical inner worlds in understandable mythic language and poetry. Sometimes they also bring warnings and prophecies of future changes expressed in visionary language—*but that's <u>not</u> their primary job* and such warnings and prophecies are often mis-understood and called failures. A "warning" is intended to inspire actions that will avoid the prophesized outcome and not as a "test" of the prophet—*so be grateful that the world didn't end on a prophesized date! Take shamanic warnings seriously and look within for answers that make sense in terms of cosmic purpose.*

Shamans Alter Consciousness to enter the Spirit World

Shamans talk with spirits—and *that's their job! They alter their consciousness in order to enter the non-physical Spirit World to gain knowledge and solicit the help of spirit entities for their people.* Often the shaman's "intuitive" understanding of the interface between physical and non-physical dimension have led to the development of divinatory "tools" used to bridge that gap, such as the forked stick used in dowsing, the pendulum to sense auric vibrations, crystals to focus and magnify spiritual images, and the practices of geomancy and sand-reading to bring structural understanding

of the inner dimensions of man and universe. And, yes, sometimes these divinatory tools do predict the future, but rarely with real detailed accuracy. Their greatest value in this is to forecast the effect of current trends rather than fixed events, such as what will happen to a client continuing personal patterns of activities.

Shamanism is not a religion, it has no dogma, no theology, no "priesthood"

Shamanism is eclectic and many faceted. It is personal and not institutional, nor defined by past practices or by any taught mythology. Individual shamans and often their families may have an inherited tradition of learned knowledge about herbs and symbols used in dream interpretation and divination, but shamanism is mainly about using particular states of consciousness to invoke desired spiritual knowledge, resources, and energies and applying them to help oneself, one's client or one's community. The shaman (man or woman) is a person, an individual. Rarely do shamans work together, but they may work with a partner, and may utilize the energies of a group brought together in an ecstatic activity for that purpose.

Ecstasy itself does not define the shaman but altered states of consciousness are a *means to an end.* "At the heart of shamanism lies the journey. It is this that helps distinguish shamans from other ecstatics, healers, and mystics."* "Any ecstatic cannot be considered a shaman because the shaman specializes in a trance during which his soul is believed to leave his body and ascend to the sky or descend to the underworld."**

* Walsh, R. (2007), The World of Shamanism: New Views of an Ancient Tradition. Llewellyn

** Eliade, M. (1964). Shamanism: Archaic techniques of ecstasy. Princeton University Press.

The Shamanic Out-of-Body Journey

The shaman's journey can be an Out-of-Body experience, but it can also be an In-Body experience. It is an Altered State of Consciousness (ASC) defined by the shaman's ability to enter and leave it at will, and—even more importantly—to control the experiences. The shaman's journey is always purposeful, but that purpose has included exploring the Cosmos, exploring the inner workings of the body and psyche, seeing the purpose behind things, and healing things (not just injuries and illnesses but also present relationships and past-life traumas).

The shaman's journey is an inner journey, a psychic journey, a soul journey, a spiritual journey—all these things no longer familiar to our modern understanding of what is real and non-real and beyond reality. We are so focused on what is really only the final "outcome" of apparent material reality that fail to pay attention to "how we got where we are." It is this mis-guided focus that leaves us floundering as to causes including those that are non-physical that we fail to cure situations whether of health, social, economic, political or other that characterize our modern world.

The Forgotten Inner World

Shamans and shamanism were forgotten about in our modern materialist age. Spirit was ignored by modern science and forgotten about by modern healers; spirits were relegated to superstition and horror fiction, and spiritualty was twisted by religion-ists in their manipulations for control over their human "sheep"—thus the Bishop's Crook carried in ritualistic processions.

Spirit was located in fictional "heaven" outside of physical reality and beyond human reach. Spirit became meaningless in the cosmic scheme and lost to the human perception of Self.

Entering the Space Age

We have confined ourselves to the physical world just at the time we are entering the Space Age. At the same time, we are entering the Information Age with vast reams of knowledge readily available at the tap of a finger on a keyboard. Suddenly, in this New Age, it is the individual who has free access to the "Wisdom of the Ages," and to the "Know How" to accomplish nearly anything a person can desire. The individual has the potential to become fully empowered.

Living in a World of Collective Illusion

Still, what has been missing until recent times was the awakening of the human spirit. We have been living in a world of Collective Illusion as if defined by a Hollywood stage setting. Our awareness has been distorted and constrictive, and too many people are driven by greed for money and consumer goods, and fear manufactured by political and economic powers themselves blind to reality. We live within a narrow band of half-awake consciousness, without vision.

Suddenly, in the 1960s, as the New Age energies began a new stage of manifesta-tion, hallucinogen-induced "Altered States of Consciousness" (ASC) suddenly made news headlines and filled the media with all sorts of *Alice in Wonderland* kinds of stories of hallucinatory experiences and sometimes schizophrenic behavior.

Hallucinogen-induced
Altered States of Consciousness

There were the "Hippies" and the "Druggies" of the Haight-Ashbury neighborhood of San Francisco, a city soon to replace New York's famed Greenwich Village as America's creative and artistic capital, where new philosophies and new life styles were developing and occultism gained a greater public awareness. And, like "the Village," Gay and Lesbian people found a place respectful of their lifestyle, and where the annual Folsom Street Parade carries on the Village's tradition of *bizarre* and *outré* behavior and dress, and where sex scenes are *de riqueur*.

But ASCs may be induced by means other than drugs, and they are not all "that different." We need to better understand consciousness itself to more fully recognize the value and nature of the altered states. Sleep is an altered state, dreaming is an altered state, meditation and concentration are altered states, and others are induced by lack of sleep, intense fatigue, music, drumming, dancing, yoga, sex, running, political rallies, sports events, euphoria, and also through hypnosis, astral projection, fasting, sensory deprivation, etc. The choices of intentional induction techniques relate to the purpose of the desired state. *Purpose* is the key to meaning and value.

And, note: ASCs do not necessarily include *high* ecstatic states nor *deep* trance. A "runner's high" feels *good* but is not always ecstatic! Meditation and prayer do not necessarily lead to ecstasy or trance. *But they can.* The human mind can be trained and directed, *under Will,* to accomplish almost anything. We call that "Magick" and it is discussed in Chapter Thirteen.

Shamanic Trance with a Purpose

Also, both ecstasy and trance states can be spontaneous. A visit to Yosemite National Park could be ecstatic, and even a long train ride can induce "road" trance. That which is sometimes called "sub-space" (discussed later) is trance-like but not necessarily ecstatic. In other words, "altered states" cover an extensive range of consciousness, and what defines any of these as specifically shamanic is **"trance with a purpose."** That also defines hypnosis, and such active meditation as *Path-Working,* but a major difference (and the one that also commonly does include journeying, broadly defined) is the physical body's involvement as a "leveraging" mechanism whether it be pain, pleasure, sensory overload, sensory deprivation, or fatigue.

No, such leveraging is not the only way, but is mostly common to the shamanic experience which originated during an earlier time when directed states of consciousness were rare—a time before Yoga, Tantra, and other advanced techniques for *self-control* of consciousness had been developed.

New Ways of Learning, Healing, Remembering Unfinished Business

The "Shamanic World" is the *Inner World of everything*—including all the "needs" and "desires" of ordinary people now living in an Extraordinary World of new experiences and personal opportunities. With vastly expanding awareness reaching beyond previous sensory limitations, and extended ranges of consciousness into subtle dimensions, even seemingly bizarre needs and desires may be perceived as "calls" for new ways of learning and healing, and ways of re-experiencing this-life and past-life memories as "unfinished business" rather embedded trauma.

But, do not anticipate such *unfinished business* to call for "logical" solutions. Unlike the "Old-Age" *karma* it is not a matter of "tit for tat," impulses of "New Age" energies and your own imaginative responses—even of living fantasy—work to restore lost energies and repair negative experiences. Learn to give respect to emergences from the Unconscious as clues to methods of resolving problems and needs from other times and other lives.

Shamanism is free of rigid formulae and "canned rituals" prescribed and administered by *theocratic* professionals, and able to adjust to new realities of self-administration and those shared with an active partner and interactive clients.

Shamanic Ecstatic States are not for Entertainment

Traditionally, shamanism is associated with *ecstatic* states in which the shaman *journeys* to interior places of altered time and space for specific purposes, for gaining wisdom in response to the needs and desires of clients and community. But ecstasy, by itself, isn't only for shamanic soul journeying and, particularly in group activities often involves a loss of control and self-identity. This is particularly the case of spontaneous and charismatically induced ecstasy with involuntary possession by spirits who may represent deities, spiritual entities, surviving personalities, animal spirits who may "ride" the human without any regard to that person's need or limitations.

The spread of "esoteric" knowledge that isn't so esoteric after all but awareness of what was so recently hidden and denied in the materialist culture is now opening what can be called "supersensible" knowledge with increased understanding of the human psyche, the subtle energies of chakras and meridians, awareness of the subtle etheric and astral dimensions, Out-of-Body experiences and Lucid Dreaming, and various Psychic Powers.

Training, Mind Control, Discipline, and Intuitive Shamanism

"Training" is the mental control of consciousness allowing the shaman to continue the Out-of-Body journey, and to follow new opportunities as they may appear. In many traditions, the shaman/teacher/trainer has an apprentice/assistant/student who also serves as a partner/guide in a working relationship of equals even as the roles are of leader and follower. In any case, the then "assistant" partner first helps with the induction and then keeps in contact with shaman to help guide the inner journey. Even as teacher and student, the levels of responsibility require the sense of equality because each of the partners is functioning in a different world or dimension and need each other to complete the journey.

While the appearance may be of "master and servant," there is a constant inter-change of energies and responsibilities and shared consciousness that comparable to our ever-changing roles in a marriage or other intimate partnership. Each requires the other for a fulfilling relationship even as it serves a third party as birth-child, client, patient, or community.

It is also comparable to any trainer and apprentice/student relationship as in modern fitness sessions, fashion modeling, yoga classes, massage training, golf lessons, etc. Trainer and apprentice enter into an intimate and shared "head space" that is unique and personal, and analogous to an interactive "leader and supporter" relationship in which each partner is equally responsible to accomplish the goals set by the leader, and which is generally identified with his or her name.

Even as the roles change, someone is always in charge. It is always necessary that one position is dominant and the other submissive. This is particularly true in many research and development relationships in which the assistants and associates may know nothing of the purposes of the "Head's" programs: they are just to follow orders.*

---

* In discussions that follow throughout this chapter, we have changed the rather standard abbreviations for "Dominance & Submission" and "Sadism & Masochism" (or Sado-Masochism) from all upper case D/S and S/M to combine upper and lower case

D/s and S/m to distinguish role-playing "fun & games" D/s and S/m from the clinical study and treatment to compulsive S/M Sadistic or Masochistic behavior.

Likewise, in the serious role-playing involved in shamanic practices, both in spontaneous "possession" and intentional Power Animal assumption, we want to avoid any confusion with the Clinical World.

While such D/s is also seen in modern role-playing games between romantic partners, there is more intense shamanic experience in Haitian Voodoo where the group dancing, drumming, and singing induces ecstasy among many participants, and charismatically even among observers and tourists. The individual is "possessed" by a Loa (deity) and ridden like a horse.

The Voodoo experience of being "ridden as a horse" by an *Unknown God* is suggestive of the "intuitive shaman"-like experience of D/s "Pony Play." A "human pony" is a very modern psycho-sexual phenomenon in which a submissive chooses to dress and "play" as a pony, and seeks out a trainer partner to facilitate the transition into "Pony Headspace." There are modern shaman schools offering training programs and hundreds of events across America, Great Britain, Europe and Russia for shows of related fashions, dressage, demonstrations, and "pony cart" racing in which one or two people are harnessed as a team to a lightweight two-wheeled cart driven by a single trainer.

Earlier we wrote of the need to respect prompting welling up from the Subconscious as possible clues to personal needs and resolutions of problem, and we spoke of "Intuitive Shamanism" as descriptive of this experience. Certain people have always had an urge, even a need, to go outside the "norm" either a) to explore and understand, or b) to fix and improve. Shamans do both, but historic examples do not include the *instinctual* experience where a person "knows" just what herb will fix an illness, or a particular form of sensual or sexual action will improve or fix a "relationship." The sudden willingness, particularly among women, to step outside the norm and explore various forms of role-playing in intimate relations seems to be a form of such "intuitive shamanism." Here, instead of possession by an alien or unknown god, the submissive identifies with her human partner in a two-way relationship of trust and shared consciousness.

While Role Playing Games (RPG) are common among the technologically savvy digital community, it can be said that the Role Playing described here is **"the Real Thing."** Nevertheless, the emphasis is on the word "play" as *play always in a learning experience* whether it is a child learning structural dynamics while playing with Legos or adults learning about the dynamics of intimacy in role playing games.

We use this example for the reason that it fully illustrates the shaman's temporary transcendence of human consciousness that is dependent upon the assistant/trainer to guide and manage the experience, and to bring the shaman/pony back to objective consciousness. For reasons discussed later, this partnership goes beyond that of the spirit guide and spiritualist medium relationship or that of guru and yoga student.

Ecstasy can be Infectious and Charismatic

Shamans not only directly enter into ecstatic states themselves, but often their ecstasy is infectious and *charismatic* to their helpers and supporters. Historically, the shaman's visions were shared and talked about in the tribe, and retold in story form many times to evolve into enduring myths of creation, human origin, and spiritual entities. The poetic stories were chanted and sung, accompanied by drumming and other acts that reproduced the shamanic ecstasy and renewed the visions for later generations.

With a change of vocabulary, we see some of these shamans or their followers becoming the prophets and messengers of religions that were later used in a political manner to bind people together into clans and tribes, and then new leaders politicalized the religions to form nations and build empires.*

> * But, when that occurs, it is no longer shamanic. As Michael Harner comments: "shamanism is ultimately only a method of learning and exploration, not a religion with a fixed set of dogmas."
>
> This is a vital distinction between shamanism and religion, which we will discuss in the next chapter. Shamans employ a variety of living and fluid techniques of Transcendence and Spiritual Communication, while religion is frozen in time to a particular theology claiming a single truth for all time, and thus has no need or place for *Communicating with Spirit*, and generally forbids it.

Shamans seek Answers through their Journey

We may not fully know the "inner" history of the symbolism behind the Tarot's images, or the other "mystic languages" of Oghams, Runes, and the Yi King or the many other systems of signs and symbols that translate between the worlds, but—like the story of the Norse Odin reaching *between the worlds* to bring back the runes—their origins are most likely to be shamanic. And it was the *shaman's ability to ask questions of spiritual entities and receive answers that led to the beginnings of the spiritual technologies* that were then further developed into the *sciences* of astrology, alchemy, magick, Tantra, yoga, and other ways to understand and apply knowledge of "how things work" from the non-physical to the physical dimensions.

An important distinction needs to be made: the physical dimension is mainly perceived through the five physical senses, while it is necessary to include non-physical "senses" or subtle forms of perception when we open to the multiple dimensions of the Greater Universe, or *Cosmos*. The shaman understands this, and also understands that the physical dimension is the "end product" of multi-level Cosmic influences which can be manipulated through metaphysical technologies such as alchemy, magick, Tantra, yoga, and experienced in the paranormal phenomenon of miracles, healings, etc.

But, the Greater Universe is exactly that—it's larger—and it's those additional dimensions, levels, energies, experiences, etc. that provide greater meanings to life, that provide the sources for ethical behavior and living moral codes. It is as *we* ascend in greater and higher consciousness that we understand the lower worlds from vantage of the higher ones.

Shamans seek Answers

As defined below, Shamans seek knowledge and answers to specific questions in order to help people through spiritual communication. Human questions and human needs constantly change and evolve, and so also does do the techniques of shamanism change and evolve, and adapt to new technologies in response to the interests of both single individuals, couples in relationship, and people within various communities.

People change, and evolve. We are entering a New Age of transition in which all action, all power, all *responsibility* is increasingly focused on the individual. It is no longer a time for "mass action," for massive marches and demonstrations, for massive concentrations of military power, for mass production with strikes and lockouts, for big business, big labor and big government—all locked in confrontation, all controlled by ideologies that even the leaders fail to understand.*

All Ideologies are Irrational

* All ideologies are irrational because they start from the wrong end of the stick, and develop from the top down rather from bottom up—as is necessary <u>within</u> any dimension. In other words, the ideal world fails to shape the real world, but the real world can form a realistic new deal. A building starts from the foundation, not from the top story. Quantum Theory demonstrates that the smallest particles contain enormous energies.

All MASS ACTION is political or religiously organized to "bind people together" into an irrational and hence unconscious union administered from the top down for the purposes that entirely deny evolutionary energies. There is a big difference between our collective consciousness and MASS ACTION. *As individuals we can consciously reach into the Collective Unconscious <u>but we must not let it take us</u>.* Never give your power over to another, and never let it be subsumed into a crowd no matter how noble the cause seems because that's the road to dictatorships, to mass terror, and the loss of humanness.

It is not that people can't work together and combine personal power with "people power" in a common goal, but it is only as the individual person can evolve and change that common action becomes true, meaningful, and enduring. All else is coercion at a reactive emotional level below active mind-directed consciousness.

Each of us, *each individual,* must evolve, must grow in consciousness, must learn and develop powers and skills to solve today's problems and meet tomorrow's challenges, to work alone and together as entrepreneurs and innovators, as partners in work and couples in meaningful relationship, as families living for today and building for tomorrow, as teams working together and in communities of shared values and interests. This is the New Age of "bottom up" in contrast to the past age of "top to bottom."

The New Age of Shamanism

This is the Age of Shamanism in contrast to organized Religion and Institutionalized Values!

Some Definitions:

"Shamanism = technique of ecstasy" (Mircea Eliade in *Shamanism—Ancient Techniques of Ecstasy, 2004*)

"A shaman is "a man or woman who enters an altered state of consciousness at will to contact and utilize an ordinarily hidden reality in order to acquire knowledge, power, and to help other persons." (Michael Harner in *The Way of the Shaman—A Guide to power and healing, 1990*)

Three key features of shamanism:

1. Shamans can voluntarily enter altered states of consciousness.
2. In these states they may experience themselves "journeying" to other realms.
3. They use these journeys for acquiring knowledge or power and for helping people in their community.

(Roger Walsh in *The World of Shamanism—New Views of an Ancient Tradition*, 2007)

Shamanism's origins are pre-historic and little attempt was made to describe or understand shamans and their practices until the 19th and 20th centuries because the people involved were few, distantly located, and pre-judged to be simple "primitives." Slowly western scholars began to note similar *magico-religious* practices found within various indigenous cultures and to realize their survival into modern times demonstrated their positive values. Variously, historians and archaeologists acknowledged that shamanism was a dominant *pre-religious* practice of Conscious "Better Living."

Shamans communicate between the worlds of human and spirits, and heal physical and psychological illness by healing the person's soul. They sometimes enter the spiritual worlds obtain guidance and to solve problems affecting an entire community, but never were they thought to bring answers for all humanity.

The Question of "Initiation"

The claim that the seeker must be *initiated*—whether as a shaman, a magician, a yogi, a Witch, a *chela* or serious student of esotericism—has been around for a long time but what it really means is that you won't get far without a real commitment to the study and its practice. In a time before the wide availability of <u>good</u> books and fields of information on any of these subjects, the stages of initiation functioned as levels of instruction, and the student's successful completion was often recognized by such terminology as *Master, Priest/Priestess, Swami, Doctor,* etc. and certified the graduate as qualified for professional practice or teaching.

Of course, all serious study requires organization and discipline, whether provided by an external teacher, or your own inner teacher—and common sense—but unless you want to teach or need such recognition to qualify for a "license" to practice, "initiation" is rarely meaningful. That is a statement with a qualification however—*in those "rare" instances where the student's "graduation" is an expertly administered astral world ceremony of powerfully energized symbols, <u>it can be transformative.</u>* At the same time, if you really know what you are doing, there is "self-initiation" similar to what Napoleon did when he crowned himself Emperor of France!

Always remember, *you are in charge of your own destiny and nobody can turn you into something you are not.*

Shamanism is the Practice of Spiritual Journey, Communication, and Intervention

While it began with the shaman's inner journeys into the three worlds on the Shamanic Tree of Life telling of the mythic origins of the world and of life, the inner visions revealing the subtle nature of plant and animal life leading to knowledge of herbs and of natural healing, the folk wisdom that eventually becomes natural science, and the direct precursor of magick, of occult knowledge, of esoteric wisdom, and of all religion, shamanism itself is not a religion but a *practice of spiritual communication and intervention.*

There is no shamanic theology or doctrine of faith but only a tradition of practical knowledge personally applied; there are no priests or clerics or ministers, but there are counselors and personal "Spirit Guides;" there is no shamanic church or temple or center other than your own home and your own Astral Room.

Shamans look beyond the Ordinary
and thus become Extraordinary

Shamans are individuals who look beyond the ordinary and thus become extraordinary through their own personal study and actions. They may learn, as apprentices, from other shamen—often as spouses or children to one who is a shaman. They are not limited to how they learn, so they are free to learn any way they want, to study whatever interests them, to turn within and learn from "spirits" and from the World Around.

Apprentice to all Shamans there are and ever were

You can be a shaman, and—indeed—you are if you wish for it. To become a good shaman requires that you fill the gap between desire and expertise. It does not mean you have to be an apprentice to a particular individual when you can become apprentice to all shamans there are and ever were by the desire to be so and the determination to learn, and thus *to become more than you are* and *all you can be.*

Yes, you *can* learn shamanism from books, from lectures, workshops, teachers, *and from your own direct experience.* You may learn more from live interaction with others, but that success is highly dependent on your own self-discipline and objectivity. Even when we study "subjective" subjects, we need to be objective, to exercise a trained mind in place of raw emotion and immature feelings.

Today, aside from good books, and a wide range of Internet information, there are many valid courses of instruction, study and practice groups, lectures and conferences all providing value and support to your shamanic study.

Cross Study: Study of one subject reinforces
Study of another, and another

In addition, there is even greater value in "cross study"—where interest in one subject is both broadened and reinforced by studies of another subject. In the study of shamanism, interest in the psychology of altered states of consciousness, the construction of the human brain and central nervous system, chakras and the subtle energy systems, the body's sexual system and the trigger points and psychic switches leading to ecstatic experience and those particular states "beyond orgasm," and what is known as "sub-space," provides opportunities related to Power Animals, forms of spirit and god possession, and states of consciousness shared between the inspired Lover and the Beloved.

Allied to these studies, the shamanic practice of "journeying" to other realms has been grossly neglected in modern times because many people still cannot grasp the psychic reality of Astral Projection and Clairvoyance. Nevertheless, it is your personal Out-of-Body Travel and Vision that is the foundation of the shamanic world-view. It is the shaman's direct vision and experience of non-physical spiritual realities that is the ultimate source for all esoteric knowledge.

While we're not done with this chapter by any means, we want to remind you that the real power behind all successful study is inspiration and motivation for service. As Dr. Roger Walsh writes in his *The World of Shamanism:*

The Value of Shamanism

"The more we explore shamanism, the more it points to *unrecognized potentials of the human body, mind, and spirit.* For untold thousands of years the world of shamanism has helped, healed, and taught humankind, and it has still more to offer us."

The Time is NOW

"The challenge is to optimize our individual and collective maturation. How best to do so is no longer an academic question but an evolutionary imperative. We are in a <u>*race between consciousness and catastrophe*</u>, the outcome remains unsure, and we are all called to contribute. How spiritual practices in general, and shamanic practices and studies in particular, can contribute is a crucial question of our time."

The Shamanic Initiatory Crisis and the Call to Service

In the pre-historic and indigenous worlds even today, Shamans are "called to service" by dreams or signs, after which they volunteer as apprentices to a respected shaman. In other situations, the shamanic training, wisdom, and *powers* are passed down within the family. Finally, within an indigenous culture where it is not normal to turn to a medical doctor or psychiatrist, a person experiencing a personal, death-threatening sickness may interpret it as a call to become a shaman.

The "call" for shaman's knowledge and help is not always as dramatic as a "death-threatening sickness," and it is not always "esoteric." To <u>be</u> a trained and experienced shaman is one thing—a very noble and important practice and resource of new knowledge for all us—but the "shamanic world" is not denied to the rest of us. *The shamanic world is the "inner world" of ordinary reality, including all the needs and desires of ordinary people now living in an extraordinary world of new alternative experiences.*

We are living in a New Age, filled with developing psychic powers and amazing opportunities of advancing technologies and alternative energy sources, of widening personal horizons and new life styles, broadening education and career choices, and much, much more. We are also learning that a rose may always be a rose, and that not all roses are red nor need they all smell alike. We are learning that with new opportunities and new freedoms—especially for women today—we are reaching out for new experiences of self-expression with sometimes seeming "bizarre" needs and desires.

We are also learning that body and soul have an *inner wisdom* as to what can be beneficial and helpful to physical health and psychological growth. As you become your own shaman, you will become aware of needs and the solution to those needs. In particular, *Intimate Partnerships* have taken on new dimensions far beyond those of the old order of reproductive servitude to a new age of mutual opportunities for expression and growth.

More on that later.

The Shaman and Ecstatic Consciousness

The Greater Cosmos consists of many levels of Substance and Consciousness, of which the Physical is only the bottom end of the line. At the same time, the physical is also the beginning of the "Great Adventure" of life and experience that builds incarnation after incarnation towards a spiritual culmination that can only be sensed through altered states of consciousness and vaguely described in mystical language.

Consciousness and Spirit are everywhere and in everything, but it is in the human person that Consciousness is the most fluid and can be changed—raised and lowered in its vibratory rate –through spiritual technologies of prayer, meditation, rituals and ceremonies, invocation and evocation, yoga, ecstasy inducing actions of dancing, chanting, sexual play, etc. The most important element in all of these technologies is—as practiced in hypnosis—the *intentional focus on a specific goal (and experience) within trance that excludes awareness of external stimuli.*

The oldest, and most fundamental of these, are shamanic practices that raise consciousness to induce trance and ecstatic states to take us from outer to inner worlds. Most of these were described in the "eight-fold path to the center" in the Old Religion of European Paganism. As described previously in our *Llewellyn Complete Book of Psychic Empowerment* (Llewellyn, 2011), these are:

1. **Meditation and Visualization.** A note in Gardner's* own words: "This in practice means forming a mental image of what is desired, & forcing yourself to see that it is fulfilled, with the fierce belief & knowledge that it can & will be fulfilled, and that you will go on willing 'till you force it to be fulfilled. Called for short: Intent."

   * Gerald Gardner, 1884-1964, amateur anthropologist, "father" of modern Wicca, and author of several books and the private received and the unpublished "Weschcke Papers" from which these descriptions were extracted and developed.

2. **Trance states leading to psychic powers.** A trance state is a hypnotic state of extreme focus, whether induced through a group setting or that of a solitary practice. The use of drumming, chanting, spells and rituals all bring the practitioner into access with the Sub-Conscious Mind and place its amazing power under conscious direction to achieve previously established and affirmed goals.

3. **Rites with a purpose.** In other words, rituals—rather than ceremonies—practiced to bring about a goal. Just another way to formulate a spell or a purposeful prayer. Such rituals are really self-hypnosis scripts, and in recognizing that, your prayers and spells can become much more powerful and effective.

4. **Drugs, Incense, Wine, etc.** "Whatever is used to release the Spirit." He adds a further admonition: "One must be very careful about this. Incense is usually harmless but you must be careful, if it has bad after effects, reduce the amount used or the duration of the time it is inhaled. Drugs are very dangerous if taken to excess, but it must be remembered that there are drugs that are absolutely harmless though people talk of them with bated breath. But Hemp* is especially dangerous because it unlocks the inner eye swiftly & easily, so one is tempted to use it more & more. If it is used at all, it must be with the strictest precautions, so that the person who uses it has no control over the supply—this should be doled out by some responsible person, & the supply strictly limited."

   * Here Gardner used the old word, Hemp, which at the time of his writing commonly lumped together both that industrial hemp used in rope-making and the psychoactive form now known as cannabis and marijuana. His warnings obviously refers to the later that "unlocks the inner eye" His concern for "control" of quantity and use by groups may be overdone, but there is common sense just as in the case of a "safe driver" following a party where a lot of alcohol has been consumed.

   Wine and alcohol have a long tradition of use in both religious ceremonies and communal setting to "loosen things up," and reducing normal conscious restraints. Incense, on the other hand, is a "mood enhancer" used in magical rituals tying the particular incense through "correspondences" to the function of the ritual. Symbols and colors are used similarly to reinforce the intent of the ritual.

Group use of drugs is generally forbidden because of the unreliable effects they may have, possibly leading to violence, severe depression, suicide, and other irrational behavior.

5. **The Dance and kindred practices.** The dance can be anything from a somber movement within the Circle to wild ecstatic dancing whether personally undertaken to induce altered states or experienced through participation in ritual or folk dancing. Most "folk dances" are derived from shamanic and ritual dancing.

6. **Blood Control (the Cords), Breath Control, and kindred practices.** Forms of "bondage" that involve restraint of movement and increased body awareness, loss of circulation and numbness in the limbs, forms of sensory deprivation using hoods or isolation, or the swinging "Witches Cradle," are intended to bring *focus to the "other world" rather than ordinary reality, and to access the Sub-Conscious Mind and the Collective Unconscious.*

7. **Scourging and ritual flagellation.** The controlled use of pain* has a long history in shamanic (and religious) practices that "leverage" the body to induce an altered state of consciousness.

    Numbers 5, 6, and 7 share this leveraging of the physical body to induce an altered and often ecstatic state of consciousness. All three, but especially numbers 6 and 7 must involve an experienced operator to avoid injury, both physical and psychological, demonstrating the greater safety and value in the use of self-hypnosis.

* For further discussion regarding the ritual use of pain, see *Carnal Alchemy—Sado-Magical Techniques for Pleasure, Pain, and Self-Transformation*, by Stephen E Flowers, Ph.D., and *Crystal Dawn Flowers*, 2013, Inner Traditions.

8. **The Great Rite,* i.e. ritual sex.** Deliberately controlled sex is part of Indian Tantra, Chinese sexual alchemy and Western sex magick practices involving control or denial of male ejaculation to drive sexual excitement higher and higher, particularly to induce a sustained altered state of consciousness in the female, and sometimes—with the exchange of energies back and forth—in both female and male. Under the direction of priest or priestess or other party (or guided by self-experience), this energy combined with the altered state may be directed to a magical goal (a "magickal childe"). Sometimes the sexual fluids are exchanged and mixed together for Eucharistic consumption, or used as a magickal "ink" to inscribe symbols or sigils on parchment as a talisman.

In Wicca and some magickal orders, the Great Rite* was also used within the initiation of the candidate as a High Priest or Priestess.

* Here Gardner is referencing in general to ecstatic and sexual practices, leaving some possible confusion with the Wiccan "Great Rite" in which the Goddess is invoked into the body and person of the priestess as an initiatory rite also called "Drawing Down the Moon." Less often, a "Drawing Down the Sun" was also used in the initiation of the priest.

In all of these shamanic practices, whether in solitary practice or practices requiring two or more people, the intent is to induce an altered state. Sometimes it is purely a solitary mystical state as in Dervish dancing, other times it may be used to invoke a spirit or god <u>into</u> the body as in Voudoun where the god "rides" the subject who is then called a "horse," and other times it is used to direct the Subject's consciousness and energies in applying psychic powers for a particular goal.

Always, we can see hypnosis or self-hypnosis at work.

The experience of shamanic or magickal ecstasy can be the means to going out-of-body to observe action at a distance or communicate with inner plane entities. The challenge is to retain focus on the goal, as facilitated by one person acting as a kind of "operations director" for those going out-of-body.

The Problem of Man's Ego in Spiritual Communication

This chapter is about Shamanism in Spiritual Communication. While the dominant "Western" and Middle Eastern sects of the Abrahamic Religion reject "unauthorized" contemporary spirit communication, their historic origins are based on a select few human "Prophets" receiving communication from a Father God demanding total loyalty and allowing a few of His angels to deliver messages and commandments to a select few unquestioning humans. We can only assume that these Prophets were in an altered state of consciousness enabling them to see and hear their god. Moses' vision of a "burning bush" is most suggestive of a hallucinogenic experience.

But, if we accept the "scriptural evidence" of these teachings as accurate, then we are faced with the question of "spiritual validity." All three of these Abrahamic religions (Judaism, Christianity, and Islam) of shared Middle East origin—while claiming to teach love practice hatred, have preached violence, have denigrated women, have historically used torture to enforce obedience, have fought science, and built glorious churches, mosques, and temples while poor people starve. It would seem that "Truth" is not part of a spiritual communication when it goes beyond direct and singular communication, and is instead institutionalized and politicized. Man's ego, ambition and greed get in the way. *Trust not the preacher who carries a sword!*

Ecstasy **is a technique for altering consciousness, but it is not an end in itself. Ecstatic consciousness without guidance and control—without purpose—can be like driving a car while under the influence of drugs or alcohol.** Hallucinogens can open doors and windows for visionary experiences, but the visions are like dreams that require interpretation and understanding. Otherwise, ***enjoy the High, but don't think you can fly!*** Truth is not found in a bottle nor seen in a mushroom, but *Visionary Consciousness guided by a Trained Mind is like a powerful horse reined by a trained charioteer: It can take you on a Journey of Discovery and of Truth.*

What is "Ecstasy" in the context of Spirit Communication?

"Ecstasy" is defined variously under categories of Emotion, Religion, Mysticism, Psychology, Sexuality, Exercise and Sports. Most such efforts fail because their focus is external; it's like defining Orgasm—as it was until later in the 20th century—as "ejaculation of spermatic fluid" without any mention of the feminine experience or accompanying emotion or changes in consciousness.

"Ecstasy" results from an *exhilaration* of consciousness arising from an

1. Extended focus of attention on a perceived and then visualized image, as in mediation* combined with Tratak and the chanting of a related mantra (see our *Astral Projection for Psychic Empowerment* (Llewellyn, 2012) and the earlier mentioned *Clairvoyance for Psychic Empowerment.*

   * As a mental and emotional exercise. "Meditation" is either a *passive* kind of "listening"—waiting for a message, vision, or revelation—or an active contemplative "reaching upward" as in prayer, or "projecting inward" as in a "Tattvic Conditioning" of body and psyche or a "Chakra Awakening" to progressively expand spiritual consciousness.

2. Repetitive physical and sensory actions leading towards sensory fatigue, such as extended dance, running, or whirling, prostrations, bowing, swaying, chanting, etc.

3. Extended sensory stimulation, such as flashing strobe lights, drumming (200 to 220 beats per minute), the sound of repetitive chanting or ocean waves, continuing massage or mechanical vibration.

4. Extended body awareness through prolonged but mild sexual stimulation without orgasm, restrained body movement using light bondage while moving, walking, dancing.

5. Extended sensory deprivation, as in total isolation, the use of a sleep or meditation mask, "mummification" by means of carefully placed body wrap, or the use of "sleep sack" in imitation of the traditional *Witches Cradle* (see the chapter on techno-shamanism in our *Clairvoyance for Psychic Empowerment* (Llewellyn, 2013). *All of these require an experienced guide.*

6. Repetitive pain as in "scourging" (light, ritual flagellation) often applied in ritual dance while chanting or singing, in "piercing" as in the North American Indian sun dance involving hooks into the chest, or carefully controlled light electro-shocks known as Transcutaneous Electrical Nerve Stimulator (more commonly referred to as a TENS unit), and sometimes known as erotic electro-stimulation. (Frankly, we entirely recommend against this as too easily misapplied or abused, leading to injury and even death. *Stay away from electricity, from fire, from ice, and other addictive sensual applications to sexual organs.*)

7. Continuous singing or chanting of one or a series of words, names, or mantras, most often associated with a particular spiritual or deific entity or with a particular part of the subtle body to excite its activity.

8. Tantric sex involving extended arousal through stimulation of many of the physical "trigger points" to the edge of orgasm, and then "holding back" until starting again (and perhaps again and again) to finally "explode" in long and sometime multiple orgasm. (A variation of this is not to have an orgasm. Orgasm is sometimes denied in D/s sexual practice, but the same practice as a continued series of orgasmic denials can lead to a prolonged "mystical state" or "sub-space" trance.)

9. The infusion of Kundalini energy through particular physical actions and visualizations extended to the automatic induction of a trance state. Here, Tantric guidance establishes a particular sequence of ascension through the seven primary chakras.

10. Hallucinogens in the form of mushrooms and herbs have a long history in shamanism, but always with a purpose other than having a good time. Different substances have different effects, and various indigenous traditions have carefully cataloged these.

To enter Trance of Focused
Attention and Inner Awareness

Any of these may be combined either sequentially or coincidentally. The point is to arrive beyond a climatic state, entering into a trance of focused attention and inner awareness, with either a self-conceived goal or as guided by an external trainer or partner. Ecstasy is that point beyond climax, beyond orgasm, beyond external and objective awareness to the point of "union" with something "Deific" and beyond personal limits. It may be a "going out-of-the-body" but it's not ordinary astral projection but a merger of "human" spirit with limitless "Divine" Spirit.

While we have emphasized that the shaman or shamanic trainee is purposefully seeking ecstasy to enter into trance in order to journey with a purpose, we want also to mention that these experiences have resulted in a vast resource of knowledge about herbs and substance that go far beyond the pharmaceutical knowledge of "active ingredients" to include the timing of harvesting, the communication with plant spirits, different methods of combining and applying, and more. In addition, these shamanic experiences include the effects of songs and chants on the bodies of patients, the power of touch and massage, the very special knowledge of women shamans as mid-wives, the shaman's knowledge of subtle body parts and energies and methods to stimulate and channel these energies, shamanic techniques of divination and the interpretation of dreams symbols and purposefully encountered visual symbols.

The Shaman's Role is Personal and Local—Here and Now!

All of these are parts of the world-wide indigenous shamanic traditions, but these are not brought together within a shamanic science or dogma. The role of the shaman is personal and "local" because the subtle elements vary from location to location, from tribe to tribe, and individual to individual, and from season to season and time to time. The shaman's sensitivity to "Spirit" is truly individual.

Only the basic technologies of ecstatic conscious, of trance journeying, divination, and certain elements of song and dance can be taught and learned, but the trip is personal and individual. Spiritual communication, like all real communication, is one to one.

Pre-historic Metaphysics

We can only speculate about these pre-historic metaphysical systems from what little survives in myth and the "secret" mystical practices of early religions and the esoteric practices of Gnostics, Magickians, Qabalists, Shamans, Tantrics, Taoists, Theurgists, and Witches. What follows is not a scholarly dissertation but a serious review based on more than a half century study of a tremendous range of literature and personal and group practices. However, this is not claimed to be factual, historically accurate, and representative of any one contemporary esoteric, metaphysical, or religious belief system. Rather it is just a reasoned projection backwards from today's evidence for which no religious claims are made.

Let's call the following **a *Metaphysical Myth*:**

A distant and "outside of manifestation" masculine-like projective force initiated the process of all creation, but as part of that first act, a balancing "inside manifestation" feminine-like attractor force came into being intrinsic to all creation at every level. That distant "outside force" may be called "God," but perhaps "the Force" (or more simply, the "source") would carry fewer distorting overtones. Within the Creation, the primary Feminine, or "Great Goddess," manifests a secondary male "God" (with both loving and fathering functions) to bring about balance within the Cosmos. Thus the Goddess has her Companion: "Masculine and Feminine He created them."*

* "Masculine and Feminine He created them." Male and Female exist beyond sexual gender in all manifestation, but sometimes we experience them as Positive and Negative, Active and Passive, Projective and Attractive, Electrical and Magnetic, and probably a longer list of "creative opposites that work in harmony." Still, they are not fixed as absolute opposites—they merge and they change, transforming from one to the other, but never—at least in this universe—ceasing. In reincarnation theory, the soul moves from one toward the other, and back again in the long journey of experience.

Down the range of manifested form positive and negative appear in electron and positron, and then up we encounter what manifests more as masculine and feminine first in cellular life, and then differentiation in organs and structure of male and female physiology and psychology, and even into the astral, mental, and spiritual structures of the incarnated personality.

At the same time, the further up the scale from the physical body we go, the less specific gender differentiation becomes, just as it does within the incarnate personality when we function in other ways than sexual roles. We retain our gender identity even in non-sexual functions, but we are in no way limited by either physiology or societal governance. Male and Female we are born but Human we are.

From top down,** the process of cosmic creation continued through many levels (or "planes") of being and consciousness, always with a balance of masculine and feminine, *positive and negative, substance and force,* culminating in the complex structure of the physical universe of Matter and Energy—within which the masculine force functions as *electrical* and *projective* and the feminine force as *magnetic* and *attractive.* Because the Physical Plane is the culmination of the "devolution" process, every plane and every level of consciousness above the physical is *subjectively* contained within it and accessible from it. *As Above, so it is Below.* It is the job of humanity in the "evolutionary" process to *objectively* bring together that which is "below" with what is "above" and thus to unify *what has happened and what is* with *what was projected and is the goal simply known as "the Return."*

** A very complex, but very logical, exposition of the "Fall" common in the creation stories of Judaism, Christianity, Islam, Hinduism, and other world religions may be found in the esoteric literature. See, for one source, Blavatsky: The Secret Doctrine. It involves the concept of a long descent of the human soul from a higher and more spiritual non-physical state into the physical body from which it is destined to return toward to its more spiritual origins as it actually evolves into a more developed entity through the process of reincarnation. In other words, "Life has a purpose" which is to grow, to become more than you are, and all you can be."

From the Top down, the process continued to the creation of stars, solar systems, and planets. Thus, for planet Earth, Gaia, there is the Earth Goddess who creates the near infinite variety of life forms we know and experience in our "family home." Within the planetary creation, the evolutionary process moves upward—evolving life forms developing within the planes with greater and greater complexity to fulfill the "matrix of possibilities" in which physical bodies, astral bodies, mental, causal, and spiritual grow through the combined creative drive and our individual experiences.

In the human form on planet Earth, the matrix of possibilities is completed and no new forms appear. Now existing forms evolve either towards or in the human form, or cease, to merge their life lessons into the Akashic "life bank" that is one aspect of the Earth Goddess. All evolution on Earth focuses on the Human Being—individually and as a whole. **We**, Humans, are the children of the Great Mother; **We** are the "Chosen People;" **We** are the "Co-Creators" and the "Special Agents in Charge" of the Health and Well-Being of Earth. Like the Eternal Flame from which the Olympic Torch is lit, **We** carry the Divine Program forward as the Living Goddess and Her Companion in our hearts.***

*** The "Great Sin" was not that of Sexual Pleasure as described in Genesis but of the externalization of Divinity and its projection outward as a singular male god and its relocation into physical places: the Tabernacles, Temples, Churches and Mosques. The Divine, the Holy Spirit, is everywhere but the special means of "Communicating with Spirit" is found through the Spirit Within.****

**** *That ultimate "Devine Spirit" cannot be defined nor named as it comes from outside reality and giving it any name is to humanize it within all the limits of human experience and emotion, to encumber it with human desires, hates, prejudices, and selfish goals. Somewhere it says* **"No man can see the face of God and live!"** *That "God" is outside of all creation but the Spirit is everywhere and in everything.*
In other words, it is indefinable! Yet it is more than "real" to those who experience it.

As yet, we have no way of knowing how the process may occur on other planets in other star systems, but it would be somewhat irrational to believe that "our god" (and/or goddess) runs the whole shebang that reaches billions of light years to such distant space as to be beyond comprehension. Nor do we have any way of knowing if other planets are home to their own "peoples." Some myth records advanced intelligences in the Sirius star system.

Note: These few paragraphs are only an abstract summary of the background perspective drawn primarily from Qabalah, Tantra, and Shamanism. And it is important not to let our choice of words too narrowly define what we are trying to describe. Above all, it should not be subjected to critique from any religious point of view, nor from a scientific perspective. It is presented not as any kind of "truth," but only as a "Metaphysical Myth."

BUT! There is always a "but" to any human experience

Just because spiritual experience can be so extraordinary, and sometimes may involve messages purporting to be from "God," from other gods and goddesses or angels, ascended masters, etc., go ahead and enjoy the experience but *remember you are only human!* Don't let an inflated ego turn you into a Fool, or worse—a religious fanatic!

Ecstasy is a tremendous input of psychic energy, and more than just an overload of body and brain circuitry. *Be very wary of Ego Inflation!* You have to assert your common sense against any seeming irrational directives, any seeming perceptions of devils and demons, or that you are now the personal agent of "God All Mighty," and never,

never, follow any seeming commandment to harm or kill another being, human or animal even if under the illusion of seeing them "possessed by the devil."

When you have an extraordinary experience, write it down as soon as possible in full detail, and—unless it seems to call for immediate action—carefully review it, taking it apart into all its elements, and then put it aside for later review—perhaps the next day but no later than one week from the experience. Study the elements and parts, look up the images, the colors, the shapes, the names, in reference books and on-line, but do not share the experience or consult with anyone. Review again and again until it all "makes sense." Write that up too. Then, if you wish, you can share it but do remember that it is your experience and you are a student. Learn from it.

Spiritual Experiences and Communications are <u>not</u> Religious

It is with this careful analysis that you learn and grow from the most extraordinary spiritual experiences. **They are "other worldly" so they are not of this world but have to be *translated* downward into human language.** These are often the source of great mystical poetry, mythic stories, artistic visions, the composition of music and other contributions to the beauty of this world.

Above all, no matter what the seeming message, no matter how beautiful the vision, your ecstatic experience <u>is not a "religious" one</u>. It may be called mystical and it is shamanic, but is not "religious" in the sense that word is used today. It is not a confirmation of any religion or the basis for founding a new religion. *All religion is human in origin,* despite any claims to the contrary. We will be discussing this in greater detail over the next three chapters but religion is the institutionalizing of a spiritual experience, losing the "Spirit" behind the doors of bureaucracy and turning spirituality into a theocracy of priests and ministers imposing a frozen theology on a population.

The Bicameral Mind & the Triune Brain

It is difficult for a person today to believe that his ancestors were very different from who we are today. Sure, pre-historic people presumably lacked any fashion sense about whatever clothing they may have worn, and probably did not have very nice dining manners, lacking even quality table ware, and all that—*but didn't they think and feel just like modern people?*

According to Dr. Julian Jayne, the answer is "No." His classic, *The Origin of Consciousness in the Breakdown of the Bicameral Mind,* reveals that until about 3,000 years ago, we were essentially "asleep"—just as many metaphysical thinkers (Gurdjieff, Ouspensky, etc.) say many people are "mostly asleep" even today. What is really being said is that we lacked full, alert "conscious awareness" and were *mostly reacting automatically just like animals.*

The concept of the bicameral mind recognizes the "split brain" in which audio hallucinations evolved in the right brain (alpha waves of 7 to 14 cycles per second) and were *heard* as "voices" in the left brain hemisphere (beta waves of 14 to 21 cycles per second). Today we think of those right brain voices as emanating from the subconscious mind, but earlier humans heard them as the *authoritarian* messages from gods and spirits, and as a result even today we react to "authorities" (religious, political, governmental, teachers, counselors) as *commands*, and still seek such guidance in preference to rational analysis and assuming responsibility for our own thoughts and acts.

Are Gods and Spirits any more "real" than other authorities are?

The reverse of that question is: *Are all "gods" and "spirits" invented or otherwise formed in the subconscious mind?* If we accept that the personal subconscious is connected to the Universal Consciousness, then we can answer "yes" with no loss of the value of our communication with Spirit. Rather, with such knowledge we can learn to consciously recognize the difference between good and bad, true and false spirits, and even relate to certain spiritual entities with love, acceptance, and *understanding.*

In fact, there is considerable value in "objectifying" these subconscious and spiritual communications—thus treating them as a *discussion among equals* so that we raise consciousness to the mental rather than the lower astral (reactive emotionality) level.

Shamanic Spiritual Knowledge and Technology

Create our own gods and spirits. Take that a step further: *Can we go so far as to consciously "create" our own gods and spirits* that will connect with universal consciousness to bring wisdom, knowledge, and affection, as we desire and choose? More importantly, can we communicate rationally and objectively with gods and spirits?*

* **Tulpas.** In Tibetan Buddhism, mind-created spirit entities are called "tulpas" and were the subject of Alexandra David-Neel's *Magic and Mystery in Tibet* in which she recounts her own experience of creating an entity that she then fought to get rid of. The book illustrates the need not only for mind training but emotional cleansing. See our *Clairvoyance for Psychic Empowerment* and its included text "Developing Psychic Clarity & True Vision."

Household Gods. This is, however, essentially the same technique used to create "household gods" to give connection between home and family, a small business or farm with owner/operators, as well as the familiar experience of relating to one's automobile, boat, or airplane as an entity.

Consciously project Spirit into the object, give it some identity, and communicate with "her" (it is almost always a feminine being), giving thanks for good performance and service, requesting a particular service (Be on guard against crooks in the neighborhood!), etc. Do not feel "foolish" in this for it is "real" even though it's on a different and non-objective level.

That answer is yours to make as you study the concepts of shamanism. With deliberate entry into shamanic states of consciousness, you can journey in the spirit worlds and seek answers to your questions. Shamanism is the oldest "spiritual technology" on the planet. It is the survival and revival of such esoteric knowledge and spiritual technology that today has grown and empowered men and women everywhere to live better, healthier, and longer physical lives while growing spiritually as well.

The "secret knowledge" of raising and altering consciousness

What we today can call "Shamanic spiritual technology and consciousness science" is the direct precursor to all religions and magick, the foundation for the folk knowledge that becomes physical science, and **the wisdom for interpreting the mythic origins of life and the universe** now replaced by the modern "factual" history. It is the "secret knowledge" of raising and altering consciousness, **inducing trance and ecstatic vision** that is at the core of mysticism and personal religious experience that was violently suppressed over the past several thousand years by the male dominated monotheistic religions.

Our modern world is too large, too complex, and too integrated for any sectarian religious theology or political ideology to dominate and repress human consciousness as espoused by militant and repressive religion and special interest political ideology. We must move forward, not backward <u>for world peace and human survival are at stake.</u> Let's try to see things from a conjectured "beginning."

Pre-Hindu Shamanic Tantra and the Aryan Invasion

Putting aside the probable *pre-historic and not yet fully physical** Lemurian and Atlantean "races," the oldest and most sophisticated of these spiritual technologies may be found in ancient *shamanic* Tantra, the precursor to Hinduism. We need to emphasize that this ancient shamanic Tantra was not a religion but a precursor to the Hindu Religion indigenous to southern India and believed to be the oldest and most diverse religion on the planet. Around 2,500 BCE Aryans from the north invaded India and brought changes to the indigenous religion and agriculturally based culture as they introduced a cattle and patrilineal property based economy, and a caste system of rulers, priests, and soldiers that condemned the indigenous "lower classes" to hard labor and perpetual servitude while the upper classes lived in a luxury previously unknown but "justified" and supported by the male-dominant changes made in the earlier religion.

> * "Pre-physical." There is a metaphysical myth that ancient "lost civilizations" existed on the long since submerged continents of Atlantis and Lemuria on which lived humans not yet fully devolved into physical form but functioning in astral bodies.

Despite the Aryan introduction of numerous male gods and the historic repressions of the indigenous people, the esoteric teaching and practices of pre-religious Tantra have survived and contributed to our knowledge and aptitude to work with both the physical and the metaphysical (more subtle) forces and substances of shamanic Tantra.

The Shamanic Vision

In many ways, shamanism is an *attitude,* a matter of respect for Nature and the worlds both of matter and spirit. Shamans personally experience the spiritual dimensions and know **there are no real boundaries between the worlds**. Each shaman learns to see with their inner vision, to listen with their inner hearing, to feel with super-sensual hands and fingers, to commune with the inner essence (spirit) of animals and places, to become one with a horse, a wolf, a hare, a cat, an eagle, or even another person or spiritual entity without interfering with their inner essence.

They may learn a particular tradition from parent shamans or a teacher, or an inner guide or from a personal "calling" and *need to know*—but not from any theology or dogma, and they verify their knowledge through direct experience. They heal, teach, and serve their clients and the local community through direct intervention and not by prayers to some distance and probably non-existent deity.

Shamanism is Empowering and Transformative

Shamanism is *transformative: some sha-persons* can cross the barrier between human and animal in a variation of *Animism.* One variation of this is found in Voodoo where a god (*loa*) possesses a human and is said to "ride the human as if a horse." That, however is an inadvertent possession, while others have deliberately sought to be a horse, or wolf, tiger or other "were" (as in "<u>were</u>wolves") creatures. Such "possession"—really an incorrect word—is not *demonic* as claimed by the Church—but *a means of experiential knowledge of alternate realities* that are part of the greater cosmic reality.

Partnering with Power Animals, Allies, and Totem Animals

One particular aspect of shamanic empowerment and training we haven't discussed is partnering with power animal spirits. Each species of animal has unique characteristics, and *the spirit of the Power Animal represents the species as a whole,* and hence we mostly experience the Power Animal Spirits in the form of "pure" wild animal.

While most Power Animals do take the form of the wild animal, there are three major exceptions in modern practice: the horse (or pony), the dog (or wolf), and the domestic cat. Here we are not speaking of indigenous or historic shamanism, but of modern, western practice of companion animals, including those adopted in therapeutic role-playing. (More on that later)

The Horse (or Pony), Dog, and Cat as Companion Allies

Both the horse and dog were more than prey (food) and more than predators against which humans had to defend themselves. These two animals became companions in work and in living. While the domestic cat also became a live-in associate, it is more often a pet or "barn cat" than a companion, and its "independent" spirit separates it from the devotion shown by dog and horse. Still, the domestic cat may be known as a *"Fetch,"* or the *"Witch's Familiar" serving as a magical envoy into the spirit world.*

Yet, in modern culture, the horse is more a woman's companion and *fetish,** the dog more the man's companion, and the cat makes her own choices.

---

* "Fetish." Word usage, and the emotions sometimes attached to particular words, can change as fast as women's fashions. Originally used in connection with religions, "Fetish" means an object imbued with spiritual energy. In Victorian times of Church-led sexual repression, it was used in a *negative* sense for objects imbued with feminine sexual (attractor) energy (corset gloves, ankle bracelets, pierced earrings, etc.). Freudians often saw an extreme high heel as symbolizing a man's penis—hence that the

woman was standing or walking on an erect penis and interpreting that to mean the male who found heels attractive on a woman was a *masochist* wanting to be trampled, and also very likely a *homosexual* as well.

What was then a fetish is now a fashion accessory to a look, the completion of a costume, or a purely sensual experience, or an expression of intimacy. It has little power in itself other than the feminine "attractor" energy projected into by both male and female.

The Horse as a Woman's Fetish signifying High Position. In this reference to a horse, it simply signifies the strong emotional involvement a woman can have with an animal or object with which she is personally identified, especially in an on-going relationship. In British society, the "Riding, Racing, and Dressage Culture," along with the accompanying fashions, is *Upper Class*, hence signifying that the woman has *arrived* at the top of the social ladder. Among the more Freudian-oriented analysts, it is the feeling of "horse power" between her legs that is a sexual "turn-on."

And while this close companionship forms one aspect of what we can call the "intuitive shamanic" relationship to a Power Animal, the other comes during a shamanic journey in which the shaman discovers and meets his/her power animal. Sometimes animals appear in dreams, but these are more often interpreted symbolically rather than as direct manifestations of the shaman's totem ally. Angelique S. Cook and G. A. Hawk present a usable technique that you can adopt to meet your power animal in *Shamanism and the Esoteric Tradition.* Also Mike Williams in *Follow the Shaman's Call.* See sources at end of this chapter.

In essence, the animal totem may be spontaneously encountered during ecstatic trance, or deliberately visualized during the trance state. The encounter with the Totem Animal is a direct symbolic and energy encounter in which the traditional meanings have an overall pertinence either to the person or situation, or to the moment of the experience. In modern American culture, the most favored animal totems and their spiritual wisdom qualities, are:

CAT—intuition, self-confidence, concentration, courage, independence, relaxation, playful, otherworldly, nocturnal vision, nighttime

COUGAR—leadership, smart strategies, persistence, courage,

DOG—hunter, faithful companion and protector, knows secrets of darkness, a guide to new knowledge, social animal, loyalty, care for the young and weak, strong sense of smell and hearing

DOLPHIN—joy in play with others, harmony with environment, love of community and mutual support

EAGLE—far sight, sees details, symbolized Light and Strength, messenger from spirit realm

ELEPHANT—strength, loyalty, love of family and partners, sexuality, memory, care of young and old, remover of obstacles in your path

HARE (not to be confused with Rabbit)—lust, sexuality, fertility, renewal, face your fears and don't run from them, courage to use your intuition

HORSE—strength, freedom, faithfulness, mother goddess, fertility, holds key to underworld, protector of the dead, journeys, astral travel, interspecies communication, interaction, partnerships, power through cooperation, sensitivity, psychic powers, endurance, adventurous spirit, control of environment

JAQUAR—self-empowerment, shape-shifting, psychic seeing, seeing patterns behind chaos, no fear of darkness

OWL—keen sight, shape-shifting, moon magick, stealth, messenger, link between worlds, knowledge of secrets

POLAR BEAR—strength in face of adversity, dreams and shamanic vision, introspection, communication with spirit, courage to face change

Author Raven Digitalis writes:

"The world of animals is enigmatic, fascinating, and magickal. The beauty, the adaptable behavior, and the inherent wisdom of animals gives us reason enough to admire them....

"Animals are telepathic, communicating on a vibratory level. This is natural and instinctive to all animal species, including humans, although most of us have forgotten about this inherent ability....

"Power animals have an infinite amount of energy to lend. With appropriate research and attention to detail, you can find an ethereal life partner and ally in magick. Power animals and spirit animals are also friends in astral travel. During astral projection, the animal may meet and escort the seeker through the astral landscape ... Some who practice astral projection like to energetically shapeshift into the form of the animal helper before embarking on journeys or vision quests.

"Some people identify with their spirit animal to the point where they feel themselves to be that animal. Still knowing their humanness, they observe that their actions, responses, and perceptions reflect the energy of the animal guide."

—Digitalis, R.: *Shadow Magick Compendium—Exploring Darker Aspects of Magickal Spirituality*, 2008, Llewellyn

In addition, there is the transformative assumption of the Power Animal encountered in induced role-playing "subspace"* during which one ***temporarily becomes the animal spirit.***

> * **Sub-space:** The trance-like altered state into which a Submissive "sinks" in which all control is surrendered without thought. A complete physical, emotional, and mental "letting go" to the will of another person. In an intimate B/d relationship it is a total release of personal power into the care and trust of the Beloved.

Interaction, Relationship, Thought Form, Goddess, Archetype, Matrix

The shaman's "Power Animal" can become something more: the horse, for example, can become a goddess, and an archetype. The Horse Goddess, known as *Epona* in the Celtic pantheon, is a particularly powerful presence in European and American spiritual practices.

The dog was a hunting *companion* living off the scraps of the kill facilitated by the human-canine partnership. The horse, however, was a four-legged *extension* of the human warrior, hunter, herder, traveler, and explorer. And, in modern times, "riding" is a mark of distinction, wealth, and class. In the American West, horse and cowboy were in many ways as intimate (not sexually) as a husband and wife—living together, often sleeping together on the trail, working together, sharing meals and water together, exploring together.

Epona, the horse goddess

Both dog and horse are known for their extreme devotion/nurturing care, sensitivity to human feelings, and willingness to "work until they drop." In both the dog- and horse- relationship to the human, *especially to the "one" human (owner, master, mistress),* the *action* is on behalf of the human's needs and desires. In the "one-on-one" relationship, the animal makes a ready distinction between the one person and the other members of the family or clan, also separating that one animal from its herd or pack.

Interaction Creates a Thought Form

Familiarity breeds Love and Dependency! We see this with the horse in particular. In any working relationship, <u>interaction</u> creates a *Thought Form* embodying the nature of the relationship, our feeling and our hopes. Over a long term, this creates a dependence and transfers Power to the thought form that turns it into a deity, and an archetype. *Epona* was so powerful a Goddess that the Roman military and bureaucracy occupying Britain "adopted" Her from the Celtic world into their own pantheon.

As a deity, she is also an archetype and her power can be *evoked* to help in a human need. An archetype is also a kind of "matrix" that can be *invoked* into the human psyche to empower that person in particular ways that also affect others in relationship with that person, and even events around the people involved.

Psychotherapy and Role-Playing with Power Animals

"Growing numbers of psychotherapists use guided visualization techniques to evoke images of 'power animals' or 'spirit guides' and then encourage clients to interact with and learn from them."*

* Gallegos, A. (1987) *The personal totem pole: animal imagery, the chakras and psychotherapy.* Santa Fe, NM: Moon Bear Press.

Guided Visualization

Understanding guided visualization in particular relation to role playing with power animals is an important element to the balance of this chapter. There are several points to be made:

1. Guided Visualization is a form of guided "fantasy." The psychologist Richard Noll believes that *shamans are intense fantasizers.* *

* Quoted in Nicholson, S (Ed.): *Shamanism,* 1987, Quest

2. Fantasy is "visualization," and *visualization* is intrinsic to "the Magickal Imagination" that connects us directly to the subconscious mind and to levels of the "spirit world," also known as the astral plane.

3. Guided visualization is much the same thing as Carl Jung's *active imagination,* and is similar to Kabbalistic Path-working in which the practicing magician builds up a structured inner world called "the Tree of Life"—strongly resembling the shamanic "world tree."

4. The subconscious mind is our personal window or even *a door into the Collective Unconscious,* which is, in turn, part of Universal Consciousness.

5. Humans, spirit animals, and real companion animals share consciousness at the lower astral level and can *communicate with one another through human controlled fantasy.*

6. Good hypnotic subjects enter into the *"fantasy state"—able to see, hear, smell, touch and fully experience what they fantasize.*

(Quoted from Wilson, S. & Barber, T. 1982. The fantasy-prone individual. In A. Sheikh (Ed.). Imagery: Current theory, research, and application.

7. A particular hypnotic-like state is called "sub-space"* and is experienced in certain extended shamanic actions and related to sexual role play. In sub-space, the "sub" is particularly open to suggestion and visionary experiences.

* **"Sub-space"** is a particular term used in D/s (Dominance and Submission) sexual role-playing (and we refer only to consensual relationships between mature adults) during which the submissive player/partner totally trusts the dominant to control every aspect of the "scene" without reservation. It becomes necessary for the dominant to show care and provide for the health and welfare of the "sub" during the scene and to bring the "sub" back into normal consciousness and self-control as the scene is completed.

This is even more necessary when the "sub" is restrained in any way, and the scene involves extremes of pleasure and pain triggering physiological responses including the release of natural hormones and body chemicals increasing pain tolerance to the point of pain becoming pleasure and inducing a trance-like state of detachment, exhaustion, and incoherence. Extreme care must be provided by the "dom" to avoid injury—including self-injury as the "sub" may seek still more of body/chemical produced pleasure.

The depth of the trance can be so extreme that "commands" given can have long-term enduring effects just as in professionally administered hypnosis. Even in terms of mystical or spiritual dimensions, the "sub" or "subject" (to use a term from hypnosis) can assume levels of consciousness beyond that which the whole personality is prepared for with a total disconnect from reality.

A Carefully Scripted, Open-ended, Ritual Drama

The footnote provides a warning, but it also describes the ordinary situation as may be variously encountered in prolonged orgasmic Tantra, sexual role play or the extended shamanic experience that can be developed in a carefully scripted drama (sometimes referred to as a "ritual drama") that is open-ended so that new psychological and spiritual experiences can occur for both partners whether as shaman and assistant or as sexual partners and role players. Similar altered states are sometimes experienced in other situations involved sensory overload as in concerts, political rallies, sports events, etc. in which the "submissive" participants become emotionally devoted and nearly dependent upon the "dominant" leader. (For further understanding of this, refer to standard texts on the roles of Hitler, Stalin, Mussolini, Peron, etc. in recent fascism.)

Let's not get hung up with the use of the word "Submissive." Even in sexual role playing, the "sub"—either man or woman—is not submitting to a secondary role either in a relationship or in society. Rather, it is an *"opening up"* and being *"receptive"* to *"developmental experiences"* that can **bring new knowledge, growth, and actual transformation.**

Ways to Growth and Expansion, and Strengthening the Partnership

And, if "dominance and submission" role-playing brings enjoyment and joy into the relationship, that too opens the way to growth and expansion in areas of life and self beyond the sexual while strengthening the partnership.

We are entering into a New Age where we are increasingly free of social, religious, and other attempts to impose outdated standards and expectations on our freedoms of choice whether in what we do, or what we wear, or how we relate to one another. In asserting our independence we are "growing up" no matter how old we may be or what obligations we voluntarily assume. Removing superficial *external* societal rules opens *internal* experiential doors to give meaning to play and fantasy.

True spirituality comes with freedom of choice and expression, with self-respect and self-responsibility, with looking forward rather than backward or over the shoulder, and "surrendering to life, growth, and happiness.

Role-playing and Spontaneous Interaction

A further point can be made that "role playing" can be a form of *live* active imagination programs (somewhat similar to drama therapy and path-working programs as mentioned in an earlier footnote in relation to "mind training") in which two or more players adopt defined *fantasy* roles as human/human or animal/human within the context of a <u>minimal script</u> *calling for their spontaneous interaction.* In the case of such play within a consensual sexual relationship, one action evokes feeling reactions in both partners. They are actually having a shamanic-like journey together in which the one partner can become one with the spirit of the animal totem, or *both relate archetypally to each other in inter-related roles.*

One type of such live role-playing is the "Human Pony Play" previously mentioned. In the case of the animal/human play, *the presence of the human partner keeps the fantasy within human bounds.*

The Mythic, and Submissive, Eve

Another form that has likewise become increasing part of our new sexual culture is that of "Sensual Magic" involving bondage and dominance and submission. D/s imitates the age-old mythic instruction to *Eve* to submit to her husband in all ways. Take the falsity of the religious myth out of it and you perceive the mythic and historic role a woman in love adopts to give of herself just as the man in love wants to care and protect his beloved.

Throughout the ages, in myth and life, these roles have been re-enacted in all cultures so as to become instinctive when not subsumed in religious theology and practice, regulated and enforced by both "church and state," and translated into systematic abuse and "justified" violence against women in tribal societies.

Sexual Energy is Healing, and Transformative

Again, we answer the logical question: *what has "Sex," or rather, "adult sexual role-playing games," have to do with Spirit Communications?*

It is our intention to fully survey the "field" in all our books, and not just "teach" a single technology as if it were "the only way." We've established that Spirit and Consciousness are everywhere and in everything, and we've discussed the interplay of Energy and Matter. *Energy is vital to all we do*—whether in regard to industry, lighting our cities, or our own internal functioning: physically, emotionally, mentally and spiritually. ***All intentional activity demands a source of particular energies vibrationally pertinent to the intended action.*** At the very core of the body, at the base of the spine, there is source of biological/spiritual energy known as *Kundalini.**

As defined in Tantra and Hinduism, **Kundalini is the creative energy of the universe.** "As Above, so Below," as *in the Universe so it is within body and soul. Kundalini* is our internal source of energy that is both Life sustaining and transformative when consciously raised and directed to the various etheric centers known as *Chakras*. In addition, there is an external source of Life energy known as *Prana*.*

> * *Kundalini* and *Prana* are *Sanskrit* words, and we use them for the simple reason that they are the most precise and now familiar words for these concepts generally unrecognized in Western "materialistic" culture but rapidly becoming more familiar with the widespread interest in Eastern esotericism and practices such as Yoga, Tantra, Meditation, and Spiritual philosophy. In addition to Kundalini, sexual activity (and even fantasy and foreplay) mobilizes biological energy both towards the pelvic array and the brain.
>
> As we have discussed elsewhere, "words" create their own problems. Various authors, teachers, schools, esoteric or scientific systems often invent their own terminology or insist on using vocabularies of Sanskrit, Hebrew, Greek, Latin, and even ancient Egyptian for specific esoteric functions, organs, energies, etc. when there are already familiar words more readily understood. Rather than clarification, obscure words are used for the purpose of impressing the student and thus proclaiming the expertise and importance of the teacher. Even though many esoteric terms today originate as Sanskrit, they are so universally familiar that we should resist efforts to "Westernize" those same words into Greek or Latin or Hebrew, if not into English.

We've previously mentioned the practice of Sexual Tantra and Sex Magick to invoke and evoke spiritual entities and even gods and goddesses. These are *Spiritual* practices of intentional communication requiring energy in raising and directing consciousness to intentional goals. All Spirit Communication requires energy, and the "higher you go, the more the energy you need."

Sexual Energy and Sexual Fantasy (a particular aspect of the Imagination) are extremely powerful "tools" for Consciousness Work.

Sexuality is not contra to Spirituality

Despite a long tradition from millenniums of male-dominated religious teachings, and from Theosophy, Yoga, and certain other Metaphysical traditions, "SEX" is not something that must be suppressed for a person to become "more spiritual." Everything is a matter of focus and intent. You can be sexual tonight and spiritual tomorrow morning—but sex is not anti-spiritual nor is it sinful. Like all else, it's a matter of *attitude.* Sex is beautiful, and it is fundamental to all Life. And human Sex is not—as some still claim—*only for Reproduction.* But, all "sex" is not the same. For some—men mostly—it is often simply little more than an "itch" easily satisfied by masturbation and even spontaneous emissions (wet dreams). For others, and for most women, sex can be an extended sensual and emotional experience with overtones that relate to her self-worth and image, her sense of "belonging," her approach to personal appearance and fashion, her care for home and family, to romance and love, and to her desire to be a mother. Her *fantasy* life is real and deep, and a source of her creativity and the beauty she makes and brings to her world and that of others.

It is the woman's Joy and Love of Life that makes us Human and it is Woman who makes Life worth Living. It is woman who is the core of the family and the foundation for civilization. It is the Feminine Force that is the Heart of Nature, of the Earth, and of the Material Universe.

Sexuality is fundamental in Human Life and Consciousness

"Sex" is fundamental to Life. In the Human person, it is *not* limited to reproduction but permeates all levels of consciousness and all aspects of culture. Understanding "sexuality" is fundamentally important to human psychology, but until <u>very</u> recent times the many intrinsic but important differences between masculine and feminine were neglected just as they had been in modern medicine in which women were seen as a kind of "inferior" man. Now we know more of human physiology, and are beginning to understand and value the extent and importance of the differences between the male and female genital *systems* (not just the sex organs) and their relationship to areas of the brain and aspects of personality and consciousness.

These difference should have nothing to do with religion, but throughout history both Christianity and Islam have not only placed women in an inferior and submissive position, but taught her intrinsic sinful nature as the "daughter of Eve who disobeyed the Lord" and that she was mentally inferior to a man as well as physically so. Even back to Aristotle we find a (so called) scientific basis for the Church's claim that the male sperm is the active procreative agent while the female egg is only passive "raw material" to be incorporated into the developing child. Making such archaic claims today is both scientifically ignorant and intellectually absurd.

Intimacy is archetypally fundamental to the "established" relationship between two people

At the same time, there are "women's issues" and needs that should be recognized in Politics and Law. Women are now successfully competing with men in every area of modern life, in Business, Science, Politics, the Professions, even in Athletics, Sports, and the Military, etc. That success has also brought recognition of the differences in male and female psychology and how those gender differences are specifically reflected in the *core* nature of our personal lives.

Yet, it is vital to ignore them in public and private life where those differences have no significance. Or, rather, not to ignore them when individually can be beneficially recognized and made functionally important to personal and organizational success. Just because either a man or a woman can become a General doesn't mean that the job description must be neutral. Each makes the job, rather than the "uniform" making the man (or the woman.)

Reproduction has a fundamental meaning for a woman far different than it has for a man. Her *conscious* awareness and knowledge of the ability to conceive and reproduce is unique to humanity in contrast to all other biological life. The desire and ability to attract the interest of a suitable mate and to reproduce in a safe environment is biologically and psychologically instinctive, and this instinct is often complicated and exaggerated by age-related hormonal drives. In youth, the "heat" is on and passion easily leads to mistakes or "accidents." In early middle years, the woman may fear losing her chance of family life.

Her modernity and life in a democratic society today encourages and provides her with choices of higher academic and professional education that enable her to make decisions about career and lifestyles that free her of the old economic dependence on a mate. And socially, today, she is enabled to personally choose her potential mate outside of race, class, caste and religious restraints or family alliances.

Her increased sense of self brings with it the desire for uniqueness, to be seen and known as an individual person in charge of her own life and not as a reproductive "machine" or "sex object." Modern life brings her choices in personal style and fashion, in self-expression and emotional enjoyment, in intellectual interest and education, in location and career, and more.

A Woman's Life is Complicated!

No matter how modern we are, male and female, we still relate to our biological and psychological heritage. We think birth is a "starting point," but even if you don't believe in reincarnation, it is only a "New Beginning," and we are conditioned and influenced by everything that has been part of all life up to this moment.

As humans, we carry with us the history of all we have ever been, with slight cultural modifications carried in the genetic system. An African American carries an intrinsic cultural/psychological heritage different from his British American cousin. And, Women and Men are different both in this specific genetic heritage and in what that culture has been in relation to gender. A Japanese American woman carries a cultural heritage different from her Indian American female cousin. Yes, a family that reaffirms its cultural heritage may strengthen those genetic memories in their children, but that's only part of the story.

It isn't only genes that carry history, but as a Japanese American Woman, she triggers psychological response from the Universal Collective Unconscious to her Femininity, her Japanese heritage, her American heritage and current life, and even more minor factors related to family history of class, caste, earlier migrations, etc. Each life begins with unconscious memories forming our subconscious mind.

Gender Rules!

But, above all, *Gender Rules!* As a women, she carries a unique *Archetypal* memory that reflects the entire history of women as the bearer and care-keepers of children, of the gatherers of fruits and vegetables, of the preparers of food and clothing providers for the family, the person who kept the home fires burning, the early gardeners and herbalists, and all the other things women have done down the ages. Of course, men have their own history reflective of their masculine gender and strength—as hunters for food, as defenders against predators, as fighters defending territory, as protectors of women and children, as explorers looking for new territory, and then as aggressors fighting to extend territory, and all the things men have done down the ages.

And Rules reflected Gender

Included in this gender heritage is the distinction that these roles have made that today we can recognize as factors reflected in instincts of male dominance and female submission, regardless of political or religious implications. Historically it wasn't called that but it simply remains that for many, many generations men <u>ruled</u> and women <u>obeyed,</u> and the only differences were related to the status and profession (often inherited and otherwise related to class or caste). Further differentiation occurred in families of higher status in how women dressed and behaved to reflect the man's position. With greater wealth and status, women's bodies were fashionably exaggerated to specifically attract the dominant male, and then adorned and constrained to reflect both sexuality and social position. Fashion and Etiquette, along with the basics of reproduction and child care, of "servitude" to home and to her "*Lord and Master*," conditioned her life and was reinforced by the rules of Church and State. Even women in the more advanced societies were "virtual slaves"—*even as not recognized*—bound by rules and fashions, and raised to serve their husbands in all manner but with no joy since *a woman's sexual pleasure was deemed "sinful"* by all three monotheistic religions, and increasingly so by other religions as well as their institutions became dominated by men.

New Sexual Freedom and the <u>New Feminine</u>. It's a New Beginning!

Modern life has changed all that. Modern life has not only freed her of those external rules and provided her with political and economic freedoms, given her education and profession, and control over her own life but has brought her opportunities of self-discovery to be who and what she wants. But, remember that even woman's right to vote was recognized less than 100 years ago in America, and is still denied in many parts of the world.

Sexual Superiority

And, regardless, she is still biologically and psychologically a woman. No longer seen as the "weaker sex" distinguished only by her reproductive organs and lack of the male penis, science has suddenly shown her to be sexually *superior* to the male with pleasure triggers more numerous and powerful than his, her orgasmic capacity far greater than the male's limited by his easily exhaustive ejaculatory function, and with contraception she is no longer fearful that sexual intercourse will lead to undesired health debilitating multiple pregnancies.

These psychological and biological heritages don't control us or limit us, but their unconscious memories *do* affect us. Few relationships these days in modern societies exist strictly in accord with the old traditional roles of dominant man and submissive woman, and yet in *any* relationship, be it heterosexual, homosexual, or non-sexual, there is a more dominant partner and a more submissive partner. These roles can change from time to time, moment to moment, and relationship to relationship, depending on circumstance, needs, desires, and individual dynamics and interests. What's important to note though is that these roles of submission and domination are grounded in biological and psychological instinct, and archetypal energies that are a part of our individual and cultural heritages as men and women.

She Rules the Roost

From an outsider's perspective, a woman who considers herself a sexual "submissive" and is interested in being sexually "dominated" by a man might appear to be weak, subservient, and repressed; the inner and magickal reality, however, is quite the opposite. In truth, **the submissive partner is typically the one in control.** Submission leads to action: the submissive partner incites the dominant partner to *do* things—call me, talk to me, want me, kiss me, touch me, caress me, hold me, penetrate me, love me and cuddle with me—while the more "dominant" partner complies in doing everything they're enticed to do by the more "submissive" partner. **Dominance and submission are simply a means to an end**, an expression of instinctual, biological, psychological, and emotional realities factored by karmic and genetic memories. Sex play, be it in domination and submission, in fantasy or role play, fashion or costume, or other enhancements, can be an effective medium for the both the sexual and the shamanistic experience. In expressing these realities through a sexual context, both partners are able to connect with spirit, bridging the gap between feminine and masculine by creating a cooperative exchange of energies between the two.

Polarities are the means to Synthesis and New Worlds of Mind and Spirit

Shamanism is exactly this—forging and traversing connections between concepts and realities that seemingly exist in polarities: male and female, objective and subjective, inner world and outer world, mundane reality and spiritual reality. Polarities are not only opposites but also the means to synthesis and new worlds of mind and spirit.

Sensual Magic, Sex Magic, and an S/m Culture

Modern feminine sexual freedom has led to the widespread practices of many kinds of more overt sexual expression in dress ranging from such "fetish fashions" as stiletto hi-heels, knee-high boots, corset belts, long opera gloves, leather dresses and skirts, skin-tight latex and other materials, and many other attractive and sensually enjoyable and now fashionable items once associated only with *sexual "perversity" and Victorian repression* and now to the acknowledged enjoyment of alternative sexual play between consensual adults in established relationships. There is no compulsion in B/d role-playing when it just an exercise of the constitutional right to "Life, Liberty, and the *Pursuit of Happiness*," which is purely individual and has nothing to do with Church or State or other people's social or political views.

Whatever She Wants

Today, women wear what they want when and where, and for their own practical needs or their sensual and fashion enjoyment and in private sexual play. With a growth of acceptance and enjoyment of "exotic" practices in established relationships, "fashion" has subtly entered the erotic scene with attractive bondage-suggestive jewelry and belts, items called "slave" bracelets and anklets, "Story of "O" rings," and "collaring" in which the submissive partner wears a collar with the same basic symbolism of the engagement and wedding rings by which a woman is stating that she is in an *antici-pated* permanent relationship with a man. Collaring is a two-way street in which *both dominant and submissive are willingly bound together by the same symbol.*

The Mutuality of Orgasmic Pleasure, and the Quest for Ecstasy

Once again, we feel we have to justify bringing "Sex" into the discussion of Spiritual Communication, and—in particular—why, what we prefer to call "Sensual Magick" or simply S/m is given prominence. As previously established, humans are uniquely sexual in nature. While at the unconscious levels it is still biologically driven as in other "animals," there is also both a purely human emotional and a mental involvement that generally brings it into the conscious level where Love, Romance, the Desire for a Family, the mutuality of Orgasmic Pleasure, and the quest for Ecstasy become decisive. **Sexuality that is <u>conscious</u> has the power of transformation, and the greater the sexual energy the greater the potentials for self-transformation and spiritual development.** *Sex is a powerful shamanic and magical tool that stimulates creativity and enables particular forms of communication beyond normal human limitations. And, Sex is a powerful means to the blending of two unique persons in a complementary partnership.*

"Sub-space" in Sensual Magic and Sexual Play—and shamanic possession

One of the newly encountered Altered States of Consciousness that S/m couples are experiencing in their sexual practice is known as "Sub-space," in which the submissive person (most often the female, less often a male) totally submits to the dominant's control for her (the "sub's") pleasure, and then into other aspects of their consensual dance. She let's go of objective awareness to turn within—sometimes to pure nothingness as in deep meditation, other times to a wealth of fantasies, and—then—under his guidance or her own intention, she awakens feminine archetypes in her subconscious to communicate directly her needs and questions. These may take the form of goddesses and spirits in communication with her at high spiritual levels or just a flow of mostly unconscious awareness.

There are two aspects of this:

1. The more common "automatic" experience of "sub-space" results from some of the same shamanic ecstatic induction techniques already discussed: *externally* directed dance—often accompanied by mild flagellation—to near

exhaustion, sexual stimulation in bondage without orgasm, sensory deprivation while suspended as in Japanese rope bondage, or the old European Witches
Cradle, etc. Combinations of pain and pleasure, sensation and denial, movement and restraint, trigger the release of natural endorphins and epinephrine
leading to a kind of drug high and a morphine like tolerance to pain—which
can have the unfortunate result of the "sub" requesting more pain to the point
of endangerment.

It also resembles the involuntary possession by an entity as in a Voodoo
ritual as quoted here:

> "Sub-space, it turns out, is not so different from the Voodoo idea
> of 'possession.' When people become possessed during Voodoo cer-
> emonies (called *danse-lwa*), Haitians say that their identity, spirit, or
> essence goes to Gine (the Voodoo equivalent of heaven) and their
> bodies are taken over by the *lwa* (the gods and goddesses). In psy-
> chology, we'd say that the primary identity (the person we think we
> are) is relaxed so that other potentials and possibilities (the multiple
> personalities we really are) are given an opportunity to shine. Most
> psychologists would agree that this is very healing—and that most of
> don't do it enough."
> —*Charlotte, K.: Wicked Voodoo Sex, 2008. Llewellyn*

2. The *internal* intentional entry into an altered state of being in which one partner fully engages in a shamanic role-play to become some other entity such as
a mythic goddess, cartoon super-heroine, Japanese anime character, and more
commonly moving into an animal's consciousness—"to become one with the
horse" or wolf, tiger, or other. The reality of this transition into an animal role
is suggestive of the lore concerning werewolves and other "were" animals.

While "Possession" was a somewhat common experience in the Spiritualist séance
in which a Surviving Personality directly spoke through the medium and sometimes
carried out physical actions—such as the expert playing of a musical instrument—
beyond the capability of the medium, deliberately induced shamanic possession by an
animal spirit was mostly outside Western European experience.

The alternative possibility, however, is that the *Werewolf* and other "were" creatures were real and not just fiction or fantasy folklore.

Pony Play and Role Playing

We've chosen to discuss Human Pony Play in this alternative sexual/shamanic practice because of its dramatic nature and suddenly increased popularity. Today there are literally hundreds of Pony Play events* (modeling of fashions for both the human Pony and Trainer, demonstrations of pony "gear" and gaits, dress parades, derby races, dressage demonstrations and various contests) across the country every year, and in Europe as well. In addition, there are clubs and groups offering classes to both ponies and trainers in major cities, and ranches and resorts where couples can enjoy their Pony Play in a supportive and sometimes communal environment. And, with this increasing commonality, there is an expanding discussion, exploration, and understanding of the interactive roles played by pony and trainer, the nature of the sub-space necessary for the pony experience, and what that experience really is. Some of these are sponsored by various shamanic and Pagan groups as well as in sexuality classes and shops.

> * The key words for Internet Search are "Pony Play Events," "Pony Play," and "Human Pony."

It takes "Two" to make a Relationship

While outside observers often presume it's the Dominant's choice that determines the S/m relationship. It actually is common acknowledgement that it is *the Submissive who rules.* The point is that the success of the relationship is conditioned by her enjoyment, just as it is increasingly in "vanilla" love-making. It is her pleasure that will determine his; it is her orgasm that may trigger his; the more "bliss" he can provide her, the more he will receive; the "higher" he can push her orgasmic ecstasy, the greater his. But, that's not all: in every equation of two opposite energies, a third is created by their fulfillment. In sexual intercourse it can lead to a baby; in Sex Magick it can lead to a "Magickal Childe" which is not a human baby but the accomplishment of a pre-determined goal; in Shamanic Magick it can lead to the companionship of Power Ally.

We also see this same drive for transcendent "bliss" and orgasmic ecstasy in the popularity of Tantric workshops. Note this observation:

> "What does tantra have to do with BDSM? The answer, we discovered, is everything. What we found was that the people in the tantra workshops were traveling to ecstasies that felt just like the SM ecstasies, only using different technique.

"The unusually, altered states can be triggered by various kinds of intense physical or mental activity, including dancing, running, or prolonged concentration. These states … point to a clear link between the autonomic nervous system and the brain's potential for spiritual experience.

"This feels to us like a very clear description of the relaxed—but revved-up way we feel during our ecstatic BDSM experiences."

—Easton, D. & Hardy, J.: *Radical Ecstasy SM Journeys to Transcendence*, 2004, Greenery

An additional factor of interest is introduced by the following quotation from *Carnal Alchemy—Sado-Magical Techniques for Pleasure, Pain, and Self-Transformation*, by Stephen E. Flowers, Ph.D., and Crystal Dawn Flowers. 2013, Inner Traditions:

"Experience will show you how Sadean sexuality is not oriented toward the orgasm. In Sadean sessions orgasms often seem 'anticlimactic.' The slow, yet steady and powerful release of sexual energy throughout the session is often far more satisfying and fulfilling than any orgasm. This is so for the dominant. This is because so much of the sexual or erotic energy is constantly being transmuted throughout the session that it may indeed feel like an orgasm that goes on for hours. Because the dominant is so strongly polarized between sexual desire and mental/spiritual creativity—by virtue of the very nature of the activity—the conduit between the physical/sexual center and the intellectual/spiritual center becomes wide open in ways that are difficult to obtain otherwise."

However, Dr. Flowers adds one caveat:

"It is usually advisable to have the submissive achieve orgasm by whatever means seem right. The reasons for this are manifold. First, it gives a sense of "physical closure," which may be necessary for the submissive to get out of the persona assumed for the session. Also, the orgasm may be used by the dominant to 'anchor' certain symbols or carnally alchemical reactions. This can be a major tool for transformation used by the dominant. Finally the orgasm is after all, the elemental Fire of the alchemist—in it the transformations that have taken place in the session are crystallized and made solid."

Both quotations strongly apply in the committed partnership in which it is vital that the Dominant must be *the fully aware and actively responsible "care giver" for the Submissive entering into altered states in which normal rational judgment and self-awareness are mitigated* by nature of the trance and the altered persona. Similar responsibilities are involved when other altered states are achieved by such tools as sensory deprivation, restraint of movement, sensory stimulation, complex postures, etc.

Don't Drink and Drive!

In all Shamanic Work there is more psychic/psychological activity than in most other systems of spirituality. In the above quotations involving the shamanic partnership we can readily see both transformation and *transmutation* activities requiring careful "management" of the process. Where great power is *invoked,* still greater awareness must be assumed and greater responsibility accepted. We call some activities "play," while others assume the façade of normality, but the reality is that it is like playing with dynamite, or finding that the gun presumed loaded with blank cartridges had real ones instead. For the Dominant, *don't drink and drive,* but stay alert.

Fetishes are an integral aspect of adult human sexuality

During the 19th and early 20th century, psychologists and psychiatrists called many things "deviant" and "symptomatic of dangerous emotional imbalance"—fantasies that today are readily practiced in video and computer games, activities that are readily talked about and practiced in classes in Tantra, indulged in as body tattoos and piercings, fashionably worn as stiletto high-heels and waist cinchers, read about in women's popular romance books and magazine, and popularized in television and motion pictures. Among these "dangerous psychiatric concerns" were sexual fetishes: objects worn by women that *felt good to the wearer* and sexually aroused men. Just as proclaimed by the Church, sexual interest other than for reproduction was considered not merely "sinful" but "decadent" and even criminal.

Such were the mores of the <u>recent</u> past age.

One element of fashion that is rarely acknowledged but important to our discussion of role-playing can be simply stated as:

Women become how they dress. Clothes make the man, but women make the clothes. He merely puts clothes on the body, but she puts her body into the clothes and becomes how she is costumed—*becoming more than she is.* When she dresses as a Queen, she is one, as a Princess, she is one, as a Seductress, she becomes one. A woman nearly always dresses the part whether as the CEO or as a tennis player. A man simply puts on a different pair of pants to mow the grass, and wears the same pants to paint the windows, fix the roof, take the kids to the park, or out for pizza.

But even if the man costumes himself as a General or a King, he doesn't become one in the inner way a woman becomes a Queen or a Princess. His Superman costume will not enable him to fly or even give him the delusion of being impervious to bullets.

A woman experiences joy in becoming another—from kitchen maid to Cinderella at the Ball. If she dresses as a dominatrix, she becomes one, while if she dresses in a collar and bondage bracelets she becomes the submissive. How great the transformation is her choice: from fantasy to reality, for the moment or for the day or night or week or more.

As Lee Harrington writes:

> "Anytime we become someone or something else, we can learn something about ourselves or the nature of the universe from a new perspective."
> —Harrington, L.: *Sacred Kink—The Eightfold Path of BDSM and Beyond,* 2009. Mystic

Fashion can be a Shamanic Tool for Entering States of Magickal Consciousness

Of course, these are generalities—many women couldn't care less about fashion, while some men are highly aware of the transformative power of the clothes they wear. Generally speaking though, women have far more options to choose from fashion-wise, and they tend to have a greater awareness of the power and symbolism inherent in such clothing choices, even when that awareness exists more on the subconscious level than at the conscious level. For both men and women, fashion can be a matter of conformity, it can be a matter of practicality, it can be a matter of expression, or it can be a matter of *magick*, transforming the wearer in a way that allows desired energies (or *spirits*) to be invoked, utilized, and projected. In short, fashion can be used as a shamanistic tool that can aid in communication with spirit, and it can help us also to become *more than we are*, entering a state of magickal consciousness where we are able to form connections between inner world and outer world, masculine energies and feminine energies, anima and animus, human experience and animalistic instincts.

Self-Transformation

The very essence of shamanism and of spiritual communication is *Self-Transformation*. We transform aspects of Self in order to discover more of who we are and to enter into new relationships with our world and with those with whom we have "growth" relations.

Dog & Pony Show

We know the phrase "Dog and Pony Show" but here we are going to give it new meaning. Of all the animals we encounter, Dog and Horse have certain "spiritual" qualities that are important to us. Both are distinctly intelligent pack or herd animals that actively *partner* with others, seemingly in telepathic communication with their animal and human companions and have instinctive awareness of their needs and care for their well-being.

As our companions, they know our needs often before we do! They nudge us in the right direction, they alert us and our other human companions to special situations, to threats to our health and well-being, they protect us from attacks, and they demonstrate all the emotions of humans: love, jealousy, desire for caress, loyalty, and they respond unselfishly and unambiguously to our requests and commands. They will sleep next to us, snuggle and nuzzle with us, and lay down their lives for us.

Deified in Myth & Religion

In other words, they are *noble* animals that have been deified in myth and "primitive" religions. Of the two, the Horse seemingly has the greater spirit powers, moving beyond the amazing but purely sensual extended awareness of the Dog. We are transformed by acts in which we share consciousness with them. Becoming a Human Pony is a near "alchemical" experience in which the most negative human characteristics are *subsumed* by the most positive of the horse.

Transformed by Costume & Acts of Imitation

We are transformed by costume and imitative acts that identify us with the horse. Some humans, women in particular, wear "skins" of black or brown rubber, shoes or boots imitating hooves, some wear hoof-like gloves, and even masks or hoods to cover their human identity. And, then, in the important relationship between the human pony and the human partner (lover, trainer, driver), it is the bondage of special harnesses and the bridle and bit that transfers control to the human partner.

Inducing the Pony Experience

Donning Pony Gear <u>induces</u> the Pony Experience which can be sexual or not. The more complete the costume, the more complete the transformation. Both awareness of her appearance and the sensual experience of each item—from pony mask, bridle and bit, latex second skin, harness, and pony hooves to the final addition of a pony tail—adds to the transformation.

Driver & Pony—<u>Together</u>

The Human Pony is harnessed to a light weight two-wheeled cart in which the driver is seated, and it's "off to the races" in which pony and driver compete with others in matters of dressage, gait, and speed. In addition—for the more enthusiastic pony players—there are "fashion" shows in which both driver and pony are judged for dress, style, and manner. In intimate relationships the pony's costume and harness may be augmented with sexually stimulating accessories to further pass control to the human for later consummation in ecstatic union with magickal purpose.

Connecting to the Unconscious

While the relationship has all the appearance of Dominance and Submission, players say otherwise, and that the "sub-space" entered into by the pony leads into a state of altered consciousness and connection to the deep personal unconscious and the Collective Unconscious. For some this is extended to include the driver-trainer-partner. This is facilitated when the partners are male and female regardless of which plays which role. For some, exchanging roles enriches the entire experience.

Pony Play

Many, if not most, Human Pony role players, participate in multiple Pony Play events and competitions around the country that further enriches the experience. As noted earlier in the quote from Lee Harrington, "Anytime we become someone or something else, we can learn something about ourselves or the nature of the universe from a new perspective." It's the same age-old wisdom about "walking in someone else's shoes" to better understand the world beyond ourselves.

Role Play as "Intuitive" Shamanism

Why become a Pony, or a Pony Trainer? Why play Dominant and Submissive? Why get all tied up and suspended in Japanese style rope bondage? Why wear a bondage collar and cuffs in public, or secretly wear a chastity belt with stimulating didoes on a romantic date? Why play games at all?

Simply because, for the people involved, it is fun and pleasurable. They release stress and increase creative energy, often leading to inspiration and developing the intuitive mind. In Role Playing Games, no one is making a lifestyle commitment or an advocacy statement. At the same time we ask: *Why are these choices rising now?*

Why? We can only guess, but surveys show that role playing B/d is a rapidly increasing pleasure practice among couples' aged from twenty to forty—ranging from 10 percent in America to nearly 30 percent in some European countries. At the same time, we've seen rapid and progressive changes in women's culture while our news is filled with reports of domestic violence, disintegrating marriages, and expressions of yearning for a depth of relationship seeming to have been lacking during the past age of sexual repression, marriage defined by reproduction and property, suppression of the individual by mass thinking and massive organizations in contradiction to the Constitutional right of every <u>individual</u> to Life, Liberty, and *The Pursuit of Happiness*.

There's something going on that has its origins in the unconscious level, and it relates to 1) the awareness of and desire for alternative states of consciousness beyond "the norm"—whether as ecstatic experience or attainment of specific vibratory levels; 2) the use of magickal imagination in active journeying or creative fantasy in "sub-space;" 3) to realize the new potentials in intimate partnering and to explore individual feeling and styles or to confirm a cohabitive relationship; or 4) an instinctive desire to express the empowering of the New Feminine self-consciousness. Role playing is not "one-sided," but a constant interplay and "power exchange" that brings new maturity to the repressed *Anima* and *Animus* of both partners.

The Power of the Self-Image

All is not how it looks from the outside. In Pony Play an outsider may see a woman in a peculiar form of bondage that would be very reprehensible to a "women's libber," but let's give the apparent submissive a true "magick mirror" in which she sees her fantasized self transformed into a horse of immense strength, goddess beauty, and a wonderful playful nature. The "harness" she wears is not bondage but the means of conveying her strength into service for a cause.

Instead of being a "sub" her magickal image has given her power and the means to transform that power for both pleasure and purpose. Fantasy turns into mythical transformation. The use of a Magickal Mirror enables the active imagination to move from material objectivity to spiritual subjectivity in which astral substance and energy provide a different reality. Again, all is not as it appears, and while someone once remarked that "appearance is everything," we've learned that subjective appearance has a dynamism in the intimate relationship.

The Magick Mirror is not an ordinary mirror with a silvered back reflecting material reality but a special glass with a painted black back that properly used provides a kind of entry to astral vision. For an *active* use, a visualized image—as in the case of a projected fantasy –can be experienced as an altered reality. For a *passive* use, a vision of a summoned spiritual entity appears and communication can be established. Instructions for making and using a mirror will be found in the appendix.

In either usage, it is the controlled use of the imagination that bridges between physical and astral dimensions, and between the personal unconscious and the universal, and between the subconscious and conscious minds. The role of fantasy and the active imagination in personal myth construction was the foundation for the new psychology of Dr. Carl Jung in which both patient and "student" (and we are all students) become self-empowered "individuals" capable of responsible life decisions.

Spirit Moves in Mysterious Ways

"Whither thou goes, there go I" is a familiar quotation from the Hebrew Bible, Book of Ruth. That same expression tells us that where we go in imagination, is where we are. Spirit follows attention, and we mentally open a door into the astral. In our materialist culture, the result is perceived mostly as fantasy. However, for today's awakened and **empowered woman**, it can become her power of Creative Fantasy through which she becomes how she sees herself.

Going beyond matters of costume and fashion, such self-imagery can be turned into the Power of Assumption or Magical Invocation. When a role-playing woman enters "sub-space" and strongly identifies herself as a pony or horse, she can become a vehicle for the Spirit of the Power Animal, or even for the Horse Goddess, Epona.

The Shamanic team learned a lot as one temporarily became "possessed" by such a Spirit. What once was, can be again today for the Pony Playing couple.

Male & Female in Dynamic Power Exchanges

It is this, the *new* partnership between Man and Woman in a confirmed cohabitive relationship that is the objective in all these new elements in sexual play. We are developing a near "mythical" understanding of the self-empowerment involved in these exchanges of personal power in a dynamic relationship built on polarity, magical power, and goal-directed sex magick. *It is a refinement of the archetypal meaning of Anima and Animus at the core of every human personality.*

Dr. Jonn Mumford has remarked about the practice of Tantra within modern Western Society in an interview with Chris Burgess:

> "Tantra is relevant today because it represents a holistic view of the universe as a cosmic dance personified through male (Shiva) and female (Shakti) principles.
>
> This Tantric approach currently blends nicely with some feminist paradigms and the revival of paganism in the West. Mother, divine Shakti or Kali reigns supreme as a cosmic power, incarnate, enshrined and evident in women. Consequently each woman is a living altar for the worship of divine Mother."

There is a *Great Mystery* here for which we have so little understanding that many tend to suppress what are truly natural desires out of fear, and to keep them *secret* when it may be the communal experience with like-minded couples that completes the refinement process and liberates men and women from a "bondage" of religious, social, and even intellectual repression.

There are many ways to the center: *you can learn from a teacher or from a book, and you can discover for your own self.* And what play may be private and personal can become a transformative learning experience when shared and discussed with others of similar interest and experience. No matter whether mystical and spiritual or sexual and fun, you can get more out of it by sharing and discussing. By making the *subjective objective* we see more and experience more. Likewise, we can take the *objective* and turn it into a *subjective* experience for alternative and deeper understanding.

Cosmic Principles in Every Woman & Every Man

What is totally missing from most discussions of spirituality is the *human* dimension. When we speak of *As Above, so Below,* the concept is usually interpreted in terms of the "Big Cosmos" of all that is and the "Little Cosmos" that is primarily the subtle nature of the individual person.

With the *human* dimension, we see the Cosmic principles repeated in humanity as a whole and in the individual—so when we refer to Shiva and Shakti, the Tantric Male and the Tantric Female, we are speaking of dual cosmic principles existent throughout all humanity and all manifestation, and in the individual psyche. The male principle manifests as Consciousness and the female principle as Energy/Matter, and these principles are universal in all there is. In humanity and in the human person both principles co-exist not only as *Anima* and *Animus* but in every bit of matter and flow of energy, and in every aspect of consciousness within body and psyche.

Put in another way: ***Every Man is a god, but with a goddess companion; every Woman is a goddess, with a god companion. And it is the ultimate goal of every human to become Deity, only possible as each becomes fully mature and empowered.***

In our partnerships, we develop the inner divinity in every way, whether in sexual play or in what we say, and all we do day after day. The constant interplay of consciousness and energy is physical and spiritual, emotional and mental, and—above all—magical, mystical, and alchemically transformative. When we live in ***Awareness,*** we are awake and alive in every sense.

Shamanism: the Direct Experience of Spirit

We've established that shamanism is the direct experience of "Spirit" and of communication with spiritual consciousness. We've also established that shamanism is not a religion, does not conform to ancient theologies or repressive dogmas, even as, in contrast, individual shamans inherit and add to a living and growing repertoire of traditional knowledge of spiritual technologies, vast catalogs of healing and consciousness altering herbs and plants and understanding of their subtle energies beyond their "active ingredients," and a substantial lore about spiritual consciousness and spiritual entities.

More importantly, ***shamans learn to <u>listen</u> to Spirit, to their inner voice, to their subconscious mind as it communicates personal needs and suggests resolution of those needs through dreams and fantasy, and so can we when acting upon those inner prompting within a consensual cohabitive relationship bring strength and creativity to the intimate partnership.***

No, we are not defining shamanism by Sex Magick, Role-Playing, hanging in Japanese rope bondage or swinging in an old European Witches Cradle, or any other specific spiritual technology or method for ecstatic experience, nor recommending them to anyone. Nor are we proclaiming that Shamanism requires an external male/female partnership. Rather we are recognizing the resurgence of the individual in spiritual search and self-expression, and in psychic development, and in spiritual empowerment and communication.

Shamanism should not be studied as a primitive religion, or thought of as mere indigenous practices involving mushroom-induced ecstasy. At the same time we can realize the living shaman's contribution to new understanding of "the varieties of consciousness experience" and value the shaman's contribution to a different kind of knowledge about herbs, plants and animals. The greater need is to recognize shamanism as the embodiment of the individual, and see this as the driving power in this New Age of Person-based Information-sharing, Knowledge-acquisition, and Wisdom-acquirement.

Love is the Creative Facilitator

To paraphrase Aleister Crowley, Love is not just the Law but is itself the Creative Facilitator for this, the New Age of Transformation and Growth through Personal Knowledge and Personal Experience. It was also Crowley who said, *Every Man and every Woman is a Star.*

Not meaning to take anything away from Crowley, for he was a great pioneer in opening these ideas and initiating the New Age (which he referred to as the Age of Horus) but we need know-how to take the Next Step and actually turn these ideals into reality in the ordinary world—not just inside secret initiatory orders.

As we mentioned earlier in connection with *Anima* and *Animus* archetypes: *Every Man is a god, but with a goddess companion; every Woman is a goddess, with a god companion. And it is the ultimate goal of every human to become Deity, only possible as each becomes fully mature and empowered.*

Much of preliminary "work" for this and other aspects of universal Human and Personal evolution is happening at unconscious levels that we see reflected in social, psychological, and political dimensions of current affairs, but there are advantages to accelerating these happenings through conscious awareness and intentional programming. We might ask: "How can a man experience his Anima "Goddess Companion?" and "How can a woman experience her Animus "God Companion?"

One such program was developed in our *Astral Projection for Psychic Empowerment* book, and we offer it here even though it is slightly out of context.

Sexual Interchange Program—Procedure

Introduction. Sexual Interchange requires approximately one hour in a comfortable private setting with no distractions. A comfortably lying-down position while preferably nude is recommended. Here is the program:

Stage 1. Preliminary Considerations. At this stage, the interchange partners, having already been introduced to the procedure, engage in open discussion, in which they share their deeper feelings and concerns. The complete consent of both partners to practice the procedure in private is critical to its success.

Stage 2. OBEs Induction. Having mutually consented to practice sexual interchange, the partners concurrently induce the out-of-body state as they lie comfortably together in close proximity, but without physical contact. Induce the out-of-body state by following steps 1 through 5 of Astral Levitation as previously discussed in this book and presented again here for convenience. Since partners often find that they achieve the out-of-body state at different rates, sufficient time must be allowed to ensure that both partners are in the out-of-body state. Experienced partners will sense the mutual emergence of the out-of-body state.

Step A. While resting in a comfortable, reclining position, mentally scan your total body from your head downward, pausing at areas of tension and letting them relax. Slow your breathing, taking a little longer to exhale, until you develop a relaxed, effortless breathing pattern.

Step B. Focus your full attention on your physical body and imagine it becoming lighter and lighter, until finally, it seems to become weightless.

Step C. As the sense of weightlessness continues, imagine your physical body, as light as a feather, beginning to rise slowly. Next, envision your physical body momentarily suspended in space, then slowly returning to its original position, but leaving your consciousness behind in astral form, still suspended over your physical body.

Step D. From overhead, view your physical body, now resting comfortably below. Notice your sense of weightlessness and separation from your physical body.

Step E. Invoke the positive energies of higher astral planes by visualizing your projected astral body, as well as your physical body below, surrounded by white radiance, then affirming:

> *My total being is now enveloped in the powerful radiance of cosmic energy. As I travel beyond my body, I will be empowered and protected, mentally, physically, and spiritually, by the positive energies of higher astral planes. I will return to my physical body at any time by simple intent alone.*

Stage 3. Astral Embrace. Once a mutual out-of-body state has been achieved, the partners engage in an astral embrace while suspended over their physical bodies which remain comfortably at rest below them.

Stage 4. Gender Exchange. At this critical point in the procedure, each partner first envisions and then astrally engages the biological body of the other partner. In the male-female dyad, the astral male assumes a female biology while the astral female assumes a male biology, resulting in a gender reversal state which we could call *out-of-one's-own-body-but-in-the-body-of-the-other.* Because they are outside their own bodies, the partners, while temporarily possessing the physical body of the other partner, remain in the astral projected state. Periodically throughout the procedure, imagery of the possessed body may be required to maintain the gender reversal state.

Stage 5. Interchange Arousal. While in the projected, gender reversal state, with each partner in possession of the other's body, the partners engage in sexual foreplay, typically through erotic expressions involving physical touch as well as mental and verbal communication. As sexual arousal emerges and throughout the ensuing sexual interchange, the gender reversal state is carefully maintained.

Stage 6. Sexual Interchange. With the female partner in astral possession of the male body, and the male partner in astral possession of the female body, sexual interchange as a *combined form of astral and physical sexual intercourse* is initiated. The sexual interchange experience typically culminates in mutual orgasm.

Stage 7. Interchange Resolution. Following sexual intercourse and while retaining the *out-of-one's-own-body-but-in-the-body-of-the-other* state, a period of reflection and relaxation is recommended, during which the partners share feelings and thoughts concerning the experience.

Stage 8. Astral Embrace and Return. At this stage, the partners simultaneously engage in a brief period of quiet relaxation, and then exit each other's body by intentionally shifting astral awareness above the two physical bodies which remain at rest and in close proximity. While in that levitated out-of-body state, the partners embrace, after which they re-engage their own physical bodies. Each partner then focuses attention on the physical body and its various sensations, such as breathing, tingling, and so forth.

Stage 9. Post-Interchange Embrace and Resolution. The partners conclude the sexual interchange experience by physically embracing and again sharing their innermost thoughts and feelings while giving particular attention to the empowering relevance of the experience.

Summary of Purpose & User Benefits: The out-of-body experience of temporary gender exchange between sexual partners is useful in understanding and overcoming various dysfunctions and inhibitions. Additional benefits include is a better appreciation of our inner self that has opposite gender psychological elements. In some cases, the OBE gender exchange has resulted in desired pregnancy.

This and additional procedures may be found in complete detail in *Astral Projection for Psychic Empowerment—The Out-of-Body Experience, Astral Powers, and their Practical Application,* 2012, Llewellyn, by Joe H. Slate, Ph.D. & Carl Llewellyn Weschcke.

In conclusion, we want to point out that once we become aware of such potentials for personal growth and development, we will find that we are able to initiate many such happenings without specific programming. At the same time, we may encounter such programs as seem specific to our needs and desires.

Simple meditations like we give at the end of each chapter are invitations to such discoveries.

MEDITATION

"How is it that Shamanism can be both Ancient and Modern techniques for human interaction with Spirit?"

Sources and Recommended Reading:

Charlotte, K.: *Wicked Voodoo Sex,* 2008, Llewellyn

Cook, Angelique S., and Hawk, G.A.: *Shamanism and the Esoteric Tradition,* 1992, Llewellyn

Crowley, R.: *The Vodou Quantum Leap—Alternate Realities, Power and Mysticism,* 2000, Llewellyn

David-Neel, A.: *Magic and Mystery in Tibet,* 1971, Dover

Digitalis, R.: *Shadow Magick Compendium—Exploring Darker Aspects of Magickal Spirituality,* 2008, Llewellyn

Easton, D. & Hardy, J.: *Radical Ecstasy SM Journeys to Transcendence,* 2004, Greenery

Eliade: Shamanism—Archaic Techniques of Ecstasy—"shamanism = technique of ecstasy," 1964, Princeton University Press

Flowers, S. and Flowers, C.: *Carnal Alchemy—Sado-Magical Techniques for Pleasure, Pain, and Self-Transformation,* 2013, Inner Traditions

Gallegos, A.: *The personal totem pole: animal imagery, the chakras and psychotherapy,* 1987, Moon Bear Press

Harner, M.: *The Way of the Shaman—A Guide to Power and Healing,* 1992, Bantam

Harner, M.–1985 in *Current Anthropology.*

Harrington, L.: *Sacred Kink—The Eightfold Path of BDSM and Beyond,* 2009, Mystic

Jayne, J.: *The Origin of Consciousness in the Breakdown of the Bicameral Mind,* 1976, Houghton Mifflin/Manner Books

Kaldera, R.: *Dark Moon Rksing—Pagan BDSM and the Ordeal Path,* 2006, Asphodel

Kaldera, R. & Krasskova, G.: *Neolithic Shamanism—Spirit Work in the Norse Tradition,* 2012, Destiny

Konstantinos: *Werewolves—The Occult Truth,* 2010, Llewellyn

Lupa: *New Paths to Animal Totems—Three Alternative Approaches to Creating Your Own Totemism,* 2012, Llewellyn

Michaels, M. & Johnson, P.: *Great Sex Made Simple—Tantric Tips to Deepen Intimacy & Heighten Pleasure,* 2012, Llewellyn

Michaels, M. & Johnson, P.: *The Essence of Tantric Sexuality,* 2006, Llewellyn

Michaels, M. & Johnson, P.: *Tantra for Erotic Empowerment—the Key to enriching your sexual life,* 2008, Llewellyn

Mumford, Dr. Jonn: *A Chakras & Kundalini Workbook—Psycho-Spiritual Techniques for Health, Rejuvenation, Psychic Powers & Spiritual Realization,* 1995, Llewellyn

Mumford, Dr. Jonn: *Ecstasy through Tantra,* 1995, Llewellyn

Mumford, Dr. Jonn: From an interview with Dr Jonn Mumford *(Swami Anandakapila Saraswati)* by Chris Burgess, 1998, manager of Adyar Esoteric Bookshop, Sydney, NSW, Australia

Nicholson, S (Ed.): *Shamanism,* 1987, Quest

Parma, G.: *By Land, Sky & Sea—Three Realms of Shamanic Witchcraft,* 2010, Llewellyn

Rosales, O.: *Elemental Shamanism One Man's Journey into the Heart of Humanity, Spirituality & Ecology,* 2009, Llewellyn

Sargent, D.: *Global Ritualism—Myth & Magic Around the World,* 1994, Llewellyn

Sheikh, A. (Ed.). *Imagery: Current theory, research, and application, 1982,* New York: Wiley

Sjoo, M. & Moore, B.: *The Great Cosmic Mother—Rediscovering the Religion of the Earth,* 1987, 1991, Harper One

Slate, J. & Weschcke, C.L.: *Astral Projection for Psychic Empowerment,* 2012, Llewellyn

Slate, J. & Weschcke, C.L.: *Clairvoyance for Psychic Empowerment,* 2012, Llewellyn

Slate, J. & Weschcke, C.L.: *Llewellyn Complete Book of Psychic Empowerment,* 2011, Llewellyn

subMissAnn: *Pony Play with subMissAnn,* 2013, subMissAnn Productions

Tedlock, B.: *The Woman in the Shaman's Body—Reclaiming the Feminine in Religion and Medicine,* 2005, Bantam

Tyson, D.: *Familiar Spirits—A Practical Guide for Witches & Magicians; A Unique System of Power Glyphs,* 2004, Llewellyn

Tyson, D.: *Scrying for Beginners—Supersensory Powers of Your Subconscious,* 1997, Llewellyn

Varrin, C.: *Erotic Surrender—The Sensual Joys of Female Submission,* 2001, Citadel

Walsh, R: *The World of Shamanism—New Views of an Ancient Tradition,* 2007, Llewellyn

Wilcox, R.: *The Human Pony—A Guide for Owners, Trainers and Admirers,* 2008, Greenery Press

Williams, M.: *Follow the Shaman's Call—An Ancient Path of Modern Lives,* 2010, Llewellyn

Wolfe, A.: *In the Shadow of the Shaman—Connecting with Self, Nature & Spirit,* 1998, Llewellyn

RELIGION AND SPIRIT

Where Spirit is No Longer Found!

We're devoting three major chapters to the discussion of religion and Spirit simply because religion is where most people think they can find "Spirit," and where—unfortunately—it's not any longer to be found. No doubt, it once was, but as with human aging, what we have in youth is gone in our old age. As institutions, these religions devote their energies to institutional affairs and not to matters of Spirit.

Religion is mistakenly confused with spirituality. Rather than some form of Spiritual *Communication* with a loving and accessible power, the religions that dominate half the world's populations today instead <u>demand</u> *worship* of a far off deity through institutional intermediaries. While some effort is made to provide some *personal intermediaries*—as with Jesus in Christianity and Mother Mary and the Saints in Catholicism—any unbiased analysis will show that both Deity, and SPIRIT, remain distant and institutional, used as much as a product "brand" as a true focal point for worship and less, or not at all, for *Communicating with Spirit.*

Human Bondage through male-dominant monotheistic "religion"

The word "religion"* derives from *ligare* meaning "to bind together" as the Roman Empire used early Christianity (hence, the *Roman* Catholic Church) to assert political (and military) control over the various populations of Europe and the Mediterranean. Belief Systems defined this way are almost all *political, monotheistic,* and <u>male-dominated</u>. The emphasis is on humans serving the distant *One God* (always represented in masculine human form) through institutional facilities with *enforcement* through His male-dominant hierarchical organization of Church, sometimes partnering with State, sometimes *used* by the State, and sometimes merged together with state in a Theocracy.

> * "Religion" refers to "an organized collection of beliefs, cultural systems, and world views that relate humanity to an order of existence. Many religions have narratives, symbols, and sacred histories that are intended to explain the meaning of life and/or

to explain the origin of life or the Universe. From their beliefs about the cosmos and human nature, people derive morality, ethics, religious laws or a preferred lifestyle. According to some estimates, there are roughly 4,200 religions in the world.

Many religions may have organized behaviors, clergy, a definition of what constitutes adherence or membership, holy places, and scriptures. The practice of a religion may also include rituals, sermons, commemoration or veneration of a deity, gods or goddesses, sacrifices, festivals, feasts, trance, initiations, funerary services, matrimonial services, meditation, prayer, music, art, dance, public service or other aspects of human culture. Religions may also contain mythology.

The word religion is sometimes used interchangeably with faith, belief system or sometimes set of duties; however, in the words of Émile Durkheim, religion differs from private belief in that it is "something eminently social." A global 2012 poll reports that 59% of the world's population is religious, and 36% are not religious, including 13% who are atheists, with a 9 percent decrease in religious belief from 2005. On average, women are more religious than men. Some people follow multiple religions or multiple religious principles at the same time, regardless of whether or not the religious principles they follow traditionally allow for syncretism. Quoted from http://en.wikipedia.org/wiki/Religion

Judaism, Christianity, and Islam are the prime monotheistic examples, along with various splinter groups and cults structured in the same manner. They all claim that only (One) God can solve problems on HIS pre-established terms, and that "faith" (along with money) is the means to engage God's power.

However, there are many "Belief Systems" commonly referred to as "religions" that are not theistic at all, and would be better identified as philosophies. Followers of Buddhism and Taoism are mainly classified as agnostic, atheistic, or nontheistic. Contrary to common belief, the Buddha is not a "god" but better understood as a *teacher,* or *revealer.* Even some people still classified as Christian or Jewish themselves reject the concept of religion while still accepting aspects of the teaching as moral guidance. A major distinction is a rejection of institutional adherence, rejection of myth as factual history, and bondage to their antique and inflexible theologies.

In particular, large numbers of Catholics reject the Church's definition of "superstition" as sinful, and particularly so as belief in reincarnation, psychic phenomena and practices of divination, spiritualism, the possibility of life on other planets, and other "New Age" practices are also included as superstitious and sinful. Likewise many reject the Church's claim that Catholic business owners, pharmacists, hospital administrators, and others can lawfully refuse to sell or dispense contraception to non-Catholics. A claim that puts Church law above secular law and hence beyond Constitutional law.

Theocratic and Monopolistic

But there are other religions that don't fit this concept of human bondage to an abstract deity through his privileged dominions. Let's start at the Beginning!

This book is about Spiritual Communication and Self (including Psychic) Empowerment. In earlier chapters we discussed some of the challenges and problems involved, but perhaps none is more pertinent when the subject is religion than that admonition given in the Foreword: *Don't let the Past be a limitation on your fresh thinking and independent investigation. We encourage you to "participate" in study and research, to use the programs and procedures we provide for your own direct experience, and to record and analyze your results.* Don't let the words, "religion" or "faith, turn off your intellect. In this age, *Mind* is your most powerful aid to understanding and growth.

You don't learn by memorizing the *Koran* or the *Bible* word for word, or the answers to the lessons in a Catholic *Catechism*; you don't learn by letting a Preacher yell at you, or a Rabbi tell you that the Torah is truth because it's old.

Age doesn't guarantee "Truth"

Most of the World's 4,200 religions are old, but age alone doesn't guarantee "truth" any more than old wine is good because it's old. Think instead of the label on your food product that says when it is stale-dated. Today many people see these dominant religions as stale-dated and non-progressive. Modern people want a religion, or belief system, that will provide relevant tools for our Spiritual growth, to help us understand day-to-day events from a higher perspective, to aid our perception for personal actions and reactions in ways beneficial to individual, family, and society including generally benevolent family and community services.

Without such pertinence, they prefer to remain **"Spiritual, but not religious."**

Religion claims to relate Human to Spirit. Some religions define that spirit in terms of a distant and *external* Deity; others define that spirit in terms of an intimate Spirit or Soul *within*; still others define Spirituality as a *Process of Becoming;* and others see Spirit in all things and continually evolving and transforming.

Religions may claim to give some *transcendent* meaning to life, *inclusive* of ordinary human experiences of love and life, birth and death, work and family, of giving and receiving care, and offering devotion.

But *"transcendence"* should not demand sacrifice, denial of joy, require chastity or repression, nor does it call for the blood sacrifice of "unbelievers."

Why should we respect any religion that worships Death in preference to Life? How can we accept any religion's promise of eternal life in exchange for taking life from others? How can any religion justify mass starvation by denying access to contraception? Why should we honor any religion that exploits cheap but willing "soldiers for God" with the promise of Martyrdom? How can anyone respect a religion that deploys children with suicide belts in guerilla warfare?

The Horned shaman is a familiar image of the shaman as "shape shifter.
It is part of a cave painting in Ariege, France, dating to 10,000 BCE.

Shamanism and Religion

The shamanism we previously discussed is not religion, although it is commonly called a "primitive and indigenous religion" classified by ethnic association and geographic location. Shamanism is a collection of verifiable spiritual technologies, practices leading to transformation and transcendence, a heritage of spiritual knowledge accumulated from shamanic journeying over many thousands of years, an extensive catalog of subtly-perceived botanical knowledge, multi-body healing wisdom, life-based relationship counseling, and ecstatic states of consciousness.

While not all "native healers" are shamen, approximately ninety percent of all medical treatments in the world are performed by such healers, many of whom practice their diagnosis and treatment while in an induced trance state. (Rheingold, H.: *They Have a Word for it,* 1988, Sarabande)

Shamans are not bound together in any institution, nor to an authoritative leader or subject to a "board of experts." They are individuals working alone or with partner, assistant, or apprentice. They may be part of a many generation family tradition, or have recently responded to an inner calling to become a shaman. Some are simply self-trained, others are trained and taken on inner journeys of "initiation." As a living tradition and practice, shamanism is both ancient and perpetually new.

Shamans were the first to talk with spirits. They discovered how to alter and "raise" consciousness to enter the Spirit World, obtain specific knowledge, and return with it to the physical world. That Spirit World is the "Astral" World.

The Astral ("Spirit") World is Real

The Astral World is real, but it is also illusory and its "visions" can be distorted by human emotions of fear, hope, fantasy, desire, and expectations based on myth, promises, and deceit. The astral *seeker* may expect to see a divine being, and then does so—but it may be a *Thought Form* created in his imagination, or that of others. *Yet, that same illusionary entity can still give a valid answer to the seeker's question.*

Know-How brings power and access

By *imaging* that thought into form, the seeker creates an astral or spiritual "search engine" that can access the Universal Consciousness (also called the Akashic Records, the Collective Unconscious, or the Mind of God). Unless the seeker clutters his thought form with fantastical storybook preconceptions of who or what this entity should be, his search engine can perform the job decently well.

Our seeker could as easily create a thought form of a vast physical library or a huge file room, or a giant computer in the sky, or a god or goddess of wisdom. Or a Spirit Helper or Guide, or attract one already existing. Human consciousness, as Mind and Feeling, connects us to that universal consciousness, and as humans we uniquely have the ability to identify needs, to frame and ask questions, to learn from the answers, to ask further questions and go beyond past limitations for ever new knowledge.

Never doubt the capacity of the Human Mind! The whole purpose of spiritual practice and study is to ***become more than we are*** and ***all we can be***—which is potentially ***all there is***. And since consciousness is everywhere and in everything and every being, the best thing we can do is to understand and train our own consciousness to go everywhere and enter into anything, to communicate with any being as we perceive need and value.

Shamanism has taught us of that potential. We don't need to adopt the methods of individual shamans or their traditions as those often carry cultural limitations of time and place. By understanding them we can adapt and improve our own spiritual technologies to suit our own time and place, and our individual needs and capabilities. At the same time, the better our mind is trained, the more disciplined we are emotionally, the better and more broadly we are educated (while remaining *open-minded*), the greater will be our ability to gain knowledge and know-how, to innovate to meet new challenges and opportunities, and to transform experience into wisdom. That wisdom attained by many seekers over many millennia, has been collected, developed, and structured into Esotericism.

Learn from history, learn from others, but realize the "Power" is in you and it's your responsibility to use it *beneficially* and *ethically.* There is a cosmic law that basically says that however you apply the Power it will reflect back to you multiplied threefold—cause harm, and sooner or later you will be harmed; bring genuine benefit to others and you will also benefit. This is not a religious "law," but a principle of Nature and of the Structure of the Cosmos.

How Religions Evolve

We previously described how an astral thought form becomes a vehicle of communication that with appropriate changes in consciousness enables personal communication with a chosen spiritual entity or thought form. It is these two functions that characterize spiritual communication: 1) Raising of consciousness to match the level of the target astral form; and 2) intentional inter-communication. It takes two to have a conversation, and it takes two to have genuine spiritual communication. It is not a matter of listening and obeying.

The mythic origin of many religions is that someone once talked with a spiritual entity appearing as a god or goddess, or "the God." The next step was developing the story of that encounter into a comprehensive myth. For most of the four thousand world polytheistic religions, the myths remain myths as part of the descriptive "qualities" distinguishing each deific form from another. In fewer cases, the myth becomes a sophisticated and comprehensive metaphysical description of the Cosmos, the physical universe, of life, and of the deity and its messenger. To varying degrees, these myths and the spiritual technologies involved in their creation, have been adapted by teachers to found institutions formalizing them into a theology and curriculum of self-improvement and spiritual development.

Symbolic concept of The First Day of Creation.

In the case of a very few myths—mostly those based on "One God"—that God was a *jealous* God brooking no competition and in whose name wars have been fought and mass killings instituted in the process of carrying out "God's work" to bring the whole world under "HIS" dominion as administered by HIS priests and clerics. Because the history of these wars and their horrors have been factually recorded, *the original myths have been treated as historic* fact even when the various elements are readily seen as derived from yet older myths, and are contradicted by verifiable facts and common sense.

These old religions are organized belief systems with a "theology" and "laws of behavior" frozen in time. Some religions are more monopolistic than others and seek to bring all humans into their fold and then to impose their theology and religious laws on everyone by dominating education, politics, government, economy, and military while denigrating all independent thought and any behavior contrary to their ancient code. These religions forbid all spiritual communication other than prescribed rote prayer and public ritual. All monopolies seek to eliminate competition, and hence lead toward destructive conflict. These religions have generally taken the form of *theocracies* with no place for democracy nor modernization of its laws and precepts.

All Religions are "Man-made," but Spirituality is Real

We can only imagine how men and women hundreds of thousands if not millions of years ago (not the mythical six thousand proclaimed in the Bible) first experienced Spirituality. No Incarnate God led them out of the wilderness and instructed them how to plant and cultivate fruits and vegetables. No Star Person from a galaxy far, far away taught the arts of cooking and animal husbandry. No Prophet, no Messenger, no Deity, no Messiah taught them the realities of human health and reproduction, or about Nature and the universe. No Angel picked out a few "chosen" people for special favors.

Instead, we can only assume that the long evolutionary "program" initiated by the Creator/Source many billions of years ago at the Beginning led to a dramatic point in human development when personal consciousness and self-awareness emerged and early men and women felt that they were part of something greater than themselves.

The Wonder of Life and the Evolution of Mind

They saw LIFE all around them, and wondered at the sky above and felt the Earth beneath their feet. They were nourished by the fruits and vegetables growing in Nature's Garden they shared with animals and birds. They learned from their observation of growth, death and rebirth; they experienced the cycles of day and night and observed the seasons and their interaction with the life of plants and animals; they invented tools to extend their reach and strength, and adapt Nature's bounty to their benefit.

They learned by observation that some plants were harmful and some animals were predators and these became natural enemies; some plants were easily cultivated to become reliable food sources and some animals became companions and members of the family. Some animals that were neither enemy nor companion became resources for food beyond that of plants and trees, and enabling survival during times of drought and changes in habitat.

Ceres: the Roman goddess of agriculture.

Woman and Earth, as the Source of Life

They felt the power and pleasure of sexuality and rejoiced in the reproduction of their bodies and sorrowed at the death of their loved ones. They saw women give birth to new life just as did the Earth, and felt awe towards Woman and the Earth as the <u>Source</u> of New Life. But *where did Life itself come from?* Here was some "essence" beyond the body of Woman and Earth. This essence, or Spirit, lived *within* each person and manifested *outwardly* throughout the universe.

We can say that Spirituality begins with the recognition of Spirit within all things, and of the process of its manifestation in all things. From this recognition came the "worship" of the <u>visible</u> Feminine as mother of human and animal life and of the Earth as the Great Mother of all Nature. Spirituality identified with the inner feeling of the Feminine as the Source of All, and sexuality was the direct experience of the <u>invisible</u> spirit moving within woman's and man's bodies. From sexual pleasure men and women discovered love, and with understanding of their shared involvement in reproduction arose the joy of family and the realization of the fundamental partnership of man and woman in committed relationship. *It was this experience of intimate partnership that started the long road we now call "Civilization" and experience in Family, Community, and Culture.*

"Worship" as Adoration, and the binding together in Community

"Worship" at this point was simply an *adoration* of this invisible spirit moving within that somehow produced Life, was Life, and gave Life to the Family of man, woman and child, and that created a sense of Community beyond the family. This led to the social aspect of the neighborhood community that remained a primary function of religion into modern times: the local "meeting place."

As populations grew, and moved, it was that sense of community that was translated into the political function of the Church and its relationship to the State—with one or the other in the Driver's Seat. And it was and is this partnership that has been instrumental in inspiring and facilitating War and Terrorism as larger communities came into conflict, and it was and is the basis for the persecution, torture, and killing of minorities within and across communities.

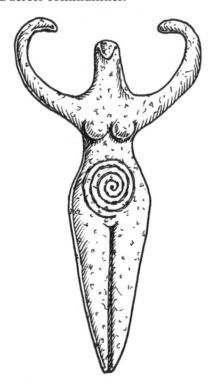

The Mother Goddess

Separation of Church and State

It is the reason Church and State must remain separate as was first established in this New World and New Age in the Founding of America with Freedom both <u>from</u> and <u>of</u> religion, of the rights to assembly and development of democratic laws, and the rights of defense against foreign kings and gods.

To represent the non-physical spiritual connection between Human and Cosmos, and the "Source," which is probably knowable only in symbol and abstraction, calls for new religions that are mostly, but not exclusively, multi-*theistic** and non-political. The emphasis is on helping humans to live better lives. Gnosticism, Chinese Taoism, pre-Aryan Indian Tantra, Druidism and modern Paganism are the prime examples. Some, like Deism, are purely intellectual and believe human rationality can solve all problems.

> * The use of the term, "<u>multi</u>-theistic" here is different from poly-theistic—meaning many deities. In multi-theism, "gods" are not necessarily perceived as deities but more often as natural forces, spontaneous thought forms reflecting human feelings about a place or activity, a composite of the spiritual essence of a herd of animals or of the species itself, a carefully constructed thought form (almost always in human form) that functions as a "formula" for evoking or invoking the ideal action represented in that god or goddess including—usually—one overall male and one female deity whose mythic union created all the manifest world, and sometimes a single representation either in bi-sexual form or as a non-human symbol to represent all creation above and beyond manifestation. Generally speaking, it is more feminine than masculine, and functions to serve Life, including humans, with a primary ethic of "Harm none."

But Worship as blind, compulsive, unquestioning, groveling, adoration is not the only kind of worship. In contrast, there is "worship" that really is *Magickal Invocation to bring that* deity <u>within</u> to become more like that deity in particular characteristics—whether Love, Wisdom, Beauty, Courage, etc. In polytheistic religions, there can be a deity matching every human need. More about this in a later chapter.

The Three Kinds of Religion

We've speculated on the origin of Spirituality, and we've described Shamanism as the oldest form of Spiritual Knowledge and Spiritual Communication. And we determined that it was some shamanic communication with spirit or spiritual entities that is the source for all religions. But we have given only the "official" definition of religion that really applies only to one kind of religion: that which *binds a people together* in a community. That is a materialistic "political" definition and not a definition of the spirituality experienced by individuals nor of the true Holy Spirit that lies at the foundation of life itself and of all that exists.

It is in our speculation on the origin of spirituality in early humanity—resulting in the worship of Life manifesting in earthy plants and animals and in Woman's reproduction of human life—that we see the foundations of the first form of human community centering around the communal cultivation and harvesting of plant life, the development of plant-based crafts, and the honor and care provided to Woman and the Feminine Force of reproduction and respecting the *bliss* ("blessing") of sexual pleasure. Here we had the rise of matrilineal agricultural food and craft civilization based on a culture of Love and Nurture rising in the "Garden of Eden" Indus Valley of ancient India, inhabited—as some claim—for 470,000 years before its invasion by Aryan warriors.

Our first type of religion was that of the Earth Mother, the Great Goddess, the primacy of Woman as the Head of the family, and the Sacred Source giving and rejoicing in sexual pleasure. And, at its source, the role of Sexual Ecstasy in altering and raising consciousness.

This first kind of religion was female-dominant and based on Love, not Law. And, while not coercive, Love and Community does "bind people together" to establish that worship of the Earth Mother and the Great Goddess does meet the official definition of religion.

One key element in this and the next type civilization is in the relation of animals to humans. In the religion of the Goddess, certain animals became companions and virtual members of the family. The wolf/dog was a partner to man, the hunter who chose certain animals for food; the cat protecting the household food against mice and rats; the horse becoming an extension of man as hunter and defender of the community; the cow, the goat, the sheep, the chicken as living associates providing nourishing milk and eggs, and wool for early clothing. Upon their maturity, certain of these animals were killed to become direct sources of food—leading to the next development.

With population expansion came a change from hunter-gatherer economics and communal sharing of land and animals to that of cattle-herding economics and property ownership. Based on their need for territorial expansion of the grazing range, the Aryan invasions of India and Europe led to imposition of their patrilineal religion and caste/class system of a male priesthood at the top, supported by a male military and a mostly male merchant class dominating the original women and farmers at the bottom. In the Indus Valley, those at the bottom were the Dravidians; in Europe they were the original Pagans.

As the Aryan warrior nomads settled into the conquered lands, they asserted patrilineal property inheritance from father to son, women became property too in order to assure the "purity of the blood line," as required in the Abrahamic religion of the invaders. The priest class subtly (and politically) merged the indigenous Goddess worship into their Abrahamic religion, but supplanting goddess with god, always praising the male warrior, asserting the superiority of the herder over the farmer, and denigrating the female into submission and servitude to the male.

This second kind of religion is male dominant and based on Law instead of Love.

Where is Spirit in these two forms of religion?

In the first, the matrilineal, Spirit is incarnate in all there is and manifesting primarily in the Life-supporting Earth, and in the Feminine nourishing side of Nature and the continuing and repetitive Reproduction of Life. This Spirit is everywhere and worshipped and directly experienced as a feminine deity. Spiritual communication is enabled by meditational practices and ecstatic states of consciousness attained though seasonal and other celebration, spontaneous and sometimes ritual sex, certain herbs and psycho-physical practices, and both stylized movement and joyful dancing.

This type of religion and spirituality in practice and lifestyle, primarily derived from Eastern origins and re-discovered European Paganism, is resurfacing today in neo-Paganism, Wicca, Yoga and Martial Arts, neo-Tantra and renewed Shamanism.

In the second, the patrilineal, Spirit appears to a male shaman to deliver a series of laws and commandments requiring obedience to this One (Male) God who immediately institutes war between father and son, between man and woman, and between one tribe and the neighboring tribe in order to usurp that tribal land. This Spirit is nowhere in this world, and is worshiped as a distant and other-worldly male god who is jealous and vengeful. Spiritual communication is limited to a dedicated priesthood so protective of its status that it soon forgets its "secret and proprietary" techniques of communication and hides that fact behind closed doors and curtains, and complex ceremonies. This type of religion exists today primarily as the three male-dominate Middle-East derived Abrahamic religions of Judaism, Christianity, Islam, and a few minor sects of each.

What of Spirit and the third type of religion?

The first two types, the matrilineal and patrilineal religions, had *accidental* shamanic origins; so does the third type—but with a major difference: *the learned principles of those old matrilineal religions and shamanic techniques are applied purposefully in 21st century adaptations for Self-understanding, Self-improvement, Psychic Empowerment and the Spirituality of Self.*

In what we are describing as the third type of religion, the revivals and living shamanic techniques of spiritual communication are adapted and applied by individuals and "voluntary" groups for personal spiritual development and growth, not by proclaimed leaders and institutional priests and entrepreneurs. This third type of religion is based on *choice* rather than birth and coercion, and will be further discussed in a later chapter. The next chapter will mainly review these old time religions that were largely imposed on the populations, and whose theologies and codes are mainly frozen in time.

Nevertheless, we must always deal with the present, look for the impact of current actions on the future, and plan to do better. We can't go back in time to correct past errors; instead, we learn from the past not to repeat those errors or continue actions we can now recognize as abusive, harmful, short-sighted, and negligent in the emerging larger picture of our reality.

Spirituality and Materialism are not necessarily contradictory

Materialism and Spirituality do not have to be contradictory each to the other. As humans, we have a *potential* capacity to see broadly and incorporate multiple perspectives and goals into our active physical existence. The spiritual dimensions (astral, mental, and causal) are associated into our physical/etheric vehicle of action. Through our growing personal *Psychic Empowerment*, we are able to not only see more broadly but to act with greater understanding of the spiritual as well as broader physical factors involved.

We need to look beyond the limiting material perspective, and particularly so with that presented to us "second hand." Our history books are still much *distorted* when it comes to the subjects of Spirituality and Religion because historians, archaeologists, psychologists—and even paranormal investigators—have mostly continued to perpetuate the official written history and orthodox theology of the three dominant Western and Middle Eastern religious establishments. Anything out of conformance with the dominant *weltanschauung* of these adopted myths is still rejected out-of-hand even when it is contrary to common sense, rejected by scientific studies, contradicted by practices and teachings of other religious and esoteric groups around the world.

Religion is <u>not</u> the same as Spirituality

More people now see that official history as no more truthful and complete than the propaganda of a political party or the commercial story behind the launch of a new diet program or other "for-profit" business products. It's intended to influence people in the target market to see the product (whether religious, political, or commercial) in the most favorable light and emotional appeal so that they <u>buy</u> into it. It is further hindered by the sheer size and political power of the Catholic Church and other Christian sects, the Jewish religious establishment, and totalitarian Islam's pervasive militant presence—all three deriving from the same Middle Eastern Abrahamic origin represented in Bible-based patriarchal myth.

Political parties and the politicians reflect the interests of the power players in their communities in their own desire for power and re-election. Agents are employed by *Special Interests* (including churches, political action committees, Big Labor, Public Employee Unions, and Big Business) to protect their "turf" and secure benefits regardless of public interest and need, individual rights and values, and the effects on small business, small farms and individual entrepreneurs.

It is often argued that religious "faith" is *above* and *beyond* science and rationality, but that doesn't prevent those religious organizations from trying to impose their theology into the secular world of public and higher education, constitutional and statutory law, medical research and practice, the use of public money to support sectarian celebrations and religious construction, nor in securing for itself public financial support through tax deductions and subsidies, credits and exemptions, school vouchers to finance sectarian education, and to use their pulpits to promote their sectarian political views.

But, we are taught that "nice people" don't talk about religion or politics in polite company—so the problems are left out of the dialogue where it can count the most!

Manipulative & Controlling Religions

By its very definition, *to bind people together,* the intention is <u>control,</u> and that means to manipulate belief (emotional) to gain *authority.* Authority comes in all manner of form—from the authority of expertise to that of law enforcement. By identifying supernatural belief systems with religious laws, the Abrahamic religions took on the role of God to enforce its laws on the people.

Historically, this was not a matter of voluntary choice of either religion or submission to legal authority but one imposed by threat, fear, terror, war, and continued by birth, bondage to the land and often to the owners of land and people, assertion of strength over weakness, imposition of perpetual ignorance, and proclaiming mythic beliefs in demons and Satan.

In modern times, the goal is often the same: to use a dominant religion to control a population through emotional manipulation, and—in some areas—threats and violence. Regardless of the "reality" of the supernatural, of belief in a single mythic creator or many gods and goddesses, it remains a dictatorship of authority whether by church or state or a partnership between church and state.

Religion is, by the nature of "faith," emotional, irrational and undemocratic. Churches having become more sophisticated in their techniques of manipulation and control, and in their partnership with politicians and wealthy individuals, have adopted the methods of Big Business and have become *Big Businesses* in fact, with huge "customer bases" requiring substantial investments in land, buildings and equipment, sometimes instead of locating in residential neighborhoods within convenient walking distance they build mega churches in prime suburban locations requiring long travel time but assuring a large audience on television as well as within the glorified temple.

These new churches have more and more lost many of the old appeals of the neighborhood social center for summer picnics and pot-luck suppers, offering a place and time for parents to socialize and for their children to play and learn to socialize with other children, a place for education and discussion, a retreat for solace and comfort, a place of family generational burial, a place of welcoming arms.

But, it doesn't have to be that way! Take away that emotional bondage, and then there are many new convenient neighborhood services, social and public or non-profit, where all are welcome "regardless of faith," offering classes and open discussions on spiritual subjects without coercion and where questions are welcome and respected, where there are opportunities to observe and participate experimentally in various traditions.

Today, there are places and opportunities, and the means for their discovery, where intelligence and rationality are a welcome part of spiritual development without onerous commitments; where psychic interests can be explored and practiced, bookstores and libraries where questions can be asked and intelligent answers received. And, there is the World Wide Web where information is voluminous and blogs and other resources can answer your questions, meet your special needs, and provide communication directly with people of like interests.

And there are New Age spiritual practices that do not involve emotional bondage and control by personal or distant authority. We will discuss many of these, but first let's start at the beginning. Some of the words and concepts that follow may at first seem obtuse, but the intention is for clarity and that will happen.

Myths—Religious, Political, Historical, and "Otherwise"

In religions, the words "soul" and "spirit" are often used interchangeably, other times they are defined as one thing and then those definitions are reversed. In all our discussions, we try to avoid such confusion and follow established esoteric practice. In Tantra, Taoism and Alchemy, "Spirit" is one of the five primal *elements* from which the other four: Air, Fire, Water, and Earth, are derived and together compose the World as we know it. Spirit is therefore the *primary substance* through which the Cosmos manifests and all Life and Consciousness expressed. Consciousness is inclusive of Mind and Emotion. We use "Soul" to mean the ultimate essence of the person, incarnating via a series of separate Causal Bodies (expressing "Will") in a continuous chain of being. Spirit, as both "substance" and "units of consciousness" is shared at many levels of being, but Soul is shared only with its past, present, and future Incarnations, and its Source.

The word "inspiration" means *to be in Spirit* so that the inspired individual is communicating from his/her highest level of consciousness. But, it is important to realize that such inspiration is *personal* and while "true" for that person at that moment of time and place, it may or may not be *pertinent* or *meaningful* to others. It's *pertinence* to others depends on "the question" asked (subject, etc.), the "purpose" of the question while being *meaningful* may only apply to the one individual or a group as defined by the nature and purpose of the question. *Ask, and ye shall learn! But also ask again and again to question the answers until you know that the details and pertinence to your specific needs can be correctly applied to your situation.*

Most myths result from such moments of inspiration, and are "stories" in response to the Seeker's questions in terms of his/her Culture, level of consciousness, degree of maturity, and breadth of general knowledge (education). As *inspired*—being in Spirit —*there* is the factor of the "state of consciousness" and the source, and the extent and quality of the Seeker's ecstasy. In addition, no matter that the Seeker is in a state of Inspiration at his/her highest level of consciousness, the *Intention* of the Seeker will influence the answer, and hence of the story.

Spirit, as substance, is basic to the highest level of human consciousness we call the "Causal Body." That Casual Body is also the instrument of personal Will, and if that person's consciousness reaches high enough, it may reflect the Cosmic Will—but that is very rare and it is only pertinent to the specific circumstance.

The story may remain only a personal story, no matter how deep or broad the subject, or it may attract the interest of a big audience, or, instead, it be projected outward to a big audience. Never presume just because the source is Spiritual that the Myth is true, pure, untainted by human emotions of greed and ambition, and <u>never presume</u> the "Blessings of God" or any other claim of authority to be meaningful no matter who transmits the message.

A Creation Myth (which may later be made into a "religious" myth) is a story-like presentation answering the Big Question on the origins of the Universe and the People, the nature of Life, Love, Suffering and Death. No matter how the question is asked, the answer will reflect the culture and the language, the time and place, and the person of the seeker. It will be in highly dramatic, symbolic, and even poetic form because that is the nature of Inspiration, of Spirit. If the seeker lives in the far northern countries of Europe in 1,000 BCE, the resulting creation myth is going to reflect the Land of Fire and Ice, the Viking marauders, the strong Nordic women, particular animals, and perhaps even the drinking of lots of ale.

The environment at hand forms the myth. A different environment, a different time, a different language, a different culture will produce a different answer presented in a familiar drama of symbols, images and words. A Land of Desert, or one of Jungle, a land of islands, or one of mountains and high plateaus, a place with active volcanoes and plentiful floods, or one of steppes and plains, each generates its own images and symbols. The structure of the cultures of the indigenous people and the natural environment, the peaceful or warlike relationship with neighboring peoples, and the nature of the Seeker all will be factors in the Myth.

Who is the Seeker asking such a Big Question? By whatever other name—Prophet, Holy Man, Wise Woman, Healer, Visionary or Seeker—he or she is a shaman, and one who has entered into a particular state of ecstatic consciousness induced by any of the techniques discussed previously. Certainly the technique itself has some influence on the shaman's visionary journey.

The shaman's vision, while intended only for his/her immediate family and clients, sometimes spreads and becomes the creation myth for a local culture. When adopted by an entire culture, it is a religious myth. The ways of the culture in turn affect the interpretation of the religious vision. A culture of greed and envy will produce a vision of war and aggression. A Land of Milk and Honey will lead to a vision of peace and plenty. The presence of volcanoes is likely to produce a vision of fire and thunder, and sudden anger from a powerful god. The cultural leaders become religious prophets and interpret the vision in ways to extend their power.

What of Creation Myths for today? Perhaps we've already seen them as in the *Star Wars* and *Star Trek* movies and television series. Here you see the effect of dramatization on a global culture opening to Space, to a future dominated by technology and freed of Earthly limitations. What we see now as pure entertainment may condition tomorrow's perceptions and even shape future realities.

The Coming of the Political Myth, "History," and Path to Power

What was originally a simple shamanic vision, pertinent only to a few people at a particular time and place, has now become extended, expanded, and interpreted to form a theology and set of laws as a religion. By whatever name, the Seeker's Myth is transformed into a religion that is in turn adopted as a "Politician's" Message that becomes re-written and edited and declared to be *"historically accurate."* No questions can be considered because the story is now a sacred vision! *"History" is always written by the victor!*

No matter what the politician is called—King, Emperor, Messenger of God, Emir, or Great Leader—the "sacred vision" is used to manipulate the people into fulfilling his vision of High Destiny for himself and "his" people.

With the greater power of banded together tribal leaders, priests and soldiers consolidated behind the Great Leader, the vision is further transformed and empowered through rich oratory, public ritual and drama rich with militant song and music, and symbols of the New Order. The vision becomes the people's religion. The Leader's great victories expands the population under his control, and makes the religious vision even more powerful. A theocratic empire results. Soon one empire is in conflict with another empire, and the winner's religious vision is proof of his god's blessing.

This was the history of the Middle East and Western Europe for 4,000 years of tribal conflict consolidating into larger units and then into nations and empires. The Roman Empire and its successor in the Roman Catholic Church's domination of European monarchies continued from 27 BCE to 1804 CE when Napoleon crowned himself. Even as democracy replaced monarchy, the Christian churches still dominated Western politics and continental law from Portugal on the West through Imperial Russia into the Far East into late 19th century. In the 20th century, this same formula of a vision turned into movement was responsible for the rise of German Nazism and the Soviet Union's (Russia) Communism—one leading to World War II, and the other to the occupation of Eastern Europe and the Cold War. Both used the *accoutrements of religion* to control the people, and—in fact—Hitler's Nazism and Soviet Communism were both religions to those populations.

The same formula led to the rise of the Islamic Ottoman Empire (1299-1923 CE) occupying much of the Middle East, northern Africa, parts of eastern and southern Europe and into parts of Russia. In the 21st century, Islamic extremists are still seeking to restore and impose what they refer to as the "Emirate" on all of the Middle East, northern Africa, and wherever Muslims live and have lived. An Emirate is defined as a dynastic Muslim monarchy ruled by an emir and governed by Islamic religious law.

In essence, the story is always the same: religion is used to dominate reason; the individual is subverted to the group whether a nation, a church, an empire, or emirate. Control passes from the individual to the representatives of the group, and the group's laws are imposed on the individual. His "spirit" is repressed and is replaced by the Holy Spirit of the Church/State under its Fuhrer or Great Leader.

Let's look at the example of "Birth Control," as personal a matter as there can be, yet the Church still attempts to deny that choice. *Why? What "sin" can there be in preventing conception?* The real reason is that the Church, or the State, wants more people to control. Think like a business—the bigger the population, the more customers you can have. It's greed for power. Contraception is a Woman's right, and it's her choice to bring forth a new life for which she has the ultimate personal responsibility no matter the support of father, family, state or church. It's the ultimate "Pro Life" statement.

The Matter of Self and Control

In the last chapter we ended our discussion with a note on the vital importance to every person NOT to hand over control of any aspect of his/her life to another person or entity—*no matter who.* Unless you are responsible for your individual choices, decisions, and actions, you cannot grow, you cannot become more than you are and all you can be, and you cannot fulfill your own life plan and destiny. *Self-responsibility is the key to all self-empowerment and to Humanity's evolutionary future.*

What is today called religion is NOT "spiritual." A growing number of people respond to questions about religious affiliation with "Spiritual, but not religious." In our New Age, the word "religion" must be re-defined if we continue to use it, rather than letting it use us.

We weren't put here just to worship some far off Creator, whether mythical or real. The only belief that makes sense is that we are here to grow and thus to participate in on-going Creation as we increase in understanding and become empowered. We are not apart from, but are a self-conscious part of Nature, a self-conscious part of this World, a self-conscious part of this Creation.

At birth, a human is already growing into self-consciousness even as still and always a part of his/her family consciousness. With growth we enter into other relationships—always retaining our self-consciousness within a self-determined participation in the consciousness of the relationships. The individual can "submit" him or herself to one degree or another in the relationship, but always retaining ultimate control of his/her person in the obligation of self-responsibility.

No matter the relationship: child and parent, spouse and spouse, lover and beloved, employee and employer, teacher and student, professional and client, soldier and commander, citizen and government, even prisoner and jailer—there is always an obligation, always a situation, where the individual still must assert responsibility and hence control his/her actions. Simply put, an order to shoot is not excuse for killing a person known to be innocent.

The more we *become*, the more active we must be, and the more control over and responsibility for our actions we must assert and accept.

"Alone, and together" is an esoteric mantra. The more we *become* as individuals, the greater can we function together as partners in the ever evolving Cosmos that we also know as the ever becoming Creation. Nothing is static, everything is alive filled with energy and spirit, and expressing consciousness. The more we grow as an individual, the greater we are in Spirit. Never *submit* your Spirit to that of the group, no matter how "holy" it is claimed to be. Spirit may be shared, *but should never be submitted to domination by another.*

What New Age "Religion" is and must be!

This is what the New Age Religions—and "Spiritual but no religious"—are about. It's not in following this leader or that teacher but in learning from life through growth, study, observation, and experience.

But first, we have to tie up a few loose end.

About Myth...

"Myth" is not bad or wrong because it isn't "fact." A "good" Myth is the attempt to make sense of apparent reality at a given time and place for a specific person or persons related to a particular situation. You won't find that definition in any dictionary, but accept it for now as a working definition.

A "bad" myth is a deliberate *lie!* Currently, in America, fundamentalist Christians have made the claim that America was founded as a Christian nation—completely ignoring the facts and the statements of the founders. George Washington, called the "Father" of the country, affirmed: *"The government of the United States is not, in any sense, founded on the Christian religion."* (The Treaty of Tripoli, 1796, approved by Congress June 7, 1797, and endorsed by then President John Adams June 10, 1797). As noted by Jim Walker, "most of our influential <u>Founding Fathers</u>, although they respected the rights of other religionists, held to deism and <u>Freemasonry</u> tenets rather than to Christianity." (Wikipedia, Dec. 26, 2004) Further, "The United States <u>Constitution</u> serves as the law of the land for America and indicates the intent of our Founding Fathers. The Constitution forms a *secular* document, and nowhere does it appeal to God, Christianity, Jesus, or any supreme being. The U.S. government derives from people (not God), as it clearly states in the preamble: 'We the people of the United States, in order to form a more perfect Union....' The omission of God in the Constitution did not come out of forgetfulness, but rather out of the Founding Fathers purposeful intentions to keep government separate from religion." (Clarification of Deism will be provided later in Chapter Eleven)

Myth is usually expressed as a story involving symbols and expressed in poetic language, sometimes in dramatized actions. Such a myth is often made into a "fairy" tale for children, a folk tale to remind adults of their heritage or of a particular way to handle a problem. Sometimes a larger myth is expanded into great art—as in a Homeric Odyssey, a Wagnerian Opera, a New World Symphony, a Bolshoi Ballet, a cinematic saga like "Star Wars," a television dramatization of futuristic possibilities and problems like "Star Trek."

Sometimes a historic event or person is turned into a myth that has meaning even when the facts have been distorted or completely fictionalized. There was a real Paul Revere immortalized in 1861 by Longfellow's famous poem, but he was not alone in signaling that "the British are Coming." He was the first observer who alerted an established crew of 60 men and women, express riders with special horses, and a code of church bells, drum riffs, trumpet blasts, beacon fires, and gun shots all to alert patriot militias from communities around Boston to meet at Lexington and Concord to route the invading British before they could get organized. Thus, "the Shot heard 'round the world"* turned 13 British colonies into the first true democratic nation. Not "one nation under god" (a phrase added to the Pledge of Allegiance in 1954 by fear-mongering politicians) but a nation of man-made laws based on common, rationally determined, principles.

* The opening stanza of Ralph Waldo Emerson's "Concord Hymn" published in 1837.

Thus used, myth does not become religion but memorizes human heroism, intelligence in action, a description of something outside the known science of the time, and a means to communicate with Spirit.

Human Spirit

And here's the point: It takes Intelligence to ask the right questions of Spirit that is the source of inspiration. We don't know how Longfellow or Emerson sought the inspiration for their poems and odes, but the principle behind all myth creation is the same: the more rationally developed and logically organized the question, the more will Spirit inspire intelligible answers in emotionally stirring form. Spirit brings together Thought and Feeling in service to the human quest. "Spirit" inspires us to move forward; Fear and Repressions pull us backward. Religion binds us to the Past; Spirituality frees us to Grow and Progress into the future.

But, remember this: just as with "Creative Materialization" where your goal may be to create the circumstances for a better job or the opportunities for a new relationship, or where your goal may be to develop a new advertising campaign, even here in Myth Making, whether you are a shaman or a poet, know how it is that you want to inspire and raise the Human Spirit. That's your goal. The Human Spirit is in everyone. It's the ultimate vehicle for consciousness and our goal is to move it forward.

Inspiration

It's not your Soul, and it's not the Holy Spirit of the Church. It's the Spirit in you, in each of us individually and shared in all of us. Inspired Myth is the foundation for morality and understanding of who we are and where we're going. Myths are timeless, but their understanding is time and place factored. Still, when rendered in art form, they continue to inspire regardless of time and place.

And now, what New Age "Religion" and Spirituality must become in order to fulfill the "promises" made in the 1967 musical *HAIR*. No more lies and distortions, no more fear instilling myths of evil and Satan, no more pleas that only "God" can solve human problems, no more pronouncements that natural disasters are God's punishment for insufficient faith, no more promises of heavenly reward for those who die for God.

New Worlds of Mind and Spirit

Instead of that old Age of Myth and Faith, of religious law rather than laws of reason and principle, of denial of science and learning, of persecution, torture and religious war, we've entered a New Age opening to **New Worlds of Mind and Spirit.** Minds that are informed and educated, people who think for themselves, and the Human Spirit that each of us has and shares. *Why hate when you can love? Why "only believe" when you can learn and know? Why march when you can dance? Why shout in anger when you can sing in joy? Love isn't the law, it's an unending gift.* **All acts of Love are rituals of Adoration.** *A glass half empty is really half-full—see Life in its fullness, not just in parts. Giving expands, taking shrinks. Pleasuring another brings mutual pleasure; abusing another will bring mutual pain and suffering. Don't punish another for past hurt, but serve one another and the hurt goes away. Kiss and make-up and you'll both wake-up happy.*

GENERAL CONSIDERATIONS

There are many different functional factors usually considered in the academic discussion and study of each religion, as listed below. They may find little specific application in our "catalog" descriptions of their functions and characteristics in the next two chapters, but they are listed here as a reminder both of inclusion and exclusion.

Functional Factors:

After Death—survival, in what form, communication

Art, Celebrated & Forbidden

Behaviors—both obligatory and prohibited

Belief Requirements

Belief Systems

Birth Rites, Baptism, Naming

Clergy, Roles of

Cosmology

Cosmos

Cultural Systems

Community, Services provide for and demanded from

Dance

Deity

Divorce

Dress Codes for Clergy and Public

Ecstasy

Education, Secular—attitude towards

Ethics

Faith

Family—Demands & Expectations

Festivals & Feasts

Forbidden Thoughts

Funding, Private (tithing, donations, required) & Public (tax supports, subsidies)

Funeral & Burial Rites

Holy Places

Hostility, defined & required towards who and what

Human Nature

Initiations

Lifestyle

Magic, Belief in, Attitude towards, Denial of

Marriage Rites

Meaning of Life

Meditation

Miracles

Morality

Music

Mysticism, Attitude towards

Myths & Legends

Narratives

Occult Practices, Attitude towards

Origin of Humanity

Origin of Life

Origin of the Universe

Personal Growth, tolerance towards

Places of Worship

Political Action and Sermonizing

Possession

Prayer, Personal & Private, Public & Required (policed)

Proselytizing, Conversion techniques

Psychic Phenomena, Attitude towards

Puberty Rites

Public Service demanded & expected (police & fire, subsidies & grants)

Public Services offered & provided (education, medical, shelter, etc.)

Reincarnation

Relationship to Community & State (degrees of separation)

Religious Laws vs. Secular Laws

Reproduction—Demands upon women, rights to contraception, abortion, life of mother or fetus

Rituals

Sacred Histories

Sacred Language & Gestures, Postures, Movements –clergy and participants in public ritual

Sacred Objects, Places and Things

Sacrifices

Sacrilegious Acts and Beliefs, Defined

Scripture

Sermons

Sex, other than for reproduction

Social Life, Segregation, Demands for a closed community

Soul—belief, definition,

Spirits, Angels, Guides, Demons

Spirituality

Superiority, Claims for "us vs. them"

Supernatural, concept of

Symbols

Theology

Tolerance towards other faiths and their sacred objects

Traditions

Trance

Words of Power, Secret Names

World Views

Women in relation to Men

Worship, Practices & Demands

It is also common to assign the religion under study a *Geo-Cultural* classification in recognition of the shared elements of geographic origin and cultural tradition. In the case of many "modern" religious movements it isn't always practical to identify even a relatively specific geographic origin nor a well-defined cultural tradition. Despite the fact that some of the recent sects of a major religion may be found far distant from historic place of origin, that is only a minor note. No doubt, some of these listings will be debated.

Geo-Cultural Classification:

Indo-European, Ancient—Armenian, Celtic, Germanic, Greek—(includes Gnosticism, Neo-Platonism), Illyria-Thracian, Roman, Slavic, Vedic Hinduism.

Middle Eastern, Abrahamic—Baha'i (19th century CE), Christianity (1st century CE—includes Anglicanism, Catholicism, Orthodoxy, Protestantism, Mormonism—(19th century CE), Druze, Islam (7th century CE—includes Sunni, Shia, Sufi, Ahmadiyya, Quraniyoon), Judaism (19th century BCE includes Conservative, Karaite, Orthodoxy, Chassidic, Charedi, Noahidism, Reform, Samaritanism), Mandaeism, Rastafari (20th century CE, Jamaica)

Middle Eastern, Iranian—Ahl-e Haqq, Bahai Faith, Manichaeism, Mazdak, Mithraism, Yazidi, Zoroastrianism (15th century BCE), Zurvanism

Near, Ancient—Egyptian, Mesopotamian, Semitic

Southern Asia, Indian—Ayyavazhi, Buddhism (4th century BCE—includes Theravada, Mahayana, Vajrayana), Hinduism (ancient—includes Shaktism, Shaivism. Smartism, Vaishnavism), Jainism (9th century BCE), Sikhism, Lingayatism, Ravidassia

Southern Asia, Vietnamese—Chi Dai (20th century CE)

Far East Asia, Japanese—Church of All Worlds (20th century CE), Seicho-no-Ie (20th century CE), Shinto, Tenrikyo (19th century CE), Zen

Far East Asia, Korean—Cheondoism (19th century CE),

East Asia. Chinese—Confucianism, Taoism

General Global, New Religious—Discordianism. Eckankar (20th century CE, America), Moralism, Nontheism, Satanism (20th century CE), Scientology (20th century CE, America), Unitarian-Universalism (20th century CE, America, but Unitarianism itself originated in 16th century CE Transylvania), Unification Church

General Global, Shamanic—Candomble, Santeria, Spiritism, Spiritualism, Tibetan Bon, Voodoo

Indigenous—African, Afro-American, Aztec, Australian Aboriginal, Chinese, Finnish-Estonian, Gurung, Inca. Javanese, Lepcha (Mun), Maya, Native American, Philippine, Polynesian

Western, New Age Metaphysical—Alchemy, Anthroposophy, Christian Science (19th century CE, America), Deism, Esotericism, Freemasonry (18th century CE), Gnosticism (modern), Goddess Worship, Hermeticism, Kabbalism (not Judaic—17th century CE), Magick, Neo-Paganism—including Druidry (18th century CE, Britain), New Thought, Objectivism, UFO—Raëlism (20th century, France), Rosicrucianism, Secular Humanism (20th century CE, America), Spiritual but not Religious, Stregheria, Thelema, Theosophy (19th century CE, America & India), Unity (19th century CE, America), Wicca (20th century CE, America & Britain), Witchcraft (Europe)

A further Typing of religions is Theistic in which they are variously classified into one of six categories:

Theistic Categories:

Monotheism is a religion that claims the existence of only one single all powerful god. There may be such lesser spiritual beings as angles, demons, and spiritual entities or forces, but are subordinate to the one god. "Worship," however described, is required by the one god, and not allowed for the subordinates.

Dualism recognizes the existence of exactly two deities representing opposite forces—those of Good and Evil—in perpetual conflict.

Polytheism recognizes more than one deity but in a dualistic relationship. There can be any number of deities, each representing or embodying specific characteristics or powers that may be individually or collectively (such as god & goddess pair) worshiped, the characteristic qualities evoked, or the powers and the entity itself invoked into the practitioner.

Atheistic religion denies the existence of any divinities, and presumably rejects any "supernaturalism" as beyond scientific knowledge and rational thinking.

Non-Theistic neither accepts or rejects the existence of deities but generally acknowledges the possibilities of supernatural phenomena. A non-theistic religion may include a belief in a god while at the same stressing humanistic beliefs and personal responsibilities for a moral and ethical life based on common sense, rational thinking, and knowledge of human experience.

Personal Development Movements focus on techniques of self-improvement in both worldly and spiritual domains while acknowledging responsibilities to self and society.

WORSHIP

Another distinguishing feature among religions is the style and function of Worship. If one of the dynamics of relationship between the human person and the deity or deities, or an acknowledged non-deific "source," or Nature, or even Humanity itself is an energy transfer between the two poles, then worship, and "sacrifice," is the primary method, while prayer, meditation, and rituals are generally considered secondary and often particularly beneficial to the practitioner.

In this short essay we are only introducing the concept of worship, and then will mention further specifics in the individual religion treatments.

Worship is said to be an act of devotion towards just one deity, even in a polytheistic religion. The word essentially means "worth-ship," the object of worship is worthy of the particular action. Worship asserts the reality of an object and honors that object with emotion.

In Christianity, worship was "adoration" expressed through formalized *liturgy* meaning a "public service" or "work of the people." It is basically a formal set of petitions (called prayer) that are spoken or sung by a leader with set responses from the people. The prayers express, teach, and govern the formal beliefs of the community. As in Islam and Judaism, these prayers were to be repeated at set times throughout the day, week, and year.

Additional acts, such as the Catholic communion service, celebrate the basic myth concerning the object of worship—whether as Allah, Jesus, or Jehovah.

Additional elements of the service may variously include a sermon reminding people of their duties to fulfill the "Will of God," music to set an emotional stage, communal singing to induce some level of ecstasy, and with that there can be a healing or a baptism service for those suitably entranced.

Other services—used to hold the flock together—include baptism of a child, coming of age rituals following a period of theological study, marriage, and a celebration of death. It may include the confession and absolution of sins.

Worship takes a multitude of forms depending on community groups, geography and language. There is a flavor of loving and being in love with whatever object or focus of devotion. Worship is not confined to any place of worship, it also incorporates personal reflection, art forms and group. People usually perform worship to achieve some specific end or to integrate the body, the mind and the spirit in order to help the performer evolve into a higher being.

There are also rituals related to otherwise ordinary activities such as a Tea Ceremony, the Blessings before a meal, and even before marital sex in which various mantras or scriptural texts may be recited. In true Spirituality, all life is the manifestation of Spirit, and so even the most mundane of activities should be seen as inclusive of Spirit, and hence special occasions or events should be marked with recognition of Spirit and the evocation of a spiritual blessing or presence.

Worship can also involve evoking higher forces to assist in spiritual and material progress and also invoking devotion and love whether towards a deity or human kind. In more fundamentally shamanic practices it can include invocation of a deity into the worshipper's own body or into that of another participant.

Worship in Hinduism and Buddhism often includes devotion to one's teacher or *guru* which may command absolute obedience and self-sacrifice.

Worship in Islam refers to ritualistic devotion which is ordained by and pleasing to Allah, primarily consisting ritual prostration and prayer five times daily. The inner meaning is the worshipper's conscious willingness to conform to their perception of His will and plan.

Worship in Wicca commonly takes place during a full moon or a new moon. Such rituals are called an Esbat and may involve a magic circle which practitioners believe will contain energy and form a sacred space for magical protection and a focus for magical action. In Gardnerian Wicca and Old Witchcraft, worship included deity invocation called "Drawing Down the Moon" in which the Great Goddess is manifest in the Being and Body of the High Priestess. In some covens, this is also an initiatory rite, and in a few there is also an invocation of the Horned God into a male. In rare practices there may be a sexual union of Priest and Priestess manifesting the Horned God and the Great Goddess.

MEDITATION:
"On your discovery of Spirit Within"

Sources and Recommended Reading:

Judith, A.: *The Global Heart Awakens—Humanity's Rite of Passage from the Love of Power to the Power of Love,* 2013, Shift Books

Leeming, David: *The Oxford Companion to World Mythology.* 2005, Oxford University Press

Melton, J. Gordon: *The Encyclopedia of Religious Phenomena,* 2008, Visible Ink Press

Vernon, Mark (Ed.): *Chambers Dictionary of Beliefs and Religion,* 2009, Chambers

10

THAT OLD TIME RELIGION, BUT WHERE'S SPIRIT?

As we discussed in the last chapter, the word "religion" derives from *ligare* meaning "to bind together," and that perfectly describes how religions have been used to bring a people together and then to assert political control over them. The outstanding example is that of the Roman Empire bringing the diverse populations of Europe and the Mediterranean under the combined control of Church and State.

Serving the "Plan"

These Western/Middle Eastern Religions are all *monotheistic* and *male-dominated*. The emphasis is on humans serving the PLAN of a distant masculine *One God* as interpreted, and *enforced, by* His male-dominant hierarchical institutions of Church and—during much of the last three thousand years of Western history—the State under religious control.

Judaism, Christianity, and Islam are the dominant and dominating religions of the Western World even today—together being the religious affiliation of half the world's population. Even though modern civilization—led by Western thought—is today based on Science, Rationality, Democracy, and Business Enterprise—these old time religions all claim that only God can solve problems on HIS pre-established terms, and that "faith" not "thought" is the means to engage God's power.

The Coming Global Civilization

As we move towards a Global Civilization, we encounter other religions—older and newer—that don't fit this concept of human bondage to an abstract deity through his privileged operating personnel. And yet we are still encumbered by these old time religions trying to control populations everywhere by dominating primary and secondary education, public service, local and national governments, and even by turning back the clock rejecting science, claiming myth as fact, and trying to replace modern constitutional law with archaic and regressive religious laws.

Refuse to be Limited!

Don't let the Past limit your fresh thinking and independent investigation. Don't let "religion" turn off your intellect. The challenges coming at us from accelerating population growth straining natural resources to meet human needs, encountering the planetary stresses producing climatic, environmental, geological crises, adjusting to the "hangovers" from the recent and older past actions and mistakes, the political and economic consequences from evolving technologies, and the religious conflicts throughout the Islamic world all present enormous ethical and spiritual challenges that require our best mental, psychic, and spiritual resources.

Think! Look ahead. Study and research. Go on-line and look at sites dealing with Global Challenges. Discuss with others. Appeal to your spiritual resources. Meditate. Ask what you can do. You are a multi-level being capable of many levels of communication. Use them.

We encourage you to refer to the lists of suggested reading material and to use the programs and procedures we provide for your own direct experience, and to record and analyze your results.

New Age Spirituality vs. Old Time Religion

People who are free to choose a religion want more than an antique myth, something other than a stale-dated morality that defies common sense and imposes irrational and anti-scientific claims on their day-to-day lives. People today expect more of a religion than mind control, more than denial of the Spirit that they feel within themselves, other than being told to worship death rather than life and to joyfully kill and sacrifice their own lives to impose one religion on people. They lose respect for a religion that tells them how to dress, who to talk with, that denies education to women and children, that rejects science, that practices terror and murder in place of personal growth, that honors corruption, theft, piracy, and holding people for ransom over work, enterprise, and skill.

Spirit is within every person, and within all there is

Some religions define that Spirit only in terms of an *external* Deity. And then deny the personal experience of the Spirit within, and further deny that Spirit is part of Life itself, and part of all Existence. Some religions claim that the Earth and all life other than human exists only to serve faithful humans and that Nature can be abused and Science ignored in the expectation that "The Lord will provide." "Don't think, just Believe."

The word *Religion* fails to be meaningful in today's world of educated people with developed minds; people who can determine for themselves what to wear and when and if to conceive children; people who wish to improve public services according to their own awareness of need and vision of betterment for themselves and their children; people unwilling to merely "follow the leader" when they can see he (never a "she") will lead them over a cliff towards an ideological disaster.

For some people, the word *Spirituality* defines spirit in terms of Spirit or Soul *within*; for others *Spirituality* is defined as a *Process of Becoming;* and others see Spirit to be in all things and continually *evolving and transforming all Life.*

The sense of Spirituality gives some *transcendent* meaning to life, including the ordinary human experiences of love and sex, of birth and death, of work and family, of giving and receiving care and devotion. *Transcendence* does not demand sacrifice, self-denial, abstinence, or repression, nor does it call for the death of "unbelievers" or of self in a battle for their conversion to "the One True Way." Spirituality does not promise eternal life of sensual delight in exchange for taking life from others and rejecting their right to sensual pleasures in this life.

Mind and Spirit, and Evolution

As we continue our study and practice of Spiritual Communication, Self-Empowerment and Psychic Development, we want to repeat our earlier affirmation:

> *Never doubt the capacity of the Human Mind! The whole purpose of spiritual practice and study is to become more than we are and all we can be—which is potentially all there is. And since consciousness is everywhere and in every-thing and every being, the best thing we can do is to understand and train our*

own consciousness to go everywhere and enter into anything, to communicate
with any being as we perceive need and value.

Perhaps the most misunderstood and the most important concept in any study of Cosmos and Life, of Spirit and Consciousness, and of Spirituality as a Process of Becoming is that of "Evolution."

Biblical Truth?

Even today, most people think of Evolution and Darwin's natural selection and "Survival of the Fittest" as applied to only plant and animal life. And they see it as involving long passages of Time long, long ago, and no longer occurring. And for many it was primarily a dispute over "Man" as a perfect form made in God's image, or "Man" as descended from an ape or monkey. For the Church, it was a contradiction of "Biblical Truth" in which Adam and Eve, the first humans, were created in 4,004 BCE, and the world—just as it is today—was created directly by God 6,000 years ago—and that all evidence to the contrary exists only as a test of faith.

Evolution began at the "Beginning," and continues to this day. Science generally confirms this, as does most Esoteric teaching. Evolution is not limited to Cosmology and Biology, but includes Sociology, Psychology and Spirituality. In other words, everything continues to change, evolve and "progress"—even as we experience it as a kind of "trial and error," or as "trial under fire." Yes, even human institutions are evolving, even our psychological nature continues to evolve, and so it is with the Human Spirit as the fundamental elemental *substance within the whole human being*, Spirit manifests in "structures" that change and evolve, enabling individuals to evolve, grow, and *become*.

The same thing is true of the other "parts" of the whole human being: the physical body evolves and so do the etheric, the astral, the mental, and the causal bodies. And so does our thinking, our feeling, our ability to empathize, our ability of understand, our intuition, the extent of our love, our psychic abilities, and all the things we can do. Our knowledge evolves, science evolves, our culture evolves, our civilization evolves, and we evolve, we grow, we become more of what we can be.

Those Old Time Religions

The Old Time Religions tried to "hold back Time" and freeze their myths and theologies in the past. The Church persecuted free thinkers, the wise women known as Witches, the healers known both as wizards and heathen, the astronomers who said the Earth rotated around the Sun, and tried to confine education only to its priests. Even into the mid-twentieth century the Church prohibited its members from reading books that offended its censors.

Shamanism, because it isn't institutionalized and frozen into the past, also continues to evolve. While it is still a "collection of verifiable spiritual technologies, a heritage of spiritual knowledge accumulated from shamanic journeying, an extensive catalog of subtly-perceived botanical knowledge, multi-body healing wisdom, life-based relationship counseling, and ecstatic states of consciousness," it grows and evolves because shamans themselves continue to grow, evolve, and serve today's clients who have modern perspectives and needs.

Old, and New, Technologies of the Sacred

No matter who else we are, we can each practice shamanism, exploring different levels of consciousness, the world of natural healing, traveling the inner worlds, talking with sprits, working with thought forms, accessing the Akashic Records, combining Eastern and Western (and Southern and Northern) "technologies of the sacred" into new practices—always learning and growing and becoming more than we are. And we can call it something else, if we want—such as "Spirituality." And instead of being identified as a shaman, we can be a "seeker," or a student of metaphysics, a magician, a yogi, a Tantric practitioner, a philosopher, or life scientist.

In this New Age, we each must learn to assert our own authority and not merely follow others—whether scholars, teachers, researchers, priests, gurus or doctors—like a herd of sheep. Yes, we turn to others, and to books and other sources, for information and knowledge, but we can only derive real wisdom from personal experience. And it is that personal experience that accelerates personal evolution. The species evolves only as individuals evolve and transfer their new development via the "field" to others ready for it and prepares the way for others not quite ready for it.

The Three Kinds of Religion

In the previous chapter we discussed how religions evolve and introduced the concept of the three most prevalent kinds of religion existent in the world today. In this chapter we will primarily discuss the Old Time Religions whose "use by" date has expired. In discussing the "old" and the "new," it is also important to recognize the cyclical nature of most things. As we remarked about the early beginnings of religious experience:

"Spirituality begins with the recognition of Spirit within all things, and of the process of its manifestation in all things. From this recognition came the "worship" of the <u>visible</u> Feminine as mother of human and animal life and of the Earth and Mother Nature. Spirituality was the inner feeling of the Feminine as the Source of All, and the sexual experience of the <u>invisible</u> spirit moving within woman's and man's bodies. From sexual pleasure men and women discovered love, and with understanding of their shared involvement in reproduction arose the joy of family and the realization of the fundamental partnership of man and woman in committed relationship. It was this experience of partnership that started the long road we now call "civilization."

"Worship" at this point was simply an *adoration* of this invisible spirit moving within that somehow produced Life, was Life, and gave Life to the Family of man, woman and child, and that created a sense of Community beyond the family. This led to the social aspect of the neighborhood community that remains the primary social function of church as of the local "meeting place."

In rural and village life, the local church was not perceived as denominational but purely as a place of acknowledgement of the Divine in life, as the place where men and women met, and married, and where their children were accepted into the community to repeat the cycle. It was the place where respect was given to the dead and where they were buried in a continuing sense of their presence in the community.

It was a place of *unity*, an opportunity for learning, and for mutual respect and support as perhaps best expressed in Unity and Unitarian-Universalism today. We will explore these further in the next chapter.

Today, we also see the Feminine "returning" and taking on new roles—not merely in equality with the Masculine but—as we will later discuss—transformative in both outer institutions and in the re-balancing of the inner dimensions of Man and Woman. Keep that in mind as we continue our discussion of religions in this chapter and the next.

As this first kind of religion, the matrilineal, was described as based on Love, so the second kind, the patrilineal, is based on Law.

Where is Spirit in these two forms of religion?

In the first, Spirit was seen everywhere, in the second it was seen nowhere, or "elsewhere." Spirit that first appeared to the lone prophet next appeared to the priest behind closed doors or hidden by closed curtains. What had been open to all was now closed to all but the few. In the third, as we will later see, Spirit can be not only seen but invoked and experienced by all.

The first two types, the matrilineal and patrilineal religions, had *accidental* shamanic origins; in the third type the learned principles of Spirituality are applied purposefully in 21st century adaptations of spiritual techniques and the universal awareness of Spirit, and the social valuation of Spirituality in community and neighborhood. The living shamanic techniques of spiritual communication are adapted and applied by individuals and "voluntary" groups for personal spiritual development and growth, not by institutional priests and clerics. This third type of religion is based on *choice* and defined by personal interest rather than birth and coercion, and will be further discussed in the next chapter. The rest of this chapter will mainly review these old time religions that were largely imposed on the populations, and whose theologies are mainly frozen in time.

Nevertheless, we will mention some very old religions whose lessons are as timeless as those of shamanism are.

Religion and Spirituality

We've previously reviewed the current "official" definition of the word "religion" as derived from *ligare* meaning "to bind together." From this we have the "political" concept of *binding* a people together as the Roman Empire used Catholicism to assert *control* over the people of Europe and the Mediterranean.

But this political use of religion did not start nor end in Rome. The three monotheistic religions founded in the Middle East: Judaism, Christianity, and Islam all have the same emphasis on humans serving the one God with enforcement through *His* institutions of Church and State.

In Europe, the medieval Church's rigid political, economic, and intellectual domination began to slowly decline starting about 1500 AD with the advent of the printed book, the spread of scientific knowledge contradicting the erroneous theology of the Church, and the decline of its political control over monarchies.

While humans are believed to have souls, communication with surviving souls of the deceased is still forbidden under the guise of protecting the innocent from the mythic dangers of "possession by demons," and communication with spiritual entities is allowed only by "authorized personnel." In the case of medieval Christianity, this dictum was enforced by the Holy Inquisition's burning to death of an estimated 7 million "heretics" (mostly women and free-thinking scientists) over a 700 year period finally ending in 1834.*

> * The Inquisition was just one example of "crimes against humanity" resulting from the politicizing of religious control over populations. Others include the religious wars ranging back to 4,000 BC and up through the Roman conquest of Europe, the Crusades, the European invasions of the Americas, Africa, and the Middle East, the Persian and Ottoman Empires, the more recent wars by German Nazi and Italian Fascism, Soviet Communism, and Islamic Terrorism. Yes, not only were Nazism and Soviet Communism developed with effective religious-styled techniques, but Hitler maintained to the end that he was a Catholic carrying out "Christ's work to exterminate the Jews." (See *The Great Cosmic Mother*)

Today we see *Spirituality* as a personal matter that may involve participation in any of the 4200 institutional "religions," or in "spiritual but not religious" programs involving personal study and practice of spiritual and esoteric systems, and the practices of self-improvement, psychic development, and the general study of psychology, quantum physics, philosophy, and developmental practices such as yoga, the martial arts, magick, Tantra, and other transformative growth systems.

This Church's formula for control of its people was adopted in the 20th century by both German National Socialism (Nazi fascism) and the Soviet Union's World Communism to intrude another particular worldview and belief system on an entire people, surrounding them with a unifying symbol, stirring music and public drama to inspire acts of devotion, and to enforce adherence through rewards and punishments to establish the superiority of the "faithful" over all *Outsiders* who were therefore to be defeated, converted, or enslaved and eliminated.

At its worst extreme, the failure to publically demonstrate one's faith, has led to imprisonment, public torture, and execution, sometimes as official acts by theocratic governments. This happens "even today" in some *tribal areas* of Bangladesh and Pakistan.

Materialism vs. Spirituality?

Until recently, modern culture was described as "materialistic" because we've been taught to perceive and value things primarily through a *materialist* perspective that says: *if you can't measure it, weigh it, photograph it, or otherwise demonstrate a physical impact, then it must be "psychological" in nature and perhaps exists only in your "imagination."*

Why should "psychological" be denigrated? Why was/is "imagination" devalued? Why were/are psychic skills and personal "spiritual communications" described as dangerous and "demonic?" Is "demonic" anything other than mythic? "Psychological" refers to the human psyche which is as real as the human body; the ability to "imagine" is essential to psychological health and is the foundation to all creativity; the word "demon" derives from the Greek *daimon* and essentially means a spirit or divine power as a source of *inspiration.* "Demonic" is an invention of myth and religion little different from the "ghost" of a scary story.

"That's one way to look at it"

Materialism is only one perspective of several that we can have simultaneously, and is not necessarily contradictory to or exclusive of Spirituality, Art, Beauty, Rationality, Love and other perspectives. It is just one way we have to look at the world: a practical perspective in relation to pure material phenomena such as: *How many miles from here to there? How much does that back pack weigh? What's the profit margin on that product? Etc.*

A materialist perspective has brought wealth and benefit to the world. It alone cannot be condemned for the accelerating challenges of our time: population growth, urbanization, proliferation of weapons, increased religious terrorism, obesity, destruction of the environment, climate change, the approval of greed, short-term corporate profiteering, etc. At the same time it must be seen that rapid population growth has been with us from the beginning of human history long before anyone thought in terms of the materialist benefits of an increased customer base for business, or a larger potential for religious conversion, or a political opportunity. Villages became cities long before the modern era, the history of war is largely one of religions in conflict, and yet—even as we face the materialist challenge of rapid population growth we have acknowledge that without the benefit of chemical fertilizer, half the world's current population would starve. We also recognize that the average span of human life has more than doubled in the last hundred years. And the millions of people who die each year from lack of a *naturally* clean water supply can look towards a future of water purification plants supplied by materialist technology.

Alternative Views, Values, and Choices

Every perspective has value, and challenge, and potential solutions to problems not only of its creation but also of the world as it is. We can't go back in time to correct past errors; instead, we learn from the past not to repeat those errors or continue actions we can now recognize as abusive, harmful, short-sighted, and negligent in the emerging larger picture of our reality. And it is other perspectives that give us alternative views and values as evolution continues not merely to bring us into higher spiritual states but to work towards a better world and a better life for all. Nevertheless, we must always deal with the present, look for the impact of current actions on the future, and plan to do better.

The Dangers of Sectarianism

A return to religious sectarian dominance is a serious threat to rational thinking, and to ignore science would be to literally plunge us back into the Dark Ages without renewable energy resources, without the means to feed our increasing populations, without medicine to treat disease, without power to meet natural catastrophes, and without the ability to make common sense decisions amounting to life and death choices.

We, the public, need to understand the realities behind all the elements in our culture in order to play the responsible roles we and the founding fathers of not only American democracy but the entire global civilization now replacing the ugly heritage of past imperialism, colonial impositions on local cultures, the "Holy" Inquisition and other tortures in the name of this god or that one, the religious wars, and the reasons that there is a necessary separation of "church from state."

The Times—they are changing!

Thankfully, today's secular culture is undergoing both rapid expansion and rapid change. The continuing industrial revolution is bringing benefit to "emerging economies," the technology revolutions is facilitating innovation and entrepreneurial development of small businesses with growth of the middle class, the ongoing agricultural revolution is increasing food production worldwide and reducing areas previously in starvation zones, the evolving social awareness is bringing health benefits to disease-prevalent areas and immediate relief to areas stricken with natural disasters, mass communication and information have "opened eyes and minds" to possibilities beyond previous dreams, and the desires for "progress" has brought quality education to what were only recently called "backward" nations.

Still, governments and cultures fail in the most basic ways: one in five babies born worldwide are in India where the bulk of women are denied instruction and means for contraception; in areas of Africa the genitals of young girls are still mutilated and sewn together; chemical pollution of water and soil is rampant because farm chemicals are not regulated in developing nations; women are commonly still beaten, raped, and mutilated in many Islamic areas, and real education is denied other than required scripture memorizations.

Common sense solutions to major problems are ignored: universal availability of contraception to reduce population growth is denied by religious obstruction; real solutions to climate change are obstructed by anti-science politicians; healthier living opportunities are prevented by short-term corporate strategies; and corrective regulation of banks and leveraged funds has been prevented through corruption; and long term solutions to budgetary problems prevented by favors extended to wealthy donors representing "special interests."

Nevertheless it is important that we recognize emerging areas where respect is given to cultural diversity in both old and new ways, colonialism and imperialism have mostly given way to democracy and local control over natural resources, and materialism is no longer seen as a necessary alternative to spirituality. Both exist side by side, and increased understanding of what each means provides for an expanding awareness of physical interplay with spiritual dimensions.

The Need for Personal Responsibility and Action

The most important dynamic of personal responsibility is yet to evolve even in the most advanced communities where people taught to be obedient to God's Will tend to sit back and say, "put your faith in God," "there's nothing we can do about it," "let our leaders take care of it," "trust to the will of God," "tomorrow's another day," etc.

When you let go of all responsibility you are giving up your humanity, abandoning the power of rational thinking to instead be led by instinct and manipulated by emotion. This New Age is happening and change is coming regardless of what preachers, politicians, paid "authorities," and experts say; the real point of leverage, the real center of political power, and the true spiritual authority is that of the Individual. *It is Individual against Institution!* Institutions are <u>not</u> citizens. Churches are <u>not</u> God. Preachers do <u>not</u> know the Creator's "will." Don't just join some group and tithe or pay dues. *It is YOU who must learn and act, personally and responsibly.* The entire purpose of physical incarnation is to fully manifest the Creative Force that is within YOU. *You can't just "pass the buck" because world peace, the survival of humanity, the potential for evolving smarter, healthier, and longer-lived, men and women depends on YOU.*

No, this is NOT a book about Religion in modern society, but this chapter is about spiritual communication *as NOT experienced in the dominant religions*. Each of the three dominant religions denies the ordinary person the right to communicate with spiritual entities. We need to break free from the hold their false myths have on thought and feeling, break their institutional hold on government and culture, and deny their grab for sectarian education and "display rights" in public places and events, and block their efforts to impose "religious" law in place of democratic *people* law.

We need to explore the new non-institutional spirituality that actually draws upon age-old practices of proven value. There are alternatives in the less dominant religions as well as *"spiritual but not religious"* practices, and we will explore those in the next chapter.

Spirituality is the perception of Spirit manifesting in all things. From this came the "worship" of the <u>visible</u> Feminine as mother of all life: human and animal, and of the Earth itself as Mother Nature. Spirituality then was the inner feeling of the Feminine as the Source of All, and the sexual experience of the <u>invisible</u> Feminine Power (Kundalini) moving within woman's and man's bodies. From sexual pleasure men and women discovered love, and with understanding of their shared involvement in reproduction arose the joy of family and the realization of the fundamental partnership of man and woman in committed relationship. It was this experience of partnership that started the long road we now call "civilization."

As populations grew, and moved, it was that sense of community that was translated into the political function of the Church and its relationship to the State—with one or the other in the Driver's Seat. And it was and is this partnership that has been instrumental in inspiring and facilitating War and Terrorism as larger communities came into conflict, and it was and is the basis for the persecution, torture, and killing of minorities within and across communities.

"Worship" as Adoration, and the binding together in Community

With the experience of the invisible Kundalini Power within male and female arose a sense of awe, with the experience of sensual joy and sexual enjoyment arose a new of adoration of each for the other, and with the harmony of their togetherness arose the sense of community that is the true "binding together."

It was that sense of community that was translated into the political function of the Church and its relationship to the State—with one or the other in the Driver's Seat. Love was twisted into repressive laws used to condemn personal acts of pleasure and re-direct those energies to church and state. It was and is this partnership that has been instrumental in War and Terrorism as larger communities came into conflict, and it was and is the basis for the persecution, torture, and killing of minorities and "unbelievers" within communities. It's the reason Church and State <u>must</u> remain separate as was first established in this New World and New Age in the Founding of America with Freedom both from and of religion.

The dominant religions have nothing to do with the *Raising of Spirit, Communicating with Spirit,* and the *Teaching and Practice of Spiritual Technologies.*

Shamanism arouse out of the inner experience of joy and ecstasy, and the discovery of means in addition to ecstatic sex, psychoactive mushrooms and herbs for its achievement. Through ecstatic experience, the shaman learned to raise consciousness and to journey out-of-body and communicate with spiritual entities to gain information of value to individuals and the community. Shamanism was the beginning not only of what we call "religion" but defines what religion today is not. Shamanism was and is the founding of the sciences of Spirit, of Consciousness, of Physics, Medicine and Psychology. Shamanism is not the political control or manipulation of people.

Spiritual Communication is older than any religion

While recorded history, by definition, starts with the invention of writing around 3200 BCE in Sumer in today's southern Iraq, archaeological and biological evidence currently projects the "birth" of humanity to perhaps seven million years ago in Africa, and the appearance of *anatomically modern* humans to about 500,000 years ago. However, there are many disputes to that dating in both directions.

All dating is constantly being pushed back as new technologies enable further refinement of the evidence. As of 2013, science estimates the age of the physical universe at 13.77 *billion* years; the age of the earth as 4.6 billion years, the age of tool making and tool using "early-humans" to 5 million years, and the earliest organized "civilizations" to 30 thousand years ago, Again, there are disputes to those figures, especially to the dating of "civilization" and the definition of what civilization is.

But, the "Bible" says . . .

In contrast, according to Biblical interpretation of the carefully constructed mythology drawn from many older sources to create a political play script, "Creation" occurred just 6,000 years ago, Adam and Eve were "created" in 4,004 BCE, Abraham (the father-ancestor of Arabs and Jews) was born 2000 BCE, *and people in the rest of the world are not mentioned at all.*

"Mythic" history* reaches further back from the time of the Biblical Flood (conjectured to have occurred 2,348 BCE) to **Atlantis*** (occupied by civilized humans 200,000 BCE to 10,000 BCE) and **Lemuria*** (about 800,000 BCE to 10,000 BCE)—both disappearing into rising ocean levels during cataclysmic earth changes—pushes the probable ages of humanity and civilization much further back while changing the concept of what constitutes pre-historic human incarnation.

* Time after time, *non-politically distorted* myth proves more accurate, and history is then corrected—as so well demonstrated in the story of Troy—presented as a Homeric myth, but then dug up by persistent archaeologist Frank Calvert in 1865. Similarly, following myth led to the discovery of the largest and most sophisticated pyramid in the Western Hemisphere at Cholula hidden and forgotten in the jungle of Central Mexico. Indeed, myth is as often factual pre-historic memories as it is story-form speculation of our human origins in the creation of local cultures.

However, there is not enough geological evidence nor sufficient archaeological evidence to support the lore regarding the "lost continents" of Atlantis and Lemuria. Indigenous "memories" say that Atlantians settled in the Bahamas around 20,000 BCE and in southern Egypt around 14,000 BCE, while Lemurians settled in Central and South America from 50,000 BCE to 10,000 BCE, and in India, Tibet, and thence to Upper Egypt about 15,000 BCE. (See http://www.atlantisinsights.net/Timeline.html)

The greater challenge here is the esoteric belief that Lemurians, and to a lesser degree Atlanteans, were not as <u>fully physical</u> as today's humans. Lemurian bodies were still primarily astral and etheric while Atlantians were still strongly etheric. This represents the concept of "devolution" as humans <u>descended</u> (or "fell") into physicality from which we are to <u>evolve</u> as we fully learn the lessons of fully incarnate material life. See *The Secret Doctrine* by H. P. Blavatsky for an understanding of this complex philosophy which is also present in the mythic legends of Hinduism, Polynesia, Egypt, Greece, and others,

"The Bible says"—Few people realize that the present scriptures referred to as the Old Testament began being written about 621 BCE while the New Testament was formulated around 400 CE from many hundreds of "books" telling the stories of Creation, Man's origins, the history of the Hebrew people, the life of Jesus, and various prophecies by a committee appointed by the Roman Emperor entirely for the political purpose of "binding" together the European peoples under Roman rule. Books not included in the final selection offer contrasting views and different stories. All the earlier writings were "edited" to reflect the desired changes—replacing feminine with masculine, changing historical references to reflect the superiority of the Hebrews over their neighboring tribes, etc. In other words, *the phrase "Biblical Truth" is meaningless.* Even beyond that problem, the Hebrew Bible consists of 24 books, the Christian Bible ranges from, 66 books of the typical Protestant version to 81 books in the Ethiopian Orthodox Christian *Tewahedo* version. None of these versions include any of the "Dead Sea Scrolls" and recent findings of older historic texts that may have had less political re-writing.

Fundamental Differences in Religions

One definition of Religion is a "belief system," but we also have an "attitude" towards other humans, and—separately—towards the non-human world. At the one extreme of the monotheistic religions, <u>Man</u>kind is proclaimed supreme over all Nature and all the Earth as <u>his</u> to be used and abused for his own benefit regardless of harm to other life. At the other extreme of indigenous shamanic and polytheistic religions, we are all of One Life and as self-conscious and intelligent humans we have greater responsibility in the care of one another, of Nature, and the Earth.

All religions provide some mythic *story* of the creation of cosmos and of humanity, and each particular religion usually provides some narrative about its origin, the functional goals of an individual's life and of the religions' service to the individual, and what the religion's organization *demands* from the individual. Usually there is a unique image identifying that worldview and sometimes serving as a symbol for meditation or object of worship, such as Cross, Crescent, or Six-pointed Star.

All religions are man-made, and unfortunately some men have projected their worst prejudices into the fundamentals of their beliefs–including sexual and racial discriminations, territorial ambitions, even economic and political ideologies. In this regard, *the male-dominant religions today are mostly hate-filled, irrational, anti-sex, chauvinistic, militaristic, teaching greed and practicing corruption* while pretending to be based on love, charity, and peace.

There are many interesting differences among the world's religions, but most of them are political and historical. And it is not those differences that are important but what we can learn of their spiritual and transforming technologies and how to adapt and apply them to our modern needs and tomorrow's goals.

Religion = A Belief System

In a modern sense we use religion as one cultural delineation among others. With over 4,200 distinct contemporary religions in the world, there really is no suitable overall definition of what "religion" is, and even less about what it should be to fulfill people's basic expectations. We can say that basically a religion is a particular belief system presenting a unique worldview inclusive of the origin of the Cosmos (all that is, including the physical universe), that of all life, the meaning and purpose of individual human life, the respective roles of the religion to human life—the believers, individually and as a group, and all humanity.

The truth is that we don't know how old any religion is prior to the development of writing 5,200 years ago in the Middle East. Archaeological evidence is not much help, even with scientific dating systems because the identification of artifacts before written history is rarely conclusive. Yes, there are images of apparent deities carved into stone, but obviously the stone is older than the carving. All the can really be said is that Hinduism (50,000 years old) and the ancient Egyptian religion (perhaps 6 to 10 thousand years old) are older than Judaism which is about 3,800 years old, Buddhism about 2,500 years, Christianity 2,000 years old and Islam about 1,500 years old.

The oldest *formal* religion is probably multi-theistic Hinduism originating 50,000 years ago in Dravidian India, long before the Aryan invasions that turned it upside down. But, the practice of animism, a non-theistic religion, reaches back to at least 70,000 years ago in Africa and Australia.

Religions of the World

Basically, we perceive various major religious streams. There are many minor sects and variations of each, but the following "catalogs" presented in this chapter and the next are either population dominant or otherwise uniquely relevant to the subjects of our discussion of Spiritual Communication.

Religions that Dominate

Some scholars classify religions as *universal religions* that seek worldwide transcultural acceptance and actively proselytize for new converts, or culture specific religions that are often indigenous and identified with a particular ethnic or nationality group and do not seek converts, or new religious movements that are sometimes using religion as a cover for political or *commercial* purposes.

Religions of Choice

The real issue is what any religious or spiritual set of practices can do for its followers. We need no longer merely stay in a religion because we were "born" into it. Instead of being dominated by it, we can choose what we want, what we believe in, what we feel will help us, etc. Instead of being "bound" to the "state religion" we make choices, we move about, look for alternatives, and determine what serves our spiritual, emotional and social needs.

Abrahamic Monotheism

The three male-dominant monotheistic patriarchal religions date back 3,800 years to their Middle Eastern Hebrew origin. Each has a single all powerful *father* deity—actually the same god under three different names of Jehovah, God the Father, and Allah which each religion claims as unique to itself although in the last half century it has served certain interest to speak of their common "Judeo-Christian heritage" despite two thousand years of Christian persecution of Jews.

All three pantheons include many spiritual entities, saints, angels, and spiritual forces serving the Father god, but any *active* communication with these entities is forbidden, and the roles any of these may play is commonly subjected to ridicule and denial. Some of the Catholic saints are adopted Pagan deities, just as many Christian celebrations replace Pagan events, and many churches and cathedrals, and "power places" simply overlay their Pagan predecessors. In viewing these, think "political strategies" of the conquerors transitioning the people to a new order of things: replace their temple and sacred places with yours; substitute your deities for theirs; destroy their monuments and historic artifacts so they won't be reminded of past glory.

When the Spanish conquistadores described the Aztec City of Mexico as the most beautiful in the world, the Church ordered them to destroy it all, to burn the libraries and wipe out all evidence of a heritage that far surpassed their own. The Hebrews did it in their time, the Christians did it in theirs, the Nazis and Soviets did it in theirs, and even today Muslims destroy religious and cultural antiquities when they occupy a territory.

God-fearing People

Why should we be taught to fear God? Because the Abrahamic God is a jealous God demanding obeisance to Him alone; obeisance which is tested as when God orders Abraham to murder his own son as proof of his faith, as when Lot's wife looked back and was turned into a pillar of salt, and then the promise: "...for those who don't obey the gospel of our Lord Jesus: They will be punished with eternal destruction."[3] And in Islam: "Anyone who disobeys God and His messenger will abide in the fire of hell foreve..."[4]

We're instructed to fear God's punishment because we are all "born in sin." While Christianity promises that Jesus' death on the cross redeemed all humanity, today's preachers still thunder that we must fear God, and obey His message. *But what of Love? What of Mercy, What of Justice and Goodness?* No, in essence, we must beg for favors from His interpreters. And to follow orders from our governments who are the managers on Earth for God's Will.

Each has a history of requiring rigid adherence to a political theology enforced by law and threats of violence. Historically, all three theologically prescribe male dominance over a "sinful" female whose major function is to serve her husband and reproduce the species (with preference for male children) regardless of personal health or desire. All three, have at times been imperialistic, seeking to enlarge their territory and enforce their theology on others through military conquest. Their theology, in practice, should be described as more materialistic than spiritual and human "goodness" has become identified with worldly power and/or wealth.

One major difference between these three "newer" religions and the older ones is that they are purely theological and declare that man must serve the "one God," whereas the older religions are *magickal and* spiritual as well as theological, and show the ways spiritual forces can help humans to better meet life's challenges.

Judaism

Judaism claims to be one of the oldest religions existing today, completely ignoring Hinduism and other religions of Asia, Africa, and indigenous peoples around the world. It identifies itself specifically with Jews as the "chosen people," and prides itself with the continuity of suffering and persecution that Jews have endured over thousands of years. While people do convert to Judaism—particular in America through inter-marriage—the people and the religion are considered identical.

Essentially, the myth of Jewish history was the creation of Abraham who felt a call from a Spirit who led him to found a nation in exchange for the promise of exclusive worship. When Abraham was old, his barren wife Sarah arranged for her maid servant Hagar to cohabit with Abraham. Their son, Ishmael, is credited as the father of the Arab people. Later, at age 90, Sarah miraculously became fertile and bore a son named Isaac who is credited as the ancestor of the Jewish people.

Thus, the age-old conflict between Jews and Arabs may simply have started as sibling rivalry between Abraham's two sons born of different wives.

The central religious belief of Judaism is that there is only one God. Monotheism was uncommon at the time Judaism was born, but according to Jewish tradition, God himself revealed it to Abraham, the ancestor of the Jewish people. Later God revealed the Ten Commandments to Moses, credited as the Law Giver of the Jews, and many more religious and ethical guidelines are given in the Torah ("the Law"). Many of the guidelines emphasized ritual purity and the importance of remaining set apart from the surrounding polytheistic cultures.

Jewish identity arises primarily from belonging to an ancient people and upholding its traditions. Aside from its staunch monotheism, Judaism has few essential beliefs, and those vary widely on such matters as human nature and the afterlife, normally of prominent concern in other theologies.

To recognize the role of God and the Jewish community in each person's life, numerous life cycle events are observed with traditional rituals. At the first Sabbath after the birth of a child, the father comes forward in the synagogue to recite blessings for mother and child. Eight days after birth, baby boys are circumcised, a mark of Jewish exclusivity.

At the age of 13, a boy becomes a Bar Mitzvah, or "Son of the Commandment." In a recent attempt at modernization, a girl at age 12 becomes a Bat Mitzvah, "Daughter of the Commandment." The occasion is marked by the youth's first public reading of the Torah in the synagogue (only boys may do this in Orthodox congregations), followed by a large and joyous celebration.

Jewish wedding ceremonies incorporate many ancient traditions and symbolic gestures (including the well-known breaking of a wine glass). At death, a Jewish person's body is washed and prepared for burial. The deceased is treated with great respect and never left alone. After burial, the deceased's loved ones enter a formal period of mourning, which gradually decreases over the course of a year. The dead is then remembered and honored each year on the anniversary of death.

Moses with Ten Commandments

In addition to these special days and ceremonies, Jewish life is marked by regular religious observance. Major religious holidays include Passover, Rosh Hashanah and Yom Kippur. Hanukkah, a minor holiday, is now common for Jews living in areas where Christmas is celebrated. In Judaism, all days begin at sundown and end at sundown.

The Sabbath is observed each Saturday by ceasing work and spending the day in worship at the synagogue and at home with family. The study of Torah and other Jewish scriptures is considered very important, and many Jewish children attend Hebrew school so they can study in the original language. In everyday life, traditional Jews observe the laws of *kashrut*, eating only foods that God has designated "kosher." Among non-kosher, or prohibited, foods are pork, any meat that has not been ritually slaughtered, shellfish, and any meal that combines dairy with meat.

All in all, it can said that Judaism is less a religion than a tradition of racial and cultural exclusivity (as the "chosen people") based on myth bolstered by religious celebrations, laws and commandments.

Christianity

While Christianity can be said to descend from Judaism, it is described in terms of the mythic life and teachings of Jesus as recounted by various writers at second and third-hand in the Biblical New Testament. In reality, there are few "teachings," but instead various stories in which Jesus is supposedly quoted and various miracles described. The religion is really based on a doctrine of faith that Jesus is the Son of God, literally, is charged as the Savior of Mankind, and is "Christ"—which means *the Anointed One*, hence the Messiah or Savior. The Church also proclaims the "Trinity" described as the uniting of "Father, Son, and "Holy Ghost" (or "Spirit").

The story of Jesus' virgin birth, and even of the crucifixion, is modeled after many earlier myths of a religious messenger born of a virgin, several of which are given below.

There is a separate esoteric tradition of "Christ Consciousness" attained through evolutional growth and communication with Spirit (not necessarily the same as the "Holy Spirit") and not defined in terms of Christianity. One description is:

> "Christ consciousness is the state of awareness of our true nature, our higher self, and our birthright as children of God. Christ consciousness is our living expression as a child of Spirit as we unfold our own divine life plan onto the earth plane: bringing heaven to earth. Living in the reality of our "christed" self is actually being fully alive and invested in who we truly

are. In our "christed" self we live as inspiration for others to seek this for themselves so we can collectively move our planet forward into the divine plan for planetary transformation and glorification."

For some esoterics, the life of Jesus—as represented *from* New Testament writings—is a model of living that will lead to this Christ Consciousness. Here Jesus is said to be the embodiment of Love, Goodness, Peace, and Understanding. Because he was God-centered, he understood the nature of the universe and could produce miracles centered on Love.

This Christ Consciousness cannot be taught per se, and has no direct relation to Catholic or other Christian theology. It is attainable through practices of meditation and living. In the same way, almost any esoteric, shamanic, or occult practice centered on growth and development of personal consciousness and a life reflecting the living presence of the Spirit within is equally valid. It can be said to be identical with the ultimate goal of every spiritual system of practices.

Christianity is not a single religion but is divided into Roman Catholicism, the Eastern Orthodox Church, various splinter churches, many Protestant sects, and such smaller groups as Jehovah's Witnesses, the Latter Day Saints (Mormons), and others who can be said to be "Christian" only in their own proclaimed identification with Jesus as Christ—the Human who became fully centered in God, the Father. Many sects do not recognize Mormonism as Christian at all.

The Mythic Jesus

Whether or not there was a historic Jesus is unknown and unprovable. What can be said is that what became the Catholic Church was invented by a minor bureaucrat named Paul, and the system was perfected under the direction of the Emperor Constantine as a method for political conversion and control over the mostly European populace of the Roman Empire. The system required keeping people ignorant, treated as children (sheep), told they were born in sin from women innately sinful as daughters of a mythical Eve who ate the fruit of the Tree of Knowledge after being told not to do so. Worse, she accepted the fruit (believed to be an apple) from a serpent, symbolically representative of the penis. Hence, a woman's sexual enjoyment is itself condemned as sinful and proof of her innate immorality and justification for her subordinate role. Women are threatened by hellish punishment for any failure to conduct their lives in accordance with ever-changing dictates from a powerful clergy aligned with local monarchies, and then forced to confess their sins and pay an ill-affordable penance to the priest.

The mythic life of Jesus is given in second-hand, sometime contradictory stories present in the books making up the New Testament as well as in others that didn't "make the cut" and deemed *Apocryphal*. Again, many of the stories repeat elements found in earlier myths. The following are just a few selections, with the familiar elements italicized for emphasis. The source for these is found at *listverse* (see end of chapter).

Krishna—*born of a virgin*, by means of a mental projection from his Divine Father, and like Jesus was called both *the Son of God* and *God*, and a *savior sent from heaven*. A *ghost* (obviously "holy") was their instrument of the fathering, and hence both were born "without sin." Krishna's adoptive father was a *carpenter* as was Jesus' father, Joseph. Both Krishna and Jesus were visited at birth by *wise men* and *shepherds,* guided by a *star;* for both babies, *Angels warned of a murder plot*; the parents fled and the names of the hiding places were nearly identical: for Jesus, *Muturea;* for Krishna, *Mathura.* As adults, both Jesus and Krishna *withdrew to the wilderness and fasted.* Both were called God and Man; both performed similar miracles: *healing diseases, making a leper whole, casting out demons, raising the dead;* both celebrated a *last supper,* both *forgave enemies,* both were *crucified* and *resurrected.*

Krishna

Dionysus—*born of a virgin*, on *December 25*, called a *Holy Child* and *Only Begotten Son*, placed in a *manger*. He was a *traveling teacher*, riding on an *ass*, who performed *miracles*, turning water into wine. He was *killed*, hung on a tree as if *crucified*, and *his body eaten in a Eucharistic ritual*. He *rose from the dead* on March 25 and was called *king of kings*.

Dionysus

Zoroaster—*born of a virgin, baptized in a river*. In his youth, he *astounded wise men with his wisdom*, and *withdrew to the wilderness* where he was *tempted by the devil*. Her performed miracles of *casting out demons* and *restored sight to a blind man*. He was killed, his religion had a *Eucharist*. His followers expect a *Second Coming* on 2341 CE ushering in a *Golden Age*.

Attis—*born of a virgin* on *December 25*. He was considered the *savior*, slain for the *salvation of mankind* and his body *was eaten as bread by his worshipers*. On "Black Friday," he was *crucified* on a tree, his *Holy Blood* fell to *redeem the earth*. He descended to the Underworld, and after *three days he was resurrected*.

Horus—*born of a virgin*, the *Only Begotten Son* of the God Osiris. His birth was heralded by a *star*. Ancient Egyptians carried a *child in a manger* through the streets on the Winter Solstice December 21 (the *real* December 25). As with Jesus, there are "lost years"* between the ages of 12 and 30, after which he performs miracles of *walking on water, casting out demons, healing the sick, restoring sight to the blind.* He was *crucified, descended to the Underworld,* and *resurrected after three days.*

* The "Lost Years" of Jesus have been variously reported to have been spent studying with the Essenes, that he traveled to India where he was known as Krishna (see above), that he studied in Tibet and in Kashmir, etc. Just as interesting are stories that after the Resurrection (really just a "swoon" from which he recovered with aid of the women), he returned to Kashmir where he died at age 120 and is buried under the name of Yuz Asaf in Srinagar, India at the Roza Bal shrine. According to the Book of Mormon, after his resurrection, Jesus came to Mexico to preach.

As we will discuss later, there is nothing wrong with "myth" <u>other than when it has been treated as fact</u>, and then used in a theology frozen in time. As seen in the above few examples, the "life of Jesus" is more likely to have been conceived in myth than in "fact." In his book *The Quest of the Historical Jesus* first published in 1906, famed historian Albert Schweitzer criticized most researchers for constructing portraits of Jesus as they wanted to see him, and *not as based on historical methods.* He concluded that the values of Christianity are not depended on whether or not the Biblical Jesus was real.

What we hear from the Catholic priests and evangelic preachers is their own projection of what they want Jesus as "ruler of the Universe" to say and do to reinforce their own prejudices and beliefs. It's a political view couched in powerful emotional theatrics free of any historic validity, without rational foundation and filled with polemic distortion. Nowhere is either Divine Spirit or human spirit invoked.

Such historian perversions will be further reviewed in our discussion of the Abrahamic denigration and persecution of women.

Islam

Islam is not a religion in the same sense as Christianity is today, or other world religions. Rather than being an "adjunct" to one's life that can be freely chosen, the most fundamentalist teaching is that one is born Islamic or becomes converted—but cannot ever choose to leave it except through death. As quoted from "Free Inquiry" (August/September 2013):

"Becoming a Muslim is a one-way street. Neither those born into it nor those who convert are permitted to renounce it. As decreed and, in his day, enforced by the warrior-prophet Muhammad, the penalty for apostates who fail to recant is death. These days one can view beheadings or apostates on the Internet if one so chooses."

—(Dr. Madeine Weld: *Islam—A Totalitarian Package of Religion and Politics*).

While time changes everything, the Middle East was relatively stable for many centuries. The Persian Empire long controlled much of the area from Egypt on the west nearly to China. The Turkish Empire then expanded to include still more, including most of North Africa and southern Europe. Finally with the end of World War I, the European colonial powers set up the rather artificial states comprising the Middle East today.

Just as Christianity largely dominated the Roman Empire, so Islam was the dominant religion of the Turkish Empire. Democracy was unknown, and religious freedom was likewise unknown. With democracy, cultural and educational change came about in Europe and America, and slowly elsewhere, but not in the Middle East dominated by monarchy and dictatorships, and theocratic Islam.

Islam is based on the Koran (Quran), the holy book believed by Muslims to have been revealed by God, and on the life and teachings of the prophet, Muhammad, a 7th century CE political and religious figure whose main source of income was raiding of rich caravans.

When Muhammad was about 40 years old he began to have visions and hear voices. While seeking refuge in a cave above the rich merchant city of Mecca, he had a vision of an angel who ordered him to recite a religious verse. Fearing that he was being attacked by an evil spirit, he fled down the mountain but the voice followed him and claimed to be the angel Gabriel and that Muhammad was to proclaim to be God's chosen messenger to redeem the people.

As he preached against the polytheism and materialism of the day, he attracted the enmity of the then ruling elite who expelled him and his small band of followers from Mecca to live in Medina. Lacking resources, they robbed traders passing through the area and taking captives for ransom. As the number of his followers increased, so were their raids and attacks on the rich caravan traveling through Mecca, resulting in open war with the city's merchant class.

Following his military victory, he was treated as a political and religious leader by other Arabs, who then expanded the Arab (and Islamic) state by continual warfare initially financed largely acts of piracy, war and terrorism on "unbelievers."

Most messianic religions begin as theocracies, some more aggressive than others. The Koran instructs it followers: "Make war on them (the unbelievers) until idolatry shall cease and God's religion shall reign supreme." It further instructs the believers that it is glorious to die in the war to bring about the world-wide caliphate (a single Islamic state) and promises them eternal life and heavenly rewards. Terrorists are happy to blow themselves up when they know they will kill unbelievers; they see no problem with using innocent children in the same manner; and Islamic people have willingly entered into modern warfare unarmed when so ordered by a religious authority. While some Muslims today continue to ascribe to this belief, most do not.

Muhammad died, aged 60, on June 8, 632 CE. His followers revere him as the embodiment of the perfect believer and model their lives on his.

The "Five Pillars" of Islam are five personal acts in Islam obligatory for all believers. The Quran presents them in a framework for worship and commitment to the faith. They are (1) the Creed, (2) daily prayers, (3) alms giving, (4) fasting during Ramadan and (5) the pilgrimage to Mecca at least once in a lifetime. Public daily prayers are part of worship, and the mosque is not only a place for communal worship but for political discussion and activism.

The Last Prophet

While Islam acknowledges the Hebrew prophets and then Jesus and his followers as predecessors, Muhammad is declared to be the last and final prophet, and the Quran the final word of God. As a result there is no successor person or institution to in any way modify or modernize the governing Law for all Muslims, and by their definition, all people everywhere.

Sharia (Law)

Sharia is the moral code and religious law of Islam including many topics normally addressed by secular law, including crime, politics, and economics, as well as personal matters such as sexual relations, hygiene, diet, prayer, and fasting. In its strictest definition it is the infallible law of God—as opposed to the human interpretation of constitutional and legislative laws.

There are two primary sources of Sharia law: the precepts set forth in the Koran http://en.wikipedia.org/wiki/Quran, and the example set by the Muhammad in the Sunnah. Where it has official status, Sharia is interpreted by Islamic judges, with varying responsibilities to religious leaders. For questions not directly addressed in the primary sources, the application of Sharia is tentatively extended through the consensus of religious scholars thought to embody the conscience of the Muslim Community.

Since its scriptures proclaim their own immortality and infallibility, there is no way to bring Islam and Sharia forward from the dark ages of its origin. As former Pakistan president Pervez Musharraf indicated, Muslim countries are among the poorest, most ignorant, and most retrograde in the world. (BBC News, Feb. 16, 2002) Incidentally, in 2011, two Pakistani politicians were murdered for advocating the abolition of the country's draconian blasphemy laws. Modernization is difficult when not founded on mass education and economic and political freedom.

More than 100 years ago, Winston Churchill said:

> "Individual Muslims may show splendid qualities, but the influence of the religion paralyzes the social development of those who follow it. No stronger retrograde force exists in the world. Far from being moribund, Mohammedanism is a militant and proselyting faith. It has already spread throughout Central Africa, raising fearless warriors at every step, and were it not that Christianity is sheltered in the strong arms of science, the science against which it had vainly struggled, the civilization of modern Europe might fall, as fell the civilization of ancient Rome."
> —(Churchill, W.: *The River War, 1st ed., volume 2,* 1899)

It is commonly accepted that one source of Muslim enmity towards Israel is the obvious fact that Jews made the desert bloom and created an advanced economy and powerful nation exactly on that same land formerly occupied by poor Palestinian farmers and merchants.

The concept of justice embodied in sharia is different from that of secular law. In Islam, the laws that govern human affairs are proclaimed as identical with the laws of nature as described in the Koran. It is believed by many that this has held back both scientific and technological progress when Islamic fundamentalism is strongest.

Sharia is Incompatible with Democracy

Sharia, and religious law in general is, by definition, incompatible with modernity and democracy. Courts have generally ruled against the implementation of Sharia law, both in jurisprudence and within a community context, based on Sharia's religious background. In 1998 the Constitutional Court of Turkey banned and dissolved Turkey's Refah Party on the grounds that "Democracy is the antithesis of Sharia", which

Refah sought to introduce and replace secular law. On appeal by Refah the European Court of Human Rights determined that "Sharia is incompatible with the fundamental principles of democracy". Refah's Sharia-based notion of a "plurality of legal systems, grounded on religion" was ruled to contravene the European Convention for the Protection of Human Rights and Fundamental Freedoms, and would "do away with the State's role as the guarantor of individual rights and freedoms" and "infringe the principle of non-discrimination between individuals as regards their enjoyment of public freedoms, which is one of the fundamental principles of democracy."

Jihad to bring all nations under Islamic Governance

In 2012, Egyptian citizens, elected a Muslim President, who then proceeded to appoint only Muslims to office and produced an anti-democratic constitution. The Military intervened in 2013 to restore political and economic order to the nation, Many Muslims responded by declaring that Jihad (religious war) is the only way to accomplish the goal of bringing all nations under theocratic (Islamic) governance. Does this mean that the world is divided into the world of Islam and the world of unbelievers, and that there can be no peace until the whole world is united under Islam?

The Muslim Plan to Control America

In 1991 the Muslim Brotherhood published their General Strategic Goal for gaining control of North America "in a … grand jihad in eliminating and destroying the Western civilization from within and sabotaging its miserable house by their hands and the hands of the believers so that it is eliminated and God's religion is made victorious over all other religions." "It is a Muslim's duty to perform Jihad and work wherever he is and wherever he lands…" (The English version of entire document can be found by scrolling halfway down at http://www.investigativeproject.org/documents/misc/20.pdf)

Muslims must Live Apart

"Let not believers make friends with infidels … do not make friends with any but your people." (Quran 3:28) Many Muslims choose not to integrate into European and American communities but keep themselves apart. Without integration, there can be difficulties in communication and understanding of one another's culture.

Human rights under Sharia

Several major, predominantly Muslim countries have criticized the Universal Declaration of Human Rights (UDHR) for its perceived failure to respect the cultural and religious context of non-Western countries. Iran claimed that the UDHR was "a secular understanding of the Judeo-Christian tradition," which could not be implemented by Muslims without trespassing the Islamic law. In 1990 the Organization of the Islamic Conference representing all Muslim majority nations adopted the Cairo Declaration on Human Rights in Islam in which democratic principles, protection for religious freedom, freedom of association, freedom of the press, and equality in rights and equal protection under the law are declared (Article 24) "subject to the Islamic sharia."

It must be noted that the modern Western concept of innate individual human rights developed in reaction to the old entrenched, largely inherited, hierarchy of class and privilege seen as holding back economic and scientific progress. Sharia rejects the democratic concept of "Equality under law, and instead justifies formal inequality of individuals subject to the collective goals of the theocratic state.

Freedom of Speech denied under Sharia

Islam has little respect for freedom of speech, and specifically regards any criticism or expression of humor in regard to God, Muhammad and religious figures as blasphemy, punishable by death. Similar judgment has been extended to any non-respectful handling of the Quran. Under Islam, there is no protection from violence against anyone accused of such blasphemy.

LGBT and Sharia

Homosexual sex is illegal under sharia law, though the prescribed penalties differ from one jurisdiction to another. Muslim-majority countries of Iran, Nigeria, Saudi Arabia, and Somalia may impose the death penalty for acts perceived as sodomy and homosexual activities.

Women and Sharia

There are no priests or clergy needed to perform rites and sacraments in Islam. The leader of prayer is known as an imam. Men can lead both men and women in prayer, but women do not lead men—only women. In practice. Islam does not prohibit women from working in a servile and secondary state to men, as it says, "Treat your women well and be kind to them for they are your partners and committed helpers."

Islam allows single and married women to own property in their own right, including the right to inherit property from other family members. However a woman's inheritance is different from a man's, both in quantity and attached obligations. A daughter's inheritance is usually half that of her brother's.

Modern Women's Rights in Democratic Countries

Up until the 20th century, Islamic law granted women certain legal rights that Western legal systems did not. Western common law long denied married women any property rights and any legal personality apart from their husbands. Since the 20th century, Western legal systems have been modernized to provide more women's rights than does Islamic law, allowing women to hold equal positions in society, employment, and government.

Holding back Economic Development

Sharia recognizes only natural persons, and has no concept of a legal person, or corporation, that limits the liabilities of its managers, shareholders, and employees; and that can own assets, sign contracts, and appear in court through representatives. Interest prohibitions impose secondary costs by discouraging record keeping, and has delaying the introduction of modern accounting. Such factors have retarded economic development in the Middle East.

The Movement to Impose Sharia in non-Islamic Nations

Since the 1970s, the Islamist movements have become increasingly aggressive in promoting their goals to establish Islamic states and to impose sharia everywhere. The Islamist power base is the millions of poor, particularly the new urban poor crowding into cities from the rural areas who generally oppose western culture and western power. Groups wishing to return to more traditional Islamic values are the source of current threats to secular movements in Turkey and other multicultural states in the Islamic World.

Extremists use the Quran and their own particular version of sharia to justify war and terror against Western individuals and governments, and against other Muslims believed to have Western sympathies. http://en.wikipedia.org/wiki/Sharia—cite_note-103

Islam today is a World-Wide Religious Practice, second only to Christianity. It is the most widely practiced religion of the Middle East, North Africa, and Southeast Asia, and spreading to other areas of South Asia, Sub-Saharan Africa, and Southeast Europe. The two major sects are Sunni and Shia. Islamic theocracies include Iran,

Pakistan, Mauritania, and Afghanistan, while Turkey, Syria and Egypt are Islamic dominated democracies, and Saudi Arabia, Jordan, and a few others are Islamic dominated monarchies.

Smaller regional Abrahamic groups, include:

Baha'i

The Baha'i Faith is an Abrahamic religion founded in 19th century Iran and since then has spread worldwide. It teaches unity of all religious philosophies, that humanity is one single race, that the age has come for its unification in a global society, and —in contrast to Islam which says there can be no prophet after Muhammad—accepts all of the prophets of Judaism, Christianity, and Islam as well as additional prophets including its founder, Baha'ih'llah. His claim to divine revelation resulted in persecution and imprisonment, and a 24-year confinement in a prison city located in Palestine where he died in 1892.

In 1844, a 25-year-old man claimed to be the promised redeemer of Islam, taking the title of the Bab, or the "Gate." The Bábí movement quickly spread across the then Persian Empire against widespread opposition from the Islamic clergy. The Báb himself was executed in 1850 and the community was almost entirely exterminated.

The Báb claimed no finality for his revelation and spoke of a Promised One, "whom God shall make manifest," would soon establish the kingdom of God on the Earth.

Druze

The Druze are a monotheistic ethno-religious community mostly in Syria, Lebanon, Israel and Jordan. It grew out of Shia Islam during the 11th century, and incorporates various elements from Abrahamic religions.

Beliefs of the Druze.

The Druze are a social group as well as a religious sect, but are not a distinct ethnic group. Druze in different states can have radically different lifestyles and tend to be separatist in their treatment of Druze-hood, and their religion differs from mainstream Islam on a number of fundamental points. Some claim to be Muslim, some do not. The Druze faith is said to be secretive and esoteric, but consistent with Islamic principles.

God in the Druze faith

The Druze conception of the deity is one of strict and uncompromising unity. The main Druze doctrine states that God is both *transcendent* and *immanent*, in which he is above all attributes but at the same time he is present. In God, there is only his essence. He is wise, mighty, and just by his own essence. God is "the whole of existence," rather than "above existence." There is neither "how," "when," nor "where" about him; he is incomprehensible.

The concept of theophany is the core spiritual beliefs in the Druze and some other intellectual and spiritual traditions. In a mystical sense, it refers to the light of God experienced by certain mystics who have reached a high level of purity in their spiritual journey. Thus, God is perceived as the divine who manifests His Light in any aspect of the material realm without necessarily becoming incarnate. This is like one's image in the mirror: one is in the mirror but does not become the mirror. Thus, Nature is not God, but Nature is not without God.

The Rastafari movement

The Rastafari movement is an African-based spiritual ideology that arose in the 1930s in Jamaica. It is both a religion and a "Way of Life." Its adherents worship Haile Selassie I, Emperor of Ethiopia from 1930 to 1974.

The name *Rastafari* comes from *Ras Tafari*, the title (Ras) and first name (Tafari Makonnen) of Haile Selassie I before his coronation. In Amharic, *Ras* means "Head," an Ethiopian title equivalent to Duke, and Tafari means a man who is to be feared, or a hero. 'Jah' is the Poetical and Biblical name of God, from a shortened form of *Jehovah* found in Psalms 68:4, King James Version of the Bible. Most adherents see Haile Selassie I as *Jah* or *Jah Rastafari*, who is the second coming of Jesus Christ onto the earth, but others see him simply as God's chosen king on earth.

Members of the Rastafari way of life are known as Rastas, or The Rastafari. Many elements of Rastafari reflect its origins in Jamaica with a predominantly Christian culture. Rastafari holds to many Jewish and Christian beliefs and accepts the existence of a single god, called Jah, who has sent His Son to Earth in the form of Jesus and Selassie. Rastafari accept much of the Bible, while at the same time saying much of its message has been corrupted.

The Rastafari way of life encompasses themes such as the spiritual use of cannabis and the rejection of the degenerate society it calls "Babylon" with its materialism, oppression, and sensual pleasures. It proclaims Zion (Ethiopia), the original birthplace of humankind, and the *Promised Land and Heaven on Earth*. Rastafari also embrace various Afrocentric and Pan-African social and political aspirations. Many Rastafari encourage one another to find faith and inspiration within themselves.

By the late twentieth century, awareness of the Rastafari movement had spread throughout much of the world, largely through reggae music and the international success of Jamaican singer/songwriter Bob Marley. By 1997 there were, according to one estimate, around one million Rastafari faithful worldwide.

Samaritanism

The Samaritan religion exists primarily in Israel and the West Bank and is based on some of the same books used as mainstream Judaism. Samaritan scriptures include the Samaritan version of the Torah, the *emar Markah,* the Samaritan liturgy, and Samaritan law codes and biblical commentaries. Samaritans appear to have several ancient texts of the Torah.

Religious beliefs:
There is one God, YHWH, the same God recognized by the Hebrew prophets.
The Torah was given by God to Moses.
Mount Gerizim, not Jerusalem, is the one true sanctuary chosen by Israel's God.
At the end of days, the dead will be resurrected by *Taheb,* a restorer.
There is a "place" called Paradise or Heaven.
The priests are the interpreters of the law and the keepers of tradition; scholars are secondary to the priesthood.
The authority of post-Torah sections of the Tanakh, and classical Jewish rabbinical works (the Talmud, comprising the Mishnah and the Gemara) are rejected.
They have a significantly different version of the Ten Commandments (for example, their 10th commandment is about the sanctity of Mount Gerizim).

The Dominant Characteristics of Monotheism

We've reviewed the three primary monotheistic religions and four lesser ones so we can determine their main characteristics. Together, their adherents total nearly 4 billion out of the 7 billion of the world's total population.

The following list of reasons to account for this plurality is simply a summary of various historical factors suggested in a wide range of literature:

- Both Christianity and Islam are active proselyting faiths with well-financed and organized missionary programs.

- Over the previous centuries, those nations in which Christianity and Islam were dominant have been expansionary and imperialistic, establishing colonial empires for merchant trade, development and extraction of natural resources (including human slavery), piracy (including holding captives for ransom), and organized robbery.

- Colonial empires created the modern diplomatic bureaucracy, with exchanges of ambassadors (originally hostages held to assure promised actions would be completed). With every "visit" between nations there came the missionaries.

- Islam, even more than Christianity, is bent on the conversion and domination of the world's population. Their religious education (often the only kind allowed) teaches that the Whole Earth belongs of Allah, and to die in His cause is glorious.

- Symbols and Words are important signals to the basic interaction between the religion and the people. Note the prominence of the birth and love in Christianity vs. death and violence in Islam. Even to the extent that the meaning of these respective symbols are not fully expressed in the everyday relation between religious authority and the faithful, their influence is present. The soldier who places greater value on death than life is himself a willing weapon of death and destruction. And armed with explosives, he even becomes a weapon of mass destruction!

The Role of Male Dominance in Monotheism

The following are the age-old instructions common to the Abrahamic religions with regard to male dominance and female subservience. While the last two hundred years have seen considerable change in Europe and America as education of women became normal, and particularly so in the United States where public education is secular and women are employed in higher positions in business, government, science, and the professions, there is less to no change in eastern Islamic countries. Even with modernization, the effects of centuries of repression still are evident, and the battle for equality continues.

- The God of all the seven religions and their sects is male, and is, in fact, the same God. The clergy is almost exclusively male dominant. As evidenced in the Bible and Apocrypha, men have been establishing their dominant hegemony over most religious and spiritual practices for at least 5,000 years.

- Beginning with ancient Judaism, the populace was taught the story of Adam and Eve where Eve "sinned" by accepting an apple (fruit of the Tree of <u>Knowledge</u>) from the serpent, (symbol of the penis representing <u>sexual pleasure</u>). Based on that myth, women for centuries were denied education and access to knowledge, and men and women were both told that any *sexual pleasure for women was evidence of sin and depravity.* Even in Europe, clitoridectomy was practiced to save women from this *compulsion* of sin! Various forms of genital mutation are still performed in 28 countries in northern Africa, the Middle East, and parts of Asia, all for the purpose of controlling women's sexuality to assure the lineage of her children as that of the husband.

- With men dominating women and controlling the religious rites, all ritual terminology was phrased in male terms: God is male, references in ritual and religious instructions is masculine, i.e. "kings," "kingdom," "lord," "master," "his priests," etc. Since the male presides at all religious ceremonies, women can only access God through his male representatives.

- The primary "job" of women was to "go forth, and multiply." Where there is no education to the contrary, that role is dominant and enforced by rape if necessary. Women are instructed that their role is reproductive, and once they reach menopause they no longer have any value other than as servants.

- Women's sexual attractiveness is dangerous—tempting both herself and men into sin and un-wed sex. Thus there is no celebration of women's sexuality and of their power to create new life. Until very recently, it was believed that the total "reproductive seed" was only in male sperm.

- Wedding ceremonies are designed to celebrate the woman's virginity and *pristine white* purity, and her future servitude to the husband. Only in recent years, mostly in North America, is there now a mutual exchange of rings and a mutual promise of faithfulness.

- The system of gender-bias in religious training and the doctrine that only the ordained male can have any direct *experience* (but not two-way communication) with the Divine is disempowering to other men and all women. Religious "Power" is held by an institution of Old Men, variously isolated from the real world. That Power is intended to enrich and benefit the institution and the old men, giving nothing back to the "tithe-payer."

- As these religions are presently practiced, the population is taught that their goal is to leave earth and go to paradise or heaven—a place supposedly clean and pure, and thus more sacred than the ground we stand on, eat from and return to. Mother Earth is seen as dirty, dark, unreliable, and uncontrollable, and of value only for exploitation. Any who experience the Divine in Nature are given denigrating labels such as *simple primitives*, and *dangerous savages*.

- These religions have long practiced sex segregation. In traditional Jewish synagogues, men do not pray in the presence of women, to prevent distraction. Sex segregation in Islam restricts any interaction between men and women. Men and women also worship separately in most mosques. In much of Christianity outside of America and Europe, the texts, leaders, experiences, and rituals are still mostly focused on men, and women remain perceived spiritually and morally deviant from "normality."

- In patriarchal religions, all the leaders are men thought to be strong and assertive, whereas women are properly subservient, passive and weak and thus unfit to be in a high position within religion, government, or business management. Even now some religious leaders consider women to be morally inferior to men, and the source of sexual (hence sinful) temptations. Since God is defined as male, men are more like God than women. Male religious leaders continue to dominate and teach the subordination if not subjugation of women, thus providing justification for much of the pervasive persecution and abuse of women throughout the world. (source: www.religiousconsultation)

- Catholic theology centers about Thomas Aquinas, who like Aristotle taught *that women were a biological mistake.* In the process of generation, these men averred, nature intended male perfection but obviously that didn't always happen and women—due to accidents in the conception process—are deficient and misbegotten. Thomas taught that children and even the insane could be validly ordained as priests—as long as they were male—but adult and healthy women could not be! The Epistle to the Ephesians tells women: "Be subject to your husbands as to the Lord: for the man is the head of the woman, just as Christ also is the head of the church … and [women must be subject] "to their husbands in everything" (Eph. 5:21–24).

- Until recently, there were no rites of passage for girls. In many cultures, and even in parts of Europe and North America, there is no formal sex education, nothing about contraception, no celebration of womanhood, no recognition of Feminine Divinity, no psychological or spiritual understanding of the animus and anima archetypes present in all humanity.

Yes, we should acknowledge changing trends in most of the Western religions as practiced in the Americas and Europe, and perhaps in some of the Middle Eastern sects, but traditions rarely change fast. Even in some of the Christian Protestant sects, women seeking to advance into leaderships positions, or actively asserting their rights to do so, find it necessary to create their own splinter groups.

But, male chauvinism is not confined to the Abrahamic religions of Middle Eastern origin but appear in nearly every *institutional* religion. Nearly all say, one way or another, that male dominance is part of the divine order. Even Hindu scripture states that it is women's nature to "seduce men in this (world); for that reason the wise are never unguarded in (the company of) females" *Laws of Manu (2:213).* "For women are able to lead ... even a learned man, and (to make) him a slave of desire and anger" *(2:214).*

This age-old chauvinism is still very much alive. As former American president Jimmy Carter spoke out on June 28, 2013: religious leaders across the world share the blame for the continuing mistreatment of women. "Religious authorities perpetuate misguided doctrines of male superiority, from the Catholic Church forbidding women from becoming priests to some African cultures mutilating young girls." He described these doctrines as theologically indefensible, and that they "contribute to a political, social and economic structure where political leaders passively accept violence against women, a worldwide sex slave trade, and inequality in the workplace and classroom." President Carter spoke forcefully: "There is a great aversion among men leaders and some women leaders to admit that this is something that exists, that it's serious and that it's troubling and should be addressed courageously." Source: Associated Press in the New York Times as reported in the St. Paul Pioneer Press, June 29, 2013.

This ancient fear of a man being seduced by a woman contrasts with the modern and ancient glorification of women's sensuality as recognized and valued in ancient shamanic Tantra and Taoism, most indigenous cultures, and as freely experienced and expressed in healthy relationships between mature men and women. While the Bible says (Ephesians 5:22): *Wives, submit to your husbands...* modern women have their own interpretation of that and other antique Bible verses.

WHAT WENT WRONG?

"What went wrong?" and "What is still wrong?" We can't change the past, but we can learn from it and better see what changes can be made and what actions should be taken.

Most people don't question the status quo: Born a Christian, die a Christian; born a Jew, die a Jew; born a Muslim, die a Muslim. Same for Buddhism, Hinduism, Shinto-ism, and any other "ism" or "none at all." That was the universal expectation until a few hundred years ago when education became general enough for people to know about other religions, to seek answers from science different than from religion, to learn to think rationally and logically, and to question "givens" and "automatic assump-tions." And with the vast migrations of people leaving ancestral lands for new worlds of opportunity, "born as" was replaced by Personal Choice.

Not only are the major Abrahamic religious dominant over half the world's popu-lation, but western culture formed around Judeo-Christian identity is itself domi-nate throughout most of the world—*despite religion not having anything to do with it.* First with the Industrial Revolution, then the Information Age and now transition into a revolutionary New Age, Euro-American systems prevail in finance, business and commerce, in communication, entertainment the arts, in science, technology and engineering, in manufacturing, transportation and energy production, in food pro-duction, nutrition science and intensive resource management, in medicine, health and life extension science, in national defense, space technology and exploration, in education, training, and knowledge management, in climate and weather science and emergency management, and more. And much of this has become international in scope and "local" in application—there is no colonialism about it in this electronically inter-connected world civilization.

Only the Islamic Middle East lags behind in this new cultural reformation, and bitterly opposes everything modern (except weapons) as Western and "Satanic." Even though the Taliban and other of the most fundamentalist Muslims claim to respect education and women, they blow-up schools and persecute girls and women seeking knowledge—just as mythical Eve was punished for accepting the "fruit of the Tree of Knowledge," and teach male children that it is glorious to die in wars to forcibly con-vert the world to Islam.

In 2012, the whole world heard about Malala, a young Muslim girl in Pakistan shot in the head because she encouraged other girls to go to school. She survived, and was able to speak before the United Nations on her 16th birthday about the importance of secular education for Islamic women. She said:

> "The Taliban thought that the bullets would silence us, but they failed. The
> extremists are afraid of books and pens. The power of education frightens
> them. The power and voice of women frightens them. That is why they

killed many female teachers and polio workers. That is why they are blasting schools every day. They are afraid of change, afraid of the equality that we will bring to our society. One child, one teacher, one pen, and one book can change the world."

In the meantime, more than 800 schools were attacked since 2009 just in northwest Pakistan, and women teachers and rights activists were murdered. In June 2013, a suicide bomber near the Afghan border blew up 14 female students.

Rather than regional resource and economic development for the betterment of their populations, the radical Islamists retain tribalism and turn to piracy on the high seas, demand ransom for ship cargos and people alike, cultivate opium over food crops, claim that payment of interest on borrowed money is evil, and challenge all international efforts for health, education, and human rights as Western colonialism.

We must call for at least universal primary school education for all children regardless of gender, race, religion or nationality

Within the Islamic dominated countries of the Middle East, there is great variation from the more highly educated populations of Iran, Turkey, and Egypt to the backwardness of the Taliban in Afghanistan and portions of Pakistan; from the economically developing Bahrain, Turkey, and United Arab Emirates to the economic unraveling of Egypt 2012-2013 under the Muslim Brotherhood, the challenge is not the variations in natural resources but Islam itself—no better illustrated than in the direct contrast between non-Islamic Israel, and then with Islamic takeover Egypt. Saudi Arabia's oil wealth has yet to be translated into an economically developing nation with an entrepreneurial middle class. Oil has made the royal family rich, but instead of real development, they passively invest their wealth in America. In Iran, the oil wealth is wasted on building nuclear "power" and supporting terrorist activities around the world. In Egypt the Muslim Brotherhood came into political power and was destroying the economy and the middle class by its sectarian bungling.

The individual is subverted to control by authority controlling the populations, and the quest is toward *Jihad,* war and terror, in the drive for world domination.

The Abraham religions claim that "God" created the Universe and all within it, and thus we are obligated to *worship* that God as our Father. Variously, they've taught that a failure to "properly" worship (per the particular religious laws) would result in punishment, and—for the most part until the Age of Enlightenment in the Western

World—that punishment was carried out by the religious hierarchy or its designated political agent, in the most barbaric manner of torture and maim.

Male and Female He Created Them

In every man there is a woman; in every woman there is a man. In psychology these are acknowledged as *Anima* and *Animus*, archetypes that are fundamental to balanced emotional, mental and spiritual development. When women are denigrated and persecuted by men, those men are wounding their own inner selves, and callously denying women self-development beyond childhood. The result is a population of physically mature but psychologically stunted adults easily manipulated by authoritarian leaders into beliefs of persecution, paranoia, meaningless and unjustifiable wars, suicidal terrorist acts, rape and mutilation of women and children, destruction of cultural antiquities, and *belief that all would be well if it weren't for them!*—*Whoever the leader identifies as "them."* There is no self-responsibility, only action on orders. One who follows orders can himself do no wrong. Without self-awareness and self-responsibility, there can be no real self-consciousness, and hence no personal growth and no spiritual development.

If we do consider that half the world's population adheres to such denigration of the Feminine, and then presume that half the world's population is women, that suggests that this old Abrahamic denial of Feminine value is a negative force that has been holding back most of humanity's full flowering for nearly all that last 4,000 years. Only in the Western world and mainly just in the last 200 years, has this ugly heritage begun to be replaced by a *Whole Spirit of Love and Growth* countering that old culture of repression, self-hate, and enforced ignorance; a culture that repressed the individual by super-imposing an institutional theocracy that led to religious wars, to the Holy Inquisition, to the Nazi and Soviet Communist movements, and that still may ignite a world war centered on the goal of world domination by one religious cult.

The Greatness that once was

And yet, once upon a time, there was greatness in the Middle East: the glories of the Ancient Egyptian Culture and Religion, advanced technology and architecture, astronomy and agriculture, and sophisticated military prowess; achievements of the early Arab culture in science and mathematics, in poetry and music, alchemy and philosophy; and of the great artistic and architectural achievements in Ancient Persia.

What greater glory there could be if we were all united in individual freedom and responsibility, with innovation and achievement, where Spirit could flower! That Greatness that once was can come again across the Whole World, blossoming in every person, releasing the human soul from the imposed bondage of sectarian denial. We <u>can</u> do it.

The Choice is Yours, and it is in truth Personal

Now we can ask what it is that people want and expect from religion and spirituality in an age where religion is no longer simply imposed by birth in a particular culture, or as the result of militant action enforcing an embrace of a religion of mental and emotional enslavement.

Christianity and Islam, together, account for half of all "believers," and even though they don't see eye-to-eye and are, in fact—increasingly competitive and endangering world peace—we need to understand their systemic failure to address the spiritual interests of their followers.

While both religions originate in Judaism, and all three Abrahamic religions source to the same One God, even though under three different names, the first fundamental difference is that Judaism is not expansion oriented while the other two are. Judaism is more concerned with the "racial purity" and defending the safety of Israel's population than it is with expansion other than economic growth. Jews are "the chosen people" and that itself is a "gift from God."

> It is this that is sought more than anything else: the feeling of being connected to a "Power" greater than Self. For the Abrahamic religions, that Power is only outside Self and beyond Humanity. For older, and newer, Shamanic religions, the Power is both within Self and beyond Self.

The Abrahamic religions, and most others, also provide a dual system of rituals recognizing birth, puberty, marriage, parenthood, and death. These rituals are both celebrations of the events, and likewise "bindings" of the individual to the faith. Thus, there is a certain "give and take," actually a kind of contractual relationship in which the religion performs a service desired by the person.

These services included: a formal recognition of the new child by gender and name; a coming of age ritual that was sometimes accompanied by actual guidance about sex, but more often in such couched language as to be meaningless of all except that girls were expected to remain chaste until married; a marriage ceremony that sometimes included certification that the bride was a virgin, and committing both partners to mutual faithfulness and separate obligations of husbandly and wifely duties; and finally a celebration of the life of the newly deceased with a place for burial and a "promise of eternal life" after death.

Variously, in earlier years, additional services might be offered: perhaps a retirement home or a place to "park" the sick and elderly unable to care for themselves; counseling services to couples or mainly to women having difficulties in married life, although such counseling often was a reminder to the woman to service the men sexually, to remain married despite abuse and neglect, and to willingly suffer and remain passive; and the opportunity to serve the Church in music and song for those with such abilities; and, of course, with money.

Many of these various services, and others, are now available through a choice of non-religious public services, and professional consultants, and some of the newer non-Abrahamic religions and spiritualties. Today, increasingly, burial is being replaced by cremation and cremation is often allowed even in Catholic funeral services.

But most importantly, as represented by the above services, there is the sense of "community" that the place of worship provided. Ideally, it was in the immediate neighborhood, within walking distance or accessible by horse. As a community center, it was a social center for picnics, sing-alongs, dances (unless forbidden by that particular sect), classes and lectures (usually religious, but sometimes cultural), and sometimes there were opportunities for question and answer sessions.

Today, particularly so in urban areas and with the increased urbanization of populations everywhere, new communities are replacing or adding to the old single choice of a religious center. Rather than a single community center, there are multiple choices based in individual interests and needs—ranging from study groups, adult and remedial education, language classes (especially in English, Spanish, and Chinese), Yoga studios, Health Studios and Gyms, Science Museums and various ethnic cultural centers, and—of course—popular bars where people mingle at the end of the work day.

With increased education, and with the experience of personal empowerment through successful work and professional achievement, "all of the above" is no longer sufficient. What is missing is the sense of personal Spirit, and answers to the bigger questions—some of which arise because the "universe" is suddenly much larger and the Earth is no longer its center—and the growing knowledge that each person is more than just a physical body. And, yes, that sex is more than reproduction of the species, and—yes—that it is pleasurable to a woman and that mutual sexual enjoyment is foundational to a good relationship and also to the health of Body, Mind and Soul. And, with people living longer and healthier, that well-being of Body, Mind, and Soul is more important than ever, and of special concern to those people now able to retire with sufficient income to enjoy the "Golden Years."

Many of these "Golden Age" retirees become interested in "spirituality" and find study groups not only for various of the world religions but even more for spiritual and psychic development through the study and practice of chakra systems, martial arts, the Kabbalah, the various new and alternative religions we will explore in the next chapter, systems of self-improvement including meditation, self-hypnosis, visualization, vibratory energy healing through touch and sound, and exploratory travels to the pyramids of Egypt and Mexico, the sacred circles of Britain, France and, the western United States, the ancient sites in Peru and Easter Island, and other tours exposing seekers to actual experiences of fire walking, transcending pain, participating in Voodoo and other Spiritist ecstatic inducing ceremonies, and other means of opening "doors and windows" to the extraordinary beyond the borders of the ordinary once the exclusive province of the priestly castes of the old religions.

In the next chapter we will look at "Spirit & the New Age Religions" and see that religion does not need to be "institutionalized," that two-way Spiritual Communication is possible and does not need "group support," and does not require a personal teacher nor a charismatic leader. And realizing that a feeling of *dependence* on an external spiritual authority or guide can interfere with your own direct spiritual infusion and communication whether with a spiritual entity or your own Higher Self.

The most important lesson we must learn from this review of what went wrong with the world's dominant religions is the necessity to take back control! You can't give control over your life to a theocratic institution nor to a distant master. You cannot abandon your own person-hood, nor can you give up responsibility for your own decisions. You need to control your own powers by not giving others control over yourself—not physically, not emotionally, not mentally, not of your will, and not of you spirit. All power must flow through your Body and Personality—under Management of your Higher Self—the incarnate representative for your discarnate Soul. Your Immortal Soul grows through your life journey—life after life and lives between lives.

Ultimately, Self-Control, Self-Initiative, and Self-Responsibility are the foundation to your Self-Empowerment—without which, you would be nothing!

RITUAL TO INVOKE YOUR HIGHER SELF

A very simple procedure is to simply relax, preferably in a semi-reclining position, in an environment as free from external distractions as possible. Establish a deep, rhythmic, but non-stressful, breathing cycle. Close your eyes, center your attention at the base of your spine and slowly feel your essence rising upward to focus in the very center of your brain.

When you feel established at this higher level, silently speak to your higher self:

> *"I invoke my Highest Self and ask for Strength and Purpose to Become More than I am, and All that I can be. I open by heart and mind to all true guidance to help me in my quest to serve and fulfill the purpose of this life. I am blessed by your presence. Thank you."*

Stay relaxed, breathing evenly and comfortable, and feel the infusion of energy and peace. Know that your Higher Self is always with you. You need not return your essence to the base. Just let be.

No complex words nor symbols were needed; no images; no words of power or names of deity. Just be clear and keep your focus. Intention accomplishes miracles.

MEDITATION

"What does it mean to you that your Spirit or Soul is continuing to evolve, and that Humanity, as a whole, is also continuing to evolve?"

Sources:

http://www.atlantisinsights.net/Timeline.html

1. Ann Moura (writing as "Aoumiel"): *Dancing Shadows—The Roots of Western Religious Beliefs*, 1994, Llewellyn

2. http://www.ctrforchristcon.org/christ-consciousness.asp

3. Source: Hurnard, J.: *The Great Book—The New Testament of our Lord Jesus Christ in Plain English*, 2005, Destiny Image Publishers,

4. Khalifa, R.: *Quran, Hadith, and Islam,* 2010, Amazon Digital

http://listverse.com/2009/04/13/10-christ-like-figures-who-pre-date-jesus/

Laws of Manu 2:213, 2:214.

Epistle to the Ephesians (Eph. 5:21-24)

Associated Press in the New York Times as reported in the St. Paul Pioneer Press, June 29, 2013

http://www.investigativeproject.org/documents/misc/20.pdf

www.religiousconsultation)

11

THE NEW AGE RELIGIONS

Spiritual, but Not Religious

What Jesus said about public prayer: "And when thou prayest, thou shalt not be as the hypocrites are for they love to pray standing in the...corners of the streets, that they may be seen of men...When thou prayest, enter into thy closet, and when thou hast shut the door, pray to thy Father which is in secret...But when ye pray, use not vain repetitions, as the heathen do: for they think they shall be heard for their much speaking." Matt. 6:5–8

We don't really know that the *historic* Jesus said this instruction to pray in private, in a closet with the door shut. It seems to contradict the *mythic* Jesus, or at least what the Church and other Christian institutions have done in building their magnificent cathedrals and mega-churches, preaching to millions via radio and television, and raising billions to send missionaries to convert the innocent.

However, if Matthew is accurately reporting the historic Jesus, then this guidance seem far more "New Age" *Personal* and *Spiritual but not Religious* than the political and financial empires of the Piscean Age constructed to bind people together in sheep-like masses. Empires without Spirit!

Some scholars believe that the "real" Jesus and that presented in Christianity are not one and the same.

Those Old Time Religions that Lost their Spirit!
The "old time religions" discussed in the previous chapter are distinguished by such characteristics as:

The Ten Characteristics of the Old Time Religions that Lost their Spirit

1. They are all *monotheistic.* Despite varying additional deific elements such as angels and archangels, personal guides and guardians, saints, spirits of place and power, various mythic demons and "satanic" powers, etc., and the Catholic emphasis on the Holy Trinity somewhat corresponding to the Kabbalistic *Ain, Ain Soph,* and *Ain Soph Aur,* these religions acknowledge only One God.

2. Their "One God" is male.

3. All have a common "mythic" origin in the Middle East, sharing one common founding "father" named Abraham. The Hebrew Bible states that Abraham was born 1812 BCE, exactly 1,948 years after Creation, and that he lived for 175 years. However, the historicity (and dating) of Abraham and other Biblical prophets and figures is increasingly held in doubt by modern scholarship. After all, *a myth is a myth,* and not always historically or factually "real," *for that is not their purpose.*

4. While each has a unique "story" of its individual beginning, all contain common mythic elements involving messengers, commandments, miracles, relationships to its followers and to its geographic neighboring unbelievers. These mythic elements lack historic and factual veracity, *for that is not their purpose.*

5. Despite various protestations of Love and Peace, all have practiced wars of aggression, territorial expansion, forced conversion, and "justified" acts of torture and murder against internal unbelievers and terror and mass killings against external enemies. *For that is their purpose.*

6. All are organized belief systems with both a "theology" frozen in time, and a set of religious laws from that same era administered by an establishment of priests and other authorities empowered to search out and punish the unfaithful. Even in democratic America, there is a movement to replace our Constitutional and human laws with Abrahamic religious laws proclaimed to be "superior" to and above science.

7. These religions are monopolistic in intent and seek to bring all humans into their fold and then to impose their theology and religious laws on everyone by dominating education, politics, government, economy, and military while denigrating all independent thought. *For that is their purpose.*

8. All monopolies seek to eliminate competition, and hence lead toward destructive conflict. These religions forbid all Spiritual Communication other than

prescribed rote prayer and participation in public ritual. In Islam, daily public prayer is so prevalent that political control over the population is easily facilitated and policed. Likewise in Islam, "Church" and State are by definition united so religious law is the "Law of the Land" in theory and intention if not always in practice. All foreign nationals are subject to the local religious law.

9. There seems to be no place for the Human Spirit in these religions. The "Immortal Soul" is acknowledged but mostly in the negative sense of something that will "burn in hell for all eternity" if the individual fails to conform to the religious law. Yet Catholicism has its "Holy Ghost" alternating with "Holy Spirit," sometimes identified as feminine but usually not. In Islam, the Soul is a secret only known by Allah after death.

10. In all Abrahamic religions, *Intellect is subordinate to required belief.* Rational thought is a contradiction to faith, and hence is "Satanic" in principle. Emotional manipulation of the faithful is managed by clergy in their roles of "Father," Mentor, Confessor, Enforcer, Administrator of punishments, Absolver of "sins," and Spiritual Leader.

The Beginnings of the New Age, and of New Age Religion and Spirituality

History of the Term: New Age

It was poet, artist, mystic William Blake who described a coming era of spiritual and artistic advancement as "New Age" in his 1809 preface to Milton a Poem by stating, " ... when the New Age is at leisure to pronounce, all will be set right ... "

In the context of modern usage, the term *New Age* appeared in Madame Blavatsky's *Magnum Opus,* "The Secret Doctrine," published in 1888. In 1894 the terms was used in the title of a weekly journal of Christian liberalism and socialism, later sold to a group of socialist writers headed by Alfred Richard Orage and Holbrook Jackson in 1907. Contributors included H. G. Wells, George Bernard Shaw, and William Butler Yeats; the magazine became a forum for politics, literature, and the arts. Between 1908 and 1914, it was instrumental in pioneering the British avant-garde from Vorticism* to Imagism. Orage met P. D. Ouspensky, a follower of Gurdjieff, in 1914 and began correspondence with Harry Houdini; he became less interested in literature and art with an increased focus on mysticism and other spiritual topics; the magazine was sold in 1921. According to Brown University, The New Age (Journal) " ... helped to shape modernism in literature and the arts from 1907 to 1922."

* Vorticism was short-lived modernist British movement in geometric and abstract art and Futurist literature in the early 20th century. It was featured in a magazine called *BLAST.*

Idealistic and Futuristic, Esoteric and Philosophical

The term, *New Age,* really has a breadth that is idealistic and futuristic as well as esoteric, philosophical, and "theosophical" in the original sense of that term:

> "The theosophist seeks to understand the mysteries of the universe and the bonds that unite the universe, humanity and the divine. The goal of theosophy is to explore the origin of divinity and humanity, and the world. From investigation of those topics theosophists try to discover a coherent description of the purpose and origin of the universe."
>
> *(From Wikipedia)*

New Age Spirituality is still called a "Western Metaphysical Movement," but it is becoming more global because of its pertinence to revolutionary developments in a wide range of applications.

The New Age: Enlightenment, Reason, and Universal Education

While its Aquarian energies began to manifest in the 17th and 18th centuries' Ages of Enlightenment and Reason, it was the spread of free, public education from its beginning with Boston's "Latin School" in 1635 and then compulsory education throughout all of Massachusetts in 1642 that marked the transition from elitist to universal education. That was followed by universal application across all of America through the political efforts of Unitarians who believed that "salvation" was not to be found in churches but attained through government provided secular, non-sectarian, free and compulsory education, freeing children from the earlier Calvinist fear-inducing religious indoctrination, and leading to reason-based moral perfectibility. The Unitarian efforts led to the enactment of laws for centralized public-funded education controlled by the states rather than churches across all of America. The whole world followed, with notable exceptions.

Among other developing influences in the early 20th century was that of American clairvoyant Edgar Cayce whose channeling and healing work led to his founding of the Association for Research and Enlightenment.

The psychologist Carl Jung was a proponent of the concept of the Age of Aquarius. In a letter to his friend Peter Baynes in August 1940, Jung wrote:

"This year reminds me of the enormous earthquake in 26 B.C. that shook down the great temple of Karnak. It was the prelude to the destruction of all temples, because a new time had begun. 1940 is the year when we approach the meridian of the first star in Aquarius. It is the premonitory earthquake of the New Age ..."

Boston's Latin School. The beginning of public education in America.

Man's Purpose is to acquire More and More Knowledge

Alice Bailey in *Discipleship in the New Age* (1944) also used the term New Age in reference to the transition from the astrological age of Pisces to Aquarius. Another early user of the term was the American artist, mystic, and philosopher Walter Russell, who wrote:

" ... this New Age philosophy of the spiritual re-awakening of man ... Man's purpose in this New Age is to acquire more and more knowledge ..."
(From his essay Power Through Knowledge, 1944)

In the "New Age"* that began to strike popular interest in the 1960s, there is no official creed, sacred book, rigid and unifying theology and liturgy, and no charismatic leadership. New Age historian Nevill Drury describes it as a spiritual movement "drawing on both Eastern and Western spiritual and metaphysical traditions and infusing them with influences from self-help and motivational psychology, health, parapsychology, consciousness research and quantum physics".

> * "New Age" has become a somewhat denigrated term by association with some *fluffy* people, but it is important to recognize it as a "changing of the guard," so to speak. *Zodiacal Ages* are cyclic realities *marking* changes in the dominant energies that influence and characterize our planet's consciousness (and all that lives in and on "her") for approximately 2,400 years. There is no sudden shift occurring exactly on a certain date and time because we are dealing with a far grander scale than your kitchen clock and calendar. Instead, we have a transition phase of several hundred years of gradual cultural and philosophical changes taking place.

Our entry into the "Aquarian Age" is reflected in the intellectual changes that began rather dramatically a few hundred years ago in the movement from the repressive, faith-bound, anti-intellectualism of Pisces into the Aquarian expectation that rationality and science will bring an age of technological progress and economic plenty. Already the "new world" is vastly different and the new times have barely begun.

Still, changes are not easy, and there will be pain to old institutions and antiquarian thinking, and there will have to be a time of healing to correct the planetary abuse done in the belief of man's (male) dominance over Mother Nature and the enslavement and murder of millions of "unbelievers" conducted by church and authoritarian state over the past two thousand years.

Spirituality without Borders or Confining Dogmas

The New Age impulse is to create, what Drury describes as "a spirituality without borders or confining dogmas" that is inclusive and pluralistic, and holding to "a holistic worldview" that includes both science and spirituality"*and embraces a number of alternative sciences considered fringe by some.

> * Drury, N. (2004), *The New Age: Searching for the Spiritual Self*, London, England, UK: Thames and Hudson

Carl Jung too spoke of rigid religious dogmas as stifling and denying to the spirituality necessary to growth and the "individuation" process he saw as vital to psychological health. Jung emphatically believed that the New Age/Aquarian Age had arrived.

New Age energies and interests dramatically increased in the second half of the 20th century and it is now recognized that many of its practices are eclectically adapted from Taoism, Hinduism, and Theosophy, as well as the Kabbalah, Hermeticism, Gnosticism, pre-Aryan Tantra, Europe's pre-Christian Paganism, various indigenous shamanic traditions, African derived Spiritism, and include modern versions of Shamanism, Wicca, Ceremonial and Ritual Magick, Practical Magick for self-improvement, Yoga, Martial Arts, the use of meditation, self-hypnosis, past-life regression, channeling, astrology, palmistry, Tarot and other divinatory systems, lunar and organic horticulture, vegetarianism, and alternative medical and health practices, and life styles that are *Nature-based*, self-sufficient, sustainable, and generally less materialistic and superficial while favoring secular and liberal thinking.

"Born Again" Witchcraft and Paganism

The Movement grew in popularity during the 1970s and 1980s through the re-birth of European Witchcraft as modern Wicca and the rediscovery of its essential shamanic roots and practices, different Pagan traditions, and the teachings of various metaphysical groups that has long existed in various esoteric forms and the secret practices of philosophers and "initiates" stretching back many millennia. Beginning with Gnosticism in the second century C.E., New Age ideas have continued through a variety of less secretive groups including Rosicrucianism, Freemasonry, Magickal Lodges, and Theosophy.

While there is no "standard doctrine" within the New Age Movement, many of the teachings focus on individual autonomy, relativism, and spiritualism. Unlike the Abrahamic and other religions, the New Age emphasis is on the *individual* and not on the "masses"* per se. There are informal and spontaneous groups of people united by an event, and there are more formal groups united by interest or purpose into lodges, covens, orders, and societies, but the greater emphasis is on individuals by themselves sharing interest through widely available books and on-line courses, or coming together in conferences, sponsored classes, lectures and discussion groups. Everyone is seen as an individual.

> * "Masses"—With this word we refer to large blocks of people—a "mass"—seen simply is an object to be manipulated, sold to, massacred, considered as a resource for money and power, or otherwise objectified without concern for character, personhood, or their own relationships, desires, etc.

Heightened Spiritual Consciousness and Personal Transformation

New Agers share an enthusiasm for the creation of a new era (or "New Age") exemplified by harmony, enlightenment, and "good will" purpose.* Even though there are few clear delineations within the New Age community, several common themes unify the movement. The most fundamental of these is that the New Age has already arrived and initiated a heightened spiritual consciousness through personal transformation, healing, and growth leading toward broad economic and social action resulting in worldwide programs to eradicate hunger, sickness, poverty, racism, and sexism, and ultimately to the end of religious conflict and war.

> * "Good will purpose"—There is a belief in "good will" energized by purpose as a positive force. Even without other action, donating of money or services, *positive thinking* is believed to have the power to bring about "change of heart," a reduction in violence, positive results, etc.

A world-wide, wake-up, Metaphysical Movement

Today (2013), there are estimates ranging from a few million New Age "followers" to many millions when others of the Metaphysical "movement" who consider their interests as Spiritual are included. Indeed, the New Age is really a worldwide movement toward *alternative spiritual practices* and concepts, many of which are ancient and indigenous, and non-militant, non-controlling, and non-proselytizing. From one perspective, the "New Age" is a fresh and eclectic look at all spiritual practices, philosophies, and sciences. It is not a "religion," and maybe not even a "movement" despite some efforts to politicize it. New Age is not something old dressed in new fashions, but something genuinely new even as it draws upon all sources for their best, and raises our consciousness to go beyond past failures.

What Institutionalized Religion cannot provide

All in all, New Age spiritual beliefs, practices and lifestyles do have a near "religious" identification for many of their followers, even as mainstream culture and most *Western and Middle Eastern religious institutions consider these same studies and practices as anathema!* Rather than the compelling binding together under authoritarian guidance, this New Age identity is "Spiritual, but not Religious." The New Age is seeking that which institutional religion does not offer and cannot provide: True Communication with one's own Spiritual Self, and other Spiritual Selves and Beings.

Origins of New Age Practices

On the one hand, the New Age is essentially an "occult" movement, while on the other hand it is the direct opposite of the old meaning of that word as *secret* and *hidden*. New Age beliefs and practices are blatantly public, open-minded, participatory and invitational. Rather than antiquarian, it is in the forefront of science, environmentalism, women's rights, life extension, democratic principles, high-tech, and all that contributes toward the modern open society.

As described in Wikipedia, the origins of many "occult" practices derive from medieval astrology and alchemy and the writings of Paracelsus, in Renaissance interests in Hermeticism, in 18th century mysticism and in the spiritualism of Swedish scientist and clairvoyant Emanuel Swedenborg. The unique discoveries of Franz Mesmer in animal magnetism and then hypnotism led toward the scientific investigation of spiritual and psychic phenomena in the 19th and early 20th centuries.

From Ancient Wisdom to Futurist Science

Authors Godfrey Higgins, Eliphas Lévi, H. P. Blavatsky, and George Gurdjieff articulated specific histories, cosmologies, and some of the basic philosophical principles that have influenced the movement. Beyond the advent of Spiritualism, there was a renewed esoteric impulse found in the work of Alice Bailey, P.D. Ouspensky, Manly Palmer Hall, Colin Wilson and organizations such as the Theosophical Society, Rosicrucian Fellowship, and the Society of Inner Light. It gained further momentum in the 1960s through rapidly increasing sales of books on self-help, serious astrology, witchcraft, practical magic, herbalism, magical philosophy, and Tarot. Books by Raymond Buckland, Scott Cunningham, Anodea Judith, Noel Tyl, Donald Tyson, Jonn Mumford, and co-authors Denning and Phillips. And then there were the various Indian gurus leaving a legacy of Hatha Yoga and Meditation practices that has endured and grown. In addition, television documentaries and entertainment led to a further opening to Eastern interest in Yoga, Martial Arts, Feng Shui, and various practices of Indian, Chinese and Japanese medicine.

New Age interests include elements of older spiritual and religious traditions ranging from Shamanism, Pantheism, Polytheism, Chinese folk-magic, Tantra and Taoism to such 19th century metaphysical movements as New Thought and the alternative medicine movements of chiropractic and naturopathy themselves rooted in Transcendentalism and Mesmerism, and then newer eclectic studies of Quantum Physics, Mythology, Jungian Psychology, the Gaia Hypothesis, Archaeo-astronomy,

Ecology and Environmentalism, UFOs, Parapsychology, and the perennial interest in Egyptian history, religion and magic, and its foundation in the mythology of ancient wisdom and technology that reappears in changing form throughout Western history.

From a "sub-culture" to a Dominant World Movement

Widespread usage of the term New Age increased in the mid-1970s as larger numbers of people began to think that the broad similarity between a wide variety of alternative ideas and pursuits did constitute a single "movement." At this same time, thousands of small metaphysical book shops, herbalists, craft people and gift stores began to identify themselves as "New Age retailers," and were soon joined by national book chains and other merchandisers under the New Age umbrella. The large-scale activities surrounding the Harmonic Convergence in 1987*, resulted in the mass-media further popularizing "New Age" as the label for all the alternative spiritual practices such as meditation, channeling, crystal healing, astral projection, psychic experience, holistic health, simple living, and environmentalism; and belief in such phenomena as Earth mysteries, ancient astronauts, extraterrestrial life, unidentified flying objects, crop circles, and reincarnation.

> * The Harmonic Convergence of August 16-17 1987 was the world's first global synchronized visual meditation. It marked a planetary alignment of the Sun, Moon, and six planets as identified in the Mayan Calendar. As the culmination of nine "hell cycles that began when Cortes landed in Mexico 468 years earlier leading to the destruction of one of the world's greatest civilization, it was intended to inaugurate a 25-year period of planetary cleansing ending December 21, 2012 that would lead to world peace. Or to the "end of the World *as we know it.*" While World Peace still seems a distant promise, that of beneficial change is still with us. With millions of people participating in meditation during the event, and others continuing to meditate with that world vision, many proclaimed it a true spiritual manifestation of the new Aquarian Age.

The Age of Aquarius

Other events further raised public awareness of the New Age subculture, but perhaps none so far reaching as *Hair: The American Tribal Love-Rock Musical* (1967). Other major factors included publication of Linda Goodman›s best-selling astrology books *Sun Signs* (1968) and *Love Signs* (1978); the release of Shirley MacLaine›s book *Out on a Limb* (1983); The appearance of channelers Jane Roberts (Seth Material), Helen Schucman (*A Course in Miracles*), and J. Z. Knight (Ramtha); the "inner dialogue" writings of Neale Donald Walsch (*Conversations with God*) contributed to the movement's growth. Other relevant New Age writers include James Redfield, Eckhart Tolle, Barbara Marx Hubbard, Marianne Williamson, and Deepak Chopra. While J. Gordon Melton has emphasized personal aspects, Mark Satin, Theodore Roszak, Marilyn Ferguson, and others have described New Age as a values-based sociopolitical movement.

An open "movement," not an Institutionalized Religion

Being non-institutional, the New Age sets no requirements or restrictions on one's beliefs about reincarnation, the attainment of psychic powers, growth into higher consciousness, and higher planes of being and manifestation. Some believe consciousness persists after death, and that the afterlife exists for further learning through the surviving personality, lives between lives, and re-birth into a new body and personality. Unlike the Buddhist or Hindu concepts, there is no desire to end this process, and there are further beliefs that all individuals can choose where they reincarnate, or that the system will choose the best reincarnation for each person. There is no belief in the traditional Christian hell or the Islamic concept of eternal damnation. There is a general abstract idea of Deity or Creator/Source superseding the need for an anthropomorphize deity.

A New World Culture beginning the First Global Civilization

Common beliefs associated with the advent of the Aquarian Age include the broad worldwide extension of democratic forms of government, of all human rights including the abolition of all forms of slavery, child labor, and abusive working conditions, the adoption of universal common law and intellectual property rights, with progress towards their enforcement by international courts and police, innovative technologies, computers and the Internet with storage of data in "clouds," widespread availability of electric power and satellite communications, world health programs and the distribution of condoms and empowering women to make birthing choices, overcoming wide-spread genital mutilation in young girls and other age-old traditions of abuse and denial of hygiene education.

Great Changes in Human Consciousness

Concurrent to many educational aid programs from developed nations to developing nations is the esoteric belief that we are living on the threshold of a great changes in human consciousness, and some perception of increases in animal intelligence and communication between human and animal. And perhaps recognition of consciousness in plant and sea life and communication of both thought and feelings.

Old Limitations on "What is Possible" are disappearing

We believe each and all Life has a purpose and there is a cosmic goal and a belief that all entities are (knowingly or unknowingly) cooperating towards this goal. We have a belief in synchronicity—that coincidence has spiritual meaning and lessons to teach those open to them. Everything is universally connected and participates in the same energy. We accept women's complete equality in all aspects of society including religious functions and leadership, and the complete acceptance of one's sexual orientation, gender identity, and all forms of fully informed and consensual sexual fantasy and play among mature and responsible adults.

Thought Creates and Emotion Energizes

Astrology and other forms of character analysis and situational forecasting may be used in understanding, interpreting, and organizing information about personality, human affairs, and other terrestrial matters. Positive thinking supported by affirmations, visualizations and energetic charging will—when properly applied—achieve success in anything, based on the knowledge that "Thought Creates and Emotion Energizes." As one begins to focus awareness and consciousness, "reality" starts shifting and materializing the positive intentions and aspects of life. A critical mass of people with focused consciousness can bring sudden change in broad areas of a society. With such realization comes individual responsibility both to take part in positive creative activity and to assure that ethical and moral considerations are applied.

Body, Emotion, Mind, Spirit—and Consciousness

Ultimately, we believe that the human mind has much greater potential than that communally ascribed to it and can even override now accepted physical reality. While we are a union of physical, etheric, emotional, mental, and spiritual bodies, it is through Mind that we focus Consciousness where and as needed. Real *Spiritual Communication* unites our being through goals of purpose and acts of intention. We communicate between our own *inner* "brains," organs, and centres as well as we do *outer* entities and beings. Intentional Communication is what identifies the *conscious* Human Person from *unconscious* autonomic activities within our being and that of external beings, entities, animals, creatures at all levels, natural forces, elementals and spiritual beings.

Mind projects purpose and intention, organizes energy and force to turn vision into reality.

Who are the New Agers?

New Age Demographics: New Age followers are generally relatively affluent and well-educated. They avoid "compulsive consumerism" and are commonly interested in living a sustainable lifestyle favoring "green" ecological initiatives that reduce humanity's negative impact on the Earth's natural resources. Even living apart, they have a sense of community through shared interests and on-line communication, and have an interest in the concept of intentional communities where people come together to live and work in a communal lifestyle. It has been estimated that as many as 30 percent of Americans share substantial elements of New Age beliefs—including the growing interest in alternative and holistic health practices, natural and locally grown foods, crafting, an increasing support for "smallness" over "bigness" in business, finance, government, and institutions that presume all individuals must fit into larger and larger rigidly defined categories. Human growth and development is more important than the focus on pure economic growth and the resulting "poverty" of ethics, personal values, recognition of personal needs, and response to signals of corporate and regulatory abuse and institutional failures.

Religion and Spirituality in a book on Spiritual Communication

Many readers of this book are "seekers" wanting to communicate with "Spirit," or with particular Spirits of the formerly living people, or with Spiritual Entities including Angels, Deities, Elemental Forces, and Spiritual Parts of their own Self.

In various ways, we have provided techniques for these various communications. However, no matter how detailed or how abstract these are, you have to do the work. And we've pointed out that it is work that is well worthwhile, that it is part of the Great Plan for your own growth and development, and that it will contribute to you *Becoming More than You Are, and All You can Be.*

But, and there is always a "but," for the simple reason that the very words, "Spirit" and "Spiritual" are commonly associated with religions, and for nearly half the world's population exposed to the dominant, male-led, monotheistic religions "of the Father," Spirit is not attainable—or, at least not in the directly and personally communicative way hoped for—religions and churches are a big social factor for many people.

Because of that, we've tried to provide a basis for the reader to explore these and other factors, and—if desired—explore some of these groups.

NEW AGE MOVEMENTS

A General "Catalog"

The following "catalog" offers short reviews of some of the major movements variously associated with the New Age with regard to their common elements. However, in discussing so many religious and spiritual practices, let's first be reminded that the *attitude* of the New Age towards religion is itself NEW! The older ways of comparative values and judgmental meanings no longer apply in a developing civilization on the move, with new ways of communication, information richness, personal independence, international business and finance, global awareness and response to natural disasters, world health perspectives, cultural respect without boundaries, and an *informal* "New World Order" beyond greed, militancy, political and religious domination.

Religion and Spirituality are still believed to have particular direct psychic, psychological, and spiritual values to the individual beyond and separate from any social values or relationships subservient to any institution, government, spiritual entity or deity.

In this respect, the absolute right to freely choose or reject any religion or practice is fundamental to Life, Liberty, and the Pursuit of Happiness, and was established as such in the First Amendment to the Constitution of the United States (otherwise known as the "Bill of Rights"):

> *"Congress shall make no law respecting an establishment of religion, or prohibiting the free exercise thereof; or abridging the freedom of speech, or of the press; or the right of the people peaceably to assemble, and to petition the Government for a redress of grievances."*

We have the guarantee that we can practice any religion of our own choice, whether part of some organization or one that is purely personal and solitary—*so long we don't infringe on another person's rights.* And we have the right to abstain from any religious adherence and practice—and *we must not infringe on another person's rights not to practice any particular religion.* In other words **we have freedom of religion and from religion.**

Likewise, note the right to speak and write about religion or no religion, and also the right to assemble with others in our religious and spiritual practice. But also know that there are reasonable requirements regarding how these freedoms of speech, press, and assembly are exercised, You cannot freely libel or slander, or create disturbances. For public events you may have to secure permits or licenses so long as the regulations and any fees or taxes are equitable, reasonable, and neither punitive nor restrictive.

And there is a "sleeping" issue that will become of some importance: *Why should public money—whether directly raised by taxation or indirectly through subsidy or tax avoidance, and whether directly or by means of various chicaneries—be granted to any religious institution or group to support any property, function, or endeavor? Why should* your *money in any way support my religion or mine yours?* That is the effect of the non-taxation of religious properties and the deductibility of charitable contributions against income taxes. Think about in terms of your role as citizen and custodian of your own and other people's money.

See end of chapter for a subject-by-subject listing of suggested resources for your additional research.

THE NEW AGE versus THE OLD AGE ABRAHAMIC RELIGIONS

We discussed the Old Time Religions pretty thoroughly in the previous chapter. Here we will try to establish the primary distinctions between them as a single group now totaling 3.5 billion people (half the world's population) of common Middle Eastern origin and what we are generally referring to as New Age Spirituality.

Not all these New Age groups refer to their beliefs and practices as "religious," nor do many of their practitioners seek to affiliate formally together in "churches" or even come together regularly for communal worship or other ritual purposes. Those that more often relate together in groups (lodges, covens, circles, temples, etc.) do so to *voluntarily* participation in seasonal celebrations, in rituals for magick, healing, and particular "initiatory" experiences and to enjoy the group energies through dance and other shamanic spiritual technologies as described elsewhere in this book.

To clarify: for the New Ager there is no compulsion to "belong" to a unique institution promising *salvation* to the true believers. In contrast, the Abrahamic religions proclaim the existence of a single all powerful male "father" deity who seems to have no other reason for the creation of the Universe and of Humanity than for his own private purpose and enjoyment of compulsory worship under threat of eternal punishment.

His "servants" enjoy special privileges among their subjects, exercising the arbitrary powers delegated to them, wearing expensive and distinctively ornate clothing, living in expensive housing, establishing irrational religious laws ordering men to dominate women and for the women to reproduce plentifully until they die, sending his subjects to kill one another, to abuse the Earth, and to live in the "fear of God."

An important distinction about the "Supernatural"

While these Abrahamic religions—as do many others—have a primary belief in the "Supernatural," there is considerable difference in definition and attitude towards what is so represented. For these religions, the Supernatural is limited to God himself and to nothing else except by his permission and intention to mislead and *test his subject's faith.*

While some modern belief systems—like Atheism—completely deny that anything is *supernatural* defined as externally objective and scientifically verified in physical form, others to varying degrees include in their cosmology dimensions that are non-physical although interrelating with the physical. For New Age and Metaphysical persons, the "non-physical" generally includes those "higher" or "inner" dimensions as the Etheric, Astral, Mental, Causal, and others commonly lumped together as "spiritual." These subtle dimensions are not beyond Nature although they are the source for so-called "supernatural phenomena."

God's Plan for Man: Worship Me and Serve Me

Another distinction is the so-called "God's Plan for Man" which was developed by theologians trying to make sense of the irrational. In Jeremiah it is written:

Know the plans I have for you, declares the Lord, plans for welfare and not for evil, to give you a future and a hope. Then you will call upon me and come and pray to me, and I will hear you. You will seek me and find me, when you seek me with all your heart.

Pastor Matthew Hagee writes "God has a very specific plan just for men. God's plan is what He created you specifically to be, how He wants for you to fully develop into someone that brings honor to Him, someone who puts Him first in all things."

An Evolutionary Developmental Program for all existence

In contrast, alternative belief systems generally accept some kind of "evolutionary developmental plan" for all life and all existence. We often call this a "program" initiated at the "Beginning"—whatever that may have been or that may be. Some also say that *Creation is continuous.* Such an evolutionary program is not limited to a Darwinian biological concept, nor is whatever initiated the "Beginning" necessarily defined as Deity, and most surely not as a Humanoid God. For the New Ager, there is the further concept that conscious and intentional actions by the individual not only shape his own evolution but contributes to that of others—*Hence: Do unto others as you would have them do unto you.*

The Universe is so immense and multi-dimensional, and yet fundamental particles of matter/energy are so minute (sub-atomic), and we recognize that so much remains beyond present human perception and knowledge, that many are comfortable referring to this presumed source of Beginning simply as the *Creative Force,* free of all gender, imagery or other characteristics.

Rationality and Understanding lead to an Ethical Life of Meaning

As we will see, most "secularists" do believe that Life has meaning, that there is some kind of evolutionary scheme, that rationality combined with understanding of physical "laws" can produce a valid non supernatural system of morality, that Science is a valid approach to Spirituality when defined differently than in the past, and that Life is beautiful and through human efforts can become richer, longer, healthier, happier, and that it is possible to use human intelligence (even allowing for some kind of spiritual intuition) combined with science, technology, entrepreneurial innovation and rational thinking to guide our "Enterprise" to diminish or avoid threatened disaster of human and natural origin and "make things better."

Now, we will look at some of the alternative spiritual beliefs and practices that are gaining New Age prominence, and see what common factors there may be.

AFRICAN SPIRITIST RELIGIONS

The term applies to the practices derived from elements of the various Spiritist traditions brought from Central and West Africa during the slave trade of the 16th to 18th centuries and sometimes combined with various parts of indigenous native traditions and overlays adapted from Catholicism to give a semblance of *respectability* for the benefit of the "masters" and "owners." The practitioners (those original slaves and their descendants) and their practices have disbursed throughout the Caribbean and the Americas including parts of the United States.

Those religions and practices are basically shamanic and animist, and the celebrants use the ecstasy-inducing techniques of drumming, dancing, chanting and ingestion of alcohol and cannabis to invoke possession by spirit entities. Animal sacrifice of a goat or chicken releases their life energies to give power to the possessing spirit who may be that of an ancestor, a power animal, or a deity known as a *Loa* in

Voodoo, an *Orisha* in Santeria and Candomble, or various Catholic saints. Men and women have equal status, and the religion is more spiritual than materialistic.

Note: These observations are not intended to characterize all Spiritist traditions, and particularly not the more recent practices and traditions in Brazil and elsewhere.

Common Factors: Alterations of Consciousness, Gender Equality, Spirit Possession, and—sometimes—mediumistic communications with the possessing spiritual entities.

ALCHEMY

There probably has been more romance, fantasy, and nonsense written on this subject than any other "occult science"—and yet there is more real practical and day-to-day value to a basic understanding of some simple facts than in most self-improvement systems.

Of course, it's all about "turning lead into gold," isn't it? Yes, except that for the most part both gold and lead are just metaphysical symbols for spiritual and material realities. But, then, real *lead has been transformed into gold* through very costly nuclear bombardment in billion dollar particle accelerators. And there is a possibility that once anything has been done "mechanically" it can be done "metaphysically." Aside from demonstrating factuality, neither has any practical value.

And, there are both historic and more recent accounts claiming actual transmutation through alchemical techniques which, while not scientifically substantiated, should not be totally cast aside. As practiced in some adaptations from Quantum Physics, *Intention* directed at sub-atomic levels does alter physical reality. We have much to learn by being open to possibilities at all levels.

You can learn a great deal about philosophical and psychological alchemy, and about its history by simple reference to the main article on Wikipedia, or in the excellent just released new title, *The Philosopher's Stone* listed at the end of this chapter.

Alchemy is basically about organized energy and consciousness in direct relationship to physical world—including the inner workings of the human body and the fundamental workings of matter. It has been well studied in Chinese Taoism, Indian Tantra, Egyptian Magick and Western Hermeticism. Anything you study about it is worthwhile, particularly as a foundation to any other esoteric, healing, and magickal practice, including Shamanism, Tantra, Sex Magick, and Sexuality.

But, what about the practical, day-to-day value mentioned above? Alchemy is the art and science of "organized energy and consciousness in direct relationship to the physical world." Every conscious act you perform has alchemical potential to transform a) things in *your* outer world, and b) things in *your* inner world. Notice the emphasis on the word "your." We're not discussing changing the world at large, but your immediate world—and that includes the kitchen, the garden, your crafts and hobbies, your daily work, your travels, your health (physical, emotional, and mental) and your psychic and spiritual development.

If you are involved in it, Craft Work* affords an easy example because it is usually something you enjoy and on which you focus attention, imagination (even fantasies), use fingers and hands, and where you have an idealized goal. To do this work, you have organized consciousness (thought and feeling, mind and emotion), and through your *will* you are organizing and directing internal energy (and often external energies), and in the process you are transforming material to match your goal.

> * Craft Work. In the sense used here, it refers primarily to the construction or modification of physical objects and materials—such as carpentry for furniture making, metal working for jewelry, weaving of cloth, knitting, crochet, leather work, and secondarily to artistic working as in sculpting of materials to change their shape and appearance—but also to the "magickal" working with physical substances as in the transmutation of lead into gold. In Wicca and Witchcraft, we also have the phrase "Craft Work" in which the recognition is that material to be transformed through physical, emotional and mental processes is the SELF as presented in Body, Mind and Spirit.

That's an alchemical process at work, but we assure you that as you transform the outer world *you are likewise transforming your inner world*, and what you have done is to train your whole being to work better, more efficiently, and more fully involving your whole person. With every new exercise, you are building new neural circuitry in the brain and other parts of the body as associated with Chakra System. That's Spiritual, Psychological, and Physical Alchemy, and it is also Ritual Magic. When you organize consciousness, focus thought and feeling, visualize and imagine, move energy and matter under will towards a goal, you are practicing Alchemy and Magick, and all the attributes for Success in whatever you do.

Please also read the section on Martial Arts as this also relates to "Chinese Alchemy."

Note: In Alchemical terms, you are working with the "Spirit of the Matter" through your own spiritual consciousness.

Common Factors: Mind Power; Visualization & Energizing with interaction between Inner and Outer; Subtle Realities; Judgment of internal success by outward accomplishment.

ANIMISM

All of Nature—animals, plants, stones, and the natural forces contain Spirit, as do humans who can communicate through Spirit to Spirit and learn the nature and magical properties of plants, animals, stones and gems, and apply them for personal and magical benefit. "Quantum Animism" adds the dimension of Mind as permeating all levels to establish a "conscious center" to every natural system from which it directs and observes its own actions, and interactions.

A further concept is that of "Morphic Fields" that animate organism at all levels, *resonating* to produce universal connections and memories between all units.

Note: The most familiar method of spiritual communication with animal and non-animal Spirit in the Natural World is through formulas involving "correspondences:" Kabbalistic, Tantric, and other Magickal traditions. Also Human to Animal emotional relationship, Human to plant "care" relationship, Human to thing "use" relationship, Human to the "managing Spirit" of the species, group, herd, family, place, and sometimes "mind-to-mind between human individual and animal individual, and even plant individual.

Common Factors: Connectedness, Magical Correspondences, Mental focus and Astral thought forms.

ATHEISM

Alternatively, see also Secular Humanism, and explore words like Non-Theism, Humanism, and Naturalism. An atheistic religion is one that expressly states that there are no divine beings. Other non-theistic "religions" may deny the existence of any deities, but do not necessarily reject their existence either. The emphasis is on objective observations, rational analysis, logical applications, and on science to solve problems.

Common Factors: Rejection of one universal male "humanoid" god and of other concepts and forms of deity; affirm the value of rationality, respect for science.

CHRISTIAN SCIENCE

The movement began with the 1875 book *Science and Health with Keys to the Scriptures* by Mary Baker Eddy which, along with the *Bible*, is the movement's central text.

In 1879, the author founded "The First Church of Christ Scientist" in Boston, Massachusetts.

The church's *practitioners, called* "Christian Scientists," believe that material reality is an illusion and only spiritual reality is "real." Thus, sickness and even death, are illusions resulting from mistaken beliefs. The practitioner treats sickness by a special form of prayer intended to correct those beliefs, and the patient should discontinue any materialist medical practice.

The avoidance of medical care and vaccination of children led to many deaths resulting in prosecutions and convictions for neglect and manslaughter. Today, the church teaches that prayer should supplement conventional medicine rather than replace it.

Christian Science is part of the New Thought metaphysical family that includes the Unity School of Christianity, the United Church of Religious Science, and the Church of Divine Science. They share the belief that the human mind is the key to physical health through "attunement with God." However, a key difference between Christian Science and the New Thought movement is that the one believes the material world is an illusion and the other sees it as real. New Thought claims to apply the methodology of science to discover new spiritual principles to improve human lives here and now. As in all Western medical practice today, this is difficult because of the domination by the pharmaceutical industry having become profit-centered rather than science-oriented.

Common Factors: The power of Mind, the power of intention to influence physical form, subtle energies.

DEISM

Deism emerged during the 17th century scientific revolution leading up to the Age of Enlightenment. Deism rejects all organized religion and their dogma, their books claiming to reveal "the word of God," and all religious mysteries, prophecies, and stories of miracles.

Deists saw a need for a new philosophy based on reason to counter the "absurdity of Christianity," and called "revealed scripture" a "well-invented flam." (Peter Gay: *Deism)* Deists believe in a single creator and that humans can only know God through reason and observation, and that each person must do that himself rather than accepting the "authority" of others. They do not ascribe any specific qualities to God other than as the creator of the universe and the formation of life using only natural processes.

Deists do not, however, believe that the Creator intervenes in the functioning of the natural world but rather humans must solve their own problems. They saw religions as corrupted by priests inventing superstitions, "mysteries," and irrational theological dogmas that only they could interpret for their "flocks" to provide for "salvation."

In the United States, Enlightenment philosophy largely inspired by Deist ideals played a major role in establishing the principle of religious freedom adopted by Thomas Jefferson and incorporated into the Law of the Land via the Constitution. Other Deist inspired Founding Fathers includes Benjamin Franklin, Governor Morris, Hugh Williamson and Cornelius Harnett.

Note: Spiritual Deists believe in an ongoing personal connection with Divinity through intuition, meditation, contemplation, and communion with Nature.

Common Factors: Rejection of organized religion and a humanoid deity, while accepting belief in a single creator knowable through observation and reason, and rejecting any belief in deific intervention as only reason can solve human problems.

DRUIDRY

Druidry is both an ancient Pagan religion and a "born-again" modern Pagan spiritual practice that promotes harmony with and worship of Nature. Today, it manifests very strongly in respect for the Environment and for all Beings.

While indeed "ancient" in its drawing upon the Iron Age Celtic priesthood for inspiration and ritual practice, it now also reflects the 18th century Romantic Movement in Britain and the intellectualizing influence of Freemasonry and various modern Reconstructionist groups.

At the present time, there are so many cross currents among the various groups that it is difficult to describe either a basic overall philosophy or standardized practices to modern Druidism which, for the most part, relates more to past then present, and more to research and discussion than to practice other than by individuals and small groups.

Common Factors: Respect for Nature, the Environment, "Romance," and history.

EGYPTIAN RELIGION & MAGIC

Why include the ancient Egyptian religion here in a chapter on New Age Spirituality? As we will see, there are elements in this religion, as in certain aspects of Hinduism, Yoga, Taoism and Tantra, that demonstrate a continuity of evolutionary spiritual technology into modern spiritual thinking and magickal practice despite its near total suppression during 40 centuries of stultifying Abrahamic supremacy only now beginning to decline.

The ancient Egyptians deified the forces they perceived behind natural phenomena, thus creating a pantheon of gods involved in all aspects of Nature and Human Life. These gods *exist* in art forms as structured symbols and formulae, and their powers are ritually evoked or invoked by priest-magicians, and by personal prayer.

A most important concept in the Egyptian religion is *Ma'at*—meaning Truth, Justice, and Order. <u>Order</u> is constantly threatened by <u>Disorder</u>. *Everyone must work to maintain balance between Order and Disorder through offerings to the gods and rituals perpetuating the correct cycles and natural rhythm.*

Egyptians believed there are three types of sentient beings: 1) the Gods; 2) Spirits of deceased humans; and, 3) Living Humans. "Life" after death was a big element in Egyptian culture, and certain acts and rituals were required of the Living for the benefit of the Dead.

The Eye of Horus

Life after Death

Death releases the *Ka*, the Life Force that sustains the body during life—in turn receiving its energies from food and drink. For the *Ka* to survive after death it must continue to receive the *spiritual essence* of food through ritual offerings. In addition, each person has a **Ba** which remains attached to the body after death. Funeral rituals are necessary to release the *Ba* to rejoin the *Ka* to live on as the *Akh.* It is also necessary to preserve the deceased's physical body so that the *ba* can return to it nightly to gain new life before again emerging as the *akh* in the morning. Sometime after death there is a final judgment called "the Weighing of the Heart" to determine if the person has lived a proper life in which case the *Akh beccomes the permanent vehicle for "life after death."*

Heka

Heka, (Magic), as "the ability to make things happen by indirect means," was the "science" of Egypt, Magic was used by many "professionals" (priests, healers, makers of magical amulets for clients, scorpion charmers) as well as ordinary "skilled workers" in the course of life and work.

And Sex

One of the Great Secrets—one unknown* (or suppressed) by the Abrahamists is the connection between Sex and Magic, and—indeed—the use of controlled and directed sexual energies, particularly those aroused and extended in feminine orgasm, for human health, success, and longevity.

> * However, there is some indication that the Catholic Church "fathers" believed that by suppressing all sex (other than for reproduction), those energies would instead be re-directed to the "higher purposes" of the Church via the Holy Spirit.

The secret of this "inner alchemy" was well known in ancient Tantra, Taoism, Shinto, various forms of European Paganism, and many Indigenous Shamanic practices. Today, this knowledge is no longer limited to esoteric practices and magic, but has been "revealed" publically in classes, lectures and in many "sex" manuals. However, these are voluntary and personal choices and not the "command non-performance" required by the Church and other ruling elitists.

The "technology" involved is relatively simple but also complex for those unfamiliar with the subtle energies of chakras, the meridian system, the relatively complex structure of the organs and nerves of the female pelvis and their neurological connections through spine and brain, and the flow of various hormones and neurotransmitters. This knowledge is combined with the practice of controlled aroused of "feel good" energies and directed through moving meditation and selected symbols and images to the magical accomplishment of visualized goals.

In Egyptian magic orgasm is "the key to eternal life." In contrast to the more familiar system of seven major chakras, there are thirteen in the Egyptian system and the structure of the Great Pyramid guides the projected orgasmic energies through the image. The complete teachings are beyond the intention of this book.

Egyptian symbolism, art, and concepts still inspire today's Magical and Masonic practitioners, as seen and used in their temples and in important governmental architecture.

Note: Spirit is *alive* and everywhere, on Earth and in the Stars, in the forms of Gods and Goddesses and in the subtle bodies of humans in life and in death, and as energies in formed structures above and below ground, in the rise and fall of waters and the movements of wind and sand. But Sustainable Life requires Law to maintain Order and keep Dis-order held at bay.

Common Factors: The necessity of human action to maintain the balance between Order and Disorder, the power of deific imagery to represent natural forces, orgasm as the key to eternal life, life after death and the subtle bodies.

ESOTERICISM

Esotericism is almost the ultimate concept of "Spiritual, but not Religious," although some practitioners among various esoteric systems like Theosophy, Rosicrucianism, Hermeticism, Anthroposophy, Gnosticism, and the mystical traditions associated with major religions tend to claim that religion and spirituality are one and the same.

Seal of the Theosophical Society.

For most purposes, "esotericism," has become the preferred alternative word to "occultism" simply because that word has wrongly been associated with "Black" Magic and its real meaning of "hidden" a contradiction to the democratic belief that no knowledge should be hidden or suppressed. Many claim that all organized religions have two divisions: the *exoteric* for the "ignorant masses" and the *esoteric,* being the real (occult) wisdom, reserved for the elite insiders whose job it is to control the masses "for their own good" while benefiting and enriching the self-same elite.

That was the Old Order of Conflict and Imposed Ignorance, now replaced by the "New World Order" in the New Age of Man and Knowledge.

Even so, esotericism, as a knowledge system, was divided into Mysticism and Magick. Mysticism involved spiritual practices to unite self with Self, or self with Divinity—"I, and the Father, are One"—while turning away from the world. In contrast, Magick, instead of turning away from the world embraces it, utilizes many of the same techniques to *become more than you are* and *all you can be,* using your increased vision, higher knowledge, enhanced abilities all in service to accelerating humanity's growth and development.

In other words, becoming a kind of Spiritual Agent, or—using a Theosophical concept—becoming an "Elder Brother," giving helpful advice in response to the younger brother's (or sister's) questions. And that, then, is a major question: even as we accept the idea that some humans do become more "advanced" than others have, *do they (or can they or should they) guide the affairs of the rest of us? Can we become more than we are without standing on our own two feet and accepting responsibility for what we do?* Or, is there a fine line between "behind the scenes" secret guidance and that of democratic selection of the fittest for responsible leadership that is *responsive* to an intelligent and educated citizenry?

Anyone can perceive the huge diversity among people, the range from minimal to extraordinary in intelligence, education, skills, and ... ethical behavior; we readily see the moral failures of "common criminals" as well as much of the wealthy and political elite who prostitute themselves on "the cross of gold" by creating false bank accounts, bundling mortgages to hide credit failures, creating drugs whose side effects sell still more drugs to cancel the side effects of the first, leading the "devout" into acts of self-immolation to induce terror and destruction and death among those on the other side of the line drawn in shifting sands, using their taxing authority to rob the already poor in order to further benefit the "special interests" of the already rich and powerful, and to subsidize the proselytizing activities of the old abusive religions.

Yes, we can see *Good* people as well as the *Bad,* but we see a system that is building on corruption and favoritism, a system that is failing the goals of the Founding Fathers, that is trying to perpetuate ignorance and to pervert secular education into sectarian nonsense. The "battle field" is as much in the West and the Far East as it is in the Middle East, and what is called "esotericism" is the very system that can bring *Clear Vision* and the enabling power to raise personal consciousness above the blindness and pettiness of the Old Religions.

But esoteric knowledge and spiritual technology cannot be reserved to the elite, else the system will fail.

Esotericism must become common knowledge and used by the growing "middle class" or the system will collapse.

An intelligent and Educated Citizenry must no longer by seduced and blinded by mass entertainment, their heads concussed by spectator sports dominated by tax-avoiding billionaires, accepting self-serving "leadership" from corrupt special interests rather than exercising the power of the ballot and fully participating in the democratic process, or we will entirely lose our way.

Esotericism is a particular systematic approach to and collection of certain principles of knowledge into these functions that are beneficial to magickal and spiritual developmental practices:

1. The knowledge of structurally defined connecting "correspondences" between all that is visible and invisible.

2. The knowledge that Nature is a continuous manifestation of a single Life Force.

3. The knowledge of "mediating factors" such as symbols, spiritual entities, gods and goddesses, natural agents and forces enabling communication and access to spiritual knowledge.

4. The knowledge empowering personal growth and spiritual transformation.

5. The knowledge that the times are critical, that change is inevitable, that planet-wide challenges must be met through intelligent actions arrived at through rational analysis as well as intuitive guidance and inspiration.

6. The Knowledge that each of us must serve as a Spiritual Agent and act on both material and subtle dimensions.

7. The knowledge that the greatest power can be managed at the smallest sub-atomic level by Intentional and Conscious action guided by Intelligence and Intuition.

8. The knowledge that at the smallest sub-atomic level each of us can join together to truly become more than we _were_ and act with greater wisdom.

9. The Knowledge that esotericism is unlimited and empowering when inclusive rather than exclusive.

10. The knowledge that esotericism is the path to the Knowledge and Conversation with the Holy Guardian Angel that takes us to the highest level potential for humanity. (See more on this in Chapter 14)

Note: Spirit is everywhere, but your personal access point is at the deepest and inner-most level of your being. It is from here that you can reach to the farthest dimensions the Space that is nowhere and everywhere and where everything may be known and found.

Common Factors: All esotericism tells us that there is a way we can, and *should*, become more than we are, that there is a plan for us to become all we can be, and a systematic set of principles and practices by which this can be accomplished. There are many esoteric groups and teachers, many books and many systems. Each offers you something that only you can recognize its value for you. But, the most important choice is that to which your intuition guides you. Listen and Learn. Follow your nose, but when something no longer smells right, move on. Forever Onward and Upward.

GNOSTICISM

"Gnosis" means the direct experience of the Divine accomplished through a process of inner exploration as described by Plotinus (205–270 CE). As simple as that seems, the earliest origins of Gnosticism are obscure and confusing, with many differed threads and practices, some religious, some philosophical, and some magical, some claiming to be true Christianity, others pre-Christian and Pagan, and others accused of being evil and satanic. Some appear to originate with Plato, others with Plotinus, and some with the Pythagorean academies. Myth claims the origin with Seth, the third son of Adam and Eve, and the early Sethians identical to or related to the Nazarenes or the Ophites. Indeed, there were so many different Gnostics that it is further complicated by those who wrote about them, either critically or favorably, without distinguishing who they were talking about, and by a complexity of terms and ideas: Nous, Demiurge, Sophia, Holy Spirit, etc., without definition.

One Gnostic belief calls the Creator the "Demiurge," defined as lesser than a Supreme Deity, and teaches that all matter is evil, that the body is a prison to be escaped from, that there is a secret wisdom code to reveal the real meaning of scriptures, that Jesus was a spirit only seeming to be human and hence that God was not in any sense incarnate into man.

Many modern occultists identify with Gnosticism without providing much in the way of logical justification. At the same time there are a few who do have a Kabbalistic and modern philosophy of practical applications of essential Gnostic principles. (See, in particular, the books by Tao Malachi listed at the end of this chapter.)

Note: Without delving into the complexity of the various "schools" of Gnostic practices, the core appears as direct communication between the Spirit in human and the Spirit that is Deity. That accomplishment requires the transformation of human consciousness through rituals and exercises with a single objective.

Common Factors: Direct knowledge of and from Deity without priestly intervention.

GODDESS MOVEMENT

The Goddess Movement, aka "Goddess Worship," is part of modern Paganism, Modern Wicca/Witchcraft, and New Age Spirituality. It is all those, but it is also unique in itself and there is good reason to study it for what it is—the genuine Re-birth of the Goddess who never left us; the return of the Great Mother who never abandoned Her children; the restoration of Human Wholeness long denied under 4,000 years of patrilineal dominance built on a myth of perpetual sin by "Eve" as the Biblical First Woman and Wife to the First Man and Husband as defined and defiled in Abrahamic religion.

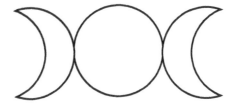

There's an inner (archetypal) Woman in every Man, and an inner (archetypal) Man in every Woman; *Anima* and *Animus* together in every Human; and part of Human Life is the discovery, the love, and the becoming each of the other. No person is whole without the other, regardless of outer gender. *Equality is not Identity, but traditional roles are not definitive and never truly were! Nor is gender a fixed thing fully understood and scientifically, psychological, and spiritually described. Change, growth, evolution, and unique individuality is intrinsic to Human Life.*

Today's Man and Today's Woman have taken on equal stature in modern life—sometimes exchanging traditional roles while mixing and blending responsibilities in dynamic partnership; and, yet, successfully expressing and fulfilling their unique biological and psychic essence. They have accomplished this without loss of the joys of being feminine and masculine beings; they have not submerged their instinctive natures under a false mask of neutered blandness; they have learned that *Every Man and every Woman is a Star,* each shining in its own light and its own colors, singing its own celestial music.

The Witch, and Wise Woman

In past European culture, there often was a wiser, older, perhaps widowed, woman living alone outside the village. Through inherited knowledge, study and experience, and sometimes involvement with a local coven of Witches, she was a healer, dispenser of herbal remedies, kinds of advices, and sometimes Magical Spells.

Often this woman <u>felt</u> a living connection to the Feminine Power that is the source of all Life, embodied in the Earth Herself, but also represented archetypally in the image of *The Goddess* and/or *The Great Mother*—they both exist, in their own way and can be evoked or invoked through ritual acts.

But, "Woman" does not need acts of ritual to communicate with the Feminine Power for she has her Intuition taping into the Collective Unconscious for collective wisdom and her special Creative Imagination that uniquely taps into her Personal Unconscious to represent her own wisdom for her personal needs, development, and service to her community as she chooses.

"Man" does not operate this way. We don't need to study men in the same manner for their ways are well represented in the dominant religions and contemporary social structures, in the systems of Hermetic Magick, Practical Magic, Alchemy, Kabbalah, and the various techniques for Worldly Success and Growing Rich (which, however, are by no means limited to the masculine gender).

The ways of both Man and Woman are directly experience in Tantra, Taoism, Yoga, and Traditional Witchcraft, and found in Esotericism and other New Age and contemporary spiritual and alternative practices.

Women are Different, and Women are Special

Men and women know this, often complain about it while appreciating and celebrating it. Men ask *"What do Women want?"* for the simple reason that women do have their own wants beyond what a man can readily identify with. George Bernard Shaw wrote the common male complaint *"Why can't a woman be more like a man?"* while showing that men are glad they aren't.

Women know that they alone have the power to reproduce life. Men can boast about their moment of ejaculating sperm, but what good is that seed without an egg and the womb that carries the fertilized egg—a man may not even know about—to birth a baby. And it is woman alone who is able to nurse (breast feed) the baby, and who alone has the immediate love and instinct to meet the baby's needs. It is woman who primarily cares for the growing child even as responsibilities are shared in modern lifestyle. If the man goes his way she remains "the Mother."

A woman's body is different from a man's, and she expresses and fulfills some of those differences by putting her body *into* clothes while a man merely puts clothes *on* his body. A woman dresses and costumes her body to express herself and sometimes to become a different goddess. A woman sees her home as an extension of herself (even of her body) and as the home of her family, while a man sees a house as a place to live and "hang his hat." They may share a bed, but what he sees as a place to sleep and sometimes to have sex, she sees as an altar to love and an opportunity for ecstasy and transcendence.

The Goddess Within, and Without

A woman can comfortably call herself a "Goddess" and other woman as "goddesses," but a man knows he is not "God" or a "god," although he sometimes *poses* as one. Either may believe that the Divine lives within, but a man has to "work" to feel the god within move up his spine; a woman can relax and just let the goddess within take charge.

The Goddess Movement is *The Women's Movement* that has restored her stature in the world after 4,000 years of "false imprisonment" under male dominant religion and resultant social ways. We believe that the male-dominated religion of the past ages (and into the present) has done harm and injustice to humanity and all of Nature. It wasn't "the feminist movement" per se, although that played an important role in Liberation, but only as Woman awakened to the Goddess Within that She could manifest again in the outer world to assert—and have recognized—both her uniqueness and her full equality with men. It's a new world in the New Age where an *individual* woman can demonstrate and execute her competency or actual superiority in a given role, job, profession, or position of power.

There must be a balancing of energies. The over-dominant male energies must diminish and the feminine must increase in order for the Goddess to empower man as well as woman. As already noted, inside of every man there is a woman, and inside every woman is a man—but after 4,000 years of male dominance, "we suffer from the absence of one half of our spiritual potential—the Goddess ... The Great Goddess was regarded as immortal, changeless, and omnipotent." For Witches, the goddess is the earth itself. Mother Earth, or Gaia, is an evolving being, as is all of nature. (Bolen: *Goddesses in Everywoman)*. Nature is hurting; The Earth is suffering; And Life's and Humanity's home is in need of healing. We are responsible for both the suffering and the healing. We have the intelligence and knowledge to see the problem and to rectify the causes and bring about a New Life for our home planet.

There is a need to awaken the reality of the Divine Feminine in every man as well as every woman. It is a different experience for each person and not just gender specific. As noted by Prof. Betty Sue Flowers "The goddess is a metaphor that reminds us of the female side of spirituality. Metaphors are important. You can't know God directly. You can only know images of God, and each image or metaphor is a door. Some doors are open and others are closed. A door that is only male is only half open."

Rituals that openly address both male and female as God and Goddess can fully open these doors *regardless of any belief in Divinity of humanoid form!* Contrary to the thundering voice of the evangelical preacher, you don't have to "Just Believe" in the sense he speaks. His "belief" is a *stance* that magically creates a reality within his imagination, but his vision is only half full and hence his reality is only "half there." Yet, his reality exists, and dominates his "flock."

Likewise, one can be an Atheist, Agnostic, Secular Humanist, or any other kind of non-Theist who intellectually denies belief in an external god—humanoid or otherwise—as necessary to the creation of the universe. The foundation of this approach is that such belief in deity cannot be proven, and hence that any premise derived from it is innately irrational and hence irrelevant. Yet, we're here.

The non-Theistic stance can exist side-by-side with the acceptance of the psychological reality of the archetypal roles that a god and goddess play in the health of the human person and in the foundation of the relationships between Man and Woman, and between Humanity, Life, and Nature. We're here too.

Goddess Worship

The Goddess, in Her many names and images, has been worshipped probably as long as there have been humans on Earth. Sometimes, She has been worshiped in secret rites hidden from public or men's view; Other times, She has been worshipped publicly or secretly by both men and women. She was the core of matrifocal worship 5,000 to

25,000 years before the rise of male-oriented religion in Europe. She was the focus for known matrilineal agricultural religions in the Mediterranean and the Indus Valley.

Goddess Worship and Goddess Magic have been part of the ancient pre-religions of Tantra and Taoism, the religious and magical practices of Egyptian Magick and European Traditional Witchcraft, and the sex-magic of modern Wicca, neo-Paganism, and the lodges of Ceremonial Magick, and in various secret orders and individual practices of ordinary couples and shamans in all time.

Balance, not Imbalance

While there is value to "woman only" rites of Goddess Worship—in rectifying 40 centuries of stultifying subjugation not merely to men but to the denigration of her as both woman and person—they can work to create imbalance in the same way that the male God religious rituals and male only social rites have been doing. Even for men participating in Goddess-only rites there can be a causal imbalance in which the Anima within the man becomes dominant and creates a *false* feminine gender for a man.

Please don't misinterpret this point as any kind of bias toward natural, so-called, "gender bending" but rather of a pseudo or false *charging* of one archetype at the expense of the other. You cannot really restore balance by imbalance. There are women who state their hope not only that "masculism" will destroy itself, but—according to a *Wall Street Journal* article—some in the goddess movement, "pray for the time when science will make men unnecessary for procreation."

Goddess rituals can be balanced with God rituals. And you can easily discover rituals with equal roles in most Wiccan, neo-Pagan and other New Age religious and spiritual movements, Spiritism, Magickal Lodges, and in ancient Tantra where both Goddess and God may be invoked.

More of this is discussed in the previous section on New Age and the following sections on Paganism and Wicca/Witchcraft in this chapter.

Note: Most rituals are of two kinds: 1) the deployment of Spiritual Power of group or individual to accomplish a specific physical world goal; 2) the invocation by Spirit of Spirit—a calling of Human Spirit to Divine Spirit to temporarily incarnate in the person calling. Other rituals serve to align and realign people with natural (mostly lunar and solar) rhythms of life and to serve the community's social needs.

Common Factors: Recognition of the Feminine Power whether seen as Goddess or Archetype, or the necessary rediscovery of the importance of Anima/Animus balance within each Man and Woman; Perception of the unique physiology, psychology, and spirituality of women, and of the creative role of "fantasy" as a real inner power.

INDIAN & HINDUISM

While some of the Indian religions could be included among the old monotheistic religions of the previous chapter, there are elements in Hinduism and its very alive and still pertinent predecessor, Shamanic Tantra, and others of the group that contribute to New Age Spirituality. Many others, do not. But the Indus Valley is one of the oldest inhabited areas of the world and has generated perhaps hundreds of different religions from pre-history to this day.

Hinduism may be the oldest religion still active today, reaching back 50,000 years, or more—older than some scientists acknowledge civilized humanity has existed! Hindu religious texts are the oldest known ancient writings treated as both myth and history. Among these are the four Vedas: the *Rigveda*, the *Samaveda*, the *Atharvaveda*, and the *Yajurveda*. Each of these is subdivided into texts dealing with astronomy, astrology, medicine, philosophy, politics, science, warfare, and day-to-day matters of life and living.

Some authorities claim that Hinduism is a *way of life,* not a "religion," but other religions—like the world dominating Abrahamic religions—proclaim the same thing and Islam further insists that their way-of-life must become that of the whole world. In contrast, Hinduism is described as the most tolerant among all religious beliefs.

Yet, that isn't really correct. Hinduism was literally overridden—just as the original Dravidian people of the Indus Valley were—by the Aryan invaders around 1500 BCE. The Aryan nomadic cattle herders and hunters introduced the caste system, with their own military and priestly leaders at the top and the original farmers—and women—at the bottom. They used the original religion in much the same way that the Catholic Church adapted and over-rode native European Paganism for its own political and social agenda. The combination resulted in a great deal of the complexity and contradictions that exist to this day. It was the Dravidian spirituality, not the Aryan that put "Spirit" into Hinduism and the other religions born from it.

Hinduism's many Gods & Goddesses

Hinduism is polytheistic and has perhaps the richest and most complex pantheon of gods and goddesses, other spiritual entities, and deified natural forces—each of which has very specific character and functions identified by unique image, name, costume, adornments, colors, gestures, postures, *mantras* (chants and words of power), *yantras* and *mandala* (geometric diagrams), etc.—all of which can be employed either in religious or magickal rituals, and perceived as psychological and spiritual realities.

Hinduism is also one of the most complex religions, and because there is no separation between "church and state," between religious belief and traditional ways-of-life, there are many rules and regulations, complex social structures of caste and outcasts, traditions that conflict with modern needs, political divisions of geography that inhibit economic development and practical operations of business and agriculture, an over-abundance bureaucracy accompanied by graft and corruption at multiple levels with little rhyme or reason, over-crowded cities and stressed infrastructures.

Let it be noted: Religion is not a good guide to state-craft, government operation, economic development and regulation, and the protection of common but essential human and property rights.

Yoga & Tantra, Magick & the Science of Life

Hinduism has contributed more to Modern Spirituality than any other religion or philosophy, and yet "Mother India" remains both backward and filled with potential. India has a rich technology sector, a vast entertainment business, a developed higher educational system, and more. And it has a powerful military and it has nuclear weapons, and remains on war-alert with neighboring Pakistan and China. It has the world's second largest English speaking population after America. (Pakistan is third, Nigeria fourth, followed by the Philippines, United Kingdom, Germany, Bangladesh, Egypt, and Canada.)

It has contributed Yoga both as a science of life and one of the most practical system for personal health development and maintenance known. It is also the foundation of various martial arts practices, nutritional science, and the most complete science of the subtle bodies and energies which still remain ignored by Western Science but are the foundation of all esoteric practices.

Yoga is actually part of Tantra—of which the modern "neo-Tantra of good and better sex" is only one very important subset. Tantra—along with very ancient Chinese Taoism—is the parent of Occultism and Magick, including inner and outer Alchemy.

We will discuss **Tantra** in greater detail separately from Hinduism.

Reincarnation, Karma and Dharma

One of the core elements of Hinduism (and most Eastern religions, and common to all esoteric systems), is that of reincarnation in which an "agent" of the immortal soul is born into a new physical body and personality to continue the endless journey of growth and transformation. In a broad sense, the surviving soul is born again and again, to master the lessons of life. Contrary to some folk lore, the primary belief is progressive and not regressive—a human does not return in a lower form. The concept is one of continuous life and of continuous learning—one life after another—with spiritual and biological advancements (*not* merely Darwinian survival of the fittest).

Karma is neither good nor bad, but is affective memory of past reactions reflected in the structuring of the new body and personality. *Dharma* is the necessary actions to balance past karma with the "master plan" leading towards a more perfect being. But, there's the challenge: Such a master plan may have been simple at the "Beginning" but now is exceedingly complex because the potential of all life is so great and yet has to reflect the total of all history from that same "Beginning" of which we can only speculate.

That Complexity!

Another of the core elements of most Eastern religions and of all esoteric systems is that of the *non-physical dimensions*. It is within the subtle bodies of human and animal life, and on those non-material "planes" we call Etheric, Astral, Mental, Causal, and Spiritual that primary transformative actions take place. While modern Science is beginning to understand more of these subtle factors through Quantum Theory, Sub-atomic Physics, and the New Psychology that goes beyond and is transcendent to a pure brain and nerve based physiology of consciousness, it still remains necessary to relieve both science and religion of any "need" for a *personal, humanoid, deity in charge.*

It is the *New Science of the Paranormal* that incorporates material science along with an expanded understanding of the subtle elements and the phenomena of past life memories that takes us beyond assuming the need for an "X-factor" within which to define our human place. We expand our vision and see all life and all existence as more complex than previously thought, and the universe and the Cosmos within which all exists and continues to "become" as meaningful without any need to "pass the buck" to an imagined Divine Manager-in-Charge.

With the New Science and the knowledge of the universality of Spirit and Consciousness, we can recognize the role and function of many "spiritual" beings beyond our selves, and comfortably give them the familiar names of Angels, and Gods, and Goddesses, Devas, and many others as units of Spirit and Consciousness in a Cosmos where we, as evolving beings, assume an ever expanding role in partnership with a Creative Source without groveling in childish dependence before an imagined super humanized being pictured as seated on golden throne high in the sky. *What Sky? Where? What Need? Put away those childish feelings and "grow up!"*

As will be better understood when we extend our studies to Secular Humanism and other non-deist but highly ethical and rational belief systems which do not necessarily reject the non-physical so much as they do the "super-naturalism" that denigrates both physicality and rationality, *nothing is purely "either/or" even though we do experience all manifest as duality moving into trinity moving on into new dualities and trinities within the evolution of life and consciousness.*

Other Indian Religions

There are many variations developed out of Hinduism. Some resulted from military or political rebellions against the Aryan imposed system, others giving greater emphasis to one or another element, or movements consolidating around a charismatic teacher.

Among those are familiar names of Hinduism, Buddhism, Jainism, Shaivism, and Sikhism—each of which has generated many variations and contributed to other religions and practices far beyond the limits of the Indian sub-continent. In reality, there is not a lot of similarity among them for the simple reason that many were rebellions against particular practices of others.

A Sikh emblem.

Note: The, "Eastern" approach to Spiritual Communication is quite different from the Western. Spirit is everywhere but "everywhere" is free of boundaries so communication is more metaphysical than physical.

Common Factors: Many gods and goddesses, with the feminine predominant. Each deity and her well-described variations expresses a real physiological, psychological, and psycho-spiritual force that can be magically evoked or invoked. More spiritual than material in belief but historically becoming more materialistic in practice. Males are favored over females in society but not in deity.

INITIATIC ORDERS

It may seem contradictory to the "New" of New Age Spirituality to include that which proclaims to be very "Old"—reaching back into ancient Greece and further back to ancient Egypt—and further back to mythic ancient Atlantis.

And yet, what these Orders offer is as modern as any structured University system of teachings by certified "master," lessons that are tested and graded, and the students certified as to their accomplishment.

While calling it "the Ancient Wisdom," it is really the integral knowledge of the evolving human psyche and the Cosmos in which we all live. Part of the process of teaching is imparted during the process of "initiation" as direct psychic transfer between Adept and Student. There are also systems of Self-Initiation.

We are only listing three groups here: *Ordo Aurum Solis,* the Hermetic Order of the Golden Dawn, and *Ordo Templi Orientis* as the best known and well respected groups. Information about them can readily be found on-line and in numerous books by such authors as Jean-Louis de Biasi, Melita Denning & Osborne Phillips, Aleister Crowley, Chic & Sandra Tabatha Cicero, Israel Regardie, and Lon Milo DuQuette. In addition, there are Initiate Schools, such as the Arcane School founded by Alice Bailey, the Society of the Inner Light founded by Dion Fortune, Servants of the Light administered by Dolores Ashcroft-Nowicki, and the Builders of the Adytum founded by Paul Foster Case to name a few.

Once upon a time, there indeed was secret knowledge hidden away, partly in the belief that those not properly trained and disciplined to ethically handle it could abuse such knowledge. In addition, at times these teachers hid from the public view as a matter of self-protection from the eyes of the Catholic Church and others not wanting such knowledge to be available either to "the faithful" or to "the unfaithful."

Today little is secret other than military, corporate, and political. Rather, it's your choice as to how you want to learn. Initiate Orders and Schools have appeals and values. Other structured and graded information is also available, and there's little if any not available in books. One value of these orders is that they provide an opportunity for responsive communal action at spiritual levels.

Here, however, is a statement directly from Jean-Louis de Biaisi, the current Grand Master of Aurum Solis to illustrate what one of the best of the active orders offers:

"Ordo Aurum Solis (*Order of the Gold of the Sun*): An initiatic Order reactivated under this name in England in 1897 by George Stanton and Charles Kingold. Focused on Theurgy, High Magick and Hermetism, it claims to descent from the Ogdoadic (Hermetic) Tradition of Ancient Egypt and then Greece. It is one of the main schools which offer a modern powerful training in the foundation of the Western Mystery Tradition. It is best known through the published works of three of its leaders, Melita Denning,

Osborne Phillips (pseudonyms of Vivian Godfrey and Leon Barcynski), and today Jean-Louis de Biasi. Together, they authored many books on magical practice, such as *Astral Projection* and *Creative Visualization*, and the comprehensive curriculum presented in *The Magical Philosophy*. Jean-Louis de Biasi nominated lifetime Grand Master perpetuates this Tradition with books such as *The Divine Arcana of the Aurum Solis, Rediscover the Magick of the Gods and Goddesses*, and more to come.

The Tradition of the Aurum Solis is defined by what is called the "Golden Chain" (of the Masters)."

This lineage is rooted in Hermetism which, a tradition associating Theurgic practices with a rational approach to the inner mysteries of the life. The tradition first describes the high origins of the human soul and how it descended into physicality and what that means; and secondly reveals the path by which the soul may again return to the Eternal and Supreme and what that involves.

This pre-Christian Tradition has given to humanity some of its greatest Scientists and Humanist Philosophers. Polytheism, the main religious expression of this time, provided the tradition of tolerance for any spiritual practice and experience. *Many are the ways!* But organization, self-discipline, and practice lead onward to the Next Step!

These progressive manifestations of non-theologic science and humanist spirituality were severely attacked during the rise of the institutionalized monotheistic religions in Europe and the Middle East, leading directly to the Dark Ages. However in the fifteenth century, the Theurgic Neo-Platonist Ogdoadic tradition) reappeared in Florence, Italy. The *Renaissance* was really a universal rebirth of the human consciousness igniting the beginning of modern civilization: breaking the religious and monarchist domination of human thought, science and philosophy and leading to the industrial, technological, and information ages, to democracy and human rights and the abolition of slavery, religious tolerance, universal education, and the metaphysical traditions, etc.

From this earlier time the Theurgic/Hermetic Tradition was secretly continued in Europe until its rebirth in 1897. Aurum Solis is a unique example of an initiatic and spiritual organization which remained rooted in the original humanist spiritual values developed by the founders. From the beginning, Aurum Solis choose to maintain a clear and unique lineage, working hard to improve the visibility of the original Western Tradition, highlighting the unique characteristics of this spiritual path, Aurum Solis is showing the urgency to see life differently. Dogmas are dangerous; chaos is risky, while rediscovering a tolerant and traditional path to the divine is paramount. This is the Modern Renaissance!"

For information: www.aurumsolis.info

IRANIAN

There were many pre-Islamic religions developed within the "Greater Iran" area we might better refer to as *Ancient Persia,* and many of these have survived Islamic persecution and are still practiced by minorities mostly within the Middle East.

Of these, perhaps the best known is **Zoroastrianism** based on the teaching of a 6th century BCE prophet teaching of a constant battle between Good and Evil under a single creator named *Ahura Mazda.* It is a belief in an immanent self-creating universe with consciousness as its special attribute. It is a form of pantheism sharing origin with Indian Brahmanism. The entire universe is dualistic with Order and Chaos in conflict. (This is the same concept recognized in the section on Egyptian religion, distorted into a "war between Good and Evil." Order out of Chaos is an everyday fact of life—file yesterday's receipts, clean last night's dishes, pick up the toys, mow the grass—it's Law and Order versus Crime and Violence, it's Civilization versus the "Jungle.")

Emblem of Zoraster.

Humanity must play an active role in resolving this conflict through good deeds that ensure happiness and keep chaos at bay. This active participation in a full life is a central element in Zoroaster's concept of free will. Ahura Mazda will ultimately prevail over the evil Ahriman, at which point time will end, the cosmos renewed, and a savior will bring even the dead back to life.

Ahura Mazda is immanent in humankind through which the Creator interacts with the world, and humans are aided by "Bounteous Immortals," who each represent one aspect of Creation. These Immortals are in turn assisted by a league of lesser principles, each "Worthy of Worship" and each representing a moral or physical aspect of creation.

Another is **Mandaeism**, a monotheistic religion with a strongly dualistic world-view sometimes identified with Gnosticism. Its belief system is concisely summed up by Wikipedia. As paraphrased and adapted:

1. There is a supreme entity without form, expressing itself through an Archetypal Man who produced a self-modeled Cosmos or numerous spiritual, etheric, and material worlds and beings.

2. The manifest Cosmos is a dualism of a cosmic Father and Mother, Light and Darkness, Right and Left in cosmic and microcosmic form.

3. Also a dualism of counter-types, a world of ideas.

4. The soul is portrayed as a captive exiled from her home and origin in the supreme Entity to which she eventually returns.

5. Planets and stars influence fate and human beings, and also serve as places of detention after death.

6. There are guardian spirits to assist the soul on her journey through life and after it to 'worlds of light'.

7. There is a cult-language of symbol and metaphor through which ideas and qualities are personified.

8. There are sacraments to help and purify the soul, to ensure her rebirth into a spiritual body, and her ascent from the world of matter. These are often adaptations of existing seasonal and traditional rites to which an esoteric interpretation is attached all based on the Abrahamic myths.

9. Initiates are sworn to secrecy about the full story of creation and our Divine origins, and the details of the sacraments.

Mandaeans believe in marriage, procreation, and family life, the importance of leading an ethical and moral lifestyle. They see the world as a "prison," and view the Torah as evil in origin.

Still another is the mystical tradition of **Sufism** best known through the ecstasy inducing actions of the "Whirling Dervishes." While sometimes considered as a mystical and esoteric form of Islam, it is opposed by the Wahhabi and Salafist Muslims just as most

Christians oppose Gnostic mysticism. The belief is that a man can become a perfect incarnate channel of Divinity, yet knowledge of God is neither necessary nor desirable. Rather, it is *knowledge of the heart* that enables one to become a Sufi master.

In this regard, "self-knowledge" is not possible, and only the master can read another person's heart. It is a mysticism that demands total withdrawal from the world and constant practice of prayer, and as a result certain Sufis have been persecuted for not publically supporting the Iranian Islamic Republic.

Common Factors: Little can be said about Sufism and Mandaeism because of the secrecy surrounding their practices. Zoroastrianism seems to have more resemblance to Judaism and Christianity.

Sufism emblem.

KABBALAH

The Kabbalah is many things, but it is not a "religion," and it is not Judaism despite its origins and its involvement with modern mystical sects like Hasidism. Along with pre-religious Taoism and Tantra, it is a comprehensive intellectual and spiritual scheme describing the Cosmos and Humanity's position within it, and of the techniques the *individual* person *must* employ for growth, transformation, and transcendence. We *must* do this because that's what we are here to do. Man is incarnate in the physical world because it is the *Foundation* (Malkuth) of the "Serpentine Path" to the *Crown* (Kether) that is also "the Path of Return."

The *Tree of Life*, with its 10 + 1 Sephiroth and 22 Paths, is an esoteric representation of the structure of the Universe and a guide to its transcendent fulfillment. It can be divided into four worlds (or levels), into three columns, three triads, circles within

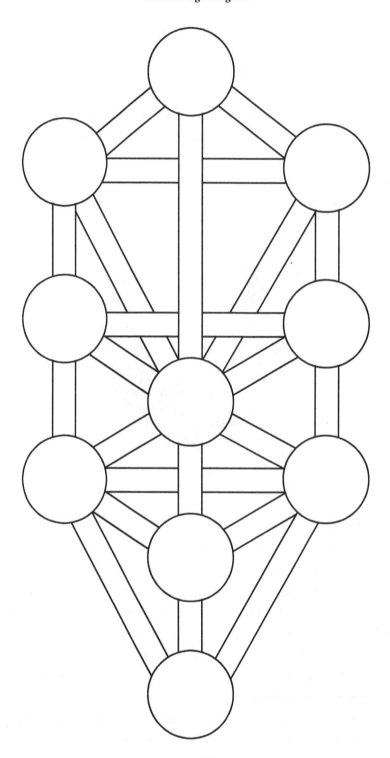

Tree of Life

circles, globes within globes, triangles and pyramids, it can be reversed front to back and top to bottom, it can be imposed in whole or parts on the human body and is used in many ways and forms of Spiritual Techniques.

It was used to give structure to the Tarot from which the meditational practice of Path-Working was developed; It is used to give structure and guidance to visionary meditations for Kundalini awakening and movement through the chakras; it is used to develop and study God Names and Words of Power used within Magickal systems; it provides structure for systems of numerology and scriptural interpretation; it provides structure for the system of correspondences used in practical magic; it provides structure and definition for forms of magickal invocation and evocation; and it provides guidance to Spirit realms, Spirit beings, access to Akashic Records, and Spiritual Communication with your own Higher Self, and other entities.

It has been "suggestively" useful to scientists of various disciplines from quantum physics to analytical psychology to parapsychology; to self-help and self-improvement practitioners; and to students of other esoteric and spiritual systems. It is eclectic and useful in all systems and practices. In this New Age personal interests are recognized as signals to opportunities for growth and development.

There is a particular value for New Age inspired study of such older systems as Kabbalah to reacquaint modern man with the nature and structure of the mythical dimensions of the old to make it dynamically personal and subjective in nature in the new. As Charles Ponce writes:

> *"Each of us must become a hero for ourselves and experience the tension of the mythical drama of fall and redemption in ourselves. In order to mythically reconstruct the universe, we must reconstruct or rediscover the original unity within us by calling forth and constellating the total man, the whole man, the new Adam who each of us has the potential to become."*
> —(From Kabbalah—see source list)

Note: Whatever "knocks at your door" may be a key to transcendence—but, remember to apply intelligence, common sense, and *wariness* before inviting a stranger into your spiritual home. You are wise to explore many paths before adopting one, or several in appropriate combination, as your Path to Transcendence. In particular, Kabbalah, Tantra, and Taoism provide intellectual structure and discipline to shamanic, mythic based Paganism, divinatory systems including the Tarot and Yi King, and disciplined meditational practices.

Common Factors: Perhaps more than any other "mapping" system, the Kabbalistic philosophy, Tree of Life diagrams, and encyclopedic references to correspondences is a true *key* to not only unlocking meanings but to opening all the gates, doors, windows, and hidden passageways in any magickal operating system, divinatory system, intellectual discipline and their essential meaning. From the Non-manifest and Premanifest to the Cosmic Unity behind all manifestation, and then through every level and sphere of manifestation and even the cast-away left-overs from manifestation, the Tree frees both Intellect and Intuition to reveal the "secrets of the universe" to the Seeker. Even more, the Seeker is free of all externally applied psychic and psychological restraints to explore each Path and Sephiroth to bring ultimate realization through any system of self-knowledge, self-development and spiritual attainment. It is the "tool of tools," the master switch, the crystal door.

MAGICK AND TRANSFORMATIONAL PRACTICES

Magick, Alchemy, Kabbalah, Martial Arts, Psychic Empowerment, Tantra, Tarot, and Yoga. While each of these subjects is further discussed in this "catalog" or in the next chapter, we want to say something here about their commonality that unites them in practice.

While not "religions" per se, many people do see these studies as that of a spiritual practice that resembles a religious choice. These are all studies and practice of human relationship to the non-physical dimensions of the Universe. The "student" seeks understanding of both physical and non-physical elements involved in what we can simply identify as "the Pursuit of Life, Liberty, and the Pursuit of Happiness." The student seeks understanding to better gain success in career, in personal and social relationships, in relationship to Nature and the Earth as a whole, and to Spirit as a whole. The premise is that the responsible individual will act to beneficially affect the future of humanity and our planet.

Alchemy, as related to Magick and Transformation, is the study of subtle energies in relation to focused consciousness. There is a "hidden" inner anatomy of the physical body, and all matter, that is consciously organized to move towards and accomplish specific goals.

Kabbalah is a set of esoteric teachings meant to explain the relationship between an unchanging, eternal and mysterious *Ein Sof* beyond all manifestation of the mortal and finite universe. Kabbalah seeks to define the nature of the universe and the human being, the nature and purpose of existence, and presents methods to aid understanding of these concepts and thereby attain spiritual realization. We discussed some particular aspects of Kabbalah earlier, and will do so again in Chapter Thirteen on Magick.

Magick is nothing more and nothing less than applied Mind Power by means of techniques of focused intention and visualization involving a systematic organization and movement of symbols and forces to accomplish specific psychic and material benefits. At the foundation of the symbol system are "correspondences" based primarily on relationships perceived on the Kabbalistic Tree of Life. Other practices are derived from Tantra, particularly that of transformative visualizations of the Tattvas. (See the included "Tattva Connection Meditation & Visualization Program" in our *Clairvoyance for Psychic Empowerment* for further detail and actual practice.)

Egyptian Magick and Religion was discussed previously and is noted here because of its importance to Modern Magick and to the fundamental concept of Spirit. Magick has been with us just as long as has Shamanism but its history is readily associated with ancient Egypt. When people think of Magick, particularly that practiced by various secret and not-so-secret Hermetic Orders, many readily turn to scenes and imagery of ancient Egypt. The term, *Heka,* means "the ability to make things happen by indirect means." *Heka,* itself was believed to be natural force by which the Universe was (and is) created. The gods use it in their work, but human also can learn to use it. As a side thought, perhaps this is the source of the old expression "By Heck!" then meaning "By Magick." Also "What the Heck!" even though believed to be an alternate for "Hell," but remember the Church said anything magical came from the Devil, hence from Hell.

The Egyptian priests taught that practical magic was a way for humans to prevent or overcome negative events. That would be ethical, but to use it for personal gain would, apparently, not.

Words are part of *Heka*, and Thoth, the god of writing, is likewise a god of magical incantations and their use in ritual along with objects naturally imbued with *Heka* or especial charged with it.

From these early beginnings we have the major divisions of High Magick and Low magic, also called Ceremonial and Practical. Ceremonial Magick is mostly *transformative* and *spiritual* in its purpose, while practical magic is intended for personal gain (success), healing, and to attract love, money, and power. It's often takes the form of "spell casting."

And, then, there is **Sex Magick** in which male and female magickians bring together *Tantric* sexual energy in an empowering ritual of visualization and intention to accomplish material benefits.

Martial Arts will be discussed later in some greater detail, but the subject is noted here because of the general importance of relating inner energies and their flow through the subtle channels called "meridians," to some forms of magical practice. While these "Arts" are an effective and very controlled projection of inner power through aggressive and defensive physical movement, they are also another form of **"Yoga"** involving postures and positions with precise movements and visualized energetic transfers from artist to target.

Tantra is more than the teaching of sexual mechanics so familiar today. It is essentially the source for the science and practice regarding kundalini and the chakras, and the meditation/visualizations that guide the ascent of kundalini through the chakras to bring about human transmutation. However, it is by means of the various practices of extended sex and the prolonged female orgasm that man and woman join together in the fundamental intimate partnership that awakens body, mind and soul to the Next Level. Tantra sees the Divine as both immanent and transcendent. Tantric practices transform the passions, instead of transcending them. We discuss Tantra further later in this chapter.

Tarot consists of an organized structure of symbols in combination with pictures of people representing life experience and action. The organizing structure is itself based on the Four Worlds and the Spheres and Paths on the Kabbalistic Tree of Life. While commonly used in divination, the Tarot also provides a system of **"Path Working"** which is a program of systematic *moving* meditation/visualization leading toward an **Alchemical** transformation of body, mind and soul. While the Tarot is not discussed in further detail in this book, it is important to see it as an element that is increasingly recognized as important to the practices of Magick and as a complete system in its own right.

Common Factors: Symbolism, Correspondences, Subtle Bodies and Energies, Psychic Empowerment.

MARTIAL ARTS

We call them "martial" and also "arts," but they're more than either word conveys. Even though they are primarily perceived as systems of *combat*—more often defensive than offensive—and some are also *performance* oriented nearly like dance or competitive gymnastics, they cover a vast range of Fighting Systems and Sports.

Commonly we think of just a few martial arts from China and Japan, mostly based on the subtle energy system of Taoism, but there are actually over 100 different styles and practices from around the world. Some have a very sophisticated underlying philosophy and a formal code of ritual and practice while others are just little more than rough and tumble, kill 'em if you can. At their core, they can resemble religious ritual and embody esoteric spirituality.

When it comes to attempting to describe them, the complexity of style, technique, and purpose, we see much more than muscle and brawn. Armed vs. unarmed; simple to elaborate movements; weapons include swords, sabers, foils, knives, clubs, sticks, spears, javelins, throwing disks, boomerangs, daggers, brass knuckles, steel gloves, hard-toe boots, and spiked elbow and knee guards; types of combat include wrestling, grappling, punching, boxing, kicking, striking, throwing, etc.

We're not used to thinking of *wrestling*, for example, as a performance "art," but then examine the elements demonstrated in a televised match that make it exciting for the audience. Japanese *Sumo* wrestling is even more choreographed. The more familiar forms include Aikido, Judo, Jujutsu, Karate, Kendo, Taekwondo, and Tai chi ch'uan, and others in which the mental state is as important as the physical training. But we must not entirely overlook those arts that include weapons. Probably the most familiar of these, at least for Westerners, is Fencing with foils—which is much choreographed, every aggressive and defense move follows very specific rules, and the advances and retreats have specific movements of feet, hands, and arms.

Keep in mind these two points: Performance, and Choreography. Those combine outer awareness of the performance with interior conformance to established rules and criteria as rigid as that for a ballerina.

But, these arts are more than performance: the familiar Oriental martial arts employ a vast knowledge of internal energies and pathways for directing those energies for maximum effectiveness. That's why a seeming "90 pound weakling" can easily toss a 200 pound man into the air, place him into and then hold him in a rigid posture, until he acknowledges defeat. That's also why those arts derived from Taoist and Tantric principles are just as much a Spiritual practice as a Martial Art.

Go back, and re-read about Alchemy to better understand the transformative interaction between inner and outer when the actions involved are consciously driven with full awareness of the Spiritual factors.

Common Factors: Conscious awareness of Inner and Outer; Controlled and Choreographed movements; "Performance" awareness of the "Watcher" (whether an audience or that of a Higher Self); Ritual honoring of the adversary, the teacher, and the Watcher; Understanding of the subtle energies, pathways, and centers.

METAPHYSICS

The word "metaphysics" derives from the Greek words *μετά (metá)* ("beyond,") and *φυσικά (physiká)* ("physics"). It commonly describes any non-traditional spiritual science and practice, and thus includes most forms of esoteric and alternative belief systems, particularly those also classified as New Age, Eastern, Occult, Oriental, and Non-conformist.

Metaphysics is a traditional branch of philosophy concerned with explaining the fundamental nature of being and the world, although the term is not so easily applied. Essentially, it attempts to clarify how we perceive and understand the world, e.g., existence, objects and their properties, space and time, cause and effect, and possibility. But, that overlooks the *meta* part of the word referring to beyond physics, or the greater than the purely physical dimension. In other words, *metaphysics* is inclusive of both the physical and the non-physical, the natural and the supernatural, the exoteric and the esoteric, outer and inner.

However, contrary to the way some people use the word, it does not exclude the physical, nor does it see it as separate: Metaphysics is the Greater Reality and the "whole ball of wax!" Just as it recognizes the inner reality of etheric, astral, mental, and spiritual, it is also concerned with how they relate to the physical. You cannot deal with one part by itself because everything is *entangled* with everything else!

The general claim is that prior to modern times, scientific questions were part of metaphysics then known as *natural philosophy,* whereas what we now apply as the *scientific method* transformed natural philosophy into an empirical activity based upon experiment, observation, analysis, and testing by further experiment *without regard to the greater questions of relationship to "higher" dimensions.*

One branch of metaphysics is ontology, the investigation into the basic categories of being and how they relate to each other. Another branch is cosmology, the study of the totality of all phenomena within the universe.

Today, metaphysics denotes all enquiry into both the non-physical and the physical nature of existence, including that of man, *visible* and *invisible.*

Modern metaphysical cosmology and cosmogony try to address questions such as:

What is the origin of the Universe? What is its first cause? Is its existence necessary? Explore such subjects as monism, pantheism, emanationism and creationism.

What are the ultimate material components of the Universe? Explore mechanism, dynamism, hylomorphism, and atomism.

What is the ultimate reason for the existence of the Universe? Does the cosmos have a purpose? Explore teleology.

New metaphysical ideas have come from quantum mechanics, where subatomic particles do not have the same sort of "individuality" as the larger particles of the "old" plain physical world with which philosophers, scientists, and the rest of have traditionally been concerned. In addition, the old determinism is replaced by the uncertainty principle at the subatomic/energetic level seemingly related to the subtle dimensions of traditional occultism. At the deepest and smallest levels of physical reality, the barriers between physical and non-physical disappear and the old "clock works" picture of the universe is replaced by the "Greater Reality" that is truly comprehensive of all that is "Heaven and Earth."

Common Factors: Holism, Scientific Method of Inquiry and Analysis, the involvement of Mind in Cosmological Reality.

MORPHIC FIELD

While the biochemist Rupert Sheldrake's "Morphic field"* is not usually discussed in a "spiritual" context, it does demonstrate the growing *metaphysical* coming together of physical, biological, and psychological sciences with esoteric and paranormal concepts so characteristic of the New Age.

In actuality—whether knowingly or not—Sheldrake is essentially attempting to provide a scientific platform for established esoteric and metaphysical concepts. And that has considerable value in bridging the gap between the two "camps" of science and metaphysics. In providing a foundation for discussion we have the means to better understanding the objectives of both and providing a better exposition of metaphysical concepts for the New Ager.

Sheldrake proposes that there is a holistic field within and around a "Morphic Field"* which organizes its characteristic structure and pattern of activity. This "Morphic Field" underlies the formation and behavior of "Holons"** and "Morphic units,"*** and can be set up by the repetition of similar acts or thoughts. The hypothesis is that a particular form belonging to a certain group, which has already established its (collective) "Morphic field," will *tune into* that "Morphic field." The particular form will *read* the collective information through the process of "Morphic resonance,"**** using it to guide its own development. This development of the particular form will then provide, again through "Morphic resonance," a feedback to the "Morphic field" of that group, thus strengthening it with its own experience, resulting in new information being added (i.e. *stored* in the *database*). Sheldrake regards the "Morphic fields" as a universal database for both organic (genetic) and abstract (mental) forms.

> * A Morphic Field is that field around which a Morphic Unit organizes its characteristic structure and pattern of activity at all levels of complexity. That pattern is shaped and stabilized by Morphic Resonance.
>
> ** A Holon is a whole field that can be part of a larger whole. Holons, in turn, are organized in multi-level nested holarchies (a term for hierarchies used by Arthur Koestler in his 1967 book, *The Ghost in the Machine).*
>
> *** A Morphic Unit is any form or organization—an atom, molecule, cell, pattern, group, system, planet, or galaxy—containing similar units in a hierarchical structure existing independently of other units with which it may be connects.
>
> **** Morphic Resonance is the continuing memory of previous structures acting as a causal influence on the formation of subsequent similar units.

That a mode of transmission of shared informational patterns and archetypes might exist did gain some tacit acceptance when it was proposed as the theory of the collective unconscious by renowned psychiatrist Carl Jung. According to Sheldrake, the theory of "Morphic fields" might provide an explanation for the concept of Akashic records (the "library" of all the experiences and memories of human minds through their physical lifetimes since one's *past* consists of *thoughts* as simple mental forms all processed by the same mind. Sheldrake's view on memory-traces is that they are non-local, and not located in the brain.

Morphic resonance. Sheldrake views the universe as a swarm of matter waves, spiraling down the gradient of their synergetic constructive interference. When two matter waves become connected by mutual quantum entanglement, they *intuit* each other. This form of intuition interconnects matter waves instantaneously, regardless of their separation.

Sheldrake thinks that all humans are connected to everybody we think of and to all the places we are attached to. Our minds are vast, far-reaching, and spatially extended networks of connections in space and time in which the brains are but a portion.

The greater the degree of similarity, the greater the constructive interference, the greater likelihood of persistence of particular new forms. Sheldrake suggests that matter waves' synergetic (energetically favorable) interference is the mechanism by which simpler ensembles of matter waves self-organize into more complex ones, and that this model provides the true explanation for the process of evolution.

Morphogenetic fields are the subset of Morphic fields which influence, and are influenced by living things. They generally refer to a "collection of cells by whose interactions a particular organ formed." Morphic fields have a more general meaning and includes other kinds of organizing fields which contain an inherent memory, such as the organizing fields of animal and human behavior, of social and cultural systems, and of mental activity.

Healing Field? We might speculate that the imposition of an organized collective field of healthy persons on to those suffering illness might experience a healing.

Common Factors: Connectedness of units within a holistic field; Endurance of personal memory; "Intuitional" sharing of similar information systems through the Collective Unconscious.

NEW THOUGHT

The earliest recognized proponent of what we call New Thought was the American philosopher, mesmerist, healer, and inventor Phineas Parkhurst Quimby (1802–66). He believed illness originated in the mind as a consequence of erroneous beliefs and that a mind open to God's wisdom could overcome any illness. He wrote: "The trouble is in the mind, for the body is only the house for the mind to dwell in … Therefore, if your mind had been deceived by some invisible enemy into a belief, you have put into it the form of a disease, with or without your knowledge. By my theory or truth, I come in contact with your enemy, and restore you to health and happiness. This I do partly mentally, and partly by talking till I correct the wrong impression and establish the Truth, and the Truth is the cure." (Quimby, P.: *Christ or Science—the Quimby Manuscripts, 2008*, Forgotten Books)

John Bovee Dods (1795–1862), another early practitioner of New Thought, wrote that disease originates in the electrical impulses of the nervous system and is therefore curable by a change of belief. Another contributor to the 19th century metaphysical healing movement was a Swedenborgian minister, Wayne Felt Evans using the term "Mental Science" to describe his practice.

In 1906, William Walker Atkinson (1862–1932) added Dods' premise about the electrical nature of the nervous system to his own idea of mental states and the new scientific discoveries in electromagnetism and neural processes. He wrote and published *Thought Vibration or the Law of Attraction in the Thought World*. Atkinson was the editor of *New Thought* magazine and the author of more than 100 books on an assortment of religious, spiritual, and occult topics. The following year, Elizabeth Towne, the editor of *The Nautilus Magazine, a Journal of New Thought*, published Bruce MacLelland's book *Prosperity through Thought Force*, in which he summarized the "Law of Attraction" as a New Thought principle, stating "You are what you think, not what you think you are."

New Thought was popularized by a growing number of spiritual thinkers, many of them women, from a variety of religious denominations and churches, such as the Unity Church, Religious Science, and the Church of Divine Science. Notable among these were Emma Curtis Hopkins, known as the "teacher of teachers," Myrtle Fillmore, Malinda Cramer, and Nona L. Brooks. Many of the churches and community centers were led by women, from the 1880s to today.

New Thought is also largely a movement of the printed word. From the 1890s and through the 20th century and into the 21st a growing number of New Thought/New Age books focus on "Mind Power" in relation to self-help, financial success, positive thinking, creative visualization and will power. Ralph Waldo Emerson, Napoleon Hill, Wallace Wattles, Dale Carnegie, Robert Collier, Wayne Dyer, Emmet Fox, James Allen, Perry Joseph Green, Frank Channing Haddock, Louise Hay, Joseph and Michal Murphy, Carolyn Myss, Norman Vincent Peale, Joe Vitale, Thomas Troward, and many, many more are extremely popular in various aspects of the New Thought movement.

The chief tenets of New Thought are:

The Infinite Intelligence of the Creative Source is omnipotent and omnipresent in all Life and Matter.

Spirit is the ultimate reality.

True human self-hood is divine.

Attuning personal thought with the Creative Source is a force for good.

Mind, is the means to focus Spirit on Will-determined Goals.

All disease is mental in origin.

Right thinking has a healing effect.

As thought evolves so does everything guided by thought.

Adherents also generally believe that as humankind gains greater understanding of the world, New Thought itself will evolve to assimilate new knowledge. New Thought is a "process" in which each individual and even the New Thought Movement itself is constantly advancing to ever higher levels of perception and understanding. *We are constantly becoming more than we are!*

New Thought publishing and educational activities reach approximately 2.5 million people annually. Divine Science, Unity Church, and Religious Science are organizations that developed from the New Thought movement. The largest New Thought-oriented denomination is *Seicho-no-Ie*. Other belief systems within the New Thought movement include Jewish Science, Religious Science, Centers for Spiritual Living and Unity. Past denominations have included Psychiana and Father Divine.

Religious Science operates under three main organizations: the United Centers for Spiritual Living; the Affiliated New Thought Network; and Global Religious Science Ministries. Ernest Holmes, the founder of Religious Science wrote that Religious Science is not based on any established belief "authority," but rather on "what it can accomplish" for the user. Unity, founded by Charles and Myrtle Fillmore, focuses on "Christian idealism," with the Bible as one of its main texts, although not interpreted literally. Another core text is *Lessons in Truth* by H. Emilie Cady.

Common Factors: *Mind Power—clear of "garbage" thinking and identified with the Creative Source and strongly focused on defined goals is potentially the greatest power in the universe.* While prayer and meditation are common practices in the movement, newer elements include the techniques of Self-Hypnosis and Tattva Meditation

(see our books *Self-Empowerment through Self-Hypnosis* and *Clairvoyance for Psychic Empowerment* for Tattva Meditation guidance)

NON-THEISTIC

A non-theistic "religion" or Belief System does not center upon the existence of any deities, nor does it deny their existence either as real or possible. Non-theist groups and individuals can easily associate with Theists as well as atheists and agnostics and other open-minded students exploring questions about ethics and morality, the responsibilities of individuals and societies, deities and spirit entities, natural forces and powers, the origins of life and of the universe, the physical and the metaphysical, the nature of evolution, the possible meanings of life and personhood, the *non-religious* values of techniques—such as prayer and meditation—often associated with religion.

Theist believers often integrate their beliefs in a deity or deities with the non-theistic religions, rather than dealing with the two "stances" as separate entities. People often comfortably identify with Unitarian Universalism for the social values, studies and discussions of world religions and spiritual practices, and various social service programs sponsored by the churches for the benefit of local residents.

Common Factors: Intellectual, Respect, Open-minded discussion, Social services.

NONE

One of the fastest growing "religious movements" in the United States today is "None" or "No Religion," as shown in response to surveys and questions as to religious affiliation. That's the choice of 20 percent of the population, and is the highest it has ever been since the surveys started in the 1930s. This is not Atheism nor Agnosticism, but the *rejection of organized religion*. According to the Pew Research center, a third of U.S. adults under the age of 30 do not identify with a religion, nor are they looking for a religion. "Overwhelmingly, they think that religious organizations are too concerned with money and power, too focused on rules and too involved in politics."

Indications are that the growth has come about because of the extreme views of the Religious Right, anti-gay attitudes, sexual conservatism and even denial of sex education and access to contraception, and its involvement in conservative politics. The perception is that "religion equals conservative politics equals religion."

While some people, particularly those who are young and starting new families, appreciate the social connections of church, they prefer the intellectual approach of Deism, Freemasonry, and Unitarian-Universalist membership.

Common Factors: Intellectual, Respect, Open-minded discussion, Social services, Rejection of "conservative" values.

NOVUS ORDO SECLORUM—A NEW WORLD ORDER

On that memorable day in American history, July 4, 1776, the Continental Congress of the new nation of the United States of America established a committee to design the official seal used as a *signature* on the work of the government. The initial members of the committee were Benjamin Franklin, John Adams, and Thomas Jefferson—all of them signers of the Declaration of Independence, and two of them future Presidents.

Today, this is known as the ***Great Seal of the United States*** and both sides of the Seal are shown on the back side of the dollar bill. All the symbols and words on these two sides, reflecting the Masonic interests of many of the Founding Fathers, have elicited controversy and endless speculation and conspiracy claims ever since their first appearance, but perhaps none so much as the wording beneath the image of seemingly unfinished Great Pyramid: *Novus Ordo Seclorum,* translated from the Latin variously as <u>A New Order of the Ages</u> or a <u>New World Order</u>.

Many sensational books have been written on the esoteric meanings of the symbols: the Pyramid, the unfinished Capstone, the All-seeing Eye in the Triangle, the great Bald Eagle with outstretched wings and claws holding—on the left a bundle of 13 arrows and on the right, an Olive Branch with 13 leaves, in its beak the Eagle holds a banner with the words *E Pluribus Unum* (Out of the many, One), over its breast is a shield of 13 stripes and above its head are 13 Five-Pointed Stars (Pentagrams) arranged in the shape of one Six-Pointed Star (a Hexagram), both used prominently in Magick and Pagan practices.

People searching for more evidence to support the various conspiracy theories proclaimed over the years have added to the list. Some claim that the whole thing is a secret message revealing a Jewish plot, others—in a time warp—have found evidence of Nazism, but one of the more interesting may be that the year 1776 inscribed in Roman numerals at the base of the Pyramid refers not to the founding of America but rather to the May 1, 1776 founding of the Order of the Illuminati by Adam Weishaupt.

The far more logical explanation is the one already mentioned: the use of Masonic symbols so familiar to Masons Franklin and Washington, John Hancock, Edmund Randolph, Ethan Alien, Edmund Burke, John Paul Jones, Paul Revere, and others. Of the 56 signers of the Declaration of Independence, eight were known Masons and seven others are believed to have been. Of the 40 signers of the Constitution, nine were known Masons and 13 more are believed to have been, and six more later did become Masons.

In addition to being a Masonic Grand Master, Franklin was also a Rosicrucian Grand Master, and it is claimed that he was Agent 72 of the British intelligence agency created by Dr. John Dee and Francis Bacon.

Interesting, but *what in particular does it all have to do with New Age Spirituality?* There are some who believe that there are "inner (spiritual) governments" of the most important nations of the world composed of *Elder Brothers* and *High Adepts* working at non-physical levels to influence the progressive evolution of those societies towards a democratic, classless, justice-for-all, rationally guided, non–aggressive, and benevolent global civilization.

Above these inner governments is believed to be the N.O.S., the *Novus Ordo Seclorum,* a secret group of incarnate and non-incarnate humans working towards a New World Order to last down the Ages.

True or not, there does seem to be movement in which American democracy and idealism are increasingly emulated by other nations—despite the regressive falterings of the Iraq and Afghanistan invasions, the recent institutionalizing of corporate and financial greed, and the corruption of pure science to the benefit of special interests in modern medicine and corporate farming.

Even if N.O.S. is but a dream, it is an example of New Age Spirituality. As a master ideal anyone can support, you can identify yourself with it by simply adding the initials N.O.S. after your signature in letters, e-mails and other non-legal and non-financial communications.

In summary, The New Order of the Ages represented in the Great Seal of the United States. N.O.S. is the spiritual unity behind the nation and the container for all the ideas represented by its founding. It has the potential to function as the 'over soul' of the nation should people turn inward to its inspiration. As we turn to the N.O.S. for inner guidance it aligns the person with those high ideas and guides their translation into their practical and contemporary manifestation. It is the repository of the high aspirations of the founding fathers and those thinkers and leaders who have sought to create a <u>new</u> nation based on principles rather than geographic and tribal boundaries. It represents the Spirit of America.

PAGANISM

As "native" to the European psyche, we have seen a considerable rebirth of interest and practice of those religions suppressed in the 2000 year rise and fall of Roman Christianity. In America, the United Kingdom and throughout Europe, ancient shamanic Witchcraft has both revived native traditions and been "born again" in modern Wicca and Goddess Spirituality. Several of the mythic religions have re-emerged in forms of Neo-Druidry, Asatru (Norse), Huna (Hawaiian), Celtic, Germanic, Greek, Baltic, Semitic, Strega (Italian) and Slavic neo-Paganism.

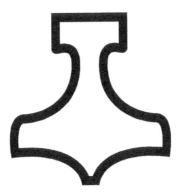

Hammer of Thor.

The movement has been far more than either revival antiquarianism and reconstruction, but a blending of old with new in response to an archetypal "re-surfacing" as people have studied their ancestral history, folklore, and crafts, have participated in past life regression, and now reject the regressive political, sexual, and fundamentalist demands of the dominant monotheistic religions. Further, more intellectual developments are occurring with Magickal interests in Ancient Egyptian, Greek, Roman, Tantric, and Mayan systems and actual participation in indigenous or "native" shamanic African, Native American, Shinto and other cultural practices.

While these are fascinating developments, particularly worth exploring for people of those cultural heritages, their full exploration is beyond the range of this book. Yet, while the various mythologies are deeply distinctive, there are elements in common with Wicca and Shamanism we do describe. Also read earlier sections on New Age Religion and Spirituality and the Goddess Movement.

Common Factors: Rejection of Abrahamic myths and values and rediscovery of those related to family cultural heritage, along with the explosion of interest in one's family tree, revivals of native crafts for personal enjoyment and sometimes small business development, and the direct experience in non-institutional spiritual practices.

PERSONAL RELIGION

Many people today define themselves as spiritual but not religious, and specifically not interested in "following the leader" of some group or organization. We believe there are many different "paths" that can lead towards real growth and development, and we feel a need to find, or develop, *the* individual path unique to our own body, psyche, mind, soul, and spirit that we can follow to *become more than we are* and *all we can be*. We may explore many growth exercises such as yoga, martial arts, meditation programs, self-hypnosis training, psychic development, paranormal skills, and study many subjects to increase understanding of self, history, spirituality, and personal transformation.

With increased understanding of the world we live in and on, and of the body and psyche we use to traverse each lifetime, we discover and embrace deeper meanings of physical and non-physical reality. Through own studies and growth we adopt our own deeply felt morality and rational foundations for an ethical life. Through our own spiritual discoveries we can have our own "religious experience" not beholden to any church or institutional belief system intended to *herd* us to proselytize on its behalf and supports its political purposes.

Common Factors: True Freedom of Belief.

PSYCHIC EMPOWERMENT

Many religions, both Western and Eastern, Old and New, make a point of denigrating psychic powers as a *distraction* from the student's <u>devotion</u> to Spiritual Attainment. There may be some truth to that point of view for the student who retreats from the world and all worldly responsibilities and single-mindedly follows the guidance of a Master or Guru.

However, we disagree!

We believe that we grow by participating in the life of "this world," and accepting responsibilities for our actions, and *non-actions!* We also believe in a continuing evolution of growth and development of all our innate powers, transforming them into skills, employing them in daily life just as we do with other talents and skills, and thus *becoming more than we are* and *all we can be.*

To use the phrase coined by author Anodea Judith in *The Global Heart Awakens:*

Evolution is the Gods' way of making more gods to which she adds: "Autonomy is essential for personal responsibility. If we cannot see ourselves as separated beings, we cannot take responsibility for our actions." In other words, the perpetual disciple is little more than a kind of indentured servant (and some gurus demand exactly that) and remains a sheep just as did the followers of the Church led by the bishop's crook.

To which we will add "There's something fishy about that free labor concept" of guru devotion just as there was in the old feudal system of free labor to the land barons and bishops of mediaeval Europe. That's all part of the past Piscean Age, for which the symbol is of two fish swimming in opposite directions, and getting nowhere!

We're in the Aquarian Age, aka the Information Age and the New Age. And that Age of Democracy and of an entrepreneurial middle class employing the newest quantum-based information and nano-technologies; of expressing personal vision through arts and crafts of a new cultural movement; which calls for every kind of self-development and self-empowerment for the vision to see new ways to meet the otherwise terrifying challenges of the population explosion, climate change, chemical pollution, and guns and guns and guns everywhere.

Yes, we are evolving toward becoming gods and co-creators, with the powers to create and destroy, but our "salvation" can only come through the exercise of personal responsibility and of participation for the good of the community rather than following corrupt and ideologically motivated politicians and self-serving "leaders."

Common Factors: Growth in Consciousness, Awareness, and Responsibility; Development of innate powers and skills; Rejection of Party Politics and Group control of thought and belief; Belief in personal and cosmic evolution; and Action to transcend old limitations and to *Become more than you are and all you can be.*

QUANTUM METAPHYSICS/QUANTUM MYSTICISM

Mind and Spirit establish Physical Reality

According to Avi Rabinowitz, the universe emerged into reality when there were "Moral Beings" able to exercise free will and thus it is that Mind and Spirit come before any physical reality. But this is also—in some manner—equating Humanity (perhaps as "co-creator) with the Creator Source, whether as an external deity or one coincident with the Creation.

True Reality is Spiritual

Also note that Mind and Spirit come before Body and Feeling. Mind is <u>not</u> a product of Body, but Body is a product of Mind. Both are, in the same send, products of Spirit.

In Rabinowitz' words "From the Kabbalistic perspective the true reality is the spiritual realm: the physical cosmos is God's precision-crafted instrument for achieving spiritual goals ... the physical universe is a shadow of the spiritual world, the illusion perceived by limited beings who are in contact with the spiritual cosmos but can directly sense and perceive only its shadow. Human free-willed moral choice connects the two realms, and this moral activity gives meaning to the existence of the universe."

The Human, potentially, controls the Spiritual

" ... the human body, rather than being a hindrance to spirituality, is a potentially holy physical tool which can control the spiritual ... every action/thought/word affects the spiritual cosmos, and one's life when correctly lived is designed to resonate with the spiritual and to correctly utilize the physical order to elicit the fusion of ultimate spirituality with the physical."

"Just as according to quantum physics (or metaphysics) nature has delegated to humans the ability to determine the nature of physical reality within the limitations of natural law, similarly God, the Creator of nature, delegated to man alone the ability to determine the nature of spiritual reality, which then influences the physical."

We Think, therefore We Are!

According to quantum physics, physical reality is *fixed* by the act of *conscious* observation, but the truth is that we know very little about **consciousness,** and what could be more important? *We think, therefore we are!* But, what are we? Everything we are <u>is</u>, or <u>is a function</u> of consciousness! We also say that everything is energy, and we know that being conscious requires energy.

Observation affects sub-atomic Reality

With the emergence of Quantum Physics we've learned that the mere act of observation affects reality at the sub-atomic level; in technical terms, "consciousness caused collapse" to change physical reality. That leads to the conclusion that the observer and reality are not separate and neither are mind and body truly separate at the subtle energy levels affecting long-term health but also providing an understanding of how non-physical healing (spiritual, energy, laying on of hands, etc.) may work.

In his 1988 book, *Quantum Healing*, Deepak Chopra explained psychosomatic healing using quantum concepts, and, then, in his 1993 *Ageless Body, Timeless Mind*, he provided studies of healing, age reversal, and longevity using specific practices derived from a "quantum worldview."

In *Shadows of the Mind*, physicist Roger Penrose wrote that consciousness may be a quantum phenomenon, that quantum forces affect neural processing. Physicist Fritjof Capra's *The Tao of Physics* explored parallels between Eastern concepts and quantum physics, broadening the discussions still further. Robert Anton Wilson's *Quantum Psychology* explained psychologist Timothy Leary's *Eight Circuit Model of Consciousness* in terms of "Quantum Mysticism."

Consciousness extends infinitely through Space

What we have is the idea that Consciousness (and potentially Intelligence) connects everyone through quantum fields that extend infinitely through space. Note, that we are acknowledging that consciousness and intelligence are not necessarily the same, but that we cannot gain and exercise intelligence without consciousness. To be conscious, to be aware, to think, to train the mind to process observations analytically and rationally are the foundations of intelligence. Inspiration, intuition, clairvoyant vision, even "feeling," all feed into Intelligence to enable the human mind to function richly beyond the mere neural processing of the physical brain.

From Small to Bigger, From Bottom Up

The realization that we are more than a physical body, that the "cosmos" is more than the physical universe, that as humans we have the power—infinitely—to **Become more than we are!** And most important of all, smallness can be more important than bigness in the physical dimension which is where we plant our feet. Ideas start off big in the higher dimensions, but unless you build "from the ground up, they won't amount to the proverbial "hill of beans."

Common Factors: The Importance of "smallness" and "building from the ground up." Consciousness is in everything and the key to all we do. Yes, even such realizations of this sort count as part of our growing spiritual consciousness, and the assumption of personal responsibility that we each must assume to grow and ***Become All we can Be!***

RAELIAN MOVEMENT

Sometimes listed as a variant of Atheism because it rejects and formally renounces all previous religions and all gods. The Creation of Humanity is credited to advanced life forms beyond Earth who seek our betterment.

Common Factors: ETs, belief in "betterment," and life and consciousness throughout the Universe.

SCIENCE AND SPIRIT

Yes, Science does belong here in a discussion about Spirit. Some writers do talk about the reconciliation of Science with Religion, but—given the definition and history of religion—that's quite a challenge.

But we do want a dynamic reconciliation of what each represents: Science brings understanding to the Physical Universe, and Religion *should* bring meaning to the Universe. Science studies the particular aspect of <u>Substance</u> that is the Universe, but that same Substance is Spirit physically *incarnate*, and Spirit and Consciousness are also two sides of the same coin.

What should we call this interdisciplinary subject that deals with three that are usually treated separately—Science, Spirit, and Consciousness—each necessary to understanding the substance and meaning of the totality we live in and through, where we love and grow, and within which become all that we can be and grow up to become gods and co-creators?

For the present, let's just call the unifying category "Science and Spirit" and hope to come up with something better. Because there is distinction here between Science and Spirit, we're not comfortable merging this study into "Quantum Metaphysics."

The Challenge

When you read books by scientists, for the most part they write in the same competitive vein as do religionists: the "other side" is treated only as an enemy, one who is blind to the "revealed truth," etc. If religion truly spoke of Spirit, and Science was open to larger realities than the purely physical, dialogue would be possible and productive.

Common Factors: The Search for Understanding and Meaning.

SCIENTOLOGY

Sometimes referred to as a "new" religion, Scientology has a lot of the old "command and control" about it.

Pulp-fiction writer, L. Ron Hubbard, wrote *Dianetics—the Modern Science of Mental Health* in 1950. The basic teaching was a distrust of emotions, ways to free an individual from restricting unconscious memories, and enabling them to become more rational. Later, Hubbard added a belief in past life memories and an expensive process of counseling involving hypnosis, memory recall, and emotional release.

In 1952, Hubbard—after stating that the quickest way to wealth was through starting a religion—released a re-named set of teachings as *Scientology, a religions philosophy,* and in 1953 he incorporated as a Church of Scientology. At times, law suits have been filed against the Church in various countries around the world. Despite that, Hubbard died a multi-millionaire in 1986, and the Church continues to serve some 8 million members.

Common Elements: The importance of Past Life memories, and the use of Hypnosis.

SECULAR HUMANISM

"Secular Humanism," in one sense, is just a way to give a name to the second largest (American) "religious" group after Christianity, and the fastest growing, "non-religious or secular" (group). (From www.adherents.com/rel_USA.html)

Secular Humanism affirms an ethical system based on rational analysis of human experience that is objective, equally accessible to every human being regardless of gender, race, class, wealth, or position. It specifically rejects religious dogma or supernaturalism as the basis of morality and decision making.

It does not assume that humans are inherently bad through some "original sin," nor that they are innately good because of "divine origin." Nor are humans seen as superior to Nature or that Nature was created to "serve man." Rather it emphasizes human responsibility for our individual and collective actions and our unique role as custodians of at least that portion of Earth where humanity interfaces with it. Aside from what we learn from pure science, we must consider the ethical consequences of human decisions.

It is also the responsibility of the secular humanist to rationally analyze all ideology, whether religious or political, to accept nothing on the basis of "faith," and to speak against attempts to violate the established principles of the Constitution and Bill or Rights. Vigilance is an obligation. In 1943 the Archbishop of Canterbury publically warned that the "Christian tradition ... was in danger of being undermined by a Secular Humanism."

In contrast to such warnings, the International Humanist and Ethic Union states:

> *"Humanism is a democratic and ethical life stance, which affirms that human beings have the right and responsibility to give meaning and shape to their own lives. It stands for the building of a more humane society through an ethic based on human and other natural values in the spirit of reason and free inquiry through human capabilities. It is not theistic, and it does not accept supernatural views of reality."*

According to the Council for Secular Humanism, the term "secular humanism" describes a world view with the following elements and principles:

> **Need to test beliefs**—A conviction that dogmas, ideologies and traditions, whether religious, political or social, must be weighed and tested by each individual and not simply accepted by faith.

> **Reason, evidence, scientific method**—A commitment to the use of critical reason, factual evidence and scientific method of inquiry in seeking solutions to human problems and answers to important human questions.

> **Fulfillment, growth, creativity**—A primary concern with fulfillment, growth and creativity for both the individual and humankind in general.

> **Search for truth**—A constant search for objective truth, with the understanding that new knowledge and experience constantly alter our imperfect perception of it.

> **This life**—A concern for this life (as opposed to an afterlife) and a commitment to making it meaningful through better understanding of ourselves, our history, our intellectual and artistic achievements, and the outlooks of those who differ from us.

Ethics—A search for viable individual, social and political principles of ethical conduct, judging them on their ability to enhance human well-being and individual responsibility.

Justice and fairness—an interest in securing justice and fairness in society and in eliminating discrimination and intolerance.

Building a better world—A conviction that with reason, an open exchange of ideas, good will, and tolerance, progress can be made in building a better world for ourselves and our children.

And, the Council offers this statement:

The Affirmations of Humanism:A Statement of Principles

- We are committed to the application of reason and science to the understanding of the universe and to the solving of human problems.
- We deplore efforts to denigrate human intelligence, to seek to explain the world in supernatural terms, and to look outside nature for salvation.
- We believe that scientific discovery and technology can contribute to the betterment of human life.
- We believe in an open and pluralistic society and that democracy is the best guarantee of protecting human rights from authoritarian elites and repressive majorities.
- We are committed to the principle of the separation of church and state.
- We cultivate the arts of negotiation and compromise as a means of resolving differences and achieving mutual understanding.
- We are concerned with securing justice and fairness in society and with eliminating discrimination and intolerance.
- We believe in supporting the disadvantaged and the handicapped so that they will be able to help themselves.
- We attempt to transcend divisive parochial loyalties based on race, religion, gender, nationality, creed, class, sexual orientation, or ethnicity, and strive to work together for the common good of humanity.
- We want to protect and enhance the earth, to preserve it for future generations, and to avoid inflicting needless suffering on other species.

- We believe in enjoying life here and now and in developing our creative talents to their fullest.

- We believe in the cultivation of moral excellence.

- We respect the right to privacy. Mature adults should be allowed to fulfill their aspirations, to express their sexual preferences, to exercise reproductive freedom, to have access to comprehensive and informed health-care, and to die with dignity.

- We believe in the common moral decencies: altruism, integrity, honesty, truthfulness, responsibility. Humanist ethics is amenable to critical, rational guidance. There are normative standards that we discover together. Moral principles are tested by their consequences.

- We are deeply concerned with the moral education of our children. We want to nourish reason and compassion.

- We are engaged by the arts no less than by the sciences.

- We are citizens of the universe and are excited by discoveries still to be made in the cosmos.

- We are skeptical of untested claims to knowledge, and we are open to novel ideas and seek new departures in our thinking.

- We affirm humanism as a realistic alternative to theologies of despair and ideologies of violence and as a source of rich personal significance and genuine satisfaction in the service to others.

- We believe in optimism rather than pessimism, hope rather than despair, learning in the place of dogma, truth instead of ignorance, joy rather than guilt or sin, tolerance in the place of fear, love instead of hatred, compassion over selfishness, beauty instead of ugliness, and reason rather than blind faith or irrationality.

- We believe in the fullest realization of the best and noblest that we are capable of as human beings.

As a kind of final admonition, Paul G. Bell wrote in Mensa magazine, Feb. 2002 the higher the intelligence or level of education, the less religious people are. Should we presume the reverse corollary: that *the less religious people are, the higher their intelligence and level of education?* No, not without scientific evidence, and even with such data there is not a logical correlation between levels of intelligence and levels of education, but there is one to the effect that education facilitates opportunities for higher intelligence and rational thinking and behavior.

Common Factors: Rejection of Abrahamic myths and values, and of all theological presumptions to impose religious concepts as morality and "law."

SHAMANISM

We discussed this subject in Chapter Eight, and refer to it here mainly to trace the common elements of "Spirit" and "Spirituality" as they function in *Spiritual Communication* and in *Psychic Development* and *Self-Empowerment* in New Age religious, spiritual, and related ethical living, systems.

What we set out to establish in that chapter is:

Spirit is the *substance* of consciousness just as matter is the *substance* of energy.

Consciousness and Energy move the Universe.

Spirit, and *Spirits*, are everywhere—and *Spirituality* is Universal.

Spirit is fundamental to all existence, even at the most basic physical level.

Spirits are fundamental to all life, even at the most basic botanical, biological, and elemental levels.

Spirituality is fundamental to all levels of consciousness.

What it comes down to is that the universality of Spirit enables communication across the universe and between all Spirit containing things, however it is Spirituality combined with Intelligence that further enables the inter-communications that are the primary interest in this book.

Shamans were and are the "direct experiencers" of ecstatic union with "Spirit" and the gods and goddesses and other entities ruling the inner world and influencing the outer world. They were and are the witches and "wise women," the medicine men and women, herbal and spiritual healers, the travelers to and messengers from the spirit world, and the visionaries able to describe the non-physical inner worlds in understandable mythic language and poetry.

Shamanism allows relatively easy access to altered states, a fact that may partly account for its renewed popularity today. Shamanism offers what it has offered for hundreds of thousands of yesterdays; namely a relatively rapid means of controlled transcendence. As such, shamans can be considered as the founders of both religious and spiritual movements.

Shamanism Today

Shamanism is ancient—the oldest system of spiritual practice known—and it has continued down through ages and is widely practiced today. But, even though it was the forerunner of religions it never was and is not a religion, per se. Regrettably some people today are attempting to make it one, but the core of Shamanism is that of the individual's *attitude* of respect for universal Spirit in all things. It is the individual sha-man's ability to relate and use that Spirit in healing, magical operations, information gathering, and personal transformation that is Shamanism's continued *raison d'etre*. It can be taught and it can be learned as a living experiential and intuitive science, and the individual can become a shaman, but it should not be "churchified" and made into a static theology controlled by a hierarchical bureaucracy. We've had enough of that in the "Old Age" still continuing to fight against change and individual spiritual empowerment.

Controlled Transcendence

What is distinct about Shamanism is that it allows easy access to altered states—essentially a rapid means of controlled transcendence. In Chapter Eight we described many of the techniques for ecstatic consciousness—and it is this that sets Shamanism apart from religion which denies transcendent states to its followers.

The Shamanic Journey

At the heart of shamanism is the journey. It is this that distinguishes shamans from other ecstatics, healers, and intuitive counselors. The shaman enters into a trance during which his/her consciousness leaves his body and journeys through the three Worlds to see, learn, and transfer information and knowledge.

The lower world is often a place of personal tests and challenges, but it is also where power animals are acquired and the shaman is guided and empowered. The upper world is where teachers and guides can be found, and journeys experienced and mystical ecstasy attained. The middle world is this world and shamans journey over it to gain information for self, client, and community.

Spiritual Road Maps

Shamans are hardly alone in seeking altered states—meditators, yogis, mystics, practitioners of magick, and others—do so and attain valuable personal realizations that have been further developed into technologies of transcendence. Spiritual traditions serve as road maps for beneficially applying these technologies. Religions and spiritual traditions are created, and their higher reaches preserved, by people who access transcendent states and then provide practices for others to learn and follow.

The shamanic tradition transmits information and techniques that allow novices to re-create the altered states and abilities of their predecessors, and even add to its accumulated treasure of wisdom and techniques, and transmit them to future generations.

Ritualization of Religion leads to its failure

But that transmission can fail for many reasons, including the invasion of indigenous territories by proselytizing churches, destructions of communities and the local shamans with it, and cultural disrespect for "the old ways." When this occurs, the technology of transcendence may be lost and, with it, transcendent states and direct experience of the sacred. Transformative techniques now give way to mere symbolic rituals, direct experience yields to secondhand belief, and knowledge decays into doctrine and dogma. This is a process of 'the ritualization of religion' of which the *Tao Te Ching* laments: 'Ritual is the husk of true faith.'"

A prime example of this is found in the history of Japanese Shamanism, once rich in tradition but few contemporary Japanese shamans enter altered states and actually journey. "Today this trance occurs only rarely. The capacity for this kind of dissociation, and for the visionary journey which goes with it, seems to have diminished in recent centuries and today the journey is most commonly accomplished by symbolic action in fully waking consciousness." (Reference Blacker, C. (1986), *The catalpa bow: A study of shamanic practice in Japan*, Boston: Alllen & Unwin.)

Shibari and Kinbaku

The once honored trance inducing technologies of *Shibari* and *Kinbaku,* otherwise known as "Japanese Rope Bondage," have been largely reduced to a *Performance Art* practiced in night clubs where women volunteer to be tied in codified forms of turns and knots and then suspended to spin and turn freely in the air. Both sensual enjoyment and trance are commonly experienced. Today the practice is reappearing as a studio art and shamanic practice.

The Value of Shamanism

The more we explore shamanism, the more it points to unrecognized potentials of the human body, mind, and spirit. For untold thousands of years the world of shamanism has helped, healed, and taught humankind, and it has still more to offer us.

The Time is NOW. The challenge is to grow up and function in ways using the Trained Mind as well as Disciplined Body and Spirit. It's an evolutionary imperative. We are in a race between consciousness and catastrophe and the outcome remains unsure. A universal and cohesive effort is called for, but in these divisive times of conflicting patterns of self-interest and religious terrorism, it is difficult to see how spiritual practices in general can resolve the looming crisis in time.

Some modern religions and psychologies do recognize the possibility of accessing wisdom from inner sources that seem wiser than the ego. Religious methods include diverse rituals, prayers, and altered states of consciousness. These altered states include possession, soul travel, or quieting the mind so as to be able to hear the 'still small voice within.'

Hypnosis

"In psychology, major techniques include hypnosis and guided imagery. In fact, it is relatively easy to create an experience akin to channeling such hypnosis, as Charles Tart describes:

"From my studies with hypnosis I know I can set up an apparently independent existent entity whose characteristics are constructed to my specifications and the person hypnotized will experience it as if it's something outside of his own consciousness talking. So there is no doubt that some cases of channeling can be explained in a conventional kind of way. There is nothing psychic involved." (Quoted from Klimo, J. (1987). *Channeling*. Los Angeles: J. P. Tarcher)

Note: "Spirit" in the body is the mechanism of the Spiritual Journey by which the shaman observes physical and non-physical phenomenon, but the emphasis is not on communication with entities other than guides.

Common Factors: There are many ways to identify the common factors of New Age Spirituality, but the following is quoted from *The World of Shamanism* by Roger Walsh, M.D., Ph.D.:

There are seven essential practices for living life to the fullest:

1. Living ethically.
2. Transforming emotions
3. Redirecting motivations.

4. Training attention

5. Refining awareness

6. Cultivating wisdom

7. Serving others.

These are not factors held in common by New Age Spiritual systems, but recognized goals. What Shamanism offers in easy access to techniques of transcendence that may provide the means of insight to lead to such self-realization—if practiced by enough people—that might resolve a crisis of planetary dimension? We need wisdom rarely seen on a large scale.

SPIRITUALISM and SPIRITISM

"Modern Spiritualism" refers to the Anglo-American religious movement having its greatest presence between the 1840s and 1920s, still continuing to this day although with lesser influence. The Nine Principles of the National Spiritualist Association of Churches, USA affirms:

We believe in Infinite Intelligence.

We believe that the phenomena of Nature, both physical and spiritual, are the expression of Infinite Intelligence.

We affirm that a correct understanding of such expression and living in accordance therewith, constitute true religion.

We affirm that the existence and personal identity of the individual continue after the change called death.

We affirm that communication with the so-called dead is a fact, scientifically proven by the phenomena of Spiritualism.

We believe that the highest morality is contained in the Golden Rule: "Do unto others as you would have them do unto you."

We affirm the moral responsibility of individuals, and that we make our own happiness or unhappiness as we obey or disobey Nature's physical and spiritual laws.

We affirm that the doorway to reformation is never closed against any soul here or hereafter.

We affirm that the precepts of Prophecy and Healing are Divine attributes proven through Mediumship.

Spiritualism most commonly has as its primary purpose communication with "spirits of the dead," or—in our preferred terminology "the Surviving Personality of the recently departed." Since such communication is often facilitated by a "Spirit Guide" and God as *Father* or *Son* is generally acknowledged in Spiritualist services, we might consider this as a minor but officially unapproved and unacknowledged sect of Christianity. While both men and women function as mediums, the female generally has a superior status to the male.

In addition to Spiritualist churches, there is the much older Church of New Jerusalem founded in 1787 based on the visionary writings of the Swedish scientist and clairvoyant, Emanuel Swedenborg. We will discuss this more thoroughly in Chapter Twelve.

Spiritualist phenomena consists mainly of prophecy, clairvoyance, clairaudience, speaking in tongues, laying on of hands, healing, visions, trance, apports, revelations, raps, levitation, automatic and independent writing and painting, photography, materialization, psychometry, direct and independent voice, and any other manifestation believed to prove the continuity of life after death.

While Spiritualism is currently a very minor religion in the United States and the United Kingdom, it is much more prominent throughout the Caribbean, South America, West Africa, India, China and Japan—each with distinct variations. A more specific variation from Spiritualism is "Spiritism" and ecstatic/charismatic religions like Pentecostalism, Candomble, Voodoo, and Umbanda. With the appearance of "*religious* ecstasy" there is usually the *occurrence* of such paranormal phenomena as spontaneous trance, speaking in tongues, voluntary and involuntary possession by spirit entities (not usually those associated with the deceased), movement of objects at a distance, levitation of objects and persons, direct automatic writing, and the appearance of apparitions.

Among the more important Spiritist movements are Voodoo, Santeria, Candomble and Umbanda in which spontaneous contagious ecstatic states invite possession by spirit entities, and other practices involve controlled inductions of possession.

Location, Location, Location!

One important distinction between shamanism and spiritualism is that of "location." The shaman travels to the spirit world, while in spiritualism the spirit travels to or manifests in the physical world.

Pentecostalism

The largest and fastest-growing segment of Christianity today is Pentecostalism with an estimated 500 million adherents worldwide. While the modern expression of Pentecostal Christianity began in America in the early 20th century, the movement has gained significant strength in Africa, Asia, and South America as well.

What unites Pentecostals is the testimony of having experienced a unique gifting of the Holy Spirit. They believe the Holy Spirit is the divine, third person in the Catholic Trinity, co-equal to the Father and Son. Unlike some Christians, Pentecostals believe that after the Holy Spirit applies Christ's salvation to the *sinner* another experience is available to the *believer* where the Holy Spirit fills them, empowering them to speak in tongues and other distinct capabilities which should then become the norm for all *born-again* Christians.

"The Charismatic Movement" describes the Pentecostal message of baptism in the Holy Spirit and the experience of speaking in tongues, occurring in certain Protestant and Roman Catholic churches first reported in the 1960s.

In 1983, the Pope John Paul II's delegate to the Charismatic movement told priests and bishops to welcome the movement. Some priests even performed "charismatic masses." The Pentecostal message was particularly welcomed by Roman Catholic churches that were predominantly Latin in makeup.

Snake handling is a rare activity practiced by a small number of Pentecostal congregations as a demonstration of their faith in God.

While advocates of snake handling come out of Pentecostal churches, no major Christian denomination, Pentecostal or otherwise, supports the practice. Most snake handlers are located in Alabama, Georgia, and Kentucky, Tennessee, and West Virginia. Some states such as Alabama, Kentucky, and Tennessee, have made the activity illegal, punishable by fine, but it still occurs in rural settings.

Common Factors: Communication with Spirits; Spiritist phenomena, more spiritual than materialistic.

SPIRITUALITY

"Spirituality" today has a new meaning separate from religion, as in "spiritual but not religious," or SBNR. A "USA Today" April 2010 article stated that 72 percent of Generation Y so identify themselves. Note: many of these still have a belief in some *higher power* or *transcendent reality*, but they find religion and religious institutions as lacking or limiting. They reject organized religions as a means to furthering spiritual growth. Instead, they relate to esoteric traditions east and west, and a growing interest in psychology and the paranormal in their desire to discover their True Self through meditation, self-study and self-expression.

Prominent in these studies are Kabbalah, Tantra, and technologies of self-improvement. Personal well-being, physically, emotionally, and mentally are important aspects of modern spirituality.

Spirituality has come to mean an *internal* experience of the *individual* in contrast to the organizational approach to mold people into some uniform ideology that may actually repress and deny any kind of personal experience. Ralph Waldo Emerson (1803–1882) pioneered the idea of spirituality as a distinct field, and became a prominent figure in Transcendentalism.

Common Factors: A non-religious and generally a non-institutional interest in higher consciousness and a non-materialist Humanist ethical system based on rationality; An emphasis on psychological well-being often inclusive of practices of meditation and yoga; interest in eastern and western philosophy.

TANTRA

Taoism and Kabbalah both have similarities to Tantra when all three are viewed in a non-religious but spiritual perspective. All three focus on "inner alchemy," working on subtle energies and images to transform physical and subtle bodies. Tantric meditation begins by visualizing the inner central column of *Shushumna* that follows the spine upward to the crown of the head. Progressing upward from the base are a series of wheel-like *chakras*.

While there are many minor chakras throughout the body, it is the Spinal Seven that are used in very detailed visual meditational procedures that include both singular visualizations and moving ones. For each chakra there are associated colors, geometric diagrams, deific images, chants, and programmed experiences to be realized. At the base of the spine is the lowest chakra where *Kundalini* (the Serpent Power) sleeps, coiled around the *lingam* (the inner phallus, unrelated to external gender), with the tip

346

of her tail in her mouth. When Kundalini awakens she uncoils and enters the bottom of the *Sushumna* and moves upward to the crown chakra at the top of the skull.

The Sri Yantra The Most Important Meditational Power Symbol
in Tantra & Hinduism

In one form of Tantric yoga, the body is visualized as a structured tree, the *Tree of Life,* on which the seven chakras sequentially represent planets. The first, or root chakra, represents the Moon; the second, sacral chakra, represents Mercury; the third, solar plexus chakra, is Venus; the fourth, heart chakra, the Sun; the fifth, throat, Mars; the sixth, brow chakra, Jupiter; and the seventh, crown chakra, Saturn. A "Climbing the Tree" meditation is a way of enlightenment.

More than a religion, Tantra is a lifestyle whose goal is "salvation," or—to put in a less religious perception—"completion and liberation." The performance of Tantric techniques and rituals facilitates access to the divine energy, enabling their practitioners to empower themselves and others associated with them—especially man/woman couples.

The knowledge, and <u>correct</u> application, of Tantric techniques and rituals utilize cosmic energies for material as well as spiritual goals. Real Tantra is much more than "great sex" (important as that is) and involves Yogic *asanas* (postures), exercises, and controlled movements, as well as *mantras* (chants), *yantras* (symbolic diagrams), disciplined meditation, self-hypnosis, and other techniques for the fulfillment of worldly needs and desires, and for the attainment of spiritual goals.

The goal of Yoga is "Union with the Absolute, or with the True Self." Other, supposedly identical goals expressed differently include *to see correctly, the direct experience of the mind, the realization of truth, Self-realization, Enlightenment, stilling the mind, Liberation from suffering, ultimate peace, and the pure and unobstructed experience of Spirit.* Perhaps they are all the same, or perhaps each reflects the goals of different moments in our lifetime.

The Goddess is the Creatrix

Hinduism sees the Supreme Being, Brahman, as actionless and outside of Creation, while it is Shakti, the Creatrix, who is constantly active within Creation as the Great Mother Goddess who creates the endless variety of forms in this world. In Her rituals and worship, humans (Man and Woman) share in Her Work and creations. In endlessly varying our rituals and erotic play, we are fulfilling Her deific power within each of us.

One of the forms of Tantra is the union of Man and Woman with the Infinite. In Sexual Tantra, deity is feminine and union comes through the extended bliss and ecstatic consciousness of prolonged and multiple orgasm of the feminine partner as accomplished through devotion and adoration by the masculine partner. In contrast to other teachings calling for repression and denial of sex, Tantra expressly and artfully cultivates aroused sexual energy, and then channels the enhanced energy for personal transcendence of the partners in mutual ecstasy.

Sexual Tantra can take as many forms as there are Goddesses, and some say their number is infinite and others say there are only millions, and still others say, "All Goddesses are One Goddess." Wikipedia lists nine major Hindu goddesses but their forms, names, colors, adornments, addresses, and rituals all add variations. Dr. Jean Shinoda Bolen describes ten goddess archetypes in "Everywoman." Just as one woman can become many different women with changes in dress, style, self-expression, etc., the variations of goddess worship and Tantric rituals can fulfill every need, desire, dream, and fantasy—and in that world everything is magically and spiritually real.

Every woman is the Goddess in any and all Her manifestations. Her male partner should ask (overtly or subtly) *What does Woman want?* They construct their ritual to fulfill that roadmap from the mundane to bliss, from ordinary consciousness to ecstatic consciousness, from feel-good pleasure to out-of-this-world ecstasy.

While Tantra is commonly assumed to be an offshoot of Hinduism, it is more likely just the opposite. Dr. Clifford Alford, writing as "The Naked Shaman" claims that Tantra derives from the Kali Naga Shamans in the Himalayan Mountains. "Mahakali Tantra is the oldest form of Tantra on the eart, and dates back over 60,000 years." "There are many misconceptions about Tantra in the Western world where the belief is that Tantra is all about sex. This is because free sexuality is what is used to sell everything in this part of the world, and yet it is the single greatest thing that is feared by all of patriarchal society. Only about 20% of Tantra involves sexual exercises and rituals while the other 80% consists of breath work, meditation, mudras, mantras, and a philosophy of life that includes living in balance with all of Creation with intense power raising activities and a very powerful form of group shamanic practice."

Common Factors: In some sense—whether as Tantra, Kabbalah, Taoism, various traditions of Shamanism, and "secret practices" of various religions and magickal orders, ecstasy is sought and sex and other practices used for its attainment and *deployment* for the energies aroused, the consciousness transformed, the ego that is transcended, and the "magick" that is attained.

Sexual practices, whether Tantric or not, are as varied as are the 4,200 religions of the world. Energy, Consciousness, Spirit, and—actually—Love are all facets of the "One Thing" that we experience through Life and what lies beyond.

TAOISM

Taoism is the fundamental non-theistic Chinese Philosophy and ethical system that dates back at least to the 4th century BC. Like other basically shamanic systems, its origins are truly surrounded in mythic mystery. Traditionally Taoism is attributed to Lao-tzu, but he is said to have been immaculately conceived by a shooting star, carried in his mother's womb for 82 years, and then born as a fully grown wise old man. It may well be that the historic Lao-tzu was a "student" of older shamanic systems, and simply wrote down the essentials of the philosophy attributed to him in the book we know as the *Tao Te Ching*. Legend says he did that in three days, and then disappeared forever.

The teaching is that there is a basic unity behind the manifest universe that is itself a mysterious and undefinable force called the *Tao*. The *Tao*, the Power, is the Source producing all things, and all things go back to it to become the One Thing again. The teaching says that Life is the greatest of all possessions, and that the goal of human existence is to attain the fullness of life by attunement with the Tao. The teaching says that we should live a simple and ethical life, letting all things take a natural course. The teaching says "The Tao that can be told is not the eternal Tao." The Tao can only be learned through honest reflection on experience. The philosophy has never been institutionalized as a religion.

It is most commonly identified with the unified dualistic concept of Yin and Yang, the Five Elements, and the "Book of Changes," or *I Ching*. It is the "Path" of living in harmony (or Flow) with the eternal Life Force (the Tao), which every person can observe in Nature and find within themselves. It emphasizes practical and non-political benefits through physical, mental and spiritual exercise and ethical living in harmony with Nature.

In Taoism, there are no irrational threats of hellish punishments or promises of "heavenly rewards." Through various exercises (martial arts), transformative rituals (alchemy and ecstatic sex), and the ritualistic "worship" of non-theistic figures, Taoists enjoy a life of "action through non-action" bringing many practical benefits (health, longevity, peace, success, and comfort). Male and female are equality honored and sexuality is taught as desirable and beneficial. A balance between spiritual and material values is the goal realized in the Three Treasures: compassion, moderation, and humility.

Taoist schools teach reverence for one's ancestors, along with practices of divination, exorcism, and achieving ecstasy, and long life. From these teachings such systems as Feng Shui, Chinese Traditional Medicine, several martial arts, Chinese astrology, and various magickal and meditational techniques developed.

Common Factors: A universal source of power manifesting in an inseparable duality, five elements, movement, ecstatic techniques.

TRANSCENDENTALISM

An "intellectual" philosophy that believes in inherent goodness of people and Nature, and that various social institution—especially organized religion and political parties—corrupt the individual. People are at their best when truly self-reliant and independent. Only from such individuals can a true community be formed. Following the skeptical philosophy of David Hume, transcendentalists reject any concept of predestination and deny that empirical proofs of religion are possible.

They do, however, believe in *the power of the individual and divine messages deriving from the inner mental and spiritual essence.* Transcendentalism directly influenced the Mental Sciences movement of the mid-19th century, and the later New Thought movement.

Ralph Waldo Emerson wrote in 1837: *"We will walk on our own feet; we will work with our own hands; we will speak our own minds ... A nation of men will for the first time exist, because each believes himself inspired by the Divine Soul which also inspires all men."*

Common Factors: Rejection of institutional religion and politics with emphasis on self-reliance, self-responsibility, and independent social action.

TRANSHUMANISM

Perhaps an unfortunate term for a concept still being developed and hence subject to a wide range of debate. For our purposes, it could as well have been "Super-Humanism" in the sense that we are transforming mind and body with artificial joints and replacing age-declined natural substances with fresh artificial ones to extend life and expand abilities. However, it also includes futuristic technologies of artificial intelligence, nanotechnology, genetic engineering, as well as accelerated biological and psychic evolution by means of age-old spiritual technologies.

Spirituality has always included the potential for humans to grow, develop and transcend biological limitations. *Where else did Ascended Masters, Inner Plane Adepti, Spirit Guides, etc. come from?* We say and believe Spirit is in everything, so does it matter that we adapt mechanical and biological resources along with the etheric, astral and spiritual? *Our need and our goal is to accelerate human evolution which is itself a fundamental spiritual concept and process.*

Transhumanists affirm the possibility and desirability of transforming humanity by slowing or eliminating aging, making available technologies to enhance our physical, intellectual, and psychological capacities, evolving into a new species. Or—to use Theosophical terminology—a new "sub-race."

There are some who fight against the use of such technologies as being non-equalitarian as if only death makes us equal. There are some who believe life extension will result in an over-population of the old and infirm, draining the economic resources of the young to care for the old—a sort of "get out of the way, you *old fuddy duddy!*" Instead, realize the benefit of a healthy elder citizen with a wealth of intellectual and financial resources in an age of advanced technologies that actually reduces drains on land and natural resources that have been the age-old cause of war and conflict (other than that of religious proselytizing). It may not seem like a religion or a spiritual movement, but it is more so than many others because *success requires belief, and a mass movement in its support.* It requires a transition from a faith that calls old age and death "God's Way" and instead sees an increasingly ageless society as an expression of the divinity in all of us.

Common Factors: Belief in Life Extension, alternative technologies to enhance natural resources, bio-engineering and life enhancement technologies, transcendence of biological limitations, and fulfillment of spiritual purpose.

UNITARIAN UNIVERSALISM

Unitarian Universalists believe individuals are free to search for their own truth about the meaning of life, their connection to Nature and the Cosmos, the Creation and its Creator/Source, the Afterlife, Moral issues, etc. There is no binding theology or dogma identifying Unitarian Universalists other than an emphasis on personal growth and development, and the ideal of "the direct experience of that transcending mystery and wonder, affirmed in all cultures.

In many ways, *Unitarian Universalism is the ultimate "Spiritual but not Religious" religion for intelligent, liberal, middle to upper class modern Americans.* It provides the comforting social environment of a church with a spiritual culture related in talks, discussions, "Sunday School" classes, the transitional ceremonies of birth celebration, marriage, and death. There are no "preachings" and no proselytizing. The churches are supportive of earth-centered traditions celebrating the sacred circle of life and living in harmony with the rhythms of nature, they discuss the guidance of reason, rational analysis and debate, the importance of science, the dangers of idolatry, and the value of good citizenship. They are perhaps the successors to the Deism of the "Founding Fathers" and the Transcendentalists of Emerson and the New England Intellectuals. They are "New Agers" without calling themselves as such.

Unitarian Universalists place emphasis on spiritual growth and development. The official statement of Unitarian Universalist principles describes the "sources" upon which current practice is based:

> **Direct experience** of that transcending mystery and wonder, affirmed in all cultures, which moves us to a renewal of the spirit and an openness to the forces which create and uphold life;
>
> **Words and deeds** of prophetic women and men which challenge us to confront powers and structures of evil with justice, compassion, and the transforming power of love;
>
> **Wisdom** from the world's religions which inspires us in our ethical and spiritual life;
>
> **Jewish and Christian teachings** which call us to respond to God's love by loving our neighbors as ourselves;
>
> **Humanist teachings** which counsel us to heed the guidance of reason and the results of science, and warn us against idolatries of the mind and spirit.

Spiritual teachings of earth-centered traditions which celebrate the sacred circle of life and instruct us to live in harmony with the rhythms of nature.

We do not, however, hold the Bible—or any other account of human experience—to be either an infallible guide or the exclusive source of truth. Much biblical material is mythical or legendary. Not that it should be discarded for that reason! Rather, it should be treasured for what it is. We believe that we should read the Bible as we read other books—with imagination and a critical eye. We also respect the sacred literature of other religions. Contemporary works of science, art, and social commentary are valued as well. We hold, in the words of an old liberal formulation, that "revelation is not sealed." **Unitarian Universalists aspire to truth as wide as the world**—we look to find truth anywhere, universally.

Common Factors: Freedom to seek inspiration and wisdom from all human experience and resources; Freedom of and from religion; Freedom for personal growth and development, and direct experience of Spirit; Freedom to celebrate the sacred circle of life to life in harmony with Nature's rhythms.

Witchcraft, the "Old Religion"

According to those who believe in the Great Goddess, Europe was once inhabited by a matriarchal, egalitarian society worshipping a matrifocal, sedentary, peaceful, art- loving goddess 5,000 to 25,000 years before the rise of the first male-oriented religion. They maintain that this egalitarian culture was overrun and destroyed by semi-nomadic, horse-riding, Indo-European Aryan invaders who were patrifocal, mobile, warlike, and indifferent to art.

Just as happened in the Indus Valley (see earlier section on Hinduism), these Aryan invaders saw themselves as "above" the peaceful goddess worshippers because of their

354

superior military ability. The matriarchal religion was eventually assimilated into the patriarchal religion of the invaders. As the invaders imposed their war-loving patriarchal culture on the conquered peoples, stories and myths involving male warriors raping women and killing serpents (symbols of the goddess worshippers) appeared for the first time. As the assimilation of cultures continued, the Great Goddess fragmented into many lesser goddesses.

According to Merlin Stone in *When God was a Woman,* this displacement of the Great Goddess was completed by the Abrahamic religions denying the feminine both in deity and in dignity of women. Women were "marked with the sin of the mythic Biblical Eve."

In the world of witchcraft the goddess is the giver of life. Jean Shinoda Bolen, M.D., writes in *Goddesses in Everywoman:* "The Great Goddess was worshipped as the feminine life force deeply connected to nature and fertility, responsible both for creating life and for destroying life." She continues: "the Great Goddess was regarded as immortal, changeless, and omnipotent" prior to the coming of Christianity.

The environmental movement is greatly influenced by those who practice witchcraft or hold neo-pagan beliefs. In *The Spiral Dance,* Starhawk writes "the model of the Goddess, who is immanent in nature, fosters respect for the sacredness of all living things. Witchcraft can be seen as a religion of ecology. Its goal is harmony with nature, so that life may not just survive, but thrive." The witch views Mother Earth as a conscious, evolving, and ultimately spiritual bio-system.

Witchcraft is the New Age movement reintroducing the sacred aspect of the earth that was destroyed by the Christian worldview. The goddess is a direct counter to the male-dominated religion of the Abrahamic God. While Christianity teaches that God is transcendent, separate from nature, and masculine only, Witchcraft is pantheistic, seeing God in nature, in all things and all things are a part of God. However, this God is in actuality the Goddess, and it's time for that to be known.

The Goddess comes First

A fundamental belief in witchcraft, as in Tantra and other pre-institutional belief systems, is that the goddess predates the God. The goddess is the giver of all life and is found in all of creation. Starhawk writes: "The importance of the Goddess symbol for women cannot be overstressed. The image of the Goddess inspires women to see ourselves as divine, our bodies as sacred, the changing phases of our lives as holy, our aggression as healthy, and our anger as purifying... Through the Goddess, we can discover our strength, enlighten our minds, own our bodies, and celebrate our emotions. We can move beyond narrow, constricting roles and become whole."

Another aspect of New Age spirituality is the blending of the sexes. The feminist movement seeks a common mold for all of humanity. Jungian psychotherapist John Weir Perry believes that we must find our individuality by discovering androgyny. He states, "To reach a new consensus, we have to avoid falling back into stereotypes, and that requires truly developing our individuality. It is an ongoing work of self-realization and self-actualization. For men it means growing into their native maleness and balancing it with their femaleness. For women, it's the same—growing into their full womanhood, and that includes their masculine side."

Starhawk writes: "The Goddess is also important for men. The oppression of men in Father God-ruled patriarchy is perhaps less obvious but no less tragic than that of women. Men are encouraged to identify with a model no human being can successfully emulate: to be mini-rulers of narrow universes. They are internally split into a 'spiritual' self that is supposed to conquer their baser animal and emotional natures. They are at war with themselves: in the West to 'conquer' sin, in the East to 'conquer' desire or ego. Few escape from these wars undamaged."

Jungian analyst Jean Shinoda Bolen answered the question, "*what ails our society,*" *by* saying "we suffer from the absence of one half of our spiritual potential—the Goddess." Male-dominated religion, still dominant in this period of transition into the Age of Aquarius, has done an injustice to humanity and the ecosystem. There must be a re-balancing of energies: male energies must diminish and feminine energies must increase in order for the goddess to empower the individual.

The New Age promises to become an age of peace, harmony, and transforming progress, whereas the passing dark age of brokenness and separation continues to bring war, conflict, and disharmony. It is the goddess' feminine aspects of unity, love, and peace that offers opportunity to resolve man's dilemma and circumvent his, and our, movement towards self-destruction.

For the pagan, "The Goddess religion is a conscious attempt to reshape culture." This reshaping is nothing less than viewing man and his understanding of reality from a feminine perspective in which the Divine is female. Therefore considerable emphasis is placed on female attributes, ultimately focusing on eroticism and sexuality. "Women are clearly the catalyst for the formation of the new spirituality. It is women above all who are in the process of reversing Genesis ... by validating and freeing their sexuality." (From Donna Steichen, "The Goddess Goes to Washington," *Fidelity Magazine,* Dec. 1986)

As this revival of the goddess continues, a growing lack of traditional distinction between male and female will become the norm. Jungian psychotherapist John Weir Perry believes that "both current psychology and ancient history point to an emerging transformation in our sense of both society and self, a transformation that includes redefining the notion of what it means to be men and women."

The Witchcraft described by Margaret Murray in her 1921 *The Witch-Cult in Western Europe* (claimed by some other historians as being in error) and further described in her 1931 *The God of the Witches, was* confirmed by Gerald Gardner in the 1950's and later by Kenneth Johnson and Ronald Hutton.

Wicca, the New Witchcraft Religion

Interest in historical Witchcraft was given a modern impetus is 1954 with Gerald Gardner's publication of *Witchcraft Today* in which he described a form of witchcraft quietly continuing the ancient ways since medieval times, still worshipping Nature and sexuality in the New Forest area of England.

The *Wicca* that Gardner initially taught was a witchcraft religion having a lot in common with that described by Murray who claimed that the witch trials held in Europe and North America by Christian churches were an attempt to fully extinguish the still existent pre-Christian pagan religion of a Horned God. In fact, Murray wrote the introduction to Gardner's book.

But Gardner's Wicca was recast as a modern Nature Goddess religion with little reference to the Horned God. It was less an antiquarian revival and more a *Liberation Movement* celebrating the naked body, sexuality, ecstatic states, equality of the sexes, combined with ritual invocation of the Goddess and possession by Her, and the ethics of personal honesty, responsibility, and life affirmation. As now practiced, it is more of an initiatory secret society based on shamanic ecstatic practices than a modern "religion." Rather than a binding together under the single theology and institutional hierarchy characteristic of most religions, this Wicca is organized into *autonomous covens* each led by a High Priesthood. Both men and women are called "witches." Wiccan writings and rituals are heavily influenced by pre-Christian religions, medieval grimoires, ceremonial magic, and Aleister Crowley's *Ordo Templi Orientis.*

Gardner's Wicca has attracted many initiates, and is believed to be one of the largest of the various witchcraft traditions in the Western world. There is also a large "Eclectic Wiccan" movement of individuals and groups who share key Wiccan beliefs but have no initiatory connection or affiliation with what is now called traditional Wicca.

One of the distinct features of "the Craft Movement"—another name for Wicca—is that practice of numerous crafts as spiritual, magical, and practical. Crafts involve visualization employing both psychic and physical skills to bring a visual image into physical reality. "Crafting" is not *manufacturing;* it is a personal practice producing the entire item, not just a part of a whole, or doing just step in a production line. Crafting is like gardening in that it involves the self, and the Spirit, in the process, and thus the crafted object becomes "alive" with character and feeling.

Wiccan Worship Practices

Wiccans believe in voluntary possession by the Goddess, connected with the sacred ceremony of Drawing Down the Moon. The high priestess solicits the Goddess to possess her and speak through her.

Wiccan worship commonly takes place during a full moon or a new moon. Such rituals are called an *Esbats* and may involve a magic circle which practitioners believe will contain energy and form a sacred space, or will provide them a form of magical protection.

Wiccan worship commonly takes place during a full moon or a new moon. Such rituals are called an *Esbats* and may involve a magic circle which practitioners believe will contain energy and form a sacred space, or will provide them a form of magical protection.

The Wiccan woman learns to visualize herself, and as an expression of the Divine within. Through Wicca she learns to be her own self and not what others expect or desire her to be.

Naomi Goldenberg, a Jungian analyst in her ground-breaking book, *Changing of the Gods—Feminism and the End of Traditional Religions* (Beacon Press, 1979), writes:

> "Perhaps the emergence of the Goddess is one sign that the cultural movement back to earth has begun. In our present situation, in which women are the ones who nurture us, natural life can probably only be imagined with female symbols. The Goddess of feminist witchcraft, with her love of life, her acceptance of death and her presence within the tangible reality of animals, plants and humans, could be an indication that the human race is beginning to grow up. She could signify that more of us are achieving

enough psychological maturity to accept mortality and yet to keep our sense of wonder and affirm that life is good. In any case, she is surely a sign that Western religion is beginning to change. For witches, God has moved from an image of a celibate male above and beyond humanity to an image of a vibrant female who is part of our physical and psychic life.

"This movement should not be trivialized as a mere sex change for God. Modern witchcraft represents a profound shift in the human tendency to imagine gods, goddesses and divine beings as forces outside human selves and to conceive of these beings as interior experiences. The psychological importance of witchcraft cannot be overlooked whatever one may think about pagans, witches or feminists."

Wicca is the only Western religion to recognize Woman as divine in her Self, and in the "Feminine Myth" that is part of Her psyche.

Common Factors: Invocation of and possession by the feminine deity; the Practice of Magic; Emphasis on Sexuality and Ecstatic States; Gender Equality.

Witchcraft: the Triple Goddess

While the Great Goddess manifests in many forms and many ways, as the Triple Goddess She represents the three unique aspects of Woman-hood: the Maiden, the Mother, the Crone.

Don't let the common interpretation of these three words limit your understanding of the real nature and reality of what they are. The Maiden, also called a "virgin" is not necessarily sexually innocent but is simply young and unattached and able to function as a woman. Essentially, she is of any age from puberty until marriage or other serious attachment. In other words, she might be ten or eleven years young or younger to thirty, forty or fifty years old, but pre-menopausal, psychologically as well as physically. What's important is the special sense of vitality and joy of expression that she has, and that in this age includes preparation for the next phase in her life through education, travel, experience, exploration, but most especially the unique attitude of "play" and excitement that fully involves her imagination and creative fantasy.

The Mother is not necessarily any age other than "adult" and functioning in the broadest sense of motherhood. This can a matter of giving birth to a human child or birthing and "mothering" any form of personal creation—a marriage or relationship, a family, a home, a business, a movement, a book, a job or profession, an invention, etc.

The Triple Goddess.

The Crone could be thought of as a "retiree" but in the modern world that doesn't necessarily mean sitting back in a rocking chair as the world goes by. It's more a change from personal responsibility to the "distance perception" that allows her accumulated and "embodied" wisdom of life experience to be expressed and respected.

Yes, each of these stages in a woman's life has an approximate equivalent to less defined stages in a man's life. But, in general, the differences are as distinct as is their physical gender. Fatherhood is the other side of parenthood, and men are performing and enjoying many things once traditionally only performed by mothers, but fathers and mothers are still as different as boys and girls and men and women, and perhaps as an old grump is from a wise crone.

Witchcraft's Feri Tradition

Unlike traditional institutional religions and spiritual developmental systems, with very few sects truly identified with the rigid and controlling dominant groups, Witchcraft and Wicca have perhaps hundreds of practicing variants started since Gardner's 1950's. We can't possibly explore them all beyond what we've already described. However, one of the most interesting of those variants is the *Feri Tradition* founded by Cora and Victor Anderson in the 1940s.

Sexual Mysticism and Sensual Awareness

It is an initiatory and ecstatic tradition of sexual mysticism with emphasis on sensual awareness and experience derived from such diverse influences as Ozark kitchen folk witchery, Shamanism, Italian *Strega, Huna*, Voodoo, Hoodoo, Kabbalah, and Tantra.

Perhaps the most distinguishing element of the tradition is "Feri Power," intrinsic to the experience of "becoming" as thinking changes from materialist to spiritual with a deep respect for the wisdom of Nature, a love of Beauty, an appreciation of artistic creativity, and of ecstatic experience.

Trance leads to a personal connection to the Divine

Feri teaches the existence of three separate interdependent "souls" forming the human psychic structure: 1) the "Talking Self" or middle or conscious mind that is self-aware, deals with language, communications, knowledge, and rational thinking; 2) the "Fetch" or lower or subconscious mind that is the source of dreams, drives, and desires, that are instinctual and physical; 3) the "God-Self" or super-conscious mind or Higher Self. The goal of Feri practices is to integrate the three souls or selves so they communicate in a holist sense of Self and communion with the Divine perceived as the Goddess.

The Three "Energy Tools"

Feri teaches the use three symbols or "energy tools": 1) the "Iron Pentacle" whose five points represent Sex, Pride, Self, Power, and Passion—those aspects of human life often distorted in the current culture; 2) the "Pearl Pentacle" which appears when the five points of the Iron Pentacle are transformed from Iron into Pearl—Sex into Love, Pride into Law, Self into Kno wledge, Power into Liberty, and Passion into Wisdom; 3) the "Black Heart of Innocence" in which all souls are truly connected to reality and liberated from all social restraints in a state of *innocent* sexuality.

The Four Classes of Deities

Feri deities are: 1) the ecstatic feminine "Star Goddess," perceived as the Egyptian *Nuit,* the androgynous creative source of Being and the Intelligence of the Great Void; 2) the "Divine Twins," as the Goddess represent Unity, her two consorts represent all Duality; 3) the erotic and seductive "Peacock God" born of the reunion of the Divine Twins back into Unity; and 4) the seven "Feri Guardians" associated with the seven directions of north, east, south, west, above, below, and center.

Note: It is Trance that enables Spiritual Communication with the Divine.

Common Factors: God and Goddess manifest through five elements and experienced through the ecstatic union of Love and Sex.

YOGA

Yoga is another marker for the New Age. Introduced to the West in the late 19th century, it slowly transformed into a mass movement with yogic "missionaries" traveling from India to America and Europe teaching meditation and postures, appearing on television, lecturing, founding institutes and centers, and inspiring research into brain and neurological changes induced by these practices.

Yoga is familiar to everyone, and while it is more than what most perceive, that is enough to make it one of the most efficient forms of physical health maintenance there is. Through posture and movement, the subtle energies move through the chakra system, conditioning the body-unity inwardly and outwardly. While Yoga evolved out of Tantra, the general perception is the reverse, and practices of Kundalini Yoga and Neo-Tantra are more and more common.

The Yoga taught and practiced in Yoga Studios across much of the Western word is *Hatha* Yoga dealing primarily with the discipline of the physical (and etheric) body. There are other schools of yoga for emotion, mind, and spirit, which when combined made a way of life, and one of Spiritual Growth.

Note: The Yogic "vision" is one of balanced growth and development without any particular interest in Spiritual Communication. Yet, the development of the subtle bodies accompanying all forms of Yogic practice is an enabler psychic skills including communication between levels of Self and other entities.

Yoga meditation pose

Common Factors: The chakra system and subtle energies; Meditation as a daily practice, and posture and movement for health.

Spiritual, but Not Religious

What can we say in summary?

"Religion," by definition of *binding together,* is "institutional." And, while participation in an institution can be a voluntary group association of mutual interest or an organization to mobilize group power for specified purpose, an institution is a hierarchical structure to *establish order* and *govern behavior* of the participants whether voluntary or not—as with the person who has been *institutionalized* because of criminal behavior, destructive emotional behavior, or medical need.

Religion is institutional. It is an imposition of behavior and belief, and an organization for the benefit of an established hierarchy. There is no place for "Spirit" in a religious institution no matter what the words, disciplines, roles, teachings, and regulated behavior proclaims.

While there are multiple definitions of "religion," such multiplicity is no definition at all. What we call "Spiritual" and "Spirituality" is about Spirit. And Spirit is not about required beliefs or regulated behavior. Spirit is in you and in everyone, and in everything. That, essentially, is what is recognized by the word "Spiritual." "Spirituality" is about what Spirit is and about techniques for communicating with Spirit and for making Spirit an organizing principle within our own person.

Because Spirit is ultimately a "substance" and the element from which all other elements and substances are derived and hence the Source of all that is manifest—physical and non-physical—it is likewise the Resource for Energy, Matter, and Consciousness. The study of Spirit and Spirituality is our means of learning about the exterior and the interior Cosmos (As Above, so Below) and using Personal Consciousness under Will (the Soul as one with Creative Source) to evolve and to aid in the continual evolution of the Cosmos (As below, so Above).

As discussed previously, the studies of Science and Spirit do belong together to bring mutual understanding and meaning to our lives. Religion has become a negation of both.

Question: *Why be part of a controlling and stultifying institution when, instead, you can act freely and individually to study Spirituality and freely participate for mutual benefit with other individuals of shared interest in voluntary groups organized for your need and purpose?* That's the New Age choice.

"The End of Religion, The Rise of Spirituality"

That's the title of an article in the September-October 2013 *The Futurist* magazine. The author, Alan Nordstrom (professor at Rollins College in Winter Park, FL), predicts:

> Society will outgrow doctrinaire belief systems accepted on traditional 'faith' and inculcated by authoritarian intimidation.
>
> By 2010, the pervasive power of communications systems will enable human beings collectively to achieve a higher level of common sense, informed by advanced sciences (physical, social, and spiritual) that make the world of 2013 seem neo-Medieval.
>
> We will have stabilized our population sustainably. Our former penchant for exploitation and domination will have been sanitized by education, informed by humane values promotion cooperation and collaboration on common interests and mutual benefits. Aggressive, acquisitive, exploitive behaviors are deemed pathological and regressive, even primitive.

Yes, we do believe that education about the realities of history, the truth about myth, the perspective of science rather than blind faith, rational thinking and logical analysis, and plain common sense along with the improved social choices of modern society will bring an end to "religion," and replace it with a growing spirituality without the necessity of a mythical all-powerful deity and creator.

Common Elements:

Ethics & Morality. "Spiritual traditions view ethics not in terms of conventional morality, but rather as an essential discipline for training the mind. Contemplative introspection makes it painfully apparent that unethical behavior—behavior that aims at inflicting harm—both stems from and strengthens unhealthy, destructive motives and emotions such as greed, anger, and jealousy."

Wisdom. "Wisdom is much more than knowledge, and Taoism is very clear that *'he who is learned is not wise.'* Whereas knowledge simply requires information, wisdom requires understanding it; knowledge informs us whereas wisdom transforms us; knowledge is something we have, wisdom is something we must become."

Spiritual Science. Shamanism was the earliest spiritual tradition to emerge, and it allows relatively easy access to its altered states, a fact that may partly account for its current popularity in the West. Shamanism continues to offer today what it has offered for hundreds of thousands of yesterdays: namely a relatively rapid means, and for most of human history perhaps the only means, of controlled transcendence. As such, shamans are the founders of the 'great tradition' that is the sum total of human-kind's religious-spiritual wisdom.

Spiritual Technology: Hypnosis. "Many religions and some psychologies recognize the possibility of accessing wisdom from inner sources that seem wiser than the ego. Indeed, considerable effort has gone into refining methods for facilitating this access.

Religious methods include diverse rituals, prayers, and altered states of consciousness. These altered states include possession, soul travel, or quieting the mind so as to be able to hear the 'still small voice within.'

Spiritual Challenge: The challenge is to move from externally controlled thought and behavior to personal thinking and self-responsibility; from externally imposed systems of morality based on myth to rationally determined systems of ethics and law; and to the separation of myth from history for the value of each.

Integration: *We must integrate Genders and Classes.* We are familiar with the integration of the races and the tremendous social and *human* benefit that resulted; we are experiencing the same thing as we remove those elements that restrain the full flowering of the Feminine, and the benefits when men and women truly join in partnerships; we are still working to eliminate so-called "class" distinctions that deny the benefits of higher education to everyone—and that includes a mis-understanding of what "higher" education really is; and we are still working from ignorance when it comes to the all-important integration of the human psyche, the balancing of anima and animus, the bridging of conscious with unconscious, the distorted rule of un-recognized archetypes.

Compartmentalized knowledge is wasted knowledge. Knowledge integrated with meaning becomes wisdom. Science integrated with technology produces wealth and benefit. Quantum study of the smallest particles becomes the nano-technology that creates a future freed of ties to land and natural resources, freed of pollution and shortages and distorted economics. Economic study integrated with politics can free us from the corruption of special interests and restore common sense to taxation and regulation.

The Time is NOW

"The challenge is to optimize our individual and collective maturation. How best to do so is no longer an academic question but an evolutionary imperative. We are in a race between consciousness and catastrophe, the outcome remains unsure, and we are all called to contribute. We need to understand how spiritual practices in general, and shamanic practices and studies in particular, can contribute is a crucial question of our time."

From the Collective to the Personal, From the Institution to the Individual, the Next Step is yours to take

You can communicate with Spirit and spirits by using and adapting any of the shamanic techniques we've discussed in the previous chapter. You can talk to the spirits of the dead, to spiritual entities of Nature, and to those that function as "managers" of natural forces. You can communicate with conceptualized images we have imposed on the natural structure of the universe, with those that are or have been gods and goddesses of ancient and modern religions, and most importantly to the spirit that is your own Higher Self.

The most important "step" is to use human intelligence to analyze what we've observed and learned, and to adapt to our needs and purposes. **"Communicating with Spirit" is communication between the incarnate human spirit and other spirit entities.** Whether you use a "medium" as a conduit, or raise your own consciousness to match that of the desired contact is a matter of choice and personal development.

Shamanism demonstrates a whole range of consciousness altering techniques, any of which can be emulated or adapted. All religions are derived from such communication, and many of them contain **magical formulae of invocation and evocation**—whether in the form of meditation (and self-hypnosis), rituals (a form of active meditation), sexual relations empowering masculine and feminine in partnership, worship (properly performed as evocation or invocation), and shamanic "intoxication" (i.e. reaching ecstasy) from which direct contact and communication can be accomplished, and more.

Our goal, in this chapter, and others, is to show you "A Way," provide examples, empower you to adapt and go your own way, and in other chapters to provide specific exercises and programs.

There is no "One Way," and yet all ways are—in essence—one way. Realize you have "the Power," and *learn to use it!*

Simply speaking, *Consciousness* as focused *Awareness* follows *Intention*. Determine the entity you want to contact, establish the purpose for your communication, list the questions for which you want answers, and *go for it!*

Program: *The Ultimate Formula for Spiritual Communication*
Now, fill in the "blanks," starting from the ending (your purpose):

1. *Make the questions very specific* and your sentences very short. Memorize them and *feel* their importance to you. List no more than three questions per session.

2. *Know the purpose for your communication.* The questions you ask are the means to accomplishing the purpose.

3. *Who is your desired communicant?* If a known entity, describe it by name, character, color, costume, adornments, function, etc. Fill in the information using an encyclopedia or other reference. Make sure that the entity corresponds to your purpose and the nature of the questions asked. In other words—that you are addressing the right "person."

4. *How are you going to focus your awareness?* All focus is a form of hypnosis, either facilitated by a companion or self-administered. Use such means as ritual, incense, candles, etc. to establish your "astral room." (See our *Astral Projection for Psychic Empowerment* for helpful details). Establish your intention in a concise statement, visualize your communicant, and see yourself making contact and asking your questions. See and hear the response.

5. *Who are you?* That may seem dumb, but it is not. You have an identity. Either use your given name or a *magickal name* that defines your spirit self. Put it in carefully constructed English sentences, or use a "magical language" like Latin, Greek, Sanskrit, or Celtic. The point is to create an identify that is "one step" more than you are, i.e. that represents a goal for your becoming. Establish a self-image fitting the magical name. Some people will "dress for the occasion," either actually or in their imagination. A consistent imagined simple robe is by far the best: You are, after all, working at a non-physical level. However, don't let the dress substitute for reality—you are not the Queen of Sheba or King Arthur and such pretense will short-circuit you're magickal work.

Every operation has a structure—but keep it simple, yet fill it with feeling of importance and purpose.

All of this is to raise your consciousness to that of your communicant. Nothing more is needed than what we've listed here. It is all accomplished through your *Intention. Surround the image of your Communicant with <u>Light</u>.* That "Light" is a particular kind of energy combined with intention that automatically defines and refines higher consciousness—both yours and that of your communicant. Don't worry about it—just "see the Light" and it is there, and the more often you do this the stronger will be your vision and the higher the rate and quality of the vibration surrounding it.

It doesn't matter, really, if you think of yourself as a *Medium* or a *Conscious Channel,* or as a modern *Shaman.* Just know that you are *special,* know that you have *the Power,* know that the *World of Spirit* is open before you, and that the *Way* is clear.

"Repeat as necessary!"

That may sound like a medical prescription, and it is. You are healing and transforming yourself, you are initiating yourself, you are becoming your SELF. You are working to *Become more than you are,* and *All you can be.* That's what this is all about.

MEDITATION
"What do you want in any form of New Age Religion or Spirituality?"

Sources and Recommended Reading—subject-by-subject:

Afro-centric Spirituality:

Bird, S.: *Four Season of Mojo—An Herbal Guide to Natural Living,* 2005, Llewellyn

Bird, S: Sticks, *Stones, Roots & Bones—Hoodoo, Magic & Conjuring with Herbs,* 2011, Llewellyn

Gonzalez-Wippler, M: *Santeria—the Religion,* 1989, Llewellyn

Santana, A. & (Art) Palumbo, G.: *Afro-Brazilian Tarot,* 2006, Lo Scarabeo/Llewellyn

Zolrak & (Art) Durkon: *Tarot of the Orishas,* 1990, 2013, Llewellyn

Alchemy:

Regardie, I. & Cicero, C. & Cicero. T.: *The Philosopher's Stone—Spiritual Alchemy, Psychology, and Ritual Magic,* 2013, Llewellyn

Stavish, M: *Path of Alchemy—Energetic Healing and the World of Natural Magic,* 2014, Llewellyn

Animism:

Andrews, T.: *Animal Speak—The Spiritual & Magical Powers of Creatures Great & Small*, 2010, Llewellyn

Conway, D.J.: *Animal Magick—The Art of Recognizing and Working with Familiars*, 1995, Llewellyn

Lupa: *New Paths of Animal Totems—Three Alternative Approaches to Creating Your Own Totemism*, 2012, Llewellyn

Morrison, L.: *Healing Wisdom of Birds—An Everyday Guide to their Spiritual Songs & Symbolism*, 2011, Llewellyn

Buddhism:

Meyer, F. H.: *Don't Give up until You Do—From Mindfulness to Realization on the Buddhist Path*, 2012, Llewellyn

Celtic Studies:

Blamires, S.: *Magic of the Celtic Underworld*, 2005, Llewellyn

Conway, D.J.: *By Oak, Ash & Thorn—Modern Celtic Shamanism*, 1994, Llewellyn

Conway, D.J.: *Celtic Magic*, 2002, Llewellyn

Hildago, S.: *Healing Power of Trees—Spiritual Journey through the Celtic Tree Calendar*, 2010, Llewellyn

McCoy, E.: *Celtic Myth & Magick—Harness the Power of the Gods & Goddesses*, 2002, Llewellyn

Woodfield, S.: *Celtic Lore and Spell Craft of the Dark Goddess—Invoking the Morrigan*, 2011, Llewellyn

Christian Science:

Quimby, P.: *the Quimby Manuscripts*, 2011, Amazon

Druidry:

Billington, P.: *The Path of Druidry,* 2011, Llewellyn

Hughes, K.: *To the Cauldron Born—Exploring the Magic of Welsh Legends & Lore,* (Druidry) 2013, Llewellyn

Monroe, D.: *21 Lessons of Merlin—A Study in Druid Magic & Lore,* 2002, Llewellyn

Monroe, D.: *Lost Books of Merlin,* 2002, Llewellyn

Sutton, M. & Mann, N.: *Druid Magic—The Practice of Celtic Wisdom,* 2000, Llewellyn

Wolfe, A.: *Druid Power—Celtic Faerie Craft & Elemental Magic,* 2004, Llewellyn

Egyptian Magick:

Ancient Egyptian Sexual Ankhing, by Drunvalo Spirit of Maat, Vol. 1, No. 9

Clark, R.: *Sacred Magic of Ancient Egypt—The Spiritual Practice Restored,* 2003, Llewellyn

Egyptian Religion from Wikipedia *Main article: Ancient Egyptian deities*

Page, J. & Biles, K.: *Invoking the Egyptian Gods,* 2011, Llewellyn

Page, J. & Milique, J.: *Pathworking with the Egyptian Gods,* 2010, Llewellyn

Richardson, A. & Walker-John, B.: *Inner Guide to Egypt—A Mystical Journey through Time & Consciousness,* 2010, Llewellyn

Esotericism:

Blavatsky, H. P.: *The Secret Doctrine*—any edition

Freemasonry:

Buckland, R.: *Signs, Symbols & Omens—An Illustrated Guide to Magical & Spiritual Symbolism,* 2003, Llewellyn

De Biasi, J.: *Secrets & Practices of the Freemasons—Sacred Mysteries, Rituals, and Symbols Revealed,* 2011, Llewellyn

Greer, J.M.: *Secrets of the Lost Symbol—The Unauthorized Guide to Secret Societies, Hidden Symbols & Mysticism,* 2010, Llewellyn

Stavish, M.: *Freemasonry—Rituals, Symbols & History of the Secret Society,* 2007, Llewellyn

Gnosticism:

Malachi, T.: *Gnosis of the Cosmic Christ—A Gnostic Christian Kabbalah,* 2005, Llewellyn

Malachi, T.: *The Gnostic Gospel of St. Thomas—Meditations on the Mystical Teachings,* 2004, Llewellyn

Malachi, T.: *Gnostic Healing—Revealing the Hidden Power of God,* 2010, Llewellyn

Malachi, T.: *Living Gnosis—A Practical guide to Gnostic Christianity,* 2012, Llewellyn

Malachi, T.: *St. Mary Magdalene—The Gnostic Tradition of the Holy Bride,* 2006, Llewellyn

Goddess Worship:

Bolen, Jean Shinoda, M.D.: *Goddesses in Everywoman—Powerful Archtypes in Women's Lives,* 2004, Harper

Flowers, Prof. Betty Sue, speaking at the International Conference of Women's Spirituality in Austin, Texas.

Monaghan, P.: *The Goddess Companion—Daily Meditations on the Feminine,* 1999, Llewellyn

Monaghan, P.: *The Goddess Path—Myths, Invocations, and Rituals,* 1996, Llewellyn

Sjoo, Monica & Mor, Barbara: *The Great Cosmic Mother—Rediscovering the Religion of the Earth,* 1987, 1991, Harper One

Hinduism:

Badlani, H.: *Hinduism—Path of the Ancient Wisdom.* 2008, iUniverse

Doiniger, W.: *The Hindus—An Alternative History,* 2009, Penguin

Judith, A.: *Wheels of Life—A User's Guide to the Chakra System,* 1986, Llewellyn

Stone, M.: *When God was a Woman,* 1978, Mariner Books

Kabbalah/Qabalah:

Andrews, T.: *Simplified Qabalah Magic,* 2003, Llewellyn

Barrabbas, F.: *Magical Qabalah for Beginners—A Comprehensive Guide to Occult Knowledge, 2013, Llewellyn*

Christopher, L.: *Kabbalah, Magic, and the Great Work of Self-Transformation—A Complete Course,* 2006, Llewellyn

Denning, M. & Phillips, O.: *Magical States of Consciousness—Pathworking on the Tree of Life,* 2012, Llewellyn

Dennis G.: *Encyclopedia of Jewish Myth, Magi and Mysticism,* 2007, Llewellyn

Godwin, D.: *Godwin's Cabbalistic Encyclopedia—A Complete Guide to Cabalistic Magic,* 2002, Llewellyn

Ponce, C.: *Kabbalah—An Introduction and Illumination for the World Today,* 1973, Theosophical

Regardie, I. & Cicero, C. & Cicero, T.: *A Garden of Pomegranates—Skrying on the Tree of Life,* 1995, Llewellyn

Magick:

Culling, L & Weschcke, C.: *The Complete Magick Curriculum of the Secret Order G∴B∴G∴—Being the Entire Study, Curriculum, Magick Rituals, and Initiatory Practices of the Great Brotherhood of God,* 2010, Llewellyn

Kraig, D: *Modern Magick—Twelve Lessons in the High Magickal Arts,* 2010, Llewellyn

Regardie, I. *The Golden Dawn—The Original Account of the Teachings, Rites, and Ceremonies of the Hermetic Order, 6th Edition, Revised and Enlarged, with New Comp0rehensive Index, under the editorship of Carl Llewellyn Weschcke,* 1971, 1989, Llewellyn

Regardie, I. & Cicero C. & Cicero, T.: *The Tree of Life—An Illustrated Study in Magic,* 2001, Llewellyn

Skinner, S.: *The Complete Magician's Tables—The Most Complete Tabular Set of Magic, Kabbalistic, Angelic, Astrologic. Alchemic, Demonic, Geomantic, Grimoire, Gematria, I Ching, Tarot, Planetary, Pagan Pantheon, Perfume. Emblem and Character Correspondences in more than 800 Tables,* 2012, Llewellyn

Tyson, D.: *Portable Magic—Tarot is the Only Tool You Need*, 2006, Llewellyn

Tyson, D.: *The Power of the Word—The Secret Code of Creation*, 2013, Llewellyn

U.D., Frater: *Practical Sigil Magic—Creating Personal Symbols for Success*, 2012, Llewellyn

Martial Arts:

Carnie, L.: *Chi Gung—Chinese Healing, Energy and Natural Magick*, 2002, Llewellyn

Morphic Fields:

Sheldrake, R.: *Chaos, Creativity, and Cosmic Consciousness*, 2001, Park Street Press

Sheldrake, R.: *Science Set Free—10 Paths to New Discovery*, 2013, Deepak Chopra

Sheldrake, R.: *The Presence of the Past—Morphic Resonance and the Memory of Nature*, 2012, Park Street Press

New Age Spirituality:

Drury, N., *The New Age: Searching for the Spiritual Self*, London, England, UK: 2004, Thames and Hudson

Sutcliffe, S. & Gilhus, I.: *New Age Spirituality—Rethinking Religion*, 2014, Rutledge

Paganism:

Campanelli, P.: *Wheel of the Year—Living the Magical Life*, 1988, Llewellyn

Higginbotham, R. & J.: *Pagan Spirituality—A Guide to Personal Transformation*, 2012, Llewellyn

Higginbotham, J. & R.: *Paganism—An Introduction to Earth-Centered Religions*, 2013, Llewellyn

Moura, A.: *Grimoire for the Green Witch—A Complete Book of Shadows*, 2012, Llewellyn

Psychic Empowerment:

Judith, A.: *The Global Heart Awakens—Humanity's Rite of Passage from the Love of Power to the Power of Love*, 2013, Shift Books

Slate, J. & Weschcke, C.L.: *Astral Projection for Psychic Empowerment*, 2012, Llewellyn

Slate, J. & Weschcke, C.L.: *Clairvoyance for Psychic Empowerment*, 2012, Llewellyn

Slate, J. & Weschcke, C.L.: *Llewellyn Complete Book of Psychic Empowerment*, 2011, Llewellyn

Quantum Metaphysics/Quantum Mysticism:

Capra, F.: *The Tao of Physics—An Exploration of the Parballs between Modern Physics and Esoteric Mysticism*, 2010, Shamballa

Chopra, D.: *Quantum Healing—Exploring the Frontiers of Mind/Body Medicine*, 2009, Bantam New Age

Chopra, D.: *Ageless Body, Timeless Mind—the Quantum Alternative to Growing Old*, 2009, Harmony

Kafotos, M. & Nadeau, R.: *The Conscious Universe—Part and Whole in Modern Physical Theory*, 1990, Springer-Verlag

Penrose, R.: *Shadows of the Mind—A Search for the Missing Science of Consciousness*, 1996, Oxford University Press

Wilson, R. A.: *Quantum Psychology—How Brain Software Programs You and Your World*, 1990, New Falcon

Science & Religion:

Kieffer, Gene: *The Secret Teachings Unveiling the Luminous Sun Within*, 2000, Bethel Publishers

Scientology:

Hubbard, L.,: *Scientology—The Fundamentals of Thought*, 2007, Bridge Publications

Wright, L.: *Going Clear—Scientology, Hollywood, and the Prison of Belief,* 2013, Vintage

Secular Humanism:

Flynn, T. & others: *Secular Humanism and its Commitments,* 2012—Selection from *"Free Inquiry"* magazine published by the Council for Secular Humanism.

Force, James E.: *Introduction (1990) to An Account of the Growth of Deism in England*

Gay, P.: *Deism: An Anthology,* 1968, D. Van Norstand Co, Inc.

Shamanism:

Johnson, K.: *Witchcraft and the Shamanic Journey—Pagan Folkways from the Burning Times,* 1998, Llewellyn

Walsh, R.: *The World of Shamanism—New Views of an Ancient Tradition,* 2007, Llewellyn

Spiritism:

Aizpurua, J.: *Fundamentals of Spiritism—The soul, the afterlife, pschic abilities, mediumship, and reincarnation and how these influence our lives,* 2013, CreateSpace

Bragdon, E.: *Kardec's Spiritism—A Home for Healing and Spiritual Evolution,* 2004, Lightening Up Press

Spiritual, but not Religious:

Fuller, R.: *Spiritual but not Religious—Understanding Unchurched America,* 2001, Oxford

Spiritualism:

Buckland, R.: *Buckland's Book of Sopirit Communications,* 2013, Llewellyn

Gallagher, M.: *Why the Victorians Saw Ghosts—An Illustrated Guide to 19th Century Spiritualism,* 2014, Seventh Rainbow

Owen, A.: *The Darkened Room—Women, Power, and Spiritualism in Late Victorian England*, 2004, University of Chicago Press

Owens, E.: *Spiritualism & Clairvoyance for Beginners—Simpple Techniques to Develop Your Psychic Abilities*, 2005, Llewellyn

Tantra:

Feurestein, G.: *Tantra—The Path of Ecstasy*, 2012, Shambhala

Michaels, M. & Johnson, P.: *Great Sex Made Simple—Tantric Tips to Deepen Intimacy & Heighten Pleasure*, 2012, Llewellyn

Michaels, M. & Johnson, P.: *The Essence of Tantric Sexuality*, 2006, Llewellyn

Mumford, J.: *A Chakra & Kundalini Workbook—Psycho-Spiritual; Techniques for Healthy, Rejuvenation, Psychic Powers & Spiritual Realization*, 1994, Llewellyn

Mumford, J.: *Ecstasy Through Tantra*, 2002, Llewellyn

Wallis, C. & Ellic, E.: *Tantra Illuminated—The Philosophy, History, and Practice of a Timeless Tradition*, 2013, Mattamayura Press

Taoism:

Yudelove, E.: *100 Days to Better Health, Good Sex & Long Life—A guide to Taoist Yoga & Chi Kung*, 2002, Llewelllyn

Yudelove, E.: *Taoist Yoga and Sexual Energy—Transforming Your Body and Spirit*, 2000, Llewellyn

Tarot:

Dugan, E. & Evans, M: *Witches Tarot*, 2012, Llewellyn

Huggens, K. & Dunne, E.: *Tarot Illuminati Kit*, 2013, Llewellyn

Kenner, C.: *Tarot and Astrology—Enhance Your Readings Wit the Wisdom of the Zodiac*, 2012, Llewellyn

Louis, A.: *Tarot Beyond the Basics—Gain a Deeper Understanding of the Meanings Behind the Cards*, 2014, Llewellyn

Moore, B. & Fell, A.: The *Steampunk Tarot*, 2012, Llewellyn

Moore, B.: *Tarot Spreads, Layouts & Techniques to Empower Your Readings*, 2012, Llewellyn

Transcendentalism:

Gura, P.: *American Transcendentalism—A History*, 2008, Hill and Wang

Transhumanism:

Horn, T. & N.: *Forbidden Gates—How Genetics, Robotics, Artifician Intelligence, Synthetic Biology, Nanotechnology, and Human Enhancement Herald the Dawn of TechnoDimensional Spiritual Warfare*, 2011, Defender Publishing

Kurzweil, R.: *The Singularity is Near—When Humans Transcend Biology*, 2005, Penguin

Unitarian Universalism:

Buehrens, J., Church, F.: *A Chosen Faith—An Introduction to Unitarian Universalism*, 1998, Beacon Press

Church, F.: *The Cathedral of the World—A Universalist Theology*, 2009, Beacon Press

Voodoo:

Crowley, R.: *The Vodou Quantum Leap—Alternate Realities, Power and Mysticism*, 2000, Llewellyn

Wicca:

Cunningham, S.: *Cunningham's Encyclopedia of Magical Herbs*, 2012, Llewellyn

Cunningham, S.: *Wicca—A Guide for the Solitary Practitioner*, 1993, Llewellyn

RavenWolf, S.: *Solitary Witch—The Ultimate Book of Shadows for the New Generation*, 2009, Llewellyn

Sabin, T.: *Wicca for Beginners—Fundamentals of Philosophy & Practice*, 2006, Llewellyn

Witchcraft:

Buckland, R.: *Buckland's Complete Book of Witchcraft*, 2002, Llewellyn

Goldenberg, N.R.: *The Changing of the Gods—Feminism and the End of Traditional Religions*, 1979, Beacon Press

Hutton, R.: *The Triumph of the Moon—A History of Modern Pagan Witchcraft*, 1999, Oxford

Murray, M.: *The God of the Witches*, 1931, Oxford

Murray, M.: *The Witch-cult in Western Europe*, 1921, Oxford

Yoga:

Butera, R.: *Meditation for Your Life—Creating a Plan that Suits Your Style*, 2012, Llewellyn

Butera, R.: *The Pure Heart of Yoga—Ten Essential Steps for Personal Transformation*, 2012, Llewellyn

12

THE SPIRIT, THE MEDIUM, THE CHANNEL, AND YOU

The Medium is <u>not</u> the Message!

We are all Spirit Communicators

All the time we are unconsciously broadcasting all kinds of "messages" to the Universe, and all the time we are unconsciously receiving messages from the Universe that is everything and everybody, including each and every one of us. It's not just the visible "out there" of Earth, Sun, Moon and distant Stars, nor the invisible spirits in higher dimensions, for we too are Spirit as well Body, Mind, and Soul. We all are made of the same stuff which is Spirit, the universal *subtle element* that is the foundation and source of all the other elements manifesting in both visible and invisible dimensions, inwardly and outwardly. We, and everything physical and non-physical, all possess "spiritual" qualities and are, in fact, mostly composites of physical/etheric, astral, mental, causal, and spiritual substance, energy, and consciousness.

You are—potentially—a Power House

Each living person incarnates Body, Mind, and Spirit, *and* Feeling, Will, and Purpose within a single multi-level vehicle. Each person is a "power house" of near infinite potential, *but*, most people are barely "awake" at the physical level of conscious awareness, and have little control over the non-physical levels of feeling, thought and will. Our bodies are alive at the deepest and most minute *quanta* levels where we are constantly *broadcasting* messages from and between body cells and organs, and radiating it all from *inner* selves to all selves everywhere.

In addition to receiving these messages from all other people, and the natural and spiritual worlds around us, we also receive and automatically *respond* to a constant flood of physical stimuli and radiation inducing emotional and unconscious mental "meandering," generating nerve impulses, producing stress hormones, and compounding chemical agents that lead to reactions in the tri-level brain one part of which is divided into two halves. The brain is all lit up, *but for what purpose?* Without conscious *intention* those messages serve no purpose—they are a waste of your energies and injurious to your long term health (and "wealth").

Reacting without Thought

Mostly, if not entirely, we *react* without thought or full awareness to physical events. Our attention is drawn to news stories of crime and disaster, to political and "religious" grand-standing, celebrity-studded entertainment, crowd-thrilling spectator sports, and the bizarre antics of young people in search of their personal identity—all tending to produce unintentional emotional reactions with unforeseen consequences to our own health and well-being and in our immediate family and social environment, and the world around us.

We *react* unconsciously rather than acting consciously with understanding and intention, and don't even know the difference. We react because most of us are "asleep at the switch" and don't know it, and don't even know that we have a switch. We're like a hot race car, all gassed up, engine roaring, and no driver, no map, no guidance, no flag to drop. Our physical self is up, the potential for greatness is with us, but the only direction to go is nowhere. You have to wake up, understand who and what you are, discover and activate that switch, and take charge of your own life. Don't let others, not their institutions nor their automated systems, rob you of purpose and your precious assets and life energies for their self-serving benefit.

Know, and Take Charge!

It's all very complex, yet you are the one who can understand and must take charge, and the fact of reaction vs. action results from what little you really know about yourself and the Universe in which we all live and have our being. *But you must decide that you want to know about both, accept the facts that you are more than a physical body, that your real self is the actor, that you live in an <u>interrelationship</u> between your whole self and the whole universe and all there is.*

Your acceptance of this defines your *Attitude* towards Life and your relation with the Universe, and your attitude reflects and incorporates your knowledge and becomes your own *inner Belief System*. No belief system imposed from without by Church or State, or Parent or School gives you the knowledge and strength to be an active partner with the Universe around you and thus enabling you to *become more than you* and *all you can be.* You, each of us, is the Microcosm to the Macrocosm; we are all that the Cosmos is, but on a different scale and still lacking the whole knowledge and awareness to become full partners in this universe.

It's Small Thing that Control Big Things

The modern world is a *New World of Mind & Spirit* in a *New Age of Higher Human Consciousness.* It is a New World of what we increasingly know of our own Body, Mind and Spirit, of the world about us and within which we live, and of our role with the Universe. The "World" is bigger than we are and constantly growing through knowledge and understanding, but *it is the small things that control bigger things.* Modern Quantum Physics reveals a fundamental dimension of smallness that switches back and forth between manifesting as Particles or Waves, Matter or Energy in response to human attention and intention. In other words, each person does have the power to introduce change (beneficial or otherwise) at the most fundamental levels of Reality as she or he lives it.

Every cell in your body has consciousness and awareness of its purpose within the structure of your physical body. That consciousness is a manifestation of Spirit, and through the disciplines of Mind and Emotion you can willfully communicate through Spirit to heal the body and extend its lifespan.

The More you know, the Deeper you can go

The more you know the deeper you can go and the better you can do these things, and more. That's the value of the full range of the Yogic Sciences—not just the Hatha Yoga of gym studios. *It's not just physical control, but emotional control, mental control, spiritual control, and life control that must become your goal.* That's the value of gaining the full range of psychic empowering skills, and the value of gaining the full range of self-empowering knowledge and understanding.

All Big things start with small things. Big things may be beyond your control and direct influence, but small things are not. Small things are points of leverage from which you can influence and change Bigger things. No, you can't change the entire world all by yourself, but you can plant seeds that can grow and perhaps reach other people and "start the ball rolling" to bring about corrective changes in those big institutions that are out of harmony with the natural world in which we live and the fundamental cosmic purpose of individual growth and evolutionary development.

The Deeper You Go, the more You Know.

The more you know, and the deeper you go, the more control over your world you have. The Big World is composed of many small worlds. Big Worlds are the Organizations and Institutions of the modern world, but all organizations and institutions are composed of individuals. Individuals *can* control the big organizations and institutions, but they have to understand their nature and structure, and know their purpose—and hence where and how to apply leverage.

Big Institutions and Organizations thrive on individuals' ignorance of their nature and purpose, and dominate YOU by your faith in the "Big Picture" they've drawn for you and for which they ask for your money and your "vote." They need you, but *claim that you need them.* Often they reflect antique ideologies based on out-of-date beliefs about reality, serving only to benefit their self-serving leadership who use their immense power to support lavish life styles of the wealthy and powerful special interests.

It's up to you to gain the knowledge, to train your mind, and to raise your "frequency"* to see things for what they really are. Don't be guided by their fear-inducing slogans that are really *selling* you a "bill of goods" contrary to your best interests, contrary to the natural order, and contrary to the cosmic directive calling for your personal development.

* A measure of vibrations. More about this in reference to your states of consciousness later.

It's All in YOUR Attitude

Your *attitude* towards the world determines the way you look at things, and is either passive and reactive or active and cooperative. The truth is that *"WE are the World."* We and the World; Humanity and Nature; Body and Emotion, Mind and Spirit; Individuals and *their* Institutions—all are *partners* and must work together in cooperative understanding of our interdependent relationship. But it is now essential that we do this consciously and become more and more fully aware. We must *BELIEVE* in our own power to do so. It is "We, the People" who must assert our Freedom and take responsible control over our institutions that serve as communities of public interest.

In the past, "Belief" was largely imposed by Church and State, and both demanded and enforced obedience regardless of science, law, or personal belief.

That Belief—imposed in the West by the dominant religious institutions—precluded people from *all* individual communication with Spirit and Spiritual Entities, basically defined as anything non-physical, hence *not of this world!* The *Other World* was literally owned by the Church, and only their *authorized personnel* could *legally* (since the Church dominated the State) communicate with other world entities.

Conscious vs. Unconscious Communication

What the Church knows is that we are all *communicators* as already discussed earlier in this chapter. Body, Emotion, Mind, and Spirit are always radiating and broadcasting subtle messages to the subtle fields of the Universe about us. But all that is at the automatic, *unconscious*, levels for most people. It is *unintentional* communication without conscious messages, and that's the way "they" want to keep it.

Real Communication must be done consciously with a deliberate message intentionally targeting the desired communicant. Even if it is a message to an out-of-balance physical organ or energy center within our own body, it is *Intention* that focuses the power to knowingly bring change to heal disharmony and disease.

Everything and every entity *vibrates,* and the numbers assigned to that rate of vibration is a measure of speed and size of the energy keynote constantly radiating outward from the whole being—physical and non-physical. That keynote *frequency* is not absolutely fixed but does operate in a narrow enough range to serve as a kind of cosmic address for each person. Other people and other entities of both the physical world and the spiritual worlds likewise have such cosmic addresses—just like we use for "e-mail."

Getting in Sync!

But, to be fully effective, *Communicator* and *Communicant* need to be "in sync" with one another; be "on the same wavelength," the same frequency or at least in "parallel harmony" with each other. We'll explain shortly.

The human being can intentionally alter the wavelength of the messages he or she consciously wishes to send to a communicant whether in this world or others in order to reach the designated target. But, it's not as easily done as said. Within this physical world, e-mail (or postal mail or a telephone call) is more reliable because there is a vast and dedicated support system to transfer the message in its purity and reach the target communicant free of interference.

Most of us are still unable to readily free our consciousness of the interfering incessant "noise" and "garbage" from within our own mind and emotion, and then to reliably raise the level of our frequency to specifically focus our awareness on the target so as to communicate accurately across the divide between the physical and spiritual (astral/mental/causal) worlds and reach a desired entity. Without a dedicated support service we need:

1. To bring our own mind under un-ambivalent control, and
2. To understand how to address any particular entity.

Absent a trained mind and such self-empowering techniques as meditation and self-hypnosis, and psychic empowering skills as astral projection and clairvoyance, just as we do to reach across the divide of physical distance by the use of an intermediary (today mostly by means of electronic devices that have replaced the older roles of the pony express and before that of the town crier and long-distance runners) we need some form of intermediary to communicate with any non-physical entity.

Intermediaries between the Worlds

While various gadgetry and "black boxes" have been pitched over the years to allow spirit voices to be heard, deliberate two-way communication is largely dependent on human intermediaries who have the ability to raise their level of consciousness and focus their awareness on the desired communicant. Aside from shamans, we know these intermediaries as Mediums and Channels.

Both the Medium and the Channel function between the Worlds of Physical and Spiritual Life, yet Spirit and Consciousness are everywhere and in everything. "Spirits" are non-physical entities, each *embodying* a unique and particularized consciousness, or "personality," and some of these also represent a larger Cosmic power and function. Each Spirit entity is as individual as is a living physically incarnate person like you, also embodying a particularized consciousness. In each of these worlds we have individuals seeking to communicate with one another.

Even though this chapter is about the use of intermediaries, we want to remind readers that every physically incarnate person is more than a body with a physical brain. We all are physical (<u>and non-physical</u>) beings currently expressing ourselves primarily through our multi-layered physical vehicle. Even as you may use an intermediary to communicate with non-physical entities, this experience will help build your own ability to eventually communicate directly with non-physical entities through your own non-physical self. The use of the trance state, whether self-induced or aided by another person or entity, is a means to focus the mind and exclude external distractions in order to have a clear focus on the desired communicant and the messages being communicated.

The Ambassador between this world and the "Other Side"

Just to give us a way to better understand the challenge of communication between the Physical and Spiritual Worlds, let's think of them like two countries on opposite sides of the planet—speaking different languages and having different histories and cultures, but sharing a common goal of world peace. Nations exchange ambassadors, and it is the job of each ambassador to not only accurately translate the languages but fully understand the difference in cultures so that every communication is founded on common ground.

Our ambassador, (we'll call her "Eartha Brown") is the intermediary or "medium" between our Physical World on This Side and the Spirit World on the *Other Side*. The common ground is the universality of spirituality and consciousness. The difference is in the "vibratory" rates or states of consciousness. Ambassador Brown has to move between these two levels, and this is usually facilitated by her entry into a self-induced *trance state*. It is by means of this trance state that our Ambassador Brown has focused and raised her consciousness to the level for communicating with the desired Spirit Entity on the Other Side—in this example we will call the surviving personality "Tom Smith." Ambassador Brown translates and communicates our messages to the Other Side, and then does the same for messages from the Other Side to This Side. In our theoretical example, it is Tom's daughter, Sarah, who wants to ask her deceased father what do about the library of old and valuable botanical books he so dearly loved. Both her sister who now lives in Portland Oregon and a distant nephew now living in Atlanta are asking about the collection. Should Sarah sell the books or give them to one or the other person? Eartha Brown is able to bring Tom Smith through and he says to sell the books and split the money between Sarah and her sister.

Such exchanges between the Physical and Spiritual Worlds has gone on for many millennia, but was large denigrated and forgotten in the Western World until a few hundred years ago, culminating in the Spiritualist movement today.

Mediums and Dead People, Spiritualist Churches and Camps

In previous chapters we've already given a short history of Spiritualism as it arose in the 19th century with the advent of physical phenomena in the Fox family's small cottage in upper New York State. The newspapers of the day spread the news across the nation and across the seas. The associated physical phenomena became dramatized with exaggerated cases of levitation of objects and people, the appearance of apparitions, the production of ectoplasm, voices speaking through floating trumpets, and more.

The seeming proof of survival after physical death and communication with the spirits of the deceased led to the birth of the religion of Spiritualism, to the birth and rebirth of interest in esotericism, the founding of the Theosophical Society, the Hermetic Order of the Golden Dawn, the Ordo Aurum Solis, and many other groups and movements advancing the non-physical dimensions, and to the involvement of science with the Societies for Psychical Research.

Séances and amateur practices of table tipping and spirit boards were popular forms of both stage and home entertainment. Some of the staged entertainment led to proven cases of fraud resulting in the general isolation of mediumship and séances into the Spiritualist Churches and the location of practitioners in "camps," such as Chesterfield in Indiana, Cassadaga in Florida, Lily Dale in New York, Lake Pleasant in Massachusetts, and many others. Now, like anything else, an online search will quickly provide a list of local mediums.

Channels and Channeling,
Ascended Masters and Spiritual Entities

After World War I, the interest in Spiritualism, mediums, séance phenomena, and communication with dead people seemed to falter, and then be replaced by "channeling" in the latter part of the 20th century which developed into the two basic types of *Conscious Channeling* and *Trance Channeling*. The basic differences between channeling and the earlier mediumship seems to be:

- The focus of Spiritualism is mostly on private messages and paranormal phenomena—demonstrating that the material world is not all there is.
- The focus of Channeling is mostly on the public and esoteric character of the messages—often reflecting the greater Cosmic Reality.

While the most popular recent channel was Jane Roberts who in 1972 published *Seth Speaks,* it should be noted that the famous founders of modern occultism, Madame H. P. Blavatsky, Dion Fortune, and Alice Bailey, consciously channeled Cosmic level teachings from spiritual masters—some believed to live in the Himalayas. Others have described such teachers as "Elder Brothers of the Human Race," "Ascended Masters," "Inner Plane Adepti," and simply "Great Spirits." Some also are described as the collective intelligence of many beings merged into a single voice.

Edgar Cayce in Trance, and the Unconscious Mind

An important transitional figure between 19th century Spiritualism and later 20th century Channeling was that of the "Sleeping Prophet," Edgar Cayce (1877–1945), who in 1901, while in hypnotic trance, diagnosed his own long-standing severe laryngitis and prescribed its cure. Subsequently, Cayce was able to provide diagnosis and prescribe treatments while in a hypnotic trance, using only a letter from the "patient" or just the person's name and location.

Newspaper and magazines told the story of Cayce's trance readings which eventually included not only personal health matters but metaphysical subjects such as Past Lives, references to Atlantis, Crystal Energies, the Akashic Records, Aura Reading, and Forecasts of Future Events.

As his fame grew, the readings—of which 14,000 were recorded—were analyzed and cataloged under the subjects discussed, and books and articles spread the information. That work led to founding of the Cayce Hospital and the non-profit Association for Research and Enlightenment (ARE) in Virginia Beach, Virginia where research, publishing, and educational work continues to this day.

"We have the body"

For a reading, Cayce would lie down, and enter into trance facilitated at first by professional hypnotists and later by his wife and son. Persons requesting a reading would normally not be present but their requests and questions would be read to Cayce and his readings recorded in short-hand by his secretary. Almost all the readings would be prefaced by the statement "We have the body" meaning that Cayce's unconscious source (or sources?) was in clairvoyant contact with the spiritual essence of the subject. From this, diagnosis was made, a treatment prescribed, and sometimes specific directions were given as to where obscure medicines could be found. Some of these were antique patent medicines no longer on the market, but the reading would give a location where the medicine could be obtained.

The Unconscious Mind

Cayce never claimed to channel Spirits or other beings. He explained that the unconscious mind—addressed under hypnosis—has access to information from sources that the conscious mind does not. Whether this involved the Akashic Field so named by Ervin Laszlo, the Collective Unconscious of Carl Jung, or the ancient concept of Macrocosm and Microcosm, Cayce's readings individually match the vast, complex and logically comprehensive metaphysical system revealed in the channeled material transcribed by esotericists H. P. Blavatsky in the late 19th century and Alice Bailey in the early 20th century, and by many others.

This recognition of the "unconscious mind" as a source of information both personal and impersonal, and beyond, that was accessible to Cayce, as well as the later readings accessing information about broad metaphysical subjects validates the _inner Self_ as the source for wisdom and "answers" in contrast to the belief that only _outer_ Spirits and High Spiritual Entities could do so.

Metaphysics is not religion

Neither Blavatsky nor Bailey claimed either personal or religious authority, only that the material they transcribed originated with "Master Teachers"—highly evolved spiritual beings no longer incarnating into physical bodies or even the lower of the "spiritual" planes. Many Channels and writers have expanded and up-dated their metaphysical systems to include ancient practices of self-understanding and cosmic attunement as astrology and geomancy, systems of divination to include palmistry and handwriting analysis; studies of shamanism and alchemy; revivals of the Old Religion of Witchcraft and European Paganism; new interpretations of Gnosticism and Middle Eastern mysticism; new explorations of Tantra and Yoga; of Taoism and the Martial Arts; and studies of the ancient Egyptian, Mayan, and the still earlier Goddess religions and practices.

From East to West, from Old to New, from Feudalism and Slavery to Freedom and Democracy, from Dogma to Science, this has been an evolution moving from religious dictates to practices of self-knowledge and self-development.

Subjective/Objective Realities

Over the 20th and into the 21st century, this evolution has coincided with the transition of physics from the Newtonian of a "clockwork" mechanical universe into the quantum physics of particles and waves, of Freudian psycho-analysis with its negative view of the subconscious and feminine sexuality into Jungian analytical psychology with its positive view of the Collective Unconscious, and of the study of paranormal phenomena from physical trickery into statistical analysis and now into a growing perception and acceptance of non-physical realities. At the same time, the dynamics of the material world have moved from the "Big Picture" and management "by the numbers" to the reality of the very small as high technology miniaturized power transfers down to the sub-atomic level.

The perception of material energy/matter transfers at the sub-atomic and sub-cellular levels, and the *expansion* of our view of consciousness *to include awareness at sub-conscious* levels has enabled our "awake" consciousness to focus at both physical and non-physical levels. Physical and Spiritual are aspects of the same cosmic reality requiring only a change of focus to empower intentional changes at the sub-atomic, sub-cellular and "subjective" levels which are—in turn—foundational to objective levels. And, perhaps, a slow evolution and exchange of terminology recognizing where the new physicist may be describing the same things as the old esotericist.

Our awakened consciousness and our new command of the subjective/objective entwinement brings individual empowerment. We have moved from the unconscious participation of herd and tribe into semi-conscious systems of institutional control, *and now we must assert more fully aware consciousness and personal authority, and accept personal responsibility for our own actions and those of our participatory community in this New World emphasizing Mind and Spirit, and a New Age of Human Resources.*

The New Age is NOW, and it is transitional

No matter what name we want to use, or what mythic belief system we may use as a subjective background to our intellectual study of "what's happening" in the world around us, all the messages are similar and easily summed up as "The end of the World—**as we know it!**" The trouble is, of course, that we know very little of what this "world" *really* is, what it really has been, and how it fits into the greater realities of human evolution, planetary consciousness, our solar system, and on up to the Cosmos as a whole. But, we do know that everything is inter-related with everything (and everyone) else. And, that we are here, now.

*But the messages are clear that **the time is** NOW. But, time for what?*

Energies and radiation from the Sky Above, the Earth Below, and the Universe Around are bringing *evolutionary* changes to the cells of our bodies and reflecting into consciousness with accelerating stimulation leading to excitement, belligerence, and reactive behavior, and increased mental and spiritual intelligence—but behind these cellular changes is the loosening of the barriers between the planes. Psychic awareness increases as the astral images and mental thought forms become more easily perceived and we become more aware of our creative abilities. *Opportunity knocks even as warning sirens wail.*

Personal Empowerment is a necessity

Much is happening, currently beyond our full awareness of the subtle energies behind the material events, and hence of our full understanding and ability to act positively rather than reacting negatively. The need is to *wake up* and know, to wake up and understand, and to wake up and act with knowledge and understanding of the causes and effects of the influx of these subtle energies and messages. Our spirit communication must be more than between two entities, and include the increasing sensitivity for conscious perception and understanding of these subtle energies of solar, planetary, and universal origins.

We exist, and therefore we are, and therefor the world is. We walk on the ground (or pavement), we mostly ride (or drive) to our daily work (and everywhere else), we mostly live with our families in (mostly good) housing, the kids go to (mostly good) schools, most of us live in relatively peaceful and safe areas.

Critical Times, or Real Change

We are also aware of increasing dangers from crime and terror and threats of war from distant lands ruled by religious zealots bound by old theologies; of increasing planetary disturbances, extreme weather, and climate changes; of abusive financial practices leading to massive economic hardship and new threats to our wealth and savings; of environmental health hazards, abusive agricultural practices, and costly medical corruption and errant regulation; and the constant presence of scams and a loss of faith in programs that were supposed to help us from being victimized by corporate (and other) greed.

We live in a world of rapid technological change and progress in communications, in information resources, in educational opportunities, in the promise of a longer and healthier life, in a culture of greater sexual freedom and understanding, and of respect for sexual pleasure and ecstasy. We are promised that science, technology, and resource management will provide sufficient food and opportunities for a growing population, but we're also threatened by growing unemployment in the face of more efficient production, by changes in consumer preferences for goods and e-commerce over local stores, and by the rapid spread of disease and increased accidents in transportation and recreation, of corruption in government and its agencies, of the domination of greed in financial transactions and regulation.

Personal Responsibility is also necessary

We enter a New Age that brings both great promise and threat, and we're caught in the middle and have to give direction to achieve that great promise. We seek understanding of where we really are, and increasingly look beyond the physical world for guidance—but we also find the old institutions of "faith" are equally as corrupt, greedy, and out of tune with reality as are the institutions of government and business, and that their theologies are inadequate and wrong to meet the obvious challenges and the obvious hazards of these and future times.

We realize that "Institutions" put distance between people and these same institutions, and place barriers between vendors and their customers and clients. Responsibility is no longer direct and so greed replaces honesty and honor because there are no direct repercussions. Old ways are inadequate and new ways are still uncertain.

We have to find our own Answers

But we do know enough to understand that the past zodiacal ages, each approximating 2,400 years in length, have transitional phases of several hundred years of which we are perhaps at more than two-thirds through from the Age of Fish (Pisces) to the Age of Man (Aquarius). No matter how specific such calculations can be, an open-minded approach recognizes the beginning Aquarian influence can be seen in the phases of Enlightenment, Reason and Democracy in the 18th century, while interpreters of the Mayan calendar might suggest that the "tipping point" occurred December 21, 2012 more fully leaving the Piscean influence behind.

This transition into the Aquarian Age of Human Knowledge may coincide with the advent of even greater cosmic level cyclical changes, but all the messages say the same thing: *we must find our own way and we do have the power to do so.* We have to learn for ourselves what we must know and what we must do. We have a World Wide Web of Information Resources beyond anything available from libraries, traditions and teachers before the 21st century. At the same time, our global network of news constantly warns of weather and climate change, of threats of religious inspired terrorism and war, of the hazards to our electronic networks and power grids from Solar Flares and changes to the magnetic fields in and around our planet, and perhaps even of planetary effects on human behavior leading to transportation accidents, unpredictable crimes against women and children, bizarre religious and political beliefs, and diversions of resources from public need to private greed.

The End of the OLD World

Is all of this what was meant in the Mayan Prophecy "as the End of the World—*as we know it?*" Well, the world didn't end on 12/21/12, *but it is different.* The same message has been repeated from indigenous cultures around the world and also in the never ending gloomy predictions of religious prophets and psychics. The prophecies are always ambivalent in interpretation, and always—so far—get the dates wrong. But the fundamental message is that change is inevitable and that the need for change in thinking and attitude is obvious.

When we turn to spiritual sources we have to accept the challenges of both interpretation and timing. The higher the source the greater the challenge because we move beyond familiar words to mystical expression and symbols. Yet, each of us can—to turn to the mystical for the moment—see "the warning signs in the sky," "feel the earth shaking at our feet," and "read the writing on the wall"—or in books.

The Beginning of the NEW World

No, this is not a book of prophecies, and it is a book about Spirit Communication. We've traced some history of both Mediumship and Channels, and now we will get into discussion of specific technologies of both.

We've tried to demonstrate that we are all communicating with the Universe at all times, and made the point that it is every person's responsibility to "wake up" and communicate consciously and purposefully with specific communicants, thus: the **How**, the **Why**, and the **Who**.

As to the **Need,** in this chapter we've demonstrated the importance of the *Individual's* active role in place of the passivity previously taught by those old *Institutions* once intended to serve our needs. As described previously, *the Need is historic.* There is no choice about the critical changes happening in the Earth below, in the Space above, in the world of Humanity around, and in the Human Person here and now. There is choice, however, in the opportunity we all have, individually and communally, to work with the Forces behind change. The New Age is one of *Individual* and *Community* vs. the old age of *Institutions* and *Collectivism*. Individuals can *form* voluntary communities for common actions. Institutions work to *force* individuals into a single massive collective led by a few persons sharing one ideology under a single leader. The old age required the submersion of the individual into the mass for *other*-determined collective action; the New Age calls for the emergence of the individual from the mass for *self*-determined communal actions.

Desire, Determination, Discipline

It is your intelligence that is needed; it is your knowledge that is needed; it is your understanding that is needed; and it is your emotional drive and commitment that is needed. Real learning requires **Desire** and **Discipline**, but the need is so extreme that you must feel **Determination** to—*literally*—"Save the World." We must all awaken and act both together and alone, but *remember* that "all" is you, and me, and every individual in every community. Every voice counts, just as does every vote. It's just as important to "spread the word" as it is to act "alone and together."

Above all, it is your two-way spiritual communication with the Earth, with Life, and with the Universe that will bring understanding and guidance for individual and communal actions at the local levels where things happen. It is that exchange that is needed to bring awareness of the needs for a new paradigm of human harmony with the natural order, with understanding of the impact humanity's actions on the Earth and the essential partnership between Humanity, Nature, and the Universe.

Reading the Signs

We abuse Nature to our own detriment and endangerment. Rivers and ponds foam with chemical waste and fertilizer runoffs. Drinking water is not drinkable in many parts of the world. Americans cannot smugly sit back and think "not in my backyard" for the contamination is so great that what happens in Japan shows up in California. Food prices soar because corn is turned into tax-subsided fuel. Family farms are turned into rodent-ridden factory farms. Animals are pressed tightly together in feedlots where disease can spread so easily that the antibiotics used virtually contaminate the food we eat. The alternatives of natural, organic and lunar culture are expensive but show the way to sustainable, self-sufficient, healthy communal cultures. Such "healthy living" may be cheaper when factor in the benefits. We cannot continue in ignorance of the inter-connectedness of all Life but must become intelligently and consciously aware of our spiritual unity and opportunity to change.

The Earth is so unstable that houses are disappearing into sinkholes. The Sky is filled in glorious colors of Northern Lights indicative of dangerous levels of solar activity. Ice melts in Greenland and Antarctica raise sea levels and increase the strength and number of hurricanes at sea and extreme weather on land, while oil-polluted waters kill and poison seafood. Ocean-floor volcanoes lead to Seaquakes that lead to tsunamis that kill hundreds of thousands. Droughts and Floods lead to failed food crops and constant threats of wild fires and insect infestations.

The Failures of Communication and the Neglected Resource

Governments are so dominated by "Special Interests" and their lobbyist-fed corruption as to be incapable of reliable regulation of food and drug safety, repairing our broken infrastructure, investing in education, and providing for safe travel and efficient transportation. And more and more Governments and Business operate with short-term goals without thought of "tomorrow."

Humans fail to communicate with one another and instead wrap themselves in narcissism and isolate themselves with narcotics. They fail to listen to Nature and fail to read the signs of Earth's agonies and the Ocean's pains, they ignore the signs in the sky and the troubles in the atmosphere and the flying debris burning in space and falling to earth.

The Spirits of Nature, or the Earth, and Gods and Goddesses

We must learn to communicate, consciously, deliberately and with full awareness of the universe all around us: the people, the animals, the forests, the fish, *and the spirits*. There are more spirits than those surviving personalities of dead people, or the angels of other dimensions. There are spirits of Nature, of the Earth, of the Mountains and Rivers, the Gods and Goddesses of Life's Functions, the places of Man's habitat and the Forces of Life. Spirits are everywhere and can be evoked, invoked, communicated with, questioned, and their attributes brought to bear on place and circumstance.

Spirits are the Matrix interlacing and embracing the visible and invisible reality. They are the neglected resource of Intentional Consciousness. When we communicate with Spirit we connect with Spiritual Power and Inner Wisdom.

Many are the Ways

People have been communicating with Spirit and Spirits for eons, and many are the ways of Shamanic travels between the worlds, Mediumistic interaction and exchanges between physical and astral entities, and Channeled knowledge teachings from Ascended Masters and Elder Brothers. *And channeling from our own selves*—un-conscious, sub-conscious, super-conscious, and even our very highest self and soul. Spirit itself is the "medium" and the communicant is spirit everywhere.

We've previously discussed Shamanism extensively and will now do so with Mediumship and Channeling, and in later chapters discuss Magick techniques and Rising into Higher Consciousness.

No One Way!

The first point to be made is that there is *No One Way!* Humans are not "factory made" and stamped out of one *Edenic* mold as per the *Book of Genesis.* Despite all the efforts of modern science, we are not absolutely certain of our common origin as someplace in Darkest Africa although the evidence is nearly overwhelming. There are many myths of varied origins, of seedings and landings from Space, and of "devolution" through the Cosmic Planes and esoteric races and sub-races, of *Lost Continents* and emigration from the planet Venus. All interesting, but the obvious fact is that we are all different whether of different historic origins or genetic mutation and cultural variations, and individuals with unique talents. Yes, perhaps all could learn just one way just as we all could and may eventually learn just one language, but there is proven value to diversity.

There are many values to be found in study of these multiple ways, the many technologies of spiritual communication and applications of spiritual information, knowledge and power. Learn, and adapt to your own needs and interests, not those of others. Learn and practice, and serve the interests of all the others too. You have the Power.

THE WAYS OF MEDIUIMSHIP

The Intermediaries in Mediumship

Mediums are "Intermediaries" between "this world" and the "next world," most commonly enabling communication between a "loved one" communicator on this plane" and a "surviving personality" communicant on the astral plane—usually thought of as the Spirit World. As discussed previously, mediums commonly enter into a self-induced trance state which enable two particular functions:

1. The exclusion of outside distractions so the medium can better focus on the pre-established goal;
2. The ability to *raise* their level of "vibration" to meet that of the intended communicant. This is a largely unconscious process involving the name and relationship of that communicant.

Spirit Guides

Historically this process was often facilitated through a second Intermediary from the astral level called a "Spirit Guide" who located the intended communicant and sometimes performed a needed task of guiding both parties in their communication, including guiding the recently deceased into the realization and acceptance of their physical death and survival in the Next World.

Often the initial communication was marked by extreme emotion on the part of the "Seeker," which creates many problems in turn—exaggerated because the astral substance is "emotional" in the same sense as material substance is physical. This astral/emotional substance is very responsive to emotional energies, fantasies, fears, feelings, sexual and religious fetishes, religious beliefs and dis-beliefs, illusions and charged thought forms, etc. Emotions are very powerful—think of E-Motion as "Energy-in-Motion," and realize it as the motive power behind *Ambition-in-motion, Armies-in-motion, Creativity-in-motion, Crime-in-motion, Discovery-in-motion, Hate and Terror-in-motion, Innovation and Invention-in-motion, Love and Passion-in-motion, Research-in-motion, and Success in itself.*

By connecting the subject with the phrase "in-motion" we mean to emphasize that such emotion can be *infectious,* leading to Crowds and Masses-in-motion, often destructively so with complete loss of rationality and self-control. At the same time, Emotion is the foundation of Magick and the *enabler* for the manifestations of Mind and Spirit into the Physical World including powerful thought-forms, deific images, healing imagery, the evocation and invocation of empowering symbols and images, and a great deal more than can be even casually mentioned within a single chapter on another subject.

The Phenomena of Hauntings and Séances

In the beginning of modern Spiritualism, Hauntings and Séances were most often accompanied by a range of psychic phenomena—from rapping to movements of objects and the appearance of apports, voices and sounds including music without apparent source, the appearance of ectoplasm and apparitions, levitation of objects and even people and sometimes of the Medium herself. The phenomena became so interesting that it was often the main objective of séances, and that led to stage performances some of which involved trickery and fraud.

Nevertheless, Spirit Communication and psychic phenomena led to the formation of psychical research societies and the founding of modern parapsychology and the new science of the paranormal in which psychic powers and their development are researched and studied separately from Spirit Communication.

Types of Mediumship

Sometimes the importance of the actual Message was overlooked in the excitement of Séance phenomena, while at the same time the practices evolved into several types. In most cases, the communicator on This Side may address the spirit on the Other Side directly by speaking or writing. The medium may repeat the message, read it aloud, or hold the written message to her forehead. Towards the end of the 19th century, the complete two-way communication was in written form by means of hand-writing from this side and the response from the other side by Automatic Writing. In mid-20th century, the electric typewriter was adapted, and then the personal computer, and even the use of voice-activated software.

Here are some of the variations in mediumship:

Mental mediumship: in which communication between spirits and the medium is in the manner of telepathy or clairaudience. The medium addresses the spirit either vocally or silently and the spirit addresses the medium and the medium hears the spirit and repeats the message vocally.

Trance mediumship: in which the medium, once in trance, "steps aside" and allows the spirit to speak through her, using her "voice box." (This terminology was used to emphasize the disengagement of the medium from the message.

Unconscious trance: in which contact and trance are facilitated by a Spirit Guide who speaks through the medium and usually speaks on behalf of the spirit. Such "unconscious" mediumship is often aided by the playing of slow rhythmic music or singing of sleep-inducing hymns.

Direct Voice Mediumship: sometimes involving a trumpet, in which the spirit speaks independently of the medium who may herself participate in the conversation.

Physical Mediumship: in which the energies of the medium are manipulated by the spirit or spirit guide to produce physical phenomena such as raps, movement of physical objects, the production of ectoplasm, and the materialization of objects.

In addition to séance communication and associated phenomena, similar experience are found in relation to the more Shamanic practices of "Spiritist" religions such as Candomblé, Macomble, Umbanda, Voodoo, and some of the older variants of

Christianity such as the Shakers and Pentecostals, and in some New Age groups where ecstatic "speaking in tongues" and testimonial healings occur.

Types of Phenomena

Apparition. The appearance of an object "out of nowhere" has been seen by many observers, and photographed. The materialization of a human form of a recently deceased person has also be been observed and photographed.

Direct Voice. In the early years, spirits spoke through a trumpet, sometimes made visible with luminous paint so it could be seen in a darkened room. In later years and more commonly in channeling, the entranced medium (or channel) allows the communicating spirit to speak using her voice and directly responding to questions from participants.

Ectoplasm. The word means "exteriorized substance." That substance, exteriorized from the medium, is at first invisible and intangible, but can be seen and photographed under infra-red light and can be weighed. At a second stage, it can be seen, appearing as vapor, becoming liquid and solid, and having an odor like ozone. In a third stage of manifestation, it feels like a moist and cold cobweb and looks like muslin. Its appearance is accompanied by a 40 degree (Fahrenheit) drop in temperature. Analysis shows it composed of white blood cells.

Baron Schrenck Notzing in his *Phenomena of Materialization* writes: "We have very often been able to establish that by an unknown process there comes from the body of the medium a material, at first semi-fluid, which possesses some of the properties of a living substance, notably that of the power of change, of movement and of the assumption of definite forms."

It can be very sensitive to light, and a flash of light can cause the substance to snap back into the medium's body with sufficient as to bruise. On the other hand, the extrusion of ectoplasm has also occurred in full daylight.

Levitation. Levitation of objects and persons has occurred in full light. Among the common objects in earlier years were tambourines, trumpets, tables, chairs, books, accordions, and various personal objects. Perhaps the most famous levitation was that of the medium D. D. Home who was seen to levitate and then float out one window and in through another.

Materialization. Hands and faces were commonly seen in Victorian era séances. Sometimes hands were only felt, not seen. Sitters would feel fingers moving through their hair and touching their faces.

Ouija and Talking Boards. While not commonly part of séance phenomena, the movement of the planchette (or a wine glass) about a board marked with letters has to be included in the list of spiritualist phenomena, and was sometimes a pre-cursor to the development of full mediumship.

Possession. Another kind of phenomena, particularly in the religious settings of Spiritism occurs when the spirit or "loa" takes over the body of a participant—whether willing or not—and speaks, sings, dances, drinks quantities of rum or other intoxicants without affect, and responds to requests for information or sometimes promising a particular action—such as returning a wondering lover home.

Raps and Knocks. These and other common noises such as footsteps, doors opening and closing, sounds of pots and pans clanging together, single words spoken, etc. often announce the presence of spirits. Raps are heard that later become coded messages between spirits and observers.

It was *phenomena* of this sort that came to dominate the late 19th century séance and led to more fabulous staged events of which many were later proven to be fraudulent trickery. It also led to some theatric methods either claimed as necessary to the production of ectoplasm or as a means to demonstrate the authenticity of the medium. Included in this were the tying of the mediums limbs to the arms and legs of a chair or to the ankles and wrists of persons seated on either side. Another yet more dramatic method was to isolate the medium in a "Spirit Cabinet"—again with her limbs tied and only her head protruding as was common in a steam cabinet. *Greed is always opportunistic!*

Psychic Powers. While not a prominent feature of Spiritualist phenomena, some mediums do demonstrate psychic abilities that are almost exclusively related to their séance work or personal consultations. One such power is Clairvoyance ("clear seeing"). It is usually related to the Spirit's communication in which the medium may say something like "Spirit is showing me a particular object. It is an antique broach that belonged to your grandmother," and similar messages.

Other Psychic powers demonstrated by mediums may include Clairaudience ("clear hearing") in which the medium hears the voice of the spirit or a guide;

Clairsentience ("clear sensing" and "clear hearing") in which the medium "feels" what the Spirit wants to convey—often feels the physical problems including mortal disease before physical death; Clairalience ("clear smelling") in which the medium smells a prominent odor—such as a perfume or pipe tobacco—strongly associated with the Spirit during physical life; Clairgustance ("clear tasting") in which the medium has taste impressions from the Spirit; and Claircognizance ("clear knowing") in which the medium simply "knows" something either related to the Spirit or that the Spirit is trying to convey but lacks the words.

The distinction between these mediumistic psychic powers and those powers and skills otherwise exercised by a "psychic" is that are almost always limited to spiritualist work. But, it is also a clear identification of the "psychic" with the "spirit" bodies of the living person as that which communicates with spiritual entities.

The Medium and the Message

Many years ago, a well-known Canadian scientist coined the phrase, "The Medium is the Message" in recognition of the importance and power that the new forms of media had in relation to the new generations of readers, viewers, listeners, and users. Particularly, at that time, the media was so respected that whatever was said was accepted as true.

But that was only one effect of the new media, a second effect was an explosion of news, photographs, reports, analysis, books, magazines, and more. And this was just before the birth of the Internet and the Information Age which has enormously magnified all of the above.

At the opening of this chapter, we inserted this phrase:

The Medium is not the Message!

Why? Because we can no longer trust the media and especially the "information" on the Internet the same way as previously. Not only is dangerous information—like instructions on bomb-making—readily available but people with bias and personal agendas go on to valuable and respected sites to "correct" information to conform to their own bias, religious beliefs, racial and gender prejudices, and political agenda along with inserting gossip, hateful lies, doctored photographs, and phony resumes into the various social media. Email arrive daily advising that the viewer is a winner of a multi-million dollar lottery, an heir to a fortune, offered participation in an undercover transition worth millions—all in exchange for credit card or banking information. Thousands are victimized and then threatened with bodily harm and financial ruin.

And then there are the "hackers," professional spies and thieves who hack into governmental, defense, and commercial sites to steal information, patents, and processes and sometimes replacing it with false information. People fear "regulation" as *censorship* and *loss of privacy*, but the Worldwide Web is becoming a vehicle for crime and fraud, and politicians will not address the problem.

What does this all have to do with Communicating with Spirit and Mediumship?

A lot!

First, let's turn back the clock to the mid-19th century and the explosion of news and photographs about séance phenomena. Even through spirit communication and psychic phenomena is nearly as old as humanity, it had been seriously repressed for 2,000 years and so suddenly we had the most powerful medium of the day, print newspapers and a growing range of magazines and journals, revealing a "proof beyond faith" of survival after physical death, and then photographs of an amazing range of psychic phenomena demonstrating that the physical world was not "the final frontier."

The media, and in this case, the *medium,* was not as important as the Message and the Revelation that direct experience and knowledge would replace faith, and unfetter Spirit from domination by religion.

The New Age was in the process of becoming.

THE WAYS OF CHANNELING

As discussed earlier, the major differences between Mediumship and Channeling is the size of the "Platform" and the purpose of the communication.

Mediumship is primarily considered as communication between one person on "this side" and one entity on "the other side." Most of the messages are personal, even when the conversation expands to the spiritual entity offering advice—as was the case of one or more of the séances held in the White House for President Lincoln in which he received guidance to the conduct of the Civil War and the necessity of ending of Slavery.

If the "surviving personality" on the other side is that of a once recognized *authority* on a particular subject dispensing requested advice on the treatment of a disease as was most often the case with Edgar Cayce's clients, the message given was still personal and intended only for the one person on "this side." In Cayce's situation, the answering entity was not a spirit but Cayce' own subconscious (or "unconscious") mind. And, while those "prescriptions" were collected and published, and have often been used by readers for their own treatment of similar conditions, they were originally personal messages for the benefit on one client.

While Cayce never claimed to be either a medium or a channel in the sense these words are commonly used today, the two "paths" of his communications—specifically Personal and broadly Informational—offer a comparison of the one to mediumship and the other to channeling. Cayce's "source" for each was his own consciousness rather than a personal message from a "surviving personality" or impersonal message for a broad audience received from a proclaimed higher level entity or a highly evolved "Elder Brother" no longer subject to human limitations.

All is Spirit, and all is Consciousness. Both are universal and both are experienced at many different levels. It is mostly the communicator who accesses that communicant—but in the trance state "dominant" operator may switch roles.

That Old Time Religion!

One of the more ancient historic channeling was the dream communication to the Egyptian pharaoh Akhenaton involving a vision of Sun worshipping monotheistic religion. Other examples of ancient channeling involve the consultation of entranced "oracles" (usually priestesses) delivering messages from "gods" of either personal or larger importance. It was only when Moses proclaimed that he communicated with the one supreme God, YHWH, through a "Burning Bush" that the Hebrews and then the later Christian and Muslim followers were prohibited from channeling spirits other than Yahweh under pain of death. Later, only certain priests (some of them inheriting their position from their father) were authorized to communicate with Yahweh, and this became limited to one way conversations in which the one God delivered "commandments" from *He who must be obeyed.*

Thus we moved from shamanic channeling of many spirits in response of personal needs, to polytheistic religions of many gods and goddesses responsive to priests serving both individual people and tribal leaders, and on to a monotheistic religion of one god and one leader and his authorized priests, and thus to a religion fixed to a single historic "message" in the form of theology taught by old priests to young priests to administer (not interpret) that message to the religion's involuntary followers who are to serve the religion and its hierarchy.

With very few exceptions, interest Spiritual Communication, mediumship and channeling declined until the late 20th century, and remains condemned as "satanic" by the most fundamentalist followers of Christianity and Islam.

Channeling Defined

"Channeling is a method used to access information from entities that are supposedly more evolved and could therefore enlighten us as we move through the evolution of consciousness and back to source."

"Channeling has always been part of the human connection to a higher vibration of though so isn't a total new process. What's new is how it is perceived and received nowadays and its quick expansion in recent decades."

—*(SpiritLibrary.com)*

Channeling Described

"Everything is vibrational. When one channels, they are tapping into, plugging into, the frequency of the grid program in which we experience. It's like tuning in a radio. Each station, or energy plug-in, brings a specific frequency of information that we sometimes associate with colors, chakras, and tones and specific evolved beings such as angels, archangels, ascended masters, and teachers."

— *(SpiritLibrary.com)*

Types of Channeling

There are various names applied to channeling—intentional and spontaneous, conscious and unconscious, mental and physical, sleep and dream state, light and deep trance, clairaudient and clairvoyant, open and direct, inspired and prophetic, invocation of a god or goddess, evocation knowledge states, and such phenomena as possession, accession to akashic records, and more. Also, the various forms of automatic writing, table tipping, mediumship. Spirit boards, and other forms of communication with spiritual entities including one's own Higher Self.

Basically, Channeling is either Conscious Channeling or Trance Channeling, with further consideration given to how either of these forms is induced, and what they are accessing. Conscious Channeling is mostly self-induced through meditation, prayer, ritual, and can be generally categorized as "mental;" while Trance Channeling, often induced through forms of spontaneous, or intentional hypnosis (whether self-induced or other-induced), is generally understood as "physical."

Channeling is communication with Spirit in any of its many forms. What is important is "self-determination," i.e. conscious, personal choice through knowledge and understanding of the Spirit being accessed—including your conscious access to your own subconscious and super-conscious minds.

Vibration is identity

Everything and every entity has a unique range of vibration. The higher on the "evolutionary ladder" an entity may be, the greater the *range* of vibration accessible in that field of identity, and the more specific the identity can be "called" of that entity is. Intentionally, the entity can enter into two-way communication with another specified entity, and *tune in* to any object—such as the beneficial vibration of a jewel or a sacred site.

Everything vibrates, and it is wide field of those vibrations that functions as a kind of "carrier wave" for intentional communications. While we can communicate with anything and with other entities, "channeling" is usually defined as communication with a consciousness not in human form with the intention of gaining information or knowledge otherwise not immediately available to the communicator. In general, the "message" desired is impersonal and broadly educational and "esoteric."

While channeling can be seen as a successor to older forms of shamanism based on ecstatic states of consciousness to achieve the personal connection with a higher level being or source, modern channeling is direct and dependent only on adjustments of vibratory rates between the two parties involved in the communication, and that communication is most valued when it is bi-directional—that is, when the communicant is responsive to questions directed from the communicator.

Levels of Consciousness, Focus of Awareness

What are we talking about? It's all interesting, you may say, but it's old stuff and *where's the practical applications?* Yes, it is "old stuff," and it is by studying old stuff that we learn, and with learning we adapt and meet new needs and develop "new stuff" to meet contemporary needs. That's very much what we will be doing in the rest of this chapter.

There are practical benefits to be found in all learning, but it is mostly you that must find them because they apply to you. What is important to understand in this discussion of the ways of Mediumship and other forms of Spirit Communication is that these all represent "levels" (or, if you prefer, "states") of consciousness. That's just the start. Within any level of consciousness there is the opportunity for intentional "focus" to control the phenomena and direct the communication.

Psychic Development

Let's consider, for a moment, phenomena like the levitation or movement of objects. We call that "telekinesis," or "psychokinesis," the spontaneous or deliberate movement of objects or persons at a distance by unknown means. In the beginning of the Spiritualist movement, such phenomena was passively, and wondrously, observed. And given a semi-religious status. Later, some mediums and researchers applied it as a skill to influencing events and in healing of the body.

Further practice has led to such variations as "teleportation" in which the object, or person, disappears from one location and reappears elsewhere. That, however, is still a phenomena under investigation. No matter what, we will learn from research and investigation, and hopefully will develop new "technologies" for beneficially applying the psychic power involved.

But psychokinesis is only one psychic skill, and it along with clairvoyance, astral travel, aura reading, divination, and others had long been known and practiced before the repressive domination by the Church and the Church-controlled State over the last 2,000 years of the Piscean Age. With the coming of the Age of Enlightenment, the birth of Democracy, universal secular public education and the new Freedom to pursue the Happiness of personal learning and self-development, the exercise of psychic skills and spiritual powers has flowered and is leading to new forms of Self-Empowerment and increasing Spiritual Awareness.

Cultural Prejudices

Even as a global culture, we still suffer from a basically "outdated" materialist perception of physical cause and effect. In matters of health we look for an alien germ, a nutritional deficiency from a failure in the food we eat, a hormonal imbalance caused by age and stress, clogged arteries from a bad diet, etc., and ignore not only emotional and mental factors but denigrate concepts of energy healing, the curative possibilities of attitudinal changes, the demonstrated benefits of meditation and self-hypnosis to do more to bring about *long-term* stress reduction than prescription drugs (often with dangerous side-effects), changes in dietary habits and addictive behavior.

Not only do most still see the body as a "machine," most also treat thought and feeling as limited attributes of that machine. On the whole, we don't communicate with our own body, nor actually with our own mind or emotions. We don't understand that we are the driver of the vehicle that is called the "body, mind and spirit" of our physical world identity, and that the "I AM" driver is the rightful owner who should be "in charge." We don't talk with our "body, mind and spirit," either in its parts or in its whole. We don't ask and we don't listen. We don't realize that we mistakenly confuse that "mind and spirit" with our true emotional/*astral* self, and we mistakenly identify emotion as "mental," and actually neglect Spirit altogether.

"Mental Illness" has rarely anything to do with Mind but is Emotional Imbalance. We can call upon Mind to communicate directly with the physical/*etheric* (energy) body and the emotional/astral self and learn their needs and bring about healing and a genuine integration that can lead to greater health, fulfillment, and longevity.

Whether in mediumship or channeling, we still looked outside ourselves rather than toward our own Higher Self. A séance commonly began with the question: *Are there any spirits present who want to communicate?* A channeling session basically asks the communicating spirit: *What do you want to tell us?* We are still waiting for someone else to tell us what to do rather than seeking the answer from our own Higher Self.

We don't call upon Spirit as the Spiritual and Causal Self we are, and we confuse Spirit with Soul. Each person is a Spiritual Entity composed of mortal Physical/Etheric, Astral, and Mental/Causal selves, and is itself the current incarnation of an immortal Soul that has incarnated in many past lives and will continue to so in many future lives. What we call "Spirit" is the *Commander-in-Chief* of who we wholly are in this lifetime.

As Spirit we are the "I AM" of this incarnation. As Spirit we can take charge of the "vehicle" of this life time. And that is the ultimate goal of our Spirit Communication. But, we have much to learn and many smaller steps to take on the Path to true Self-Empowerment. Each kind of communication we practice is a step forward. We will gain from the study of forms of Shamanism, types of Mediumship and Channeling, learning to communicate with different kinds of spirits and Spirit Entities, learning to communicate with our own bodies, feelings, and thoughts. Learning from attaining higher states of consciousness and increased breadth of awareness and through the Evocation and Invocation of Gods and Goddesses as we will do in future chapters. But our goal is to communicate with our Higher Self (also known as our Holy Guardian Angel) who is also the Divinity Within.

We grow by learning and by practicing, accomplishing smaller steps before bigger steps, but always *becoming more than we are* on the road to *being all we can be.*

THE WAYS TO THE FUTURE

To open the opportunities of the Future, we need to learn from experience with other forms of Spirit Communication, to communicate with our own Higher Self, and to bring into our Conscious Mind the resources of the sub-conscious and super-conscious minds, and eventually to raise our consciousness to the highest level of our Spiritual Self.

With what we have learned, with the experience we have gained, with the benefit of New Age Aquarian and other dynamic incoming energies, we can do this. We can become more than we are. We can move forward and become all that we can be.

In the past, channeling was mostly one-sided from the higher level communicant to a lower level communicator and took the form of instruction and commandments. Without the benefit of true bi-directional communication, such instruction was easily interpreted in terms of the human communicator's own prejudices and personal ambitions for power and glory.

Often the human communicator was a leader of his clan or tribe, or the direct "employee" of the leader as a priest or other functionary. Even when the intent of that leader was benevolent on behalf of "his people," it became a means for the limited gain of the community and for his control over its members.

As "time marched on," communities often grew in population, their dependency on resources expanded, and human relationships became more complex. Individual tribes often came into conflict over territory and resources, and the leaders found it necessary—at least in their view—to manipulate and consolidate control over their people through fear and desire, using propaganda about their superiority over the inferior "enemy" tribe, and going to war. Thus, the original message became the basis for organized "religion" *to bind the people together* under the direction of their "commander in chief."

The pattern was repeated over and over again, on larger and larger scales to create vast nation states united regionally with treaties and trade. Human beings, being what they are, some leaders sought full domination over larger territories and their religions were the instrument by which the people were motivated to the sacrifice of lives and property for the greater power and glory of "the God" even if purely represented in symbolic form such as a swastika, the hammer and sickle, rising sun, lunar crescent, or other image now holding the magickal power of religious idolatry.

The Choices we face

Today, we may have a choice: to repeat patterns of the past, or to move beyond sectarian conflicts in recognition of the now existent near worldwide common culture that could lead to a unity of nations in a true global civilization.

How will that choice be made? Who will make it?

The best answer is that WE can make it, but only if YOU open the doors to a spiritual communication with all the participating parties of the People, the Planetary consciousness, all Life, Solar and Lunar energies, and Universal Consciousness, and the guidance of your own Higher Self.

YOU can channel all these entities. Their message is for you and for us. Because we are all channels, *there is no need for you to broadcast your personal understanding of the universal messages.* Remember that—no matter what contacts you have made and the messages you have received, you are still "Only Human," Each of us will have their own personal "spin" pertinent to themselves, and not to others. Together and Alone, we can choose peace and progress and move to the next evolutionary level. We can create a New World for the New Age. It won't happen overnight, but now is the time to start the process and that process will itself raise and expand your consciousness in response our need and to the influx of energies from all the universe around us.

There's no previous time in human history when this has been possible on this planetary scale. What you do, what we do, Alone and Together, we share and fulfill destiny.

MEDITATION

"What does it mean that 'Spirituality is not passive?'"

Resources, and Suggested Reading:

Buckland, R.: *Buckland's Book of Spirit Communications*, 2001, Llewellyn

Dennis, L. L.: *New Consciousness for a New World—How to Thrive in Transitional Times and Participate in the Coming Spiritual Renaissance*, 2011, Inner Traditions

Hopkins, R.: *The Transition Handbook—From Oil Dependency to Local Resilience,* 2008, Chelsea Green

Klimo, J.: *Channeling—Investigations on Receiving Information from Paranormal Sources,* 1987, Tarcher

Mor, B. & Sjoo, M.: *The Great Cosmit Mother—Rediscovering the Religion of the Earth,* 1987, HarperOne

Owens, E.: *How to Communicate with Spirits,* 2001, Llewellyn

13

MAGICK, EVOCATION & INVOCATION

MIND AND MAGICK

Magick is nothing more and nothing less than applied Mind Power by means of techniques of focused intention and visualization involving a systematic organization and movement of symbols and forces to accomplish specific psychic and material benefits. At the foundation of the symbol system are 'correspondences' based primarily on relationships perceived on the Kabbalistic Tree of Life. Other practices are derived from Tantra, particularly that of visualizations of the Tattvas.

—Chapter Eleven, *Communicating with Spirit*

Wake up, and Live!

Magick is many things, and it is actually how we live our daily life whether we realize it or not—and *most people do not*. Most people are barely "awake," going through life more unconscious and reactive than conscious and "in charge," and unaware of their autonomic functions—and yet they are still living a magickal life, even though *very inadequately*. In other words: *We can Wake Up and Live Better, Happier, and More Fulfilling Lives through Applied Mind Power and the Principles of Magick.*

Mind is not the Brain!

Most people confuse "Mind" with "Brain." The brain does not *think* by itself, it only operates automatically and reflexively, reacting to stimuli received either directly from the physical body, the external physical world, or through non-physical psychic perceptions. The Mind thinks and initiates actions beyond mere physical reflexes that are carried out by the brain. The Mind functions mostly through the brain and some through the heart while we are physically incarnate, but Mind also works within the Mental Body to construct ideas and to structure thought forms in the Astral World to affect things in the Physical World and Physical Body. The Mind and the Mental Body are the connection between Will and Soul and Feeling and Physical Being.

The untrained and undisciplined Mind

When people speak about only using a small portion of their "brain," they are describing a real situation but speaking incorrectly since the brain is only a neurologically networked tool for consciousness just as a computer is only an electronically networked tool connected with an internal or external memory and the Internet. Most people don't fully utilize their computer, and even fewer fully utilize their brain and their mind hardly at all.

Not only are they more asleep than awake, but their mind is untrained, undisciplined, and *wasted* through lack of understanding of its nature and potential, and its domination by emotions of fear, hate, worry, fantasy, and the insatiable desire to be entertained. As a result, most minds are mostly "asleep" and uninvolved—the greatest waste of natural and human resources there has ever been. *How wonderful it will be when we all wake up and live consciously, actually applying Mind Power to solve problems, and transform our world and ourselves!*

Magick!

Magick, whether spelled with or without that "K," is not something to be practiced only in darkness and hidden places except for those who prefer blindness to vision. It is not a secret and obtuse practice except for those that make it so. It does not require mastery of archaic languages except for those who adore the sound of their own voices pronouncing *barbarous* words. Its practice is not limited to people *initiated* behind closed doors and drawn curtains and sworn by dreadful oaths except by those who love good drama with themselves in the starring role.

Yet, such practices can be matters of personal choice and meaning in terms of a magical operation at hand. The point is that none of them are necessary nor are they definitions of real magic. Art and drama can add energy and "flavor" to any work, magical and otherwise. You can make life exciting, but never lose sight of your goal and the intention to master your skills, your practice, and your profession.

Nor, it must be said, are the immense *potential* powers of Magick so easily learned that its knowledge and *self-transformative* techniques must be denied to "ordinary" folk because "they would surely abuse it and blow up the world!" It is more likely that the more Magickal study and "real" work one does, the more conscious, aware, and ethically responsible one becomes. It is ignorance and arrogance that leads to childish and malicious behavior, and *"real Magick" is not easily mastered by a child!*

Magickal Power is a Skill to be Learned

Even though life is naturally magical to us, Magickal Power is a skill to be learned like any other through study, practice, and experience followed by self-analysis and development. It can be applied to many things but it should first be applied to daily life to make every day better in every way. "Think and Grow Rich"—that's applied Mind Power; "The Secret of Attraction" is applied Mind Power; "Love, Power, Money" all can be had through Applied Mind Power. Even "Peace in Our Time" and "Security at Home" and "Freedom from Fear" can be had through applied Mind Power if enough people work harmoniously together to bring it about. And it's not a leader that is required but people working together at the same level. That's a distinction and practice not easily understood and undertaken, but it is our goal.

You may ask, *"How can I learn to apply Mind Power?"* Ah, that's the **Great Secret**, isn't it? And like most secrets, the answer can readily be found—like the old saying—right in front of your nose!

Yes, you can join secret societies, subscribe to lengthy courses, become a devoted student to a Great Guru, read many wonderful books (some old and beautiful, and very expensive), develop your psychic powers, travel out-of-body to many locations, and converse with many spirits—all without learning to fully develop and apply Mind Power.

When you look for Mind Power in all the wrong places, you simply end up in a Blind Alley. When you waste your precious resources chasing Power Balls and Jack Pots with lucky numbers and other fantasy formulae, you're just another Loser. When you devote your life to serving a Great Guru, you join the great crowd behind the saying, "There's a sucker born every minute."

The Great Secret will not produce instant wealth or bring you the Love of your life or pay all your bills. Nor will it free you from spiritual poverty, turn you into an ascended master, or make you a master teacher.

Balancing present Skills and Goals

But when you understand the simple principles of balancing your present skills and what you want out of life, determining your goals realistically, scheduling your time to what is more important, organizing your work to your schedule, applying your skills to your prioritized work schedule, and extending from short term goals to long term goals and your possible accomplishments, you are opening the doors to a magical life. Or, call it "a life plan for successful living," or "the Next Step Program," or "the determination to become more than you and all you can be." Choose a name that contains meaning for you and that condenses your goals into a single formula. And write that formula in *your* brand new Magickal Journal that you will use to record your practices, experiments, and your analysis of the results.

Magick is a Way of Conscious Living

The point is that real magick is not something you do occasionally or only on Sundays. It's not something to fantasize about or play around with using beautiful tools and wearing fancy robes. It's not a game or a hobby or something to talk about. *It's something to do all the time as your way of life.* It's an "integration" of your spiritual, mental, emotional, energy, and physical bodies under personal will to change and transform your life and the world around you, to develop your innate powers, and become more than you are toward becoming all you can be. A "magickal life" is a well-lived life, a life of purpose and fulfillment, a life rich in love and accomplishment. A life that is the result of hard work and never saying "No" to what you can do better.

Magick is an Art, a Science, a Philosophy, a set of Psychological Principles, a collection of Consciousness-changing Technologies and their many applications in both what we call "high" and "low" forms, and theory for further development.

Magick is not a single subject like an encyclopedic entry. It is "Life Science" and it can be specifically studied under many different names ranging inclusively from Alchemy through Yoga—each of which can itself be totally comprehensive, or holistically comprehended with others. Magickal living is a matter of holistic choices, but to live that life we have to understand more about those choices and the challenges they present.

The Three Challenges

The first challenge we have is with the word "magic" itself for it automatically conjures up fairy tale images of a wizard waving his wand and performing miracles. That's not reality, and we know it—but the fantasy is something to challenge and better understand in terms of the real power within intentional fantasy and the constructive imagination. *Real magick deals with the real world, which is one seen in a broader perspective than either the purely sensory model of ordinary perception or that of nonsensory perception and pure uncontrolled fantasy.*

The second challenge is to recognize that all magick involves change and transformation, and calls for the human resources of energy, imagination, intelligence, will and dedication. *Real Magick involves the realistic acceptance of change and transformation of self within life and not as an assumed escape from it.*

The third challenge is that there is more than one kind of magic/magick. Commonly they are referred to as "Low Magic" and "High Magick." Beyond those two classifications are other forms, categories, subjects, and sub-subjects more or less inclusive within these two which are also known as "practical" or "mundane" and "esoteric" or "spiritual." There's spell craft, candle magic, love magic, sex magick, nature magic, sympathetic magic, ceremonial magic, ritual magic, talismanic magic, divinatory magic, and so on, and so on. *Real Magick draws upon both day-to-day skills and the learned Life Sciences (from Alchemy through Yoga).*

Applied Mind Power requires Energy and Focus

But many of these terms are basically descriptive of the tools and techniques for raising, directing, and applying the "power" necessary to bring about the change and transformation of matter and form desired. And, while the same tools and techniques, and/or others, can be used in both practical magic and esoteric magick, it is essential to remember that the *POWER* is in you and not in the tool or even in the technique. A tool can magnify and direct power—a hammer does a better job than a closed fist, rock, or club, while a technique raises and focuses consciousness either as self-directed or externally imposed—but the POWER comes from you.

The common elements in all magic-magick, as in all human endeavor, is energy as power, and consciousness, focused on the specific goal.

Additional Energy Resources

Still, your present *inner* power may not be sufficient for a Big Job—*where and how can you tap into additional sources?* One is to extract it from other human resources: a group working collectively together as in "ritual" focusing their consciousness on the same goal; two people in partnership as on in sex magick raising and attracting inner power and sharing it focused on a common goal; an excited crowd as in a mass event (sports, concert, rally, etc.) ready to respond to something that triggers as collective action (often violent); an ecstatic crowd aroused by a charismatic leader or a shared shamanic experience leading toward individual "possession" (sometimes resulting in healing); a small sympathetic group focused to help an accident victim (sometimes enabling an act of heroic physical strength), and so on.

The size of the focused group is one measure of the power available. Without direction—as at a sports event or concert—the raised power either dissipates or leads to distributed ecstatic behavior (wild dancing, reactive sex, drugs),—or, unfortunately, sometimes turns into mass violence.

And, one additional and unfortunate method of extracting power has been human and animal sacrifice, almost always in a religious setting.

Lost Knowledge?

Some magickians, particularly as portrayed in legends, have found ways to extract power from natural phenomena—lightning bolts, volcanic activity and geysers, earth currents and internal heat, the moon and ocean tides, the sun and air currents, storms and winds, and natural springs and sacred groves. *It almost sounds like the same list being developed for alternative energy sources today, doesn't it?* Anything that moves either uses energy or generates energy. Earth currents have been tapped by structures in particular locations and with particular designs—pyramids, monoliths, great statues, stone or wood circles, and—perhaps—long causeways and deep wells.

Some knowledge may have been lost, other may be kept secret from all but an elite circle of initiates, and yet—in this New Age—the more we know the better can we meet the great challenges affecting us all and every individual. We need to reveal those old secrets and to discover new ways and sources. Old ways, like old wine that turns sour, are not necessarily better. Innovations apply in magickal and spiritual technologies as well as in "high-tech," nano- and other transformative technologies that "change everything." The exploding world population, the dangers of religious conflict and inspired terrorism, the global challenges and opportunities, and more—all demand new thinking in all areas but fundamentally in what we identify as the Magickal Way that involves all that a person can be. No matter the source, the "transformer" and the "control panel" are in you and directed under your conscious will power.

"Theory" invites the Acquisition of New Knowledge for New Times

This is where the word "theory" comes in. Some will insist on using the word "science" and others "art," and still other will speak of the "practice" of magic. When we don't know all the answers and how it all works, "theory" is the better word just as we speak less often today of quantum *physics* or quantum *mechanics,* and more commonly relate to "quantum *theory.*" With theory, we think we know what we are doing, and why, but we're always testing, examining, and analyzing so that we are constantly learning and developing our theory into practice and developing applications for real life benefit.

That's what life is all about: learning, growing, changing, transforming, and continually *evolving.* And Magick is, in many ways, the culmination of all that we do and much of what this book has been about. Spiritual Communication is about communicating between the middle self or Conscious Mind, the lower self or Subconscious Mind, and the higher self or Super Conscious Mind. It is under the direction of the Conscious Mind that we communicate with spiritual entities through the Subconscious Mind or the Super Conscious Mind. The more we understand each of the primary levels or worlds that these three selves occupy, the more power each gains, the more integration of the three we create, and the more effectively our magical Mind Power can be applied to our magical living and our evolutionary goal.

Enabling Action to follow Intention

Of course, this all reads complexity, but *the* operational process enables *action to follow intent,* just as reaching your hand out to grasp an object is a very complex process in which everything happens automatically to accomplish the intention set by the Conscious Mind operating through the autonomic nervous system. All this "hardware" and "software" enabling *action to follow intent* is the result of billions of years of purposeful evolution set in motion at "the Beginning."

We can't possibly cover all the forms and styles of Magick in this one chapter or even one whole book. We will list some recommended books at the end of the chapter. But there are two particular magickal practices specifically related to *Communicating with Spirit* and *Self-Empowerment* that we must discuss here: **Evocation** and **Invocation**. They are among the most powerful and specific techniques of overall Psychic Development and Spiritual Communication possible.

To Change and Improve requires
Understanding and Communication

Magick, like shamanism, is very old and has been part of human life and of our evolving psyche from the first beginning of conscious awareness. It's intrinsic to our desire to understand and improve our world, to change and transform our selves, and to control our own destiny.

Magick is the basic impulse behind communication and expression; the foundations of the search for understanding through mythology, philosophy, psychology, and science; the search for meaning through art, exploration, conversation, and the development of psychic powers; the need to have an active relationship with the natural world led to the technologies of agriculture, animal husbandry, food management, seasonal planning; and then to the transformative nature of the industrial age by resource extraction and manufacturing; and on into the present ages of information management and hi-technology, and the rapidly developing newer nano-technologies and local and immediate 3-D printing/manufacturing along with home-based (solar, wind, and thermal) energy sourcing; community gardens and markets, and to individual and family proprietorships; and to democratic citizen participation to replace the present *top-down* political party dictatorship.

Change and transformation is coming, and coming fast. The New Age demands that we re-invent and up-date many institutions and social, economic and political structures *before it's too late!*

"Before it's Too Late?"

Yes, time is a demand factor because the "old ways" of delay, wilful ignorance and ideological obstruction have failed to meet the accelerating challenges of climate change due to atmospheric and oceanic pollution; the unwillingness to develop alternate and more cost effective technologies; the growth of population resulting from life extension (good), religious obstruction to sex education (bad) and contraception (bad), and the massive and unregulated deployment of farm chemicals (bad); the development of increasingly powerful personal-sized weapons (bad) and ideological refusal to control their access has facilitated an explosion of local and organized crime (very bad); the failure to control weapons of mass destruction in the face of major religious conflict between the two dominant male-controlled monotheistic religious sects is threatening world peace (awful); the failing educational system as resources have been mis-directed towards sports mania (worse), and many other forms of destructive thought and behavior threaten human survival.

Magick can help show the way. Magick—as the technology of change and trans-formation—permeates human culture, still mostly at the unconscious levels. Now it is time to make Magickal Thinking conscious and to fully integrate Inner with Outer, Subjective with Objective, and Cosmos with Psyche. No, it won't happen overnight but it is the dynamic of the New Age and the transiting into the 2,400 year Age of Aquarius as symbolized in the traditional Zodiacal Sign of Man pouring "something" onto Earth. We will explore that *something* later.

Before Time Began

Before time, when the devolution of Spirit into incarnation was incomplete, there was much interaction between spiritual entities and forces and "proto"- humans. Here we had the appearance of Gods and Goddesses, elementals, angels and other forces in fundamental relationships. Here, too, was the beginnings of Magick, the foundations of spirituality and of religions with the development of symbols with their attributes and qualities and their associations of deific accessories. Thus began the long history of "correspondences" for magical control and verification of deities, entities, forces and powers. Here we have the functions of Worship as Invocation, Meditation as Evocation, Communication as the *conscious interaction between Inner and Outer, Lower and Higher, and of Humans with Deities.* In order to bring Spirit Power down into the Mental & Astral realms to initiate effects on the Etheric/Physical level, we have to reach up to the Spiritual. *As spiritual beings, we have to access not only the powers within but the limitless powers beyond. Magick is what Humans do.*

Before time, the devolution of spirit into matter led towards the ultimate struc-ture of the Universe we know today, with "layers" of Matter, Energy and Conscious-ness. Within this structure certain conscious entities began to function in ways that brought about a more complex structure within which the evolutionary process began. And continues.

As the Evolutionary process continued those conscious entities took on specific creative functions guiding the development of Energy into Matter and Energy and Matter into Conscious forms evolving into greater and greater complexity and *Self-manifestation.*

Each "higher" level of form takes on higher levels of consciousness leading toward *Self-consciousness* and *Self-realization.*

Higher levels of conscious beings assume interactive roles in the continuing evolutionary process in the seeming fulfillment of some mythic "Great Plan" of which we can have only glimmerings at this point in our own level of *Self-awareness.*

Nevertheless, we "know" that there is meaning and purpose to life and being, as we more consciously experience the evolutionary process becoming more specific and individualized. We are becoming *Self-knowing.*

With the advent of self-conscious humans there comes levels of awareness of the existing higher creative entities, later called "Powers," and interaction with these Powers and the natural energies resulted in the burgeoning human imagination (often aided by natural clairvoyance) forming elemental beings around natural places and even historic events. Some of the higher entities became identified as *local* or *native* Gods and Goddesses, and so did lesser beings recognized as processing manifest energies and functions in on-going creation become identified as Gnomes, Sylphs, Undines, and Salamanders, and still other names and other beings.

Mythic Times

These were Mythic Times, and as human consciousness became more complex so did the world of human perception. Mythology "explained" creation and the phenomena of life and the world around. Legends described that nature of the Gods and Goddesses and lesser beings. Mythology was the "science" of the day.

If worldly phenomenon could be conceptualized, then the natural powers and forces could be explained in story-form, and either deified or demonized to explain their relationships to humans. If things were beneficial, the credit went to God; if they were harmful, the blame went to the Devil.

Gods and Goddesses

As human consciousness grew in complexity and increased awareness of the world around, and within, these Gods and Goddesses became totally human in form and ever more detailed in their functions and their appearances. Some became very specific in their representation of human function like love, attraction, reproduction, plant growth; activities like fishing, hunting, farming, fighting; concepts like beauty, leadership, intelligence; natural phenomena such as thunder, lightning, rain, and other very specific functions and happenings. All could be represented by images (mostly humanoid), gender, names, colors, costume and ornaments, even postures.

Here was the beginnings of Magick, the foundation of religion, the development of symbols and their connections, and the long history of "correspondences" for magical control and verification.

Mythology is Alive and Well, Today

Mythology is a natural form of Human Perception. Gods and Goddesses, Angels, Fairies, Spirits of all kinds, and even devils and demons are *imagined* into human form, and given human-like stories to explain their origin and function. And it is their "humanity" that makes them approachable and establishes the magical ways to interact with the powers they symbolize and represent through their correspondences, attributes, and stories.

Myth-making continues as a natural human instinct—giving birth not only to comic-book super-heroes and heroines, but in the mythic auras we project on to celebrities and the people we work with and relate to everyday, and even in the personalizing ways we relate to pets and animals, environmental phenomena, our homes and automobiles and other objects. We project human personalities in lesser or greater detail on to everything we experience. *It's the human way!*

And it's the magical way when we consciously accept the unconscious reality of what we do so that we can practice it both as an art and a science.

INVOCATION and EVOCATION

Moving from the generally ineffective *external* religious forms to the *interior* "scientific" forms of spirituality and magick, worship takes on a different role than rote prayer and the *unconscious* groveling and posturing before "graven images," often ordered and led by priests and tribal chieftains. Instead, *conscious* worship becomes an active method of *assumptive* meditation and visualization we call Invocation, and a method of active and intentional prayer and focused meditation we call Evocation. Both are forms of communication with "spiritual entities" of all types ranging from functional aspects of the Universe to human created thought forms both deliberately and spontaneously imagined.

Vehicles of Energy, Consciousness, and Spiritual Substance

Just as individual human units of consciousness function through a complex of *vehicles* of varying duration and compositions of substance (physical and non-physical), so do all spiritual entities function through vehicles of energy and consciousness formed of "spiritual" substance. That *substance*, depending on the level of the entity's consciousness (vibration), ranges from higher causal and mental down through astral and even etheric. Those that are strongly etheric require "feeding" such as those provided by burnt offerings and blood sacrifices to sustain their form, and—thankfully—rapidly decay without such truly primitive sacrificial feeding. Those entities working through primarily etheric and near physical substance can become very demanding, expressing base human emotions of anger, rage, and desire to punish. Even though they have called "gods" and "demons," there were of entirely human invention and rapidly died away when supplanted.

Philosophically, Magick is based on our visions of the structures of the Greater Cosmos connecting with those of the Human—"As Above, So Below"—with distinctions of Masculine and Feminine and other dualities manifesting as Archetypes, Aspects, Deities, Elemental Forces, Entities, People, Psyches, etc., and of their Unity through their progeny (children, thought forms, spirits, etc.)

Active Communication with Spiritual Forces

Meditation as Evocation, Worship as Invocation: each is a way of Active Communication with Spiritual Forces. If we're drawing down Spirit Power into the Mental and Astral levels to bring about effects on the Etheric and Physical, we have first to raise our consciousness and harmonize with the Spiritual. *As a Spiritual Being, we have access to not only the powers within but the limitless powers beyond.*

From mostly unconscious beginnings in the distant past, increasingly spotted through time with great intellects and mystics, artists and composers, philosophers and scientists, we emerge into a New Age of more conscious and responsible interaction with the Planetary Being and Cosmic Forces. Now, as we invoke deific powers into ourselves, we activate the nascent powers within and in the world outside; as we evoke those powers around us we integrate inner with outer and outer with inner to bring about unity of the planetary family.

Integrating Visions from East and West

In this particular magickal program, we deal with two major visions—East and West—of Tantra and Kabbalah in their non-religious "science" aspect. We further recognize the influence of ancient Egyptian Magick, Chinese Taoism, the Greek and Roman pantheons, the Celtic-Druidic, and other traditions from around the world as all contributing to our integrated worldview, but it is primarily Tantra and Kabbalah that offer magickal and psychological organizing principles and structure that serve our contemporary personal needs with a means of connecting to the Universal. And it is the Tantric and Egyptian pantheons, supplemented mainly by Kabbalistic correspondences that offer the greatest detail and variety of deific forms to match the variety of modern spiritual and practical needs and interests for evocation and invocation magickal work.

Nevertheless, while particularly recommending the Tantric and Egyptian deities along with Kabbalist tools for a your later magickal studies, because of the relatively wide range of deities and the richness of symbol and detail for each, we want to keep our examples simple and familiar to make the principles of practice easier to understand. We will work with the Roman goddess *Libertas* so familiar to us in the Statute of Liberty located at the Gateway into America, and with the Greek *Athena*, goddess of wisdom, law and justice, courage, inspiration, crafts and skills, and patron of education, her statute seen in the reconstructed Parthenon in the city of Nashville, TN, home of Vanderbilt University. We'll get to the magical process later.

Are Gods, Goddesses, and other spiritual entities real?

Rather a good question to ask, and the answer is both Yes and No, and then new questions *who knows for sure and does it matter?* One prominent magician simply answered those questions by saying: *If something works for you, use it. If it doesn't, then don't.* No single *procedure* (process, technique, system, drug, or whatever) works equally well for everyone, or even works the same for everyone. In contrast, most *tools* work as intended if they are used correctly.

So, we have a distinction. Magick (or Religion, or any other system) may not seem fully valid for you, but change your procedural perspective and see individual aspects as *tools* and you can learn to apply them to accomplish your specific goals. We've become conditioned to think of gods and goddesses as spiritual entities to be "worshipped" from afar, but that's the error of religion. And it's a serious error on the part of historians, scholars and theologians to see all deities as functional only within a "religion" and even worse to classify all these systems that have deities as "religions" within the same definition of what are essentially political and business institutions as we've seen in the previous chapters.

Deities don't have birthdays!

No matter what the religious story tellers claim, deities are not *born* ("virgin" or otherwise) as "finished products" but have mythic origins over time, and often are conglomerations of many previous similar entities. But, *where did those previous entities come from, and why is the nature of their origin important to our magickal discussion—or, for that matter—to modern psychological understanding and even to the newly developing considerations in quantum physics?*

We can only speculate, but that's better than nothing! Never denigrate the process of speculation (other than *financial!*) or the use of theory in the process of experiment and verification. Just as deities weren't born whole, neither were ancient humans. "Evolution" is real, but vastly mis-understood, and then abused by religionists out of ignorance and for their own bigoted purposes. Early humans were as intellectually naive, emotionally immature, spiritually unaware as other animals, but somehow as part of evolving consciousness humans grew and changed in ways other animals did not.

Ancient Ways and Modern Magick

All deities are ancient, and all were man-made in a time when the creation of such deific thought forms was natural and spontaneous.

Early humans saw things that they didn't understand, things to which they responded emotionally, and slowly they created stories that "humanized" these things to give them a human perspective. Thunder became a loud, perhaps angry, god. Lightning, too, became a deity, but most likely without a perceived connection to thunder until later. Over time, different tribes of humans in different locations and environments developed different gods of thunder and lightning, and as populations expanded and brought different tribes into contact with one another, these humanized perspectives of natural phenomena became more sophisticated and developed into more complex stories that we call myths. And as the process was repeated again and again, those myths merged and became yet more complex and detailed and inclusive—with elements combining human experience with observation and respect for other viewpoints. Thunder gods were given names, places where they lived (and after the phenomenal connections were made) from where their lightning bolts were hurled, they were given parents or other forms of origin, children or other kinds of progeny, joined into families with other gods and goddesses, perceived to have enemies just as humans did, and life stories just as humans do.

Deities live! And become complex compounds of energy and meaning

Myths became complex stories to explain natural phenomena in terms humans could understand. At the same time, as the myths became more complex, the gods and goddesses gained in stature and power, and some ceased being just local deities and instead became regional and even worldly, beyond cultural limitations. Over time, the various "assignments" or "rulerships" given to each became both more extensive and more complex as human history became more complex and *involved*. And humans evolved and tried to explain more of what they observed and experienced, forming school from which great thinkers taught students the rudiments of what later we called philosophy, and then science.

Still, this was a time when Mind was still more subjective than objective—a time before science. Instead of describing physical phenomena in terms of scientific "laws" of attraction and repulsion, energy exchanges, chemical analysis of herbal compounds, biological understandings of birth, death, and hormonal drives, humans still resorted to the legends and stories about the anger, lusts, fears, kindness, teachings, hates, ambitions and other mostly emotionally driven actions of the gods and goddesses—in their increasing interaction with humans—to explain human observations of history and the phenomena of the natural world.

All this means that each major deity became and remains a compound of psychic energy, emotional (astral) images and powers, and an organized collection of knowledge and "facts" related to their assigned "rulerships" nearly like an entry in a magickal encyclopedia that the magician can access, study, and employ in carefully choreographed programs to accomplish appropriately related goals.

Deity as a "magickal formula of psychic procedures"

Think of any simple formula. It tells you the ingredients needed, the procedures to be followed, the process to be expected, and the actions to be accomplished. The encyclopedic entry for a goddess tells us the actions ruled by her, the things associated with her identity, her various symbols which themselves are formulas of various energies, her favored activities for which she is patroness, it shows us a representation of her image, how she is dressed, her adornments if any, her names and, her songs, mantras, yantras, associated animals and places, and so on. Every aspect of the formula can be adapted into a procedure used in magickal evocation or magickal invocation.

Why a "formula" in human, or mostly human, form? Because we are human, and it is innate for us to "humanize" things we love, things we fear, things we hate, things we want, things in the Sky, things hidden in the Earth, things in the Sea, things in Nature, things in the Cosmos, and even more the things we feel as we do about a lovely forest glade or natural spring, the mist of a waterfall, the smoke of a volcano, and everything else including our pets and the projects and problems we work upon.

The human person in all its dimensions has the "circuitry," the "structures," the "spaces," the "zones," the "cells," the "energies," and the awakened and unawakened "correspondences" to all there is known through the Hermetic principle *As Above, So Below.* And equally as imaged in the Kabbalistic *Tree of Life* which provides the organizing principle worksheet for all magickians.

Magickal Evocation and Invocation

There are two primary ways for an individual to relate to a specific deific force as recognized in a long established god or goddess: Evocation and Invocation. In both operations, we make use of Name, Image, Symbols and Attributes to evoke the primary myth and surround ourselves the energies and qualities of the deity.

In the case of evocation, we can do this with either ritual or meditation, or a combination of those two procedures. The choice is personal and the greater power is in a personal "script" rather than a "professionally prepared and packaged" one. Let's take a moment to discuss that statement. Yes, you can find all sorts of spells and rituals in books and on-line, and you can purchase packaged incenses, tools, and other aids described as beneficial in many specified operations live Love, Protection, Success, etc., but when it comes to Evocation and Invocation we believe the more you do for yourself, the better.

You are Human, and deity is humanized; the personal actions you take build on your mutual human qualities. But, don't make the mistake of *personalizing* the particular deity to fit your self-image—don't change the gender, name, or anything else. The result would be a "short circuit" and potentially a psychological disaster. Such personalizing is not the same as invoking the deity into you person.

Writing your own script and preparing your own incense, determining how you can involve the important associated symbols, adding appropriate chants or declarations that you've discovered in your research or been inspired to write all help impress them deeply into your own personal unconscious mind. The more specific the "formula" becomes because of your own work the more does it function in your personal unconscious to tap into the universal (aka "collective") unconsciousness.

Obviously there is a difference between *conscious* and *unconscious,* and to fully explain this difference and even just its pertinence to this limited discussion would take more than this short aside. For simplicity, think of your "conscious mind" as the active intelligence making managerial decisions and carrying out the necessary actions. Now think of the universal unconscious as a vast information resource of every kind of memory there ever has been, and then think of the personal unconscious as containing just your own memories. Most of these memories are not on active recall, but they are there and the conscious mind can recall them even if we have to make a lot of effort for those of childhood and past lives.

All those memories, in both the personal and the universal unconscious resources have "smart tags" that enable the conscious mind to recall those memories desired from the personal unconscious along with those triggered by those smart tags from the universal. To the degree that the conscious mind is trained in magickal thinking and techniques, the detail can be amazing and those that are "just right" can be selected for the work desired.

Just to offer an alternative way of seeing this, think of the information resources of your computer: you do have both a personal memory drive and access to the World Wide Web (universal memory) and the computer's Operating System which functions like a trained mind.

Evocation: The Calling Forth

From the Latin word *evocatio* means the "calling forth" or "summoning" of a Power or Quality. In earlier monastic practice this was often a full-time lifestyle that combined intense devotion to the divine with the summoning of a personal cadre of spiritual advisers and familiars. In modern practice a Spirit is evoked by a human to carry out a function with which it is identified.

In the context of this discussion, a "Spirit" is any kind of Spiritual Being from the smallest "blind" (unconscious) elemental and natural forces up to aware and responsive (more conscious) gods and goddesses, and even to the all-seeing (wholly conscious) Creative Force generally called "Deity" or "God"*

> * But not in an anthropomorphic or humanoid form, and specifically not the Abrahamic "Father God" called Jehovah or Allah as that would supersede the individual gods and goddesses of magickal and true *religious* work of any religion or sect! The ultimate Creative Force is beyond description, and even any attempt at definition has to be considered as purely speculative, and a limitation imposed upon your inner Deity, and Consciousness.

We consider "Deity" to be *everywhere* and in *everything*, as *outer* and *inner*, as *above* so *below*—but so, also, is Spirit everywhere and in everything, and likewise with

Consciousness. Spirit is our unconscious connection with everything, and our means of communicating with the *Deity Within* and other spiritual beings. The Deity Within each human is the unconscious Life Force and the Conscious Presence of the Creative Force. The Deity Within is the source of our free will and conscious creativity. It is the Deity Within that makes us a "Co-Creator"—even though presently still mostly unconscious and unaware and hence "blind" and thus the source of many of our own destructive actions that bring harm and terror to other humans and harm and error to the environment that is the global home we share with all beings on this planet.

Only by becoming conscious do we become constructive rather than destructive. Only by *becoming more than we are* do we fulfill our obligation to the Creative Force that programmed the evolutionary drama from the Beginning. It is by making conscious the many blind forces within our body and psyche through the practices of Invocation and Evocation of associated deities that we become wholly "all that we can be" to fulfill the role assigned to us as co-creators.

All esoteric teachings have been dedicated to advancing humans as "Gods in the Making." This is the Dawning of the Age of Aquarius, when East and West come together in the New Age of Awakening Humanity. The call is to everybody, not the elite few. Everyone must be responsible both to himself and his neighbor as brother and sister, not as leader and follower. We begin now.

Invocation: The Calling In

From Latin *invocare*—"to call in" a Power or Quality taking the form of <u>possession</u> or <u>self-identification with certain spirits.</u> A Spirit is invoked* into a human to enable the person to identify with the associated character and power.

> * We are not discussing the common use of the term as a public prayer asking for Divine blessing or guidance before the opening of official business at any political or governmental institution (a practice generally deemed unconstitutional and a violation of the principle of separation of Church and State in America that is essential to Democracy.)

Libertas and Athena, Goddesses of Liberty and Wisdom

We've chosen these two ancient but modern deities because of their long established presence in images and literature throughout the world identified with the full range of Modern, American and New Age Aquarian ideals: Freedom and Independence from religious, ideological and political oppression; Liberty and Opportunity to pursue self-improvement through Education, Training, and Mastery of arts, crafts and skills

428

of all kinds, agriculture and forestry, the breeding and training of oxen and horses; the cultivation of Reason and Intelligence applied to human benefit through science, invention and innovation; person driven Business, Commerce, and Transportation; personal and communal health and strength, strategic planning to avoid purposeless war; Justice and Equality for all including women's' rights through democratic and citizen centered government within our global civilization and culture.

THE GODDESS ATHENA

Athena's Mythic Origins

Athena's mythical parents are *Zeus,* king of the gods living on Mt. Olympus, and *Metis,* goddess of crafty thought and wisdom. Zeus, fearful of a prophecy that he would be overthrown by the second of her children, settled the matter by swallowing pregnant Metis whole. As a result, she bore only one child and that birth occurred *inside the Godly head!* Zeus' skull was split open and *fully grown* Athena burst forth with a shout, wearing a *helmet* and a *suit of golden armor,* and carrying a *spear.* Because of her manner of birth, Athena has dominion over all intellectual things and remained a virgin. She is also identified with the Roman Minerva and with *Neith,* the Egyptian goddess of war and weaving.

Athena's Attributes & Rulerships

Athena's primary attribution is Intelligence applied to human benefit, wisdom, philosophy, and inspiration. She is the goddess of personal strength, courage and freedom, and patron of many arts, crafts and skills including sculpture, pottery, architecture and building; business and commerce, cities and their government, civilization, law and justice, horses and oxen, medicine and healing, music and dance, psychic and physical protection, mathematics and the sciences; shipbuilders and all forms of transportation, trees and pillars; renewal, writing and literature. And, because she did not approve of fighting without reason she is the goddess of diplomacy, peace, and prudent military strategy, soldiers and weapons making.

Athena is credited as the inventor of the flute, loom and spindle, plow, rake, the chariot, bridle, ox yoke, and for teaching women the arts of sewing, dressmaking, embroidery, spinning and weaving; teaching men agriculture, gold and other metal working, and to breed and break horses. In modern times she is well known as the goddess of wisdom and rationality, the patron of universities throughout the world, and also the patroness of career women and women's rights.

Athena's Symbols & Feast Days

Athena's traditional feast day is celebrated on August 15th. However, in her Roman manifestation as Minerva, her feast day was March 19th and was especially celebrated by artists, artisans, craftspeople, and school teachers.

A number of objects are associated with Athena. As seen in her most famous representation, the giant statute in the Greek Parthenon (there is a full scale reproduction of both the temple and the goddess' statue in Nashville, TN, home of Vanderbilt University and many musical productions), the most important are her Serpent child, the Helmet, and the Spear. In addition, she is also commonly seen in armor and carrying a small round shield, with an owl either seated on her shoulder or flying just above her head.

Athena's most common symbols and their meanings include:

Helmet (not always worn but sometimes carried in her hand), symbolizes that wisdom and strategy are the keys to victory in war, and the helmet protects their source.

Lance or Spear is a "targeting" weapon separating the warrior from the victim, demonstrating strategic action.

The large, man-sized **serpent** at her feet, partially risen, is *Erichthonius*, the serpent child of the Earth Goddess, *Gaia* and Hephaestus, the unwanted would be lover of the virgin goddess Athena. His lust was so great that he prematurely ejaculated while chasing her, and a blob of semen landed on her thigh and then fell to the earth, immediately becoming a child that was adopted by Athena. The serpent also symbolizes protection and rebirth, knowledge, wisdom, and Kundalini power.

The **Owl**, either on her shoulder or arm, or flying above her head—signifying wisdom and watchfulness.

Aegis, the round shield represents the Goddess' protective power. It shows the snake-covered Medusa head said to petrify enemies on sight.

Armor, symbolizes both soldiering and common sense self-protection sometimes forgotten by those aggressively "looking for a fight."

Cloak. As a virgin goddess, she is modest and not seductive. At times, she was held as the model for "prime and proper" young ladies. Her cloak hides her feminine body, and you should visualize her so modestly covered, and you may utilize such a cloak to assimilate your persona with hers regardless of gender during ritual and meditation.

Sandals. As a strong and active goddess, she is never barefoot, so always see her (and if you wish, dress likewise) in plain, unornamented leather sandals.

Intertwined Snakes, represent creative power and wisdom in common endeavor.

Mulberry and olive trees are valued both for their fruit, juice and oil, the beauty of the trees in landscaping, and the unique beauty of their wood in small wood-working. In addition, the extended olive branch is an established gesture of peace.

Other symbols associated with Athena are the bowl symbolizing harmony and utility, the dove symbolizing victory, the eagle symbolizing imperial power, a spindle symbolizing utilitarian knowledge, and the oak tree symbolizing endurance and strength.

Colors associated with Athena:

Blue (knowledge and power), cinnamon (success and power), gold (supreme power), green (ambition), orange (joy), ruby red (immortality), and yellow (intellect).

Incense, oils and substances associated with Athena:

Olive, Pomegranate, and the almost universal compounding of Frankincense, Myrrh, and Storax.

Chants associate with Athena:

While various poems and chants dedicated to Athena can be found in books and in on-line resources, when it comes to magickal evocation and invocation, these are best constructed in your own words in specific regards to those qualities of the goddess you are seeking in direct association with your needs and desires.

An example might go something like this:

> Oh Athena, Athena, be with me now,
> Goddess of strength and courage,
> I see thee in golden armor and helmet,
> With spear and shield, owl and serpent.
> Oh Athena, Athena, be with me now
> Goddess of Wisdom and Invention,
> I know thee through guidance and training,
> In arts and crafts, science and numbers.
> Oh Athena, Athena, be here with me now,
> Give me Strength within and without and all about,
> Goddess of inspiration, leadership, and power,
> I seek thy aid and protection, now and ever,
> To bring about _____.
> *(Describe the work or need, concisely in symbol)*
> Oh Athena, Great Athena, my gratitude is forever.

Athena's Invocative Characteristics: Self-Development, Self-Improvement and Self-Empowerment

Based on the above attributions, Athena may be magickally called upon for inspiration relating to acts of judgment, diplomacy, mediation, strategy, innovation and invention, matters involving business and commerce, building and architecture, Law and justice, city management, health and healing, the training of horses and ponies and their riders and trainers, the training of soldiers and their commanders, inspiration for courage, instruction in psychic and physical self-protection (including martial arts), education and career choices (especially for women), instruction in traditional women's crafts, music and dance, arts and writing, mathematics and science, and metal working. She also taught agriculture and horticulture to men and women, and can be said to be the patron of community gardening. By extension and in summary, we can say that *Athena is the goddess of choice for self-development, improvement and empowerment.*

Athena's Intuitive Character:
Defensive Military Weapons and Strategy

Even though Athena is perceived as a warrior goddess, she disapproves of aggression without purpose—her aid should be sought to create an atmosphere for diplomacy and defense strategy. As an inventor and patron of the sciences, soldiers, transportation, metal working, all forms of protection, we can consider her as the magical inspiration and resource for modern hi-tech defensive weapons and strategies, and likewise for modern commercial technology. Perhaps because of the flying owl we should also think of her in terms of air and space.

Doing Magickal Work

Doing magickal work with any deity, you must decide what specific aspect is your objective because every deity has more than one strength or rulership as you see from that we've already described for Athena. When working with Athena, it is important to decide on what aspect of her you wish her aid: the strength and leadership of the Warrior Goddess, the inspiration and foresight of the Creativity Goddess the intelligence and rational thinking of the Wisdom Goddess, etc.

Magickal Working with Athena

There are many aspects and qualities to choose from and you need to do so with two objectives in mind:

1. The clear and specific association of the listed item with your need;
2. The clear and specific Athena's role and "persona" with your objective and your own "persona." *You must feel a total sympathy between the two of you.*

Desired Aids: an altar, or small table, and chair; statue of the Deity or a photo or other image (or just this book opened to the illustration above); a private location for that image which you see often, but others do not; a statue or image of an owl; a statue or image of snake, preferably coiled with head raised (but not threateningly); a helmet or image of one; a round shield or image of one; a cloak, shawl, or simple scarf; a burner and incense associated with Athena; a short chant or mantra; and other symbol associated with defensive strength, innovation, art and craftsmanship, and any other qualities of the deity's rulership. Other aids or tool may be added or deleted, depending on the purpose of your ritual and whether it is evoking or invoking, BUT never let your tool dominate your procedure!

Procedure: Sit before your altar, with the cloak or shawl or scarf draped over your head and call the Goddess to you. A simple way to do this is by repeating her name slowly, over and over, using it like a mantra. Each time you repeat her name, visualize the Goddess standing before you. When you have finished chanting the mantra, feel the energy of this powerful Goddess around you and ask her to assist you in your creative aspirations or whatever else you desire she assist you with.

Proceed with the main evocation or invocation, using the personalized chant you have written or adapted.

When finished, thank the Goddess you are working with and you may like to leave her an offering, such as a feather you have found to represent her wisdom and intellect, or a particular crystal that you feel is appropriate. Carefully put away your cloak for it is to be worn only when you need work this particular deity's energy. Carefully and respectfully put the other aids and tools away.

After our discussion of the goddess *Libertas,* we will describe the special adaptations of procedure related to the operations of Evocation or Invocation.

THE GODDESS LIBERTY

Libertas, the ancient Roman goddess of liberty, is also known as *Columbia, Lady Liberty,* and the *Goddess of Democracy.* She was adopted in 1793 during the French Revolution as *Lady Liberty* and patroness of the "Cult of Reason," replacing depictions of the Virgin Mary on several altars in the Notre Dame cathedral. She was also known as *Britannia* in the United Kingdom, but is best known as *Liberty* in association with America, the "Land of the Free and Home of the Brave," in the words of the national anthem.

Libertas' Symbols & Meaning:

Torch: The torch is the primary symbol in this rendition of Liberty reflecting the actual name of the Statue—*Liberty Enlightening the World.*

Crown: The crown has seven spikes representing the seven seas and the seven continents of the world—thus Liberty is for all.

Windows of the crown: The 25 windows represent heavenly rays of light shining over the seven seas and continents of the world.

Tablet: The tablet in her left hand is a book of law representing that this nation is founded on Human Law.

The Tablet's Keystone Shape: The keystone at the acme of a stone gateway keeps the others together. Without it everything would collapse. The keystone of this nation is its foundation on law. Without law, freedom, democracy, and justice could not prevail. Liberty Island is the Gateway to America for those who came here to escape religious and monarchial tyranny.

Writing on the Tablet: This shows the date of America's independence: JULY IV MDCCLXXVI. The date is given in roman numerals which have been commonly symbolic of law.

Robe: Liberty wears a free-flowing robe called a *stola*, which refers back to the Roman influence of the goddess who was worshipped by freed slaves.

Sandals: The Statue show Liberty wearing sandals for walking. She is not standing still. Even though the Statue stands on a pedestal, Liberty is actually walking ahead, always moving forward. Liberty is lighting the path to freedom through peace, not violence. Wearing footwear her stature as a free person. Slaves commonly are barefoot.

Broken Chains: The broken chains at Liberty's feet symbolize freedom from the slavery and bondage common in the old world that immigrants, including the African slaves and some European and Oriental indentured servants brought to America in actual slave chains, finally have left behind.

Shields: The shields on each side of the pedestal symbolize the states in the Union.

Pedestal's Granite Brick: The 13 layers of granite that comprise the body of the pedestal represent the 13 colonies that joined together to form the American nation in 1776.

As *Columbia*, she is hailed in the official song for the Vice President of the United States.

> Hail Columbia, happy land!
> Hail, ye heroes, heav'n-born band,
> Who fought and bled in freedom's cause,
> Who fought and bled in freedom's cause,
> And when the storm of war was gone
> Enjoy'd the peace your valor won.
> Let independence be our boast,
> Ever mindful what it cost;
> Ever grateful for the prize,
> Let its altar reach the skies.
> Firm, united let us be,
> Rallying round our liberty,
> As a band of brothers joined,
> Peace and safety we shall find.

America's Goddesses

It is these two goddesses, *Athena* and *Libertas*, that best represent not only **American ideals** but those of the New Age Aquarian person: **Freedom and Independence** from all oppression, the **Liberty of personal opportunity**, the **pursuit of Education**, the **qualities of Reason and Intelligence**, mastery of **Crafts and Skills**, of **Innovation and Invention**, the wisdom of **Strategic Thinking**, **Courage in Defense**, but Avoidance of Wars of Aggression, and the potential **transforming power of the inner Kundalini.**

While neither Liberty nor Wisdom are commonly thought of in terms of *personal* Magick, and Magick is generally thought of as *personal* rather than communal, we need to come to some new realizations.

1. We are all *interconnected* at all levels and dimensions but the dominating culture has led us to think in terms of separateness: of individual against individual and institution, institution against institution, class against class, party against party, falsely empowered corporations against people, heart against brain, and even highly intelligent academics and professions neglecting or actually falsifying research analytics in wars of ideas and ideologies.

2. Separateness is *disconnectedness* and leads to anointed and proclaimed *authority* vs. individual, the "top down" concepts of academic primacy and organizational structure, "trickle-down" economics, "vested" special interests against commoners, and to unelected leadership of faceless mass movements manipulated against "the people."

3. "Communal" is a recognition of *connectedness.* Within a body there is a community of interests in which cells work together, heart and brain function together, and all the organs, complexes, ganglia work together in support of the health of an individual. But, "communal" also means that improving or healing one organ benefits the whole body; improve one individual and the whole community benefits; improve one community and the whole nation benefits; improve one nation and the world benefits.

4. "*Connectedness*" is the beginning and culmination of "integration"—communal, social, organizational, financial, international, psychological, spiritual, and magickal. Magickal Power (Applied Mind Power) comes from the integration of the individual's physical and emotional energies through mentally visualized thought forms guided by personal will with spiritual purpose. Integration is a "bottom up" process in contrast to a "top down" falsity.

5. *Liberty* and *Wisdom* are individual attributes best expressed communally. They are not "political" forces won by military or institutional actions although historically it has been made to appear that way. Liberty and Freedom are only meaningful when founded in the individual person and re-enforced every day through personal actions and decisions. Wisdom doesn't exist in nationhood and then trickle down to individuals, but wise individuals inform a whole nation.

6. The personal invocation of the goddesses of Liberty and Wisdom reinforces their presence throughout the community by means of the *connectedness* of the individual with all others to the degree of their closeness to the originating individual.

Magickal Evocation and Invocation

As previously discussed, there are two primary ways for an individual to directly and personally relate to a specific deific force—one that is recognized in the form or a long established god or goddess: Evocation and Invocation.

In both operations, we make use of Name, Image, Symbols and Attributes in order to connect the primary myth and the energies and qualities of the deity.

In the case of evocation, we can do this with either ritual or meditation, or a combination of those two procedures. For an individual, we prefer meditation; for a small group, a ritual may be practical but has certain challenges that we prefer to avoid in the case of deities outside an established religious or other spiritual practice.

Why? In the case of an established practice, its own *egregor* (defining thought form) will influence or even dominate the intent of the operation. In contrast, individuals will establish their own intention by their own actions and choices of associated symbols and aids. By choosing the specific deity for meditation the individual is establishing the intent to evoke the known character and qualities the deity, or a stated selection among those characteristics and qualities.

Focus is a Magical Necessity

For either Athena or Liberty, there is a considerable range of attributes from which the individual may choose to focus upon. Athena "rules" both horses and oxen, but they are quite different animals even though they share the primary function of transportation of goods and people, but the horse is also further specialized as a race horse, a work house, a riding horse, a show horse, a breeding horse and any of those should be specified in the meditation. In contrast, it may be that meditator chooses to evoke Athena for her primary identification as the Goddess of Wisdom, or may choose Liberty as the Goddess of Freedom from religious domination.

In other words, define what you want, and be specific about it

Writing your own script and determining how you can involve the important associated symbols, adding appropriate chants or declarations that you've discovered in your research or been inspired to write all help impress them deeply into your own personal unconscious mind. If the correspondences suggest a particular incense, see if you can make it yourself. Likewise with any of the aids and tools—like, for example, a magical mirror. A personally made tool—especially one created in direct connection with a *dedicated* evocation—is worth far more than a very expensive purchased item.

The more specific the "formula" becomes because of your own work the more does it function in your personal unconscious to tap into the universal (aka "collective") unconsciousness.

Conscious and Unconscious working together

It should be said that the goal of all magical work—and also of life itself—is the enable to conscious mind to exploit the powers of the unconscious. Even when we tell you to work with long lists of symbols and correspondences, chanting names and mantras, visualizing forms and images in colors and particular dress, we are enabling the conscious mind to draw upon the memories and knowledge of the person and universal unconsciousness. Some people refer to this as "integration," but we reserve that term for a more personal form of psychological work.

While some would-be "master magicians" tell you to memorize all these long lists and to learn to pronounce everything in "sacred" languages, that is not necessary or practical any more than memorizing all the information available on the Internet. The real need is to learn where to find desired information when you need it and how to employ it. That's the guidance given to young law students.

Obviously there is a difference between *conscious* and *unconscious*, and to fully explain this difference and even just its pertinence to this limited discussion would take more than this short aside. For simplicity, think of your "conscious mind" as the active intelligence making managerial decisions and carrying out the necessary actions. Now think of the universal unconscious as a vast information resource of every kind of memory there ever has been, and then think of the personal unconscious as containing just your own memories. Most of these memories are not on active recall, but they are there and the conscious mind can recall them even if we have to make a lot of effort for those of childhood and past lives.

All those memories, in both the personal and the universal unconscious resources have "smart tags" that enable the conscious mind to recall those memories desired from the personal unconscious along with those triggered by those smart tags from the universal unconscious. To the degree that the conscious mind is trained in magickal thinking and techniques, the detail can be amazing and those that are "just right" can be selected for the work desired.

Just to offer an alternative way of seeing this, think of the information resources of your computer: you do have both a personal memory drive and access to the World Wide Web (universal memory) and the computer's Operating System which functions like a trained mind.

When the Spirit is with you

Sometimes, even those lists of names and correspondences aren't needed when the "Spirit" is strong as it was in the case of the brave 15-year old Pakistani girl, Malala Yousafzai, who had the courage and belief in education for women to stand up against threats of assassination by the strict Islamic Taliban, the strength to survive two bullets fired at close range into her brain, to endure nearly a year-long painful series of surgeries, and finally to speak before the United Nations on behalf of all women with the courage and conviction of their right and their need for genuine non-sectarian education. Malala may not know anything of *Athena* but that Spirit of Courage, the Belief in a Woman's Right to Education, the Protection of her arms and armor, and the Power and Strength of a Goddess, but the "Spirit" was with her without the need of an Invocation of the Goddess Herself.

There are times and places where a particular Spirit is strong and seemingly permeates a culture as did *Libertas* in the founding of European and American democracies. It may that a particular individual invokes a deity and become the trigger for a massive evocation of the same deity. As Patrick Henry spoke out "Give me Liberty or give me Death" it may be that Malala's manifestation of *Athena* is empowering more young women to stand up and free their sisters and even their mothers from the ancient repression of women's spirit in the Islamic world.

And the Spirit of Liberty Today

The world was strongly reminded of the power of Liberty to transform a nation and to inspire many with the 2013 celebration of the life of Nelson Mandala in South Africa. Here was a man who emerged after 27 years of imprisonment for daring to challenge apartheid with a wondrous smile on his face and the ability to finish his mission as a freely elected president of the nation.

The power of these two goddesses and the ideas and ideals they represent are incarnate in the Spirit of the Times, but no matter how powerful that spirit may be it must manifest through courageous human people who *act with the full strength of belief and conviction.*

Spirit and the Times

Approximately, every 2,160 years there is a transition from one zodiacal age to the next in an established sequence. A total round of the twelve zodiacal ages equals approximately 25,920 years and has been various named a "Platonic Year," the "Great

Year," and other names depending on the culture and different approaches to the determination of the starting and transitioning times. The current Great Year began about 10,858 B.C.E.

Now is not the time or place to get into the details of the concepts involved. The fact remains that these historical cycles are characterized by evolutionary changes in the dominant cultures and individual psychological reactions. Even without belief or understanding of astrology, a cursory reading of history brings a perception of transitions in most aspects of personal and public lives, of the dominance and submission of groups and classes of people, of major changes in the economics of land and labor, of climate change and migrations of people, of earth changes and the rise and fall of civilizations, and more.

How much of this is causally related on associative, we don't know, and really it doesn't matter anymore than switches in time zones from standard clock to daylight time. The fact remains that these cycles do happen, and the symbolic associations do give understanding and the basis for projecting further developments within the symbolically defined pattern.

Human Influence

The Age of Pisces is ending and the Age Aquarius has progressively dominated the "spirit of the times" for the last few hundred years. In each Age, particular energies rise and fall and characterize "the influential Spirit" over particular areas of space and time. Whereas we can think of earlier Age as more dominantly characterized by the "ruling Sign," the human power is increasing a modifying factor as we grow in consciousness.

In many historic turning points, human factors may have progressively coincided with the spiritual, as with America's Founding Fathers and very possibly with those of the heroic Pakistani girl Malala Yousafzai and South African President Nelson Mandala. Such acts are invocative of higher spiritual forces and are not ritualistic but their power is even greater. And the Spiritual power being invoked by powerfully motivated human action is not always so benevolent. There have been many gods who have brought horror and terror, repressing knowledge and spreading ignorance, gaining strength through human pain and suffering as witnessed in the recent eras of the Nazism and Stalinism, and the current era of Fundamentalist Islamic Terrorism.

The Difference when Human and Cosmic Intertwine

That's why a conscious and deliberate Invocation of deities like *Athena* and *Libertas* are again important at this time in human history. The person who has invoked the Goddess is like a flame spreading Her evocative power to others. That's the real difference between genuine Magical Invocation and Evocation speaking the energies of the times in contrast to archaic religious acts from a time long past.

But, humans must do their part in this New Age. The *Aquarian Couple* is pictured pouring forth not merely knowledge and information but the power to transform both into Enlightenment and Personal Empowerment. We are active partners—but as we assume conscious responsibility for our action in awareness of its permeations.

The Aquarian man and woman together as one.

RITUAL & MAGICAL INVOCATION OF ATHENA

Why <u>Invoke</u> the Spirit of Athena?

Why? Why anything? Conscious living involves purpose, and effective magical action is dependent on firmly establishing your objective as specifically as possible, setting the parameters of your action. Go over the list of Athena's characters and rulerships and choose <u>one</u> that you feel is important for individual human support at this time and in your place as defined by your perception of how far your influence can extend, or should be limited.

Go over the lists of symbols and correspondences and choose those to go with the Athenian image compatible with your objective. How is She to be visually represented?

Write a chant or statement around Her name, image, and the objective you've chosen.

Build a script of how you are going to invoke Athena into your essential being, and how you are going to act as her direct representative. You are not inviting "possession;" it is vital that you remain fully conscious and self-aware, but also be aware that you are representing this Goddess-Power in the field of human action to accomplish a goal of your "mutual" decisions. You are direct representative, and agent of the Goddess Athena for the duration of this operation, and a continuing support-person until you judge the objective is fully accomplished.

And, yes, the operation can be repeated, or you can follow the same procedure to accomplish another objective.

A final choice. In the preceding drama, we said you were going to invoke Athena into your "essential being." We didn't define that, but you have to. When you <u>invoke</u>, you either *become* Athena, or you *speak for* her. There is a danger to "becoming a deity," a danger of "ego inflation." With experience, you can learn how to handle that temporary phenomena.

If you feel able, then you can invoke the Goddess into your being, but still not possession. Maintain your dual awareness of being both human and divine. That itself is a goal of your magical work: to knowingly know that you are divine and human, and to more manifest both inwardly and outwardly without inflation and with humility and awareness of your primary humanity as long as you are incarnate. And the longer that, the greater benefit to all humanity.

RITUAL & MAGICAL EVOCATION OF ATHENA

Why <u>Evoke</u> the Spiritual Power of Athena?

With evocation you are "spreading the word." Malala may have unconsciously invoked Athena—even at the same time that she was invoking courage and determination and the ideals that are the goddess with her aspirations—but now she is speaking out and her friends are speaking out too—all saying "I am Malala" in answer to that question posed by her would-be assassin: "Who is Malala?"

Yes, Malala is unique. You are too—but your invocation is deliberate in a different way than the friends of Malala now speaking and spreading her word. The initial procedure for evocation is the same as for invocation: make your selections and write your statement or chant representing you objective.

But instead of invoking the goddess into your essential essence your spread the word as far as you can. Visualize a color and soft imaged that represents your objective, and as you chant or speak see that image reaching out, and feel its influence upon people. Know that they are becoming infused with qualities you are projecting.

It's not the same as ordinary magical evocation or invocation

No, it's not the same as your ordinary magical evocation where the goal is to surround yourself with the same images, colors and qualities as you are projecting. With ordinary evocation, you are filing your aura with the magical qualities you are seeking, but in this book we are dealing at a higher level with deific powers. While Spirit is everywhere and in everything, the Spirit in a deity is much higher and more transformative. It is, perhaps, the most highest and most advanced form of Spiritual Communication and Empowerment.

One approach to invocation is to write a play with you starring as the "Goddess Incarnate"—but never "incarnate" an entity of a lower nature than yourself. And, do not worry about invoking a deity of the opposite gender because each of us, archetypally, has both masculine and feminine elements in our psyche.

RITUAL AND MAGICKAL INVOCATION AND EVOCATION OF LIBERTY

We're not going to be redundant and largely repeat what was written for Athena because the procedures are the same for these two deities, and for others. These are not ordinary magical operations, and the importance of specificity cannot be overemphasized. Select the lists with care and awareness that you are doing some of the highest value.

THE INVOCATION OF ATHENA AND LIBERTY

As seen in the illustration above of the Aquarian Man and Woman each "blessing" the world with the transforming powers of Enlightenment and Empowerment, this New Age is also the first time in known history when *Anima* and *Animus* are each equally and fully empowered in every Man and Woman, whether acting singly or together, to meet the challenges of the times with human strength, intelligence, courage, and wisdom.

The spirits they invoke are those we have long projected into these deific images, and now we can fully draw upon their powers in fulfillment of our destiny to become more than we are and all that we are to become.

Not only are you working with deity Spirits, but with these two Goddesses you are working with the Spirits of the Age, and in doing so participating in the *coming in of the* energies of both Aquarius and the New Age. To our knowledge, this opportunity of being a conscious participant in the "incarnating" of the qualities and transforming energies on a global level has never happened before. Working together and alone, we are building a global civilization in which all the attributes of Libertas and Athena as deific powers are the primary characteristics. Yes, we can simply state it as "Life, Liberty and the Pursuit of Happiness" while knowing that with any magical mantra, the meaning and actual energies are far broader than just seven words.

ASTRAL POWERS BASIC TRAINING

This is a book on Communicating with Spirit and this chapter is on Magick—both involve the Cosmic dimensions of Astral, Mental, and Causal as well as the Physical/Etheric and the personal human vehicles associated with each.

With most books and most discussion on Spiritual subjects, both the Cosmic and the personal levels are variously neglected. It's all a matter of "attitude" in which—East and West—one or the other have been neglected or pushed aside. Spirit is universal, and as *Consciousness* we can explore both. To do so requires both purpose and development. The following procedures and exercises are intended as a "Basic Training Program," some of which has been touched on previously and will be noted again later in the book.

The Astral Powers Basic Training Program is inclusive of the Etheric Training Memory Stations Procedure, Advanced Astral Training, the Qabalistic Cross Exercise, the Magic Circle Exercise, the Four Elemental Winds Exercise, Creating the Body of Light Procedure, and the Transfer of Consciousness to the Body of Light Procedure.

The Astral Powers Basic Training Program
The Etheric Training Memory Stations Procedure

Introduction. System, Memorization, and Visualization are key factors in *all* "training for success" no matter what the goal may be.

Step One: the Route. Starting from your sleeping area, plan a route in your home and memorize it from your act of getting up from bed, slowly walking to the end destination, and then slowly returning to lie down in your bed. The route should be long enough so that you can establish six distinctive "Memory Stations," preferably out of sight each from the next. You should actually draw a map of the route with the six stations indicated and described. Review that map at both the beginning and ending of the exercise described below.

Step Two: Observation of Details. Carefully study each memory station in turn for at least ten minutes each for ten days. The more distinct the characteristics of each memory station, the better. For that reason it will be helpful for you to place a differently colored object at each station. You can strengthen the sensual references by adding a distinct odor at each station—such as vanilla, chocolate, anise, peppermint, lemon, cinnamon, etc. If you can secure a pitch pipe or other instrument, and memory-record a distinctive sound at each station to recall each time you return to the station. Add something with a distinct feel—like pieces of felt, silk, leather, wool, glass, a sponge—and perhaps even something you can taste that is different at each station. Involving all your senses makes memorization easier and richer.

Step Three: Awareness Extension. Look at each memory station, smell, listen, feel, taste. And realize that you are looking not only with your physical eyes, but also your etheric and astral eyes. Likewise you are listening with you physical, etheric and astral "ears," and so on. As an extension of this part of the exercise, try dreaming about each station, one at a time on successive nights.

Step Four: Visualization. At each station, close your eyes and visualize every detail while consciously experiencing it all with your other senses.

Step Five: Reversal. Do dry runs over the route, stopping at each station to exercise your senses, and then turn around and do it all in reverse. See the entire route both going and returning, including the look and feel of the floor under your bare feet, the colors of the walls, passages through doorways, past windows or pictures on the walls, down and up any steps, and so on.

Step Six: "Test & Verify." Next, test yourself by closing your eyes and "walking" the route from start to finish entirely in your memory, visualizing and sensing everything at the memory stations. *Test and verify* until you do it perfectly, without error. Make sure to take the same length of time for your memory trips as required for your "awake" trip.

Step Seven: Astral Walking. Do this action for several weeks, and then augment it by imagining, seeing and feeling yourself getting up from bed or chair and walking the route, always from start to finish and back in your bed. When you fully _feel_ that it is you making these trips, not an image, then attempt to transfer your consciousness to that etheric image of yourself.

Endeavor to realize that the image is of your Etheric Double and *you are seeing it with the "eyes" of your Astral Body,* i.e. the body *above* the Etheric Double. Hold your consciousness in the Etheric Double and see it perform all the actions with the etheric counterparts of your physical arms and legs. At some point, you will feel your two bodies merge and you will be conscious of both the Etheric Double and the Physical Body at the same time. When you return to the starting point, be sure to transfer your consciousness back to the physical body. Always do these actions with awareness and completion. As long as you are incarnate in your physical body it is your home.

Step Eight: Dream Walking. As a final exercise, try to fall asleep while seeing yourself get up and walk the memory path. It should turn into a dream, and you should realize you are dreaming and then move on into astral consciousness.

Summary of Purpose & User Benefits: Through memory and visualization, you are integrating you physical, etheric, and astral faculties. By dreaming the same exercise, you are doing a controlled (and verifiable) astral trip.

"Check & Verify." This phrase was made famous by U.S. President Ronald Reagan in Cold War negotiations with Soviet Prime Minister Michael Gorbechef, but it is a vital part of your astral training. Astral consciousness includes the faculties of imagination and dreaming and untrained they lead to fantasy and even delusion. Magicians have various methods to verify their astral visions, but we start with this simple program: remember and record you dream, and compare with the physical experience.

Advanced Astral Training Programs

The next step in our training is for you to produce a *Body of Light* that can be used as your vehicle of consciousness on the inner planes.

Unlike the basic training we adapted from Ophiel's "Little System," the Body of Light has a long history in all esoteric traditions and is described in religious terms as well as magical and shamanic. Nevertheless, it is not common knowledge and it does involve some very detailed and time-consuming study and practice. *It's well worth your effort!*

There are two basic preliminary exercises that are well-known rituals, long used in magical training. The First is called the *Qabalistic Cross* and is adapted from "The Middle Pillar" by Israel Regardie. See end of chapter for details.

Astral Projection—Magickal Training— The Qabalistic Cross—Exercise

The Qabalistic Cross Exercise

Introduction. The *Living Light* of the inner planes is key to our development of "forms" for our particular functioning on the astral and higher planes. This exercise and those that follow function to awaken particular psychic centers and sensitivities before proceeding to the full procedure to form your own Body of Light. The gestures are a variance of the ordinary Christian Cross, making use of the last few phrases of the Lord's Prayer. It is utilized in magical work because it is an ideal method of equilibrating the personality and raising the mind to the contemplation of higher things.

The words employed are Hebrew because the magical system evolved from the Qabalah. We've provided their meaning, but please only say the Hebrew. Rather than "speaking," you want to *vibrate* the words syllable by syllable, centering your voice at the back of the mouth and at a pitch slightly lower than normal, and feeling the sound projecting forth to the far reaches of the universe.

Here is the Qabalistic Cross Exercise:

Stand in a comfortable position, feet together. Take a few breaths to make yourself relaxed and receptive. Using your right hand,

1. Touch the forehead; vibrate:

   A-TOH (meaning "Thou art")

2. Bring the hand down and touch the breast, vibrate:

   MAL-KUTH (meaning "the Kingdom")

3. Touch the left shoulder, and vibrate:

   VE-GE-DUL-AH (meaning "and the Glory")

4. Touch the right shoulder and vibrate:

   VE-GE-VUR-AH (meaning "and the Power")

5. Clasping the fingers on the breast, vibrate:

   LE OLAHM AMEN (meaning "forever, Amen")

As an advanced step, you may visualize a line of Light following the motion of your hand, forming a cross of Living Light before your body like a protective shield.

Summary of Purpose & User Values: While there are various esoteric factors at work in this simple exercise, the primary function is to link the four psychic centers together in a protective (non-Christian) cross.

The Magic Circle Exercise

Introduction. Most magician draw, or "erect," a circle about themselves and their place of working. This is both a circle of protection and a container for psychic energies, and rather than a simple circle it is a miniature three-dimensional "world"—a sphere—with the magician at the center.

Both of the tracing of the pentagrams and the circle should be visualized in Blue Flame—the model for which you can establish by placing a <u>small</u> amount of rubbing alcohol or brandy on heat resistant plate in a dark room, and igniting it. Memorize both the color and the wavering of the flame. This is the color often seen in etheric and séance phenomena. It is sometimes called "Electric Blue" and visualizing it stimulates the throat chakra.

Banishing Earth Pentagram

Here is the exercise:

Face East. Extend your right arm before you, and with your index finger trace a "banishing earth pentagram:" a five-pointed star drawn in one continuous motion starting at left bottom point, up to the top point, down to the right bottom, up to the left, across to the right, and back down to connect at the bottom left starting point.

Pull your partly back and then still using your extended index finger "stab" the pentagram in the center while vibrating YHVH:

YOD-HEH-VAV-HEH

Face South. With you arm and index finger still extended in front of you, turn to face South. Trace another pentagram just like the first, stab it, and vibrate ADNI:

AH-DON-NAI

Face West. In the same manner turn to face West, trace the pentagram, stab it, and vibrate AHIH:

EH-HE-YEH

Face North. Turning to the North, trace the pentagram, stab it, and vibrate AGLA:

AH-GAL-LAH

Face East. Rotate back to face the East, extend your arms out to the sides to form a cross, and say:

> *Before me is Raphael; behind me is Gabriel; on my right is Michael; and on my left is Auriel. Before me flames the Pentagram and behind me shines the Six-rayed Star.*

Repeat the Qabalistic Cross:

1. Touch the forehead; vibrate:

    A-TOH (meaning "Thou art")

2. Bring the hand down and touch the breast, vibrate:

    MAL-KUTH (meaning "the Kingdom")

3. Touch the left shoulder, and vibrate:

   VE-GE-DUL-AH (meaning "and the Glory")

4. Touch the right shoulder and vibrate:

   VE-GE-VUR-AH (meaning "and the Power")

5. Clasping the fingers on the breast, vibrate:

   LE OLAHM AMEN (meaning "forever, Amen")

Relax and mentally close the circle.

Summary of Purpose & User Benefits: As previously mentioned, the Qabalistic Cross and Magic Circle exercises place the user in the center of a sphere that is both protective and a container of energy. It is also a container of magical (astral) consciousness, of awareness and intention within which magical rituals are performed to their completion without outside disturbance.

The Four Elemental Winds Exercise

Introduction. Once you have mastered these two exercises, and before closing with the second Qabalistic Cross, you will be standing in the middle of the circle. We are adding another exercise recommended by Ophiel in his "The Art and Practice of Astral Projection." This exercise helps to awaken and balance the elemental forces in your own persona. Once you are familiar with the imagery and the feelings invoked, you may choose to modify the imagery—but (1) keep it simple and (2) keep it archetypal and abstract.

Here's the exercise:

Facing East. You are still facing the East from the Magic Circle Exercise. Vibrate EURUS (E-U-RUS), the name of the East Wind. Enlarge the blue flame pentagram. Visualize a scene through the pentagram of a beautiful dawn with pink and rosy clouds. The East is the quarter of Air whose Archangel is Raphael. Feel AIR. Feel this Air wash over you and flow through you. Imagine and feel a soft and cool morning breeze coming from the dawn clouds and passing over you.

Facing South. After a few moments finish with the East and gently erase the image and feeling from your mind. Turn to face South. Vibrate NOTUS (NO-TUS), the name of the South Wind. The south is the quarter of Fire whose Archangel is Michael. Enlarge the blue flame pentagram and through it visualize a tropical scene. Visualize blue seas and white waves dashing upon rocky coral reefs with palm trees swaying in the warm breeze. Feel the gentle, warm almost hot, heat coming from this quarter. Feel it warm you through and through. Finish and erase from your mind.

Facing West. Turn and face the West. Vibrate ZEPHYRUS (ZE-PH-ER-US), the name of the West Wind. The West is the quarter of Water whose Archangel is Gabriel. Enlarge the blue flame pentagram. Visualize a waterfall with clouds of mist arising from it. The water-laden mist rising from the bottom of the falls is gently blowing towards you. Feel the misty wetness on your face and then feel it flowing into your consciousness.

Facing North. Now turn and face the North. Vibrate BOREAS (BOR-US), the name of North Wind. The North is the quarter of the element of earth whose Archangel is Auriel. It is in the quarter of Earth and in Earth itself, that all the other forces end. Hence Earth is the great final storehouse of all things and forces. You will find in Earth all the physical things you desire and all the things that you need to make you happy.

Enlarge the blue flame pentagram and see many immense fields of food crops feeding all the populations of Earth. See great fields of ripened corn, of wheat, barley and other grains, of rice, and other food crops. See vast orchards of trees loaded with fruits and nuts of all kinds. See the oceans and rivers with fish and other sea foods. Then visualize great herds of animals grazing on the green grasses. Everywhere there is Peace, Prosperity and Plenty. Beyond these fertile lands stretch great forests of trees that furnish lumber for our homes. Beyond these forests rise mountains containing mines of metals that supply other of our needs. And on the tops of these mountains is ice and snow which gather there and then melts and flows down to the plains through streams and rivers to nourish and water the growing things below.

See, too, the many factories transforming natural resources into the goods that meet our needs and desires, see that laboratories where new technologies are created, see the ships, trucks, trains and planes that transport the goods, see the many warehouses and stores that distribute the goods, and also see the hospital and doctors, and other services that make modern civilization possible.

Feel the bounty and great beauty of the Earth, feel the benefits of employment and wealth creation, feel the pleasures and happiness that life brings to all of the people, and feel, too, the role you play as a steward for all that is in the Earth Plane.

Turn to the east and close the exercise with the Qabalistic Cross.

Remember that all the actions you do on the physical plane extend "up" and through the Etheric, Astral, Mental, and Causal planes—all at once—to become causes of physical world effects. These rituals primarily benefit you, but also affect conditions in the physical world although mostly close to you.

Summary of Purpose & User Benefits: These quarters have no relation to the usual ideas of Air, Fire, Water, Earth, but are concerned only with the <u>qualities</u> of them. Connecting to the qualities of the elements gives you a principle role in directing material forces from the inner planes. Once you have completed the exercise of building your Body of Light you will be able to place your consciousness in position to direct these forces in relation with your visualized programs.

Creating the Body of Light Procedure

Introduction. This is a tedious but very powerful procedure that builds upon the previous three exercises. Remember, these exercises have no religious or other sectarian associations—instead they are programs of particular actions that utilize established inner plane connections to ideas and energies that add power to your mental and physical actions.

First we have to develop a deep connection between you and your physical body. It may seem redundant at first, but as you proceed with the exercise you will realize how little you really know your own body. Here's the procedure:

Outer Actions:

- Look at your right hand, turn it both ways, and note the appearance, the lines and marks, and movement and actions carefully.
- Holding the hand up, palm facing you, bend the thumb over the palm and say "Thumb." Speak it aloud if at all possible, but if not say it silently and feel the meaning.
- Bend the first finger down over the thumb and say "First Finger."
- Bend the second finger down over palm and say "Second Finger."
- Continue with the third finger and say "Third Finger."
- Then finish with the little finger, and say "Little Finger."
- Do these actions slowly and watch the movements carefully. *Feel* them.
- Now, reverse the process from little finger back to thumb. Do these actions with the same care and concentration as you did moving from thumb to little finger.

Repeat the complete exercise several times daily.

After a few weeks, expand the exercise to include the left hand in the same manner.

- Next extend the exercise to the right leg, and then the left leg. If you can do it bare-legged, look at the toes, and move them as much as you can. Then flex the foot, rotate the ankle, bend the knee. Speak the appropriate words with feeling.

- Sit in a chair, and bend forward and backward and sideways as far as you can and say appropriate words as you do.

- While sitting, slowly nod your head back and forth, and then rotate it in both directions. Speak the words.

- Stand up and raise your arms to form a cross, and then rotate your hands one way and then the other. Speak the words.

Inner Actions:

After doing this exercise for a couple of weeks, sit or lie down, close your eyes and "see" an image of your "inner" hands (appearing as grey-white-transparent shadows) doing the same actions with your "inner" eyes as you do them physically. After a few days, extend the closed eye exercise to the feet and legs, and then step-by-step to the whole body. See these actions just as you would with the eyes open but in transparent shadow.

After some time, sitting or lying down, with your eyes closed, see your entire inner body before you and mentally command it to do all these actions while your physical body remains still. This is important. The inner body must do every action, taking the same amount of time, as did your physical body. If you don't see this, then you must repeat the previous exercises until you do.

<u>Summary of Purpose & User Benefits:</u> While the ultimate value of all this work—the Etheric Training Memory Stations Procedure, the Qabalistic Cross, Magic Circle, and Four Elemental Winds exercises, and then the Creating the Body of Light Procedure—culminates in the next procedure, they have been immensely valuable in developing the inner resources of the physical/etheric complex and integrating that into the astral form. The net effect is truly summed up in the phrase "Mind over Body." You now have the ability to effect mind control over the physical and energy body for health and healing purposes.

Transfer of Consciousness to the Body of Light Procedure

Introduction. *This is the ultimate astral technology.* Transferring consciousness to the Body of Light enables you to exercise astral powers often presumed to be mythic or possible only for high spiritual beings. And, to an extent that is true—but it is also true that you will now have the potential to become such a being. It's like suddenly finding that you have the physical body of a super athlete able to excel in most sports, able to defend yourself against attacks, and capable of heroic feats.

Yes, you still have a lot of work ahead of you, but you're now in the home stretch. With great power comes great responsibility. You will need to gain direct experience at the astral level to develop the ethical understanding that goes with such power. Be honest and humble and realize this is the true second birth.

Here's the procedure:

Do the Qabalistic Cross Exercise with the physical body. Then sit in a chair facing east and visualize the Body of Light you have created standing in front of you, facing east. Command the Body of Light to go through the Qabalistic Cross Exercise. Watch carefully to see that all the actions are correctly performed.

End the program by withdrawing the Body of Light back into yourself.

Repeat the complete ritual, first with the physical body, and then with the Body of Light many times.

Always withdraw the Body of Light back into yourself.

Your next step is to transfer your consciousness to the Body of Light. This is no small accomplishment! You must feel and know that you are conscious in the Body of Light, seeing with its eyes, moving its parts, etc. Then extend the exercise to first include the Magic Circle with banishing pentagrams and finally the Four Elemental Winds.

You need to unite your consciousness with the consciousness of the Body of Light by transferring to that Body your physical senses, and then functioning on the inner planes through those senses. Perform the Qabalistic Cross and Circle of Flames. Sit in the center of the circle, facing east. See the Body of Light in front of you also facing east. Visualize yourself moving across the intervening space and enter into the Body of Light. Then attempt to see about you.

At first, you will see on the Etheric Plane. After learning to see, learn to feel. What you see are etheric counterparts of physical things. Learn to feel those things (but do no attempt to feel living things). Then continue on to develop senses of tasting, smelling, and hearing.

With the completion of this program, you will be tempted to think of yourself as a "Master of the Universe." *Don't!* Don't give in to the temptation. Such hubris will isolate you from reality and wipe out all you've accomplished. You have the means to tremendous possibilities, of which the only limits are your own. That means that the dangers of abuse and self-destruction are even more enormous.

When you are not using the Body of Light, you must keep it inside your Aura by a conscious act of will.

<u>*Summary of Purpose & User Benefits:*</u> Your purpose is to create a Body of Light. This is more than a Thought Form, discussed in another chapter, but there are many similarities. But you also must transfer your consciousness to this Body, and that is a considerable achievement with many ramifications. To some extent, you do this when dreaming, and even when day dreaming, but a complete transfer of consciousness under direction of your will is mastery of the highest order. You now have conscious vehicle with which to explore the non-material universe.

You can also use the Body of Light as a Familiar, *i.e. an extension of yourself on the inner planes, made of the material of those inner planes. It can be used as A Watcher and sent to any place to watch and record what is going on and then to report the information back to you. You can create A Guard in the form of an animal or other form and set it to guard something. If attacked, it will fight back as appropriate to its form. The Body of Light can be A Healing Agent—you identify the particular illness in the physical body and transfer it into the Body of Light, and then through your imagination you change the pictured illness into health. It can be used For Rejuvenation—transfer images back and forth between the imaged physical body and the Body of Light where you make the changes into the youth you had, or make it even better than when you were young. And you can use it as A God Image—Image a particular mythical God and merge your body of Light with the God Force represented.*

Perhaps the most interesting possibility is that of **Merging with a Counterpart**—*all physical things have counterparts on the inner planes. Using your Body of Light, merge yourself with the counterpart and thus know it and control it. Think what it might mean to merge with a super computer and understand how to increase its power and speed. The possibilities border on science fiction, and there may be no limits.*

This and additional procedures may be found in complete detail in *Astral Projection for Psychic Empowerment—The Out-of-Body Experience, Astral Powers, and their Practical Application*, 2012, Llewellyn, by Joe H. Slate, Ph.D. & Carl Llewellyn Weschcke.

<u>MEDITATION</u>
"The Experience of Past Life Memories"

Sources and Suggested Reading:

A.L. Soror: *Western Mandalas of Transformation—Magical Squares, Tattwas, Qabalistic Talismans*, 1996, Llewellyn

Almond, J. & Seddon, K.: *Egyptian Paganism for Beginners—Bring the Gods & Goddesses of Ancient Egypt into Daily Life*, 2004, Llewellyn

Barrabbas, F.: *Magical Qabalah—A Comprehensive Guide to Occult Knowledge*, 2013, Llewellyn

Clark, R.: *The Sacred Magic of Ancient Egypt—The Spiritual Practice Restored*, 2003, Llewellyn

Clark, R.: *The Sacred Tradition in Ancient Egypt—The Esoteric Wisdom Revealed*, 2000, Llewellyn

Conway, D.J.: *Magick of the Gods & Goddesses—How to Invoke Their Powers*, 1997, Llewellyn

Greer, J. M.: *The Celtic Golden Dawn—An Original & Complete Curriculum of Druidic Study*, 2013, Llewellyn

Kraig, D. M.: *Modern Magick: Twelve Lessens in the High Magickal Arts*, 2010, Llewellyn

Kraig, D. M.: *Real Tantra*, 2014, Llewellyn

Kraig, D. M.: *The Truth About Evocation of Spirits*, 1994, Llewellyn

Masters. R.: *The Goddess Sekhmet—Psycho-Spiritual Exercises of the Fifth Way*, 1990, Llewellyn

Monaghan, P.: *The Goddess Path—Myths, Invocations & Rituals*, 1999, Llewellyn

Mumford, J.: A Chakra & Kundalini Workbook—Psycho-Spiritual Techniques for Health, Rejuvenation, Psychic Powers & Spiritual Realization, 2008, Llewellyn

O'Neill, J. F.: *Foundations of Magic—Techniques & Spells that Work*, 2005, Llewellyn

Page, J. & Biles, K.: *Invoking the Egyptian Gods,* 2011, Llewellyn

Ponce, C.: *Kabbalah—An Introduction and Illumination for the World Today,* 1973, Theosophical

Reed, E. C.: *Invocation of the Gods—Ancient Egyptian Magic for Today,* 1992, Llewellyn

Regardi, I.—with Cicero, Chic & Cicero, Sandra Tabatha: *The Philosopher's Stone—Spiritual Alchemy, Psychology, and Ritual Magic,* 2013, Llewellyn

Richardson, A. & Walker-John, B.: *The Inner Guide to Egypt—A Mystical Journey Through Time & Consciousness,* 2010, Llewellyn

Woodfield, S.: *Drawing Down the Sun—Rekindle the Magick of the Solar Goddesses,* 2014, Llewellyn

14

BECOMING MORE THAN YOU ARE

EVOLVING TO ALL YOU CAN BE

You're not Finished!

"Becoming more than you are" is not simply a *motivational* phrase, nor is "Evolving to all you can be" only a statement of possibility—it's all about what you can do to accelerate your own <u>multi-dimensional</u> evolution. *And what you should do!*

A Complex Multi-Dimensional Being

The first step is the fundamental need to recognize, and *remember,* that the human person is a far more complex being than commonly perceived as just the physical body, brain, and the familiar personality. As we've discussed throughout this book and other writings, this complex being is made up of several *subtle vehicles,* each of which is also multi-dimensional and expresses consciousness in unique ways related to the substance and nature of the particular coincident cosmic dimension or "plane," (and "sub-plane" which likewise conditions particular aspects of consciousness). Yet, all these vehicles and "sub-vehicles" of consciousness are functioning together, as well as separately and *unconsciously to us* at different levels of "awakening." Mostly, we are *asleep at the switch,* and have little or no idea of what being even a little more awake would be like.

Asleep, or Awake, what's the difference?

You are more than you think you are, but your degrees of unawareness limits your abilities to function at greater levels. Learn to see yourself differently and things begin to change. Look around you and see that there are other people who have more developed physical bodies and skills, some through training and exercise, and others through genetic and past-life inheritance. And note people with better education and more developed mental skills—and then realize that the two are only partially coincidental. Some well educated people are not really as "smart" as someone less well educated is, but you can also see where a good education could benefit even those "born smart." Truly smart and aware people are not emotionally reactive to biased ideologues and extremist theologies.

Reactive Emotionality, or …

Look around and see that some people readily fly into a rage and others don't; others fall into depression and others stay positive even under the worst challenges. Some people fall in love every other day while others are well-balanced and emotionally mature. Some people latch on to every kind of charismatic leader, politician, preacher, and guru, while others "keep their head" and remain objective to find value if there is any. Look some more, and you see people who live with a purpose, who know what they want, and who may accomplish great things.

Developed, Balanced, and Reliable

And, then, there are people who have learned to use their Astral (emotional) and Mental powers, and others who also have developed their natural Psychic powers into reliable skills and dependable abilities. The more we develop our "lower" vehicles in a natural and balanced manner, the more accessible become the powers of the "higher" vehicles to develop the Intuitive Mind and other faculties of the Super-consciousness. Well-balanced people can experience spiritual insights and are not blinded by professional religionists who actually have none.

Look Within

Many of these differences cannot be simply accounted for by the physical or social environment, nor can every problem be solved with a new pharmaceutical "pill" or a better job, a change in relationship, a new home, another car, another refrigerator, a new dress, or a vacation trip to a wonderful place with opportunities to meet new people, to engage in temporary flirtations, to attend some exciting lectures, etc. With development comes greater experience and maturity.

Other Bodies, Other Lives and Memories

Each of our subtle bodies—etheric, astral, mental, causal and spiritual—do, in a sense, have their own lives, their own memories, their own substance and their own logic. Our need is to integrate these under conscious awareness and control, to "de-condition" our responses to others that lead toward "inappropriate" behavior and drives, destructive feelings and urges, and irrational thoughts led by others rather than rationally arrived at through our own mental processes and led by our Higher Self.

A Life of Purpose

Instead of passive acceptance and response to "whatever comes your way," you can act with understanding of your needs and true desires and plan ahead and live a life of purpose, with growth and development to become all you can be.

Many Lives, Multiple Vehicles, Growth & Development

Most people reading this book already believe in reincarnation, and many have spontaneously remembered past lives in dreams and awakened memories during meditation, or experienced them through hypnosis and guided meditation. Others do know how their whole "person" is a composition of many vehicles and levels of consciousness, and many more are learning as students of Yoga, Magick, Shamanism, and other programs of psychic and spiritual development.

Real Human Growth is through Intentional Self-Improvement

The next step—it is the second, but since it is the essence of all the many steps that follow we prefer to call them all "next"—is the recognition that *real* human growth and development is *intentional and purposefully transformative*. It marks a shift from simple biological "passive" evolution that happens within a *mass* (or species) *context* to that of a willful and "active" drive for *self-improvement* at an <u>individual and personal context.</u>

From Species to Individual

This shift from a species or even racial contest to the singular drive has been gradual but accelerating, and particularly so over the last few centuries as we transition into the New Age as partially symbolized in the passing of the Age of Pisces into that of Aquarius—from the Age of two fish swimming in opposite directions to that of the mature human communicating knowledge and information to the World. It's a move from unconscious participation in the planetary process to conscious awareness and action. We can no longer simply *live <u>on</u> the earth but must become active life-partners with the Living Earth.*

The Evolutionary Plan

Not everyone fully understands that we are the unfinished products of a vast evolutionary "program" or plan that for all practical purposes can be described as endless—that is without beginning and, more importantly, without an ending. We are born out of the Divine, are ourselves Divine, and will return to the Divine—but all is endlessly Divine without Beginning or End. Some theorize a time will come when time itself pauses and the Divine sleeps only to awaken again in a new time and a new cosmos, but further speculation along that line is meaningless to us when we still have our own lives to live, our own assignment to complete.

We are All Evolving

What we do need to understand now is that evolution, growth and development is not only physical but non-physical as well, that it is Cosmic in extent but also specific to humanity, that for the human "chapter" it is singular and multiphasic, and that it is not uniform in all vehicles, sub-vehicles, levels, states of awareness, etc. Much growth is spontaneous and driven by the cumulative effects of past decisions and actions, while other growth is developmental programs. Some growth is causally responsive to events and actions involving other people and—sometimes to a very minor extent—other entities in interactive communication with humans.

The Great Plan

But, and this is important, our evolution, growth and development is **part of a "Great Plan"** and it *should be **our own plan** to individually undertake our growth and development consciously and purposefully.* As humans, with self-awareness and free will, that is what we are supposed to do: to knowingly and deliberately improve ourselves knowing that what we do for ourselves will have effects on everyone.

Waking Up!

Without some experience of more wakefulness at any of these other levels of conscious awareness you have no way of knowing and hence no obvious reason for seeking to become more than you are. But, as you've read in this book and others as well, there are many altered states of consciousness that you probably have experienced to some *partial* degree in those ecstatic states related to music and dance, sports events, political rallies, religious inspirations, the joys of romance and sex, the love of family, breakthroughs in understanding, academic and other achievements, scientific discoveries, triumphs of innovation, meditation, chakra awakening, energy healing, and other happenings that are becoming more familiar rather than exceptional.

Small Steps

Those "partial" awakenings are just that—partial glimmerings, samples of what can be—small steps on the path towards what becoming fully awakened in all levels and sub-levels of our multiple vehicles will be like.

Bigger Steps

Throughout history, in many cultures, there have been more fully awakened individuals who have left us guidelines and examples by their teachings and in the lives they lived. Some are known to us only through surviving folk tales and myth and history, but certainly many more never "made the headlines," at least in this world but do continue in other worlds and other dimensions, serving the Plan in many ways unknown to us.

Many are the Names, Many are the Ways

Many of the "Awakened" who became known figures attracted great numbers of followers, and often the followers recorded and analyzed the "teachings" and the life experiences (embellished with myth and enhancements) to develop them into stories and lessons. Many such stories, often with important lessons, are known to us only by means of historic artifacts of such ancient religions and magical practices as those of the Egyptians, the Mayans, the Incas, the ancient pre-Aryan indigenous occupants of the Indus Valley and the Isle of Crete, while others have survived in complex myths such as those of the Norse and the Celts complete with "working tools" (symbols, alphabets, god images and names, songs and gestures, and systems and tools of divination and magick).

"Teachings," and Religions

Certain of the Awakened are known primarily by the "titles" given them by their followers: *the Buddha* and *the Christ*, by which the teachings turned into religions are named; others, where the religions are identified with their personal names of the founders, include: *Zoroastrianism, Confucianism, Manichaeism,* and many lesser known names; still others where the names of those credited as founders have are less identified with the system but known as the historic person, such as *Taoism* with Lao-tzu, *Raja Yoga* with Patanjali; and many more where the system has demonstrated merit beyond that known of its founder. Most of the 4,000 world religions have anonymous origins, and other powerful transformative "systems" (such as pre-religious *Tantra*) are well known through scholarly studies, free of any religious associations or personal identities.

The Awakened States

The awakened states of consciousness have many names: *Ascension, Attainment, Awakening, Buddhahood, Christ Consciousness, Cosmic Consciousness, Enlightenment, God Consciousness, Liberation, Moksha, Rising on the Planes, Salvation, Samadhi, Self-Realization, Super-Consciousness, Transcendence, Union with the Divine, Way of Return,* and others. The methods and techniques themselves vary and the best known mostly reflect the historic achievement of one person, such as the Buddha or the Christ. Then, in most these systems now known as religions, the later followers organized the teaching and associated mythic stories into a unique theology and personality-cult administered and controlled by a hieratic priesthood that subsequently has spent much of their time and effort to denigrate other religions and transformative systems—casting themselves as the "one and only true Way."

Eastern Ways, Western Ways

Interestingly, those systems that came to dominate the Eastern World are truly transformative to the students who adhere to the teachings, while those that dominate the Western World are not, and instead seek to suppress personal transformative experiences to the non-initiated and the followers of competing systems—whether priests, magicians, philosophers, students, or solitary mystics. Some of the solitary mystics were accepted back into the system, declared as *saints* after their death. Some later called saints were never alive as humans but were popular local deities specifically associate with an identifiable function much as were the gods and goddesses of ancient Greece and Egypt.

You Gotta Believe, but—first—You Gotta Belong!

For the Western "seeker," it's not merely a matter of *"You gotta believe!"* but also of *"You gotta belong!"* Under different terms: *Baptism* or *Immersion, Initiation* or *Gradation, Degrees* or *Grades, Certified* and *Recognized, Members* and *Subscribers,* etc. access to whatever was promised by the institution became organized along systems involving the exchange of power or money with the assurance that thus "chosen" you are part of an elite few who will be "saved" or "empowered." Yet, there is no evidence of chosen becoming better, or becoming something "more," demonstrating "powers," or anything other than becoming an "insider." Western Ways lost their Spirit. Training systems suited to Academia, Business, and Professional Practices are not the same as those applied to Spiritual Development.

Different Strokes for Different Folks

There is little uniformity among the transformative systems other than the belief that the human person is something more than a physical entity and that what is in the non-physical is of considerable transforming power and glory such that the one transformed becomes a "Super Person" able to perform miracles of a paranormal nature. Yet, within the mainstream of Western religion there is no encouragement to the individual person to *become more than they are,* and of the many teachers of non-religious transformative systems most will caution their students that the development of paranormal powers is a diversion from the true path of Attainment. In other words, *don't compete with the master!*

The Developmental Map

Others disagree. All intrinsic powers (psychic, mental, spiritual) should be developed and become reliable skills to *fulfill the potential for all you can be* as provided for in the "matrix" that itself is the plan for both personal and species-wide human attainment. That matrix is the map around which each of the individual's bodies is formed following conception as a basic structure of its potentials based on genetic programming and the carry-forward karmic memories from past lives and as planned prior to conception. The structure is formed for each body from causal down through mental, astral, etheric and physical, and then developed within each body as the current life progresses through the natural cycles of growth, maturity, and decline.

From the "Beginning"

Each of the five lower bodies of incarnate lives has seven "sub-levels" mapping both the karmic memories and the matrix of potentials that are the very nature of the particular body itself. To fail to develop the potential is to fail the opportunities provided by life and to ignore the evolutionary program for the development of the Higher Self set in to motion at "the Beginning."

"Beyond" is also More

Beyond the physical body and familiar personality are the non-physical vehicles commonly known as Etheric, Astral, Mental, Causal, Intuitional, Spiritual, Monadic and Divine. Each of these vehicles (or bodies) is composed of the substance of the corresponding cosmic plane (or dimension) and each has its own unique "laws of nature and function." Each cosmic plane is populated with beings—some unique and limited to it, and others able to manifest and function on one or more other dimensions.

The Ways of Growth are Developmental through the Higher Dimensions

What is important to us is that the ways of personal evolution, growth and development are through these upper dimensions by means of consciousness functioning in the coincidental vehicles. All transformative techniques are systematic programs involving the etheric, the astral, and the mental vehicles in their several levels—sometimes specifically, sometimes progressively, and sometimes collectively. With further development, we move on into the causal level where all becomes one. Beyond that there is no need for physical incarnation.

The Great Work—You are Many Splendored

Contrary to some impressions, the object of the Great Work is not your soul but *all that you are* now—and you are all the memories retained within those subtle bodies: etheric, astral, mental and causal, and their functional collectives of the sub-conscious mind, the conscious mind, and the super-conscious mind (otherwise known as the lower self, the middle self, and the higher self). Your real soul is beyond your present conscious incarnating being, and only functions passively to receive and collect the abstract lessons of your many life times. Once you have passed into the upper world, then the Soul will be your only vehicle—*but that lies far beyond anything you can do now!*

Your Assignment—that You must Accept

And, *beyond that which must be your objective now!* Your "assignment" now—that you must not refuse—is the "wholeness" of your being that will be brought to the point of transition between the lower and middle worlds, still below what is called the "Abyss" that eventually must be crossed into the higher world where we *awaken* in the soul. But first we have to leave behind the "garbage" otherwise known as *karma* that clutters the astral and mental bodies together called the "Spirit" to then center consciousness in the causal body which when united is called the "Soul"—although not yet the ultimate individuality also known as the *SOUL*. Your goal for now is to transform and perfect the essential natures of the lower bodies including that of *Intuitive Intelligence* so that you become "master of your own destiny," no longer dependent on others for the knowledge that empowers the Self in daily life.

Self-Empowerment leads to Freedom from Dependence

Please think carefully about all that means: that "independence" is freedom from dependence, but it does not mean you will not interact with other people and other entities. All of creation is composed of "social animals" that do interact and share with one another—not always limited to their species, herd, tribe, or family—but your goal is to become a complete human being in every dimension, a "powerhouse" in your own right, able to meet all your needs free of dependence on consultants, doctors, lawyers, administrators, teachers, preachers, politicians, organizations, churches, covens, lodges, temples, groups of any kind, and—ultimately—even of governments of all kinds and sizes. Yes, a far-off "dream," but it is the goal of human life. Beyond that, we move into a "life" free of the need for incarnation.

You do "take it all with you!"

It is the "whole self," in which the Lower Self has been "alchemically" purified and transformed into the Higher Self in the process the Jungian psychologist refers to as "Integration."

Referring back to that word "transformation," realize that you are in charge of a particular piece of the Cosmos that actually is a "matrix" or "memory pattern" that continues and evolves, incarnation after incarnation, to control the formation of the lower bodies in each life—the physical, etheric, astral, mental, and causal—out of the substances specific to each of those five planes. To become an "integrated whole" you have to purify and transform the lower complex of physical and etheric bodies as well as the middle complex of astral, mental and lower causal bodies, and then unify them into the higher causal body. This is your purpose and your assignment that must be completed before you are ready to call your Holy Guardian Angel, and hold conversation with that entity to prepare to cross the Abyss.

Where do we go from here?

Thus, what we call the Ascension, the Attainment, the Awakening and the Becoming, is what ends the "human" phase of your continuing evolution. But. That's not where we are now, and it is now that we must act with purpose.

The choice is yours. There is no "one way" and that which is right for you is that with which you now most comfortably identify. In this Age, you don't need to join the Church, enter a nunnery or monastery, or abandon family and fortune to fly off to an ashram. You don't need to join a secret order, master a sacred language, dress in expensive robes and buy or make expensive and ornate tools. You don't need rites of initiation, immersions in baptismal pools, undergo painful tests and arduous retreats. If you want these things, do them wisely and sensibly, realizing that they are not necessary but may be helpful if engaged in constructively and without any kind of compulsion.

The Choices are Yours—Seriously!

Anyone telling you that theirs is the only way, or even the best way, is thereby admittedly limited and defective. "Wholeness" means without limitation. Over many lives you have and will have processed many ways, learned many things—and, yes, eventually the many become one but the one does not start as the many.

The choices are yours—as long as you adopt a serious program of study and development. You can learn all you need from books, from classes, from study and practice with or independent of teachers. Choose from Yoga, Martial Arts, Meditation, Tantra, Magick, and Psychic Development; learn self-hypnosis, astral projection, chakra awakening, aura reading, and scrying with a magick mirror. Study, analyze, apply, practice, develop, experiment to understand what you know, grow, and "repeat as necessary." When done with the purpose of growth and development, all techniques count.

What You Do is for You

What you do is for you, not for God or Church, and not for other institutions or in any kind of service to another person—with one exception: working with a life partner is of powerful benefit because it is a form of completion and balancing of *Anima* and *Animus.* Yes, it is true that each person does contain both these archetypes—better understood as *spiritual parts*—and a solitary seeker or striver is not inhibited in the Great Work but still may be somewhat limited or inhibited by the lack of a supportive partner. That we work best in partnership is just a fact of life, but partnerships can take many and multiple forms including parent and child, siblings and life-long friends, one-on-one co-workers or assistants, work and professional relationships, and even human with spirit helpers.

The Most Sacred Relationship

Lucky is the committed couple who find completion with each other. But that is rare and its lack should not inhibit either or both partners working with others in respect to particular studies or interests so long as commitment continue to the heart-felt partners and their partnership. A fully realized committed partnership is the most "sacred" relationship a human can have—at least equal to that between parent and child—and far more so than any commitment to deity or institution or guru of any kind.

To put it "crudely" but logically, an all-powerful God does not need and should not want your help in anything, but religionists will often claim that the deity needs your help—mostly money or some form of servitude—to carry on the good work of converting those of other faiths to theirs, or to support the parochial and biased charitable work better provided by public and professional agencies.

"The Knowledge and Conversation of the Holy Guardian Angel"

The <u>ultimate</u> goal for each person has been called *the attainment of the "Knowledge and Conversation of the Holy Guardian Angel"* (abbreviated as "HGA") sometimes also known as one's Higher Self *experienced as a separate being.* Other names for the HGA include the "Genius" in the Hermetic Order of the Golden Dawn, the "atman" in Hinduism, the "Augoeides" by Iamblichus, and the "Daemon" of the ancient Greek philosophers.

Crossing the "Abyss" ends the Human Stage

Even that Attainment is not the end of the process but it is the end for the pure "humanness" of the seeker. In magickal terms, that next (and last step in purely human terms) is called "crossing the Abyss" and is beyond the purpose of this book.

A Single Journey with many Rest Stops and Side Trips

Like any journey, any process, any "Path," there is a beginning and at least a projected ending. We start from where and who we are and map our journey ahead which may include numerous rest stops and side journeys on to individual paths identified by the techniques involved as steps in the overall process. Even as many guides will proclaim that their path is complete it is more likely that you will move on from one to another—from (only as examples) Hatha Yoga to Tai Chi, on to Tantra, over to High Magick, to Raja Yoga and Meditation with and without form, cleansing the subtle body through Tattvic Visualization, Raising Kundalini through the Chakras while chanting Mantras and visualizing Yantras, and also learning and using the valuable tools of Correspondences (Kabbalistic and Tantric), practicing the Tarot (which is more than just divination), Kabbalistic Path-Working and other Guided Meditations, using various forms of Divination to develop your Psychic Skills, Rising on the Planes (through the Four Worlds of the Kabbalistic Tree of Life), regularly projecting Out-of-Body and communicating with Spiritual Entities.

Some authorities and teachers will insist on not mixing systems, and that's fine if that's where you find "your bliss," but it's not the "Path" but the "Goal" that counts. Keep the Goal as your Life Purpose, and the Path and paths will be parts and means of the *Becoming more than you are, and all you can be.* In other words, your map becomes your Path even to the point of "blazing your own trail."

The "Signs" of the Times Condition the Trip

We've referred to the zodiacal ages as conditioning factors that last approximately 2,200 years each. We're transitioning from the Age of Pisces to the Age of Aquarius. Each age is represented by a symbol that characterizes the broad movements of history and the development of human consciousness during those periods.

Sharing Ideas

Our discussion starts almost 10,000 years ago with the last age symbolized by human images, albeit twin children, the Age of Gemini approximately 6900 to 4700 BCE (Before the Common Era), we had a time when people began sharing ideas. Gemini is an Air Sign, and marked the beginning of written communication, the development of myths and the telling of *stories* suited for young minds. It also was the beginning of recorded history, the recording of observed facts and information for sharing with others, and the exchange of philosophic speculation. It was still a time of nomadic cultures, with people moving with the seasons and migrating animals, to hunt and gather food for sustenance, a time when the Feminine Spirit (the Great Mother Goddess) dominated culture.

Developing Ideas

Next, from approximately 4700 to 2500 BCE we had the Age of Taurus, an Earth Sign symbolized by a Bull, marked with the discovery and development of agriculture, animal husbandry, and Earth Science (mining of minerals, refining of metals, building of structures). Also a time of settling into villages and towns with the ending of nomadic culture. But town and villages needed protection from the remaining nomads and hence fortress walls were built and someone had to be in charge—leading to local chiefs and then on to the time of hereditary kings and a culture increasingly dominated by the Bull-headed Masculine Spirit. It was also a time of building of pyramids and other huge structures.

Imposing Ideas

From 2500 to 300 BCE we have the Age of Aries, a Fire Sign symbolized by the Ram, and marked by wars of conquest and acts of violence (rams butt heads). Villages and Towns became cities within empires, and empires expand their territory through conquest requiring standing armies led by soldier kings and emperors. The culture becomes even more male dominated and religions more "fiery" and expansionist.

Enforcing Ideology

Coming closer to the present, from 300 BCE to approximately 1900 CE (the Common Era), we were in the Age of Pisces, an emotion-ruled Water Sign symbolized by two fish swimming in opposite directions (and hence getting nowhere), and marked by Big Religion and Bigger Wars, by religious persecution and fear. It is the age of exploration by sea and of emotion, with the discovery of the subconscious mind which dominated the final acts of the age—the Holy Inquisition, oly Inquisition,. Hitler and Nazism, Stalin and World Communism, acts of genocide, and mass-minded politics and warfare.

The Age of Ideas—Aquarius, and its Meaning for You and Me

Finally, with the progressive transition (lasting two to four hundred years) into the Age of Aquarius, a Mind-ruled Air Sign symbolized by an androgynous–appearing human person (or Couple) spreading information and intelligence across the earth. While it is far too early in the transition phase to foresee with exactitude, it should be an age of gender equality and the rise of the New Feminine to balance the Old Masculine, of mind-based spirituality rather than emotion-laden religion, of rationality in politics rather than fear-mongering, of science and technology based economics in place of ego-aggrandizing consumerism, of individuality rather than massive special interest supportive organizations, politics of the person and not that of an ideology-driven political party, and a move from geographic empires to a true global culture.

Free Spirit is without Bounds

Speaking of Spirit, the focus is individual and personal and not of organizations promulgating an imposed impersonal theology. Spirit is everywhere, Spirit is fundamental to all existence, but the dynamic is now centered on the evolution of the individual rather than of humanity as another species.

More importantly, what we might call "spiritual science" and hence the practices of spiritual growth and transformation <u>will</u> no longer be dominated by *group dynamics* ranging from organized religion led by ordained clergy, churches led by preachers, magical orders led by priests and priestesses, schools centered around gurus "who-must-be-obeyed," and unquestioned theologies delivered from "masters" on high, to various therapeutic practices centered on group discussions—the "blind leading the blind."

Self-Responsibility, Self-Authority, and Self-Judgment

No, it can't happen overnight, or even next year and perhaps not totally by next century. But the movement from massive organizations toward smaller groups and then down to the level of couples-in-partnership and solitary practitioners is happening now as individuals awaken into greater self-awareness and higher consciousness.

What this means for you is *Self-Responsibility!* All the knowledge and information you need is available to you in print and online, in classes and lectures, and through question-and-answer courses. But, not only must you seek out that information and knowledge, but you must learn to qualify and judge its importance and direct value to you. The responsibility is on you to ask the right questions and seek out the right answers. Your growing Intuitive Mind must recognize "right from wrong."

The Un-Conscious Rises into the Conscious Mind

The intelligent and benevolent human spirit in contrast to bull-headed and ram-butting animals and blindly conflicted fish swimming in opposite directions going nowhere symbolizes the New Age. It is the conscious mind rising above the unconscious, drawing strength from the past but building for the future. Our new curriculums are not dictated absolutes imposed in graded form by "masters" from above and marked by degrees and initiations as rewards for a "good job." You must know yourself, and determine your needs, set your goals, and know that your reward is growth and accomplishment. It's an astonishing concept with many ramifications: political, economic, educational, and social as well as personal and intimate.

Great Size Brings Abuse

Each New Age brings challenges to those who cling to the past. Gone is the era of "Top-down" Dictators and Military Leaders, of Kings and Emperors, Bishops and Popes, Prophets and Masters, of Oracles and Diviners; and gone too is the "too big to fail" giant corporations with their irresponsible and over-compensated CEOs, the huge regulatory agencies run by often incompetent political appointees, the too large lost purpose "non-profit" and non-taxed foundations, the huge untaxed and very profitable Mega Churches, and the educational system that favors sports over academics. Each of the above has a too huge "separation" between producer and beneficiary so that there is no personal connection to remind the distant Executive of *ethics rather than just metrics*. Greed increasingly dominated the last age, and when the perpetrator no longer even sees the victim, the pull of the trigger, the push of the button, or the signing of the order is merely the execution of the mission for which no one is responsible.

Great Power Corrupts

With Power there is always potential for abuse, but when "distance" is diminished, judgment is immediate and personal—there is *no passing the buck*. No orders from above, no dictates by policy, no voices in the dark, no divine orders, no word of god ordering death to unbelievers. You're on your own, and new technologies will enable smallness to replace bigness with even greater intimacy between giver and receiver, and person-to-person transactions will replace ignorance of consequences with face-to-face awareness.

Without awareness of the consequences for your decisions and actions, there can be no growth. You cannot live in a cave and simply dream your way to saint-hood. The world is multi-dimensional and each dimension brings its own obligations and opportunities for growth. Self-Knowledge and Awareness show you the ways you must take provided you look for them with your eyes wide-open. Your journey is yours alone, but the ways are well-traveled and well-marked. You benefit from all who have gone before.

Everything NEW builds—one way or another—on the PAST

Sometime we see error in the past and have to correct for it as we build for the future. Other times we can adapt from past procedures to meet the needs of the new conditions and ways of today and the foreseeable future. When—as we are now—in a time of radical transition we have to draw upon the past but make our own decisions based on our own understanding of new directions to take.

Old ways die hard. We can see the building conflicts in the Big Religions, Big Governments, Big Academia, Big Institutions, Big Business, and more—but what is important to us in our personal growth program is the realization that the old religious rituals, those of ceremonial magick, and even of the reconstructions of Pagan rituals reflect much that is unnecessary, undesirable, and often intentional obfuscation of the Piscean spirit in which our goals are lost in the fuss over garments and gestures, expensive religious edifices and costly ceremonial implements, invented words drawn from antique languages, intentional dependencies on hierarchal leaders—all of which are contrary and negating to the Aquarian Spirit.

Our challenge is to work with others without "choosing sides" and succumbing to dependency on a new leader. Each group participant—when you choose that route—still must be their own guide, accept full responsibility for their actions and choices while contributing to the growth and success of others. It's the "spirit of the household" in which all give and receive, help and accept help, where love is a two-way thoroughfare. If you are to grow and become "more" you have to stop depending on others. Move onward to a higher dimension of Spirit and your Higher Consciousness, communicate with your Higher Self, listen to your Intuitive Mind, and discover your True Will. These are not empty phrases, but real challenges to overcome the Past and welcome the Future.

Of course there is great value in techniques and programs from those great, mostly nameless pioneers whose practices and systems were at the source of pre-religious esoteric wisdom. Our need is to simplify those old ways back to their pure essence for effective spiritual experience. We have mostly adapted from models based on the Kabbalah and Tantra—the core wisdom of East and West. Most will be familiar to students of both, and it is that key familiarity of terms and systems, symbols and images that opens the doors to the perennial wisdom that is both ancient and still living.

In the techniques that follow, we have attempted to do that, but it is up to you not to merely follow the formula but to directly <u>experience each step of the way</u> *under your own authority. That's what we are trying to accomplish in this work of <u>Becoming More</u>*

than You Are. As you continue the work, you may intuit the need for some specific modification to meet your own changing needs as you grow—but be careful in staying within the established *intent* of the programs. Focus on Intention, and do not be distracted by people creating proprietary systems for personal gain.

With this objective in mind, we can establish a basic formula for

THE WAY OF ATTAINMENT

Your True Will, Your True Path, Your True Love

1. The discovery of your True Will. It starts with your acknowledgment of Purpose, supporting it with thought and feeling, and <u>calling</u> to your Highest Self. You won't "hear" an answer, but your Intention is to align yourself with the Highest Aspiration.

2. The discovery of your True Path. With the recognition of Life Purpose your Path unfolds before you. Keep your focus. Avoid distractions from you goal.

3. The discovery of your True Love. Even though we have Love Partners, your True Love is for your Higher Self that is part of your Incarnating Self.

4. *Energize!* Practice techniques to keep your enthusiasm high and methods to increase your energy. Recognize that your health is both necessary and a commitment to keeping your True Will.

5. *Invoke often!* Invoke Gods, Goddesses, Angels, and other Higher Beings (never lesser ones than yourself). Each will strengthen and purify corresponding elements in your astral, mental, and spiritual bodies. Reach higher and higher, but don't neglect who and where you are now on the True Path. You can't skip the steps in between.

6. Sing Praises to your Holy Guardian Angel. Develop your "magickal voice," vibrating it with power. Even if you think your voice is horrible, sing and it will become a communication between you and your Angel. Find Words of Power, Mantras, and Magickal Invocations that express your True Love of your Higher Self that you are becoming.

THE ASTRAL ROOM

Ritual for Establishing Your Astral Room & Work Place

We all need a distinct "work shop" no matter what kind of work we're doing. It is a place—even if created solely in your imagination—set aside to be free from disturbance and conflict. If possible, utilize actual physical space even on a limited occasional basis, and make it private and personal—*it is not a "public temple."* It is where you can locate your psychic, divinatory, magickal, and spiritual tools to keep them separate from contact with other people. Put your tools away when not in use; put your journal under cover; keep your thoughts and feelings focused on your magickal and spiritual work. Your Astral Room is a reflection of your highest goals, so keep it free of day dreams, fantasies, and worries. It's a place for meditation and visualization, but not for sleeping or the reading of books not related to the "work."

The Astral World where Spirits Live

The astral world is where spirits live, and it's more than right next door because it truly "connects" via your mind even though it may be founded in a physical room even as it is also beyond your mind as part of the Greater Universe that is all inclusive. The "mental" images that you create are made of astral substance and are part of the astral world, but they are also *your* astral images and just as with computer software you can create a "firewall" to control what entities can enter into your astral room. Visualize the walls, floor and ceiling in that uniquely blue color characteristic of electrical sparks. It is the "Astral Light," and your *intention* charges it as a psychic shield against all uninvited entities.

Establishing Your Astral Room and Work Place

And it is here, in your astral room, that you create the special environment favorable to your astral work and where your divinatory, your mediumistic, your magical and your spiritual activities take place. It is the place for your clairvoyance, and other paranormal actions. It is your psychic lab and workshop.

Note, it's your astral room and only you can create it. And here's how.*

* Some of the wording and the ideas that follow are developed from Donald Tyson's excellent *Scrying for Beginners—Tapping into the Supersensory Powers of Your Subconscious,* 1997, Llewellyn

Always remember that an astral room is not limited by *physical* space, and yet your room is centered in your space. The Greater Universe is infinite in all directions and dimensions—as a result its center is everywhere and anywhere you want it. But because you, yourself, are anchored in your physical body, the center of your astral room is your center and it's geometric center and boundaries are limitless but nevertheless defined by you to control access to your room. And even as it may be founded in a physical space, it is like a tablet computer working from "cloud-based" software and memory: you can take it with you. Wherever you may be physically, you can center yourself and create a *simulacrum* of your "home base" Astral Room.

We start with establishing the infinite extension and the place of the geometric center:

1. Standing (or sitting) in what is or will be your work room, extend your arms straight out from the sides and know* that a straight line continues from each hand to the "infinite no-ends" of the universe.

2. From the point in your body where that line changes from left to right, know that a vertical line extend up through your head and down through your feet to the "infinite no-ends" of the universe.

3. From that same point in your body, know that a line extending forward and another backward to the "infinite no-ends" of the universe.

Now know that those three infinite lines become three infinite *planes* and where they intersect at the center of your body you will visualize a *globe* of white, pulsing light becoming larger and larger to become infinite, but within that infinite globe is your personal globe just comfortably enclosing your work room. *See this personal globe become a translucent silvery demarcation of your personal space from infinite space, a demarcation of your consciousness from the universal consciousness, a demarcation of your spirit from the infinite Holy Spirit.***

* Know. The way we use this familiar word is crammed with special meaning. To know is an *action* use of the verb to establish the object as *real* in the subtle dimensions of Astral (feeling), Mental (knowing), and Causal (willing). It is the same concept connoted by "Visualization" but with the added power of *Will* which changes potential into actual at all levels.

** This Holy Spirit is not identified with that of the Roman Catholic Church or other Christian or Abrahamic religions. Rather, it is the impersonal Universal Spirit permeating all dimensions of the Cosmos at the Highest Level from which all other elements and powers are derived.

Your Astral Room is the psychic space you control, into which you can admit spiritual entities as you wish, but not those whose intentions are out of harmony with yours. It is multi-level psychic space where action leads to completion from one level to the next, in all five lower dimensions.

Working with Intention

The firm declaration of Intention *charges* "potential" with the capacity to b*ecome* that described *in the specific declaration.* It is a statement that "means more than mere words."

The Declaration of Intent to Establish

Say these words, and feel them reaching to the infinite no-ends of the Universe:

> By my act of will, I establish this sacred space.
> The Light of Spirit* creates it.
> The Fire of *Spirit* surrounds it.
> The Air of *Spirit* expands it.
> The Water of *Spirit* cleanses it
> The Earth of *Spirit* sustains it.

> * Spirit is the core element (Tattva) in Eastern Tantra and Western Alchemy from which the other elements are derived. Spirit empowers the Elements, and exists in all things.

Within this silvery globe are the astral reflections of your physical room, furniture and tools. It is now your job to carefully and thoroughly examine the walls, ceiling and floor of the room and each one of the objects and commit their feature to your memory. Then close your eyes and re-create it all in your visual memory. One by one, check and verify the accuracy of your vision, and repeat until you can accurately and knowingly see only the astral reproductions within which the physical ones are mere shadows.

Next you should choose a scent, either an incense or an essential oil, and memorize that scent so that you can reproduce it astrally to purify both the physical room and the astral room. Whether working in ritual, or inducing an altered state through trance, use the astral and physical scent to purify the atmosphere of your astral room and establish it as your private domain where only the "invited" gain entrance. *Do not use that scent for other purposes! Do not wear the scent, and do not "generalize" it other rooms in your home.*

Finally, you can also establish guardians at the six spherical power points of your personal globe corresponding, roughly equivalent of the four quarters and above and below as matched with the reach of the human body on the six-pointed star as illustrated here. Know that you, yourself, are the Seventh Point around which the Six Points are located.

The six-pointed star of completion.

The Question of Security

Just as the Personal Globe can go wherever you go, so can the recreated Astral Room. At the same time there is value in adding to the security of the physical room that is the foundation of your Astral Room. The Astral Room's security against negative energies and entities is entirely dependent on your Strength and the Detail of your Visualization. If you have done a good job, nothing more is necessary. Yet, there is value beyond that of pure security to adding Guardians at the four quarters and those points representing Earth and Sky. Note: In this situation, there are only Six Guardians at the external points.

RITUAL FORMING THE QABALISTIC CROSS

A tried and true traditional method for opening and closing sacred space comes from the Magician's "tool box." In most of the programs and "rituals" that follow, you (sometimes called "the Magician") can carry out the action physically, or imaginatively. There are certain advantages to both, but if you do the physical actions do them imaginatively as well just as you did in creating your Astral Room. *Many practicing magicians overlook this.*

When ritual actions are physical only and without imaginative awareness, the astral thought forms lack the same strength as when consciously imagined. One way to understand this is to realize that *we live <u>on</u> physical Earth but with conscious enactment we move and speak <u>in</u> all five of the lower dimensions.*

We want to act and live <u>fully,</u> not partially. That means to act and react physically and also consciously with feeling, vision, and purpose in full awareness of intention and consequences.

The Lesser Ritual of the Pentagram
Part One: Creating the Qabalistic Cross

<u>Introduction.</u> The *Living Light** of the inner planes is key to our development of "forms" for our particular functioning on the astral and higher planes. This exercise and those that follow function to awaken particular psychic centers and sensitivities before proceeding to the later procedure to form your own Body of Light. The techniques are an ideal method of equilibrating the personality and raising the mind to the contemplation of "the higher mysteries."

The words employed are Hebrew because this particular magical system evolved from the Qabalah. We've provided their meaning, but you should only pronounce the Hebrew, and rather than "speaking," you want to *vibrate* the words syllable by syllable, centering your voice at the back of the mouth and at a pitch slightly lower than normal, while feeling and visioning** the sound projecting forth to the far reaches of the universe.

> * This "Living Light" is an aspect of astral and mental plane substance we intentionally visualize as *focused* and *concentrated* "electric blue **"pulsating** Astral Light. Almost all magickal and paranormal phenomenon occur in this astral substance also call "astral light." The difference between paranormal and magickal is that between passive experience of phenomenon and active, intentional, focus of will and visualization of the desired goal to knowingly bring about its accomplishment.

> ** "Visioning" is something more than just imagining and visualizing something as already accomplished. In "visioning," we see the *process as it is happening*—in this case

it is of the vibrating sound moving through space to fulfill that which is the subject of the image.

1. Stand in a comfortable position, feet together, at the center of an imagined circle itself at the center of your Astral Room. Face East. Take a few breaths to make yourself relaxed and receptive. Bring both hands upward in a wide sweeping movement to your brow and place the palms facing inward, the fingers just touching. Vibrate the word *A-TOH* (meaning "Thou art")

2. Visualize White Light descending to form a sphere of white brilliance above the crown of your head.

3. Lower your Hands, still together, to your chest over the heart centre. Vibrate the word *MAL-KUTH* (meaning the Kingdom). Visualize a beam of Light extending downward from your crown centre through your heart centre and continuing to the center of the Earth.

4. Drop your right hand, palm inward, and place it just over the Solar Centre. Raise your left hand to touch your right shoulder with the finger tips. Vibrate the words *VE-GE-VUR-AH* (the Power). Visualize a beam of Light extending to the ends of the Universe from below your right shoulder.

5. Drop you left hand, palm inward, and place it just over the Solar Centre while raising the right hand to touch the your left shoulder with the finger tips. Vibrates the words *VE-GE-DUL-AH* (and the Glory). Visualize a beam of Light extending to the ends of the Universe from below your left shoulder.

6. Cross both arms over your chest, fingers touching the shoulders. Vibrate the word *LE-OLAHM* (for ever and ever).

7. Clasp both hands, one over the other, firmly over your heart centre. Vibrate *AMEN*. See yourself at the center of a great cross of white light.

You have formed the Qabalistic Cross.

Part Two: Ritual Forming the Pentagrams Ritual for Creating & Energizing the Magick Circle

8. Still standing, facing east, form a "wand" with the first two fingers of your right hand, and draw a human-size *banishing pentagram* of Earth in the air before you. Begin the pentagram from outside your left hip, then up to a point that is level with the top of your head, and down to outside the right hip. Then straight

up diagonally across to outside of your left shoulder, and horizontally straight across to outside your right shoulder, and then down and across to the point of beginning. The two lower points are roughly outside the left and right hips, the apex level with the crown of your head, the other two points outside the left and right shoulders. See the pentagram **burning** and **flaming** before you. Bring the point of your "wand" to the center, project energy as if you are "stabbing" it, and vibrate the Divine Name **YOD-HE-VAU-HE**. See the Pentagram become even more energized—not merely "glowing," but **flaming** and **vibrating** with power.

9. Continue to hold your arm and hand extended as you rotate for the entire Circle back to the starting point. *Do not lower the power point wand of your two fingers throughout the ritual.* You are *visualizing* and *energizing* the Magick Circle of Light, with the fiery **Banishing Pentagrams** marking each quarter.

10. Turn 90° to your right to face South, draw another **Banishing Pentagram** and "stab" it in its center while vibrating **A-DO-NAI**.

11. Again turn 90° to your right, keeping your arm straight, to face West. Draw the **Banishing Pentagram**, stab it, and vibrate **E-HEI-EH**.

12. Again turn 90° to your right, keeping your arm straight, to face North. Draw the **Banishing Pentagram**, stab it, and vibrate **A-GL-A**.

13. Complete the circle to face East and stand in the **Tau Posture**, arms extended so as to make a T-cross with the whole body, palms upward. You should now see a circle of brilliant light around you, studded with four bright flaming pentagram stars.

Part Three: Ritual Evocation of the Archangel Guardians In the Six–Rayed Star

14. Standing in the Tau Posture (thus forming the "column" later mentioned), facing East, as described in No. 13 above, Speak forcefully and vibrate the divine names of the Archangels: Before me **RAH-FAH-EL**, behind me **GAH-BREE-EL** on my right hand **MEE-KAH-EL**, on my left hand **OR-EE-EL**. For about me flames the pentagram, and in the column stands the six-rayed star!

15. See the archangels clearly, standing before their Pentagrams. *Raphael* wears robes of yellow and violet, while golden rays of the **Air element** pour through the pentagram from the East.

16. See *Michael* in robes of scarlet and emerald, while red rays of the **Fire element** pour through the pentagram from the South.

17. See *Gabriel* in robes of blue and orange, while the blue rays of **Water element** pour through the pentagram from the West.

18. See *Auriel* in robes of citrine, olive, russet, and black, while the green rays of the **Earth element** pour through the pentagram from the North.

19. See yourself surrounded by a circle of ***pulsating*** light studded with four ***flaming*** pentagrams, with the Archangels (standing very tall and towering) guarding the quarters. Above you and below you appears the ***six-rayed star***, the golden hexagram.* It is the floor and roof of the palace for the Indwelling Spirit that you have built.

* Note, however, that the hexagram is actually two triangles—one point up and male, the other point down and female.

20. Repeat the Qabalistic Cross as at the beginning.

21. After mastery of this ritual, you can go one step further by visualizing the Hebrew names in the actual Hebrew letters as in the table below. The important

need is to see those letters as composed of *FIRE*. They *flame* in constant *vibratory* movement in direct response to the spoken words.

Stand in the center of the place of working, or as nearly the center as the arrangement of the chamber will allow.*

i.   Facing East, assume the Want Posture. Vibrate אתה

ii.   Raise the arms at the side, vibrate מלכות

iii.   Touch the right shoulder with the left hand, vibrate וגבודה

iv.   Touch the left shoulder with the right hand, vibrate וגדולה

v.   Keeping the arms crossed, bow the head and vibrate לצולמועך

vi.   Advance to the East. Beginning at the point and retruning thereto, move widdershins round the place of working, with hand outstretched tracing the circle.

vii.   After completing the circle, return to the center. Facing East, make the Gesture Cervus: at the first point vibrate אהית at the second יהות

viii.   Turn to face North: make the Gesture, vibrating אגלא at the first point, אדני at the second.

ix.   Face West: make the Gesture, vibrating אגלא, then אל.

x.   Turn to face South. Make the Gesture, vibrating אהיה and אלהים.

*If the Bomos is stationed at the center of the place of working, begin Eat of Bomos.

In Summary

With the Qabalistic Cross, you have invoked the divine presence into your heart, mind and body, and then placed yourself at the center of the *spiritual replicate* of the Universe. You have cleansed the four quarters of this replicate Universe with pentagrams of fire, affirming that Man is mirror of the Divine Image, Microcosm to Macrocosm, and hence with the ability to control the elements through spirit.

The deity names are *visioned* as <u>thundering</u> through "Greater Space"* to the Ends of the Universe and back again. *Your* Magical Universe is thus defined by the circle of light.

* "Greater Space" describes Space that is not empty but filled with potential. It is also the *Chaos* from which *Order* emerges, the *Spirit* from which all the other *Elements* emerge. It is the *Nothing* from which *Everything* emerges. It's the *Pre-manifest*" from which *Manifestation*" emerges.

The drawing of the four pentagrams automatically invokes spirit, the fifth point, and so raises the microcosmic consciousness to the level of the macrocosm, having completely sealed the circle against the Outer Darkness.

The column is the shape of the space created by the circle extending vertically above and below the magician. The construction of the circle banishes the four Elements and thus the column is the Element of Spirit extending into the infinite above and the infinite below.

* The *Centre* is both an alternate spelling of "Center" and a word with a distinct meaning of its own as used here. Used descriptively as in "at the center of the circle" it merely establishes a geometric point. As used here, it is the name of a psychic organ, the *Heart Centre,* and does not refer to "the center of your physical heart" organ. Nor does the metaphysical phrase, "the *Centre* of your being" refer to any obscure geometric point in whatever may be your "being." As a metaphysical phrase, "the Centre of your being" is a symbolic reference to the "core" of your "essence," and is not something that can be defined in reference to anything that is *physical.*

"Metaphysics" is *beyond* or *above* physics, hence the non-physical dimensions in general. However, this is a good opportunity to point out a common religious abuse of the word "Spiritual" wherein religionists proclaim they are *above* physical laws including those of Natural Science" and those of "the People" as administered by Government and the Courts. and that the church is not bound by the Constitution.

RITUAL FOR THE AMERICAN MIDDLE PILLAR & AURIC ENERGIZER (Also known as the Ritual for Activating the Six Centres on the Body)

Introduction. This is, in many ways, one of the more complex procedures described in this book because you need to memorize and visualize the various items listed in the following tables before the actual exercise is undertaken. It is also one of the more interesting procedures bridging from the older magical training practices of the Western Magickal Tradition to a blending with the Eastern Tantric Tradition utilizing the Chakra system.

Do not be concerned with this usage of six psychic centres in contrast to the usual seven chakras familiar to Eastern systems. Each has its own purpose.

While the basic exercise has been part of the training program of the Hermetic Order of the Golden Dawn, the Aurum Solis program given here uses American imagery and names in Latin rather than Hebrew. Thus it is more New Age, reflecting the incoming influence of Aquarian energies and a more global feeling in contrast to the old Middle Eastern heritage of the Hebrew language and imagery.

The psychic Centres are truly psychic (non-physical) and located in the Etheric Double but their positions are associated with areas of the physical body, and their nature symbolically reflects the associated physical organs.

Note, also, that this is an exercise that can be undertaken individually or in group practice as a fundamental ritual of unification among the participants. The ideal procedure is for the High Priest or Priestess (or solitary practitioner) to open with the three parts of the Qabalistic Cross, and then to follow or lead in the American Middle Pillar & Auric Energizer Procedure. Sometimes the leader will follow with a group practice called "The Blessing of the Land" which can encompass any area from local to global in size.

Psychic Centres: Locations, Names & Sephirothic Correspondences

Location	Name*	Sephiroth
1—Above the Crown of the Head	*Magnus Spiritus*	Cosmic Centre, Kether
2—Brow, between the Eyes	*Mater Stellarum*	Control Centre, Binah/Chokmah
3—Throat	*Puer Maris*	Bridge Centre, Daath
4—Heart	*Aquilla Bellatrix*	Sun Centre, Tiphareth
5—Genital area	*Alba Domina*	Moon Centre, Yesod
6—Feet together, at the insteps	*Mater Libertas*	Earth Centre, Malkuth

The language used for the psychic Centres is not important in itself. Hebrew and Greek are often preferred because of long usage as "sacred languages" and the ease of numerical associations in Qabalistic practice. Latin was used here because of its basic familiarity to English language speakers and yet it is not "common" to them and hence it has more *magical*, or sacred, potency than would plain, ordinary English. And, of course, Latin was long the sacred language used by the Catholic Church, adding that potency as well.

Yet, as even in the American Catholic Church where the use of Latin has increasingly been discontinued, there is New Age value to open understanding of all that is spoken in common language. The ritual use of a "foreign" language puts distance between the priestly functionary (the acting leader) and the group participants. Distance reduces communication whether common or spiritual, and reduces the group to the level of a mere herd of childish lambs to be guided by the Bishop's Crook. Hardly desirable to this New Age of classless democracy and open communication among intelligent people!

There is also the value of familiarity with the language as we associate the words with actual American images, as in the table below:

Psychic Centres: Names & Associated Images

Psychic Center Name	Common Name & Associated Image
1—*Magnus Spiritus*	"Great Spirit"—the 'Manitou,' Sky Father
2—*Mater Stellarum*	"Mother of the Stars"—the Star Goddess
3—*Puer Maris*	"Child of the Waters"—the Child of Potential
4—*Aquilla Bellatrix*	"Warrior Eagle"—the American Bald Eagle
5—*Alba Domina*	"White Lady"—the Moon Goddess
6—*Mater Libertas*	"Mother Liberty"—the Earth Mother

These images are not the same as the particular symbols to be associated with the body locations of the psychic Centres themselves, which will be given next. However, these images should be sensed appearing in front of you as if "invoked" by the names used as *sacred names of power.* The images should appear facing the same direction as you are for *they are part of you.*

A note on pronunciation of these names for they each invoke a particular vibration that should be felt in the associated body area. In each case you want to break the words down into syllables, and—giving each syllable the same weight—*chant* each syllable the same length of time. Always take a full and deep breath before pronouncing the name, and try to be at the end of that breath as you complete the word/phrase. As you speak the name, you want to *vibrate*** each syllable in a tone that is slightly lower than your normal speaking voice.

** Vibration is accomplished by a 'quiver' at the back of the throat to energize the word.

The Psychic Centres themselves are not to be visualized as images or symbols, but rather as colored spheres of intense light, each about one and one/half inches in diameter, located—as indicated—either as a full sphere external to the body, or as a half sphere partially within the body and partially projecting out in front of the body. Nevertheless, you know and feel the half sphere as a whole one—the other half being internal. The actual Centre should be perceived as glowing as colored light.

Psychic Centres: Names, Locations, & Colors

Name	Location	Color
Magnus Spiritus	1—Sphere—six inches above head	Intense White light
Mater Stellarum	2—Half sphere—center of brow	Pearl Grey
Puer Maris	3—Sphere—just in front of throat	Purple
Aquilla Bellatrix	4—Half sphere—center of chest	Yellow/Gold
Alba Domina	5—Half sphere—genital area	Lavender/Violet
Mater Libertas	6—Sphere—at feet, half below ground, half above ground.	Rainbow of Colors

The Centres are to be activated sequentially from just above the crown of the head down to just below the feet. As they are activated, a beam—or pillar—of white light is to be seen and felt to descend from above the head down through the center of the body and just into the earth at the feet. This "Middle Pillar" descends sequentially to the point corresponding to the area of the Centre being activated, and remains there while you are vibrating the name of that Centre (which responds in size and brilliance), and then descends further as you proceed to the next Centre in the sequence.

Once completed, the Middle Pillar is to be seen and felt to have circulation both upward and downward as it connects the Heaven and Earth poles of the human electrical circuit. The pillar of vibrating light simultaneously descends from above the Crown to below the Feet through the center column in the body following the spine and rises upward to "fountain out" and descend through the outer aura back to the feet and in to rejoin the rising pillar. This is further described in steps 13, 14, and 15 below.

There is one more set of correlations we would like to provide for these six Centres that will illustrate the further possibilities inherent in the system. These are familiar American symbols with very powerful energies attached to them.

Psychic Centres: Names, Symbols, & Elucidations

Name	Symbol	Elucidation
Magnus Spiritus	A Spirit Power in the Sky	Possibly "Uncle Sam" might be associated here, but it would seem more appropriate to have a stern "presidential" head in clouds.
Mater Stellarum	The Star Spangled Banner, or a woman soldier with flag leading troops into battle.	Could also be thought of as the Egyptian sky goddess, Nuit.
Puer Maris	The embryo shown at the end of the "2001" sci-fi movie.	New Beginnings
Aquilla Bellatrix	The American Bald Eagle.	Great strength and far vision.
Alba Domina	Woman in white robes reclining on a crescent moon	A Huntress. Woman of allure. Woman as Lover.
Mater Libertas	Earth Goddess in the form of the Statute of Liberty.	Earth Mother is always pictured showing benevolence and concern.

THE SIX PSYCHIC CENTRES ON THE BODY

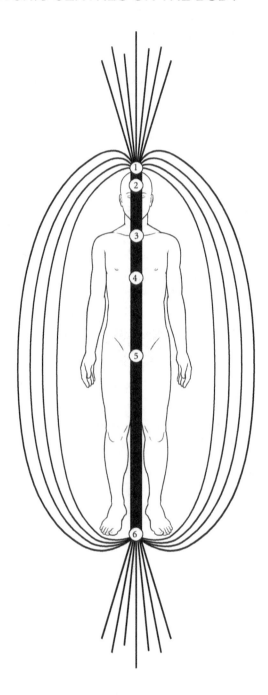

Now that you have the "picture" and all the instructions, let's do the exercise step-by-step.

The American Middle Pillar Exercise

1. Form the mental image of a sphere above the Crown of the head in intense white light. *See it, feel it, hold it!* Take a deep breath and vibrate **Mag-nus Spir-it-us** as you exhale. Inhale and reform or reinforce the sphere and vibrate the name again. Repeat a third time. As you vibrate the names, feel the Centre itself vibrating. In your mind's eye, see it vibrating. Feel the power in the Centre.

2. Upon an exhalation, see the Middle Pillar of white light descend from the Crown Centre to the level of the Brow Centre. See it, feel it, and continue to hold it there.

3. Form the image of the sphere of pearl gray light in the Brow Centre—half in and half out. *See it, feel it, hold it!* Take a deep breath and vibrate the name **Ma-ter Stell-ar-um** as you exhale. As you inhale, reform and reinforce the sphere of light at the Brow Centre, and then again vibrate the name for a total of three times.

4. On an exhalation, bring the Middle Pillar down to the throat level.

5. Form the Throat Centre sphere in purple—totally outside just in front of the throat as indicated. *See it, feel it, hold it!* Vibrate the name, **Pu-er Mar-is.** Repeat as previously for a total of three times.

6. Bring the Middle Pillar down to the Heart Centre as previously instructed.

7. Form the Heart Centre sphere in yellow/gold in the center of the chest. *See it, feel it, hold it!* Vibrate its name, **A-Quil-lah Bel-la-trix,** three times as previously instructed.

8. Bring the Middle Pillar down to the Genital Centre as previously instructed.

9. Form the Genital Centre sphere in lavender/violet in the genital area. *See it, feel it, hold it!* Vibrate its name, **Al-ba Dom-in-a**, three times as previously instructed.

10. Bring the Middle Pillar down to the Feet Centre as previously instructed.

11. Form the Feet Centre sphere in a spinning rainbow of colors in the insteps. *See it, feel it, hold it!* Vibrate its name, **Ma-ter Li-ber-tas**, three times as previously instructed.

12. Finish at the Earth Centre between the feet, and see the Middle Pillar extending as a column of white light and vibrating energy from just below the feet up through the center of the body and out the top of the head.

13. Now, as you inhale your breath, see and feel energy rise up the Middle Pillar from just below the feet to 'fountain out' just above the head as you exhale. See light descending from above your head to join that from your Middle Pillar, flowing down on all sides of the body to sweep back in at the feet so that you have an egg-shaped oblong sphere around you. *See it, feel it, hold it!*

14. Again inhale, see and feel more energy from the earth rising up the Middle Pillar adding more and more strength to the power you are circulating. Likewise, see and feel more energy and light added at the crown as you start each exhalation.

15. Circulate the light and energy up the Middle Pillar and out and down the egg-shaped aura for as long as you can feel energy still being added to the circuit you have developed. Make this such a positive image that you can form the aura about you at any time without going through the whole exercise.

A Daily Morning Ritual

Repeat daily: If working alone, you can end the exercise at this point, but it should be practiced daily, preferably as a morning ritual.

Ritual for Unifying & Empowering a Group

If you are working with a group of individuals, each doing the Middle Pillar together in concert following the pattern as set by a leader, you can now bring the individuals together in a circle, arms joined shoulder to shoulder or hand to hand as you prefer, and form a single Middle Pillar at the circle's center for the entire group and a common aura about the group. Raise energy from the common Earth Centre of the group Middle Pillar to fountain above at the Sky Centre of the group and, to join both with the descending light down though the center pillar and with that fountaining out from above to flow down the group's outer aura and back in at the Earth Centre.

Ritual for a Group Blessing of the Earth

Upon common agreement, you can change the direction of the circulating energy from vertical to horizontal moving clockwise around the group, expanding the circulating group aura outward to the far horizons of locale, region, nation, and the world as desired.

See the far horizons in the mind's eye, and pour blessings upon the Earth as if rain falling upon parched soil. Continue for as long as you feel comfortable, and then bring the aura back to the group, identify with the Middle Pillar of the group, and then separate and re-identify with your personal Middle Pillar and aura, and then close down.

Ritual for Exercising the Power of the Group Mind

It is possible for the group leader to visualize the entire exercise without the members being together if the group is firmly established and the members have given their individual permission. It's better if those members know of the Leader's plan so they can participate in absentia. This will be more completely treated in a separate book on the Group Mind.

Ritual for Establishing the Group Mind of the Intimate Couple

The exercise can also be modified for use by an intimate couple in a procedure basically like that for the group. Standing face to face, arms on each other's shoulders, with the Middle Pillar visualized between you and a single aura around you, circulate the energies as before, first vertically and then horizontally. You can expand your joint aura to encompass family, home, the entire home property, a family business, and your financial estate. You may want to relate this back to the discussion in Chapter 10 ½ of our book, *Astral Projection for Psychic Empowerment*. This will be more completely treated at a future date in a separate book for the Intimate Couple.

It is possible to perform the Middle Pillar exercise for the Intimate Couple even when they are separated by distance, visualizing each other and circulating the energies as if the visualized person was present. It does not require the other person to do the visualized exercise simultaneously but is desirable that each know that the other partner may do it, particularly if the separation will be lengthy, as in the case of military assignments.

Here the benefit is not only for the strength of the partnership but a re-enforcement of distant partner's personal strength and spiritual resources "under fire."

Ritual for Establishing the Group Mind before Sexual Union

You can also modify the Middle Pillar for the Intimate Couple prior to sexual union. After building the Middle Pillar and Aura separately, standing face to face, come together as above with the Middle Pillar visualized between you, your arms on each other's shoulders, circulate the energies vertically, and then the male should focus on the Brow Centre and project energy to her Brow Centre. She receives it and brings it down through her spinal column to her Sex Centre where she projects it to his Sex Centre. He brings it up through his spinal column to his Brow Centre, and projects it to hers as before. Repeat as long as desired, and then complete with sexual union.

Grounding

It is desirable to end the exercise, whether group, couple or solitary, with some positive act of body consciousness such as stamping your feet on the ground, shaking your hands, calling out "It is finished!" or having a long drink of water.

Visualizing Images with "your mind's eye"

A major value in the Middle Pillar and Group Mind exercise is the expansion of consciousness that comes with expansion of the aura. In that sense it's similar to other exercises that train the physical senses, that strengthen and stretch muscles, and that train your ability to observe and remember scenes in your imagination along with the ability to accurately visualize images with "your mind's eye."

And Remote Viewing

It is also interesting to reach out with your aura to any specific location to observe activities as in remote viewing.

And Psychic Empowerment

There are many other variations that can be practiced as you gain experience, remembering that you are—particularly as practiced regularly by yourself—increasing your psychic sensitivity and developing your Super-Conscious Mind. You can, for example, center your awareness on any particular Psychic Centre and *feel* it for its own power and character. This is particularly of value in connection with the Brow Centre. Learn to feel the "space" that is back of the eyes, see that space fill with "light," learn to project light out from the Centre, etc. Each Centre has its own Power, and as each is activated this power becomes yours in expanded skills. Because you are working within a balanced exercise, you need not be concerned with any danger of "ego inflation" or coming into contact with forces you can't handle.

Wait—there's more to come!
The combined Middle Pillar and Group Exercise is a powerful developmental program for the Group Mind which will be treated in full in a future book in this series.

In Limitation, there is Strength, not Weakness
But note: While there is great value in groups of individuals coming together in this manner for specific defined projects, there are hazards to avoid. Even if all, or most of the participants repeat, *do not make the error of continuity* regardless of the specific purpose. Dedicate one group for this operation, another group for that operation, etc. Give each such group a separate name and defined "charter" that is very specific as to the singular purpose of the group's operation. *Do not make the mistake of "Bigness for Bigness sake"* which will dilute the strength of purpose and lead to ego inflation and bureaucratic weakness.

Note: This and additional procedures may be found in complete detail in *Astral Projection for Psychic Empowerment—The Out-of-Body Experience, Astral Powers, and their Practical Application,* 2012, Llewellyn, by Joe H. Slate, Ph.D. & Carl Llewellyn Weschcke.

Ritual Invoking Your Holy Guardian Angel
This is only a small step towards establishing your relationship with the HGA. But, a Beginning is a Beginning, and once the door is opened, more will follow. This is true for all serious work whether "exterior" or "interior." It is one of the great mysteries for which many theories have been offered, but we can think of it as each strong action modifies brain or some psychic circuitry so that it acts like a broadcast antenna to attract similar ideas. It is, as we just wrote, when a particular door is opened to an invited guest idea, a crowd will follow.

The Theory

First, we do need to discuss who, or what, is the Holy Guardian Angel. As for answers, there are so many traditional ones framed in the personal experiences of many, many people that we will simply offer two variations on a single theme.

1. The HGA, as it is commonly abbreviated, is an external spiritual aspect of oneself that *may* choose to act as a guide to further knowledge and to your development.
2. Instead, The HGA is your Higher Self acting as an external entity that on your request or particular need offers guidance both as inspiration or in direct response to questions.

In either case, the HGA is addressed as a separate entity to establish the communication as objective and authoritative. In addition, whether as the Holy Guardian Angel or the Higher Self, this is an aspect of Self that operates at the highest dimension of incarnate existence beyond which we cease to be ordinarily human. But, full integration with that state is a long ways away, and to gain the "right" to communication with that high self we have to actually *become more than are and all we can be* at these lower levels. There are very few such (fully integrated) "Advanced Souls" and it is very unlikely that any of us will run into one of them in the normal course of events, and most certainly not among those who claim to be such an entity. *Beware of anyone making such claims, and hold on to your wallet or purse.*

Some distinguish between the Higher Self and the Holy Guardian Angel as the one being on this side of a point identified as the "Abyss" and the other as what the Self becomes after crossing the Abyss to actually become a fully integrated higher being. On the Kabbalistic Tree of Life, the Abyss lies above the Sephira Tiphareth but on that Tree located as the world of Briah (the Archangelic World) becomes Atziluth (the World of Archetypes).

All of that is a theoretical discussion of little importance to us now. We need to know that by *becoming all that we can be* we then move onward and upward to *become more than we are* on our way *to all we can be.* Our goal is to grow and develop our innate powers, to master the resulting skills, and to unfold our spiritual potential. To accomplish that we can follow many paths or focus on a few but always with the singular purpose summed up in the familiar expressions: Self-Knowledge, Self-Improvement, Self-Development, Self-Empowerment, and Self-Realization. Five "Stepping Stones" matching the Five subtle bodies and the Five lower cosmic dimensions.

Ritual Practice for the Presence of the Holy Guardian Angel

Seated in your physical Work Space at the foundation of your Astral Room, place a single lighted candle before you. While gazing at the candle flame, visualize and sense a human-like presence standing several feet behind you. Build a complete and sustained *mental impression* of this, your Guardian Angel without <u>imposing</u> your own ideas of his or her appearance.* If your Guardian Angel presents an image of himself in your mind, accept it.

> * The matter of gender: It is common to see angels as feminine and archangels as masculine—but such appearance is a matter of choice rather than "inner reality." Still, per the practices of grammar, we use the masculine to avoid further confusion of gender and plurality.

Do not turn your head or attempt to look at this entity in any manner, including the use of a mirror to see behind you!

Mentally invite your Guardian Angel to step forward and visualize him raising his hands to place them very lightly on your shoulders. Feel the shape of his fingers, their weight, their pressure, their warmth.

Say these words:

> *By my act of will, I welcome the illuminating radiance of my Holy Guardian Angel into this sacred sphere and into this Astral Room.*

From his hands, feel an energy flow into your body like a cooling **Fluid Fire**. This vitalizing energy is known by many names, but we most often simply refer to it as Psychic Energy or Life Energy.

The Blessing

Gratefully accept this blessing. This is more important than you may think for in gratitude we acknowledge a specific channel to this entity. That channel grows in strength and capacity as it is used.

What's the point of such a simple practice? It is to consciously extend the Invitation, and thus to open the door for more to follow.

Invoke often, and be open to communication but do not force anything. At some point you MAY see an image, a symbol, or hear a name. Make notes, and if it feels right to do so, repeat the name aloud. If you feel a response, address the name as if it is that of your HGA and ask the simple question: *Are you my Guardian Angel?* No matter what the response is, treat it seriously and respectfully but without excitement or ego inflation. Write it down and the session.

When you have the next session, call the HGA by that name, and if there is a satisfactory response be ready with another question. Let your intuition be your guide. Build the relation slowly, one question at a time, don't push. Record the answers and meditate and analyze. Treat them respectfully, but *accept nothing on faith! TEST! ANALYZE! Use your mind and your intuition. You are done with Feeling.* Note: Be very cautious about what teachers, writers, and other authorities may say about this process.*

When you reach this point in your development, you are essentially on your own. You are a unique individual and other peoples' experiences most likely will not apply to yours no matter who they are or what they claim to be. You are beyond any magical order grade system or any initiation offered by one guru or another teacher. You are on your own Path, and it is only as you *master your own destiny* that you become a "master"—finishing that particular course of life lessons that must be complete before you take the "Next Step." To put it another way—a very old fashioned Abrahamic way—*Salvation is not given, it is earned!*" Most things in life must be earned—free rides are rare, and probably have a hidden price you won't like!

> * Note: It is not that old ways or other ways were or are wrong, it's that they are dated, and/or operating within a vastly different cultural background than is likely for any readers of this book. Background, particularly that of the educational system and any previous discipleship—particularly if founded in eastern Buddhism or western mysticism—will mostly likely have created a barrier of dependency and of "withdrawal" rather than the active "participation" that is now the Aquarian way. *These cycles make a difference in just about everything!* The next few decades promise radical, and beneficial, change to successfully meet the challenges of the times—most of those left over from the previous Piscean energies.

ADDENDUM TO THE INVOKING OF THE HOLY GUARDIAN ANGEL

There are many more practices that can be added to your personal curriculum. Many of these will be found in the recommended texts at the end of this chapter as drawn both from the Tantric and the Kabbalistic systems. You must both continue to study and practice, and learn to listen to the promptings of your inner self as to what to do next. Two Kabbalistic practices, in particular, are those of "Path-Working" and "Rising on the Planes." Two of the recommended texts from the Tantric system are *Wheels of Life* by Anodea Judith and *A Chakra & Kundalini Workbook* by Dr. Jonn Mumford.

The following exercise is particularly recommended for follow-up from your Invocation of the Holy Guardian Angel as re-enforcement of our belief that *Psychic Development* must be combined with *Spiritual Development* for comprehensive completion of the evolving Personality, or Psyche.

PROGRAM & PROCEDURE FOR OPENING THE THIRD EYE*

Ajna Chakra, (the Brow Centre), is the "Control Center"

Allow the **Fluid Fire** to circulate throughout your body, feeling every part tingle with vitality. Mentally, direct it to concentrate in the space on your forehead above your nose and between your eyebrows. This is the place of your third eye, the *Ajna Chakra* that is the means to spiritual vision and clairvoyance.

> * This particular Third Eye Opening is just one of the several techniques as on-off switches for clairvoyance developed in "Clairvoyance for Psychic Empowerment."

Visualize an eye opening in this place on your forehead. This eye is smaller than your physical eyes (about the size of an almond), and it is *vertical* rather than horizontal.

Say these words:

> *By my act of will, with the Fluid Fire of my Guardian Angel, I open and illuminate my third eye of second sight.*

Often, your astral sight, *clairvoyance,* will seem the same as physical sight because third eye visions are automatically converted into images familiar to your ordinary consciousness. Other times these images come in the form of symbols and representations of the archetypes requiring *in situ* interpretation.

Program & Procedure for Closing the Third Eye

Because you live in the physical world, you should close down your astral vision at the end of your session.

Say these words:

> *By my act of will, I withdraw the illuminating fire of my holy guardian angel and close my third eye of second sight.*

Mentally, feel the kundalini energy flow out of your Ajna chakra and out of your body though the hands still resting on your shoulders. Visualize the energy returning to the unseen body of the Guardian Angel standing behind you.

Say these words:

> *By my act of will, I release the illuminating radiance of my Holy Guardian Angel from this place of spirit, my Astral Room and work space.*

Feel your Angel's hands leave your shoulders as he withdraws away from your chair.

The Act of Withdrawal

At this point, some advocate a complete withdrawal of the Astral Room by reversing your visualizations in creating. Otherwise, if you feel that your workspace is going to be used for spiritual work nearly every day, than a simple act of closure would be sufficient.

RITUAL FOR CLOSING YOUR ASTRAL ROOM & WORK PLACE

Say these words:

> *The Earth of Spirit sustains it.*
> *The Water of Spirit cleanses it.*
> *The Air of Spirit expands it.*
> *The First of Spirit surrounds it.*
> *The Light of Spirit creates it.*
> *By my act of will I close this sacred space.*

The act of closure is completed as you snuff out the candle, respectfully put away your divination tools, clean up any incense or oil residues, actually dust and clean the furniture and put everything away. Such closure is a principle that should be observed in all your activities, whether in the kitchen or the office, the garage or the barn, no matter what your work or play, never leave the things at "loose ends" and open to negative energies or entities—even if it is just flies feeding on food leftovers. Take seriously the admonition that "Cleanliness is next to Godliness."

PROGRAM & PROCEDURE FOR RAISING CONSCIOUSNESS

Rabbit Holes

There's probably as many way's into Alice's Wonderland* as there are Rabbit Holes in the forest, and there are probably as many ways to raise consciousness as there are people. But, some of these ways have been developed and proven, and more or less standardized over many centuries.

> * *Alice's Adventures in Wonderland,* the novel by Charles Dodgson has amused children and adults since 1865, and taught bits and pieces of esoteric lore unbeknownst to the readers. In the story, the young Alice accidently tumbled down a rabbit hole to enter a hidden world that could be a model of the Astral World. There are many rabbit holes in the natural world.

It is from these that we have adapted those presented above. They don't come with guarantees, but they will work and they are solid mind and subtle body training.

But we are individuals, each uniquely different in subtle and fundamental ways, and no one way is the "only way" to psychic growth and spiritual development. For some people the simple process of "raising consciousness" is effective. By this we mean simply:

1. Relax and prepare yourself for psychic work as you normally do.
2. Close your eyes, clear your mind, breath slowly, comfortably, and in a regular pattern.
3. Feel yourself gently float upward.
4. If you can, without any strain, augment the feeling of rising upward with a very subtle and objectless vision of rising as through a slowly thinning mist or mountain cloud.*

> * Alternatively, you could imagine yourself slowly ascending from the bottom—outside—of a mountain, or you could imagine yourself ascending from beneath—inside—up through the Great Pyramid to emerge just above the top. See the picture on page 11 of our *Self-Empowerment and your Subconscious Mind,* or that on page 234 of our *The Llewellyn Complete Book of Psychic Empowerment.*

5. If you can, without any strain, augment the feeling of rising upward with a very subtle and nearly soundless "white noise" (without any pattern) that *seems* just vaguely to rise with you.

While the goal is to emerge above the top of the pyramid or the mountain, or just a sense of momentary completion, or—most commonly—just passing into the sleep state, this "Raising of Consciousness" exercise is a gentle meditation that can grow into a Communication with your Higher Self.

And, just as likely, it can serve as an effective preparatory exercise for the other programs described in this book.

MEDITATION
"How does the phrase 'Different Strokes for Different Folks' apply to personal evolution?"

Recommendations for your continued
Study and Development Curriculum:

OTHER BOOKS BY JOE H. SLATE &
CARL LLEWELLYN WESCHCKE

Astral Projection for Psychic Empowerment (Llewellyn 2012)

Clairvoyance for Psychic Empowerment (Llewellyn 2013)

Doors to Past Lives & Lives Between Lives (Llewellyn 2011)

Llewellyn Complete Guide to Psychic Empowerment: Tools & Techniques (Llewellyn, 2011)

Psychic Empowerment for Everyone (Llewellyn 2009)

Self-Empowerment through Self Hypnosis (Llewellyn 2010)

Self-Empowerment & the Sub-Conscious Mind (Llewellyn 2010)

AUDIO PRODUCTS BY JOE H. SLATE &
CARL LLEWELLYN WESCHCKE

Astral Projection for Psychic Empowerment CD (Llewellyn 2012)

Self-Empowerment through Self Hypnosis CD (Llewellyn 2011)

Vibratory Astral Projection & Clairvoyance CD (Llewellyn 2013)

BOOKS BY CHIC CICERO & SANDRA TABITHA CICERO

Self-Initiation into the Golden Dawn Tradition—A Complete Curriculum of Study for Both the Solitary Magician and the Working Magical Group (Llewellyn 1995)

Tarot Talismans—Invoke the Angels of the Tarot (Llewellyn 2006)

The New Golden Dawn Ritual Tarot—Keys to the Rituals, Symolism, Magic & Divination (Llewellyn 1991)

BOOKS BY MELITA DENNING & OSBORNE PHILLIPS

Foundations of High Magick—The Magical Philosophy (Llewellyn 1975)

Magical States of Consciousness—Pathworking on the Tree of Life (Llewellyn 1985)

Mysteria Magica—Fundamental Techniques of High Magick (Llewellyn 2004)

Planetary Magick—The Heart of Western Magick (Llewellyn 1989)

The Sword & The Serpent—The Two-fold Qabalistic Universe (Llewellyn 1988)

BY DONALD MICHAEL KRAIG

Modern Magick—Twelve Lessons in the High Magickal Arts (Llewellyn 2010)

BY ISRAEL REGARDIE

The Golden Dawn—The Original Teaching, Rites and Ceremonies of the Hermetic Order (Llewellyn 1989)

BOOKS BY ISRAEL REGARDIE—EDITED AND ANNOTATED WITH NEW MATERIAL BY CHIC CICERO & SANDRA TABATHA CICERO

A Garden of Pomegranates—Skrying on the Tree of Life (Llewellyn 1970)

The Middle Pillar—The Balance Between Mind and Magic (Llewellyn 1998)

The Philosopher's Stone—Spiritual Alchemy, Psychology, and Ritual Magic (Llewellyn 2013)

The Tree of Life—An Illustrated Study in Magic (Llewellyn 2001)

15

Excellence as Continuous Growth

Excellence as Continuous Growth:

A concept that views Spiritual Excellence as a dynamic, endless process of Personal Development and Self-Improvement

Promoting Spiritual Excellence through continuous growth is essential to our existence as spiritual beings.

Rather than an end product, object, or another subject, excellence—from the spiritual perspective—is a continuing process that is always at our command. Through the belief in excellence for continuous growth, all barriers to our personal development and fulfillment can be dismantled and replaced with new resources that accelerate growth and generate personal empowerment. As a dynamic, driving force existing in everyone, excellence then embraces our imperfections and empowers us to transform them into new growth possibilities. It challenges us to overcome all barriers and to turn failures into stepping stones. On a much broader scale, it motivates us to reach beyond ourselves by contributing to the greater good and making the world a better place for all.

Humans have become limited by what physicist Gary Zukav refers to as "five-sensory perception" in which we see only the purely physical dimension. The evolutionary imperative requires that we move on and become multi-sensory humans to recognize the full range of human opportunities in the multi-dimensional universe. (Zukav, G.: *The Seat of the Soul,* 1989, Simon & Schuster)

There's an old saying: *Seeing is Believing,* but a more meaningful saying could be: *Unless you believe, you cannot see!* Embracing the concept of Excellence opens the doors of perception to the universe that is in contrast to that of limited expectation. Expectation is like a cause, and for every cause there is an effect. We grow, the universe grows, and we expect more, and more becomes new reality.

The Nature of Spiritual Excellence

Spiritual Excellence as a dynamic growth process is cumulative and self-empowering in nature. It is a positive force that centers on possibilities rather than limitations. By recognizing the incomparable worth of each individual and the potential for greatness existing in everyone, it generates conditions that are essential to progress and personal fulfillment.

Once embraced, the dynamic of Spiritual Excellence can actively banish negativity, insecurity, feeling of inferiority, and all self-imposed limitations. It can build a powerful expectancy effect that is essential to self-empowerment and the successful achievement of personal goals.

Once recognized as inherent in your spiritual makeup, excellence becomes a driving, developmental force that can identify dormant potentials and manifest them to conscious awareness as totally new growth possibilities. As a universal force existing in everyone, Spiritual Excellence reaches beyond the inner self to become a personal link to the unparalleled resources of the higher spiritual realm of the *Spirit World*. Typically accompanying that linkage process are increased feelings of self-worth and security along with positive expectations of success in achieving even highly complex personal goals.

Vision opens the Doors to the Higher Self for greater access to Dimensions without limit. Spiritual Excellence, as an unfolding growth process, is both bi-directional and endless. It is an evolving force that reaches into your endless past and future alike. As a consistently positive force, it knows no limits. It can retrieve past experiences, including those of past lifetimes, and use them as resources with current relevance. It can transform perceived past failures into new growth possibilities. It can engage the illimitable power of the spirit realm and apply it to increase awareness and add quality to life in an instant.

Resolving conflict, unleashing dormant aptitudes, overcoming depression, extinguishing phobias, increasing feelings of self-worth, and building positive expectations for success, to list but a few, are all possible through the power of excellence as an active growth force.

Activating Excellence

While excellence, as a continuous growth process, is spontaneously empowering, it is consistently receptive to deliberate intervention. You can purposely focus it on specific objectives, including a wide range of personal goals. By exercising excellence as a goal-related process, you can replace limited expectations with a new awareness of your inner resources as well as those existing beyond yourself. You can literally dissolve barriers to your growth and ensure success in achieving otherwise unattainable goals. Excellence as spiritual growth thus becomes the most powerful motivational and empowering force known.

Spiritual excellence is both general and specific in nature. As an endless growth process, it can weave the threads of experience into the greater fabric of your life. It can take the simple threads of kindness toward persons and animals alike and interweave them in ways that renew frayed edges and restore brightness. Once embraced, spiritual excellence becomes an energizing, sustaining force that brings new hope, inspiration, and success into your life.

The spirit realm with its limitless wealth of growth possibilities is consistently receptive to your spiritually focused interactions. Motivated by personal growth and self-improvement, you can discover a totally new world of resources including spiritual planes of specialized power as well as advanced spirit entities such as enlightened guides and growth specialists. You will experience the unexpected rewards of discovering the higher sources of power and your intrinsic ability to interact with them. Motivated by excellence, you can master the techniques required to engage their powers and apply them as spiritual resources. You will find that nothing is beyond your reach once you become spiritually empowered through your interactions with the spirit realm.

By exercising your potential for excellence through continuous improvement, you will discover ways of focusing spirituality both inwardly and outwardly to achieve otherwise unattainable goals. You will discover how to accelerate the growth process and direct it toward specific goals. At a deeply personal level, you will discover how to liberate blocked inner potentials and reverse all negative inhibitors to your growth. You will find ways to facilitate a continuous flow of spiritual empowerment that enriches your life and the lives of others. Though it may seem overly idealistic, it becomes increasingly plausible that the possibilities for global peace and progress could become dramatically enhanced through the positive application of spiritual enlightenment and power.

Excellence as Onward and Upward

Excellence, as a spiritual growth process, is not carved in stone. It is proactive, constructive, and practical. Rather than a tablet of fixed demands, it is flexible and forever evolving. It is dynamic, adaptable, forgiving, and consistently positive. Although it can be repressed and denied expression, it remains in potential form within everyone. As spiritual beings, developing that potential is our major challenge both in this life and the beyond.

As a proactive, vibrant force, spiritual excellence is forever onward and upward. Through that force, you can take mistakes and turn them into learning experiences. You can finds way of using your strengths to overcome your weaknesses. You can banish arrogance and discover the rewards of humility. You can discover greater quality of life through acts of kindness toward persons and animals alike. You can become increasingly aware of the spiritual resources available to you and ways of using them to gain insight, solve problems, conquer fears, enrich relationships, break unwanted habits, maximize your will-power, manage stress, and add meaning to your existence. Every facet of your life is receptive to this empowering force.

Building Excellence through Spiritual Interaction

Whether spontaneous or deliberately induced, authentic spiritual interactions are essential to our spiritual evolvement. From the simple awareness of a spirit presence to the profound intervention of a protective spirit guide, spiritual communications are consistently empowering. *Building Excellence through Spiritual Interaction* (BESI) is a step-by-step program designed first, to generate a productive spiritual interaction and second, to focus that interaction on specific objectives. The wide-ranging results can include goal-related interactions with familiar spirit guides and specialized growth facilitators as well as so-called *spiritual repositories of power* which include numerous power sources often called *domains of spiritual power*. Among these are the so-called *spiritual planes* and *spheres* as well as highly personalized domains that include your individual records that reach endlessly into the past and to some degree, into your future. The program can retrieve important records of past-life relevance as well as records of events that are seemingly predestined while recognizing that even highly predictable events are subject to change through personal intervention.

At a highly practical level, the program has been especially effective when applied in the academic setting. It can identify hidden potentials and facilitate their development. It can accelerate the learning process and improve memory for material learned. Along other lines, the program can be applied to enrich social interactions, build feelings of security, stimulate creativity, and promote effective stress management. Aside from these, there is strong evidence related to the program's effectiveness in promoting the personal development of paranormal potentials. Both precognition and clairvoyance often occur during the procedure, particularly at Step 7 during interactions with the spirit domain.

Program: 9-Steps for Building Excellence through Spiritual Interaction

Preparation. *Expectation, like Intention, is Causal and expands your world of opportunities.* Set your goals both realistically and expansively. Your universe of opportunities expands as your imagination soars. Here's the program which requires approximately 50 minutes in a quiet, comfortable setting free of distractions:

Step 1. Relaxation. While in a comfortable seated or reclining position, close your eyes and mentally relax your body, beginning with your head region and progressing slowly downward. Take plenty of lime to become fully relaxed.

Step 2. Reflection. As you remain deeply relaxed, remind yourself of the spiritual nature of your being. Mentally affirm in your own words your personal worth and the endless nature of your existence as a spirit entity. Reflect on the spirit realm, not as some distant place, but as a present spiritual reality that is receptive to your interaction. Picture the spirit realm and reflect upon it as a limitless, timeless dimension without limits. Sense your connection to that dimension and its relevance to your existence—past, present, and future.

Step 3. Life Review. Review your life and *reflect on the purpose of your existence.* As images of past experiences unfold, take ownership of your present lifetime and affirm: *I am here in this lifetime at this moment to learn and grow.*

Step 4. Visualization. Visualize the spirit realm as a vast domain. Note its specific characteristics to include structures and functions as you experience oneness with them.

Step 5. Affirmation. Affirm your oneness with the spirit realm in your own words. Note the energizing presence colorful planes, bright orbs, gardens, fountains, and other structures. Note the illimitable vastness of the spirit realm.

Step 6. Spiritual Awareness. Sense the loving presence of spirit beings, including caring guides and benevolent growth specialists. Note the complete absence of evil or any other negative force. Remind yourself that the existence of evil or any other negative force in the spirit realm is inconsistent with the intrinsic nature of that realm.

Step 7. Spiritual Interaction. Give yourself permission to interact with the spirit realm and its vast wealth of resources, from its spirit guides, guardians, and developmental specialists to its vast planes and other repositories of power.

Step 8. Goal Embracement. Reflect on your goals. As you state them positively, sense them becoming an integral part of your spiritual being. Embrace them as an integral part of you at the moment.

Step 9. Affirmation. Affirm: *Excellence as continuous improvement is my destiny.*

Reflection. Upon completing the exercise, reflect upon the experience. Note your sense of self-empowerment and remind yourself that spiritual excellence as a continuous growth process is a present reality in your life. Review your stated goals and affirm your complete success in achieving them. Note your feelings of *security, success,* and *self-empowerment.* Let them together become your *3-S Formula for Excellence!* Affirm as needed, "I am Secure, I am Successful, I am Self-empowered!"

The Spiritual Element

The expression "I was in my element," which is often associated with either the accomplishment of an important task or an experience of profound enlightenment, suggests the existence of a highly personalized element of spiritual power that is readily available to us. Our case studies showed that experiencing that personal element often led to increased awareness of an extended *spiritual space* and our personal existence within it as a place for endless growth and personal empowerment. To experience that spiritual element, according to our studies, was to experience the core of your personal spiritual identity and the spiritual context within which you learn and grow.

The experience was often described as a *peak experience* that included instant contact with the spirit realm and increased awareness of its empowering nature. More specifically, personally experiencing the spiritual element often included interactions with its host of guides, teachers, and growth specialists as well as with the departed. Our studies also found that being in that spiritual element was receptive to out-of-body travel to the spirit dimension and astral interactions with its diverse sources of power. Among the common results were spiritual enlightenment, accelerated growth, and better quality of life to include successful achievement of stated goals.

Here are a few other conclusions of our studies regarding the spiritual element and its empowering functions:

- Your spiritual element with its enveloping interactive space embodies the totality of your spiritual being. It is often perceived as the energizing force underlying the bi-directional endlessness of our spiritual existence.

- Your spiritual element reaches to infinity. It embraces physical reality while reaching beyond it to become your connection to the higher spirit realm.

- Your spiritual element is an interactive expression of the spiritual nature of your existence and the context in which the spirit evolves.

- Your spiritual element is consistently receptive to your interactions.

- Increased awareness of your spiritual element adds quality and meaning to your existence as an evolving spirit.

- Your spiritual element embraces the totality of your spiritual being as uniquely different from that of any other soul. Although you may have lived many lifetimes—and, should you choose to do so, you may live many more—your unique makeup as a spirit entity is forever constant.

- Your existence within your spiritual element with its extended energy space knows no bounds other than those you impose upon it.

- Like your spiritual identity, your spiritual element is an integral part of your total being. Rather than limited by physical reality, it exists independently of any perceived physical constriction.

- It is within your spiritual element and its encompassing energy space that you experience spiritual excellence through continuous growth and progress.

Experiencing Your Spiritual Element

To fully experience the spiritual nature of your existence can be a profound growth experience that adds new meaning and power to your life. The step-by-step program that follows was developed in our labs to achieve that important goal. It is designed to increase awareness of your personal spiritual element and to facilitate empowering interactions with it. Discovering that central element within its spiritual space can enlighten, empower, and inspire. It can activate dormant inner potentials and focus them on designated goals while connecting you to the unlimited resources of the spirit realm. It can generate powerful feelings of security and personal worth.

Program: 8 Steps for Experiencing Your Spiritual Element

Preparation. Here's the program which requires approximately one hour in a quiet setting free of interruptions. It should never be used while driving, operating machinery or engaged in any activity requiring alertness or focused attention.

Step 1. Oneness Within & Beyond. While in a comfortable seated or reclining position, take a few moments to join your hands as a symbol of inner harmony and balance. Next, turn your palms briefly upward as a symbol of your connection to the highest sources of spiritual enlightenment and power. Relax your hands and affirm in your own words your oneness within and beyond.

Step 2. Personal Orb of Energy. Visualize an orb of bright energy with yourself situated comfortably at the center of it. Take time for the image to slowly unfold. As you visualize yourself at the center of the emerging orb, note your feelings of security and wellbeing.

Step 3. *My Element.* Think of the orb of energy as your spiritual element with yourself at the center of it. Note your sense of oneness with the orb as the essence of your spiritual being, and let yourself become fully infused with its powerful energy.

Step 4. Spiritual Enlightenment. As you remain enveloped in the bright orb and infused with its energy, specify your spiritual goals and affirm your commitment to achieve them. Focus on *spiritual excellence as continuous improvement* and take time to sense the power of excellence permeating your total being.

Step 5. Spiritual Affirmation. Affirm in your own words that spiritual excellence as continuous improvement is presently unfolding in your life.

Step 6. Distance Spiritual Interacting. As you remain at the center of the orb, focus your attention on distant sources of spiritual enlightenment and power. You can interact directly with them as empowering resources by simply deciding to do so. Reflect on your personal goals as previously specified while deliberately engaging the spiritual resources related to them.

Step 7. Spiritual Travel (Optional). At this optional step, you can by intent travel spiritually beyond your physical presence with the orb as a spiritual vehicle to interact directly with distant sources of spiritual power, including personal guides and other growth facilitators as well as such sources as cosmic fountains, gardens, and horizontal planes of concentrated spiritual power. Upon deciding to do so, you can by intent alone return to your physical presence and fully re-engage it.

Step 8. Conclusion. Visualize again as in Step 2 your personal orb of energy enveloping your total being. Sense as before your feelings of oneness with the orb as the essence of your spiritual being. Review your spiritual goals and affirm you success in fulfilling them. Remind yourself that spiritual excellence as continuous growth is a present reality in your life.

Our review of case reports showed repeatedly that personally experiencing the unique spiritual element through this program can activate your inner growth potentials while connecting you to the highest resource of the spirit realm. Once situated within the energy orb as your unique spiritual element, you can stimulate the spiritual growth process and focus it on personal goals. You can activate dormant inner potentials while accessing the outer sources of spiritual enlightenment and power. You can generate a state of spiritual balance and attunement that is essential to your success.

Not infrequently, the program identifies blockages to spiritual growth, including those of past-life origin. Among the common examples are phobias resulting from un-resolved past-life trauma. For instance, fear of crowds was associated with public execution before a jeering crowd, fear of darkness and enclosed spaces was associated with long-term imprisonment in an underground dungeon, and fear of heights was associated with death by falling from a cliff into a deep cavern. Each of these examples was later validated by past-life regression using hypnosis. Taken together, our studies showed that past-life enlightenment regarding the source of a phobia is almost always sufficient to extinguish the fear.

Obsessive-compulsive conditions were found to be likewise receptive to past-life enlightenment through this program. A striking example was that of a student whose obsession with time and a strong compulsion to count were both found to be associated with long-term imprisonment during which he repeatedly counted the days remaining until his release. The condition was spontaneously extinguished upon his discovery of its past-life source.

Interactions with personal spirit guides can be likewise empowering through this program. These interactions can occur either from a distance or through astral travel that directly engages the spirit realm. Recovery from grief appears especially receptive to comforting interactions with supportive spirit guides and so-called *recovery facilitators.*

The discovery of missing persons was found likewise to be receptive to this approach. A criminal investigator, for instance, used this program in his effort to discover the exact location of a missing child. Fortunately, the child was safely rescued, thanks to the investigator's use of this program. By his report, he continues to use this program in his search for missing persons as well as in gathering crime-related evidence.

Spiritual Excellence Forever

Spirituality is the multiversal force that both defines and sustains our existence as endless spirit beings. It is the energizing core of our being that gives meaning and substance to life. Achieving spiritual excellence through continuous growth is the major challenge of our existence—past, present, and future.

Fortunately, spiritual growth by its nature is integrative and irreversible. Past growth achievements, whether in life on Earth or the afterlife, become forever woven into the fabric of our spiritual genotype. They become empowering resources that are self-sustaining. While spiritual growth peaks with intermittent decline, the peaks of growth are sustained. Upon our transition at death, the peaks of past growth remain, a concept we call the *preservation of peak growth*. While unfulfilled past-life purposes and unresolved past-life issues may remain, they are receptive to our afterlife efforts to resolve them. The preservation of peak growth, along with the assistance of spirit guides, is essential, not only to the success of those efforts, but to our continued spiritual growth.

Essential to our spiritual growth is a commitment to contribute to the spiritual growth and wellbeing of others. Spiritual growth when self-centered becomes spiritual baggage that hinders our progress and inhibits personal fulfillment. Among the strongest accelerants of spiritual excellence are our contributions to the greater good. Acts of kindness contribute not only to the good of others, they promote our personal spiritual progress as well. They add to the quality of life while making the world a better place for all.

Conclusion

Spiritual excellence is based on the concept that spirituality is an endless process of personal discovery and development. Rather than a *part of you*, spirituality is the *essential you* without which you would not exist. It is through spiritual excellence as continuous growth that you fulfill the purpose of your existence—whether in this lifetime, a previous lifetime, or lifetimes yet to come. Add to these your continuous growth between lifetimes and the possibilities are without limits. A major challenge is to live in the moment while embracing the endless opportunities for excellence through continuous grow and self-improvement.

<u>MEDITATION</u>
"What does 'endless process of Personal Development and Self-Improvement' mean to you?"

Suggested Reading:

Slate, J.H.: *Aura Energy for Health, Healing & Balance,* 1999, Llewellyn

Slate, J.H.: *Connecting to the Power of Nature,* 2009, Llewellyn

Slate, J.H.: *Psychic Empowerment for Health and Fitness,* 1996, Llewellyn

Zukav, G.: *The Seat of the Soul,* 1989, Simon & Schuster

16

REWARDS OF SPIRIT INTERACTIONS

Communication, Interaction, Growth, Integration

Spirit interactions are essential to our spiritual growth. Without them, spirituality becomes merely a concept with little relevance to our existence as spirit beings. Fortunately, the spirit dimension with its enormous wealth of empowering resources and rewards is constantly receptive to our interactions. Only through spirit interactions with the accompanying energy and information flow can we discover the true nature of spirituality and the immense rewards of spirit interactions.

Spiritual Growth: Endless yet Uneven

The primary goal of sprit interactions is spiritual growth. *We exist in the world as we know it to learn and grow.* Our spiritual growth, whether in each lifetime or between lifetimes, is *endless yet uneven*. In the real world, progressing onward and upward is often followed by slipping backward and downward.

Fortunately, both *progression* and *regression* can be important learning experiences that facilitate spiritual growth. While progressing can provide feedback on what works, regressing can provide feedback on what does not work. Past perceived failures thus become important growth resources with critical relevance to spiritual excellence as continuous growth and improvement.

Over the years, our studies investigating the rewards of spirit interactions often revealed the purposeful presence of spirit guides, not only at times of peak advancements but at times of peak retreats as well. Both were seen as "peak experiences" that contributed to spiritual growth and knowledge. Through interaction with spirit guides, retreats or so-called "failures" were reversed and integrated into successful advancement at the moment. The past growth peaks, whether seen as successes or failures, were thus preserved to became critical resources that promoted spiritual progress and growth. Put simply, through spirit interactions the totality of our past can become significant resources for progress in the present and future alike.

The Growth Plateau: Review, Refection, and Integration

Often following periods of rapid spiritual advancement are the unfolding spiritual plateaus in which past growth experiences are stabilized and integrated as future growth resources. The growth plateau experience is a balanced and attuned state that is typically active and receptive to spirit interactions with comforting guides and growth specialists. It is a state in which both mental and physical healings often occur, not as earned rewards, but as benevolent spiritual gifts.

The plateau experience, while often brief, is essential to our continued spiritual growth and progress. It provides opportunities for reflecting on past accomplishments and integrating them as present growth resources. It provides time for reviewing personal goals in progress while facilitating the formation of new ones. It can generate a so-called "success orientation" with realistic expectations for future growth and accomplishments. It can initiate a totally new growth process that includes empowering interactions with highly advanced spirit guides as specialized growth facilitators.

New Insights, Solutions to Growth Barriers, Therapeutic Breakthroughs

The plateau experience can set the stage for new insight to unfold, often in spontaneous and detailed imagery form. Solutions to growth barriers, including those of past-life origin, often occur effortlessly as "therapeutic breakthroughs" with important relevance to future growth. These breakthroughs frequently include vivid imagery of the past-life sources of phobias, emotional conflicts, and other conditions that impede our progress. The plateau experience can spontaneously provide the enlightenment required for successful resolution, often instantly. A striking example of such a breakthrough is that of a college student whose persistent fear of being close to tall structures such as high rise buildings was instantly extinguished by a dream experience in which her death in a past life resulted from the collapse of a towering building. In her own words, "The dream, which I immediately recognized as past-life related, provided the insight required to totally eradicate the fear." In a similar instance, a student majoring in elementary education discovered during dreaming the past-life source of her fear of the number eight, a condition called *octophobia*. In the dream, she experienced the death of her 8-year old child during an 1888 typhoid outbreak. The dream with bold images of the number 8 appearing repetitively provided the insight required not only to explain the otherwise irrational fear but to fully extinguish it. "Upon awakening," she reported, "I knew that my fear of that number had vanished." Interestingly, in *numerology*, which is the study of numbers and coinciding events, the number eight commonly represents either power or its polar opposite, sacrifice.

In yet another example of dreaming as a critical breakthrough event commonly occurring during the plateau experience, a retail specialist for a technology firm experienced instant recovery from a long-term fear of spiders through a dream in which an invasion of spiders fully covered her body, some crawling in and out of her mouth, nose, and ears. Upon suddenly awakening in panic from the dream, she felt a comforting spirit presence accompanied by a slowly fading of her life-long fear of spiders. The implosive effects of the experience together with the comforting spirit presence illustrated her capacity to cope with even the most extreme conditions related to her growth. In her words, "I am today totally free of all fear of spiders."

Resolving Disempowering Relationships, New Growth, Self-Discovery

Traumatic experiences, including those involving disempowering relationships, are likewise often resolved during the plateau state. The balancing, attuning function of the plateau can build a positive mental state that becomes a foundation for empowered independence, increased self-confidence, and when needed, constructive assertiveness. The plateau state provides a powerful foundation for new growth and self-discovery.

Conflicts are often resolved and growth barriers fully eradicated.

The plateau experience often becomes a creative canvas upon which relevant insight and creative solutions to challenging problems emerge. Not infrequently, future events of spiritual relevance are revealed, often in striking detail. The plateau experience can also include the activation of both clairvoyance and precognition as sources of information of spiritual relevance not otherwise available. Examples include clairvoyant awareness of dormant or undeveloped potentials within as well as enlightenment of spiritual relevance related to past lives. The results include an expanded perspective of possibilities, not only for our personal growth but for the greater good as well. Knowledge of clairvoyant and precognitive origin thus becomes essential resources for coping with present conditions and shaping future events.

Challenge, Insight, and Response

While certain future happenings are believed to be fixed and pre-determined, others are clearly influenced by present conditions that activate probable outcomes. For instance, peace oriented actions and interventions can increase the probability of global peace; whereas war oriented actions and violence can increase the probability of war. All is not pre-determined—present decisions and actions have future consequences, both on a personal and global scale. Although peace is a major reward of spirit interactions, it is a reward that requires reasonable thought and responsible action.

Becoming Spiritually Connected, Forever Evolving

Whether spontaneous or voluntarily induced, spirit interactions are consistently empowering. They collectively are the energizing and enlightening link to the *life force* that sustains your existence as an eternal spirit entity. That force, rather than a spatially distant untouchable reality, is the spiritual core of your being. Forever evolving rather than fixed, it is the unique "I AM" that gives identity, substance, and unlimited potential to your spiritual existence. Once you are spiritually connected to that life force, you become empowered to set your highest goals and achieve them. All the resources you need become readily available to you at any moment. While many of them are spontaneously active, you can deliberately access others and apply them with complete confidence. You become empowered to dissolve all blockages to your growth, from overcoming fear to banishing feelings of insecurity.

BECOMING SPIRITUALLY CONNECTED EXERCISE

Becoming Spiritually Connected is a brief, step-by-step exercise developed in our labs and designed to promote an empowered state of spiritual connectedness in which dormant potentials become activated and receptive to application. The results typically include increased awareness of spirituality as the central force that sustains our existence. The exercise recognizes the concept that we are each a unique spirit—without the spirit we could not exist. It further recognizes that, given the spirit and a state of empowered connectedness with it, our existence is without limits. We become aware of our existence as not only endless, but as forever advancing. Plateaus, peaks, and even so-called failures become crucial growth experiences.

This self-administered exercise accepts the premise that becoming spiritually connected is the *number one rew*ard of spirit interaction. It emphasizes the substance of spirituality as not *expecting* rewards but *experiencing* them. You will find that becoming spiritually connected empowers you to solve pressing problems and find ways of dissolving growth blockages that impede your progress. You will discover ways of replacing self-defeating coping strategies with effective adjustment and stress management techniques. Free-floating anxiety, obsessive-compulsive conditions, and feelings of insecurity are all receptive to this approach which builds a more positive self-image along with strong feelings of personal worth. Unleashing dormant potentials through identifying and overcoming blockages can occur at any stage of the procedure.

Exercise—Becoming Spiritually Connected and Empowered

Here's the exercise which requires a comfortable, safe setting free of distractions.

Stage 1. Beginning Affirmation. Settle back and with your eyes closed, affirm:

> *"I am spirit. Becoming spiritually connected and empowered through continuous growth is my destiny."*

Stage 2. Finger-tip Engagement. Join the tips of your fingers in a "praying hands" position, and sense the balancing, attuning effects of this simple technique. While holding the finger engagement position, sense your connection to the inner core of your being. Affirm:

> *"I am attuned, balanced, and spiritually secure. I am at one with the totality of my existence."*

Stage 3. Upward-Palm Gesture. Turn your palms upward, and while holding the upward palm gesture, sense your connection to the highest spiritual dimension, not as a theoretical concept but as an empowering reality. Visualize that dimension as you experience the powerful infusion of spiritual energy permeating first your palms and then your total being. Allow plenty of time for spiritual images and the related energy infusion to continue as you experience a powerful connection to them. Think of that connection as a state of spiritual oneness and power. Affirm:

> *"I am fully connected to the highest realms of spiritual power."*

Step 4. Palm-against-Palm Gesture. Bring your palms together as your sense of connectedness continues to permeate your total being. Affirm:

"*I am spiritually connected, attuned, and balanced. I am spiritually empowered.*"

Personal goals stated at this step can become clear precursors of future realities. From goals related to self-improvement to goals of global relevance, all are receptive to this gesture.

Stage 5. Concluding Reflection. Conclude the procedure by relaxing your hands and reflecting on the empowering effects of becoming spiritually connected, not as a temporary state, but as an actively enduring state of self-empowerment. Take a moment to refocus on the attuning, balancing effects of the exercise. Note the defusement of deep-seated self-rejection and the emergence of a supremely positive self-image.

Through the regular practice of this simple exercise and the resultant acceleration of spiritual connectedness, you will discover a higher degree of productive thinking and the power of the adaptive subconscious. Spiritual inspiration along with heightened receptiveness to the flow of spiritual energy and enlightenment almost always accompanies the exercise, particularly when regularly practiced. Through your repeated use of this exercise, you will discover the art of serenity and new ways of maintaining stability, even during times of distress and uncertainty. You will discover how to resolve deep-seated conflicts, including those of past-life origin.

Becoming Spiritually Connected, when regularly practiced, becomes a functional link to the highest sources of spiritual empowerment with seemingly unlimited possibilities. In Step 4 of the exercise, profound awareness of a spirit presence often emerges as an effective growth facilitator. Through the intervening presence of ministering guides, spirit guardians, and growth facilitators, personal objectives when stated at this step can become *future realities awaiting materialization.*

The procedure is especially effective as a stabilizing, integrative exercise when practiced during the plateau stage of spiritual development. It effectively integrates your past growth experiences into the greater whole, a process we call *sum-total effect* which establishes a firm foundation for your continued spiritual growth. The results include increased feelings of personal worth, along with powerful feelings of spiritual security.

Becoming Spiritually Connected is one of the most powerful self-therapy and healing techniques known. Our research related to this technique revealed its capacity not only to link us to the sources of spiritual empowerment but also to activate those sources in ways that infuse us with their specialized powers. In that connected state, spiritual growth processes becomes active and receptive to focusing on stated objectives, including a wide range of self-improvement goals. At any stage of the procedure, profound insight related to current life situations can emerge.

In the clinical setting, such conditions as major depression, posttraumatic stress disorder (PTSD), panic disorders, and a variety of phobias including agoraphobia were all found to be receptive to the technique. The exercise often uncovered the sources of these conditions and identified the dynamics related to them. The therapeutic results included expiation of guilt, ventilation of stress, resolution of deep-seated conflict, and increased feelings of security and personal worth. Central to the effectiveness of the exercise was a recognition of the incomparable worth of the individual accompanied by awareness of spirituality as a critical therapeutic resource.

Here are some of the spiritual rewards of the exercise as reported by our research participants. Included among them were both university students and non-students with an age range of 17 to 61 years:

- As a result of this exercise, I experienced greater self-insight and spiritual-insight as inseparable empowerment resources.
- The exercise generated for me a deeper understanding of spirituality as an endless growth *process* rather than simply an end *product*.
- Through this exercise, I discovered that "I am a spirit" rather than "I have a spirit."
- I discovered ways of overcoming adversity rather than giving in to it.
- I learned how to get back on track once derailed.
- I learned how to overcome growth obstacles.
- I experienced the pleasure of spiritual congruency.
- I experienced the excitement of letting go of non-workable ways and embracing a totally new approach.
- I learned how to discard the cycle of self-defeat and engage the cycle of self-empowerment.
- I found that spiritual interactions are essential to my personal growth and fulfillment.
- I learned how to replace failure with success.
- I went from ambiguity to certainty through this experience.

- Upon becoming spiritually connected, I discovered that nothing is beyond my reach. All things are possible through spiritual empowerment.
- Becoming spiritually connected gave new meaning to my existence. I felt a totally new sense of wholeness and self-worth.

Connecting to the Power of Nature

Possibly nothing manifests the powers of spirituality more than our interactions with nature, from its simplest life form to the multiverse at large. Rescuing an animal in distress, embracing a tall tree, climbing a towering mountain, viewing a night sky, exploring a hidden cave, strolling along a beach, and simply stroking a leaf or small stone—all are examples of interactions with empowering potentials. Fortunately, nature's resources are available to everyone. They invite our interaction by their very existence.

Our interactions with nature can connect us to the supreme energy force that both sustains and enriches our existence as spirit beings. Personally interacting with nature can generate an inclusively empowered state that gives new meaning and substance to life. Among the many specific rewards are increased feelings of personal worth and security along with a renewed sense of connectedness within the self and beyond. Awareness of a guiding spirit presence and the gentle melting away of growth barriers commonly unfold during the experience.

In his book, *Connecting to Power of Nature*, your co-author (Slate) illustrates the vast range of spiritual rewards available through interacting with nature. Among the most powerful rewards are those resulting from our interaction with trees as nature's oldest and biggest living things. While simply placing your hands upon a tree as earth's antennae to the universe and beyond can spontaneously generate a surge of spiritual energy, structured programs utilizing the tree have been developed for the express purpose of connecting us to the highest sources of spiritual power.

THE TREE POWER PROJECT

The Tree Power Project was introduced by the Parapsychology Research Institute and Foundation (PRIF) at Athens State University (Alabama) to investigate the application of trees as spiritual creations for goals ranging from spiritual enlightenment to such self-improvement objectives as simply breaking an unwanted habit. Within that vast range, exercises were developed to achieve such highly specific goals as accelerating learning, improving memory, slowing aging, enriching social interactions, promoting creativity, and exploring past lives, to list but a few.

Underlying the project's series of studies was the concept the tree is not only a repository of spiritual energy, it is also a channel to the highest sources of spiritual power. Rather than simply tapping into the tree's energies or applying the tree as an object, the project focused on the importance of establishing a meaningful relationship with the tree and then embracing the tree as a significant empowerment partner.

Among the numerous self-empowerment programs developed by the project was an interactive procedure called the *Tree Embracement Exercise*. The highly flexible procedure begins with the formulation of a single goal followed by the selection of an appropriate tree and then interacting with it. The exercise ends with an expression of appreciation for the tree as an interactive empowerment partner.

The Tree Embracement Exercise

Here's the procedure:

Step 1. Goal Statement. Formulate a specific goal and state it in positive terms.

Step 2. Tree Selection. From either close up or a distance, select a tree that seems appropriate to your stated goal. View the tree, paying special attention to its special appeal and unique characteristics such as height, size, shape, foliage, and limb structure.

Step 3. Tree Visualization. Having viewed the selected tree, close your eyes and allow a detailed image of it to emerge. Note in detail the characteristics of the image.

Step 4. Tree Connection. As the image remains clear in your mind, sense your connection to the tree as a potential empowerment partner. Allow sufficient time for the connection to emerge.

Step 4. Tree Personalization. Again view the tree as in Step 2 and, while viewing it, personalize the tree by giving it a name using free association in which you simply say the word, "Tree," and then allow a name to come to mind. Once the name emerges, call out to the tree using that name.

Step 5. Tree Invitation. Having addressed the tree using its assigned name, state your goal as formulated in Step 1 and invite the tree to become your empowerment partner in achieving it.

Step 6. Empowering Interaction. Given the tree's acceptance of your invitation, turn your palms toward the tree and engage it, either mentally from a distance or from close-up by physically placing your hands upon it. Sense the emerging interaction with the tree, first in your hands and then throughout your full being. As your connection to the tree builds, remind yourself that the tree is earth's antennae to the universe and beyond. Again, focus your attention on your stated goal and note the emerging power of success related to it.

Step 7. Success Affirmation. Affirm:

I am empowered with success in achieving my stated goal.

Step 8. Conclusion. Conclude the exercise by addressing the tree again by name and expressing in your own words your appreciation of it as your empowerment partner. Having disengaged the tree, sense your continued connection to it as your empowerment partner.

The participants who assisted in our development of this exercise almost always experienced a profound connection, not only to the tree but also to the spirit realm. For such goals as personal improvement, career success, spiritual enlightenment, and academic achievement, the tree became a trusted empowerment partner.

They reported powerful feelings of security and "oneness within and beyond" that continued long after concluding their interactions with the tree. They frequently returned to the same tree, confident in its capacity to connect them to the highest sources of spiritual power. Equally as important, the tree often spontaneously connected them to the inner sources of spiritual power. Following their repeated practice of the exercise, they discovered that by simply visualizing the tree, they could generate when needed an empowering connection to it.

The Tree Embracement Exercise has steadily gained recognition for its effectiveness in promoting rejuvenation and longevity. Interacting with a preferred tree seems to literally generate a vibrating, rejuvenating energy force, first in the hands and then throughout the full body. Although hands turned toward the tree from a distance can generate the desired vibratory effects, hands placed directly upon the tree typically intensify them. Numerous case reports suggest that this technique, when practiced regularly, can dramatically reverse the visible signs of aging while adding both longevity and quality to life. The aged oak, which is generally considered to be an all-purpose empowerment tree, is among the preferred trees for rejuvenation and longevity goals.

From the start, our research related to this exercise suggested remarkable therapeutic benefits, including breaking unwanted habits, coping with depression, extinguishing phobias, and managing excessive stress. A psychology graduate student noted that the exercise put her in touch with the best of all therapists—the one existing within her own being. In her words, "My interaction with the tree gave totally new meaning to my life." As another participant put it, "The exercise added quality to my life in the present and gave an inspiring glimpse of the splendors ahead. I became, in a word, empowered." Self-empowerment, it seems, is the ultimate reward of spirit interactions. Could anyone ask for more than that?

MEDITATION
"How can OBE Probes of the Subconscious Mind reveal Dormant Memories of Previous Skills?"

APPENDIX A: HOW TO MAKE & USE A MAGICK MIRROR

FOR SELF-EMPOWEMENT, SELF-DISCOVERY, MAGICAL OPERATIONS, EVOCATION, and DIVINATION

Magic mirror on the wall
Who is the fairest of all?
(to which the mirror always replied)
You, my queen, are the fairest of all.
(until, one day)
Queen, you are full fair, 'tis true,
But, Snow White is fairer than you.
—*The Magick Mirror—the Black Mirror*

Properly used for Self-Discovery, a Magick Mirror, can reveal important information to the "Seeker." And, *properly used,* the Magick Mirror (also known as a *Black Mirror)* is a power tool not only for *Self-Discovery,* but more commonly for Divination (also known as *skrying),* as well as the more esoteric operations of *Self-Empowerment, Self-Improvement, Evocation, and in Magickal Operations.*

It may seem that Divination and Self-Discovery are the same thing, but each has its own internal process just as do these other uses. We will only be able to give a very basic description of each application in this short appendix. More would require an entire book or a course of lessons with interactive Question & Answer provisions, but—along with instructions for making a simple <u>Black</u> Mirror—we want to provide sufficient guidance and motivation to encourage you to actively explore the opportunities opened up by this very powerful tool normally relegated to the back waters of psychic work.

Before we begin this discussion, we would like you to note two things about the Snow White story above: 1) It is really the Queen's Subconscious that is giving the answers through the magic mirror; and 2) when Snow White becomes the fairest of all, she has just turned seven years old. In other words, the Queen herself really knew the answer to her question, but she didn't know she knew it. The mirror functioned to turn subjective knowledge into object fact.

The Importance of Seven

"Seven" is a very important number, and cycles of seven years are definitive in human life. Ages of seven, fourteen, twenty-one, and twenty-eight each mark a vital transition point in human development. Astrologers know these as the quarterly aspects that Saturn makes before returning to its natal position. We recognize them as age markers on the way to full maturity at age twenty-eight. Thereafter, age fifty-six roughly approximates the high point in one's career, eighty-four perhaps as the ideal time for retirement, and one hundred-twelve as the normal age of transition.

But, don't let others put limits on your own potentials. Age 128 is only the completion of another cycle of four. With advances in health and longevity, perhaps "born again" will take on a new meaning. Why not? The Universe is infinite, life and consciousness are universal, and evolution continues.

Divinatory Tools

Many objects other than a true Black Mirror have been used in skrying: Many use a crystal ball, others just a bowl of water, a glass of wine, a piece of polished obsidian, polished metal, a faceted jewel, even an ordinary mirror and other reflective surfaces. Of course, other devices are used in divination—many along the line best represented by the modern Ouija® Board and Automatic Writing.

There are vast difference between these three basic approaches:

1. The "Talking Board," Dowsing-type instruments, and Automatic Writing are each passive aids to natural clairvoyance.

2. The Crystal Ball and other forms of reflective surfaces are mostly a "semi-active" method of inducing a light trance.

3. The Black Mirror is another matter altogether, and functions as a *doorway* into the Astral Dimension.

In addition, of course, working in a different direction, we have Mediumship and Channeling, Listening to Shells, Sand Reading, Geomancy, Dream interpretation, and more. Nearly everything and most anything can and has been used in "readings" of past, present, and future situations, but certain methods have been highly developed over the centuries.

Black versus Silver

Compare the familiar "ordinary" mirror and the black mirror: the ordinary mirror has a silvered back and the black mirror is prepared piece of cut glass that has been spray painted on the "back side" with a matte black finish. We will give complete instructions later for making your own black mirror.

What's the difference? Well, it's almost the difference between Night and Day. The familiar silver-backed mirror that we all use throughout the day reflects back *the physical reality of ordinary things as they are in the <u>exterior</u> world.* The black mirror, as mentioned, properly used, can be *a door into the astral reality of things as they can be,* and as *they are in the <u>interior</u> world.*

Exterior/Interior? This is a reminder that we are more than the physical body, that consciousness is more than the electrical activity of the physical brain, and that we live <u>in</u> a mutli-dimensional universe as well as <u>on</u> and <u>in</u> a mutli-dimension planet. Exterior reality is just the *surface* of all that we are and all that is, and the focus of our awareness on the surface is truly limiting and *superficial.*

Exterior reality is also a reminder that we are still evolving, we are unfinished products, and the age markers previously mentioned are measures on the road toward fulfillment of at least one phase of human growth. We need to live longer, healthier lives just to attain the "age of wisdom." George Bernard Shaw once said something like this: *By the time a man is old enough to be smart, he turns senile.*

Psychic Empowerment

Pre-20th century physical science has brought extraordinary benefit to us but it has tended to reduce awareness of the "spiritual" (non-physical) dimensions, as also did the pervasive and controlling actions of the monotheistic religions.

Starting early in the 20th century, both Quantum physics and the Metaphysical resurgence have brought broader public awareness of the Greater Reality, Cosmic and Personal. Now it is time to actively and *personally* explore that reality and become self-empowered through the growth and development that comes through personal experience and the application of resultant knowledge.

Psychic Empowerment is an expansion of consciousness, and the employment of psychic abilities leads towards the integration of the unconscious and conscious elements of the human psyche in to become more than we are. We call that the process of self-empowerment that results from *doing*. Growth does not come without effort, and the only logical reason for our existence is that of growing to become more than we are. Think of it as your own divinely inspired personal obligation, and the opportunity that growth provides for you to become a co-creator with the Ultimate Source.

Activating the Magical Process from Imagination into Manifestation

A Black Mirror is a magical doorway into the Astral Dimension—which also means it is a "tool" by which we can activate and guide the human imagination, itself empowered by the emotional energies of the astral plane.

We must keep certain ideas in mind as we explore this subject:

1. The *Imagination* is real! There is no room for "it's only your imagination" as a denial of something's reality. That reality may not be a *physical* reality, but whatever is imagined *can* have a physical impact, and often a particular impact on the person at the physical level. A fear of the "monster in the closet" can have repercussions on a child's health, and similar irrational or rationally justified fears can do the same for the adult.

2. Using your imagination, you can perceive a problem and work out its solution. Doing so can initiate a physical process to change physical reality. Blending that physical process with the active imagination can help continue the physical process to its completion.

3. All magickal work and most psychic work requires mental guidance of the astral process and of its "manifestation" into physical reality, otherwise you probably won't get what you asked for.

4. That mental guidance itself is empowered by the Causal Will. Be specific in what you ask for.

5. Dreams are also known as magical mirrors. Dreaming is a special act of imagination whether as a spontaneous dream or a pre-determined dream. Dream "management" is a powerful process to focus levels of consciousness on particular information.

6. Fantasy is another special form of the imagination working primarily at the psychological level to provide creative solutions to personal development and career needs. Fantasy is also a way to explore relationship connections, personal expression, and to develop your self-image.

7. Conscious "management" of Dreaming and Fantasy can provide you with real "feedback" to improve and guide all magical, psychic, and psychological work and to work visually in the Black Mirror.

8. Through the Black Mirror the Imagination can be employed in special studies and operations such as learning the Tarot and divining with it, and likewise with other major image-related divinatory systems like Runes, Tree Alphabet, the Yi King, etc. As just one rather advanced technique, you can visualize each Tarot Card, then project its image into the Mirror, and when the image is clear, see yourself in the projected mirror image acting within the scene.

9. The Black Mirror can work with any divination system to turn actual Self-Discovery into a Self-Improvement program, as an adjunct to Kabbalistic Path Working, for the active initiation and management of Past Life Regressions, and other forms of spiritual and psychological exploration.

10. The Black Mirror can be used in the Evocation of Spirits and Entities through the process of projections of Seals and Sigils into the mirror.

11. The Black Mirror can focus and aid the imagination in learning astrology and particularly the exploration of the personal horoscope, to explore the effects of transiting planets, and situational forecasting.

12. The Black Mirror can focus image-making and progression in any magickal operation.

In all of this, it can be said that the only limitation on the value of the Black (or Magical) Mirror is that of your own imagination. But, always remember that it is a *Tool* while the <u>Power</u> is with you. Many books and traditions will tell you that you must carefully "purify" this tool before use, that you must "consecrate" it to your use "invoke" protective defenses and aids by means of prayer, chants, painted symbols, and more.

There is no *real* necessity for these actions, but they do serve the real purpose of treating any tool with respect, and to dedicate any magical, psychic, psychological, and spiritual aid to your personal use. Wrap it up and put away when not in use. Don't show it off and don't let other people handle it. Otherwise, the choice is yours—don't let other people, dead or alive, dictate to you.

HOW TO USE THE BLACK MIRROR

We will later give instructions for making the Black Mirror, but what's the sense of making something unless you know how to use it?

We've given twelve ideas as to the use of this tool, but how to use it another matter. Bear in mind that:

1. The Black Mirror is a door into the Astral.

2. The Astral Universe is even more immense than the Physical Universe, and like the physical and other levels of being, it has <u>seven</u> major sub-divisions. (Keep that number, as previously mentioned, in mind)

3. In all levels of being, each person has a "presence." Some writers refer to these as "bodies," while we prefer the term "vehicle" for the active presence. But, just as we are not always active at the physical level, neither are we at these other levels in which we have a *presence.*

4. We can learn to focus our awareness at any level, in any presence, and be active or passive, projective or receptive, and—in the meaning of communication— we can talk and listen, question and answer.

5. However, each of these <u>duets</u> is a third thing. When you talk and listen, it is a conversation or dialogue. When you question and receive answers, it is a learning experience. When something is projected and received, some "birthing" experience is initiated. Active and Passive are states of Positive and Negative which combine to produce movement and transformation of particular states of reality.

6. When you look into an ordinary silvered mirror, you see a reflection of your physical body which is inclusive of several levels of *presence.* That reflection is *objective* because it is in the same dimension as is the viewer.

7. When you look into the magical Black Mirror, you may at first see nothing until you *actively* <u>project</u> an image into the mirror (remember it is a door into the astral) or *passively* prepare to <u>receive</u> an astral image or message. Either is *subjective.*

8. The process in making the objective *subjective* and the subjective *objective* is to complete a <u>duet</u> consisting of the viewer/projector person and the receptor/ entity/thing seen in the Black Mirror.

9. With a <u>duet,</u> communication is now facilitated between the objective/conscious self and the astral subjective self, or entity.

10. Such communication between the conscious self and the "other"—whether a Spirit, an Entity, a Deity, or an aspect of your own psyche, the Subconscious Mind, the Collective Unconscious, the Akashic Library—or your <u>Higher Self</u> (or, some simply call it the "Watcher") is the goal of Spiritual Communication.

11. This Spiritual Communication is one form of psychological integration by which your whole being becomes a fully realized Conscious Soul. That's your ultimate goal.

12. We are limited to the extent that we tend only to look in one direction (outward), and focus on only one dimension (physical). The Magical Black Mirror reminds and aids us to also look inward, and to also focus attention upward into higher dimensions.

Of course, the Black Mirror is only a tool on the Path or Journey you are on, and may soon be put aside. But it is a starting point, a facilitator, the beginning towards an end that is endless.

Those twelve ideas given earlier are all techniques to be employed with your Magickal Black Mirror. Each contributes to your growth and development. Put them all to work.

Know what you want

Know what you want—whether actively or passively. If you are projecting the image of a seal or sigil to contact a particular entity, be ready to do so and know what you want to ask for. If you are looking for a "sign" of things to come or information about your health or other question, have them. If you are looking for guidance towards kinds of self-improvement or particular projects, ask real questions. And learn to "switch gears" from active to receptive so you can "hear" (with inner senses) answers.

If you are studying the Tarot, Astrology, or doing a Path-Working, have everything ready to project into the mirror and what you will actively pursue in the astral frame you have created. Again, learn to switch between the active and passive phases of your communication so that you can receive corresponding instruction.

If you are undertaking a magical operation by projecting a "formula" or program of steps towards that accomplishment, have it all ready.

And, finally, always give thanks to any entity you perceive, or just express gratitude for what you've learned. Remember, that with the aid of the mirror, you are working with some particularized consciousness. Even to the point of thanking your own Sub-consciousness for remembering something, do so. At the same time, always remember that it is you, your conscious self, that's "in charge." But, be *gracious* about it.

There are details of all such workings that *you are going to work and learn for yourself.* You are your own best teacher, but only as you work at it. Providing detailed instructions for all level and manner of using the Black Mirror is beyond the reach of this one book.

Preparations for Use

When your mirror is ready (see below for construction instructions), create an appropriate environment, in the form of your Astral Room as described earlier in this book, or as you would otherwise prepare for meditation or a session of self-hypnosis. Turn off bright lights but have sufficient light to see the mirror and any symbols or sigils you will be working with. If you want, use a few candles, burn a *little* incense, any music (if at all) should be very soft and non-obtrusive in any way; isolate yourself from all distraction and possible interruptions; relax your body, loosen clothing and shoes as desirable; position your mirror upright at a comfortable distance on an uncluttered table, or lay it flat immediately before where you will be seated; sit upright on a comfortable chair in which you can mostly avoid movement.

Have any materials you will use immediately at hand. Close your eyes and continue the relaxation process. Establish a rather full but slow rhythmic breathing pattern. Clear your mind of all thoughts and feelings. Visualize White Light filling your mind. When ready, open your eyes and *passively* look at and into the mirror's black surface.

Energize and "Awaken" the Mirror

Gazing at the mirror, and "charge" it by *allowing* the white light to flow into the mirror. Don't concern yourself with how much light flows into the mirror, just know that it does and that it also remains in your mind. It is limitless and it connects you with the universal Spirit. Your mirror in now energized and receptive to your will and not to that of any other person or entity.

Do not *objectively* see any whiteness appear in the mirror at this time, but the black surface may seem to glow with energy. Do not stare, but continue fixedly gazing at the mirror until you see or, initially just sense, the outer edge begin to vibrate. Your mirror is now awake.

The Next Step

Now you are ready to take the *Next Step*. The Next Step is always the most important step in any process. The First Step in only a beginning, and the Final Step is only the ending—for the moment. But the Next Step is where the real action is.

Take that Next Step on this Journey!

HOW TO MAKE A BLACK MIRROR

Now that you know how to use this tool, it is easier to construct it to fulfill your purpose and goals. It's like "knowing where you're going before stepping out." Many times when you encounter a question in construction the answer is found as return to that knowledge.

Like anything else, there are many ways to construct this particular tool. And, you can easily buy one ready-made at a metaphysical store or from Amazon or some other on-line source. There are two factors to consider: 1) The First is the value of getting started with exploratory work right away which encourages buying. 2) The Second is the always true value of crafting an object for such personal metaphysical use yourself.

You have to make the choice but for your first efforts we urge you to spend the least amount of money if buying and to keep it simple if constructing. At a later time, when you know how it is working for you, then you can better decide what you want in any upgrade. Don't waste time or energy on fancy ornaments, painted symbols and words, expensive frames or stands, etc. until you actually know what will benefit your work. Start simple and gain experience.

Let's get started.

Step 1. Since your mirror is made of glass, you need a frame to hold the mirror for usage. You need to decide on the basic *form* and *size* of the glass to be used. One form is that of a piece of *flat* glass cut in a circle. The other is sometimes referred to as a watch or clock glass because it is slightly concave as in a traditional clock face.

There are arguments for either choice. The particular advantage of the concave clock glass is that you can buy it ready made from a clockmaker or repair shop in a choice of sizes—anywhere from six to ten or twelve inches in diameter. But, remember, you want clear *glass*, not plastic. And one argument presented for the concave shape is the theory that it can focus and concentrate your projected energy. And that's exactly the argument against it and for the flat glass: The concave shape may distort image or energy. The flat glass is neutral, but more work.

Step 2. Acquire the glass, and if you decided on flat glass you want have it cut into an exact circle of chosen size from four to six inches to as much as 12 to 18 inches in diameter. The size and form of the glass determines your need for a frame. That frame needs a stand to hold it in position unless you are going to mount it on a wall directly in front of your work table. If you do that, you need to provide a way to cover it when not in use. It is not *decorative* and should not be seen by others. You can either add a hinged piece of board on the back to hold the frame upright, or buy a triangular stand to hold it.

Step 3. Prepare an appropriate piece of quality plywood to hold it the glass. It should be to make an equal-sided triangle whose sides are approximately three times that of the cut mirror's diameter. Sand it smooth, and then paint it with flat (not glossy) white paint. When dry, sand it lightly again and paint again. When it's dry, be sure you can't detect any of the wood grain through the paint. If you can, sand and paint age. Find the exact center of the triangle and lightly mark three point to enable to center the class circle. (One easy way is to find the center of each side, and then place one end of your ruler and the other over the opposite point of the triangle. Where those three lines cross is the center of the triangle; whatever is half the diameter of your cut mirror is the distance out from the center to place each of the three pencil marks.)

Step 4. With either glass, the next step is to paint the *backside* black. In the case of the flat glass, either side can be the back, but for the concave glass the backside is the "outside," i.e. opposite the curved inside that could hold water. Wash the glass thoroughly and dry it with a lint-free cloth. You need to buy a flat black non-glossy spray paint that will adhere to glass. Spread some newspapers out and place the glass backside up, paint evenly, and let dry. It is better to apply several thin coats (being sure to let them dry thoroughly between coats) than one heavy coat, as the result may not be smooth. Do as many coats as necessary so that you cannot see through to the other side when you look at a light through the glass. When dry, look into the glass. You should see no streaks or runs in the paint. If you do, remove the paint and start again at step two above.

Step 5. With the flat mirror, the next step is to mount in on the triangular frame by placing the backside exactly in the center of the marks you previous made. Using three mirror mounts, secure the mirror in place. With convex mirror you will instead need to cut a circular hole of the correct size using the center mark as the guide. Insert the mirror through the hole so that outer rim rests on the front side of the plywood. Again secure the mirror in place with three mirror mounts.

Your mirror is ready for use.

Final Step. Feel a sense of reverence to your magical and spiritual tools. Think what they are to you—the ultimate aids to growth. Yes, some people go through rituals of consecration, purification, dedication, and what have you—but often the rituals actually obscure the intent which should be reverence rather than identification with any magical order or tradition, or dedication to a specific deity.

Extra

Once you have advanced in you usage of the mirror so that operation is definitive, that is the time for the next step in which you can attach appropriate signs, symbols, or names as a *temporary* "instruction" to whatever program you are working. It isn't really necessary when you have everything needed in your mind, but it can be useful, and hence, practical.

Rather than paint them on permanently, which then limits your action, we suggest preparing three simple labels for each kind of usage. Each label should have the appropriate signs, symbols, and words on them, and then tape or otherwise affix in place above the three sides or the triangle. Additional "codes" could be placed just outside the mirror at the triangle's three points.

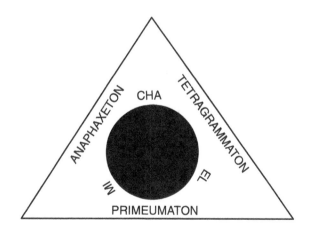

The Black Mirror with Symbols

Supplemental Instruction on Using the Mirror

These instructions are from an article in the Llewellyn on-line Encyclopedia written by Donald Michal Kraig. More articles can be found at www.llewellyn.com.

1. Begin by doing any cleansing or banishing rituals you wish to use.

2. If you work with any deities, call on them for support. If you are going to do a divination for a specific purpose, clearly identify what that purpose is. You might even want to write this down on a piece of paper.

3. Dim the lights and darken the room, save for one small light. Many people prefer a candle. Hold the mirror so you are looking into the inside of the glass, similar to looking into a bowl. That is, the painted part is on the far side of the glass from where you are looking. If you used flat black paint, the glass will make it look shiny. You should not be looking at the side with the flat black paint on it. If it is too big to hold, set its holder with the mirror on it (or in it) on a table in front of you.

4. Move the light so you cannot see its reflection directly in the mirror, but make sure that you can see the mirror.

5. Focus on the purpose of the divination and look into the mirror—not at it, but literally into it or through it.

6. Relax. Breathe. Allow yourself to be open to anything you might see, feel, hear, smell, taste, or sense. Nothing may happen the first few times you try this or you may be flooded with images. Whether it occurs right away or after a few experiments, it will come! Be open to anything. You don't need to force it or try. Just relax and allow yourself to be shown what you need to see. Eventually, it will come.

7. Observe and remember what happens.

8. Finish with thanks to any you have called and dismiss them. Cleanse and/or banish the area. It is important to immediately write down what you experienced, as divinations of this kind can fade rapidly from memory, just as even the most vivid dreams may quickly fade from memory when you awaken in the morning.

Sometimes, divination with a magic mirror opens the divination rather than completes it. You may have prophetic dreams or synchronistic experiences as a result of the work begun with the magic mirror. Don't ignore this new information.

Suggested Reading:

Clough, N. R.: *How to Make and Use Magic Mirrors, 1977,* Aquarian Press

Kraig, D.M.: *The Truth About Calling Spirits,* 2013, Llewellyn

Tyson, D.: *How to Make and Use a Magic Mirror,* 1990 Llewellyn, 1995 Phoenix, and others.

APPENDIX B:
TRAVELING IN SPIRIT

The Classic Out-of-Body Experience

That which is more commonly called "Astral Projection" today was long known as *Traveling in Spirit,* and the non-physical "Spirit World" broadly includes the Astral, Mental, and Causal dimensions in modern esoteric terminology.

A more interesting point is that it may have been a more common experience before modern times when we all became more focused on physical reality as the cultures changed and our physical needs became more demanding. This was further reinforced as the Church claimed dominion over all things spiritual and philosophy and science more and more focused on the mysteries of the physical universe.

And as populations began the expansion we today call "the Population Explosion," so did people begin to move and migrate in search of safety from territorial conflict and new food resources, mental horizons shrank to the immediacy of physical survival and satisfaction. The world of Spirit disappeared behind the closed doors of religious institutions. Personal Consciousness lost sight of the Spiritual World.

Towards Modern Times
As societies became more organized and as the Industrial Age increased the availability of goods and allowed people to enjoy more leisure time, the focus began to switch and interest in Spiritualism and the paranormal returned to awareness of that "Other World" and led to the founding of psychical research societies and to developing techniques for spiritual experiences.

Today we add the advantages of new knowledge about consciousness and the power of modern technology in audio products that guide personal consciousness to explore the astral world—the more common name of that level of the spiritual world immediately adjacent to the physical.

Announcing a Companion Audio CD

Vibrational Activation of the Astral Body for Clairvoyance &
Astral Projection

The Winged Globe. Stare, without blinking, at the center of this symbol until it vibrates; close
your eyes and see the image floating in Inner Space before your Third Eye.

Many people spontaneously experience a ***vibrational state*** in which the etheric
(energy) double moves within the physical body in a series of progressive waves moving from foot to head and back again, up and down.

With practice, these waves can be strengthened to literally *push* the etheric double
up and out, with the *astral vehicle* separating and leaving the physical body in an
induced Out-of-Body Experience.

The Induced Out-of-Body Experience (OBE) and the Development of Extra-
Sensory Perception (ESP) are not just interesting paranormal phenomena. *They are
innate to the extraordinary expansion of conscious awareness happening today.* Evolution to higher consciousness—is liberating and empowering. It's <u>the Future, Now!</u>

It's an "Awakening" that can't be turned off. Human Evolution happens in higher
levels of Consciousness, and brings changes to the physical Brain and body through
the chakra system. You can "swim with the tide" and individually accelerate this growth
and bring its benefits to all levels of your life. Through use of programs of personal
development, it is a greater opportunity and breakthrough in human advancement
than even the advent of the personal computer, the Internet, and *the coming Age of
Singularity.*

Astral Projection is NOT an actual separation of "bodies" but an expansion and
movement of Consciousness through all the subtle vehicles of the Whole Person. Nevertheless, it is useful, *and effective,* to picture the Energy & Astral vehicles moving

beyond the Physical to facilitate this proven way to develop & extend your Psychic Power.

Dr. Slate has developed and recorded the script for the "Vibrational Activation of the Astral Body for Clairvoyance & Astral Projection" to facilitate your own experience—*and further personal development*—of this powerful psychic technology.

Note that phrase: "and further personal development," because that is not something that can be done <u>for</u> you but only <u>by</u> you. You have to build your own astral "muscles" and you have to learn how to direct and apply this ability yourself.

It's all part of your own continuing "Journey of a Lifetime." but the journey itself is personal and yours alone. Nevertheless, your experience becomes part of the Collective Unconscious that adds to the resources of the Akashic Records accessible by any of us developing the ability of higher vision. Then your ventures becomes part of the Human Adventure adding depth and breadth <u>to</u> the substance of all Humanity.

About the Audio CD

This professionally scripted audio CD guides you safely through this process known as *Vibratory Astral Projection.*

The inductive script is followed by carefully developed music inclusive of a subtle audio "pulse" that will facilitate your relaxation down through alpha, theta and delta levels of consciousness—without necessarily inducing sleep. Certain sounds are subtly introduced to aid your focus on the astral level.

You may not be completely aware of your astral experiences the first time you use this CD—or even for the first several times. This is <u>not</u> like a mind-altering drug leading to an immediate but uncontrolled experience. This is a developmental process that is expansive and evolutionary. You are supposed to forever grow and astral projection is the Next Step!

Become more than you are! Become all you can be! You are intended for greatness!

This special audio program is part of a series complementing the books by Dr. Joe H. Slate and Carl Llewellyn Weschcke. Each audio program is complete and is intended to:

1. Induce or complement your out-of-body experience.
2. Provide you with a program for multiple usage that will make the preliminary astral experiences more and more familiar as to become "automatic" whenever you willfully initiate an out-of-body experience.

3. Facilitate your astral projection in particular applications of the OBE contributing to your expanding psychic development and personal empowerment.

Astral projection is *not* just a *developmental* encounter with the Greater Universe beyond the physical body and its limited physical experience but an actual *awakening* to higher consciousness. *You* are more than a physical being, and the greater universe is experienced through your "inner" non-physical levels of consciousness we call astral, mental, causal, and spiritual "bodies." The *real* you is a "whole person" and all your perceptions, actions, and experiences are inclusive of all you are. Your astral body is part of you *now*, and the astral dimension is open to you *now*, but your "awareness" has to be extended and trained to *consciously* perceive and act at this level.

Your life purpose is to grow, and thus *to become more than you are*—starting with the realization that you already are more than you've been led to believe. Even your physical body is more than its visible form for it includes the "etheric double" that is the source of your aura and the subtle energy system that flows through your chakras and meridians, and connects with astral and other subtle bodies.

You are much more than you thought! And through astral projection you are going to *become more than you are!* Your astral projection experiences will facilitate your psychic development while expanding and enhancing your field of conscious awareness to **know more of what actually is.**

Every person is composed of physical/etheric, astral, mental, causal and spiritual substance, energies and consciousness. Just as your physical body is developed and strengthened through real life experience and exercise so do you develop your astral body through conscious experience and exercise—aided by developmental programs such as this meditation companion and other meditation and self-hypnosis products in this series.

You are mostly unaware of any distinction in your etheric, astral, mental, casual and spiritual functioning, and most of your past astral experiences have been unconscious and passive while dreaming and feeling, and reacting to emotional encounters. *Now* you can begin conscious control of your astral experiences and learn to integrate astral awareness and power into your whole being. The astral world is much larger than the physical universe, and yet—together—they are only part of the spiritual Cosmos that is opening before you as you grow in astral experiences.

The astral body in combination with the etheric double—it is your "psychic body." And just as the physical body is made up of energies, and processes that are mostly unconscious (functioning *autonomically*), so is the astral body. And as the capability of the physical body is enhanced by increased understanding, and experience of its functioning, the same is true of our astral self. It is through *understanding* that we gain conscious control and can more fully benefit from the special abilities and powers opened through astral development.

The astral is the primary world of psychic and spiritual experience. All *creation* has descended *downward* through the astral from higher planes to manifest as physical reality. While some people say that "all is illusion," that illusion is the reality we know. Even on the astral where thought is given final shape before physical manifestation its astral "blueprint" can be *intentionally* altered through *disciplined imagination.* That's the Big Secret behind psychic healing, magick, and religious miracles.

The Power & Benefits of Astral Projection

- You can increase awareness of the endless nature of your existence.
- You can shape interactions with your past, present, and future that dissolve all barriers to your personal growth.
- You can awaken dormant resources from your distant past and interact with them to release growth blockages.
- You can create a dynamic force in your present life by interacting with your full life span—past, present, and future.
- You can discover ways to shape present and future events that promote not only your personal well-being, but the well-being of the planet and others as well.
- You can experience the entirety of both physical and spiritual reality, to include the complexities of the universe and the myriad dimensions that make up the spirit realm.
- You can interact with the spirit realm and its abundant sources of power that include ministering guides, growth specialists, and repositories of concentrated power such as orbs and planes of energy.
- You can promote better mental and physical health. You can even slow the aging process.
- You can facilitate your career success, enrich your social interactions, resolve personal conflicts, overcome fears, increase creativity, and accelerate learning.
- You can increase the total quality of your life.

Everything Vibrates—Movement is Life Itself

Of course, we rarely can perceive the vibratory nature of the world within and without but there are times when we feel the "vibes" of another person either in sympathy or antagonistic to our own.

In addition, spontaneously in pre-sleep experiences or during stages of meditation and other alterations of consciousness, we often do directly experience vibrations as waves during which the etheric and astral bodies move within and sometimes move outward from the physical body.

Everything vibrates. We all experience and radiate "Vibes." Life, Consciousness, Energy, Matter, and Light are all states of vibration. Our own vibratory rates constantly change as we move from wakefulness to sleep and in between, as we focus attention in study and work, as we relax and participate in entertainments, as we engage with family and friends, as we play with children or engage in love-making and other activities. We *vibrate,* and we project vibrating energies (and substance) inwardly and outwardly.

We can also consciously alter our own vibratory rates for particular "psychic purposes," going into deeper and slower states as in trance and faster and higher rates in concentration and visualization, and in such activities as active clairvoyance and induced astral projections.

With intentional changes in our vibratory experience, we see things differently and move our consciousness into other dimensions.

This phenomenon can itself be consciously directed to induce the out-of-body experience, i.e. projection of the astral body. But projection is not the only object of experiencing consciousness at the astral level. Here we want to recognize the "higher and larger" view that the astral offers, and it is at the astral and mental levels that clairvoyance functions most accurately and penetratingly to both see "behind the scenes" and to foresee the future through "the shadows cast ahead by coming events."

We can experience this expanded view of the world purely from the physical body when we climb to higher altitudes on a mountain or by airplane. The horizon moves further and further away as we move higher and higher—but the details of our view are diminished by the limits of physical reality. Not so in the case of the higher realities of astral and mental perceptions which can focus at will on distant objects and events and magnify the view as with a telescope. Or, magnify the view of things up close as with a microscope—*only to a greater degree than can be experienced with a physical instrument.*

The Vibratory State in Astral Projection

Entering the out-of-body state is often associated with a vibrational experience of a series of pulsating movements upward from the feet to the head region and then downward. Often, but not always, these are accompanied by buzzing-like sounds and fluctuating bluish light. Through an upward, downward, and then upward again progression of these movements, the vibrating waves may generate an energized integrative state of balance and synchronicity embracing not only physical reality but the non-physical as well.

Sometimes the vibrational waves are accompanied by spontaneous states of heightened psychic awareness that can include inner perceptions of physical health, various levels of clairvoyance, increased accuracy in your divinatory practices, precognition and past-life enlightenment, and other forms of knowledge and empowerment.

Aside from the spontaneously empowering effects of both vibrational waves and the synchronicity they generate is their receptiveness to stated objectives including those related to clairvoyant viewing, precognitive awareness, and distance traveling. With the formulation of specific objectives prior to the induced vibrational experience, the empowering potential of the vibration is magnified by its capacity to integrate the stated objectives into the out-of-body experience. Adding to the power of vibration waves is its capacity to generate a heightened sense of self-confidence and a positive expectancy effect related to previously stated goals. Following the out-of-body experience, the integrated nature of vibrational waves generates a state of balance and a powerful expectancy effect that virtually ensures success in achieving personal goals whether quickly perceived or experienced over extended time.

The Vibratory State, Energy Waves and PK Power

The psychokinetic (PK) powers of energy waves are believed to include the capacity not only to generate an integrative state of synchronicity, but in some instances to literally influence other realities. Here are a few examples of PK power associated with the focusing of energy waves:

- To promote health, fitness, and rejuvenation by targeting healthful energy on specific internal organs and functions.
- To intervene in emergency situations, including the influencing of objects in motion, removing blockages to escape, and initiating warning signals.

- To influence global realities in ways that will cumulatively facilitate progress and peace.

These functions of energy waves can be implemented either during the vibrational state preceding astral projection or during the out-of-body state. The formulation of PK goals prior to the vibrational state is essential to the success of this application. The growing capacity of the psychically empowered individual holds much promise for evolving humanity.

Clairvoyance, Astral Projection, and the Akashic Records

There is a lot of talk and writing about the Akashic Records without much real definition. The reality is that vast amounts of information exist as unconscious memories of all that has ever been experienced. Like the modern World Wide Web, much of this is unorganized, not necessarily "factually accurate" data that includes personal opinions as well as careful scientific and scholarly studies. Like the fabulous *Wikipedia*, the Akashic information invites serious study, editing, and contributions. Never assume that just because the information emanates from a "higher" source and is identified with a Sanskrit or other esoteric name that it is "pure" and accurate, and "spiritually" correct. It may well be, but even so it is subject to the "filter" of your own mind and present experience.

We are responsible for using any information source responsibly. For our practical usage of this information, we should remove the myth and instead substitute some familiar symbolisms under which the Unconscious is more easily organized. It's not just "Trust, but verify" as President Reagan reminded us, but "Test to verify" as Crowley and others have advised.

Think of all this as a vast, constantly updating, library of many levels and assigned subject areas. An amazing network of the most advanced quantum level computers and software automatically responds to your unconscious needs and stated goals to take you to destinations or bring you the desired information. Some areas may be "off limits" as yet—awaiting your further growth and development—but you are now "on the Path" and your progress is assured.

You can commonly access these records through meditation, or you can exercise your growing clairvoyant abilities to read them, or you can employ your imagination during astral projection to walk through this "astral library." The more you use it—just as with the Internet—the more easily will you access what you want and need, and learn to avoid the fantasy and nonsense that can be found there just as on the Internet and within the books found in any physical library and bookstore. *Information is your responsibility too.*

The Astral Adventure and Journey

Astral projection is *not* just a *developmental* encounter with the Greater Universe beyond the physical body and its limited physical experience but an actual *awakening* of higher consciousness. *You* are more than a physical being, and the greater universe is experienced through your "inner" non-physical levels of consciousness we call astral, mental, causal, and spiritual "bodies." The *real* you is a "whole person" and all your perceptions, actions, and experiences are inclusive of all you are—physical and non-physical. Your astral body is part of you *now*, and the astral dimension is open to you *now*, but your "awareness" has to be extended and trained to *consciously* perceive and act at this level.

Recommended Product:

Slate, J.H. & Weschcke, C.L.: *Vibratory Astral Projection—Your Next Step in Evolutionary Consciousness & Psychic Empowerment. A Personal Empowerment Audio Program, 2013,* Llewellyn

APPENDIX C:
LAB RESEARCH REPORTS

Science is founded on inspiration, but is developed and brought into reality through research. For years, Dr. Slate developed and led research projects at Athens State University. Some of them were funded by the United States Army and others by the Parapsychology Foundation and other private and academic sources.

The research projects discussed in this book include instruction research activities as well as controlled laboratory studies. Many of these are quite revolutionary.

The parapsychology program at ASU was introduced in 1970 as a research oriented instructional endeavor that included a research component for each instructional course. The unpublished technical reports for the instructional related research, while unavailable for distribution, are available for inspection at the Library Archives, Athens State University, 300 North Beaty Street, Athens, AL 35611.

Also available for inspection at the Library Archives are the final technical reports for research projects funded by the Parapsychology Foundation of New York, the U. S. Army Missile Research and Development Command, and the Parapsychology Research Institute and Foundation (PRIF), a research and scholarship program established at ASU in 1970. Current research efforts sponsored by PRIF, now a private organization, include global empowerment, the nature of the multiverse, and interdimensional phenomena.

GLOSSARY

A Veritable "GALAXY" of Words & Meanings & SUGGESTED READING LIST
Specifically related to "Spirit" and "Spiritual Communication"

Note: The primary intention of a Glossary is specific to words and concepts as used within this book's text. As such, it is not a comprehensive dictionary or encyclopedia and doesn't include words believed to be generally familiar to the reader unless the usage here varies considerably from "standard" definitions for reasons that will be generally obvious. For further reference, please refer to the Llewellyn Encyclopedia at www.llewellyn.com.

For most words, reference to the extensive Index will provide all the definition and details needed. However, in this glossary we have included more detail for certain words and concepts than is usual for a Glossary when we consider them important developmental steps in expanding your awareness and background knowledge in relation to the subject of this book. We want to make this book as complete as possible by providing all the tools you need for actual practice rather than only "reading about," although we believe you will find it a "good read" and an interest intellectual journey.

The occasional reference (See Index & Text) directs you to the Index because the subject is considered so important that we prefer that you review what has been written rather than any alternative.

In addition, please remember that to a limited extent, this glossary performs the third function mentioned in the <u>Detailed Table of Contents:</u> "This is what we're going to tell you, this is what we are telling you, and this is what we told you." This "Three-Fold Learning Experience" has been used over many years in various forms in many situations. Remember too that the numbers <u>Three</u> and <u>Seven</u> are recognized as powerful factors in psychological and magickal operations.

Abrahamic Monotheism: The three male-dominant monotheistic patriarchal religions date back 3,800 years to their Middle Eastern Jewish origin. Each has a single all powerful *father* deity, and all three have many "spiritual entities, saints, angels, and spiritual forces" serving the Father. Each has a history of requiring rigid adherence to a political theology enforced by (religious) law and threats of torture and death.

Historically, all three theologically prescribe male dominance over the "sinful" but otherwise weak and defective female whose major function is to reproduce the species (with preference for males) and serve and pleasure her husband regardless of personal health or desire. Today, neither Judaism nor Christianity are dominate within the Western World, and—within expanding geographic areas—women are emerging into equal status with men, becoming equally educated and politically empowered, although there remains a lag in economic equality. And sex education and access to contraception is still widely denied or restricted.

All three, have at times been imperialistic, seeking to enlarge and enforce their theology on others through military conquest. Early Christianity (primarily when the Roman Catholic Church was dominate) was totalitarian under the command of the Pope, and Islam, throughout its history and by scriptural dictate, seeks totalitarian domination of the entire world under the command of a single Caliphate.

Both Judaism and Christianity can be described as more materialistic than spiritual and human "goodness" has become identified with worldly wealth achieved through advanced technology. In contrast, Islam is concerned with military power but otherwise is "anti-modern" and looks to return its culture to the time of its founder.

While humans are believed to have souls, communication with surviving souls of the deceased is forbidden and communication with spiritual entities is allowed only by "authorized personnel." In the case of medieval Christianity, this dictum was enforced by the Holy Inquisition's burning to death of an estimated 7 million "heretics" (mostly women and a few free-thinking scientists) over a 700 year period finally ending in 1834.*

---

*The Inquisition was just one example of "crimes against humanity" resulting from the politicizing of religion to control a population. Others include the religious wars ranging back to 4,000 BC and up through the Roman conquest of Europe, the Crusades, the European invasions of the Americas, Africa, and the Middle East, the Ottoman (Turkish) Empire's invasion of Europe, the more recent wars by German Nazi and Italian Fascism, Soviet Communism, and Islamic Terrorism. Yes, not only were Nazism and Soviet Communism developed with effective religious-styled techniques, but Hitler maintained to the end that he was a Catholic carrying out "Christ's work to exterminate the Jews." (See *The Great Cosmic Mother*)

All three religions are theologically opposed to democracy since the Earth belongs to Father God to be ruled by <u>His</u> anointed servants for His glory and not the benefit of human life. Secular Law is in conflict with religious law, and in the case of Islam it must be replaced entirely by Sharia—Islamic religious law dating back to the time of the Mohamed. No modernization is recognized.

While all three religions and various sects have had "mystics," spiritual communication is essentially denied to "the common sheep," and such practices have often been proscribed as "sinful," "demonic," even "Satanic," and commonly— with few exceptions—practitioners have been persecuted, tortured, and condemned to death.

Abyss: (Kabbalah—Tree of Life) A division on the Tree of Life separating the top three sephiroth from the rest of the Tree. A separation of the noumenal from the phenomenal, and the perceived separation between the upper, *unmanifest,* trinity of Kether, Chokmah and Binah, and the lower seven Sephiroth that are manifest. It is believed that only adepts can access those higher levels.

Adepts: Some believe advanced beings from super-physical levels of consciousness— superhuman or beyond human–have previously communicated at least partial *factual* information about the inner & greater realities of the Cosmos and the potentials for our advancing development. Perhaps their work continues "behind the scenes" and is real and effective. However, rather than look to such beings today we have plenty of "esoteric" knowledge available and have every opportunity to grow and advance without supernatural intervention at this time—and *that's what we are supposed to do! Grow Up!*

African Spiritist religions (also practiced in the Caribbean and Central and South America) that combine elements of animism and shamanism. Through drumming, dancing, chanting, and sometimes alcohol consumption and hemp smoking, the participants seek possession by a spirit entity. An animal—commonly a goat or chicken—is sacrificed to release the animal essence to be used by the possessing spirit. That entity may be the spirit of an ancestor, an animal spirit, or one of many deities called a *Loa* in Voudoun, an *Orisha* in Santeria and Candomble, and other names including those of Catholic saints. Males and females have equal status and the religion is more spiritual than material.

After Life: Generally, the life we have after the physical body's death. <u>*Where*</u> *does* <u>*What*</u> *go after death of the physical body?* Many different answers to those two questions are offered depending on different belief systems. We take a non-religious perspective in which the etheric double, along with the astral, mental and causal bodies, separates from the physical body to also slowly decay over a few days. After that, consciousness awakens in the astral body and experiences the astral world.

Ajna (also see Chakras)—*Sanskrit:* "Command Center." (AKA the *Brow* Chakra, the *Eye of Horus,* the *Third Eye*) but primarily known the **"Brow Chakra"** (which see): This chakra is located between the eyes but above the brow line, and physically manifests through the nasocilicary plexus and anatomically indicted by the pituitary gland, and in terms of psycho-physiology, the pineal gland. It relates to the balancing of our higher and lower selves and inner guidance. Physically it rules our visual consciousness, emotionally our intuitive clarity. It relates to our sense of awareness. The associated psychic powers are clairvoyance, telepathy, telekinesis, precognition, remote viewing, and aura reading.

It is the terminal point where the two nadis, *Ida* and *Pingala,* merge with the central channel, *Sushumna.* With its activation, the perception of duality ceases. *Sushumna*—along with *Ida* and *Pingala*—rises up from the *Muladhara* chakra to curve over the Crown of the head and then down to terminate in *Ajna,* while *Ida* and *Pingala* continue down to the two nostrils.

It is symbolized by an indigo colored lotus with two spokes, and represented graphically in a white winged globe. Actually, each petal or wing itself consists of 48 spokes for a total of 96. One wing is rose colored and the other is yellow. The two petals or wings are identified with the anterior and posterior pituitary lobes and symbolically represent the Sun and the Moon, mind and body, *Ida* and *Pingala.* The seed mantra is *AuM.* The element is *Manas,* "mind-stuff" the energy of consciousness. The mandala of Ajna represents the "winged" (of imagination) Hermes Caduceus with the colored iris (globe), framed by the two white pennants of the sclerotic coat of the eyeball.

With its activation, perception of duality ceases. *Sushumna,* along with *Ida* and *Pingala,* rises up from *Muladhara* chakra to curve over the Crown of the head and then down to terminate in *Ajna,* while *Ida* and *Pingala* continue down to the two nostrils.

Ajna (Brow) Chakra (Correspondences)

Alchemical Planet: Moon	Alchemical Element: Silver	Tattva: Manas (Mind)
Animal: Owl	Basic Drive: transcendence	Tattva Color: Half, rose with yellow; Half, with purplish blue
Body Function: sight, consciousness	Chakra Color: Indigo	
Element: Light, Mind	Gemstone: Quartz, Lapis lazuli	Tattva form: Winged globe
Gland: Pituitary	Goddess-form, Egyptian: Isis	Tattva Sense: Mind
God-form, Greek: Apollo	Incense: Saffron, mugwort	God-form, Hindu: SShiva-Shakti[1]
Location: Brow	Order of chakra unfoldment: 6th	Goddess-form, Hindu: Hakini [2]
Part of Body: Eyes	Sense: Mind, awareness	Yogic Planet: Moon
Psychic Power: clairvoyance, pre-cognition, remote viewing, aura reading	Seed Syllable/Number: AuM (0)	
Psychological Attribute: Logical thinking		Sense: Awareness
Spinal Joint: 32nd	Spinal Location: 1st Cervical	
Tarot Key: II, High Priestess	Tree of Life Sephirah: Chokmah & Binah	

1. Male & female in union
2. Insight

Source: Slate, J. & Weschcke, C.: *Psychic Empowerment—Tools & Techniques,* 2011, Llewellyn

Akashic Records: They are believed to exist on the higher astral and lower mental planes and to be accessible by the super consciousness through the subconscious mind in deep trance states induced through hypnosis, self-hypnosis, meditation and guided meditation, or in spontaneous reaction to deep-level emotional need.

These "records," as perceived on the astral plane, are only a reflection of their causal level permanence, are "recorded" in that substance known as the "Astral Light" to retain all that has ever happened in thought and deed; hence the Akashic Records are the enduring records of people's <u>perceptions</u> of everything they have ever *experienced* (but not the actual events) and the repository of all knowledge and wisdom, and the files of every personal memory. **Being able to call up infinite information and integrate it into your present life needs is of enormous benefit—similar to but beyond the capacity of any present-day Internet Search Engine.**

The Akashic Records, at least as "recordings" of the past, are also known as the Collective Unconscious, a kind of group mind that is inherited from all our ancestors and includes all the memories and knowledge acquired by contemporary humans.

Suggested Reading:

Dale, Cyndi: *The Subtle Body—An Encyclopedia of Your Energetic Anatomy,* 2009, Sounds True

Alpha Level: See Brain Waves.

Altered States of Consciousness (ASC): Ordinary waking consciousness and sleep are the two most familiar states of consciousness. Others include dreaming, day dreaming, hallucination, hypnagogic (half-asleep) & hypnopompic (half-awake) states, and conscious self-programming; types and levels of trance induced by focused attention and exclusion of outside stimuli, chanting of mantras, fixation on flashing lights and brightly colored geometric images, listening to and feeling drumming and other repetitive sounds, sleep deprivation, fasting; ecstatic states induced by extra-sensory stimulation, extended sex and dancing; shamanic states induced by hallucinogenic herbs, sensory deprivation & isolation, restraint in fixed positions, pain, light flagellation; meditative and hypnotic states; Out-of-Body Experiences, etc. Some of these are "exclusive" and not normally recalled during waking consciousness, while others are "inclusive" and readily remembered. Once you've been 'there,' it is easier to get there again.

Altered States are the means by which spiritual communication as well as many psychic powers are enabled. Altered states do not necessarily involve the need for ecstatic induction—non-ecstatic techniques of meditation, prayer, ritual, and hypnosis likewise induce alterations. With experience and awareness, intent alone is sufficient to shift focus from a current state to another state. The choices of intentional induction techniques relate to the purpose of the desired state. *Purpose* is the key to meaning and value. It's essentially a method of moving from one band width to another. **You can do it!**

Despite early "myth," ASCs may be induced by means other than drugs, and they are not all "that different" as already pointed out above. We need to better understand consciousness itself to more fully recognize the value and nature of the different altered states. Sleep is an altered state, dreaming is an altered state, meditation and concentration are altered states, and others are induced by lack of sleep, intense fatigue, music, drumming, dancing, yoga, sex, running, political rallies, sports events, euphoria, and also through hypnosis, astral projection, fasting, sensory deprivation, etc. ASCs do not necessarily include *high* ecstatic states nor *deep* trance. A "runner's high" feels *good* but is not always ecstatic! Meditation and prayer do not necessarily lead to ecstasy or trance. *But they can.* The human mind can be trained and directed, *under Will,* to accomplish almost anything. We call that "Magick" and it is discussed in Chapter Thirteen.

Also, both ecstasy and trance states can be spontaneous. A visit to Yosemite National Park could be ecstatic, and even a long train ride, road trip, or even a long walk can induce "road" trance. That which is sometimes called "sub-space" (discussed later) is trance-like but not necessarily ecstatic. In other words, "altered states" cover an extensive range of consciousness, and what defines any of these as specifically shamanic is **"trance with a purpose."** However, that also defines hypnosis, and such active meditation as *Path-Working,* but a major difference (and the one that also commonly does include journeying, broadly defined) is the physical body's involvement as a "leveraging" mechanism whether it be pain, pleasure, sensory overload, sensory deprivation, or fatigue. No, such leveraging is not the only way, but is mostly common to the shamanic experience which originated during an earlier time when directed states of consciousness were rare—a time before Yoga, Tantra, and other advanced techniques for *self-control* of consciousness had been developed.

Anahata **(also see Chakras) (AKA "Heart"):** This chakra is located in the upper thoracic area over the heart, and physically manifests through the cardio-pulmonary plexus and the thymus gland at the "heart" of the immune system and the site of T-cell maturation. It relates to compassion, tenderness, unconditional love, and personal well-being. Physically it rules circulation, emotionally our unconditioned love both for others and for self, mentally our passionate interests, and spiritually our devotion. It relates to the sense of touch. The element is Air. The associated psychic power is hands-on-healing. *It carries consciousness to the next life.*

It is symbolized by a *yantra* consisting of a hexagram of two interlaced triangles representing the union of female and male, within a lotus of twelve green spokes or petals, and its tattva is represented geometrically in a blue hexagram (or a circle). This yantra—more than a symbol of man and woman united—is a powerful meditation device for uniting lower with higher, anima with animus, microcosm with macrocosm, and human with Divine. It is the heart of Man and the heart of the Divine manifest in Man. The audible seed mantra is *YuNG* followed by mental echo of *YuM*.

Ancient Wisdom: "The Ancient Wisdom" remains a mystery, perhaps a myth, perhaps lost history of a time when "Men were Gods." Or, was it when "The Gods walked on Earth?" or when "Space Visitors seeded the Earth?"

However we treat it, this "Ancient Wisdom" purportedly included knowledge of great powers and energies, of technologies still surpassing those of the modern world, and of wisdom that would transform our present world into one of Peace, Prosperity, and Progress. It's the real concept underlying the belief in the "New Age," and in *Novus Ordo Seclorum*—a "New Order of the Ages."

Real or not, we are pushing back the edge of known history and finding that the artifacts we see—the Great Pyramid, the Great Sphinx, the mountain monuments in Peru, and many others—are much older than previously believed and indicative of technologies still to be "rediscovered" today.

Was that Ancient Wisdom hidden away in the Tarot? Are whispers of it contained in the symbols and signs of Freemasonry? Is it waiting for us in the practices of Magick, Yoga, and the Martial Arts? Can it be glimpsed in the ecstasies of Sex Magick? The mystery remains, all our esoteric practices are founded in the belief that we can each solve the mystery and move beyond the still luminescence of the Ancients.

Angels: Astral "helpers" and "shapers" responsible for various manifestations of life in the physical world—human, animal, plant & mineral kingdoms—and also as personal "guardian angels." In Spiritualism, they are Messengers from a higher realm. As seen clairvoyantly they may appear as robed, without wings, or either sex, and *shining.* They are sometimes referred to as "the *Shining Ones.*"

Anima and Animus: Psychology now recognizes that every woman has a bit of a man in her psyche—called the "animus," and every man has a bit of a woman in his psyche—called the "anima." In other words, "Male and Female He created them" means that every human in their wholeness is psychologically, mentally and spiritually inclusive of both genders. Sexual organs are not the "end all" but the "beginning." Women and Men are equal in the eyes of creation and in the eyes of the law. It's time that all Men see likewise. *As Aleister Crowley said: "Every Man and Every Woman is a Star."*

The Woman in every man is the Anima and is mythic ideal of the feminine that a man projects on to women. It manifests in fantasy, romance, sexual behavior, the estrogen hormone, and in feminine energy. Likewise the Man in every woman is the Animus and is the mythic ideal of the masculine that a woman projects on to men, manifesting in fantasy, romance, sexual response, the testosterone hormone, and in masculine energy.

(We differ, somewhat, from the Jungian concept in which there seemed to be little evolution in these archetypes. Instead, we change, there is slow change in them as well. Memory maybe fixed, but other change is universal in particular ways.)

Animal Communication: Most often a form of Mental Telepathy by which information is transferred between the animal and a human, generally by uncharacteristic behavior.

Animal Magnetism: Etheric, or life, energy that, like *Prana* and Reich's *Orgone*, is present in all animal life and everywhere throughout the universe, like Ether. It can be concentrated, stored, transferred and projected by magical practices—essentially the use of a trained imagination. It formed the basis for many of the practices of *Mesmerism*, considered by some to be an early forerunner of Hypnotism.

Animism: Simply the belief that all of Nature—animals, plants, stones, natural forces, etc. contain "essential" Spirit and that humans—likewise containing Spirit—can communicate with that essential Spirit, learn the nature of plants and the ways of animals and the energies and properties of stones and gems, and through appropriate "magickal" actions apply those properties to personal benefit. A recent variation called Quantum Animism further postulates that Mind permeates the world at every level and that every natural system has a conscious center from which it directs and observes its action. Another variation proposes that Morphic fields "animate organisms at all levels of complexity, from galaxies to giraffes, and from ants to atoms." (Wikipedia—animism) The concept of Morphic resonance is of universal connections between like units where each benefits from the memories of repetitive behavior of past actions.

Apparition: (Psychic Phenomena) A projection of one's image that is seen by another. Unlike Astral Projection, the appearance is mostly spontaneous and does not involve the projector entering into a trance state. Apparitions are often connected with a personal crisis or intense interest in the other person. Sometimes it is coincidental with the person's death.

Apport: (Psychic Phenomena) The appearance of an object as if moved from another location by psychic means. Some suggest it involves the dematerialization and then re-materialization of the object.

Aquarian Age: (Astrology) (New Age) The zodiacal age of approximately 2,150 years length subsequent to the Piscean Age. The 'spirit' of the Age is characterized by the symbolism and astrological characteristics ascribed to the zodiacal sign. The Piscean Age, symbolized by two fish swimming in opposite directions, relates to authoritarian Christianity and Islam, and the conflicts of the last 2,200 years. The Aquarian Age is the Age of Man, of Intellect rather than Emotion, and of self-responsibility rather than the 'shepherd's crook of the Church Bishop and the harsh commands of a human authority operating in the name of God. It is associated with the "New Age" which Carl Jung believed to have begun in 1940.

While the ending of one age and the beginning of another is determined by the astronomical position of the Sun at the Spring Equinox, the exact timing on such a cosmic scale is hard to determine, and transitional influence between the old and new is active over several hundred years. The Aquarian influence has been active since the Age of Enlightenment and more and more apparent with the liberalization of science from the Church's domination, the growth of political freedom with the founding of America, and the advancement of widespread education through universal public and secular schools. The Aquarian Age *demands* that Knowledge be applied to both practical and spiritual needs, and that schools function as "places of knowledge," rather than parochial temples of indoctrination and dogma!

Aquarian Man, The *Inner* Directed: The Inner-Directed person holds independent views derived through rational study and/or intuitive processes in contrast to the outer-directed person who 'follows the crowd' or accepts the guidance of authority figures without reasonable questions. 'Inner-Directed' has also been associated with the Aquarian Age individual man in contrast to the Piscean Age with its symbolism of fish who swim in groups. The outer-directed person is perceived as easily manipulated because of his dependence on outer authority. (See Piscean Man, The *Outer* Directed)

Aquarius' symbol is the "water bearer" pouring forth new Knowledge for everyone's benefit, but the **Aquarian Age** is also that time when the student becomes the active acquirer of learning—thus the reason behind the explosion of Self-Study, Self-Help, and Self-Improvement so marked over the past half-century. Previously secret esoteric knowledge is coming out into the open so that everyone can "walk with the Gods." The World of the Mind and Spirit is the new frontier for exploration of Inner Space rather than land and sea. Our scientific and technological thrust must be directed to saving the planet and opening the inner doors of consciousness as well. People are coming together in learning knowledge once called "occult," in research and sharing of discovery of New Worlds of Mind & Spirit, in the revival of a non-institutional religion of Nature and Heart, and learning how it is that Man and Woman can liberate each other.

The physical, social, and economic dimensions of world crisis demand that we make our spiritual knowledge a living and growing culture, not a static faith. That is why we make our celebrations renewals, conventions of discovery and learning as well as festivals. We take joy in the responsibility that the Age thrusts upon us, for with it is the opportunity for a tremendous leap forward in personal and planetary evolution. Humanity is poised on a precipice from which we can fall or ascend. The choice is ours. If we choose to fly and ascend to the Gods we must, like Icarus, make our own wings of Mind and Spirit.

Archetypes: (Psychology—Jungian) A universal image and center of psychological function & energy mostly similar across nationalities, races, cultures and historical times. Generally speaking, "Mom" is the same mom everywhere. Nevertheless, there may be some minor variation across long established cultures as expressed in dominant religions, art, folklore, magickal practice, and personal experiences in dreams and visions. Personal variants that conflict with the "norm" may be the source of traumatic disturbances as when a real-life mom fails to fulfill her archetypal stature or the role proclaimed for her by religion or culture. Essentially, archetypes have no *inherent* form but their shape is projected by individual psyche in response to circumstance.

The archetypes are the foundation of major mythologies and subsequent religions, and correspond with the gods of their "prophets" and myth heroes, the gods, goddesses and spiritual entities representing the elemental forces and the dynamics of human relationships and experience. They are found in the major arcana of the Tarot, are experienced through Kabalistic path-working and shamanic trances, and are often met in dreams and projected on to real life figures in times of crisis. One of the goals in every program of self-knowledge is to gain understanding of our particular interaction with them, and possibly change those interactions from a childish to a more mature level.

As Above, so Below! The key phrase found in the *Emerald Tablet* that recognizes the dynamic formula established when "God created Man in his own image." Simply stated, the human person is the Microcosm and the Universe in the Macrocosm. Not only is their identity between Man and Cosmos but there is a continuing interaction between the two.

Each human being is a miniature cosmos, complete in every detail even though those details may exist more in energetic levels and in a matrix of potential rather than current fulfillment. In our new perspective, this means two things:

First: Each person functions through the same laws, principles, formulae, etc. as does the Universe as a whole. It means that the "Laws of the Universe—the systems by which it functions—are also the "Laws of Magick."

Second: Each person has the potential to become successively greater representations of the Universe in all its glory. We are "gods in the making!"

Each of us is in process of becoming more than we are. The life purpose of each person is to grow in our wholeness, developing innate powers into actual skills. Through the study and practice of the skills of Mind & Spirit we grow into the whole person we are intended to be, uniting the Lower Self with the Upper Self. In esoteric practice it is called "Initiation," in magickal work it is called "the Attainment and Conversation with one's Holy Guardian Angel," i.e. the Higher Self. *It is also known as Self-Empowerment because the process heals the divisions of Self enabling the Whole Person to draw upon all the Knowledge, Powers, and Skills of the entire Consciousness, the Soul uniting Past Memories with the Present Life and Future potential.*

Ask, and Ye shall Receive: There's more than one aspect to this expression:

    1. To ask is to set a goal, and with a goal little is accomplished.

    2. You cannot expect an answer to a question you have not asked.

Remember that your Personal Human Consciousness is modeled on "the Body of God," the Macrocosm. The Powers of the Universe are yours to earn and learn. You do have the Power, but you have to learn it, understand it, believe it, use it, and—above all—have *faith* in its reality.

Astral Awareness: The essential goal of astral projection is to extend awareness beyond the limitations of the physical brain to become fully conscious on the astral plane. Moving beyond single body limitation to multi-body consciousness our horizons become infinite.

Astral Body, aka Astral Vehicle: Equivalent to the Sanskrit *Kama-Rupa*. The extra-biological part of our being, which exists as a conscious, intelligent, and inde-structible entity, is the third *Vehicle* ("upward" in the general scheme) or level of consciousness, also called the Desire or Emotional Body, or Emotional "Enve-lope." In the process of incarnation, the astral vehicle is composed of the plan-etary energies in their aspects to one another to form a matrix for the physical body. This matrix is, in a sense, the true *horoscope* guiding the structure of the body and defining karmic factors.

The Astral Vehicle is the Lower Self of Emotion, Imagination, Thinking, Memory and Will—all the functions of the mind in response to sensory percep-tion and emotional reaction. It is the field of dreams and the subconscious mind. It is the vehicle for most psychic activities including the "spirit" or *Surviving Per-sonality* following death of the physical body.

Yet, a distinction must be made: The Physical Body is the field of ordinary conscious mind and the Astral is that of the sub-conscious mind, and a door-way to the super-conscious mind and the collective unconscious. It is vehicle of astral projection and the Shamanic Journey, the means of exploration of the Inner Worlds.

Astral Doorways: (Astral Consciousness) Meditation on certain objects may func-tion 1) to induce an alternative state of consciousness or 2) to bring access to certain areas of the sub-conscious mind and astral plane. Among the first are fascination devices that focus awareness and induce trance—crystal balls, magick mirrors, swinging pendulums, pools of ink, etc.—allowing the user to receive impressions. Among the second, meditation upon particular symbols such as the Tattvas & Yantras, certain decks of Tarot Cards, Rune Symbols, the I Ching Hexagrams, Hebrew and Sanskrit letters, Egyptian Hieroglyphs, Planetary and Magickal Sigils, and certain "pure" deific images can be visualized as "doorways" through which to project consciousness or the Astral Vehicle to access subjective states of consciousness and explore specific "areas" of the astral dimension.

Astral Light: (Astral Consciousness) The lowest principle of Akasha; the 'substance' of the Astral Plane that responds to emotion. It is approximately equivalent to Ether, Mana, Vital Fluid, etc. holding the impressions of thought and emotion and feeling, forming memory. It is generally perceived in that unique blue color characteristic of electrical sparks.

Suggested Reading:

Regardie, I., Cecero, S.T. & Cicero, C.: *The Tree of Life—An Illustrated Study of Magic,* 2001, Llewellyn

Astral Matrix: The astral body—in contrast to a constructed thought form—is a non-physical replica of the physical body and can be used as an organizing matrix perceived to be ideally healthy. Upon re-engagement with the physical body, health images can be transferred for healing and rejuvenation.

Suggested Reading:

Slate, J.H. & Weschcke, C.L.: *Astral Projection for Psychic Empowerment,* 2012, Llewellyn

Astral Plane (Level, World, and Dimension): The second level (third when counting the etheric level separate from the physical) or plane, sometimes called the Spirit World, Inner Plane, Emotional Plane, or Subjective World, it is an alternate dimension both coincident to our physical world and extending beyond it. Some believe it extends to other planets and allows for astral travel between them. It is that level of concrete consciousness between the Physical/Etheric, the sphere of ordinary consciousness, and the Mental and Spiritual levels. It is where dreams, vision, and imagination are experienced and magical action shapes physical manifestation.

The astral world has its own landscape, generally replicating the physical world, but is far more extensive, reaching wherever consciousness reaches. It has its own inhabitants, which include the astral bodies of the inhabitants of the physical world. Those astral inhabitants also include forms that have never incarnated into physical bodies as well as temporary inhabitants created by humans through the power of imagination, emotion and fantasy. It is also possible that some creatures, like certain paranormal entities such as UFOs, Aliens, the Loch Ness and other 'monsters' that slip in and out of the physical world have their origin in the astral, and that mythical beings like dragons also exist in the lower astral close enough to the physical that they sometimes appear to the physical world inhabitants.

Just as humans cannot fly through the air without aid so we cannot readily function at these higher levels until we ourselves are able to raise our levels of consciousness and achieve increased awareness. Your perceptions at the lowest levels of the astral plane can be as challenging as those of the lowest levels of the physical plane such as below sea level where there are creatures living without oxygen in the midst of sulfurous plumes in the ocean deeps rising from the earth's hellish volcanic interior.

Instead of physical substance the astral world has its own unique substance that some writers refer to as "emotional" because it is the foundation for our emotional consciousness just as the physical substance is the foundation for our physical consciousness, and the mental world substance is the foundation of our mental consciousness.

In this New Age, we will experience the same drive that led us to explore and adapt to the far reaches of the physical world extended to these additional worlds that make up the vaster universe that is both physical and non-physical. The astral plane is in many ways *our new frontier,* and as we focus more and more in this added dimension we hope that we will at the same time bring peace and true prosperity and full realization of the beneficial opportunities in the physical plane that is the *foundation* for our evolutionary journey.

Suggested Reading:

Slate, J.H. & Weschcke, C.L.: *Astral Projection for Psychic Empowerment, 2012,* Llewellyn

Astral Powers: Those natural powers and trained skills that arise from mastery of the particular "rules of engagement" that characterize the astral plane. With understanding the nature of astral substance & energies and the unique characteristics of the many sub-planes and resources of the astral plane, we need to train the astral body in much the same as we do the physical body—by learning and practice.

In most situations, we are interested in using the astral to explore the non-physical universe and to influence physical actions. Still anchored in the physical body, we make use of various OBE procedures to do these things. In most cases, it is vital to set specific goals, and it is through such work that we do gain skills, train our astral "muscles," and grow in consciousness.

Suggested Reading:

Slate, J.H. & Weschcke, C.L.: *Astral Projection for Psychic Empowerment,* 2012, Llewellyn

Astral Projection & Astral Travel: (Astral Consciousness) It is desirable to treat these two subjects together because of the confusion in terminology over the years. Astral projection is a particular state of consciousness in which the astral body is perceived as separating from the physical and is able to travel on the astral plane, obtain information, communicate with other beings, consciously experience distant realities, and return to the physical with full memory. In most situations, we are interested in using the astral to explore the non-physical universe and to influence physical actions. Still anchored in the physical body, we make use of various OBE procedures to do these things. In most cases, it is vital to set specific goals, and it is through such work that we do gain skills, train our astral "muscles," and grow in consciousness. Among Spiritualists, this is referred to as "spirit leaving the body."

It is commonly thought that the astral body separates from the physical during sleep, but does not travel. Non-physical movement in the familiar physical world is more likely to involve the Etheric body than the astral. But, the astral plane is not the physical world, and it lacks the 'solidity' of the physical plane even though there is replication. However, things may appear on the astral that are not in the physical. The etheric is the energy double of the physical body, able to function separately from the physical body while connected to it with the 'silver cord' that transfers energy and consciousness between the two. The etheric body can travel anywhere in the physical world, moving with the speed of thought, and can interact with the physical in a limited manner.

In recent metaphysical thinking, it is more often believed that the Astral Body does not *spatially* leave the physical body because it is not really an independent "body" but is the sub-conscious mind and 'moves' within the field of consciousness without moving at all. Consciousness is everywhere, and in consciousness you can be anywhere. To the extent you want a body, you need to create a Body of Light in your imagination and then just imagine it doing what you want, going where you want.

Suggested Reading:

Bruce & Mercer: *Mastering Astral Projection* book and CD companion, 2007, Llewellyn

Phillips: *Astral Projection Plain & Simple—the Out-of-Body Experience,* 2003, Llewellyn

Denning & Phillips: *Practical Guide to Astral Projection, the Out-of-Body Experience,* 2001, Llewellyn

Goldberg: *Astral Voyages, Mastering the Art of Interdimensional Travel,* 2002, Llewellyn

McCoy: *Astral Projection for Beginners—Six Techniques for Traveling to Other Realms,* 1999, Llewellyn

Slate, J.H. & Weschcke, C.L.: *Astral Projection for Psychic Empowerment,* 2012, Llewellyn

Webster: *Astral Travel for Beginners, Transcend Time & Space with Out-of-Body Experiences,* 2002, Llewellyn

Astral Room: A space that is, or can be temporarily isolated and designated as "Do Not Disturb" while in use. In addition to the physical space, through visualization you create a temporary (that is actually large and longer lasting than you think) astral room. You should do your meditation, magickal, and other astral/psychic work in this space and always think of it as your "Astral Room."

Attunement: Adjusting your normal state of consciousness (your frequency) to match another frequency.

Aura: (Aura) (Etheric Body): *Note: We are providing an unusual amount of detail to the subjects of the Aura even though it is not a major study in this book. The reason is to provide a foundation for a greater understanding of the "spirit in the human person" and how it relates (and communicates) with the world aound.*

The Human aura is an egg-shaped sphere of energy extending as much as two to three feet beyond the physical body and viewed by clairvoyants in colorful layers that may be 'read' and interpreted. It includes layers outward from the physical: the Etheric, Astral, Mental, and Spiritual bodies. The aura is also known as the "magical mirror of the universe" in which our inner activities of thought and feeling are perceived in colors. It is also the matrix of planetary forces that shapes and sustains the physical body and the lower personality. Clairvoyants may analyze the aura in relation to health, ethics and spiritual development, and the aura can be shaped and its surface made to reflect psychic attacks back to their origin.

Suggested Reading:

Andrews: *How to See and Read the Aura,* 2002, Llewellyn

Slate: *Aura Energy for Health, Healing & Balance,* 1999, Llewellyn

Webster: *Aura Reading for Beginners, Develop Your Psychic Awareness for Health & Success,* 2002, Llewellyn

Aura Reading: (Aura) Clairvoyant 'reading' of the aura to determine the health, character and spiritual development of the person (or animal) by the colors seen.

The main factors to consider are:

- The various fields about the body reflecting the etheric, astral, mental, and spiritual bodies or *sheaths.*
- The levels of the body corresponding to the location of the chakras.
- The colors, and their clarity, brightness and intensity.
- The presence of irregularities and patterns: such as blockages, holes, depressions or bulges, blotches, streaks, fluctuations, fissures, points of light or darkness, streams and clusters of energy, tentacles, arcs, agitation, symmetry and balance
- In some auras, there will be geometric figures.
- The size of each of the fields as distance out from the physical body.

- The overall structure, which Dr. Slate refers to as the unique *signature* of the individual.
- The observer's *feeling* or psychic impressions.

While some specific observations can be augmented with the use of dowsing rods and pendulums as well as the hands in sensing the aura, the aura visionary, or reader, should attempt to start with basic observations of the above factors, and then slowly perceive the complexity of the overall aura in which the following elements are important considerations:

- Streams of Energy. These can occur in a variety of formation and colors anywhere in the aura. They can radiate outward as brilliant streamers or meander about in a network of energy. Any blockage to these streams should be noted in relation to the color and location.
- Clusters of Energy. These intense concentrations of colorful energy can occur anywhere in the aura and typically are in response to specific empowerment needs. Color and location should be noted.
- Points of Light. These are associated with powerful forces intervening to empower the individual's life, and can signify a spiritual presence such as a guide or angel. Intensity and location should be noted.
- Points of Darkness. These may signify an attack on the aura, possibly—in rare instances—an actual psychic attack or involuntary psychic vampirism, but more often as points of severe weakness or injury.
- Voids. Larger than points, voids are inactive areas with little or no energy that often reveal psychological factors such as discouragement, feelings of hopelessness, depersonalization, detachment, etc.
- Agitation. Appearing as churning turbulence accompanied by discoloration, they suggest fractured relationships, insecurity, fear, excessive anxiety, unresolved conflicts, and when localized may indicate the site of chronic pain.
- Symmetry. This signals a healthy, harmonious mind, body, and spirit able to accommodate change and opportunities as new learning experiences.
- Fissures. These are breaks and tears that have jagged and irregular edges and are usually gray in color. They originate in the outer layers of the aura as the result of psychic injury—often from early childhood or past-life experiences. They may be indicative of physical or emotional abuse and often appear in

the auras of battered women. The effects of past-life experiences survive and are reflected in the aura.

- Tentacles. These extend outward from the aura's external boundary and are often associated with immaturity and dependency needs—a reaching out for support. They are frequently found in the auras of people who look for instant gratification, or who make selfish and unreasonable demands on others. Too, they are found in the auras of pseudo-intellectuals, self-anointed "scholars" who specialize in debunking contrary views to their own. Tentacles are often associated with psychic vampirism in which the tentacle reaches from one aura to another.

- Arcs. Arcs connect the upper regions of two auras in close and satisfying social interaction and will sometimes lead to a literal merging of the two auras.

- Geometric Forms. Geometric forms can occur anywhere in the aura as specialized concentrations of energy originating either within the subject or from an external force.

    a. Spheres. Like other aura signature forms, the color and location offer clues to its energizing role. For example, a bright yellow sphere in the upper region of the aura is associated with intellectual enrichment. A bright green sphere indicates healing energy being applied in the physical body at that location.

    b. Pyramids. Psychics often have a bright pyramid of energy in the upper regions of the aura, sometimes directly overhead.

    c. Sheath. A large shield-like ring of intensely bright energy may enclose the entire aura as a protective boundary.

    d. Asymmetrical globs, often smoky in coloration, tend to constrict the aura and suppress its energies.

Interpretation of the aura should not be based on strict *rules* following these listings of colors, brightness, size, shapes, etc., but rather a holistic synthesis characterize by the aura visionary's empathy with the subject—even when viewing one's own aura. While details count towards the whole, we must never let the details overwhelm the whole in our interpretation.

Aura readers interpret colors, their intensity, and their location through established definitions:

- **Blue**—Throat Chakra—Religious (but not limited by doctrine). Light blue is associated with balance, tranquility, self-insight, flexibility, optimism, and empathy for others. Deep blue is associated with mental alertness, sharp-wittedness, and emotional control. Dullness of blue anywhere in the aura is associated with negative stress, pessimism, despondency, and insecurity (feeling blue), whereas dark, dingy blue may indicate suicidal tendencies.

- **Brown**—Strong interests in the earth and natural resources, along with personality traits of practicality, stability and independence. Brown is also characteristic of such professionals as geologists, ecologists, archaeologists, and landscape and construction workers. Brown in the aura is commonly indicative of outdoor interests such as hiking, skiing, mountain climbing, and hunting, as well as physical fitness.

- **Gold**—Advanced spirituality. People with gold in the aura are charismatic and able to handle large-scale projects, but they usually attain their successes later in life.

- **Gray**—Usually a transient color that can foreshadow illness, adversity and even death. Small areas of gray can signify health problems in relation to their location.

- **Green**—Heart Chakra—Love, affinity with Nature, often a natural healer. Bright green signifies healing energy, self-actualization, and raised consciousness particularly concerning global conditions. Bright green is typical for health care professionals and environmentalists. The auras of psychic healers are usually iridescent, a feature not often found in the auras of other health care professionals. Dull green is associated with envy (green with envy), inner conflict, personal unfulfillment, and resistance to change. A very dull green with shades of gray is often a precursor of serious adversity, personal catastrophe, or physical illness. Associated with healing energy.

- **Indigo**—Brow Chakra—Intuition, nurturing. See also purple as indigo and purple are sometimes difficult to distinguish from one another. Associated with spiritual awareness.

- **Orange**—Genital or Sacral Chakra—Social extraverts who typically pursue careers requiring considerable social interaction, such as politics and sales. They are independent, competitive, and possess strong persuasive skills. Discoloration in the orange aura is associated with impatience, egotism, emotional instability, and a low tolerance for frustration. Associated with emotional energy.

- **Pink**—The color of youth, longevity, rejuvenation, sensitivity, humanitarians, idealism, and talent. Typically, older people with an abundance of pink in their auras have achieved prominence in their careers through hard work, have moderate political views, and are interested in the arts and such matters as historical preservation. Associated with affection.

- **Purple**—Associated with philosophy and abstract interests, purple is often predominant in the auras of ministers, philosophers and theoreticians. People with purple in their auras value intuitive knowledge, often possess superior verbal skills, and command respect from their peers. Wealth often comes easily to them and they settle into comfortable careers in which they can pursue personal interests.

- **Red**—Base of Spine or Root Chakra—Vitality, sensuality, physical energy, impulsive behavior, strong emotion, outbursts of anger (seeing red), the need for excitement, adventure, and risk-taking. While flashes of red in the aura (anger) are usually transient, more permanent strands of red woven into the aura may be indicative of violent and uncontrolled aggressive impulses. Areas of red are not uncommon among male college students active in contact sports and similarly in professional athletes in competitive sports. Red can also relate to leadership, responsibility, drive and charisma. Associated with sexual energy.

- **Silver**—While rarely seen, people with silver in their auras are often full of grand, but impractical ideas, more characteristic of dreamers than doers.

- **Violet**—Crown Chakra—Advanced spirituality and psychic skills. People with a lot of violet in their auras sometime exhibit an off-putting air of superiority and are often involved in metaphysical pursuits.

- **White**—Not commonly seen but indicative of "purity," self-effacement, peace-loving.

- **Yellow**—Solar Plexus—Intellect, mental power, creativity, strong personality. The brightness of the yellow is associated with intelligence, while the expansiveness of the color is associated with social competence and dependability. Bright yellow around the head is associated with abstract thinking, problem solving, and verbal skills, while bright yellow around the shoulders and chest is associated with superior eye-hand coordination and mechanical skills. Dullness and constriction in the predominantly yellow aura may indicate stressful conditions and difficulties in social interactions. Associated with mental energy.

Suggested Reading:

Andrews: *How to See and Read the Aura, 2002,* Llewellyn

Slate: *Aura Energy for Health, Healing & Balance, 1999,* Llewellyn

Suggested Reading—Slate, J.H. & Weschcke, C.L.: *Astral Projection for Psychic Empowerment, 2012,* Llewellyn

Webster: *Aura Reading for Beginners, Develop Your Psychic Awareness for Health & Success, 2002,* Llewellyn

Aura Seeing: (Aura) The perception of the aura, initially by means of the "subtle senses" and then by psychic clairvoyance. Mark Smith says that anyone can learn to see auras in only 60 seconds. In his book, *Auras: See Them in Only 60 Seconds!* he breaks this instruction down into a few easy steps:

1. Stand the subject eighteen inches to two feet in front of a bare white wall. Avoid walls with colors or patterns. (Joe Slate in his *Aura Energy for Health, Healing & Balance* suggests that you place a small shiny object such as a thumb tack or adhesive dot on the wall a few inches to the upper left or right of the subject.)

2. Use indirect lighting—natural ambient daylight, if possible. Avoid fluorescent light or direct sunlight.

3. View the subject from at least ten feet away.

4. Ask the subject to relax, breathe deeply, and rock gently from side to side with hands unclasped at his or her side.

5. Look past the subject's head and shoulders and focus on the wall behind.

6. Avoid looking at the subject, concentrating instead on the texture of the wall or the shiny object behind him or her, *using your peripheral rather than direct vision.*

7. As you look past the outline of the body, you will see a band of fuzzy light around the subject, about one-quarter inch to one-half inch in depth. This is the *etheric* aura.

8. Continue to look past the outline of the body, and you should see the subject as if he or she is illuminated from behind, sometimes with a bright yellow or silver color. One side might glow more strongly or slowly pulsate. Auras rarely are uniform.

9. As you progress you will soon see a second, larger band of light three inches to two feet around the body. This is the astral aura. It is usually darker and more diffuse than the etheric.

10. Joe Slate says that once you see the aura you should shift your attention from the shiny object to the aura and observe its various characteristics. Should the aura begin to fade away, shift your focus back to the shiny object, and repeat the procedure.

Suggested Reading:

Andrews: *How to See and Read the Aura*, 2002, Llewellyn

Slate: *Aura Energy for Health, Healing & Balance*, 1999, Llewellyn

Slate, J.H. & Weschcke, C.L.: *Astral Projection for Psychic Empowerment*, 2012, Llewellyn

Smith: *Auras: See Them in Only 60 Seconds!* 2002, Llewellyn

Aurum Solis: The Order of Aurum Solis is an Initiatic society which transmits the Theurgic heritage of hermetism. This means that Aurum Solis is an occult organization whose principle function is to do the necessary work utilizing the magical principles of the Ogdoadic tradition. We will begin our discussion by examining those principles that define the validity and the effectiveness of the Ogdoadic tradition's work and transmission.

The first Principle is that there is a direct link between each Grand Master and all the Grand masters who preceded him or her. That link is part of the unbroken lineage that extends back to the time of the earliest Grand Master, it is by this link that each new Grand Master of the tradition is charged with his office. In a Theurgic Order such as ours, the office of the Grand Master is not the result of an election or the personal will of an assembly. The presiding Grand Master chooses his/her successor and transmits to him/her, during a specific initiation, the occult office of the Order. This is accomplished by connecting the New Grand Master with the unbroken golden chain of the Past Grand Masters. This linking process makes the chosen Grand Master able to assume the full power of his/ her office.

The special rites of the Grand Master give him the ability to maintain the egregores of the Tradition in a living, active and dynamic state.

The second principle that establishes the legitimacy of the Ogdoadic tradition is the power to transmit and connect with the egregore of the Order. Those who are familiar with this kind of work, recognize that an initiation must be coincident with an awakening of the consciousness of the Initiate. His/Her connection with an egregore facilitates that process and protects the aspirant in his/her work. This capacity (the linking to an egregore that protects and aids in the evolution of consciousness), is a direct result of the active Initiatic chain of the Order. The act of Initiation causes these changes to occur in the aspirant, (making that person part of the unbroken chain), so that (s)he is able to perform rites using a directly transmitted material basis, (such as the Tessera, of which we will speak in the next paragraph). Initiation manifests these changes in the aspirant and links the aspirant to the golden chain.

The third principle, rooted in the Hermetic initiation, is that of the transmission of the "sacred objects" or more exactly the transmission of "consecrated objects." The Tessera, as a specific example of such a material basis, was made public by our Order. A presentation of one of the models was given in the public writings of the Order. These Tesseri constitute a direct link with the Mother Tessera and the heart of the Order; as such the Tessera forges another link for each new member to that unbroken occult chain which ensures the constant aid and protection of the egregore to each linked member of the Order. The construction and consecration of the sacred objects of the Order is specifically transmitted, and must always be made and consecrated according to precise steps and principles. These teachings have their origin in the writings of Iamblicus, Proclus, Apuleus and Marsilio Ficino.

Automatic Writing: A form of Channeling in which a person, sometimes in trance, writes or even keyboards messages generally believed to originate with spiritual beings, or with aspects of the subconscious mind. Typically the hand holding a writing pen rests lightly upon a sheet of blank paper and is *allowed* to write spontaneously. Not infrequently, meaningless scribble will precede meaningful writing that becomes the channel between consciousness and the information source.

Suggested Reading:

Wiseman, Sara: *Writing the Divine—How to Use Channeling for Soul Growth & Healing*, 2009, Llewellyn

Autonomic nervous system: The 'lower intelligence' that safely runs the body functions without conscious awareness.

Awake (Consciousness): In contrast to sleep, being awake supposedly means that we are alert and perceptive to sensory input and the ongoing functions of ordinary consciousness. Nevertheless, self-observation will clearly show that there's more to being awake than having your eyes open! It's somewhat like having a dimmer on your light switch. Learn to turn up the intensity to become fully awake. Awakened refers to an opening of personal consciousness to the "Greater Reality," which is facilitated as we gain access to the higher dimensions we most commonly call Astral, Mental, Causal, and or just a comprehensive "Spiritual" for levels beyond but inclusive of the physical/biological.

Awareness (Consciousness): Awareness is the focus of consciousness on things, images, ideas, and sensations. Full awareness is more than what we physically sense. We do have psychic impressions independent of the physical apparatus. And we can focus our awareness on memories dredged up from the subconscious; we can focus on symbols and images and all the ideas, and memories associated with them. We can turn our awareness to impressions from the astral and mental planes, and open ourselves to receiving information from other sources, from other dimensions, and from other minds.

Awareness is how we use our consciousness. It is just as infinite as is consciousness, and as is the universe in all its dimensions and planes. When we speak of expanding or broadening our awareness we are talking about paying attention to new impressions from new sources, and from the other ways we use our consciousness. Awareness is like the "Operating System" that filters incoming information, sometimes blocking "what we don't believe in."

At a minimum, awareness is our ability to perceive, to feel, or to be conscious of events, objects or sensory patterns without necessarily understanding the object. It is a cognitive reaction to a condition or event. Awareness is a relative concept. An animal may be partially aware, may be subconsciously aware, or may be acutely aware of an event or other animal. Awareness may be focused on an internal state, such as a visceral feeling, or on external events by way of sensory perception. Awareness provides the raw material from which animals develop a subjective or automatic "knowledge" of what needs to be done.

Awareness is something of a corollary to Concentration. We are used to thinking of it as passive in sensory perception but it changes dramatically when used actively. Through extended awareness, we grow and develop our latent psychic powers into reliable skills.

Your perceptions are extended and enriched, and what was invisible can become visible, or heard, or tasted, or sensed. And becoming aware is not limited to objects and people, but includes energies pulsing through and around objects, persons, and their environment.

"*Public* Awareness" may also refer to public or common knowledge or understanding about a social, scientific, or political issue, and hence many movements try to foster "awareness" of a given subject. Unlike the "Collective Illusion" (which also see), this awareness is collective, but "real."

Banishing: A ritual or meditative (visualizing) approach to shield, neutralize, ground, and dissipate unwanted spiritual energies and psychic self-protection.

***Become more than You are.* (New Age):** A phrase used by Carl Llewellyn Weschcke to express the concept of self-directed evolution. You are, we all are, a 'work-in-progress' towards fulfilling the potential of the Whole Person already existent as a 'matrix' of consciousness into which we are evolving. To "Become more than You are" is the goal of everyone who accepts the *opportunity* and *responsibility* of accelerated development and Self-Empowerment.

Before Time Began: In esoteric thinking, both the Cosmos and Consciousness (Spirit) *devolved* (the opposite of evolution) from the "Divine Idea" through a series of various forms and "layers" of Matter, Energy and Consciousness. Within this structure certain conscious entities developed and began to function in ways that brought about an increasingly complex structure within which the evolutionary process began in accordance with the initial Idea, or Plan, and culminating in the …

Beginning which is conceived as a "program" of basic instructions guiding the evolutionary process.

It is important to understand evolution as a *process* and not a series of precon-ceived objects and beings. "In God's image" does not mean that humans, angels, other beings, or even physical matter and the physical world were "created" as they appear today, or as they were in the past, or as they will be in the future.

While evolution moves within a multi-dimension scheme in which a series of matrices function as "next steps" building from the past, those steps work as experimental "trial and error" from which the "better" survived and went on while others met a *dead end*. There is a spiritual impulse, a kind of spiritual guid-ance that is relentless and continuous but it becomes increasingly *participatory* as human evolve into "co-creators." For all we know, that may lead to an even-tual merger of human with the robots and drones of their creation. Along with replacement parts that are improvements on their processors, physical immortal-ity may be achieved.

Belief System: (Consciousness) The complex of emotional and mental complex thought structures that define the way we perceive reality. Also see "Feelings" and "Operating System." Belief is also described as "Faith" that filters our perception of reality as defined by religious institutions.

Suggested Reading

Braden: *The Spontaneous Healing of Belief, Shattering the Paradigm of False Limits,* 2008, *Hay House*

"Biblical Truth:" Because the Jewish and Christian "sacred scripture" claims to be the "Word of God," it is likewise claimed that every word, statement, historical reference, and claim regarding physical phenomena is literal truth. *Nothing could be further from the truth!* The Bible is based on particular myths, folklore, tribal behavior, and stories intended to establish and affirm various political claims as historic fact. As the Bible was further "institutionalized," it became protected and used in religious laws even to the extent that "mythic" fact became substitute for historical, psychological, and scientific facts. Such absurdities as the dating for the "Creation," for the appearance of humanity, the birth of certain persons, the "proper" role of women, and more are all fictional and intended to impose reli-gious dominance on the "common sheep."

Bi-directional Endlessness: From the reincarnation perspective, the continuum for individual existence is endless, with neither beginning nor end.

Book Test: Apparent communication from a Spirit directing a person either by words or impulse to go to a particular book, to a particular page, and sometimes to the exact word that passes information known to be identified with the Spirit as a proof of survival.

Brain Waves: (Self-Hypnosis) The brain generates weak electrical impulses representative of its particular activities. As recorded by the electro-encephalograph (EEG), they fall into particular levels assigned Greek letters. Beta, at 14 to 26 cycles per second, is our normal waking state including focused attention, concentration, thinking, etc. Alpha, 7 to 14 cycles, is the next level down characteristic of relaxation, alert receptivity, meditation and access to the subconscious mind. It is at 8 cycles per second, the border between alpha and theta that Trance occurs. Theta, 4 to 8, is lower yet and occurs just before (hypnopompic) or after (hypnagogic) sleep and is characteristic of light sleep, deep meditation, vivid imagery, and high levels of inner awareness. Delta, 1 to 3, is characteristic of deep dreamless sleep. 0 to 0.5 is the state of death or unconsciousness.

Cabinet: (See Spirit Cabinet)

Causal Body: Buddhi and Manas, the incarnating self. It is the Causal Body that is what is most identified as the "Soul," although it is not the ultimate Spirit.

Causal Substance: Like the other five planes of the three lower levels, there is "substance" as well as "laws" relating to its specific nature. The Causal shares the third level with the Mental Plane—which likewise has its unique substance, but the two share the characteristic of five dimensions (in contrast to the familiar three of the Physical and Etheric Planes of the first and lowest level.

Ceremonial Magick (Also see Magick): The object of ceremonial magick is to stimulate the senses, to power-up the emotions, and to firmly conceptualize the purpose of the operation—which is to create a transcending experience to unite Personality with the Divine Self.

To this end, rituals, symbols, clothing, colors, incenses, sound, dramatic invocations and sacraments are selected in accordance with established 'correspondences' of one thing to another to transport the magician towards a mystical reality.

Chakras: These are etheric/astral energy centers located in the aura on the surface of the etheric double and functioning through etheric/astral connections to exchange particular energies between the physical and non-physical bodies, the psyche, and the higher sources of energy associated with the planets, the solar system, and the cosmos. They are interfaces between Mind and Body.

There are seven traditional "master" chakras located along the spine from its base to above the head, and dozens of minor ones located in such places as the palms of the hands, soles of the feet, joints of arms and legs, and just about any place traditionally adorned with jewelry.

Chakras are whirling centers of energy associated with particular areas of the body. In Yogic/Tantric practice, *Muladhara* is located at the base of the spine and is the source of *Kundalini* and the power used in sex magic to raise consciousness and create thought forms to carry pre-determined objectives. *Svadhisthna* is located at the sacrum. *Muladhara* and *Svadhisthna* are linked to the physical body. *Manipura* is located at the solar plexus. *Muladhara, Svadhisthna,* and *Manipura* are together associated as the Personality, and their energies can be projected through the solar plexus in such psychic phenomena as rapping, ectoplasm, and the creation of familiars. *Manipura* is linked to the lower astral body. *Anahata* is located at the heart level and is associated with group consciousness. *Vishuddha* is located at the throat and is associated with clairvoyance. *Anahata and Ajna are linked to the higher astral body. Ajna* is located at the brow and is associated with clairvoyance. *Sahasrara* is located at the crown and is associated with spiritual consciousness. *Anahata, Vishuddha, and Sahasrara* are together associated as the spiritual self.

These master, or major, chakras are as follows. While we are listing some correspondences to planets, colors and the Kabbalistic sephiroth, there is considerable debate about these and the correlations cannot be specific because the chakras and the sephiroth involve two different systems. Likewise, although not listed, there are differences between both these systems and those of Oriental martial arts and healing systems.

No.	Common Name	Sanskrit Name	Location [2]	Color[1]	Spokes or Petals	Associated Gland[6]
1	Base	*Muladhara*	Base of Spine[5]	Red	4	Ovaries, Testicles
2	Sacral	*Svadhist-hana*	Over Spleen	Orange	6	Pancreas
3	Solar Plexus	*Manipura*	Over Navel	Yellow	10	Adrenals
4	Heart	*Anahata*	Over Heart	Green	12	Thymus
5	Throat	*Vishuddha*	Throat	Blue	16	Thyroid
6	Brow	*Ajna*	Brow	Indigo	96 [3]	Pituitary
7	Crown	*Sahasrara*	Top of Head	Violet	960 + 12 [4]	Pineal

1 These are the most commonly assigned colors, but authorities differ.

2 These are the most commonly assigned locations, but authorities differ. Instead of the Solar Plexus, Theosophists identify it with the Spleen, others with the navel.

3 Commonly, this is given as two, but it is really two "wings" of 48 each.

4 Most commonly, it is identified as a thousand petaled lotus. The crown chakra has 960 spokes plus another 12 in its center which is gleaming white with gold at its core.

5 Between anus and perineum.

6 Again, there are disagreements among authorities. Remember that there is no direct physical connection between the etheric chakras and the physical body.

Source: Slate, J. & Weschcke, C.: *Llewellyn Complete Book of Psychic Empowerment—Tools & Techniques*, 2011, Llewellyn.

Suggested Reading

Judith: *Wheels of Life, A User's Guide to the Chakra System*, 1987, Llewellyn

Mumford—*Chakra & Kundalini Workbook, Psycho-spiritual Techniques for Health, Rejuvenation, Psychic Powers & Spiritual Rejuvenation*, 2002, Llewellyn

For specific detail, see each of the individual listing alphabetically by their Sanskrit Name.

Channel (as a noun): Either a spiritual entity able to communicate information from non-physical reality, or a person able to receive the communication. **Channel (as a verb):** To receive or communicate information by a non-physical and non-psychic (telepathy, clairvoyance, and divination) means.

Channeling: (Psychic Empowerment) Receiving information from a discarnate entity or a higher spiritual being. It may also refer to communication with an aspect of one's own subconscious mind. It is similar to, but not necessarily the same as, the spirit communication of mediumship. In both, however, one person serves as bridge between a spirit or spiritual intelligence and people of ordinary consciousness. In spirit communication, the medium is more often unaware of the communication; in channeling of spiritual intelligence, the channeler is more often aware and sometimes a participant.

Automatic Writing is a form of Channeling in which a person, sometimes in trance, writes or even keyboards messages generally believed to originate with spiritual beings, or with aspects of the subconscious mind.

Suggested Reading:

Wiseman: *Writing the Divine—How to Use Channeling for Soul Growth & Healing*, 2009, Llewellyn

Channeling the Sub-Conscious: (Psychic Empowerment) Similar to "channeling" and "mediumship" in technique, our intention is to open the Conscious Mind to the Sub-Conscious and experience the unity of consciousness as, indeed, there truly is.

Within that unity—just as there is in the ocean everywhere on planet earth with its layers, currents, variations in temperature, etc.—there will often be practical barriers preventing the free flow of information from the one to the other. Through mental disciplines we must do the same thing done with wireless communications technology: establish a channel of our own that is "interference free." We calm the mind through relaxation and meditation, breath control, ritual and routine. We isolate our channel from the noise of others and direct it towards known sources. In studying both channeling and mediumship we benefit from the cumulative experience of many thousands of practitioners recorded in studies, journals, folk lore, and expositions of theory, practice, and application. With either approach we must develop means of conscious control.

In studying both channeling and mediumship we can benefit from the cumulative experience of many thousands of practitioners recorded in studies, journals, folk lore, and expositions of theory, practice, and application. With either approach we need to develop means of conscious control.

No matter which approach we adopt, it is what the practitioner does that 'powers up' the actual process with defined intention to establish the *channel* and then to clear if of all interference. The 'channel' may be one of the familiar divinatory tools, or a visualized tools only using the mentally created channel. It is the practitioner's intention that matters. The conscious mind can create the channel as an act of creative imagination in which a gate, door, natural stream, road of light, tunnel, etc., can serve as an "information highway," or it can just feel the intention itself, or your own journal will itself serve as a channel (as in dream processing and in automatic writing). Find what has the strongest appeal to you, one that satisfies your sense of drama or propriety.

Clearing the channel of interference is commonly accomplished by keeping the whole operation secret, or revealed only to a group of supporters so that no expression of amusement, criticism, contrary images, or doubts interferes with your own sense of correctness. The choice of either direct experience or of a divinatory or communication tool will, to some degree, shape the remaining elements of composition, transmittal, receiving and interpretation.

Chanting: The repletion of particular words or short phrases in a vibrating voice that stirs psychic energy and may induce trance or other states of consciousness, or magickal effect. The words themselves are chosen because they have special meaning as names of deities, established correspondence with energy flows, and known healing benefit.

Suggested Reading:

Andrews: *Sacred Sounds, Magic & Healing through Words & Music,* 2002, Llewellyn

Circle: A temporary boundary within which a séance or magical operation may take place. The theory is that it becomes a kind of psychic container for the energies used in the operation and a barrier to unwanted energies from outside. Spiritualist mediums work in a circle with participants—mostly regulars—to energize contact spirits of the deceased. Participants sit in a circle or around a circular table for meditation or to call Spirits. Such a closed circle, whether in magical operations or a séance circle, or a "focus group" does do exactly that—focuses attention within the parameter of the circle.

Clairvoyance: Clairvoyance is the *direct perception of realities hidden* to normal perception by the limitations of physical senses. It is possibly the most intricate and advanced form of ESP, demonstrating the wondrous capacity of the human mind to expand its own field of awareness to encompass limitless realities. Clairvoyance isn't just about "secret" alternative knowledge, but is a means to *expanded knowledge through expanded awareness.* To understand this requires an understanding that you, every person, is more than you think you are and psychic development and empowerment is about *becoming more than you are.* It's about expanding your "objective consciousness" in union with the subjective.

We have to learn the art & practice of clairvoyance just as we do any other human skill, and there's a science to that. We believe its development should be encouraged as a matter of growth and movement into wholeness. We believe psychic empowerment should be your goal because you should be an empowered person. There will be many practical benefits to your developed clairvoyance as well—extending your inter-dimensional perceptions of reality means that you see more and are better able to judge the meaning and value of your inter-actions with the complex world in which you live. It gives you a greater foundation for the decisions you must make in life. You will gain deeper insights into your own physical and emotional reactions to both external events and internal issues.

Clairvoyance simply means "clear seeing," the implication being the particular *psychic vision* involved reveals the hidden nature of an object, event, or person. When we look at any object with our physical eyes we are limited to its three ordinary physical dimensions. We are not only unaware of the sub-atomic aspects functioning in the object, but many of us are not truly observant of the finer details of color, shape, odor, taste and feel and of **the *resident consciousness* fundamental to the object itself.** There is consciousness even in a brick, and more so in a blade of grass, a swimming fish, etc. And, where there is consciousness, there is *life. The universe is alive at all levels and in every dimension.*

On the physical level, we perceive with our physical senses. As we focus consciousness at higher levels, we don't perceive with "sense organs" but through awareness of the substance and changing vibrations emitted from the object of our attention. The higher we ascend in awareness, the greater our vision. At the astral level, we are aware of a fourth dimension, and at the mental level we perceive five dimensions.

Both clairaudience and clairvoyance, and other psychic skills, have been induced through hypnosis and self-hypnosis showing them to be innate to the human psyche.

Clairvoyance can dramatically expand our world of awareness and perception of spatially distant realities, uncover critical sources of new knowledge and power. Precognition can provide advanced awareness allowing us to prepare for future events and, sometimes, to influence or prevent them altogether. While some future events seem to be unalterable destinies, others may be probabilities subject to our intervention. Through precognition we are empowered to eliminate negative probabilities while accentuating the positive. Given precognitive knowledge, we can generate a powerful expectancy of success that literally transforms probabilities into realities. We *can* literally create the future of our choice.

Dr. Joe H. Slate, working at Athens (Alabama) State University, shows an emerging body of evidence that ESP, rather than an unexplained extension of sensory perception, is a fine-tuned manifestation of the non-biological or spiritual nature of our being, and includes interactions with spirit realm.

"As part of the unfoldment of the human intellect into omniscience, the development occurs at a certain stage of human evolution of fully-conscious, positive clairvoyance. This implies an extension, which can be hastened by means of self-training, of the normal range of visual response to include both physical rays beyond the violet and, beyond them again, the light of the super physical worlds…It is important to differentiate between the passive psychism of the medium, and even the extrasensory perception (ESP of parapsychology), and the positive clairvoyance of the student of occultism. This later, completely under the control of the will and used in full waking consciousness, is the instrument of research…to enter and explore the Kingdom of the Gods." (Quoted from Hodson, Geoffrey: *The Kingdom of the Gods*, 1953, Theosophical Pub. House, Madras, India)

Suggested Reading:

Slate, J.H. & Weschcke, C.L.: *Clairvoyance for Psychic Empowerment—the Art & Science of "Clear Seeing" Past the Illusions of Space & Time & Self-Deception*, 2013, Llewellyn

Slate, J.H. & Weschcke, C.L.: *Psychic Empowerment for Everyone—You Have the Power, Learn How to Use it*, 2009, Llewellyn

Co-Creators: (Self-Empowerment) We are coming to realize that all along we have unconscious co-creators, and now we have the growing realization that we must become <u>conscious</u> co-creators, broadly aware of our own transgressions of natural law, or else the human experiment will end in failure. In this New Age, we come to know that we are evolving toward becoming gods and co-creators, with the powers to create and destroy, but our "salvation" can only come through the exercise of personal responsibility and of participation for the good of the community rather than following corrupt and ideologically motivated politicians and self-serving elitist "leaders."

The Deity Within each human is the unconscious Life Force and the Conscious Presence of the Creative Force. The Deity Within is the source of our free will and conscious creativity. It is the Deity Within that makes us a "Co-Creator"—even though presently still mostly unconscious and unaware and hence "blind" and thus the source of many of our own destructive actions that bring harm and terror to other humans and harm and error to the environment that is the global home we share with all beings on this planet.

Only by becoming conscious do we become constructive rather than destructive. Only by *becoming more than we are* do we fulfill our obligation to the Creative Force that programmed the evolutionary drama from the Beginning. It is by making conscious the many blind forces within our body and psyche through the practices of Invocation and Evocation of associated deities that we become wholly "all that we can be" to fulfill the role assigned to us as co-creators.

All esoteric teachings have been dedicated to advancing humans as "Gods in the Making." This is the Dawning of the Age of Aquarius, when East and West come together in the New Age of Awakening Humanity. The call is to everybody, not the elite few. Everyone must be responsible both to himself and his neighbor as brother and sister, not as leader and follower. We begin now.

Louis T. Culling wrote: "Let the cynic or quibbler, who would think that this is an avoidance of realism, a kidding of one's self, practice the opposite of these trances! He would then get a well-deserved dose of his own medicine." What we build in our consciousness shapes outer reality.

Suggested Reading:

Culling, Louis T. & Weschcke, Carl Llewellyn: *The Complete Magick Curriculum of the Secret Order G∴B∴G∴*, Llewellyn, 2010.

Collective Illusion: The average person today is so subjected to a constant bombardment of distorted worldviews created in "Hollywood for the Entertainment Industry, by the "Creative People" in Advertising and Public Relations management, and Political and Religious Ideologies that we all function within varying degrees of a *Collective Illusion* based on the premises of salvation through intense consumption, prescription drugs, a party life of song and dance, fast cars, Big Sports mania, and happy pets. It's a matter of personal responsibility to breakthrough this illusion and see "things as they really are." *See also Consensuses Reality.*

Collective Unconscious: (Psychology—Jungian) A kind of group mind inherited from all our ancestors and including all the memories and knowledge acquired by humans. It is believed to exist on the higher astral and lower mental planes and to be accessible by the super consciousness through the personal subconscious mind in deep trance states induced through hypnosis, self-hypnosis, meditation and guided meditation. The ability to call up infinite information and integrate it into your present life needs is of enormous benefit—similar to but beyond the capacity of any present-day Internet Search Engine.

It is the function of the Personal Consciousness to bridge to the collective tribal, racial, cultural, national, mythic, even planetary memories and the world of archetypes of the Universal Consciousness, making them available to the Psyche mainly through the Sub-Conscious Mind.

The memories of all of humanity, perhaps of more than human, and inclusive of the archetypes. The contents of the collective unconscious seem to progress from individual memories to universal memories as the person grows in his or her spiritual development and integration of the whole being. There is some suggestion that this progression also moves from individual memories through various groups or small collectives—family, tribe, race, and nation—so the character of each level is reflected in consciousness until the individual progresses to join in group consciousness with all humanity. This would seem to account for some of the variations of the universal archetypes each person encounters in life.

The contents of the collective unconscious progress from individual memories to universal memories as the person grows in spiritual development and integration of the whole being. There is some suggestion that this progression also moves from individual memories through various groups or small collectives—family, tribe, race, and nation—so the character of each level up to union with consciousness with all humanity. This would seem to account for some of the variations of the universal archetypes each person encounters in life. Also see Akashic Records

Suggested Reading:

Dale, Cyndi: *The Subtle Body—An Encyclopedia of Your Energetic Anatomy,* 2009, Sounds True

Coming Global Civilization: As we move towards a Global Civilization, we encounter other religions—older and newer—that don't fit the Abrahamic concept of human bondage to an abstract deity through his privileged operating personnel. And yet we are still encumbered by these old time religions trying to control populations everywhere by dominating primary and secondary education, public service, local and national governments, and even by turning back the clock by rejecting science, claiming myth as fact, and trying to replace modern constitutional law with archaic and regressive religious laws.

Don't let the Past limit your fresh thinking and independent investigation. Don't let "religion" turn off your intellect. The challenges coming at us from accelerating population growth straining natural resources to meet human needs, encountering the planetary stresses producing climatic, environmental, geological crises, adjusting to the "hangovers" from the recent and older past actions and mistakes, the political and economic consequences from evolving technologies, and the religious conflicts throughout the Islamic world all present enormous ethical and spiritual challenges that require our best mental, psychic, and spiritual resources.

Think! Look ahead. Study and research. Go on-line and look at sites dealing with Global Challenges. Discuss with others. Appeal to your spiritual resources. Meditate. Ask what you can do. You are a multi-level being capable of many levels of communication. Use them.

Communicating with Spirit: We do need to make a distinction between "Spirit Communication" and "Communicating with Spirit." In the first we are communicating with various spiritual entities by various means often involving intermediaries of mediums, guides, channels, and such tools as spirit boards, writing instruments, pendulums, etc. In the second, we are communicating by means of Spirit, that quality or power innate to every person.

Spirit Communication is not just conversation with "dead people" but can *ascend* into communication with "higher" beings known variously as Guides, Teachers, Guardian Angels, Ascended Masters, Inner Plane Adepti, and—perhaps a strange thought at first—your own Higher Self. With each higher level we move from Spirit Communication toward and ultimately only to Communicating with Spirit, i.e. Spirit to Spirit by Spirit.

Communicating with your Higher Self: (Magick—Ceremonial) *I swear to tell myself the truth. I swear to regard every event (or condition) as a particular dealing between myself and the Holy Guardian Angel.* These were the two primary oaths in the work of the Secret Order G∴B∴G∴

What we're doing, of course, is building more lines of communication between the middle (everyday) consciousness and the super consciousness, or between the personality and the Holy Guardian Angel. And, we are doing one more important thing: in promising to tell the truth we are building trust between the selves that often act as if separate entities. Therein lays a mystery and an important recognition.

On this basis of trust, the Higher Self knows that its messages will be respected and attended to.

But, there remains a problem to our communications, and that is that—in part—the Higher Self doesn't speak directly in the common language. Your Holy Guardian Angel doesn't just shout: "Hey, down there, listen up! I want you to stick with the G∴B∴G∴ for six more months."

Instead, through the use of clues and symbols, you have to put effort into understanding the message, making communication a two-way street and a learning situation with direct application to your needs of the moment. In other words, despite the cautions against a pathological belief that everything is a message just for you, almost anything can be used to bridge the gap between meaningless and meaningful. A crystal ball is just a polished rock, but it can open your vision to another world. With intention, anything can become a key to unlock the doors of the Unconscious.

Before Integration there must be Communication. Divination and Meditation on the divinatory results and your dreams provide the basis for communication.

Suggested Reading:

Culling, Louis T. & Weschcke, Carl Llewellyn: *The Complete Magick Curriculum of the Secret Order G∴B∴G∴*, Llewellyn, 2010.

Conscious Mind: The 'middle' consciousness—the 'ordinary' consciousness, the 'objective' consciousness, the 'aware' consciousness—with which we exercise control and direction over our 'awake' lives.

With your Conscious Mind you can take charge of the great resource of the Sub-Conscious Mind. Information is constantly coming in, more than you can take full cognizance of, and so much of it is automatically diverted to the Sub-Conscious Mind. The Sub-Conscious Mind is more than a passive collection of memories, it is also your personal connection to the Universal Consciousness containing all that is from the very Beginning. Within this are all the potentials for all that you may become. This includes what we call "powers"—generally thought of as *psychic* powers. But before these powers are fully meaningful, they must be developed to become consciously directed skills.

But wait, as they say in television commercials, *there's more!* All that is the Conscious-Mind—with its magnificent potentials for rational thinking, for creative development, for abstract analysis, for organization, for the use of imagination, for planning, and all those skills that make it possible for the human being to manage the resources of the natural world—rose out of the Sub-Conscious Mind. Outwardly, that's what we do; inwardly, we manage Consciousness, because that is what we are. In particular, the job of the Conscious Mind is to manage the Sub-Consciousness and develop its innate powers into skills that we can then deploy consciously with awareness and intention to work with the Great Plan of evolving life. In another sense, it is to make Conscious the Unconscious through careful management of its resources.

When you take deliberate charge of the subconscious, your life takes on a new dimension of both meaning and power. Rather than a risky existential leap into a dark cavern of the unknown, your probe of the subconscious is an "inward leap of power" that clarifies the nature of your existence and reaffirms your destiny for greatness and meaning. It's a leap of progress that not only accelerates your growth, but guides you toward greater happiness and fulfillment as well.

As we became more aware of ourselves as individuals and operated more in the Conscious Mind, developing personal memory, rationality and new ways of thinking, we perceived ourselves in relationship to the natural world rather than as part of it. We learned to store knowledge in our memory rather than having immediate 'feeling' access to it. Rather than relating internally to the rhythms of Sun, Moon and Planets, we saw them externally and developed sciences of astronomy, astrology and agriculture. And we became aware of linear time.

Nature can show the ways to knowledge and understanding of her secret powers when you learn to listen. The Sun, the Moon, and the Planets, too, have powers to share with Man in his wholeness.

As Manager, it is the job of the Conscious Mind to know, understand, and direct all these resources. It's the most exciting, most gratifying, most rewarding and grandest job you will ever have, and it's one that is yours forever! You can't be fired, nor can you abdicate.

Consciousness: Everything that is, out of which Energy and Matter manifest and Life evolves. Consciousness is the beginning of all things and part of the trinity of Consciousness, Energy and Matter. "Consciousness just IS!" We can't really define consciousness because we are nothing but consciousness and consciousness cannot really define itself. "I AM THAT I AM."

Our personal consciousness includes all states of awareness and our experiences of fear, love, hope, desire, happiness, sadness, depression, ecstasy, mystical union, etc. We experience connectedness through consciousness.

Consciousness is not a 'thing' nor is it a function of a 'thing' called the brain. Killing the brain doesn't kill consciousness but it limits its expression in the familiar physical world. Consciousness is *expressed* through the brain, but it exists outside the brain. Consciousness acts upon the physical world, like a "force," as in telekinesis.

There are three levels of consciousness:

I for Instinct, a function of the lower subconscious

I for Intelligence, a function of the ordinary consciousness

I for Intuition, a function of the super-consciousness

The ancients were far more sophisticated in their understanding of "consciousness" than we give them credit. Moderns tend to judge everything from the background of technology and material sciences, believing that the lack of advanced scientific instrumentation means a lack of understanding about "how things really work."

In more than one sense, today's science is still catching up with the "Ancient Wisdom" which expressed understanding of the universe through myth and symbol. The single greatest difference is that the "old" wisdom was the property of the few and today we extend our knowledge to nearly any and every one. Modern education seeks to give everyone a basic knowledge of physical science, although there is a serious gap when it comes to "spiritual science."

One great difficulty arises because spirituality is thought to be the province of religion, and the institutions of religion limit themselves and their adherents to rigid theological interpretations of scriptures written down long ago within specific cultural environments vastly different than today. The truth is that spirituality is not religion but involves study of the higher levels of the psyche and an understanding of their role in the growth of the Whole Person and their beneficial applications to personal life and cosmic relationship.

Consensus Reality: The concept that the physical world, *as we perceive it,* is an illusion—an illusion so powerful that it we accept it as "real" and in our endeavors to understand this reality we have given it still greater "hardness" through our accumulation of history, myth, fable, and statements of physical laws. All of this has been limited to the perceptions of physical senses and rejection of the nonphysical.

Suggested Reading:

Slate, J.H. & Weschcke, C.L.: *Astral Projection for Psychic Empowerment,* 2012, Llewellyn

Control: The spirit who acts as a kind of manager through which other spirits communicate to the medium during a séance.

Correspondences: (Kabbalah) The Kabbalah, using the symbolic system of the Tree of Life and numerological associations provided through the Hebrew language, Astrology, and Natural Science identifies a wide range of *correspondences* between subjects, planets, herbs, plants, metals, crystals, colors, animals, angels, deities, etc. that allow substitutions of one thing for another, or that augment understanding about one thing by knowledge of another of corresponding value.

Suggested Reading:

Whitcomb W.: *The Magician's Companion—A Practical & Encyclopedic Guide to Magical & Religious Symbolism,* 2002, Llewellyn

Hulse, D.: *Western Mysteries—The Encyclopedic Guide to the Sacred Languages & Magical Systems of the World*, 2002, Llewellyn

Cosmic Consciousness: A phrase coined by Richard Bucke to describe his own experience of unity with the universal consciousness of the cosmos. Bucke believed this to be the goal of human evolution.

Cosmos: The Cosmos is not to be confused with the physical universe which is limited to the single physical plane, while the Cosmos is inclusive of the physical and all other planes, and is far more complex and infinitely larger than what we ordinarily see and think.

Many esoteric writers chart a Cosmos of eight dimensions within seven planes of manifestation, plus three more planes beyond manifestation that guide the process, and three more above and outside of manifestation from which it is sourced. This corresponds with the structure of the Kabbalistic Tree of Life with the seven plus three Sephiroth and the three levels outside manifestation.

Crystal Ball: A round ball of quartz crystal or glass used as focal point in skrying. Gazing at the ball, one enters into a trance-like state where dream like scenes and symbols are seen and interpreted. Similar aids are the Magic Mirror, a pool of black ink, a piece of obsidian.

Suggested Reading:

Andrews: *Crystal Balls & Crystal Bowls, Tools for Ancient Scrying & Modern Seership*, 2002, Llewellyn

Cunningham: *Divination for Beginners, Reading the Past, Present & Future*, 2003, Llewellyn

Slate, J. & Weschcke, C.: *Psychic Empowerment—Tools & Techniques*, 2011, Llewellyn

Crystal Gazing: (Psychic Empowerment) Also known as *Crystallomancy*, a technique typically using a crystal ball to induce a light trance to engage and liberate the mind's psychic powers while promoting a state of general self-empowerment. Crystal gazing opens the channels of the mind and permits the free expression of multiple inner faculties.

Suggested Reading:

Slate, J. & Weschcke, C.: *Psychic Empowerment—Tools & Techniques,* 2011, Llewellyn

Decaying Remnants: After physical death, the "surviving personality" occupies a temporary and transient vehicle commonly called a "Spirit," the entity encountered in a séance. After a time, this "spirit" loses connection with the surviving personality as it moves on, leaving behind a *decaying remnant*—not of the astral vehicle but of the "thought form" automatically created during that period in response to the communications between the surviving personality and the "earthy" communicators.

The "thought form" sometimes called a "ghost" was created in astral substance that is very sensitive and reactive to thought and emotion, and it is this fact that accounts for much paranormal, magickal and religious phenomena.

Devolution: Before time began, when the devolution of Spirit into incarnation was incomplete, there was much interaction between spiritual entities and forces and "proto"- humans. Here we had the appearance of Gods and Goddesses, elementals, angels and other forces in fundamental relationships. Here, too, was the beginnings of Magick, the foundations of spirituality and of religions with the development of symbols with their attributes and qualities and their associations of deific accessories. Thus began the long history of "correspondences" for magical control and verification of deities, entities, forces and powers. Here there are the functions of Worship as Invocation, Meditation as Evocation, Communication as the *conscious interaction between Inner and Outer, Lower and Higher, and of Humans with Deities.* In order to bring Spirit Power down into the Mental & Astral realms to initiate effects on the Etheric/Physical level, we have to reach up to the Spiritual. *As spiritual beings, we have to access not only the powers within but the limitless powers beyond. Magick is what Humans do.*

Before time began, the devolution of spirit into matter led towards the ultimate structure of the Universe we know today, with "layers" of Substance, Energy and Consciousness. Within this structure certain conscious entities began to function in ways that brought about an increasingly complex structure within which the evolutionary process began, and continues.

As the Evolutionary process continued those conscious entities took on specific creative functions guiding the development of Energy into Matter and Energy and Matter into Conscious forms evolving into greater and greater complexity and *Self-manifestation.* Each "higher" level of form takes on higher levels of consciousness leading toward *Self-consciousness* and *Self-realization.*

Higher levels of conscious beings assume interactive roles in the continuing evolutionary process in fulfillment of some mythic "Great Plan" of which we can have only glimmerings at this point in our own level of *Self-awareness.* Nevertheless, we "know" that there is meaning and purpose to life and being as we more consciously experience the evolutionary process becoming more specific and individualized. We are becoming *Self-knowing.*

With the advent of self-conscious humans there comes levels of awareness of the existing higher creative entities, later called "Powers," and interaction with these Powers and the natural energies resulted in the burgeoning human imagination (often aided by natural clairvoyance) forming elemental beings around natural "power" places and even historic events. Some of the higher entities became identified as *local* or *native* Gods and Goddesses, and so did lesser beings recognized as processing manifest energies and functions in the on-going creation become identified as Gnomes, Sylphs, Undines, and Salamanders, and still other names and other beings.

These were Mythic Times, and as human consciousness became more complex so did the world of human perception. Mythology "explained" creation and the phenomena of life and the world around. Legends described that nature of the Gods and Goddesses and lesser beings. Mythology was the "science" of the day.

If worldly phenomenon could be conceptualized, then the natural powers and forces could be explained in story-form, and either deified or demonized to explain their relationships to humans. If things were beneficial, the credit went to God; if they were harmful, the blame went to the Devil.

As human consciousness grew in complexity and increased awareness of the world around, and within, these Gods and Goddesses became totally human in form and ever more detailed in their functions and their appearances. Some became very specific in their representation of human function like love, attraction, reproduction; activities like fishing, hunting, farming, fighting; concepts like beauty, leadership, intelligence; natural phenomena such as thunder, lightning, rain, plant growth and other very specific functions and happenings. All could be represented by images (mostly humanoid), gender, names, colors, costume and ornaments, even postures.

And here was the beginnings of Magick, the foundation of religion, the development of symbols and their connections, and the long history of "correspondences" for magical control and verification, and the beginning of Science.

Different Strokes for Different Folks: There is little uniformity among the transformative systems other than the belief that the human person is something more than a physical entity and that in the non-physical is the potential to become a "Super Person" (think of mythical super-heroes) able to perform miracles of a paranormal nature. Yet, within the mainstream of Western religions there is no encouragement to the individual person to *become more than they are,* and of the many teachers of non-religious transformative systems most will caution their students that the development of paranormal powers is a diversion from the true path of Attainment.

Others disagree. All intrinsic powers (psychic, mental, spiritual) should be developed and become reliable skills, *fulfilling the potential for all you can be* provided for in the plan for both personal and species-wide human attainment. That personal plan is the matrix around which each of the individual's physical and subtle bodies is formed as a basic structure of potentials starting with genetic programming and the carry-forward karmic memories from past lives as planned prior to conception. The structure is formed for each body from causal down through mental, astral, etheric and physical, and then developed within each body as the current life progresses through the natural cycles of growth, maturity, and decline.

All systems of psychic development and spiritual growth take the "Next Step" in programs of personal transformation empowering the person to *become more than they are* and *all they can be.* There is no diversion from "the true path of Attainment" but rather the practical steps toward its accomplishment. And the actual methodology is unique to each person based on past and present, and the plan for the future, i.e. "Different Strokes for Different Folks" developed from techniques of Self-Discovery and Self-Understanding into those for Self-Improvement and Self-Development inclusive of those for Psychic Empowerment and Self-Empowerment.

The challenge is that of "self-aggrandizement" and over-sized ego. Challenges are to be overcome and not seen as "Do not enter here!"

Direct Voice: When a medium allows a spirit to directly speak through her/him, it appears to be the voice of the deceased. Sometimes during a Spiritualist Séance, a voice will be heard that does not directly emanate from a participant's larynx, but rather from an "artificial" larynx formed out of ectoplasm ejected from a medium's body. Often, the voice is very faint, and is magnified by a very light-weight aluminum "trumpet" that levitates and floats around the séance room.

Divinity Within: Esoterics believe that each of us has some form of Divinity With-in—called a Divine Spark, the Power, the Goddess Within, even—as in Quan-tum Physics—a God Particle. For some this is the same as *Spirit*, for others the Soul. Whatever name be it in Sanskrit, Hebrew, Greek, Tibetan, etc., there is this distinct core point that connects the physical body with some similar point in each of the higher bodies, and which can be activated to cleanse and transform the physical body and initiate a progression through the higher bodies. When we undertake a conscious program of self-development it is another form of *Spiritual Communication.* In yoga, it is the "awakened" Kundalini that transforms consciousness as it spirals upward through the body's centers to bring union with the Divinity within each of us and unity with Spirit and Universal Con-sciousness. Some variation of this is present in all spiritual development systems including Christianity and the image of Christ's Heart center.

Doctor Guide: A spirit guide who counsels on health and who may channel healing energies through a medium or healer.

Doppelganger: A seemingly unconscious projection of the astral body.

Drumming: One of the traditional Shamanic techniques to induce trance states lead-ing to ecstatic states of consciousness, possession by spiritual entities or pow-er animals. The rhythm is specific at 200 to 220 beats per minute, but also has "breaks" that seem to cause a kind of psychic lurch that precipitates the process.

Duality to Trinity: Within the Taoist conception, the "opposites of Yin & Yang are united in all there is. If we go back to the image of a stick where one end is Spirit and the other end is Consciousness, we have represented duality but also their unity in the center at the point of balance. Go one step further, bend the stick into a circle uniting the two ends and you have a representation of Male and Female, consciously uniting in their physical centers, reaching orgasmic ecstasy and union with the Divine at the point where biological (physical) energy merges with Spirit to find wisdom. Herein is the formula of Spirit Communication: When two communicants are brought together in the third point known as Trinity, we have the potential for greater knowledge and understanding found through partnership and intentional sharing.

Movement from Duality to Trinity always requires Action. To merge Consciousness with Spirituality requires a unity of action charged with energy and directed purpose. The culmination in Divine Union is facilitated by Intention and Vision, but always requires that additional focus of energy.

Earth bound Spirits: The belief that some spirits, especially those dying in sudden and unexpected transitions, and children, cling to the earth experience they knew and fear moving on and resist the natural process.

Suggested Reading:

Davidson: *Spirit Rescue, A Simple Guide to Talking with Ghosts and Freeing Earthbound Spirits,* 2006, Llewellyn

Crawford: *Spirit of Love, a Medium's Message of Life Beyond Death,* 2002, Llewellyn

Ecstasy: "Ecstasy" is defined variously under categories of Emotion, Religion, Mysticism, Psychology, and even in Philosophy. Most such efforts fail because their focus is external; it's like defining Orgasm—as it was until later in the 20th century—as "ejaculation of spermatic fluid" without any mention of the feminine experience or accompanying emotion or changes in consciousness.

"Ecstasy" results from an *exhilaration* of consciousness arising from:

- A series of repetitive physical and sensory actions leading towards sensory overload, such as extended dance, running, or whirling, prostrations, bowing, gesturing with arms and hands, rotating through prayer beads, etc.

- An extended experience of sensory deprivation, as in total isolation, the use of a sleep or meditation mask, the combination of restrained movement with a meditation mask, or the use of "sleep sack" in imitation of the traditional *Witches Cradle* (see the chapter on techno-shamanism in our *Clairvoyance for Psychic Empowerment* Llewellyn, 2013). Also the unique form of artistic Japanese Rope Bondage and swinging suspension known as *Shibari*—originally shamanic but now a "Performance Art" in night clubs;

- An extended experience of sensory reception, such as flashing strobe lights, drumming (often with a very slowly accelerating beat but with an overall rhythm of 200-220 beats per moment, the sound of repetitive chanting or ocean waves;

- An extended focus of attention on a particular image, as in mediation*—best if combined with Tratak and the chanting of a related mantra (see our *Astral Projection for Psychic Empowerment* Llewellyn, 2012 and the earlier mentioned *Clairvoyance for Psychic Empowerment*). Also see recommended titles at the end of this chapter.

* As a mental and emotional exercise. "Meditation" is either a *passive* kind of "listening"—waiting for a message, vision, or revelation—or an *active* "reaching upward" as in prayer, or "projecting inward" as in a "Tattvic Conditioning" of body and psyche or a "Chakra Awakening" to progressively expand spiritual consciousness. See our *Clairvoyance for Psychic Empowerment*, 2013, Llewellyn.

- A controlled experience of pain, particularly when applied repetitively as in "scourging" (light, ritual flagellation) often applied in ritual dance, or carefully controlled light electro-shocks known as Transcutaneous Electrical Nerve Stimulator (more commonly referred to as a TENS unit) and sometimes known as erotic electro-stimulation. (Frankly, we entirely recommend against this as too easily misapplied or abused, leading to injury and even death. *Stay away from electricity, from fire, from ice, and other applied force.*)

- A continuous singing or chanting of one or a series of words, names, or mantras, most often associated with a particular spiritual or deific entity or with a particular part of the subtle body to excite its activity.

- Through prolonged intercourse and visualization of woman as the Goddess Incarnate, sexual ecstasy can be made to become psychic ecstasy, the fire that excites and powers the magickal imagination. Body, Mind & Spirit are united with a transfusion of energy to transform subjective reality into objective reality.

- Tantric sex involving extended arousal through stimulation of many of the physical "trigger points" to the edge of orgasm, and then "holding back" until starting again (and perhaps again and again) to finally "explode" in a long and sometime multiple orgasm.

- The infusion of Kundalini energy through particular physical actions extended to the automatic induction of a trance state.

Any of these may be combined either sequentially or coincidentally. The point is to arrive beyond a climatic state, entering into a trance of focused attention and inner awareness, with either a self-conceived goal or as guided by an external source. Ecstasy is that point beyond climax, beyond orgasm, beyond external and objective awareness to the point of "union" with something "Deific" and beyond personal limits. It may be a "going out-of-the-body" but it's not ordinary astral projection but a merger of "human" spirit with limitless "Divine" Spirit.

That "Divine Spirit" cannot be defined nor named as it comes from outside reality and giving it any name is to humanize it within all the limits of human experience and emotion, to encumber it with human desires, hates, prejudices, and selfish goals. Somewhere it says "No man can see the face of God and live!" The God is outside of all creation but the Spirit is everywhere and in everything.

Ectoplasm: An "exteriorized misty appearing substance" emitted from mouth or nose and various other body orifices, frequently from the solar plexus and sometimes from fingers and toes of the medium and believed to originate from the etheric body. Ectoplasm is used by a spirit to give itself visibility. It is also used to give shape and visible appearance to a thought form in various magical and religious practices.

Suggested Reading:

Owens, E.: *How to Communicate with Spirits,* 2001, Llewellyn

Egregor: An autonomous thought form containing astral energy & substance and created of astral light by magical intent, focused consciousness, or religious devotion. It is often in the form of a guardian creature (such as an Eagle or Lion) to protect a building or a spiritual group. The form can originate in mythology or be adapted from folklore and can be ritually charged with additional functions such as observing distant events, carrying out an act of revenge, or to serve as a focus of devotion to unite the group.

Eidolon: Ghost

Elementals: The elemental forces of this world and possibly for the whole Universe. They are variously ascribed to the inner side of natural forces, and also to the Spirits of the four Elements of Air, Fire, Water, and Earth, along with the fifth Element of Spirit from which the four are derived.

1. Non-human nature spirits associated with the different states, quality, and character of the five elements or Tattwas.

   Spirit, Ether (underlying; universal & originating; awareness):
   Air (gaseous; mediating, embracing & pervasive; intellect): Sylphs
   Fire (energy; active, energizing & transforming; will): Salamanders
   Water (fluid; receptive & responsive; feeling): Undines
   Earth (solid; stable & enduring; sensation): Gnomes
2. A thought form charged with energy and intention by a magician to carry out a particular operation, such as a household guardian.
3. Beings that carry the elemental forces of this world and possibly for the whole Universe.
4. Elemental Spirits, or Forces, that are the Guardians of the Four Directions of the Magickal Circle, thus transforming the Circle into a miniature of the Universe.
5. Beings that function as agents-in-charge of the various manifestations of each of the "Kingdoms" of Animals, Plants, and Minerals.

"End of the world as we know it." The belief fostered by Carl Llewellyn Weschcke (and coincidental with the *Mayan Prophecy* that the world would end on December 21st, 2012) that there will be a dramatic rebirth of the human spirit and a new global civilization structured to meet the challenges of international terrorism starting in 2001, religious extremism, the financial collapse of 2008, and other common threats to planetary survival.

Coincident with this time is the continuing transition from the Piscean Age of faith, restriction and conflict (symbolized by fish swimming in opposite directions) into the Aquarian Age of knowledge and wealth (symbolized by a man pouring largess from the horn of wealth and wisdom).

New institutions and international standards are required of nations to participate in new economic, security, educational, legal, health, etc. organizations.

Essentials for Discovery & Development of Psychic Powers & Spiritual Growth:
A cardinal principle of psychic empowerment holds that psychic and spiritual potentials exist in everyone and can be developed through appropriate programs. Common to those programs are the following three essentials:

- *Motivation.* The number one essential in developing *any* of your potentials is motivation—*the doorway to power and fulcrum to success.* Given motivation, you become goal oriented and focused in your pursuit of growth and empowerment. Without it, you are like a minnow in a shallow country stream, darting about without purpose or plan.

- *Learning.* Through your exploration of various psychic concepts, exercises, and development programs, you will discover the knowledge that's essential to your growth and development. You will also discover that knowledge is power, and knowledge of psychic origin is power in its highest form. You will find that the supreme personal psychic exists within your own being as an essential part of yourself. It beckons your interaction and is constantly poised to enrich your life.

- *Practice.* In developing your potentials, there is no substitute for practice. Through practice using various exercises and programs, you will discover the tools and techniques that work best for you. Through continued practice, you will develop your psychic and spiritual Powers to their peaks.

Together, these three essentials provide the foundation for the discovery and development of your psychic and spiritual powers, including those identified as paranormal. Through motivation, learning, and practice, you will discover ways of using those powers to accelerate your growth and enrich the quality of your life. Beyond that, you will find effective ways of contributing to the greater good and making the world a better place.

Suggested Reading:

Slate, J. & Weschcke C.: *Psychic Empowerment: Tools & Techniques,* 2011, Llewellyn

Etheric Body (AKA the Etheric Double): The second, or energy body that is closest to and—in life—integral with the physical body. As with all the subtle bodies, it has two layers:

The first, sometimes called the "Etheric Double," is fully coincident with the physical body in health and extends about an inch beyond physical skin. It is the psycho-physical circuitry of the human body (the chakras, nadis, and meridians) through which the life-force flows under direction of the astral matrix. To clairvoyant vision, it is the health aura and appears as very fine needles of radiation—standing straight up in health and lying down in illness.

The second layer, along with the astral and mental bodies, forms the egg-shaped aura surrounding the human body visible to clairvoyant vision. It is an interface between the individual and dynamic planetary energies and cosmic forces that sustain life.

During life, the integrated physical/etheric complex is vital to physical, emotional, and mental health, and it is the etheric energy system that plays important roles in martial arts and physical work and sports, in energy healing, in many paranormal activities such as psycho-kinesis, dowsing, pendulum work, automatic writing, séance and poltergeist phenomena including levitation, in kundalini yoga, and is the foundation upon which many magical operations are built.

The Etheric Body can be projected (see *Etheric Projection*) and can be molded by intense thought and thus shape the physical body.

Ted Andrews writes* that the etheric body "vitalizes, energizes and protects the physical vehicle. It serves to ground the consciousness into physical life. It also filters out the more subtle energies and dimensions of life so that we are not overly distracted. Our primary focus is to be in the physical. It is this band of energy which is usually first detected by someone working to see the auric field.

"The etheric forms around the physical body anytime between birth and puberty, most often between the ages of four and eight. Until the etheric body forms entirely, the astral plane ... plays upon us and is recognized more fully. It is not filtered out. For this reason, many of the so-called imaginary playmates of young children are not really so imaginary. They are beings and entities of that plane.

"Once the etheric is formed much of the subtle plays of energy are filtered from the conscious mind, although the subconscious will still be able to perceived them. As we grow and mature we can work to reopen our conscious awareness of those subtle realms. To do so we must learn to extend the consciousness out through the etheric to the realms beyond.

"Lying between the etheric and the astral is a thin band of energy sometimes referred to as the atomic shield. It is like a thin layer of atoms that filters out the strong astral energies from physical consciousness. These are the strongest feelings and emotions that could play upon us and affect us."

*Andrews, T: *How to Meet & Work with Spirit Guides,* 2002, Llewellyn

Etheric Plane: The Energy Plane between the Physical and Astral planes. Its energies are in constant movement, like tides and currents, ruled by the Moon, Sun and Planets and moving in cycles. In theory and practice, the etheric is considered to be the upper "layers" of the physical plane and consists of substance and energy not perceptible to the "hard" physical senses. However, its substance and energy permeates the physical plane and the physical body to provide the life force—mostly "regulated" by the Moon and Planets—that enlivens all physical life.

Etheric Projection: A portion of the etheric body, sometimes along with other etheric material for added substance, can be formed as a vehicle for the operator's consciousness and projected to other physical locations in order to perceive physical information about physical events. It is also possible to use the etheric body to affect physical events, as in healing. Being of near physical substance and energy, it is sensitive to certain physical materials, like iron and silver. It can be injured, and such injuries will repercuss back to the physical body.

The etheric body can also be shaped to resemble other entities, and is a factor both in the lore of were-wolves and were-leopards.

Etheric Revenant: This is the foundation for vampire lore. As with the ancient Egyptian practice of mummification, the preserved body—hidden and protected from disturbance including the effect of sunlight—provides a base for the continued use of the etheric body by the personality of a deceased person. The etheric body has to be nourished with substances rich with life energy, like blood.

Etheric Template: In the incarnation process, the "information" needed for the whole physical body and associated subtle bodies is brought down from the Causal level, through the Mental and Astral levels to form an actual "template" at the Etheric level to guide the formation of the embryo and its birth in relation to the pre-determined birth horoscope. It is this Template that provides the blueprint for the physical life.

Evolution: Unlike the Darwinian concept that focuses primarily on the physical form, esotericism extends that concept of evolutionary change to every aspect of life and consciousness including the Soul, and sees a constant movement of growth and development throughout the Cosmos, both visible and invisible. Evolution is not a thing of the past but continues, both in physical response to the environment but also in fulfillment of a primal program set forth at the "Beginning."

Evolution began at the "Beginning," and continues through the present to the future. Evolution is not limited to Cosmology and Biology, but includes Sociology, Psychology and Spirituality. Everything continues to change, evolve and "progress" in a kind of "trial and error," or as "trial under fire." Even our psychological nature continues to evolve, and so it is with the Human Spirit as the fundamental elemental *substance within the whole human being,* Spirit manifests in "structures" that change and evolve, enabling individuals to evolve, grow, and *become.* Yes, even human institutions are evolving,

The same thing is true of the other "parts" of the whole human being: the physical body evolves and so do the etheric, the astral, the mental, and the causal bodies. And so does our thinking, our feeling, our ability to empathize, our ability to understand, our intuition, the extent of our love, our psychic abilities, and all the things we can do. Our knowledge evolves, science evolves, our culture evolves, our civilization evolves, and we evolve as we grow and become more of what we can be primarily through the growth and development of the Super-Conscious Mind.

Dennis Bushnell, NASA's chief research scientist at their Langley Center has written: "Humans are now responsible for the evolution of nearly everything, including themselve ... The ultimate impacts of all this upon human society will be massive and could 'tip' in several directions." (speech at World Futurist Society's Annual Conference July 8, 2010)

Many in the esoteric community believe that the beginning of the New Age in the 1960s coincides with the influx of Aquarian Age energies brought an expansion of awareness and an actual change in consciousness that is having an increasing effect on personal and social development.

In the personal area, this is having an immediate effect in the development of innate unconscious psychic powers into conscious psychic skills. In the social area it is developing the first Global Civilization and will translate into world government and the regulation of the global economy and financial institutions as a fundament public utility, with universal law protecting property and human rights, projecting universal education protected from impositions of religious theology and other extremes of ideology.

As a factor in human consciousness, the evolutionary impulse is not limited to the physical structure but rather can mold it as needed by the emergency psychic faculties.

Four Divisions of Soul: As pictured on the Tree of Life, these levels are:

1. Neshmah, which is itself divided into three parts:
   a. Yechidah (the superego), centered in Kether, is our Divine Self
   b. Chia, centered in Chokmah, is our True Will
   c. Neschamah, centered in Binah, is our Intuition
2. Ruach (the ego), consisting of Chesed, Geburah, Tiphareth, Netzach and Hod, is our Mind
3. Nephesch (lower self) centered in Yesod is our subconsciousness
4. Guph The lowest part of the soul, centered in Malkuth. A low level of subconscious intelligence allied to the physical body. The autonomic nervous system.

Four Functions: In Jung's Psychology, the four functions are Reason, Feeling, Intuition, and Sensation. These are also the four quarters of the Magician, grouped around the Center which is the Imagination.

The goal of magick is the integration of the four functions together with the Imagination.

Separately, the Four Functions are the Four Beasts; The Four Functions are Man on the Cross of the Elements; the Four Functions integrated with Imagination are Woman. The Four Functions integrated with Imagination united under WILL is the God-Man.

Four Minds: The personal "self" of the physical brain, the subconscious, conscious, and superconscious minds under the "rulership" of the incarnating immortal Soul.

Four Worlds: The four fundamental levels of being or consciousness as considered in the Kabbalah:

- Atziluth (nearness): the archetypal or divine world—Fire and the Spiritual Plane
- Briah (creation): the archangelic world of eternal patterns of Platonic ideas—Water and the Mental Plane.
- Yetzirah (formation): the angelic world of force and form—Air and the Astral Plane.
- Assiah (action): the physical world of matter and energy—Earth and the Physical Plane.

In relation to the Tree of Life, the Four Worlds are presented in two different ways:

- Four different levels on one Tree:
    a. Atziluth corresponds to the first through third sephiroth: Kether, Chokmah and Binah.
    b. Briah corresponds to the fourth through sixth sephiroth: Chesed, Geburah and Tiphareth.
    c. Yetzirah corresponds to the seventh through ninth sephiroth: Netzach, Hod and Yesod.
    d. Assiah corresponds to the tenth sephirah: Malkuth.
- Four different Trees one on top of the other so that Malkuth of the highest Tree is also Kether of the next Tree lower, and so on. Meditation on both these ways will be meaningful.

Fourth Dimension: (Astral) While Time is called the fourth dimension in Relativity Physics, it is also a non-spatial addition to the physical three dimensions of space found on the astral plane enabling a clairvoyant to see all three dimensions of an object at once.

Ghosts: 1) Earthbound spirits 'haunting' a particular location. 2) A psychic 'recording' of emotional energy released during such traumatic experiences as suicide, murder, accidental or painful death. The "psychic recording "is reproduced and experienced by psychically sensitive people—almost always at night when nothing competes with the reception. These experiences usually induce an emotional responses, often fear, which then reinforces the initial energy. Like other kinds of recording, the original energy can often be released or erased by 'overwriting' with other strong releases of emotion such as a ritual exorcism, happy children, shamanic practices, and even loud music.

Suggested Reading:

Danelek: *The Case for Ghosts, An Objective Look at the Paranormal,* 2006, Llewellyn

Wilder: *House of Spirits and Whispers, The True Story of a Haunted House,* 2005, Llewellyn

God-Form: The ritual construction of an archetypal images and personality of a chosen deity out of astral substance, and its "assumption" by the ritualist to connect with the deific nature and power.

Great Plan, the: Some esoteric groups believe that there is a Plan guiding the evolution of human consciousness to its eventual reunion with the ultimate Source. They further believe that Humanity has a role to play as co-creators able to accelerate the Plan in its application to human consciousness.

Great Secret: The "Higher" always controls the "Lower." What is *magically* created on the higher planes—Causal, Mental, and Astral—will precipitate action on the next lower plane, and if so "instructed" through ritual and intention will manifest as physical reality.

Suggested Reading:

Slate, J.H. & Weschcke, C.L.: *Astral Projection for Psychic Empowerment*, 2012, Llewellyn

Great Work: The path of self-directed spiritual growth and development. This is the object of your incarnation and the meaning of your life. The Great Work is the program of growth to become all that you can be—which is the realization that you are a 'god in the making.' Within your being there is the seed of Divinity, and your job is to grow that into the Whole Person that is a 'Son of God.' It is a process that has continued from 'the Beginning' and may have no ending but it is your purpose in life. It is that which gives meaning to your being.

In this New Age, you are both teacher and student and you must accept responsibility for your own destiny. *Time is of the essence!* Older methods give way to new ones because the entire process of growth and self-development has to be accelerated. Humanity has created a *time bomb* that's ticking away, and only our own higher consciousness can save us from self-destruction. But—have faith and do the Great Work for it is all part of a Great Plan.

The Great Work is not denial and restriction but fulfillment. There's not just one narrow Path, but many paths—one for each of us.

Suggested Reading:

Denning & Phillips: *Foundations of High Magick*, 1991, Llewellyn

Growth Specialist: An advanced spirit entity who facilitates the personal growth of others and promotes the full actualization of existing growth potentials. They are also known for their capacity to introduce totally new growth possibilities.

Guardian Angel: Often identified as one's *Higher Self* and sometimes as an *Angelic Being* assigned to each person at birth, or incarnation. It is not necessarily the same as the *Holy Guardian Angel* described in certain High Magick operations.

Guide: The name we apply to certain intelligences encountered through clairvoyance and astral projection, and sometimes in dreams, that appear to exists on the Inner Planes with no or rare physical manifestation.

Hauntings: Hauntings are experienced in specific physical spaces and are accompanied by such experiences as uncomfortable feelings, strange and scary sounds, sights of swirling mists, and of deceased people. The phenomena almost always occurs at night when there is no competition for the experience and most often in locations that are rarely disturbed such as abandoned houses and churches, old cemeteries, ancient religious sites, etc. There are claims that haunting experiences fluctuate with the phases of the Moon.

Suggested Reading:

Belanger: *Haunting Experiences, Encounters with the Otherworldly,* 2009, Llewellyn

Goodwyn—*Ghost Worlds, A Guide to Poltergeists, Portals, Ecto-mist & Spirit Behavior,* 2007, Llewellyn

Higher planes: 1) A general reference to levels above the physical—generally meaning Etheric, Astral, Mental and Spiritual. 2) A reference to levels above that being discussed, and generally meaning planes above the Spiritual or that are commonly grouped into the Spiritual Plane. Planes refer to a) levels of manifestation and b) levels of the Whole Person as 'bodies.'

Higher Self: The third aspect of personal consciousness, also known as the Super-Conscious Mind. As the Middle Self, or Conscious Mind, takes conscious control of the Lower Self, or Sub-Conscious Mind, the Higher Self becomes more directly involved in functioning of the Personal Consciousness. The Atmic Body, the supreme soul, the divine Monad, overshadowing the lower Ego. The Individuality that is permanent.

Even though the Higher Self is also known here as the Holy Guardian Angel, there is value in using a more easily comprehended psychological term. Words are words and there are often many names for the same thing. But each gives a particular shape or color or tone to the thing named to expand our understanding comprehension when we are relating to larger concepts.

Kabalistically, it is the Super-Conscious Mind in Tiphareth that mediates between the Divine Self and the Lower Personality.

Holy Guardian Angel: (Also the HGA) The transcendent spiritual self that mediates between the Divine Self and the Lower Personality and serves as guardian and guide. The term was used by Abramelin the Mage as the focus of the magical operation known as "the Knowledge and Conversation of the Holy Guardian Angel." The HGA is also called the Higher Self, known also as the Augoeides of Iamblichus' system, the All-Knower, the Divine Genius of the Golden Dawn, the Atman of Hinduism the True Ruler, Adonai, the Indwelling Spirit, etc. Carl Jung calls it his Daemon (not demon!) as did the Greeks.

Contact between the Higher, Divine Self and the Lower Self/Personality can only be initiated by the Personality, and then is experienced as a separate being. That contact is the first step in the Great Work that leads to integration. This is the discovery of one's True Will.

Human, potentially, controls the Spiritual, The: Ari Rabinowitz writes "From the Kabbalistic perspective the true reality is the spiritual realm: the physical cosmos is God's precision-crafted instrument for achieving spiritual goals ... the physical universe is a shadow of the spiritual world, the illusion perceived by limited beings who are in contact with the spiritual cosmos but can directly sense and perceive only its shadow. Human free-willed moral choice connects the two realms, and this moral activity gives meaning to the existence of the universe."

" ... the human body, rather than being a hindrance to spirituality, is a potentially holy physical tool which can control the spiritual ... every action/thought/ word affects the spiritual cosmos, and one's life when correctly lived is designed to resonate with the spiritual and to correctly utilize the physical order to elicit the fusion of ultimate spirituality with the physical."

"Just as according to quantum physics (or metaphysics) nature has delegated to humans the ability to determine the nature of physical reality within the limitations of natural law, similarly God, the Creator of nature, delegated to man alone the ability to determine the nature of spiritual reality, which then influences the physical."

We Think, therefore We Are! According to quantum physics, physical reality is *fixed* by the act of *conscious* observation, but the truth is that we know very little about *consciousness,* and what could be more important? *We think, therefore we are!* But, what are we? Everything we are <u>is</u>, or <u>is a function</u> of consciousness! We also say that everything is energy, and we know that being conscious requires energy.

Consciousness extends infinitely through Space. What we have is the idea that Consciousness (and potentially Intelligence) connects everyone through quantum fields that extend infinitely through space. Note, that we are acknowledging that consciousness and intelligence are not necessarily the same, but that we cannot gain and exercise intelligence without consciousness. To be conscious, to be aware, to think, to train the mind to process observations analytically and rationally are the foundations of intelligence. Inspiration, intuition, clairvoyant vision, even "feeling," all feed into Intelligence to enable the human mind to function richly beyond the mere neural processing of the physical brain.

The realization that we are more than a physical body, that the "cosmos" is more than the physical universe, that as humans we have the power—infinitely—to **Become more than we are!** And most important of all, smallness can be more important than bigness in the physical dimension which is where we plant our feet. Ideas start off big in the higher dimensions, but unless you build "from the ground up, they won't amount to the proverbial "hill of beans."

Intention: Acting with a goal in mind. However, "Intention" has become a key word in applied Quantum Theory where it is demonstrated that directed thought and image can effect changes in the Universal Field at the foundation of physical reality.

Inner Worlds: The astral and spiritual worlds accessed in Shamanic journeys and clairvoyant vision, experienced in ecstatic states of consciousness, and known subjectively in dreams and visions. The Inner Worlds are the worlds of Spirit Communication, and the Imagination is the key for their conscious exploration and for communication with spiritual entities including your own Higher Self. The Inner Worlds are where imagination is "real" and visualization is used to create and empower thought forms, make magick, and "speak with the gods."

It is through the Inner Worlds that the conscious mind can access subconscious memories, the wisdom of the Collective Unconscious and the Akashic Records.

Intuition: A blinding flash of insight answering a question or solving a problem originating at the Soul level of consciousness. Instinctive knowing without actual knowledge and sensory validation. "Our central nervous system automatically responds to events that have not yet happened and of which we are unaware in the present." (Research by Dean Radin of the Institute of Noetic Sciences quoted in Larry Dossey's *The Power of Premonitions.*) However, there are programs that teach "intuitive thinking" in relation to specific professions, such as Nursing, and in practices such as "Creative Thinking." It is considered a faculty of the High Mental or Causal Body.

Invocation: Invocation and Evocation are often, mistakenly, used interchangeably and with little appreciation of their vast difference. Invocation precisely means to actually bring a spirit or divine presence (or <u>concept</u>) *into* the psyche and even the body of the magician. Evocation, in contrast, calls a spirit or other entity (or concept) into the presence, not the being, of the magician and usually into a magical triangle placed outside the magic circle of the magician. Invocation requires psychological and spiritual strength as well as proper preparation. It's not just that there are dangers but that the opportunities are so great.

Jungian Psychology: Also called Analytic Psychology—the system developed by C. G. Jung. After studying with Freud he advanced a more spiritual approach to psychotherapy evolving out of his studies of occult traditions and practices including, in particular, alchemy, astrology, dream interpretation, the I Ching, the Tarot, and spiritualism.

For Jung, the whole range of occult and religious phenomena have evolved out of the relationship between the individual consciousness and the collective unconscious. While the personal unconscious or subconscious mind is the 'lower' part of the individual consciousness, it is through it that we also experience and have experience of the elements of the collective unconscious—most importantly the role of the archetypes.

The archetypes are 'collectives' of images and energies relating to 1) roll specific functional, formative and universal experiences such as Mother, Father, Lover, Judge, Hero, etc. 2) those that are more personal with karmic content including the Shadow (repressions), the Anima (expressions of the Feminine in men), the

Animus (expressions of the Masculine in women) and 3) the Self (the evolving Whole Person that overshadows the Personality).

Kabbalah: Kabbalah is a complete system of knowledge about all the dimensions of the universe and of the human psyche organized into 'the Tree of Life' diagram showing the inner construction and the connections between levels and forms of consciousness, energy and matter.

The Kabbalah—spellings of "Kabbalah" and "Kabala" generally refer to the original Jewish version, "Cabala" refers the Christian version, and "Qabala" and Qabalah" for the magical or Hermetic (and Greek) version—is probably the most complete purview of the world as perceived and experienced through spiritual vision that we have. It is a systematic organization of spiritual reality into a manageable formula for human study along with a methodology of "correspondences" to organize all of human knowledge.

It is a treasure trove for practicing magicians and the most expert self-study program of progressive mediation the world has ever seen.

It provides a resource for understanding and applying the principles of Magick, for understanding the dynamics of the psyche, and for interpreting human history and action.

The present day Tarot specifically relates to the Tree of Life.

Suggested Reading:

Andrews: *Simplified Qabala Magic—Easy-to-follow techniques for utilizing the transformative energies of the Qabala—including meditation, Pathworking, the Qabalist Cross and Middle Pillar, and more*, 2003, Llewellyn

Christopher: *Kabbalah, Magic, and the Great Work of Self-Transformation—A Complete Course*, 2006, Llewellyn

Dennis: *Encyclopedia of Jewish Myth, Magic and Mysticism*, 2007, Llewellyn

Godwin: *Godwin's Cabalistic Encyclopedia—A Complete Guide to Cabalistic Magick*, 2002, Llewellyn

Gonzalez-Wippler: *Kabbalah for the Modern World*, 2002, Llewellyn

Gonzalez-Wippler: *Keys to the Kingdom—Jesus and the Mystic Kabbalah*, 2004, Llewellyn

Malachi: *Gnosis of the Cosmic Christ—A Gnostic Christian Kabbalah*, 2005, Llewellyn

Regardie & Cicero: *A Garden of Pomegranates—Skrying on the Tree of Life*, 1995, Llewellyn

Regardie & Cicero: *The Middle Pillar—the Balance Between Mind & Magic*, 2002, Llewellyn

Stavish: *Kabbalah for Health and Wellness*, 2007, Llewellyn

Trobe: *Magic of Qabalah—Visions of the Tree of Life*, 2001, Llewellyn

Karma: In general, the force generated by a person's actions, many of which are created in life by thoughtless action in response to such emotional drives as lust, greed, blind hate, and particular ideologies and theologies—themselves an excuse for "not thinking about it." *Following orders* is no excuse for the killing, mutilation, rape, theft, and other crimes executed under direction of power driven leaders.

Knowledge and Conversation … This is an important concept for you are to recognize in your Holy Guardian Angel as your own teacher with whom you, the present personality or (small 's') self must actually converse, recognizing the HGA as your (big 'S') Self.

… Of One's Holy Guardian Angel. Yes, *the Big 'S' Self, the Higher Self, the Augoeides, the All-Knower, the Divine Genius, the True Ruler, Adonai, the Indwelling Spirit, your Daemon (not demon!), your Spirit Guide.* It's the BIG SHOT, the God Father, of your personal family of psychological parts you will integrate.

This *conversation* between Personality and Higher self is an art as well as an 'act of faith' that you must believe in. There are practices that will establish the reality of this Indwelling Spirit as well as that of your communications. For the moment, accept as fact that you are a 'fractured' being of sub-conscious and conscious-mind and of higher-consciousness which will eventually unite in a Whole Person as you *become more than you are.*

Yes, it is possible to converse with your Higher Self. First you have to honestly believe in the Higher Self, and that the person you think of as your self is not it. At the same time, don't let the name "Holy Guardian Angel" deceive you into thinking of a separate being that is so *holy* as to be beyond your ability to deserve the attention of the HGA.

True, the HGA is normally distant from the personality that is the everyday 'you,' but the function of the Great Work is to build a relationship between the personality and the Higher Self leading towards *Integration*—when the two become as one.

Ceremonial Magician Louis T. Culling wrote "I swear to regard every event (or condition) as a particular dealing between myself and the H G A." Culling has done a beautiful job in explaining the practical issues around this magickal oath, and his examples demonstrate its practical value and effectiveness. (See Culling & Weschcke: *The Complete Magick Curriculum of the Secret Order G∴B∴G∴,* 2010, Llewellyn)

This practicality is rather unique among magickal oaths! Many are too grand for realization within a single lifetime. While their intention is to stimulate spiritual growth and attainment, it is usually not some grand event or rare or expensive artifact but very ordinary things that call to us for our deeper awareness. Their symbolism may be obscure—normally—but suddenly they glow with meaning or practically yell at your for attention. Or, it may seem like nothing, but still your attention has been re-directed to the event as if it has a special meaning for you, *and it usually does!* It may be obscure at first, but record in your Journal and reflect on it.

But, note further: this oath directs your attention to everyday events of all kinds so that your awareness is alerted to the greater meaning and potential that each may represent. Magick and meaning may be found in the most mundane of events when there is that possibility of relationship between the inner you and the inner side of the event. The effect is to activate connections to your Higher Self, and that is the goal.

"I swear to tell myself the truth." This, of course, is very challenging. *What is truth?* Can we ever really know it? Again, Culling has given us a good but simple example. It is perhaps too simple. The real requirement is to be *honest* with yourself; to test your answers for their truth and honesty. This is more than "knowing yourself" for it is also a test of your truth and honesty in relation to others and to the world you live. We too easily deceive ourselves and once again the entire purpose of the oath is to prepare yourself to communicate with your Higher Self, the HGA.

Even though your communication with the HGA isn't always in *plain English*, it is not a game! The Great Work is serious business.

Kundalini: The Life Force rising from the base of the spine, the *Muladhara* chakra, and animating the body, our sexuality, the etheric body, and passing through the chakras to join with its opposite force descending through *Sahasrara* chakra to open our higher consciousness.

Kundalini manifests as a transforming force centered in the Base Chakra and operating within the body, driving evolution, desire, sex drive, growth and individual development. It exists on all planes in seven degrees of force.

Bringing astral experiences into conscious (physical brain) awareness requires some arousal of Kundalini and its movement through other chakras whether spontaneously aroused or consciously directed in yogic ad magickal practice.

Suggested Reading:

Mumford: *A Chakra & Kundalini Workbook, Psycho-Spiritual Techniques for Health, Rejuvenation, Psychic Powers & Spiritual Realization,* 2002, Llewellyn

Paulson: *Kundalini and the Chakras, Evolution in this Lifetime—A Practical Guide,* 2002, Llewellyn

Life-between-lifetimes: One's existence in the spirit realm between one's lifetimes in physical incarnation. It is believed there is a period between the previous life and the next life during which the past life is reviewed and the next life planned.

Suggested Reading:

Newton: *Destiny of Souls, New Case Studies of Life Between Lives,* 2000, Llewellyn

Newton: *Journey of Souls, Case Studies of Life Between Lives,* 2002, Llewellyn

Newton: *Life Between Lives, Hypnotherapy for Spiritual Regression,* 2004, Llewellyn

Newton: *Memories of the Afterlife—Life-Between Lives Stories of Personal Transformation,* 2009, Llewellyn

Slate, J.H. & Weschcke, C.L.: *Doors to Past Lives,* 2011, Llewellyn

Life Goals and Purpose: Every life has purpose: We are here to grow, to become more than we are. Each of us has the ability to apply our inherent powers and our emerging skills to the challenge of accelerating personal growth.

Individually, we have instinctive, and consciously determined goals—some inspired by outside events, such as reactions to observed poverty, gender discrimination, hate-actions, etc., other in response to observed opportunities. Some are distinctly personal—as in the drive to overcome a physical handicap—others are individual as career goals, the writing of books, and other accomplishments. Other than those that are criminal and injurious to others, the setting of life goals are both simply and expressly that which amplifies the evolutionary process. It is not enough to just express the biological force of reproduction, the fight to be king of the herd, to "feather your own nest," or even to climb the next hill. Those are givens; you must add to the givens with personal and social goals, ambitions to accomplish, to improve. It's the *management* of your life, and it comes from the spiritual level. Seek guidance from within.

Living Light: The *Light* that is characteristic of the astral and higher planes. It is this "Living Light" that is the foundation of the Cosmos itself and the source of Spirit or Akasha, the element from which all the other elements are derived. It gives meaning to the phrase "Let there be Light" that is the true beginning of all.

Love: *In giving and receiving, there is love.* Love is one of the great mysteries. We *feel* love. Love is both something we project towards another, and then something that holds things together. It is an 'attractor force' and a 'binding force.' As humans, we yearn to give and receive love, and we speak of 'making' love. As observers, we see the same phenomena 'out there' in the world—not only in living things but in non-organic things right down to the smallest particles. We think of Love as an emotion, but it is unlike other emotions such as fear and anger. We speak of "God's Love" but we don't speak of "God's Fear." Love is such a unique and powerful force that it almost takes on a physical dimension right along with the force of gravity, and perhaps it is Love that is the unifying force that Einstein was searching for.

It is "love" that holds all the many parts together in a functional unity. Love brings people together in relationships, but it is also love that holds all the cells, organs and parts of the body together, and that holds all the many 'bodies' (physical, psychic, emotional, mental spiritual and even extra-spiritual) together in the complex person each of us is. And it is love that allows our relationships with other dimensional beings and with our Divine origin. There is no limit to love as it is the creative force of the Cosmos.

You can give this love other names if you prefer: attraction, gravity, magnetism, nuclear force, and others, but 'Love' is something we know. We experience the power of attraction, and we experience the yearning to love. We want to receive love and we want to give love. Through love, we seek expansion, to go beyond ourselves, to reach out towards union with the beloved, and through union we go beyond present limitations.

Love under will: It's the second part of the phrase that begins with 'Love is the Law.' "Love magickally directed, and used as a spiritual formula," says Crowley. This is an important clarification for what otherwise has commonly been interpreted as justification for a kind of 'free love' movement. As a 'spiritual formula' it is a concise instruction for Sex Magick as practiced by the GBG. This "Will," is the True Will of the Higher Self, while sexual love arouses the energy directed by the True Will in fulfillment of our magickal goals.

Lower Astral: The lower sub-planes of the Astral Plane with vibrations close to the physical level. It is the realm of ghosts, hauntings, and poltergeist phenomena.

Lower Self: The conscious mind and the subconscious mind, together, are the Lower Self.

Magic: The power to change things in conformity with will or desire. It is a function of focused consciousness accompanied by emotional force intending change by reaching down into the Universal Field where everything exists as potential until affected by the operation of intention also known as magic. This means that magic is happening all the time, but as magicians we have the opportunity and responsibility as co-creators to direct change in accordance with 'The Great Plan,' meaning no more and no less than whatever the underlying purpose of creation is.

As "low (or practical) magic" it is the intentional ritual action supported by various physical correspondences with particular herbs, astrological factors, symbols, etc. lending strength to the visualized accomplishment through psychic powers to make things happen as a materialization of desire. As "High Magick" it is the intentional ceremonial action supported by particular philosophical correspondences to bring about self-development, including increased psychic skills, and the realization of the Whole Person. Which is what the Great Plan is all about.

"Magic it is said, is the process of producing visible, physical results determined by the trained will-thought of the magician who has found the way to communicate with the appropriate angelic Intelligences and win their collaboration. Magic has therefore been describes as the power to address the Gods in their own tongues." (Hodson, G.: *The Kingdom of the Gods*, Theosophical Pub. House, Madras)

Malala Yousafzai: The 16-year old Pakistani girl who survived a bullet to the brain intended to kill her and deter other girls and women from seeking education proscribed by fundamentalist Islamic theology. Such courageous acts by individuals are sometimes invocative of higher forces leading to widespread progressive changes. As a woman heroine, she may have initiated a deepening and far-reaching revolution in Islam that could change the course of history, even avoiding a Middle Eastern war between Sunni and Shia, and perhaps a World War. Such individual acts have amazing potential to initiate historic change.

Manipura **(the Solar Plexus):** This chakra is located in the lumbar area above the navel, and physically manifests through the adrenals, and the solar plexus. It relates to the conversion of food into energy, the expression of personal power, the formation of personal opinions, and the transformation of simple into complex emotional expression. Physically it rules our digestion, emotionally our expansiveness, mentally our personal power, and spiritually growth. It relates to the sense of sight. The element is Fire.

The associated psychic powers are clairsentience, empathy, premonitions & prophetic dreaming. This is the center of the salamander (fire-walker) whose inner life is sustained by the primal heat element. The fire-walkers of North India walking across beds of glowing embers and the Pacific islanders walking upon white-hot stones employ the Manipura chakra. Other so-called "fire-eaters" unknowingly use Manipura chakra together with Anahata chakra to perform their feats, including dipping the hands into boiling water, boiling oil, molten, and molten steel. Simultaneous mastery of earth, water, and fire with subsequent immunity to pain and searing of flesh by heat is accomplished through manipulating the forces inherent in the first three chakras and culminating in Manipura, the Solar Plexus chakra.

Manipura is symbolized by a yellow inverse triangle within a lotus with ten spokes, and its tattva is represented geometrically in a red inverse triangle. The audible seed mantra is *RuNG* followed by a mental echo of *RuM*. Like Muladhara, it contains a feminine energy.

Manipura Chakra Correspondences

Alchemical Planet: Jupiter, Sun	Alchemical Element: Tin	Tattva: Tejas (Fire)
Animal: Ram	Basic Drive: Pleasure	Tattva color: Blue
Body Function: Digestion	Chakra Color: Yellow	Tattva form: Crescent
Element: Fire	Gemstone: Amber, topaz	Tattvic Sense: Taste
Gland: Adrenals	Goddess-form, Egyptian: Tefnut	God-form, Hindu: Braddha-Rudra
God-form, Greek: Apollo, Athena	Incense: Carnation, cinnamon	Goddess-form, Hindu: Lakini
Location: Over navel	Order of chakra unfoldment: 4th	Yogic Planet: Sun
Part of Body: Solar Plexus, Navel	Psychological attribute: Power, passion, energy	
Psychic Power: empathy, psychic diagnosis	Sense: Sight	Bija Mantra: RuNG, RuM (4)
Spinal Joint: 7th	Spinal Location: 1st Lumbar	
Tarot Key: XVI, Tower	Tree of Life Sephiroth: Hod, Netzach	
Tarot Suit: Wands Authority	Yantra (internal) Green inverse triangle	

Source: Slate, J. & Weschcke, C.: *Psychic Empowerment—Tools & Techniques*, 2011, Llewellyn

Mantra: A word or phrase, usually in Sanskrit, Hebrew or Latin, repeated or chanted repeatedly as a way to still the mind in meditation, and/or to instill a particular feeling or to invoke a special state of consciousness. Mantras are usually associated with particular images which may be visualized during meditation and chanting for increased effect. Some of the mantras are 'God Names' and the associated images are of the deities.

Mantra Yoga—"man" (mind, to think) and "tra" (a tool or instrument), so literally, a "mind tool" for manipulating consciousness:" The systematic use of sound vibrations (usually monosyllables) to bring about physical, psychic, and psychological changes.

Martial Arts: A particular training of the whole person, and not just the physical body, uniting physical and psychic actions. See also "Tao."

Suggested Reading:

Carnie: *Chi Gung, Chinese Healing, Energy and Natural Magick, 2002*, Llewellyn

Master: This word, "master" should not be confused with "ruler." This *Master* is used in the sense of one who has *mastered* a subject, skill, or level of being. A *Master of Botany* is one who has become expert in the subject and now can teach it. An *Ascended Master* is expert in Life Science to the level of being a teacher or guide.

Materialism: Modern culture, worldwide, is called *materialistic* because most people—lacking clairvoyant vision or psychic sensitivity—perceive things primarily through a physical perspective resultant with the following belief: if you can't measure it, photograph it, or otherwise demonstrate a physical impact, then it must be "psychological" in nature and perhaps exists only in your "imagination."

Generally speaking—from a "moral" perspective, materialism is often judged as "selfish," "bad," even as "evil." Materialism need not be so negative when balanced within a holistic, life-affirming, planetary, and comprehensive world-view recognizing spiritual as well as material needs and values. Just as important is to also respect and understand the impact to today's actions over the long-term and merely assume that "everything will be taken care of."

At the same time, we must acknowledge the benefits our materialism has brought with it in meeting the challenges of our time—including reducing the harm resultant from the dangerous and often *criminal* hasty application of a materialist technology without thought to its effects within the greater physical and social environment. Think, for example, of the harm to the water supply from chemical and agricultural wastes that has been "cleaned up" even as the demands from "development" and energy needs introduces further harm.

We must always deal with the present, look for impact of current actions on the future, and hope to do better. We can't go back in time to correct past errors. Instead, we do have to learn from the past not to repeat those errors or continue actions we can now recognize as abusive, harmful, and negligent of factors in the emerging larger picture of our reality.

Materialism and Spirituality are not necessarily each contradictory to the other. As humans, we have an immense capacity to see broadly and incorporate multiple perspectives and goals into our active physical existence. The spiritual dimensions (astral, mental, and causal) are incorporated into our physical/etheric vehicle of action. Through psychic empowerment, we are able to not only see more broadly but to act with greater understanding of the spiritual as well as physical factors involved.

We need to look beyond the limiting physical perspective, and particularly so with that presented to us "second hand." Our history books are still much *distorted* when it comes to the subjects of Spirituality and Religion because historians, archaeologists—and even psychologists and paranormal investigative writers—have tended to perceive primarily from a purely *physical* perspective that pits experiential Spirituality against the <u>official</u> history and orthodox theology of the three dominant Western religious establishments. Anything out of conformance with the dominant view of these establishment hierarchies is rejected out-of-hand even when it is contrary to common sense, rejected by scientific studies, contradicted by practices of the secondary religious groups, and at odds with other religious teachings around the world.

Materialization: When something appears as from nowhere. The presence of a spirit perceived either objectively to physical sight or subjectively to non-physical sight through imagination and visualization. Also, the actual "precipitation" of a spirit or non-physical visualization into material objects that may or may not have endurance. Apports reappear after being de-materialized. Objects are teleported from one physical location to another and is also associated with poltergeist-like activity when stones appear in mid-air to fall on a house. There are also materializations of human forms or just of limbs and hands sometimes occur in séances, and wax impressions have been made of them.

Matrix: The background framework for all and any manifestation. It is a union of Consciousness in the Universal Field of primary energy/matter potentials. The universal matrix is the pattern for evolving universe and all within it. The individual matrix is the pattern of energy/matter guiding the development and function of each life form. It is mostly a function of Mental, Astral and Etheric levels of consciousness guided by an intention expressed at the Soul level. It functions as the Etheric Body.

Suggested Reading:

Braden: *The Divine Matrix, Bridging Time, Space, Miracles, and Belief,* 2007, Hay House

Meditation: Over the years there's been a lot of nonsense written and spoken about this subject than perhaps anything other than dieting for weight reduction. Simply put, meditation is: 1) An emptying of the mind of all thoughts and 'chatter'

often by concentration only on the slow inhalation and exhalation of breath and is characterized by slow alpha and theta waves. It induces relaxation and a 'clean slate' preparatory for receiving psychic impressions. 2) A careful thinking about a particular subject in a manner that brings access to physical memories as well as astral and mental level associations of knowledge about that subject. 3) A state of consciousness characterized by relaxed alertness reducing sensory impressions with increased receptivity to inner plane communications.

Meditation, hypnosis and self-hypnosis are all associated with special mental states which facilitate positive personality changes and connect with higher dimensions of the psyche. In addition, those particular mind disciplines being used to achieve particular therapeutic results, are receiving increasing professional and scientific attention.

Meditation, hypnosis, and self-hypnosis, all progress from the relaxation of the physical body to remove or by-pass emotional blockage and open the mind to possibilities beyond past restrictive conditioning. Meditation has a particular value in reduction of stress—considered by most health professionals as a genuine "killer" of older people because it is cumulative in physical damage and tends to become a habitual mental pattern.

Like Self-Hypnosis, meditation is mostly self-administered and can be applied entirely for physical, emotional and mental benefits. From a Mind/Body perspective, meditation is a non-drug way to lower stress levels, relax any area of the body, reduce blood pressure levels, calm the emotions, and clear the mind.

Before going too deeply into the "overlay" of various traditional yogic and religious practices and teachings, we need to discuss the single most important key: deep, regular, and relatively slow breathing. Study yourself: when you focus on many activities, physical and mental, *you tend to tense up, breathe shallowly and often hold your breath*. Don't! Practice your full and regular breathing at all times and you will improve your health, reduce stress and tension, think more clearly, and control emotional reactions to external stimuli.

This controlled breathing should become habitual, but conscious observation will enable you to restore any interruption of that fundamental pattern. Physical relation results, correcting many health "disturbances" that result from physical stress. Control breathing and you control stress. But, for a body already habitually stressed, addition programs of relation of both mind and body will deliver more results, and will facilitate psychic development and spiritual growth. You will find benefit in silently speaking the phrase "breathing deeply and evenly" in a relaxed rhythm coordinated with your breath. "Breathing deeply" as you inhale, "and evenly" on the exhale. Let it become a constant reminder.

Body/Mind Relaxation: To get started with Body/Mind meditation requires no
  training, just common sense. The keys to success are found in:

1) A comfortable posture, preferably seated in either a modest reclining or a spine upright position;

2) Deep but *not exaggerated* breathing at a comfortably slow pace;

3) An intentional stilling of the mind. While not a requirement, in most meditative traditions, the eyes are closed. In some traditions, different eye focus points have different effects, and points such as the "third eye", or gazing over the nose, help to lock the brain into a point of stillness. Different meditations may call for staring into a candle flame, or other object of focus (trataka meditation).

Often, especially when first beginning a regular practice of meditation, there is noticeable tension in the body. You can easily add a Tension & Release procedure to aid Body-Mind Relaxation.

Start by pointing the toes of both feet like a ballet dancer, and hold them pointed for 60 seconds, and then relax. Next, spread the toes of both feet apart as hard as you can and hold them that way for 60 seconds, and release. You will feel mild warmth and relief. Repeat tensing, holding and releasing with both ankles & calves. Then move upward, repeating for each muscle group: thighs, buttocks & groin, chest, upper arms, forearm & wrists, hands & fingers, neck & shoulders, mouth & facial muscles, brow & scalp.

Alternatively, you might prefer first with working up the left leg, then the right, and similarly with the arms. Either way, *feel* the whole body as relaxed while restoring the breathing rhythm, slowly and deeply. Silently or quietly tell yourself "breathing deeply and evenly, I am more and more relaxed." Repeat to yourself, "breathing deeply and evenly" in a relaxed rhythm several times as you note that your mind is only involved with that one thought.

"Mantra Meditation" is by far the best known form of meditation, and you've
  already engaged in mantra meditation as you slowly repeated the phrase
  "breathing deeply and evenly" in a relaxed rhythm coordinated with your
  breath. Instead, in mantra meditation you can repeat other words, phrases,
  and short prayers in a similar fashion. Every tradition includes such mantras

that may be used in the same way, but with effects that do reach into the spiritual dimension. Both Eastern Tantra and Western Judaic-based Kabbalah have made a science of mantra meditation, but it's not the subject area of this book per see. See the list of recommended books.

Each mantra while have similar physical and mental effects, will also produce different emotional feelings and induce unique spiritual effects identified with the particular tradition and the words or names used. Phrases containing "God Names" are especially powerful, as you would expect.

Words aside, meditation can be classified into three types according to their orientation which in turn can be distinguished from each other by brainwave patterns.

- *Concentration* is focused attention on a selected object, thought, image, sound, repetitive prayer, chant, mantra etc., while minimizing distractions and constantly bringing the mind back to concentrate on the chosen object.

- *Mindfulness* requires a non-reactive monitoring of present experience: perception, thought, feelings, etc. The meditator centers focuses awareness on an object *or* process—such as breath, sound, visualized image a mantra, koan, or on a physical or mental exercise—while maintaining an "open" focus that may lead to insight or enlightenment. The meditator must passively observe without reaction.

- *Transcendent Mindfulness* requires that the meditator is open to experiencing a *shift* in consciousness and even changes in the physical/etheric body, all the while focusing on a thought, image or object to the point of identifying with it.

Meditation can be practiced while seated or standing in particular positions (called *asanas* in yoga), but once you have broken habitual mental patterns that produce stress, you can be meditating while walking or doing simple repetitive tasks.

In a form of meditation using visualization, such as Chinese Qi Gong, the practitioner concentrates on flows of energy (Qi) in the body, starting in the abdomen and then circulating through the body, until dispersed.

Mantra meditation is also the most familiar form of concentration, particularly when you expand the definition of "mantra" to include chants and prayers. Mantras are usually associated with Hinduism and Buddhism, but the method is generic and can apply to any tradition. Chants are commonly associated with

Judaism and many neo-Pagan religions. Sometimes magical "spells" are chanted. Repetitive Prayers are found in most religions, but are particularly associated with Christianity, Judaism and Islam as forms of other-direct "Mind Control." In Hinduism. One of the oldest sacred texts, the Brihadaranyaka Upanishad, refers the goal of meditation: "having becoming calm and concentrated, one perceives the self (ātman) within oneself".

Yogic science teaches that man-tra ("man" meaning mind, "tra" to cut) helps "yoke" the mind to a more conscious and harmonious vibration. The repetitive use of mantras can aid meditation, clear the subconscious of unhealthy attachments, and break accumulated mental patterns.

While we list some of the best known Hindu mantras transliterated into English, we still need to provide phonetic pronunciation guide.

Sanskrit Pronunciation Guide

a = *a* as in *sonata*   ai = *ai* as in *aisle*

ah = *a* as in *alms*   I = *I* as in *big*

ey = *ey* as in *they*   oh = *o* as in *no*

ee = *ee* as in *reed*   u = *oo* as in *fool*

s (at the beginning of a word = *ss* as in *Ssiva*

s or sh (in the middle of a word = *sh* as in *she*

From *Words of Power* by Brian & Esther Crowley

OM, or AUM: Pronounced *Aum, or Ah,Oo, Mm.* Note: The Ah can start at the solar plexus, moving up to the heart, and then to the throat. Repeat several times, and then the Ah should commence at the throat; then move up to the brow with the Oo; and up to the crown with the Mm. The full mantra should be extended out in vibratory fashion to *Ahuu-oooo-muummm,* feeling the vibrations as indicated.

Meaning? There is no meaning as this is said to be the primal sound that initiated the universe. Still, it can be considered in three parts: the "A" as in "the beginning," the "U" as the maintenance and preservation of what was created, and the "M" as transformational power. Another perspective is view the "A" and the Physical Plane, the "U" as the Astral and Mental Planes, and the "M" as Spirit.

OM MANI PADME HUM: Pronounced *Aa-oo-mm Mah-nee-Pad-may Hoong.* Note: In extended meditative work, colors may be visualized with each syllable as follows:

Om—White, the world of the devas.

Ma—Green, the realms of spirits.

Ni—Yellow, the realm of human.

Pad—Blue, the realm of animals.

Me—Red, the realm of nature.

Hum—Gray, the realm of the underworld.

Meaning: "Hail to Him who is the Jewel in the Lotus." It is the Infinite bound within the Finite. It is used as a protective mantra, and as an attunement of person with the Divine.

OM HRIM KRIM HUM SHRIM: *This mantra is actually four mantras generally pronounced as one, but also separately. The "Four Great Goddess Mantras" bring about development and integration of the mind, body and soul. Each governs primal forms of energy.*

HRIM (pronounced *Hreem*) governs over the cosmic magnetic energy and the power of the soul and causal body. It is the prime mantra of the Great Goddess, ruler of the worlds, and holds all her creative and healing powers. HRIM awakens us at a soul or heart level, connecting us to Divine forces of love and attraction, opening the lotus of the heart to the inner Sun of consciousness. Source: *The Mantric Approach of the Vedas* by David Frawley

KRIM (pronounced *Kreem*) governs over prana as lightning or electrical energy. KRIM grants all spiritual faculties and powers—from the arousing of kundalini to opening the third eye. It has a special power relative to the lower chakras, which it can both stimulate and transform. It helps awaken and purify the subtle body. It is the great mantra of Kali, the Goddess of energy and transformation. KRIM carries the supreme life force. Source: *The Mantric Approach of the Vedas* by David Frawley

HUM (pronounced *Hoom)* is a mantra of the inner fire. It represents the soul hidden the body, the Divine immanent in the world. It both calls the divine down into us and offers our soul upward to the Divine for transformation in the sacred fire of awareness. It is used to destroy negativity and creates great passion and vitality. Source: *The Mantric Approach of the Vedas* by David Frawley

SHRIM (pronounced *Shreem*) is a mantra of love, devotion and beauty. SHRIM is a Lakshmi mantra, the Goddess of Beauty and divine grace. Yet SHRIM works at a deeper level than merely to give us the good things of life, including health. It takes us to the heart and gives faith and steadiness to our emotional nature. Source: *The Mantric Approach of the Vedas* by David Frawley

Another group of mantras are used individually to stimulate the psychic centers, or *chakras*.

LANG (pronounced *LAM*)—Mooladhara: Root Center
VANG (pronounced *VAM*)—Swadhistana: Sex Center
RANG (pronounced *RAM*)—Manipura: Navel Center
YANG (pronounced *YAM*)—Anahata: Heart Center
HANG (pronounced *HAM*)—Vishuddhi: Throat Center
ONG (pronounced *OM*)—Ajna: Third Eye Center
Silence—Sahasrara: Crown Center

There are many, many more traditional Hindu and Buddhist mantras with various applications. As indicated above, some have specific transformational effects, while others are chanted or sung to produce feelings of peace, unity and communion.

Judaism: The core of Jewish meditation disciplines are found in the Kabbalah in which the ultimate purpose is to understand and cleave to the Divine. Classic methods include mental visualization of the higher realms through which the soul navigates to achieve certain ends.

The basic belief is that through meditation one can separate his soul from his body and transcend to the upper universes. The Kabbalah serves as a map telling one how to prepare and where to go.

Meditation involves controlling ones thought process, blocking out the five senses and entering expanded consciousness. Without meditation a person uses only three to five percent of his brain. Part of the brain receives signals of spirituality, but these signals are very sublime and are blocked out by the other five senses. When one clears his head of all thought he can feel spirituality and eventually can transcend to the upper worlds.

Jewish meditations are, of course, in the native language of Hebrew, and the mantric words will be presented in transliterated English. Here is a phonetic pronunciation guide:

The Hebrew letter *chet* is pronounced "ch" as in the Scottish word *loch*.
The letter *zayin* = "dz" as in *adze*.
Kaph = "kh" as in *Khmer*.
Tzaddi = "tz" as the *ts* in *cats*.

Quf = the guttural "q" as in *Qoran.*

The proclaimed goal of Kabbalah meditation is able to answer three of life's most critical questions: who we really are, where we came from, and why we are here. The answers provide the means to achieve true joy and a deep sense of accomplishment. You are able to experience life under the light of the Higher Being of your own realization.

The central focus of Kabbalah is on the Tree of Life, a unique diagram representing the Macrocosm and the Microcosm—that whole of that which is without and the whole of that which is within, the Universe and the Whole Person.

This Tree of Life and the wisdom of the Kabbalah are the foundation of most Western metaphysics and *invisibly* of the whole of Western science and philosophy. With it, we have the means to understand and relate to the body of the Universe and of Man, and the Soul of Man and of the Universe.

While there are individual Hebrew mantras, the premier form of meditation is found in the practices of "Path-Working" often in combination with individual cards from the Tarot. These are imaginative journeys or *guided meditations* following the twenty-two paths between the ten Sephiroth which should be understood as the "God Forces" behind the universe.

From a psychic perspective, path-working has been described as *the art of clairvoyantly investigating the Paths of the Tree of Life.* The technique was largely developed by adepts of the Golden Dawn and Aurum Solis but has become a comprehensive meditative system outside the magical orders. Once the meditator has passively followed the guided meditation, he should then attempt to re-tread the Paths out-of-body following certain ritual techniques involving visualized symbols, performing certain gestures and vibrating Divine Names.

Path-working can be classified as a *Transcendent Mindfulness* form of meditation in which shifts in consciousness are the intended result. These are *astral* learning experiences that can be understood as "initiations."

Generally included in the visualized symbols used with each path are the related Tarot cards (major arcana) and/or the related Hebrew letter. Just as the individual Tarot Arcanum communicates particular information and *energies,* so do the individual Hebrew letters. That's a deep subject unto itself.

Because path-working is a visual exercise, it needs some sort of visual focus and the images of the Tarot Trumps are the most convenient for this purpose, and often serve to frame the type of vision that ensues.

We can't go into even an overview of path-working in this short article, so we refer the reader to *A Garden of Pomegranates—Skrying on the Tree of Life*, by Israel Regardie with Chic & Sandra Tabatha Cicero for a full exposition.

To the kabalistic, speech is the medium of revelation and hence language itself is sacred and an object of contemplation. The 22 letters of the Hebrew alphabet are profound realities embodying those primal spiritual forces that are, in effect, the "building blocks of Creation." Hebrew is called a "flame language" and each letter appears to be shaped out of *flames* that can channel forces connecting Heaven with Earth is special ways.

Because of the belief that these letters (the forces embodied therein) predated Creation the letters themselves and the order and manner in which they are utilized are of crucial significance, and their properly pronounced sounds transformative. Hebrew chants (mantras) were designed as special formulas able to arouse spiritual forces.

As with Hindu mantras, the purification of the divine power within is attained through the correct and persistent vibration of the sacred sounds and can result in powerful effects of a physical and paranormal nature.

Active Imagination. The pre-eminent psychologist, C. G. Jung developed a technique of meditation called "Active Imagination", which is similar to Path-working.

The meditator is instructed to choose a dream or fantasy image, and then concentrate on the image to fix it in the mind. Contemplating it serves to animate it, and the alterations that occur must be noted as they reflect the psychic processes occurring in the unconscious which appear in the form of images of "conscious memory material," thus uniting conscious and unconscious.

Instead of merely observing events, the meditator participates as a real character in drama that is taking place within his psyche. The goal is to assimilate lessons from the Unconscious into Consciousness in "Individuation"—the conscious process of psychic healing and integration of all parts of the psyche. The importance of being involved in the vision rather than just being an observer is to integrate the statements of the unconscious and to assimilate their compensatory content—thereby producing a whole new meaning.

Jung observed in his own active imagination sessions two types of fantasies: one was related to images from his own past, but the others were mythological, archetypal, spiritual, and religious". He recognized these as symbols of basic drives common to every man throughout history—leading him to form the theory of the Collective Unconscious, perhaps his greatest achievement.

In path-working, the meditator likewise must experience himself as a character fully participating in the vision he is experiencing. In addition, the symbolism of the Paths of the Tree of Life is likewise "mythological, archetypal, spiritual, and religious", and the Tarot Arcana are direct representations of the Archetypes. The path-worker has a set framework within which to explore the archetypes himself.

Likewise, we can compare the self-initiatory process of path-working with the individuation process of Jung's Analytical Psychology.

The Middle Pillar Exercise. Perhaps one of the most important magickal exercises based on the Kabbalah, and given here in Hebrew, was developed by the Golden Dawn, and described in *The Middle Pillar* by Israel Regardie (edited with new material by Chic and Sandra Tabatha Cicero). The following version is a variation practiced by Carl Llewellyn Weschcke in his personal discipline.

Essentially, it is a meditational exercise intended to open and balance the five specific psychic centers (chakras) that correspond with the Sephiroth on the central pillar of the Tree of Life as visualized within the physical body.

While visualizing the Sephirothic Centers within the body as shown in the illustration, reach up to center above the head (Kether) with both hands, see the center fill with white light from the Cosmos above, then vibrate the holy name AHIH (Eh-he-yeh) three times, pausing in between each to take a deep breath. After the third vibration, inhale and bring your hands down to the throat center (Daath) while visualizing the light descending from the crown to the throat, and vibrate the holy name YHVH ALHIM (Ye-hoh-voh E-loh-heem) three times as previously.

Continue on down the Middle Pillar in the same manner vibrating YHVH ALOAH ve-DAATH (Ye-hoh-voh El-oah ve-Da-ath) at the heart, SHADDAI AL CHAI (Shah-dai El Chai) at the genital center, and then ADNI HARTZ (Ad-doh-nai ha-Ah-retz) at the earth center.

In review, you have brought light from above down the central column of the Tree and your spine, filling each center with that white light. Each center is pulsing with the light.

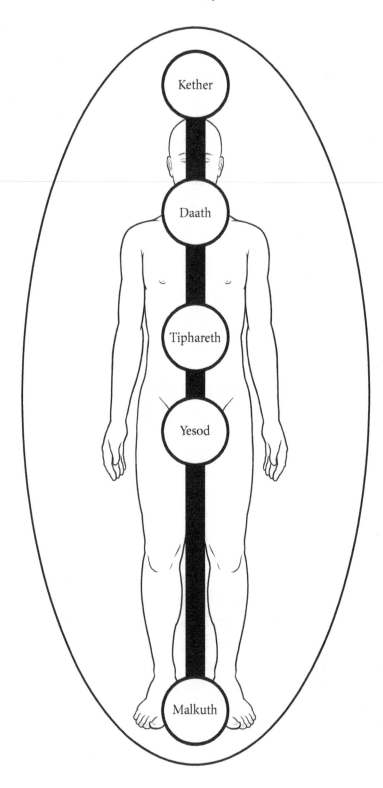

Continue experiencing the light continuing down the central column, but now slowly bring your hands from their down position (just like in the illustration) up on each side while seeing and feeling Earth energy rising upward through the spinal column in your inhalation, and when you reach the crown see and feel it fountain out and down outside your body to sweep back in at the feet. Now comes the more challenging part: With each inhalation pull energy up the center column, and with each exhalation let energy flow down the center column as well as outside the body in a complete and continuous full circulation of light and energy. It sounds more complex than it is. Continue this for several minutes, and then let it dissipate as you feel calmly energized in your body and aura.

The Open Dialogue: There is one particular form of meditation dear to writers and researchers alike—that of tapping into the Unconscious to secure answers to specific questions.

In the *Mindfulness Meditation* there is focus on a single object or idea combined with openness to insight. In the "Open Dialogue" our focus is on a specific question while we are open to a variety of answers that might be specific to the question but more often will be "clues" that can be noted and then become the object of further continued meditation, or taken up again at a later meditation.

In essence, we are entrusting the Unconscious to come up with generally non-specific answers to our specific question that may lead to further questions and further answers that are more clue-like than specific. It's a kind of inner brainstorming that can be continued over a period of time. And even though it is presented here in a discussion on meditation, the same process can be continued with the use of our Tarot cards, Tea Leaf Reading, the Pendulum, Dreaming, Crystal Gazing, Spirit Communication, etc.

The "Open Dialogue" is for Big Questions that may even be your Life Work, but more often are chapters in your "book of life."

And, in closing . . .And for our final mantra we remind the readers that the primary purpose of all meditation and all psychic work is to bring each person to union with the Divine Spirit that is everywhere but most easily found within:

SOHAM, HAMSA
(So-ham, Hahm-sa)
He Am I; I am He.

Suggested Reading:

Chadwick: *Inner Journeys—Meditations and Visualizations,* 2006, Llewellyn

Clement: *Meditation for Beginners, Techniques for Awareness, Mindfulness & Relaxation,* 2002, Llewellyn

Crowley, B. & E.: Words of Power—Sacred Sounds of East & West, 1991, Llewellyn

De Biasi, J.: The Magick of the Upper Paths, Forthcoming, Llewellyn

Denning, M. & Phillips, O.: Magical States of Consciousness, 1985, Llewellyn

Denning, M. & Phillips, O.: The Sword and the Serpent, 1988, Llewellyn

Mumford: *A Chakra & Kundalini Workbook, 1995,* Llewellyn

Paulson: Meditation as Spiritual Practice, 2005, Llewellyn

Regardie, with Cicero, C. & Cicero, S.: A Garden of Pomegranates—Skrying on the Tree of Life, 1999, Llewellyn

Regardie, with Cicero, C. & Cicero, S.: The Middle Pillar—The Balance Between Mind and Magic, 1998, Llewellyn

Regardie, with Cicero, C. & Cicero, S.: The Tree of Life—An Illustrated Study in Magic, 2001, Llewellyn

Slate, J. & Weschcke, C.: Psychic Empowerment: Tools & Techniques, 2011, Llewellyn

Tyson, D.: The Power of the Word—The Secret Code of Creation, 1995, Llewellyn

Medium, Spiritual: In Spiritualist work, a person who is able to consciously communicate with spirits or other non-physical entities, guides, messengers, teachers, etc. Most mediums enter a trance state and speak or write messages from those on the "Other Side," or enable communication with a discarnate person through the agency of a "control" or "guide," Often the Control speaks for the Spirit seeking communication.

See also "Channel." The term has either the same meaning as "channeler" or is nearly the same.

Suggested Reading:

Mathews: *Never Say Goodbye, A Medium's Stories of Connecting with Your Loved Ones, 2003,* Llewellyn

Mediumship: The study and development of the skill necessary to function as a spiritual medium facilitating communication between the worlds of spirit and the living. See also Spiritualism.

Suggesting Reading:

Eynden: *So You Want to be a Medium? A Down-to-Earth Guide, 2006,* Llewellyn

Here are some of the variations in mediumship:

Mental mediumship: in which communication between spirits and the medium is by telepathy or clairaudience. The medium addresses the spirit either vocally or silently and the spirit addresses the medium and the medium hears the spirit and repeats the message vocally.

Trance mediumship: in which the medium, once in trance, "steps aside" and allows the spirit to speak through her, using her voice.

Unconscious trance: in which is contact facilitated by a Spirit Guide who speak through the medium and usually speaks on behalf of the spirit.

Direct Voice Mediumship: sometimes involving a trumpet, in which the spirit speaks independently of the medium who may participate in the conversation.

Physical Mediumship: in which the energies of the medium are manipulated by the spirit to produce physical phenomena such as raps, movement of physical objects, the production of ectoplasm, and the materialization of objects.

Messages: Brief communications delivered by Spirit through a medium to the various participants in a séance or demonstration.

Mental Body: The fourth body. The mental body "thinks" in abstract rather than emotional form. The lower mental body unites with the astral and etheric bodies as the personality for current incarnation. The higher mental body is home to the Soul between incarnations.

Mental Imagery: The ability to visualize specific images is an acquired cognitive skill. Mental images are the language of the subconscious mind. Combining imagery with self-talk, you can successfully interact with your subconscious resources and even expand them. You can awaken your dormant resources and exercise them in ways that enrich your life with new potentials for growth and success. With the powers of your subconscious mind at your command through a combination of self-talk and imagery, literally nothing is impossible for you. Through self-talk and mental imagery you can energize your biological systems and even influence brain activity to rejuvenate and recreate yourself. You can increase the length and quality of your life by protecting and fortifying your innermost energy system.

Mental Plane: The third plane (or level or dimension) up from the physical/etheric between the Astral and the Spiritual Planes. It is the plane of abstract consciousness, where we find meaning, patterns, the laws of nature and mathematics, number and form. It is the plane where all thought is shared. It is the upper home for the Akashic records shared with the astral.

Metaphysics, Metaphysical, and Metaphysicians: Words increasingly used as alternatives to *Occult and Occultists, Esoteric and Esotericists, "Seekers," and Spiritualists* to avoid typical negative confusions with the prejudicial usage by theologians, preachers, and even scientists who really know little about the subject matter. In addition, *Metaphysical* has become a common trade term in the book industry for the full range of subjects from alchemy, astral projection, astrology, and auras down through all forms of divination, Kabbalist studies, magick, Paganism and Witchcraft, Tantra, Taoism, to yoga, as well as Alternative and Holistic Healing, Natural and Lunar based horticulture and sustainable lifestyle, and that all in various ways involve the concepts of Spirit and Spirituality. At this point, we see no need to define "Metaphysics" as your dictionary or the Internet does a good enough job.

Mind-out-of Body: Understanding that consciousness is not a function of the brain, but separate and not dependent on it. Contrary to 19th century beliefs, consciousness does not arise out of the brain but pre-exists it and survives it, and functions outside and beyond it.

Mind Power: Astral and other subtle powers applied to consciously directed projects. The Mind is the organizer, manager, and directors of such psychic powers as psychokinesis where material reality is changed.

Motivation: Simple speaking, Motivation is what empowers action. While motivation often comes from outside as reaction or inspiration, or a response and extension love, self-motivation is what drives growth and development. Growth, and becoming all you can be, is what you are here for. Do it! Never stop growing, learning, developing, stretching, climbing, and loving.

Muladhara **(Sanskrit "Base or Root"):** This chakra is located at the base of the spine about half-way between the anus and sex organs, and physically manifests through the pelvic plexus, the gonads (testicles and ovaries), and the muscle that controls male ejaculation and vaginal movement. It relates to the basic instincts of security, survival, and basic human potentiality. Physically it rules our sexuality, emotionally our sensuality, mentally our stability, and spiritually our sense of security. It relates to the sense of smell. The element is Earth. It is symbolized as a red square with 4 red spokes (petals), and its Tattva is represented geometrically in a yellow square. The audible seed mantra is *LuNG* followed by silent mental echo of *LuM*.

The associated psychic powers are pain control, psychometry, dowsing and telekinesis. Opening of Muladhara gives power over all the earth elements and metals, and the physical body. Pain control becomes a reality as demonstrated by walking on hot coals, lying on a bed of nails, insertion of pins through the tongue, etc.

It is the seat of Kundalini. From this chakra three channels—*Ida*, *Pingala*, and *Sushumna*—emerge, separate, and spiral upward to Sahasrara chakra.

Muladhara (Base) *Chakra* Correspondences

Alchemical Planet: Saturn	Alchemical Element: Lead	Tattva: Prithivi (Earth)
Animal: Bull, elephant, ox	Basic Drive: Security	Tattva color: Yellow
Body Function: Elimination	Chakra Color: Red	Tattva form: Square
Element: Earth	Gemstone: Ruby, garnet, lodestone	Tattva Sense: Smell
Gland: Adrenals	God-form, Egyptian: Geb	God-form, Hindu: Bala Brahma [1]
God-form, Greek: Gaia, Demeter	Incense: Cedar	Goddess-form, Hindu: Dakini [2]
Location: Base of spine	Order of chakra unfoldment: 1st	Yogic Planet: Saturn
Part of Body: Between anus & genitals	Psychological attribute: Solidarity	Bija Mantra: LuNG, LuM (3)
Psychic Power: pain control, psychometry, dowsing, telekinesis	Sense: Smell	
Spinal Joint: 1st, 2nd, 3rd	Spinal Location: 4th Sacral	
Tarot Key: XXI, World	Tree of Life Sephiroth: Malkuth	Yantra (internal) Blue Square
Tarot Suit: Pentacles		

1 Child-God
2 Security
Source: Slate, J. & Weschcke, C.: *Psychic Empowerment—Tools & Techniques*, 2011, Llewellyn

Natural Law: The orderly principles of nature that apply to all of us.

Nature Spirits: Spiritual beings and Elementals including fairies, gnomes, salamanders, etc. who are instruments of life.

Near Death Experience (NDE): People near death, and sometimes those who have been resuscitated after dying, report common experiences of peacefulness followed by separation from the body. At first there is darkness then seeing a source of light and moving into the light, sometimes through a tunnel. At this point, many turn or are turned to move back into the body. Sometimes they see family and friends, and other times a 'presence,' who all advise that it not yet the time for the person to pass over. Other times there may be a review of the lifetime and a decision made by the person to return to complete unfinished business. It is nearly always a very positive and transformative experience, giving the person a much greater appreciation of life.

Next Step: Advancement, growth, development, expansion all comes about when we are willing to take the "next step" out of self-imposed and societal limitations. Whether we are concerned with advancements in career, education, innovations in science and technology, or other worldly success, or projecting into the astral world, aura reading, psychic development, or spiritual growth, we have to jump over the fence, get out of the rut, breakthrough the walls.

Evolution results from the series of next steps that societies and individuals have taken and will take—for evolution is not just the past but even more the future. Without growth, without evolution, we are passé, in fact doomed like dinosaurs. *What does this have to do with you?* It is you, the individual, who is the vehicle of evolution. Unless you take the next step in your own life, growing in consciousness and psychic powers, you fail to lend your strength to our better future.

Psychic Powers and Spirit Communication are not just incidental to our evolutionary advancement; rather they are essential to the process. Undertaking their conscious development accelerates personal growth at a most critical time in world history.

Astral Projection is a vital contribution to this acceleration and to our ability to meet the challenges of this moment. Astral experiences *ignite* psychic development and the expansion of consciousness necessary for new knowledge and understanding of the cosmic adventure that is our origin and our destiny. The experience of astral consciousness is one of the dynamic "next steps" necessary to move forward, to make the transition into the real New Age that will be a reality for those willing to commit themselves *to becoming more than they are.*

Suggested Reading:

Slate & Weschcke: *Astral Projection for Psychic Empowerment, 2012,* Llewellyn

Slate & Weschcke: *Clairvoyance for Psychic Empowerment, 2013,* Llewellyn

Slate & Weschcke: *The Llewellyn Complete Book of Psychic Empowerment, 2011,* Llewellyn

Slate & Weschcke: *Psychic Empowerment for Everyone, 2009,* Llewellyn

New Age Shamanism: (See Index & Text)

New Age Spirituality: In the "New Age"* that began to strike popular interest in 1960, there is no official creed or sacred book, no rigid and unifying theology and liturgy, and no charismatic leadership. The New Age impulse is to create, what Neville Drury describes as "a spirituality without borders or confining dogmas" that is inclusive and pluralistic, and holding to "a holistic worldview" that includes both science and spirituality"*and embraces a number of alternative sciences considered fringe by some.

> * Drury, N..(2004), *The New Age: Searching for the Spiritual Self,* London, England, UK: Thames and Hudson

> * "New Age" has become a somewhat denigrated term by association with some *fluffy* people, but it is important to recognize it as a "changing of the guard," so to speak. *Zodiacal Ages* are cyclic realities *marking* changes in the dominant energies that influence and characterize our planet's consciousness (and all that lives in and on "her") for approximately 2,400 years. There is no sudden shift occurring exactly on a certain date and time because we are dealing with a far grander scale than your kitchen clock and calendar. Instead, we have a transition phase of several hundred years of gradual cultural and philosophical changes taking place.

Our entry into the "Aquarian Age" is reflected in the intellectual changes that began rather dramatically a few hundred years ago in the movement from the repressive, faith-bound, anti-intellectualism of Pisces into the Aquarian expectation that rationality and science will bring an age of technological progress and economic plenty. Already the "new world" is vastly different and the new times have barely begun.

Still, changes are not easy, and there will be pain to old institutions and anti-quarian thinking, and there will have to be a time of healing to correct the planetary abuse done in the belief of man's (male) dominance over Mother Nature and the enslavement and murder of millions of "unbelievers" conducted by church and authoritarian state over the past two thousand years.

New Feminine: Today, we also see the Feminine "returning" and taking on new roles—not merely in equality with the Masculine—but transformative in both outer institutions and in the re-balancing of the inner dimensions of Man and Woman.

New World of Mind & Spirit in a New World of Higher Human Consciousness: (See Index & Text)

New World Order: (See Index & Text)

No One Way: (See Index & Text)

None: It should be noted that one of the fastest growing "religious movements" in the United States today is "No Religion," the choice of 20 percent of the population. This is not Atheism nor Agnosticism, but the rejection of organized religion. According to the Pew Research center, a third of U.S. adults under the age of 30 do not identify with a religion, nor are they looking for a religion. "Overwhelmingly, they think that religious organizations are too concerned with money and power, too focused on rules and too involved in politics."

While some, particularly those starting new families, appreciate the social connections of church, they prefer the intellectual approach of Deism, Freemasonry, and Unitarian-Universalist membership.

Novus Ordo Seclorum: The New Order of the Ages represented in the Great Seal of the United States. N.O.S. is the spiritual unity behind the nation and the container for all the ideas represented by its founding. It has the potential to function as the 'over soul' of the nation should people turn inward to its inspiration. As we turn to the N.O.S. for inner guidance it aligns the person with those high ideas and guides their translation into their practical and contemporary manifestation. It is the repository of the high aspirations of the founding fathers and those thinkers and leaders who have sought to create a <u>new</u> nation based on principles rather than geographic and tribal boundaries. It represents the Spirit of America.

Occult: That which is, at least temporarily, hidden from our perception. In astronomy it refers to the passing of one body in front of another as when the Moon passes in front of the Sun (an eclipse). In the common culture it has been used as a category for 'hidden' knowledge, i.e. those subjects and technologies functioning to manifest psychic and spiritual faculties.

Suggested Reading:

Greer: *The New Encyclopedia of the Occult, 2003,* **Llewellyn**

Ogdoadic Tradition: (See Aurum Solis above).

Old Religion, The: The name sometimes given to the worship of the Great Mother, the Goddess of all life. While this "Nature Religion" is far older than even "pre-Christianity," it continued into modern times in Shamanic practices and European Witchcraft, and is used as an alternate to Wicca. As the Old Religion it has many fundamental similarities to *ancient* Tantra.

Open to Spirit: "*Once you are receptive to the spirit realm, nothing is beyond your reach.* Its limitless wealth of empowering resources becomes readily available to you. Protection, comfort, support, healing, enlightenment, and joy—all of these are possible through spontaneous spirit manifestations and interventions."

Sounds simple, doesn't it? Spirit is everywhere, in everything, and is within each and every one of us. Just open to Spirit. *Open the Door, Richard* was the title of a song first recorded in 1946. *Open the Door, and Let me in.* In a sense, Spirit is waiting for you to open the door, your door, and welcome the wisdom and inspiration of the higher self and spiritual entities.

Spirit is both an external cosmic dimension and an internal one. Spirit is also the primary element from which all others are derived. Spirit is with you, but you have to turn attention to Spirit and "let Spirit in." It's a very subtle thing—simply relax and "feel the presence."

Do not complicate matters with prayers and rituals. Just be, and Spirit will "be here now." Just let it happen, and over time you will feel that presence and slowly Spirit will answer your genuine needs, your essential questions, empower your love-motivated actions.

Operating System: Inside every computer there is a software package providing the instructions for the hardware to carry out the work requested by application software packages like Microsoft Word and Excel. The operating system is the interface between the computer hardware and the outer world, while the application packages are like the skills and training we learn by study and experience. Like every other computer the human brain requires an operating system that interfaces with the world and filters our perceptions to correspond to what we are conditioned to expect through parental guidance, our life experiences, education, training, and interaction with authority figures, social expectations, and to far lesser extent by our genetic heritage and past-life memories. This operating system also conditions and directs the way we respond to external stimuli. Much of this operating system functions in the subconscious mind. Like computers, the operating system can be modified, up-dated, changed and even replaced. Self-understanding is learning about our operating system; self-improvement is about modifying and changing our operating system; self-transformation is about up-dating and largely replacing our operating system. It is a vital next step for every conscious person to undertake, again and again.

Other Side: A phrase used to describe the spirit world, the location of the After Life.

Ouija™ Board: A simple board with the alphabet printed on it along with 'yes' and 'no,' and a planchette or easily moveable device used to communicate with spirits. The users, usually two people of opposite gender, rest fingers on the planchette which slides quickly to the variously letters to spell out answers to questions. To use the Ouija the partners must relax and let the Unconscious Mind operate the planchette. It is helpful to have a formal starting and ending of the session—as simply as speaking "Please, if any spirits wish to speak through Ouija, say YES." To end the session, simply say "Thank you, and goodbye for now," and put Ouija away. Do not just leave it on a table but restore it to a box or drawer where it rests undisturbed and unobserved. A spirit or spirits may operate through the Unconscious but cannot until you "let go" of your conscious objective faculty. It's sort of like "Closing Down" one aspect of your consciousness in order to "Open Up" the other which can then act as a doorway to other units of consciousness—your own or spirit entities. Have questions prepared, speak them slowly and allow the planchette to move from one letter to another to spell out the answers.

"Past," The: What's "past" is past. We build on the past, it is the foundation for the building the future, but *do not let it become a limitation upon your making a New Beginning!* The Past is filled with failures, with tired ideologies, with antique the-

ologies, and old authorities standing in the of way progress. "What's past is prologue" wrote William Shakespeare, but it is essential that we do not allow the past
to *write the future!* Everything changes, and the "Future" evolves from the Past.
Moving forward, we each can be pioneers, great innovators, discoverers of new
worlds of mind and spirit, and perhaps of new space and being.

Past Life Regression: A technique using hypnosis/self-hypnosis to recover certain
memories, and sometimes learned skills, from the memories of a previous life
that are stored in areas of the unconscious. The more specific the "probe" of the
targeted past life, the more efficient will be the technique and the more beneficial
the recovery for this life. Perhaps the greatest benefit is to uncover and mitigate
the causal relationship between a past life trauma and a current life phobia or
fear or even a physiological problem.

Also to experience preexistence and life-between lifetimes.

Suggested Reading:

Andrews: *How to Uncover Your Past Lives, 2006,* Llewellyn

Grimassi: *The Cauldron of Memory—Retrieving Ancestral Knowledge & Wisdom,*
2009, Llewellyn

Newton: *Destiny of Souls, 2000,* Llewellyn

Newton: *Journey of Souls, 2002,* Llewellyn

Newton: *Life Between Lives, 2004,* Llewellyn

Newton: *Memories of the Afterlife, 2009,* Llewellyn

Slate & Weschcke: *Doors to Past Lives & Future Lives, 2011,* Llewellyn

Webster: *Practical Guide to Past Life Memories, Twelve Proven Methods, 2001,*
Llewellyn

Pendulum: Simply a weight on the end of a string somewhat shorter than the length
of the forearm. The string is held by fingers so that the weight can freely swing over
a simple chart or map, or sometimes an object, and revealing by the direction of
the swing answers to specific question framed mostly for yes/no response. By-pass-
ing conscious control, the subconscious provides the answers. Some people believe
that spirits may move the pendulum similar to the movement of the planchette on
the Ouija™ Board. Pendulums are also used in dowsing, often over a map with a
sample of ore held in one hand or in a hollow cavity in the pendulum that serves

as a 'witness' to find a body of the same ore in the geographic location indicated by the pendulum over the map.

Working with a pendulum is a desirable practice developing psychic sensitivity and extended awareness. It is a valuable means to communication with the subconscious mind.

Suggested Reading:

Ghiuselev & Astanassov: *Pendulum Power Magic Kit.* Brass pendulum, book & Full Color Layout Sheet to develop extrasensory faculties, 2012, *Lo Scarabeo/ Lewellyn*

Slate, J. & Weschcke, C.: *Psychic Empowerment: Tools & Techniques,* 2011, Llewellyn

Person Deities: They are called *anthropomorphic* because they are "formed in man's image." It's the nature of human consciousness to *anthropomorphize* to one degree or another most of our experiences of a psychological, psychic, or spiritual nature.

We make distinctions by how deities are "seen" through intuition and imagination (and in dreams). Mostly we think of the creative sources of reality in a human-like form rather than as a pure force which can—at best—only be described symbolically or mathematically. To appreciate these distinctions, recall your lessons in mythology where most deities appear as humanoid gods and goddesses, named and costumed in certain ways to symbolize their nature and function as gods of thunder, the sea, war, wisdom, lust, or as goddesses of love, crafts, agriculture, child-birth, healing, and so on.

In some cultures, the goddesses in particular manifest in hundreds of carefully crafted forms distinctly varied by color of skin and costumes, ornaments and jewels, metals and shapes of their construction and where they are worn, postures and gestures, names, associated mantras, powers, locales, their companions, and more. Both gods and goddesses are sometimes given other attributes drawn from the non-human 'kingdoms' of animals' heads, horns and hooves; birds' heads, wings, feathers and claws; fish tails; and even insect shapes. All these distinctions are meaningful and are related to in worship and meditation, or used in prayer or magical acts to manifest the particularized powers to meet human needs and desires.

Some cultures do not humanize the creative powers, but see them only as abstract symbols such as the most familiar *Yin* and *Yang,* but also in particular symbols directly associated with a single deity, such as the Christian Cross, the Jewish Star of David, the Egyptian Ankh, the Radiant Sun, the Crescent Moon, Thor's Hammer, and others. Even mathematical formulae have taken on a near or actual religious-like significance as in the case of Einstein's famous $E=mc^2$.

In pre-history, most deities were experienced—and then more strongly visualized as feminine—in the form of the Great Mother Goddess and many other goddesses. Starting approximately around 5000 BCE, feminine deities were slowly replaced or reduced in their role and function by masculine deities as the solar-based, hunter-herder-warrior, cultures supplanted the earlier lunar-based agricultural cultures. With that change, the singular and community based magickal relationship with spirit and deity was replaced by the institutional and hierarchical male dominated myths and religions. The older personal contact and direct communication with spirits and deity was supplanted in the new role of male priests as the only "lawful" communicants with deity.

Personal Consciousness: Your Personal Consciousness that was once part of the Universal Consciousness remains forever connected to it. And thus it can be said to be created in the image of God. In *Self-Empowerment and Your Subconscious Mind,* Carl Llewellyn Weschcke describes an image of the Great Pyramid with levels for the *Lower, Middle* and *Higher* Consciousness, i.e. Sub-Conscious Mind, Conscious Mind and Super-Conscious Mind. The image is a matrix called 'the anatomy of the Body of God'. It can be visualized as the Great Pyramid with levels for the *Lower, Middle* and *Higher* Consciousness, i.e. Sub-Conscious Mind, Conscious Mind and Super-Conscious Mind. This 'matrix' is to be filled in by experience, and the goal is to ascend through the layers of physical stone through to the open cap where all the universe is seen.

Suggested Reading:

Slate, J.H. & Weschcke, C.L.: *Self-Empowerment and your Subconscious Mind,* 2010, Llewellyn

Personal Growth Facilitator: (See Index & Text)

Personal Religion (or Spirituality) and Personal Development: While not generally indexed as "religion," we feel it reflects an attitude of respect for the Life we have been given and see a responsibility for personal growth and development—of body, psyche, mind, and soul—to *become more than we are* and *all we can be.*

We include many growth exercises such as yoga, martial arts, education, meditation, self-hypnosis, paranormal studies, psychic development, and studies in all subjects to increase understanding of self, history, spirituality, and personal transformation.

Personality: The immediate vehicle of personal consciousness we believe to be ourselves. It is a temporary complex drawn from the etheric, astral, and mental bodies containing current life memories, the current operating system. It is the relatively enduring complex of attitudes, interests, behavioral patterns, emotional responses, social roles, and other individual traits. Each individual's personality is an aggregate conglomeration of decisions made throughout life. There are inherent natural, genetic, and environmental factors that contribute to the development of the personality. According to the process of socialization, "personality also colors our values, beliefs, and expectations ... Hereditary factors that contribute to personality development do so as a result of interactions with the particular social environment in which people live." (Quoted from *Wikipedia*)

The Personality is only one chapter in the full biography of the evolving Soul. And each chapter is analyzed and abstracted to secure the essential lessons and experiences of the entire lifetime, while the memories of that lifetime flow into the Subconscious Mind and become part of the Universal Consciousness providing a complete history of the Soul's many lifetimes. In between lives, the Soul absorbs lessons from the many successive personalities and thus evolves. From his now greater perspective, the Soul outlines a new chapter and sends part of his essence into incarnation to gain new experiences that will become new lessons for the evolving Soul. It is somewhat as if a mature adult could have planned the years of his childhood to get the right experiences and education for the professional life he has chosen.

Phantasm: An apparition of a living person, probably an astral projection.

Phantom: An apparition of a dead person, possibly the etheric/astral bodies after leaving the physical body.

Physical Body: We refer to the physical body as a "temporary vehicle" for the incarnating personality (which, after death is referred to as the "surviving personality"). At the same time, we need to recognize that there's "more than meets the eye"—for the physical and the etheric bodies—so long as the physical body is "alive"—are intimately joined together when the body is awake, but can drift apart (still connected by *cords*) during sleep and during certain kinds of magical operations. Even though we can call the physical/etheric body "fixed" together on the material plane, we need to understand that other subtle bodies (astral, mental, and causal) are also present as long as there is life. These can be perceived in the aura.

The physical body, along with the vital etheric *energy* body is the <u>action</u> vehicle for the incarnate personality, and any denial of the physical as "non-spiritual" is to restrict its field of action and experience—which is what we are here for! There is nothing evil, dirty, or sinful about the physical body itself, but the conscious mind should be the "manager" and bring the body and its appetites and lusts under intelligent self-control.

When awake, the physical and etheric bodies are inseparable, although it is possible to project parts of the etheric body in magical operations. Asleep, it is possible to partially separate the etheric body from the physical for travel on the physical plane. It is this physical vehicle that is the means to the experiencing of life's lessons.

Physical Phenomena: "Physical" phenomena associated with a séance, such as: movement or levitation of a trumpet, planchette, table or other physical object, the materialization of a spirit most often out of ectoplasm, voices and sounds sometimes emanating from a person or object and other times without apparent source, and other physical manifestations usually in relation to Spiritualist activity.

Physical Universe/World: We inhabit a Physical Universe* that our five physical senses experience as a solid measured by three dimensions of space plus a fourth of time. And, yes, there is a fifth dimension, and some physicists are of the belief that there may be a total of eleven dimensions as well as parallel universes to our own. The physical universe is our "home plane" during physical life, and is that which we perceive and know best as the foundation for our manifest being. While the physical universe contains matter both visible and invisible which extends beyond the physical plane into the non-physical ("spiritual) planes generally known as Etheric, Astral, Mental, Causal, and Spiritual. Each person is more than his/her physical body as our consciousness extends into the non-physical and uses bodies of etheric, astral, mental and causal substance.

We, the residents of planet Earth (also called *Gaia*), are not alone! Spirit, Life, Intelligence is everywhere, and *we can communicate with other beings at spiritual levels beyond the confines of physical space.*

* In this usage, we are also referring to the *esoteric* concept of the physical or material "plane," also called a "world" or "level." Most esoteric writers chart a Cosmos of eight dimensions within seven planes of manifestation, plus three more planes beyond manifestation that guide the process, and three more above and outside of manifestation from which it is sourced. A pretty complex system, but we don't need to get into that except to make it clear that **the Cosmos is far more complex and infinitely larger than what we ordinarily see and think.** This is important to our discussion of Communications with all Spiritual Entities, to all forms of Psychic Development, to all aspects of Spiritual Growth and Attainment. Realize that the entire Cosmos opens to you—you don't need to go through any intermediary of teacher, priest, bishop or secret chief, but *you should do the developmental work for yourself.* That's how you grow and become more than you are towards the fulfillment of each lifetime's purpose. See tables in the Glossary.

The physical universe is mainly *physical* Space, in we which experience Matter and Energy through the *motion (vibration)* of the sub-atomic particles of our physical environment and of our physical bodies while we are *alive.* We also know that physical objects, including our own bodies, are mostly empty space despite the appearance and feel of solidity. "Superficial" appearances are often deceptive relative to the purpose and nature of our observation. T*he truth may be that such "emptiness" is Spirit itself, and offers the opportunity to focus consciousness to induce healing and magickal changes in the physical manifestations.*

Piscean Man, the Outer, Other-directed: In contrast to the "Inner-directed Aquarian Man," the Other or Outer, or Other Directed person 'follows the crowd' and accepts the guidance of authority figures without reasonable questions. 'Inner-Directed' has also been associated with the Aquarian Age individual man in contrast to the Piscean Age with its symbolism of fish who swim in groups. The outer-directed person is perceived as easily manipulated because of his dependence on outer authority. (See also Aquarian Man, the *Inner* Directed)

PK: (See Psychokinesis)

PK Bombardment: A PK procedure that targets mental energies in an effort to influence the fall of a coin.

PK Channeling: An Out-of-Body procedure designed to access the healing resources of higher planes and transfer them to the physical body.

Suggested Reading:

Slate, J.H. & Weschcke, C.L.: *Astral Projection for Psychic Empowerment, 2012,* Llewellyn

PK Illumination: An imagery procedure designed to unleash inner rejuvenating energy.

Plane: The old word, still in common use, for the various *worlds* and *levels* of reality and consciousness. While there is debate on their total number and classification, the most common is that of the five planes plus a collective designation under Spiritual:

Physical (sometimes with the lower part of the etheric attached)

Etheric (sometimes considered as two layers, one always attached to the physical and the other always to the astral)

Astral (commonly divided into Lower and Higher)

Mental (commonly divided into Lower and Higher)

Causal (the Highest level of the Mental)

Spiritual (sometimes considered as consisting of two or more additional planes)

Platform: A stage used by a medium delivering messages or lectures.

Poltergeist: Literally, a mischievous spirit. A presence or energy, sometimes confined to a single room but more often associated with a particular person, that creates unintentional disturbances such as knocking over vases, clocks, mirrors, knick-knacks, and other small but generally favorite objects. At one time, it was believed that the activity was the result of unstable emotional energies, often repressed, and unconsciously projected by adolescents during puberty.

Suggested Reading:

Righi: *Ghosts, Apparitions and Poltergeists, An Exploration of the Supernatural Through History, 2008, Llewellyn*

Possession: The temporary displacement of the self by a spirit entity. Possession can be voluntary as when a medium surrenders her/his body to a spirit or involuntary when the entity takes over. In Voudoun, the god takes possession and 'rides' the person like a horse. While the person is possessed, the body is often capable of physical feats beyond the normal ability of the person.

A somewhat different situation arises when the control is involuntary. It becomes a state of possession in which a spirit or other entity such as a "Loa" in the Voodoo religion seems to push your conscious to one side and their consciousness takes over your body and personality.

Postures, and Movements, East and West: "Postures" generally refer to Eastern yogic *asana*s, along with controlled breathing, and our familiar Western postures of standing and sitting. In addition, postures involve intentional movement, even if just sitting with grace, and awareness of energy flow. There are, of course, other postures: those of the martial arts in China and Japan, belly and dervish dances in the Middle East, Hula from Hawaii, and much more. Any movement and posture that involves energy probably have an associated shamanic or sacred tradition. Every posture, movement, and gesture involves muscles and nerves, electrical currents and chemicals, energy flows and hormones along with emotional and spiritual responses, and changes in the aura. Every movement of the physical body triggers a complex of responses, but some are very specific in what they do. The important point is to understand that there is a psychic, magickal and spiritual side to all these positions, postures, movements, signs and gestures.

The Western Esoteric Tradition has adopted the Egyptian God postures as seen in paintings on tomb and temple walls. Whether standing, moving, or seated, these show positions of dignity and energy restraint. You can sense power that would be released in a simple gesture. When you assume any of the magical positions and make the movements, you should learn to be sensitive to the energy flow, and with that learn to adjust your stance and movements until the energy flow feels just right. It will help to allow yourself to "imagine" seeing those energies from outside your body, seeing them just as if viewing a schematic diagram of channels and centers.

In studying the Martial Arts postures and movements, consider how these holds, blows and movements—no matter the particular style—generate and deliver amazing power. And when you study any of the martial arts you will often find illustrations showing the many subtle body energy channels, meridians and psychic centers involved.

Now, think of your own body. A simple smile causes your body and emotions to respond to that simple 'posture.' "When you smile, the whole world smiles with you" is more than a pretty phrase because that gesture is infectious and brings smiles to other people as well. But, *what happened to you when you smiled?*

You felt better! The "smile movement" triggered not only an emotional response but through the nerves and muscles involved switched on many electrical and chemical transfers in your body. And then projected energy into your aura and broadcast it to these other people who "smiled with you."

Prana: Chi, the Force, the Power. The universal life-force flowing throughout the universe, and locally emanating from the sun as vitality absorbed from the air we breathe and the food we eat. It can be visualized as flowing into the body as you inhale, and then distributed throughout the body as you exhale.

Prana is also considered as one of the "seven elements:" Prana, Manas (mind), Ether, Fire, Air, Water and Earth, corresponding to seven regions of the universe. In Hebrew Kabbalism, Nephesh (the Psyche) is Prana combined with Kama (Love), together making the vital spark that is the "breath of life." Prana is comparable to Chi (Chinese), Ki (Japanese), vitality globules (Theosophical), Nous (Rosicrucian), Orgone (Wilhelm Reich), animal magnetism (Mesmer), Quintessence (Alchemical), and Mana (Hawaii priests).

Prayer: 1) A mantra-like series of words addressed to deity to seek particular benevolence and blessing. 2) An emotionally laden plea to deity to meet a personal or collective need. 3) A form of affirmation used in meditation, ritual or self-hypnosis to invoke the power of the subconscious mind to bring about change in personal circumstances. Prayer, too, can be understood in terms of both Meditation and Magick (including both Invocation and Evocation). However, many of the prescribed "rote" prayers of the Abrahamic religions are for the benefit of the institution, not the individual.

Suggested Reading:

Braden: *Secrets of the Lost Mode of Prayer, 2006, Hay House*

Psychokinesis (PK): The ability of the mind to influence objects, events, and processes in the apparent absence of intervening physical energy or intermediary instrumentation. An extended definition of PK includes its capacity to influence internal biological systems. The movement of objects without physical contact.

Quantum Physics, and the New Paranormal: The new science of Quantum Theory tells us that the beginning is (not just *was* but still *is*) the Universal Field of Possibilities that manifests first as Energy/Matter under the guidance of packets of information/instruction. Thus we can see an analogy with a computer with its Operating Program & its Application Programs.

The mere act of observation affects reality at the sub-atomic level; in technical terms, "consciousness caused collapse" to change physical reality. That leads to the conclusion that the observer and reality are not separate and neither are mind and body truly separate at the subtle energy levels affecting long-term health but also providing an understanding of how non-physical healing (spiritual, energy, laying on of hands, etc.) may work.

The realization that we are more than a physical body, that the "cosmos" is more than the physical universe, that as humans we have the power—infinitely— to *Become more than we are!* And most important of all, smallness can be more important than bigness in the physical dimension which is where we plant our feet. Ideas start off big in the higher dimensions, but unless you build "from the ground up, they won't amount to the proverbial "hill of beans."

The Importance of "smallness" and "building from the ground up." Consciousness is in everything and the key to all we do. Yes, even such realizations of this sort count as part of our growing spiritual consciousness, and the assumption of personal responsibility that we each must assume to grow and *Become All we can Be!*

Raps and Rapping: Noises produced during a séance, seeming to come from the surface of tables, walls, ceilings, floors. They seem to be some kind of energy materialization produced by a spirit to announce his presence and sometimes as a means of communication.

Reincarnation: The belief that the Soul experiences multiple lives through newly born physical bodies and personalities. Upon death of the physical body, the personality withdraws to the astral and then mental plane while the essential lessons of that incarnation are abstracted to the Soul.

Suggested Reading:

Slate: *Beyond Reincarnation, Experience your Past Lives & Lives Between Lives*, 2005, Llewellyn

Religion: Religion is generally defined as a "belief system," but it also—and more realistically—is an "attitude" towards other humans, and—separately—towards the non-human world. At the one extreme (primarily the three monotheistic religions), humanity (as Man) is proclaimed supreme over all Nature and all the Earth as his to be used and abused. At the other extreme, in most other religions, we are all of One Life and as humans we have greater responsibility in the care of one another, of Nature, and the Earth.

All religions provide some story of creation of cosmos and of humanity, but a major difference is that the three "newer" religions are purely theological and declare that man must serve the "one God," whereas the older religions are both theological and magickal, and provide ways their deific forces can help humans to better meet life's challenges.

All religions are man-made, and unfortunately some men have projected their worst prejudices into the fundamentals of their beliefs– including sexual and racial discriminations, territorial ambitions, even economic and political theory.

With over 4,000 distinct contemporary religions in the world, there really is no suitable overall definition of what "religion" is. We can say that basically a religion is a particular belief system presenting a unique worldview inclusive of the origin of the Cosmos (all that is, including the physical universe), that of all life, the meaning and purpose of individual human life, the respective roles of the religion to human life—the believers, individually and as a group, and all humanity. Usually there is a unique image identifying that worldview and some-times serving as a symbol for meditation or object of worship.

For each particular religion, there is usually some narrative about its origin, the functional goals of an individual's life to that of the universe, to the religion's organization and of the organization's service to the individual, or what the orga-nization *demands* from the individual.

Religion and Mythology: All religions are founded on some form of mythology pre-sented as 1) as a Creation Story; 2) as History, usually of one man's life; 3) as a philosophic (even "scientific") interpretation of reality as perceived, and usually limited to one time and place. Based on any mythology, a resultant theology and supplemental religious law, moral code, institutional activity, etc. are essentially irrational.

Religion and Spirituality: Spirituality is often mistakenly confused with religion. The word "religion" derives form *ligare* meaning "to bind together." From this we have two concepts:

1. To bind a people together as the Roman Empire used Catholicism to assert political control over the people of Europe and the Mediterranean. These religions are all *political* and *theistic,* and today are *monotheistic.* The emphasis is on humans serving the one God (always represented in masculine human form) and His institutions. Judaism, Islam, and Christianity are the prime examples. They claim that only God can solve problems and "faith" (along with money) is the means to engage God's power.

2. To represent the non-physical spiritual connection between Man and Cosmos and the "Source" which is probably knowable only in symbol and abstraction. These are mostly, but not exclusively, multi-*theistic** and non-political. The emphasis is on helping humans to live better lives. Chinese Taoism, ancient Indian Tantra, European Paganism, Druidism and modern Hinduism are the prime examples. Some, like Deism, are purely intellectual and believe human rationality can solve all problems.

* The use of the term, "multi-theistic" here is different than poly-theistic—meaning many deities. In multi-theism, "gods" are not necessarily perceived as deities but more often as natural forces, spontaneous thought forms reflecting human feelings about a place or activity, a composite of the spiritual essence of a herd of animals or of the species itself, a carefully constructed thought form (almost always in human form) that functions as a "formula" for evoking or invoking the ideal action represented in that god or goddess including—usually—one overall male and one female deity whose mythic union created all the manifest world, and sometimes a single representation either in bi-sexual form or as a non-human symbol to represent all creation above and beyond manifestation. Among examples are Druidism, ancient Tantra, European Paganism, and variations of Deism and Pantheism. Generally speaking, it is more feminine than masculine, and functions to serve Life, including humans, with a primary ethic of "Harm none."

Spirituality is a personal matter that may involve participation in any of the 4200 institutional "religions," or "spiritual but not religious" involving personal study and practice of spiritual and esoteric systems, many of them freely derived from their shamanic foundations, and the ongoing practices of self-improvement, developments in the newer sciences of the paranormal or general study of psychology, quantum physics, philosophy, and practices such as yoga, the martial arts, magick, tantra, and other transformative growth systems.

Responsible Student: Books are no longer just "about" subjects, or "how to" manuals, but the new books even go beyond "theory & practice" to fully *develop* the theoretical foundations of a subject, explain the whys and the benefits of practice &

application, often include case studies & examples, provide specific self-applied techniques for personal use, and sometimes even self-administered tests and questionnaires to affirm your understanding and knowledge.

It's not only such new books but the entire "responsible student" concept has carried over into self-study courses, on-line universities, down-loadable lessons, and has changed the style for author and conference lectures. Teachers are no longer reigning authority figures or unquestioned gurus but helpers taking their lead from students. As a result, more university classes provide for students to participate in research and experimentation on a co-equal basis with teachers for true "hands-on" study. In other words, everyone participates and everyone grows.

Responsibility, Personal: Every adult person, unless mentally or emotionally handicapped, must be self-responsible. That doesn't mean not seeking help or advice in specific matters and times of need but otherwise we must move beyond dependence whether on teacher, preacher, doctor, government, or employer. Adult relationships should be partnerships.

As with any clairvoyant experience, whether apparently sourced from the Spirit Realm or even perceived as coming from one's Higher Self, Guardian Angel, or some Inner Plane Adept, or Messenger of Deity, or as an interpretation of a Symbol, it is important to engage with the Conscious Mind to bring the message into context of the physical world and your personal environment.

You have the ultimate responsibility for rational and practical application of all other-dimensional guidance in relation to physical plane matters. Be particularly wary of all guidance regarding money, property, relationships, etc., especially those that may benefit another person, religious organization, spiritual leader, or other promising extraordinary benefits or "other-worldly" return on your investments. Remember the challenges of growing from childhood, through the hormonal 'teen years, into the early years of adult life, and then into the more mature years, and then understand that you are entering into expanded and unfamiliar areas of consciousness and awareness. It is somewhat similar to moving to a foreign culture where it sometimes is easy to mis-interpret the language and culture. We have to grow into familiarity with these new worlds and "put away childish things" to accept the new responsibilities that go with vast new opportunities

Role-Playing for Self-Discovery and Therapy: "Growing numbers of psychothera-pists use guided visualization techniques to evoke images of 'power animals' or 'spirit guides' and then encourage clients to interact with and learn from them."*

* Gallegos, A. *The personal. Totem pole: animal imagery, the chakras and psychotherapy.* Santa Fe, NM: 1987, Moon Bear Press.

A further point can be made that "role playing" can be a form of *live* active imagination programs (somewhat similar to drama therapy and Kabbalistic path-working programs, and also to "fantasy training" in which two or more players adopt defined *fantasy* roles as human/human or animal/human within the con-text of a <u>minimal script</u> *calling for their spontaneous interaction.* In the case of such play within a consensual sexual relationship, one action evokes feeling reactions in both partners. They are actually having a shamanic-like journey together in which the one partner can become one with the spirit of the animal totem, or *both relate archetypally to each other in inter-related roles.*

As Lee Harrington writes:

"Anytime we become someone or something else, we can learn something about ourselves or the nature of the universe from a new perspective."
—*"Harrington, L.: Sacred Kink—The Eightfold Path of BDSM and Beyond, 2009. Mystic*

Sahasrara (AKA the *Thousand Petaled Lotus* and the *Crown* Chakra): This chakra is located at and then just above the crown of the head. It manifests through the pineal gland, which produces melatonin—the hormone regulating sleep. Physically, it relates to the basis of consciousness—physically with meditation, emotionally with "beingness," mentally with universal consciousness. The female Kundalini *Shakti* energy rises from Muladhara to the crown to unite with the male *Shiva* energy to produce *Samadhi.* It relates to our sense of the Divine Con-nection. The associated psychic powers are astral projection and prophecy.

It is symbolized by a violet lotus with one thousand multi-colored spokes (actually 12 in the center and then 960 around the center for a total of 972), and represented graphically by an image of a red rose. There is no seed mantra. The element is "Thought."

Sahasrara (Crown) *Chakra* Correspondences

Alchemical Planet: Mercury, Uranus	Alchemical Element: Mercury	Tattva: Bindu (a dot)
Animal: None	Basic Drive: union	Tattva Color: Clear
Body Function: Super-consciousness	Chakra Color: Violet	Tattva form: rose seen from above
Element: Thought	Gemstone: Diamond	Tattva Sense: Higher Self
Gland: Pineal	God-form, Egyptian: Nut	God-form, Hindu: Brahma Vishnu[1]
God-form, Greek: Zeus	Incense: Lotus, gotu kola	Goddess-form, Hindu: Maha Shakti [2]
Location: Crown of Head	Order of chakra unfoldment: 7th	Yogic Planet: Mercury, Uranus
Part of Body: cerebral cortex, central nervous system	Psychological state: Bliss	Seed Syllable/Number: H(0)
Psychic Power: astral projection, prophecy	Sense: the Divine Connection	
Spinal Joint: 33rd	Spinal Location: none	
Tarot Key: I, Magician	Tree of Life Sephiroth: Kether	

1 Inner teacher
2 Union
Source: Slate, J. & Weschcke, C.: **Psychic Empowerment—Tools & Techniques**, 2011, Llewellyn

Suggested Reading:

Dale: *The Subtle Body—An Encyclopedia of Your Energetic Anatomy,* 2009, Sounds True

Science and Spirituality, Together: Both science and spirituality are essential to the discovery and application of knowledge, spirituality is the validating force that underlies knowledge in its purest form. When looking at science and spirituality we often see a peculiar rift between them, especially when viewed from afar. But the closer we look, the more any disjunction seems to disappear. Dormant knowledge, once uncovered, becomes an active force of spiritual origin that can work hand-in-hand with science to open totally new gateways to both personal growth and global advancement. The results include not only the uncovering of potentials but the activation of them, often through step-by-step procedures developed in the scientific research setting. By embracing the hidden powers of the mind, body, and spirit, spirituality and science together can become an interactive force that accelerates the achievement of stated goals and the full actualization of both personal and global potentials.

Scientific research into the paranormal over the years has taught us that every problem is capable of being solved. It has also taught us that every secret is capable of being unveiled, and not only unveiled but applied. A key question arises, however, when the results of paranormal research appear either to lie outside the accepted scientific map or to be in discord with the quantitative methods of conventional science. That dilemma can best be resolved when we consider ways in which science and spirituality affect humanity. Among the major challenges we face today is not only discovering knowledge, but applying it in ways that promote the common good. That, in fact, is the ultimate challenge of both science and spirituality.

Séance: The event of a Spiritualist meeting in which a medium serving as an intermediary in communication between the world of spirits and living people. It usually takes place in a private room with a circle of a half-dozen or so participants to give energy support, although some mediums will function in a large group and "work the crowd" to provide messages for most.

Search Engine-like Functions: Many things are *causally* related to Natural Forces which then function as "rulers" of those groups. In the past, those forces and their rulerships were personalized as Gods, Goddesses, and their ministering agents, and these were identified by names and images. In the course of time, Symbols have come to replace those deities while connecting more universally—beyond cultural limitations—to these forces and their rulerships of related things. Symbols now provide the means to invoke the forces and to *divine (seek)* answers *to* specific questions through "correspondences" with things related by rulership. As a result, *symbols can function like a search engine listing.* More specific addresses connect to smaller and more specialized groups, while a master address connects to the rulership. And symbols themselves become part of the system of correspondences. By means of symbols related by a system of organized correspondences on the Kabbalistic Tree of Life, we have a means—similar to mathematics—of relating parts (correctly) to the whole.

Sex Magick: *For I am divided for love's sake, for the chance of union.* Sex Magick is the whole thing—expertise in sexual arousal and in orgasmic restraint for a greater ecstasy, the exercise of the Magickal Imagination, the memorization of correspondences, the learning of concentration and visualization, and the glory of union. Sex Magick involves a carefully planned and executed ritual with a shared goal either for the attainment of a mundane goal or for the attainment of alchemical transformation. Properly planned and executed, it is the fulfillment of the spiritual promise that "Every Man and Every Woman is a Star."

Women's pleasure is the key, and orgasm is not the biggest part of it. Prolonged intercourse, with or without her orgasm, is vital to create the energy field needed for the transformation of consciousness fundamental to Sex Magick. Women are the *engines* that power-up the field whereas men are just the mechanics and the best of them learn how to carefully manage the process while she just swoons in enjoyment.

In Giving and Receiving there is Magick, and Love

Every woman should feel herself as a goddess incarnate in the lead-up to sex, during sex, and after sex. His role as a god is a secret—else his ego inflates and robs the mission. She should become filled with energy, but her energy is 'magnetic' while his is 'electric.' They should both enter into the "Borderland" state of consciousness where there is only pleasure but no climax, and hold that state for two or more hours. When the "moment is right," her magnetism should simple draw his electricity into her person, body and soul, with or without his sperm which is of no particular interest to the Sex Magick operation.

And when the "moment" comes, he projects his special intention, the magickal goal of the operation, right along with his electricity and semen. His role is primarily that of the Magician who projects the imaged goal with the release of his power into her. She receives, transmutes, and makes it happen in dimensions beyond the physical and mostly beyond her awareness. Some women claim to know when they're impregnated, but it's not likely and not necessary. Instead of a physical child, here there is a "magickal childe."

Magick is powered by energy-in-motion, i.e. e-motion. Sex itself is a powerful method of raising energy, and when guided by will towards an established goal, it can become magical. Sex accompanying romance and love expertly directed to mutual pleasuring so that energy is multiplied many times. Sex Magick employs the energies of sex in an established technology specific to several cultures. In India it is a subset of Tantra, in China it is part of the same alchemy found in the martial arts, in the Middle East it was part of the mystical practices of the Sufi, and in the west it is mostly a subset of ceremonial magick.

Yes, all this does require preparation, discipline, and restraint. And the importance of preparation precedes foreplay and should include the planning and execution of drama to elevate the feeling of importance of the ritual and the roles of the players. Sex Magick evolves from Dramatic Ritual with the staging of place, costuming, incense or aromatic oils, soft lighting, music possibly romantic or with a stimulating base beat, and possibly a non-intrusive script leading to awareness of the intended result.

Orgasm itself produces an *altered state of consciousness, and that consciousness is—for that moment at least—in the astral.* The feeling of bliss and connection to the universe is sometimes called "Cosmic Consciousness," although that phrase is otherwise used to express the goal of evolution, of meditation, and of spiritual attainment.

It is possible to grasp that moment of astral consciousness and extend it into astral travel, and sometimes for both partners to have that together.

In this case of a Magickal Curriculum, it is the Knowledge and Conversation with the Holy Guardian Angel. It can be the objective for either partner, or both.

It calls upon the Magickal Imagination to see the partner as god or goddess, or as Holy Guardian Angel. *What does the god or goddess or Holy Guardian Angel look like? Do they move? Do they speak?* Some answers can be found in reference works in religion and mythology, while others will arise from your sub-consciousness.

Do what thou Wilt. Love is the Law; Love under Will

In your planning, let awareness of pleasure and arousal be your guide. Don't neglect the possible role of fantasy role playing and fetishes in costuming. Goddesses wear anything they want, and what they want includes knowing and witnessing the arousal and lust of their partner. The challenge remains the required discipline and restraint, especially on the part of the man so that you can remain engaged for two or more hours. Even though the emphasis in a Sex Magick operation does not call for the partners to be an established couple, knowledge and understanding of each other's needs and 'turn-ons' is helpful in holding the man back from orgasm and leading the woman to the edge, and then pushing that edge beyond previous limits. The edge should not be a cliff to fall down but the start of a spiral upward to heaven. An important side note: fantasies and fetishes should be her choices, not his. We have been conditioned to think that only men have fetishes and sexual fantasies, but that's not accurate. Hers are more subjective and his more objective but in Sex Magick it is "She who must be obeyed." An important book is *She Comes First,* by Ian Kerner.

See yourselves enjoying the extended bliss of the Borderland state rather than the immediacy of satisfaction. Make Love for an Eternity! You will find that extended bliss is healthful, will rejuvenate you; will lower blood pressure, bathing your inner bodies with health-giving energies and secretions.

Love is the Law

Suggested Reading:

Culling & Weschcke: *The Complete Magick Curriculum of the Secret Order G∴B∴G∴, 2010, Llewellyn*

Kerner, Ian: *She Comes First: The thinking man's guide to pleasuring a woman,* 2004, Collins

Kraig, Donald Michael: *MODERN SEX MAGICK, Secrets of Erotic Spirituality—Learn to control and direct sexual power when it's most intense—during arousal. Increase your pleasure and enhance your relationships,* 2002, Llewellyn

Slate & Weschcke: *Astral Projection for Psychic Empowerment, 2012,* Llewellyn

Shamanism: We mostly refer to those people who long ago talked with spirits, and who still do, as *Shamans.* And, despite the "man" portion of that word, both men and women practice shamanism and the earliest archeologically recognized shamans—40,000 years ago—were often as many women as men. (An interesting note is that the male shaman often dresses as a woman.)

Shamans were and are the "direct experiencers" of ecstatic union with "Spirit" and the gods and goddesses and other entities ruling the inner world and influencing the outer word. They were and are the witches and "wise women," the medicine men and women, herbal and spiritual healers, the travelers to and messengers from the spirit world, and the visionaries able to describe the non-physical inner worlds in understandable mythic language and poetry.

One important distinction between shamanism and spiritualism is that of "location." The shaman travels to the spirit world, while in spiritualism the spirit travels to or manifests in the physical world.

Shamanism demonstrates a whole range of consciousness altering techniques, any of which can be emulated or adapted. All religions are derived from such communication, and many of them contain magical formulae of invocation and evocation—whether in the form of meditation (and self-hypnosis), rituals (a form of active meditation), sexual relations, worship (properly performed as evocation or invocation), and shamanic "intoxication" (i.e. reaching ecstasy) from which direct contact and communication can be accomplished, and more.

Shamanism and Ecstatic Consciousness: The Greater Cosmos consists of many levels of Substance and Consciousness, of which the Physical is only the bottom end of the line. At the same time, the physical is also the beginning of the great adventure of life and experience that builds incarnation after incarnation towards a spiritual culmination that can only be sensed through altered states of consciousness and vaguely described in mystical language.

Consciousness, and Spirit, is everywhere and in everything, but it is in the human person that Consciousness is the most fluid and can be changed—raised and lowered in its vibratory rate –through spiritual technologies of prayer, meditation, rituals and ceremonies, invocation and evocation, Yoga, ecstasy inducing actions of dancing, chanting, sex, etc. The most important element in all of these technologies is—as practiced in hypnosis—the *willed focus on a specific goal within trance that excludes awareness of external stimuli.*

The oldest, and most fundamental of these, are shamanic practices that raise consciousness to induce trance and ecstatic states to take us from outer to inner worlds. Most of these are described in the "eight-fold path to the center" in the Old Religion of European Paganism. See Slate & Weschcke: The *Llewellyn Complete Book of Psychic Empowerment* (Llewellyn, 2011)

The experience of shamanic or magickal ecstasy can be the means to going out-of-body to observe action at a distance or communicate with inner plane entities. The challenge is to retain focus on the goal, which may be facilitated by one person acting as a kind of "operations director" for those going out-of-body.

Shamanic Practices: The projection of conscious awareness into the astral world accomplished through trance induction by methods of physical stress including Fasting, Sleep Deprivation, Ecstatic Dancing, Flagellation, Prolonged Bondage, Sensory Deprivation, Sensory Overload, Drumming, and the use of hallucinogenic and psychoactive substances.

Suggesting Reading:

Walsh: *The World of Shamanism, New Views of an Ancient Tradition, 2007,* Llewellyn

Shaman's Journey: The shaman's journey can be an Out-of-Body experience, but it can also be an In-Body experience. It is an Altered State of Consciousness (ASC) defined by the shaman's ability to enter and leave it at will, and—even more importantly—to control the experiences. The shaman's journey is always purposeful, but that purpose has included exploring the Cosmos, exploring the inner workings of the body and psyche, seeing the purpose behind things, and healing things (not just injuries and illnesses but also present relationships and past-life traumas).

The shaman's journey is an inner journey, a psychic journey, a soul journey, a spiritual journey—all these things no longer familiar to our modern understanding of what is real and non-real and beyond reality. We are so focused on what is really only the final "outcome" of apparent material reality that fail to pay attention to "how we got where we are." It is this mis-guided focus that leaves us floundering as to causes including those that are non-physical that we fail to cure situations whether of health, social, economic, political or other that characterize our modern world.

Shape Shifting: The projection of the Etheric Body molded in the shape of an animal, or sometimes another person, to serve as a temporary vehicle for the lower self. See Etheric Projection and Etheric Revenants.

Shaping Reality: Unlike those physical spatial dimensions you can see and feel, in which you can move from a current position up or down, forward or backward, to one side or another, you can't *touch* or *see* time, and you can only measure it's movement as a seeming forever forward passage from past through present to the future. You experience the past only through memory (personal or recorded, as in books), and you can only *think* (or imagine) the future and maybe mark an anticipated future moment on your calendar.

And that something is unique: you can plan the future, hence to varying degrees you help shape the future. But there is also the possibility that the Future helps shape us. Think about that for a moment: if you have a plan of action for the future and then act upon it, each step forward in that plan already exists and takes on solidity as each step of the plan is completed.

Just as we shape (and thus change) the Future (Time) through our plans and acts, so do we shape the three dimensions of Space. We construct buildings and the cities within which we work, live and play. We construct roads and highway,

and canals and ports to connect our cities. We re-construct the land from forest and prairie into farms and ranches to feed our populations. We change the
environment through deforestation, adding chemicals to the soil and the aquifers beneath and the rivers running through the land. And we affect the air with
pollutants. But not only did we affect Space, but the changes we made *externally*
affect us *internally* not just physically in the Body but also in Mind and Spirit.
There is constant <u>interaction</u> between Time and Space, and Human Spirit.

The fourth dimension of time is a function of the non-physical Astral World
which is characterized by time, *emotional substance,* and *energies.** We refer to
time as a dimension separate from the physical, but we also *feel* and *recognize* the
passage of time as a measure of physical phenomena. In other words: separate
dimensions but with <u>interaction </u>between the two worlds or planes.

* Do make note of the repeated occurrence of *Trinities*—in the *movements* within each
dimension, and the *characteristics* of each plane or world. *Trinities* (the recurrence of
groups of three) and *Septets* (groups of seven) are so prevalent in descriptions of the
Cosmos that you should look for their occurrence. See the two tables appended to the
Introduction of our book *Clairvoyance for Psychic Empowerment,* Slate & Weschcke,
2013 for a detailed understanding of this complex structure.

How do we know that? <u>We "think," *therefor it is.*</u> The fifth dimension of thought
is a function of the non-physical Mental Realm characterized by thought, *mental
substance,* and *energies.* Again, we have separate dimensions that we—through
conscious and unconscious awareness—experience in their <u>interactions</u> between
all three levels.

The sixth dimension is experienced as unlimited love; a seventh dimension is
experienced through intuition and the eighth as union with the Divine beyond
which individuality ceases. All these higher dimensions <u>interact</u> with the lower
ones, and as we grow in knowledge and power that *action becomes conscious, causal,* and *transformative.*

Soul: *"You" are not your Soul.* The "You" you know is best understood as a partial and
temporary manifestation of "Soul" that we call "personality." This personality is
not the *whole* soul but one of many aspects of it incarnating life after life and
occupying a series of temporary vehicles each composed of the substance of one
dimension after the other. Then the essence of each life's lessons is abstracted
and eventually "absorbed" and further refined into the soul until the soul itself is
ready to move on into still higher spiritual dimensions. The soul continues on its

journey through the Cosmos, learning and/or "working" on behalf of the *Great Plan* set in motion by the "Creator Source" of all that is—which is better realized as *Unity* when not given a defining and hence *limiting* name.

The soul is the absolute ultimate and immortal essence of who you are. The eternal part of the human being, attributed Kabbalistically to Chesed, Geburah, Tiphareth, Netzach, Hod and Yesod.

Soul's Vehicles:

Causal Body (Higher Mental)	To evolve with	Ideals & Abstract Thought
Mental Body (Lower Mental)	To think with	Ideas & Concrete Thoughts
Astral Body (Upper & Lower)	To feel with	Emotions & Desires
Physical Body (incl. Etheric Body)	to act with	Sensorial Reactions & Actions
Personality, the Lower Self	Lower Manas, Concrete Mind	Mental Body
	Astral, Desire Nature	Astral Body
	Physical, Functioning Body	
	Physical/Etheric Body	
Body Consciousness	Autonomic nervous system	

Source: Jinarajadasa: *First Principles of Theosophy*, 1861

Spark of Divinity: In our core of our consciousness, we have a spark of Divinity that gives us, in our Consciousness, the power to shape the future and even to change the present. We will earn that power through the techniques of Self-Empowerment and the Self-Improvement programs presented in books on Self-Empowerment by Dr. Joe H. Slate and Carl Llewellyn Weschcke.

Spirit: See also "Ether" and "Akasha." This word has multiple meanings.

- The Spiritual Body, or Soul.
- The entity surviving physical death—believed to temporarily function on the Astral Plane.

- The fifth element from which the lower four—Fire, Air, Water, and Earth are derived.
- Entities from other dimensions or planets channeling to humans.
- A non-physical entity functioning on the Astral or other planes.
- The 'collective' of etheric, astral, mental and spirit bodies other than the physical.
- God, or an aspect of Deity.
- A collective term for non-individual spiritual power and intelligence, probably an aspect of the Collective Unconscious or Universal Consciousness.
- Non-human inhabitants of the astral plane.
- The inner reality of something—as in "the spirit of the times."
- The Alchemical element symbolized by an 8-spoked Wheel is the higher level of reality of Eight Dimensions from which other elements and levels flow.
- Symbolized by the "Egg," it is the Great Mother Goddess, the source of all physical manifestation.
- The "interdimensional" function through which all things and entities seem to appear and disappear with a change in their nature.
- Spirit is also the "Space" between things and around things. In a broad sense, it is the old, pre-Einstein *Ether* of empty space which being non-physical could not be observed.
- The 'Holy Spirit' which may be the Primal Consciousness or Matrix that can be activated by prayer or other affirmative thoughts.
- That part of the Human Being attributed to Kether, Chokmah and Binah.

There is another way to look at Spirit, and that is that some Spirits may be projections of human consciousness. "Nature abhors a vacuum" is an old adage. A modification would be that "Empty Space invites <u>active</u> Consciousness." *Thought and Feeling, guided by Will, create Forms and Energizes them.* Whether these forms are created consciously or unconsciously, they exist, and the more attention, and <u>intention,</u> is focused on them, the more Life and Power they have.

There are, then, perhaps, three kinds of *Spirits:*

1. Bodies of consciousness created by the Soul to progressively incarnate into a series of vehicles, such as now occupied by you and me, and all living people.

And then at death, these include the traditional spirits of the surviving personalities of people and—in a different fashion—animals.

2. Units of consciousness created as functioning parts of the Cosmos out of the substance and energies of each cosmic plane, such as the Sun, Moon, and Planets for the physical plane; such as Elementals and Nature Spirits and others for the astral plane; such as Thought Forms and Magickal Constructs for the mental plane; and Angels and Archangels for the Causal Plane. But, notice—contrary to materialist beliefs—we are stating the stars, their satellites, and the planets all are active forms of consciousness, and are all spiritual entities.

3. Forms of consciousness created through the human imagination, drawing substance and energies from all four of the lower planes, in varying degrees dependent on unconscious to conscious to intentional responses to initial stimulus and opportunity.

  a. In this third category we include unconscious projections via the imagination of thought forms created in response to natural stimulus—such as the energies surrounding a natural spring inhabited by water sprites and other elementals. The human response might picture a feminine deity (water being a feminine element) who then acts to further draw energies to herself to protect the spring from harm, and to create an atmosphere of love and nurture beneficial to all who come to the spring.

  b. A second form as humans respond to natural forces and earth currents (ley lines) that instinctively trigger thoughts and images of snakes and dragons. With repetition, and recognition of their importance as guides to planting and other activities, the images take on life and consciousness, and become objects of worship or magickal interaction.

  c. A third form of unconscious projection comes in response to strong and repeated emotions such as love, lust, hate, fear which take on person-like images of goddesses and gods. Here we have not only the opportunity for worship but for magick—defense again objects and causes of hate and fear, invocation for the goddesses of love and lust. With more conscious attention focused on these deities, they become multiple and specific, and are presented in detailed symbolism to represent all the variation of their manifestation.

  d. A fourth form comes with conscious projection developed from knowledge of magickal principles where abstract symbols become charged with energies of attraction and repulsion. Gods and Goddesses of the house-hold, of the city and the nation, sometimes projected on to the memories of heroes and great leaders. Many of the Christian and Buddhist saints are so charged with energies that they too function as spirits. Sometimes, animals are the matrix for projection of consciousness and psychic ener-gies—in particular the horse, the cow, the goat, the dolphin, the cat and the dog—because of their special role between Man and Nature.

Spirit as Primal Substance: "Spirit" derives from the Latin *spiritus,* meaning "breath." In Hindu and other mythically expressed cosmologies, the Cosmos comes into manifestation on the "out-breath" of the Creative Force, and is withdrawn on an eventual "in-breath" at the end of all time (until, maybe, the *next* time!). Spirit is the primal *substance. Spirit is the "beginning," and the matrix for what follows.* The Cosmos, and ultimately the physical universe, evolves, layer after layer, upon this primal immortal spirit *substance. It is the Holy Spirit* that is fundamental to, and the Hidden Reality behind, all existence even as it is also the idealist pattern for all intentional activity, the goal and culmination of all action, and the completion of our reason to be. We exist to fulfill the purpose of existence.*

> * This "Holy Spirit" is not that identified with that of the Trinity of the Roman Catholic Church. It may have been intended that way, but—if so—the original concept was lost in the theological struggle to keep everything masculine and non-Pagan.

Spirit Body or Vehicle: In the hierarchy of subtle bodies, Spirit is higher than Mental, Astral, Etheric and Physical. There is lack of specific definition, but it could be that the Spirit Body is first in the process of the descent of the Soul into physical incarnation. In this scheme, the Soul creates the Spirit Body which then serves as a kind of matrix for the Mental Body formed of mental 'substance,' then the Astral Body of astral substance, etc.

The Spirit Body is also a "temporary vehicle." Just as the physical body or vehi-cle was inclusive of that multiple composite, so does that astral vehicle include the composite of mental, causal and higher spiritual levels. That "after death" vehicle is also temporary just as was the physical body, and the surviving per-sonality continues to learn and grow just as it did in the physical world but with a new mission and set of *experiential* opportunities specific to its new "home." That temporary vehicle is made of *astral* substance and continues for as long as the personality "lives" in the astral world. The astral world is a much larger non-physical and non-spatial dimension than the physical world. You won't find it on any map, but you do see it indicated on many drawings illustrating the various dimensions of the *Cosmos:* Physical, Astral, Mental, Causal, and others variously named but more often simply grouped together as *spiritual.*

Spirit Cabinet: An enclosure in which a seated medium is isolated—usually in trance—to facilitate the accumulation of energy to produce ectoplasm. The enclosure may be anything from a curtained closet to a special "box"—most often of wood—in which the medium is seated. It must either have air holes for ventilation, or a large hole at the top for the medium's head to protrude—similar in appearance to a steam cabinet.

The function of the cabinet is both to condense the ectoplasmic energies and to protect the medium from physical contact with "investigators" which has been demonstrated as potentially dangerous to the medium's health. The cabinet also provided darkness believed necessary to the accumulation of ectoplasm and its excretion as "materialized" forms appearing in front of the cabinet.

During the "heyday" of public spiritualist performances, the cabinet also provided opportunities for fraud, and to counter this appearance, the medium was sometimes bound to the chair, or—in the most ornate "bondage cabinets" the medium's wrists also protruded through holes and were bound in full sight of the audience. Good showmanship always provides an excellent cover for fraud as any stage magician can demonstrate. Nevertheless, spectacular materializations were produced with the aid of these spirit cabinets and it can be speculated that the bondage applied to the medium may have helped induce the particular trance state conducive to producing ectoplasm.

Spirit Communication: Generally, the communication between living people and the spirits of the deceased. Also may include communication with other spiritual entities—Guides, Angels, Masters, etc. most often through a person acting as a "Medium" or "Channel" under the direction or "Control" of a Spirit Guide.

Suggested Reading:

Buckland: *Buckland's Book of Spirit Communications, 2004,* Llewellyn

Konstantinos: *Speak with the Dead, Seven Methods for Spirit Communication, 2004,* Llewellyn

Livon: *The Happy Medium—Awakening to Your Natural Intuition, 2009,* Llewellyn

Parkinson: *Bridge to the Afterlife—A Medium's Message of Hope & Healing,* 2009, Llewellyn

Slate and Weschcke: *Psychic Empowerment for Everyone,* 1997, Llewellyn

Spirit Entities: There are many levels and forms of spirit entities, but at the ultimate level of religious experience, we may perceive Spirit either as a single person-deity or as multiple person*-deities, or characterize the ultimate source of all reality only through impersonal abstract symbolism.

> * We are trying to make distinctions on how deities are "seen." Mythically and historically we have mostly thought of the creative sources of reality in a human-like form rather than as a pure force described symbolically or mathematically. To appreciate these distinctions, recall your lessons in mythology where most deities appear as gods and goddesses, named and costumed in certain ways to symbolize their nature as gods of thunder, the sea, war, wisdom, lust, or as goddesses of love, crafts, agriculture, child-birth, healing, and so on. In some cultures, the goddesses in particular manifest in hundreds of carefully crafted forms distinctly varied by color of skin and of costumes, ornaments and the jewels, metals and shapes of their construction and where they are worn on the body, postures and gestures, names, associated mantras, powers, locales, their companions, and more. Both gods and goddesses are sometimes given other attributes drawn from the non-human 'kingdoms' of animals' heads, horns and hooves; birds' heads, wings, feathers and claws; fish tails; and even insect shapes. All these distinctions are meaningful and are related in worship and meditation, or used in prayer or magical acts to manifest the particularized powers to meet human needs and desires.

Some cultures do not humanize the creative powers, but see them only as abstract symbols such as the most familiar *Yin* and *Yang,* but also in particular symbols directly associated with a single deity, such as the Christian Cross, the Jewish Star of David, the Egyptian Ankh, the Radiant Sun, the Crescent Moon, Thor's Hammer, and others. Even mathematical formulae have taken on a near or actual religious-like significance as in the case of Einstein's famous $E=mc^2$ symbolizing our entry into the "Atomic Age."

Spirit Guide: An entity manifesting on the astral or mental plane exhibiting high intelligence and wisdom with a personal interest in the welfare of the individual experiencing the more or less constant presence of the Guide. The Guide sometimes facilitates the trance, and brings spirits as "surviving personalities" to the séance.

Suggested Reading:

Andrews: *How to Meet and Work with Spirit Guides,* 2006, Llewellyn

Webster: *Spirit Guides & Angel Guardians, Contact Your Invisible Helpers, 2002,* Llewellyn

Spirit Lights: A paranormal phenomena commonly associated with Spiritualism presumed to be a means by which spirits make their presence known.

Spirit Operator: A spirit who uses the medium to manipulate psychic energy.

Spirit Realm: Rather than a distant, inaccessible dimension, the spirit realm is a presence throughout non-physical reality that is not typically available to sensory awareness. It does, however, often manifest through sensory channels. Examples include sensory perceptions of sight and sound that can announce a spirit presence.

Spirit World: The non-physical world. The subconscious is, in fact, in continuous interaction with the higher realms of power to meet your empowerment needs, including protection in time of danger, comfort in times of grief, and hope in times of despair. Through your connection to the spirit realm, you will experience the full beauty and power of your existence— past, present, and future—as an evolving soul.

What is the Nature of the Spirit World? One answer is that it is "not this, not that" meaning that it is not a place but is everywhere and that Spirit is the universal "Divinity" that is everywhere and in everything and everyone, and can be experienced both or either as "personal"* or as a "force." In other words: we are saying that the non-physical/spiritual reality—lying behind physical reality with the potential to re-shape physical phenomena—can be <u>experienced</u> in various ways as *determined by choices we make and actions* (interactions) *we take.*

Spiritual Alignment: The aligned state of attunement and balance in which you will experience the relevance of spirituality to your total existence—past, present, and future—and become empowered to meet all challenges to your growth. See Chapter Four for Spiritual Alignment Program: Spiritual Alignment through Automatic Writing

Spiritual Body: The highest aspect and consciousness of the human being. (See "Spirit Body" above)

Spiritual Communication: "Spiritual Communication" calls for an active relationship with a spiritual entity, not a passive experience. To make the choice on how you are going to relate to non-physical reality, please take note of what this means. In essence, in the modern world, the non-physical is often seen as a religious choice. For most people, religion defines their experience of non-physical reality and whether it is a passive or an active relationship with Spirit.

Before discussing the nature or those religious choices, we are going to make a definitive, un-provable, statement that may be controversial and disturbing: ***"Magick is communication with Spirits, and is the oldest and truest form of religion!"*** Elsewhere, we will write that **Shamanism is the source of all religions**. A seeming contradiction that is resolved only as we discuss "attitude" in religions. Magick is the active creation of spiritual experience to influence physical reality; **Shamanism is the active seeking of Spiritual Knowledge** that may include influence of physical reality.

Interaction with Spirits through an unconscious paranormal phenomena as with poltergeists, hauntings, rappings, etc.; the practices of mediumship and channeling; communication with saints, guides, teachers; the magickal practices of invocation and evocation; touch on the various shamanic techniques; meditation and prayer; clairvoyance and astral projection, intuition; ecstatic union; and other forms of interaction.

These methods break down into three models:

- The use of a "tool" as an intermediary between the "caller" on this side and the "recipient" on the other side. Like a telephone, an Ouija Board, or a crystal ball, pendulum, or even e-mail on your computer or tablet, is essentially "blind" and the recipient on the other side might not be the entity you are calling, and could even be your own higher or lower self.

- The use of a human intermediary, such as a medium or channel to call the recipient on the other side or to receive calls initiated by entities from the other side. These entities range from surviving personalities to guides, teachers, or advanced intelligences. You can test the identity of the surviving personality with questions, and you may be able to test those entities claimed to be higher intelligences, but you may have "to take their word for it."

- Direct contact by means of astral projection or clairvoyance or similar means where you are essentially raising your consciousness (your rate of vibration) to match or harmonize with that of the other entity. You can't really communicate unless you are on the same "wavelength." Many of these techniques originated in ancient shamanism as astral travel and in pre-religious Tantra as worship and invocation of the Goddess.

No matter the methodology of communication we use, it is important to remember that spirituality is not in the facilitating tool or intermediary but within us and in everything. It's a matter of perspective: *Look and ye will see!* All limitations are in the viewer, once you begin to open the doors of your own perception your understanding (a function of consciousness) will expand to see the spiritual nature alongside the material view.

Spiritual Genotype: The individual's unique spiritual or cosmic makeup which remains unchanged from lifetime to lifetime. See also Cosmic Genotype.

Suggested Reading
Slate: *Beyond Reincarnation*, 2005, Llewellyn

Spiritual Plane: The highest level of creative being from which the lower planes are derived.

Spiritual Substance: Every plane has its own unique substance and its own unique "laws" of operation.

Spiritual World: A generally indefinable religious concept. Likewise, most parapsychologists reject the non-physical nature of psychic phenomenon—preferring to consider only physical factors which rarely satisfy the full observation and hence the phenomenon are rejected as fraudulent or delusional.

Spiritualism: The religion that evolved around the paranormal phenomena of the Séance in the 19th century and centered about the Medium as communicator between the Living and the Once Living persons, sometimes also functioning as counselor and minister. And, also, the Christian church founded earlier by Emanuel Swedenborg.

Spiritualism and Spiritism have as their primary purpose communication with spirits of the dead. Since such communication is often facilitated by a "Spirit Guide" and God as *Father* or *Son* is generally acknowledged in Spiritualist services, we might consider this as a minor but unacknowledged sect of Christianity. While both men and women function as mediums, the female generally has a superior status to the male. Certainly Spiritualism is more spiritual than materialistic. While currently a very minor religion in the United States, it is much more prominent throughout the Caribbean, South America, West Africa, India, China and Japan—each with distinct variations. Prominent in both Spiritualism/Spiritism and the ecstatic/charismatic religions like Pentecostalism is the occurrence of paranormal phenomena such as spontaneous trance, speaking in tongues, possession, movement of objects at a distance, levitation of objects and persons, direct automatic writing, and the appearance of apparitions.

Spiritualist: Properly, a member of a Spiritualist Church. Also, a follower of the religion or an active researcher and student of spiritualist phenomena and philosophy.

Spiritualist Person: We are using this term not to identify persons interested in the practice or the religion of Spiritualism but rather persons interested in exploring spirituality and the spiritual nature of the person, of humanity and of the Cosmos itself.

Spiritualist Camps: There used to be a large number of so-called "Spiritualist Camps" scattered about the country. Camp Silver Belle in Pennsylvania and Camp Chesterfield in Indiana were two of the better known. Such a camp was a gathering place for spiritualists—a place where people could go and meet a wide variety of mediums and sit in on séances of all types. There was frequently a summer season, though some operated year-round. They filled a very real need and many families would spend their annual vacations at a spiritualist camp.

Spirituality: The study and exploration of the spiritual nature of the person, of humanity and of the Cosmos itself. The study includes the foundations and nature of religion, the nature of man in relation to Creator, and the connections of Spirituality with metaphysical subjects. Spirituality is the *supreme force* that energizes your growth and gives quality to your existence from your endless pre-existence to present moment and beyond.

Spirituality as Awareness: "Spirituality" is a particular state of awareness enabling a human person to perceive Spirit within and without his/her own self and in doing so become able to communicate across the limitations of form and substance.

Thus, "Spirit Communication" is the ability to communicate with other spiritual beings by moving from one level of consciousness to another. For convenience, we call them all "spirits" whether they are Nature Spirits, Elemental Spirits, Spirits as Surviving Personalities, Spirits functioning as gods and goddesses, Spirits that are units of consciousness imbued with character and intent by human observers, or Spirits that are humanly created Thought Forms empowered to carry out particular assignments.

Spiritual Communication is the ability to "communicate" between one conscious being and another via the animating spirit level of consciousness.

Spirituality in Action: Contrary to common thinking, Spirituality is not a *passive* attitude towards life but does call upon the individual for action and responsibility for personal growth and development. It requires an active attitude recognizing Spirit is part of everyone and everything, but also that is nascent in each of us—like a "blank slate" to be filled in with our life work.

Sub-atomic Field: Also called simply 'the Field' in which primal/universal energy and matter appear as waves and then as particles when observed. It is the foundation for the study of Quantum Physics (also called Quantum Mechanics and Quantum Theory). Packets of energy/matter are called Quanta.

Subconscious, AKA the Subconscious Mind and the Personal Unconscious: The vast inner region of experiences not ordinarily available to the conscious awareness. It is believed to be the repository of all past-life experiences. The term subconscious is used in many different contexts and has no single or precise definition. This greatly limits its significance as a definition-bearing concept, and in consequence the word tends to be avoided in academic and scientific settings.

In everyday speech and popular writing, however, the term is very commonly encountered as a layperson's replacement for the unconscious mind, which in Freud's opinion is a repository for socially unacceptable ideas, wishes or desires, traumatic memories, and painful emotions put out of mind by the mechanism of psychological repression. However, the contents do not necessarily have to be solely negative. In the psychoanalytic view, the unconscious is a force that can only be recognized by its effects—it expresses itself in the symptom. Unconscious thoughts are not directly accessible to ordinary introspection, but are supposed to be capable of being "tapped" and "interpreted" by special methods and techniques such as meditation, random association, dream analysis, and verbal slips (commonly known as a Freudian slip), examined and conducted during psychoanalysis.

Carl Jung developed the concept further. He divided the unconscious into two parts: the personal unconscious and the collective unconscious. The personal unconscious is a reservoir of material that was once conscious but has been forgotten or suppressed.

The idea of the "subconscious" as a powerful or potent agency has allowed the term to become prominent in the New Age and self-help literature, in which investigating or controlling its supposed knowledge or power is seen as advantageous. In the New Age community, techniques such as autosuggestion and affirmations are believed to harness the power of the subconscious to influence a person's life and real-world outcomes, even curing sickness.

Though laypersons commonly assume "subconscious" to be a psychoanalytic term, this is not in fact the case. Freud had explicitly condemned the word as long ago as 1915: "We shall also be right in rejecting the term 'subconsciousness' as incorrect and misleading." In later publications his objections were made clear:

"If someone talks of subconsciousness, I cannot tell whether he means the term topographically—to indicate something lying in the mind beneath consciousness—or qualitatively—to indicate another consciousness, a subterranean one, as it were. He is probably not clear about any of it. The only trustworthy antithesis is between conscious and unconscious."

As outlined above, psychologists and psychiatrists exclusively use the term "unconscious" in situations where many lay-writers, particularly such as those in metaphysical and New Age literature, usually use the term "subconscious". It should not, however, be inferred from this that the orthodox concept of the unconscious and the New Age concept of the subconscious are precisely equivalent. Psychologists and psychiatrists, unsurprisingly, take a much more limited view of the capabilities of the unconscious than are represented by the common New Age depiction of a transcendentally all-powerful "subconscious".

The Subconscious retains memories of everything through the feelings associated with that memory. In general, however, we are mostly concerned with childhood memories, fears, and misunderstandings that have been—often—repressed. As childish memories, they live on and may still influence our adult understanding and feelings erroneously and painfully. By recalling those memories, an adult perspective can replace the childish one and at the same time release energies tied up in those childish fears and misunderstandings.

The Subconscious Mind is never asleep, always aware. It is the Nephesh on the Kabbalistic Tree of Life. That part of the mind below the threshold of consciousness. Normally, unavailable to the conscious mind, it can be accessed through hypnosis & self-hypnosis, meditation, automatic writing, etc.

More importantly, in the studies of Joe H. Slate and Carl Llewellyn Weschcke, it is the *lower* part of the Personality which while containing forgotten and repressed feelings & memories and our emotional nature, it is also the fundamental Belief or Operating System that filters Reality, that collection of guilt feelings called the 'Shadow," the 'Anima' or 'Animus' collection of feelings representing our idealization or fear and hatred of the opposite gender, the various Archetypes and Mythic images formed though the history of human experience, all of which can operate as doorways or gates to the astral world and connect to the higher or super consciousness. The subconscious is also home to our instincts and the autonomic system that cares for the body and its operation.

"The subconscious is not only a content domain but a dynamic constellation of processes and powers. It recognizes that the wealth of our subconscious resources is complementary to consciousness rather than counteractive. It's a powerful component of who we are and how we function." (from Slate & Weschcke: *Psychic Empowerment for Everyone,* 2009, Llewellyn*)*

According to the self-empowerment perspective, the subconscious never sleeps—it's in continuous interaction with consciousness. It embraces the physical, spiritual, and psychical nature of our existence. Awareness of future events, telepathic communications, and clairvoyant insight are all among its powers. The subconscious, with communication to the Collective Unconscious and the Super-Consciousness has very nearly unlimited resources available to you through your Guide. Almost like a forgotten best friend or favorite mentor, the subconscious welcomes our probes and challenges us to use its powers.

The Sub-Conscious Mind has no ethics or morals; it is your Conscious Mind that must make choices and impose order on chaos, develop distinct channels to reliable resources, and otherwise understand and learn that your Sub-Conscious Mind is your key to the infinite resources of the Universe. Helping you to build the relationship between the Sub-Conscious Mind and the Conscious Mind is the purpose of Self-Empowering procedures. (See Slate & Weschcke: *Self-Empow-erment & your Sub-Conscious Mind, 2010*)

But the major message we want to give you is that the Sub-Conscious Mind is an unlimited resource, not only of memories and information but also of powers and skills. It is the foundation and matrix to all we are and all that we will become. Our personal unit of consciousness is part of the Universal Consciousness so we have unlimited potential and have yet to discover any limits to our capacity or ability to use that potential. Our goal is to become <u>adept</u> at upon calling these powers and resources to match our needs and interests, and to keep "pushing the envelope" towards yet greater capacity and ability.

Aside from the integrative process, there's evidence suggesting that the sub-conscious can literally generate new potentials and growth energies independent of our conscious interactions through processes not yet fully understood, pos-sibly through the synergistic or holistic results of the integrative process alone. What we need to understand is that the Sub-Conscious Mind is <u>not</u> a passive by-stander but always aware and always active. As you grow in consciousness and integrate more of your psychic and other powers into your Whole Person, the Sub-Conscious Mind grows and contributes more to the Whole Person you are becoming.

Understanding these creative processes of the subconscious mind is among our greatest challenges with potentials for enormous benefit. The point here, as elsewhere, is always that the greater our understanding, the greater the benefit, *but even as we face the continual challenges, the very attempt at understanding stim-ulates positive developments.*

Contrary to some views, the subconscious is "the essential you," the essence of your being as an evolving soul. Without the subconscious, you would not exist at all. It's the vast totality of your existence: the 'old you' of the past, the 'dynamic you' of the present and the 'infinite you' of the future.

There are a number of methods in use in the contemporary New Age and paranormal communities to try to directly affect the latter, such as Affirmations, Autosuggestion, Hypnosis & Self-Hypnosis, Meditation, Prayer, Pre-Sleep sug-gestions followed by Dream Analysis, Ritual, and various Shamanic techniques.

Suggested Reading:

Slate & Weschcke: *Psychic Empowerment for Everyone*, 2009, Llewellyn

Slate & Weschcke: *Self-Empowerment & your Sub-Conscious Mind*, 2010, Llewellyn

Summerland: A common name for "heaven" among older European Pagans. Most esoterics place it in the lower astral world where expectation shapes astral "reality."

Super Conscious Mind: Your subconscious mind is mostly conditioned by the past, and your conscious mind by the present. But you were born with a basic purpose, with some specific learning goals for this life time. The Super Conscious Mind is your doorway to and from the future. The super-conscious mind is the higher self and the source of your inspiration, ideals, ethical behavior and heroic action, and the very essence that is "the Light of Men" as it was in the beginning and as it is now and as it will always be...

The Super Conscious Mind is the *higher* level of personal consciousness with access to the universal of Collective Unconscious. It is where the 'gods' or powerful archetypes and spirit guides can be found, and where the Akashic Records are accessed.

Survival after Death: Most people do not really believe in a "world" or dimension of Spirit, but do believe in something called "Soul" (or Spirit) that survives the death of the physical body and that may go on to a place called "heaven" or, alternatively, to other dimensions that culminates in rebirth (reincarnation). Little thought is given to either *Soul* or the *Next World, until—perhaps—when their confrontation with death is imminent.* Rather than think about it now, at most they leave it all to Fate or Faith with the same blind acceptance as they have towards acting now to make a Better World for tomorrow and generations to come, or even to assume some responsibility of their own health, wealth and welfare.

But, if death is not 'the end,' and if you do believe in the survival of your 'soul,' why not learn about it, prepare for it, and plan on moving onward to make a better "world" for self and others? (Would you do that it immigrating to another country?) You are not going to find answers in the Bible or other religious literature because real answers come only from within as you study and learn to ask the right kind of questions.

Surviving Personality: Most people think of a "Spirit" as the person formerly living in a physical body and now in a non-physical body or "vehicle" in the Spirit World. But for Occultists and an increasing number of psychologists and paranormal scientists, the entity called a "spirit" in séance and other Spiritualist phenomena is better understood as the "surviving personality" of a deceased person in transition to another dimension, temporarily occupying a vehicle composed of the substance of the currently occupied dimension.

In other words, the person (personality) we know in daily life does not become a "spirit" after death but continues as a *personality* surviving death and occupying an astral vehicle instead of the cast-off physical vehicle. At some point, it will abandon the astral vehicle and move into a mental and then a causal vehicle. This "surviving personality" is not the *Soul* but a partial projection of the Soul seeking learning and growth opportunities by means of incarnating through a series of personalities manifesting successively again and again through physical, astral, mental, and causal vehicles—all of whom provide memories of experiences as "life's lessons" to be abstracted into the Soul.

During each life the new personality (partially shaped by its past and by its future) functions through all these vehicles (physical-etheric-astral-mental-causal-spiritual) simultaneously but with different levels of awareness and purpose. In this life, the primary focus of consciousness is through the physical *(biological)* vehicle. After death there is movement into the energy aspect of the physical known as the "Etheric Double" from which it quickly moves on to focus through progressive levels of the astral vehicle with degrees of *emotional* awareness to the mental & causal vehicles. It is an astral-mental-causal unity that is primarily focused through the astral vehicle that is generally called "spirit" in the séance and other forms of spirit communication.

Svadhisthana (AKA *Sacral*): This Chakra is located in the sacrum over the spleen and below the navel, and physically manifests through the pancreas, kidneys, and the hypogastric plexus. Like Muladhara, it relates to the gonads, the production of sex hormones, and the female reproductive cycle. It relates to relationships, basic emotional needs, and sensual pleasure. Physically it rules our reproduction, emotionally our joy, mentally our creativity, and spiritually our enthusiasm. It relates to the sense of taste. The element is Water.

The associated psychic powers are empathy and psychic diagnosis. It is the fluid control point for the entire body system, including blood flow. Vaso-constriction and vaso-dilation of the arterioles are controllable at will. Stigmata, the percolation of blood through the skin, can also be demonstrated. It is symbolized by a crescent moon within a white lotus with six orange spokes, and its Tattva is represented geometrically in a silver crescent. The audible seed mantra is *VuNG* followed by mental echo of *VuM*.

Svadhisthana (Sacral) *Chakra* Correspondences

Alchemica l Planet: Mars, Pluto	Alchemical Element: Iron	Tattva: Apas (water)
Animal: Crocodile	Basic Drive: Pleasure	Tattva color: White
Body Function: Sexuality, Pleasure	Chakra Color: Orange	Tattva form: Crescent
Element: Water	Gemstone: Coral	Tattvic Sense: Taste
Gland: Pancreas	Goddess-form, Egyptian: Tefnut	God-form, Hindu: Vishnu[1]
God-form, Greek: Pan, Diana	Incense: orris, gardenia, damiana	Goddess-form, Hindu: Rakini [2]
Location: Over the spleen	Order of chakra unfoldment: 3rd	Yogic Planet: Sun
Part of Body: genitals, kidney, bladder, circulatory system	Psychological attribute: Flexibility, equanimity	
Psychic Power: empathy, psychic diagnosis	Sense: Taste	Bija Mantra: VuNG, VuM (4)
Spinal Joint: 7th	Spinal Location: 1st Lumbar	
Tarot Key: XIX, Sun	Tree of Life Sephiroth: Yesod	Yantra (internal) Black Crescent
Tarot Suite: Cups		

1. Preserver
2. Sexuality
Source: Slate, J. & Weschcke, C.: *Psychic Empowerment—Tools & Techniques*, 2011, Llewellyn

Suggested Reading:

Dale: *The Subtle Body—An Encyclopedia of Your Energetic Anatomy, 2009, Sounds True*

Swedenborg, Emanuel: (1688-1772), a Swedish scientist and theologian who had a prolific career as an inventor and scientist. In 1741 at the age of fifty-three he entered into a spiritual phase in which he eventually began to experience dreams and visions that culminated in a spiritual awakening, where he claimed he was appointed by the Lord to write a heavenly doctrine to reform Christianity. He claimed that the Lord had opened his eyes, so that from then on he could freely visit heaven and hell, and talk with angels, demons, and other spirits. For the remaining 28 years of his life, he wrote and published 18 theological works, of which the best known was *Heaven and Hell* (1758)

Symbol: A true symbol contains power because of its shape, form, color, and its name which connects it to an established and constantly up-dating "system of correspondences" retrieved from the 'information storage' function of the subconscious mind. The tattvic symbols, in turn, are "the primary building blocks from which all magical symbols, sigils, talismans, ciphers and designs are composed." As Dr. Mumford wrote: "The Tattwa 'triggers' the psychic layers of our mind through the compressed power of its geometrical shape, the primal colors vibrating forth, and the implied numerical concepts in each shape."

When we *consciously* evoke the power of a symbol, it 'triggers' the psychic layers of our mind through its compressed power and brings forth the needed knowledge and energies to accomplish the set task. In this case, it is the awakening of the inner tattvic matrix so that the clairvoyant can more accurately "read" the external situation required by the task set forth.

Using symbols, the Unconscious is able to "invent" the means to communicate with our conscious minds, often *disguised* in symbols and strange words that we must manipulate and interpret to gain answers to our questions and to discover the wisdom to make lives not merely meaningful but also purposeful. It is through symbols and images, and icons, that we open the doors of our inner perception. The great secrets of magicians, shamans, and modern scientists are in the associations they attach to such icons, and in the power of certain signs and formulae to function as circuits and pathways—not in the brain but in consciousness.

Synchronicity: Events that appear coincidentally or simultaneously that may have a non-causal relationship.

Table-Tilting, Table Tipping, Table-Lifting, Table-Turning: The partial or complete lifting of a table in a group setting used as an intermediary device in communication (most in response to yes/no questions with one tilt or two) with spirits.

Tantric Tradition: It is not any of the more modern "religions" or yogic or sexual practices sometimes called "neo-Tantra," but a *system* of psychological, psychic, and physical practices including specific sexual techniques based upon and incorporating knowledge of both human subtle anatomies and their cosmological connections.

Tantra is the source for much esoteric knowledge of the complex nature of cosmic reality beyond physical universe, and inclusive of our physical & subtle bodies and the energetic system of chakras, nadis, tattvas, mantras, yantras, breath-regulation, kundalini, and all that is developmentally important to the fulfillment of our Divine purpose.

Of particular importance are the Tattvas, a Sanskrit word that translate approximately as "the true nature of reality." We experience them primarily as the five primal elements that are the fundamental *Energy Forms* behind the manifestation of all Matter composing the entire Physical Universe. Einstein's famous equation: $E=mc^2$, where "E" stands for Energy and "m" stands for Matter, demonstrates that every *substance* is made up of these five fundamental elemental energies: Spirit, Fire, Air, Water, Earth. Symbolically they are represented in the following table:

Name	Sanskrit	Color	Shape
Spirit	Akasha	Black	Oval egg
Air	Vayu	Blue	Circle
Fire	Tejas	Red	Triangle
Water	Apas	Silver	Crescent with horns upward
Earth	Prithivi	Yellow	Square

Unlike many Eastern and Western spiritual systems, Tantra is "world embracing" rather than "world denying," and sees the world as *real* and not an illusion and the whole of reality as the self-expression of a single Creator Consciousness in which there is no division of spiritual versus mundane. Tantric practices are intended to bring about an inner realization that "Nothing exists that is not Divine," and their goal is freedom from ignorance. We live in a holistic universe and need to live holistically with awareness of the spiritual as part of our reality. We are born into the material world to grow and develop the whole person we are intended to be. Tantric principles should be incorporated into every aspect of daily life as a continuing spiritual growth practice.

Tantric sexual practices, perceived as the union of male and female and the re-union of god and goddess, Shiva and Shakti, are a means into an intense and expanded (ecstatic) state of awareness, freed of mind-created material boundaries to reaffirm our identity with the Divine Source found within each person.

Tantra is a complete system of esoteric knowledge and practice that in its ancient purity is a personal resource for every person seeking understanding and development. It is the most radical form of spirituality, and the ideal personal "religion" of the modern world that has had a profound influence on Western Occult Philosophy and practice, and on the development of today's Neo-Paganism. It is this Tantra that is the source of our knowledge of the tattvas.

Tao: Taoism is a Chinese philosophical system in which 'the Tao' is both the ultimate reality in which all action takes place, the way by which an individual can live in harmony with the universe, and the universal energy behind all phenomena.

Tarot: A vast system of Archetypal Knowledge condensed into a system of 78 images on cards that can be finger-manipulated and then laid out in systematic patterns to answer specific questions or provide guidance to the solution of problems. While it is a form of divination, it is one of the most sophisticated and carefully developed systems of images and relationships following the structure of the Kabbalah's Tree of Life. Going beyond divination, it is also a system to access the Unconscious, and to structure magical ritual. It's a powerful Western esoteric system comparable to the Eastern I Ching.

The concepts of the Tarot cards have kept pace with the evolution of advancing knowledge, with the concepts and psychology of the European peoples. This is a very important point for it is fairly unique among occult divinatory systems for such evolution to take place. While interpretations of such systems as the I Ching will have some evolutionary change, the system and its physical representation in the 64 Hexagrams has remained static. The Tarot, in contrast, has changed, been modified, and evolved in physical form and structure, and in interpretation and application.

And there is inter-change between the Tarot deck and the person using the deck, facilitated by the artwork that—in my opinion—provides a positive aspect no other system has. The reader is *invited* to communicate with the cards, and that's one among many reasons that there are so many Tarot decks—over a thousand—to choose from.

Suggested Reading:

Amber K & Azrael Arynn K: *Heart of Tarot, an Intuitive Approach, 2002,* Llewellyn

Ferguson: *The Llewellyn Tarot.* 78-card deck and 288 page book, 2006, Llewellyn

Cicero, Chic & Tabatha: *The New Golden Dawn Ritual Tarot—Keys to the Rituals, Symbolism, Magic & Divination, 1997,* Llewellyn

Hollander: *Tarot for Beginners—An Easy Guide to Understanding & Interpreting the Tarot, 2002,* Llewellyn

Kraig: *Tarot & Magic—How to use the Tarot to do magic on a practical level, with Tarot Spells, Talismans, working on the Astral Plane, etc.,* 2002, Llewellyn

Louis: *Tarot Plain and Simple—A self-study program to do readings for yourself and others,* 2002, Llewellyn. Written by a psychiatrist, with a Jungian approach to understanding human nature and psychological conflict.

Slate, J. & Weschcke, C.: *Psychic Empowerment—Tools & Techniques,* 2011, Llewellyn

Sterling: Tarot *Awareness, Exploring the Spiritual Path,* 2000, Llewellyn– How the Tarot can be a gateway toward spiritual development by unlocking a vibrant communication with the divine.

The Time is Now: Energies and radiation from the Sky Above, the Earth Below, and the Universe Around are bringing *evolutionary* changes to the cells of our bodies and reflecting into consciousness with accelerating stimulation leading to excitement, belligerence, and reactive behavior, and increased mental and spiritual intelligence—but behind these cellular changes is the loosening of the barriers between the planes. Psychic awareness increases as the astral images and mental thought forms become more easily perceived and we become more aware of our creative abilities. *Opportunity knocks even as warning sirens wail.*

Much is happening, currently beyond our full awareness of the subtle energies behind the material events, and hence of our full understanding and ability to act positively rather than reacting negatively. The need is to *wake up* and know, to wake up and understand, and to wake up and act with knowledge and understanding of the causes and effects of the influx of these subtle energies and messages. Our spirit communication must be more than between two entities, and include the increasing sensitivity for conscious perception and understanding of these subtle energies of solar, planetary, and universal origins.

We are also aware of increasing dangers from crime and terror and threats of war from distant lands ruled by religious zealots bound by old theologies; of increasing planetary disturbances, extreme weather, and climate changes; of abusive financial practices leading to massive economic hardship and new threats to our wealth and savings; of environmental health hazards, abusive agricultural practices, and costly medical corruption and errant regulation; and the constant presence of scams and a loss of faith in programs that were supposed to help us from being victimized by corporate (and other) greed.

We live in a world of rapid technological change and progress in communications, in information resources, in educational opportunities, in the promise of a longer and healthier life, in a culture of greater sexual freedom and understanding, and of respect for sexual pleasure and ecstasy. We are promised that science, technology, and resource management will provide sufficient food and opportunities for a growing population, but we're also threatened by growing unemployment in the face of more efficient production, by changes in consumer preferences for goods and e-commerce over local stores, and by the rapid spread of disease and increased accidents in transportation and recreation, of corruption in government and its agencies, of the domination of greed in financial transactions and regulation.

We enter a New Age that brings both great promise and threat, and we're caught in the middle and have to give direction to achieve that great promise. We seek understanding of where we really are, and increasingly look beyond the physical world for guidance—but we also find the old institutions of "faith" are equally as corrupt, greedy, and out of tune with reality as are the institutions of government and business, and that their theologies are inadequate and wrong to meet the obvious challenges and the obvious hazards of these and future times.

We realize that "Institutions" put distance between people and these same institutions, and place barriers between vendors and their customers and clients. Responsibility is no longer direct and so greed replaces honesty and honor because there are no direct repercussions. Old ways are inadequate and new ways are still uncertain.

We have to find our own Answers, and we do know enough to understand that the past zodiacal ages, each approximating 2,400 years in length, have transitional phases of several hundred years of which we are perhaps at more than two-thirds through from the Age of Fish (Pisces) to the Age of Man (Aquarius). No matter how specific such calculations can be, an open-minded approach recognizes the beginning Aquarian influence can be seen in the phases of Enlightenment, Reason and Democracy in the 18th century, while interpreters of the Mayan calendar might suggest that the "tipping point" occurred December 21, 2012 more fully leaving the Piscean influence behind.

This transition into the Aquarian Age of Human Knowledge may coincide with the advent of even greater cosmic level cyclical changes, but all the messages

say the same thing: *we must find our own way and we do have the power to do so.*
We have to learn for ourselves what we must know and what we must do. We
a have World Wide Web of Information Resources beyond anything available
from libraries, traditions and teachers before the 21ˢᵗ century. At the same time,
our global network of news constantly warns of weather and climate change, of
threats of religious inspired terrorism and war, of the hazards to our electronic
networks and power grids from Solar Flares and changes to the magnetic fields in
and around our planet, and perhaps even of planetary effects on human behavior leading to transportation accidents, unpredictable crimes against women and
children, bizarre religious and political beliefs, and diversions of resources from
public need to private greed.

The End of the OLD World: Is all of this what was meant in the Mayan Prophecy "as
the End of the World—*as we know it?*" Well, the world didn't end on 12/21/12,
but it is different. The same message has been repeated from indigenous cultures
around the world and also in the never ending gloomy predictions of religious
prophets and psychics. The prophecies are always ambivalent in interpretation,
and always—so far—get the dates wrong. But the fundamental message is that
change is inevitable and that the need for change in thinking and attitude is obvious.

When we turn to spiritual sources we have to accept the challenges of both
interpretation and timing. The higher the source the greater the challenge
because we move beyond familiar words to mystical expression and symbols.
Yet, each of us can—to turn to the mystical for the moment—see "the warning
signs in the sky," "feel the earth shaking at our feet," and "read the writing on the
wall"—or in books.

As to the **Need,** in this section we've demonstrated the importance of the
Individual's active role in place of the passivity previously taught by those old
Institutions once intended to serve our needs. As described previously, *the Need
is historic.* There is no choice about the critical changes happening in the Earth
below, in the Space above, in the world of Humanity around, and in the Human
Person here and now. There is choice, however, in the opportunity we all have,
individually and communally, to work with the Forces behind change. The New
Age is one of *Individual* <u>and</u> *Community* vs. the old age of *Institutions* <u>and</u> *Collectivism.* Individuals can *form* voluntary communities for common actions.
Institutions work to *force* individuals into a single massive collective led by a

few persons sharing one ideology under a single leader. The old age required the <u>submersion</u> of the individual into the mass for *other*-determined collective action; the New Age calls for the <u>emergence</u> of the individual from the mass for *self*-determined communal actions.

It is your intelligence that is needed; it is your knowledge that is needed; it is your understanding that is needed; and it is your emotional drive and commitment that is needed. Real learning requires **Desire** and **Discipline**, but the need is so extreme that you must feel **Determination** to—*literally*—"Save the World." We must all awaken and act both together and alone, but *remember* that "all" is you, and me, and every individual in every community. Every voice counts, just as does every vote. It's just as important to "spread the word" as it is to act "alone and together."

Above all, it is your two-way spiritual communication with the Earth, with Life, and with the Universe that will bring understanding and guidance for individual and communal actions at the local levels where things happen. It is that exchange that is needed to bring awareness of the needs for a new paradigm of human harmony with the natural order, with understanding of the impact humanity's actions on the Earth and the essential partnership between Humanity, Nature, and the Universe.

Theurgy: Also called 'high' magic (or Magick) that deals with raising the level of Consciousness and the fulfillment of 'the Great Plan' of Man's evolution and reunion with the ultimate Source.

Think it, Speak it, Apply it: In the process of a meditation, ritual, or self-hypnosis procedure in self-improvement, the "once only" approach is insufficient. There are always core ideas or phrases that can be reduced to a short "mantra" and a single "culminating symbolic gesture" that expresses everything intended in the procedure. The procedure should be repeated as necessary, but the mantra and gesture can be used at any time and any place as a short-cut to the benefits of the whole procedure.

The famous example of a simple mantra is "Better and Better, Every day, in Every way." Adding a simple gesture—such as clenched fist or palms pressed together—brings the action to the physical level. Repeat three times.

Third Eye: A colloquial reference to the *Ajna*, the "brow chakra" believed to be the main etheric source of psychic powers. A mental faculty associated with clairvoyance, connected to the sixth chakra, located at the center of the forehead.

Thought Form: 1) An astral image created by concentrated thought intended to accomplish a specified objective. When reinforced with emotion and charged with etheric energy, it will become physically manifest. 2) A spontaneous image created in the imagination that is charged with emotional energy. Either is perceived by a clairvoyant and is felt by ordinary people with some degree of psychic sensitivity. A carefully constructed mental image that is charged with emotional energy can become a manipulative tool used in product marketing, political action, and religious domination.

Suggested Reading:

Ashcroft-Nowicki & Brennan: *Magical Use of Thought Forms, a Proven System of Mental & Spiritual Empowerment, 2001, Llewellyn*

Trance: A state of consciousness in which awareness is concentrated, focused and turned inward to the subconscious mind either unconsciously through repetitive stimuli or consciously induced in a similar technique in hypnosis, meditation, or religious or shamanic practice. During a trance state, carefully designed programs of suggestion and affirmation can lead to dramatic changes in conscious behavior and perceptions.

A spiritualist medium's is often a self-induced alteration of consciousness preparatory to receiving communication with spirit 'controls' or guides, summoned spirits, and other entities. The trance induction is sometimes aided by prayer, hymns, soft 'churchy' music, chanting, swaying movements of the medium's body and sometimes by others swaying in unison with the medium.

Trance Dancing: An associated phenomena and a technique common to shamanic practices, and also with recognized mystic systems like the Sufi Whirling Dervishes. It often leads to "spirit possession" (whatever that may really mean and involves another question about what that spirit is), often involuntary as with the cases of observers being caught up watching Voodoo and "ridden" by the Loa.

In modern times, young women were into trance dancing at disco clubs and such, mostly enjoying the borderland consciousness stimulated by the music, and the body movement, and the expectation of ecstatic experience as induced by sensory overload of loudness and flashing lights.

Trance Psychic: A psychic who engages in the trance state during readings.

Tree of Life: (Qabalah) A diagram with ten spheres and twenty-two connecting paths that functions as a kind of 'Interdimensional' 'cross-indexing filing cabinet' for you to relate corresponding facts and experiences with others of the same nature along with the information similarly experienced and related by millions of other students over hundreds of years.

Trumpet: A cone-shaped instrument made of very light-weight aluminum used in connection with the physical phenomena of a séance. See "Direct Voice."

"Trust but Verify": The phrase was made famous by U.S. President Ronald Reagan in Cold War negotiations with Soviet Prime Minister Mikhail Gorbachev. It is a vital procedure in all Spiritual Communications because they generally involve astral consciousness which include the faculties of imagination and dreaming and untrained they lead to fantasy and even delusion.

Unfoldment: It is believed that a person's ability to communicate with spirits will "unfold" through sitting in Development Circles and Classes. The concept is that psychic powers are innate but need to be developed into skills. The presence of fellow students is believed to be helpful.

Universal Consciousness: "In the Beginning is the Word." But before the manifestation of the physical cosmos there was the emanation of Consciousness and the Great Plan that first guided the formation of Spirit and then of Space/Time and Energy/Matter leading into the Big Bang of physical creation. With physical creation we have Universal Consciousness (or the Unconscious, or the Great Unconscious) functioning in the background of all there is, and permeating every life, visible and invisible, and everything, visible and invisible.

Universal Field of Possibilities: The Universal Field of Possibilities manifests first as Energy/Matter under the guidance of packets of information/instruction. Thus we can see an analogy with a computer with its Operating Program & its Application Programs.

Vehicle: A newer and alternate esoteric term for the word "body" in reference to the vehicle of consciousness to express the concept that "we are not the body" but only use it as a temporary "vehicle" of action and expression. Thus: the Astral *Vehicle,* the Mental *Vehicle,* the Spiritual *Vehicle,* etc.

Vibration: Everything that exists "vibrates." Vibrations are the *motion* of physical and non-physical atoms within all matter and substance, and are measured by their frequency per second. Touch, sound, odor, taste and sight are each characterized by particular ranges of vibrations and all phenomena perceived by these senses occur within defined ranges of vibration.

Further it is in our sharing of consciousness with all things that we can be aware of that motion. More importantly, however, the nature of matter and of consciousness changes as the *rate* of vibration changes. As we consciously raise our own vibrations we perceive the matter at different levels, or "planes."

And our perceptions are uniquely *tuned in* to specific ranges of vibration that we sense with our appropriate organs—physical as well as psychic although these psychic organs are different in structure and nature than the physical ones. Nevertheless, some psychic perceptions combine the physical organ with one of the chakras—which we can call "psychic" or etheric organs.

The following table is scientific and speculative. It is also visibly incomplete and begs reader input. Its intention is to provide a structure for our understanding of the position of Whole Person within the Whole Universe inclusive of all that lies outside of our physical perception. Because of the size of some of the numbers, we are providing a table of the "meanings" of standard prefixes to terms used in measurements.

Frequency (approximate Vibrations or Beats or Waves or Cycles or Hertz (Hz) per Second)

Note: the meanings of prefixes—

nano- means	**n** 10^{-9} or 0.000000001 (minus 8 zeros = milliardth)
micro-	**u** 10^{-6} or 0.000001 (minus 5 zeros = millionth)
milli-	*m* 10^{-3} or 0.001 (minus 2 zeros = thousandth)
centi-	**c** 10^{-2} or 0.01 (minus 1 zero = hundredth)
deci-	**d** 10^{-1} or 0.1 (no zeros—tenth)
	10^{0} or 1
Deca-	**D** 10^{1} or 1 zero = ten

Hector-	**H** 10^2 or 100 (2 zeros = hundred)
Kilo-	**K** 10^3 or 1,000 (3 zeros = thousand)
Mega-	**M** 10^6 or 1,000,000 (6 zeros = million)
Giga-	**G** 10^9 or 1,000,000,000 (9 zeros = billion)
Tera-	**T** 10^{12} or 1,000,000,000,000 (12 zeros = trillion)
Peta-	**P** 10^{15} or 1,000,000,000,000,000 (15 zeros)
Exa-	**E** 10^{18} or 1,000,000,000,000,000,000 (18 zeros)
Zeta-	**Z** 10^{21} (21 zeros)
Yotta-	**B** 10^{24} (24 zeros)

Infrasonic to Very Low Frequency (VLF) Waves, Magnetism and Gravity:
(Measured in **G** Gauss (not a prefix)10^{-2} or minus 2 zeros to 100 Hz)
Certain Paranormal senses and phenomena, including levitation.

.00000	.0000	.000	.00	0 gauss
ESP Field	Dowsing Streams*	Black Field	Gravity Field	Magnetic

*Described as "harmful earth rays" studied by members of the Institute of Electrical and Electronics Engineers in John Keel's *The Eighth Tower*.

Physical Senses—in vibrations per second:

Touch	2 to 16
Hearing	(from 16 in infants) 20 to 28,000
	Infrasonic Base Treble Ultrasonic
Taste	
Smell	
Sight	370 THz to 750 THz
	Infrared Red Violet Ultraviolet

Brain Waves in vibrations per second:

Delta	1 to 3
Theta	4 to 7
Alpha	8 to 13
Beta	14 to 28

Electromagnetic Spectrum, longer waves: in Hertz:

Electric Power & AC Motors	60 to 100
Very Low Frequency Radio	3 KHz to 300 KHz
Radio, AM	540 KHz to 1630 KHz
Radio, Shortwave Broadcast	5.95 MHz to 26.1 MHz
Very High Frequency (VHF)	30 MHz to 300 MHz
Television, Band I	54 MHz to 88 MHz
FM Radio, Band II	88 MHz to 174 MHz
Television, Band III	174 MHz to 216 MHz
Ultra High Frequency (UHF)	300 MHz to 3000 MHz
Television, Bands IV & V, Channels 14-70	470 MHz to 806 MHz
Super high frequencies (SHF)—Microwaves:	3 GHzto 30 GHz
Infrared, Heat	300 GHz to 430 GHz
Visible Light (visible to human, *physical,* sight:	430 THz to 750 THz

Red	400 to 484 THz
Orange	484 to 508 THz
Yellow	508 to 526 THz
Green	526 to 606 THz
Cyan	606 to 630 THz
Blue	631 to 668 THz
Violet	668 to 789 THz

Ultraviolet	1.62 PHz to 30 PHz
Spirit Light (visible to human, *psychic,* sight)	300 GHz to 40 PHz
X-Ray	30 PHz to 30 EHz
Gamma Rays	30 EHz to 3000 EHz
Cosmic Rays	10^{20} to 10^{21}

Includes levels of Psychic Projections, and of Soul Essence

Vibration (of voice): When pronouncing a word or phrase for psychic effect it must be done 1) at a lower octave than normal; 2) louder than normal but without stress; 3) with a vibratory feeling—sort of a trembling or buzzing sensation throughout the body. With practice the effect should be noticeable wherever the words are projected inside or outside the body.

Vishuddha (Sanskrit) *"With purity":* The fifth chakra, primarily known as the **Throat Chakra.** This chakra is located in the cervical (neck) area, and physically manifests through the thyroid and parathyroid glands, the pharyngeal plexus and the vocal cords. The thyroid hormones are responsible for growth and maturation. Physically it rules our communications, emotionally our independence, mentally our fluent thought, and spiritually our sense of security. It relates to the sense of hearing.

The associated psychic powers are channeling, clairaudience, and telepathy. It plays a role in Dream Yoga and Lucid Dreaming. It is symbolized by a silver crescent within a lotus with sixteen blue spokes, and its tattva is represented geometrically by a black upright oval. The audible seed mantra is *HuNG* followed by mental echo of *HuM*.

Vishuddha is considered a main alchemical transmutation point in Kriya Yoga. It is said to secret a fluid of immortality ("Amrit," meaning "against death") which is burned by Solar Plexus *(Manipura)* chakra. When this process is reversed, decay is slowed.

Vishuddha (Throat) *Chakra* Correspondences

Alchemical Planet: Venus, Jupiter	Alchemical Element: Copper	Tattva: Akasha (Ether, Spirit)
Animal: Bull, Lion, Elephant	Basic Drive: Creativity	Tattva Color: Blue-Violet
Body Function: Speech	Chakra Color: Bright Blue	Tattva form: Oval
Element: Spirit (aethyr)	Gemstone: Turquoise	Tattva Sense: Hearing
Gland: Thyroid, Parathyroids	God-form, Egyptian: Seshat	God-form, Hindu: Pancha-Vaktra [1]
God-form, Greek: Hermes	Incense: Frankincense	Goddess-form, Hindu: Shakini [2]
Location: Throat	Order of chakra unfoldment: 5th	Yogic Planet: Venu
Part of Body: neck, shoulders, arms, hands	Psychological Attributes: Communication, Empathy	
Psychic Power: channeling, clairaudience, telepathy	Bija Mantra: HuNG HuM	
Spinal Joint: 31st	Spinal Location: 3rd Cervical	Sense: Hearing
Tarot Key: III, Empress	Tree of Life Sephirah: Chesed & Geburah	
		Goddess-form, Celtic: Brigit
		Yantra (internal) white oval

1. 5-faced Shiva
2. Knowledge
Source: Slate, J. & Weschcke, C.: *Psychic Empowerment—Tools & Techniques*, 2011, Llewellyn

Suggested Reading:

Dale: *The Subtle Body—An Encyclopedia of Your Energetic Anatomy,* 2009, Sounds True

Visualization: Create a vivid image in your mind, before your closed eyes, or whatever is called for—a pictured object, person, word, symbol, alphabetical letter, deity, etc., make it glow, and then retain that image as you open your eyes. 2) Using the imagination to create vivid images of desired conditions or objects to attract those goals. 'Creative Visualization' is a practical system for personal success. This is the process of turning an imagined image or picture into an energy-charged astral "matrix" used in magickal operations, meditation, hypnosis, and prayer to in some degree modify current material reality. The same process is to create images of actual scenes rather than single objects. The scenes may be static or in motion depending upon the need.

Western Magickal Tradition: *In this now global civilization, is there a distinction between eastern and western magick?* Yes, but it is less a distinction than so sincerely proclaimed when it was assumed that the eastern mind was different than the western. We can understand that various esoteric methods have a cultural history without saying that yoga is only for people born in India just as we've learned that computer science is not the sole province of Americans.

Western Magick has a distinctive system of knowledge and application, just as does Indian Tantra and Chinese Alchemy, but anyone can learn and apply these techniques without limitation.

Western Magick is largely founded on the Kabbalah and today includes Tarot and Ritual Magick. At the same time, there are differences in different traditions as to the understanding of various correspondences and symbols. At the practical levels, one system is not necessarily enriched by another. Learn the basic correspondences and symbols of the system you practice.

Suggested Reading:

Hulse, David: *THE WESTERN MYSTERIES—Catalogs and distills—in hundreds of tables of secret symbolism—the true alphabet of magic of every Western magical tradition,* 2002, Llewellyn

Regardie & Cicero: *THE TREE OF LIFE, An Illustrated Study in Magic—Combining Ancient Wisdom with modern magical practice, developing the principles of magic that cut across boundaries of time, religion and culture*, 2000, Llewellyn

Skinner, Stephen: *THE COMPLETE MAGICIAN'S TABLES—The most complete collection of magician's tables available, documenting thousands of magical links, pagan pantheons, Kabbalah, Astrology, Tarot, I Ching, Angels, Demons, Herbs, Perfumes, and more, and how it's all connected together*, 2007, Golden Hoard/ Llewellyn

Skinner & Rankine: *THE VERITABLE KEY OF SOLOMON—Never before published material and based on one of the best-known Grimoires of the Western world, this is a complete and workable system of high magic. Over 160 illustrations*, 2008, Golden Hoard/Llewellyn

Tyson, Donald: *RITUAL MAGIC, What it is & How to Do it—What magic can do for you, and what it can't, the differences among various magical paths, and instructions for two rituals*, 1992, Llewellyn

Whitcomb, Bill: *THE MAGICIAN'S COMPANION, A Practical and Encyclopedic Guide to Magical and Religious Symbolism—The theory and practice of magic and ritual with over 35 magical models, and tables and data on Runes, the Tree of Life, Yoga, Enochian Magic, the I Ching, Symbology, Magical Alphabets, the Chakras, Planetary Spirits, Hindu Tattwas, the Wheel of the Year, Eight Psychic Channels, Geomancy, the Tarot, Astral Travel, the Body of Light, Magical Squares and Sigils, Descriptions of Major Deities, and much more*, 2002, Llewellyn

White Light: Both experienced and visualized, the White Light is believed to be a function of a higher spiritual power. When visualized as surrounding a person, it is a means of protection from harm, particularly as originating from non-physical worlds. The White Light is also visually absorbed or projected as a healing energy.

Will to Believe: The fundamental need to believe that there is Spirit and meaning beyond our pure physical existence.

Will to Matter: The fundamental need to know that we "matter" in our physical existence—that we *matter* to one another, that we attract the interest of other people (and even pets and other animals), and are recognized for our unique achievements.

Worship: Generally associated with religious practice but better understood as two forms of meditation or magick:

1. The *external* in which a person prays to a deity or other spiritual identity most often represented with a physical image and a name. It often includes rote, mantra-like repetitions of passages from scripture. It can take the form of extreme "groveling" before a statue, emotional pleading for particular benefits and promises of behavioral changes, or less extreme postures of kneeling in prayer. It is comparable to a magical *evocation* in which the called upon entity is kept outside the circle, hence outside the psyche.

2. The *internal* in which a person seeks to actually identify with the spiritual entity or force or principle by bringing its image *within* the psyche, even perceived as bringing within the physical body. Magically, it is comparable to *invocation.*

   In either operation, the practice can be relatively simple or become extremely complex. And there are variations that appear to mix the two forms—as in the "assumption of a god-form" in which the person places himself within the image rather than bringing the image within himself. And with either form the practice can be intensified with shamanic techniques of ecstatic energy charging of the image or of the practitioner.

Yantra: *Sanskrit* "Conception instrument." The prefix "yan" means "to conceive, perceive, imagine, visualize," and the suffix "tra" equals an "instrument, implement or tool"—hence a yantra a geometric style of diagram from Tantric philosophy used for concentration and in ritual to represent and contain specific psychic energies. It is a tool for focusing the mind and encouraging clarity of conception. When used as a focal point in meditation, visualization or as a charged magical talisman, it initiates the process of invoking elemental forces that will induce specific consciousness experiences.

   Dr. Jonn Mumford describes the function of the tattva yantras as "information storage and retrieval devices' of amazing potency. They are the primary building blocks from which all magical symbols, sigils, talismans, ciphers and designs are composed. The Tattwa 'triggers' the psychic layers of our mind through the compressed power of its geometrical shape, the primal colors vibrating forth, and the implied numerical concepts in each shape."

Though mostly rendered in two dimensional art forms, yantras are then visualized in multi-dimensional images and may be presented in three dimensional objects. In meditation and trance, the visualized image generates the yantra in the subtle bodies. Because a yantra is composed of archetypal forms common to all existing phenomena, the process of drawing or otherwise representing the form actually reaches down into the genetic structure to make it an energetic reality. The drawing act activates the right brain.

In its most extreme form, a yantra becomes the "body" of a particular deity.

As derived from the Tantric tradition, such figures are used to balance the mind or focus it on magical, psychic or spiritual actions. The act of wearing, drawing, tracing or concentrating on a yantra evokes spiritual or talismanic or magical benefits.

"Ye are Gods in the making": While common in esoteric literature and teachings, old and new, East and West, it is a phrase said many times with many different meaning depending on the context. The most common interpretation is within the contexts of reincarnation and continued human biological and spiritual evolvement. A further concept includes that of continued cosmic evolution— of a universe starting with either a Big Bang or a Soft Whisper (who knows for sure!)—and evolving in continuous waves of expansion and complexity inclusive of all life and consciousness from the most minute to the most huge, and both visible and invisible. Still other concepts include a hierarchy of divine and semi-divine beings from "elementals" through angels, and then also of those Gods and Goddesses believed to have initiated with human thought forms nurtured by emotion, devotion, sacrifice, and prayer.

Another aspect of the concept is that of "Success Magick" (also known as "Creative Visualization") in which the trained human magician shapes his or her own destiny in the material environment.

Yoga—*Sanskrit* "Union, to Yoke": An Indian system of Tantric origins which, like Taoism and Western Magick, is intended to develop the whole person including the psychic and spiritual bodies. The Sanskrit root not only implies a linking with cosmic forces but also suggests the harnessing (a yoke is a harness) and control of our own energies. Yoga is a total art and science of living leading to "skill in action."

The Sanskrit root "yug" gives rise to the following meanings:

1. Yoking, team; vehicle; equipment (of an army).

2. Performance, employment; occupation.

3. Use, application, method.

4. Remedy, cure, wholeness.

5. Means, device, instrument producing a result.

6. Spell, magic, dexterous feat.

7. Opportunity, undertaking, task performed perfectly.

8. Union, contact with, relationship.

9. Combination, mixture, bringing together of polarities or complementaries (e.g., arrow with target, key with lock).

10. Acquisition of, gain, profit (alchemy).

11. Order, succession, correctness.

12. Aggregate, sum, conjunction (of stars); constellation.

13. Fitness, propriety, strenuousness, exertion, endeavor, zeal, assiduity.

14. Mental concentration, systematic abstraction, system of philosophy.

15. Unity of soul (Purusha) and Nature (Prakrit) (alchemical marriage).

16. Connection of a word with its root, etymological meaning of a word, deriving one word from another.

Suggested Reading:

Muni: *Yoga, the Ultimate Spiritual Path, 2002,* Llewellyn

You are more than you think you are: Every person has immense undeveloped potential. The familiar phrase that we use only 10% of the brain's capacity is itself a minimal recognition of the reality of not only our cranial potential but of the non-physical aspects of personal consciousness and its connections with universal consciousness. Your goal must be to ***become more than you are!*** That's the purpose and function of all training and work of Psychic Empowerment and Self-Empowerment.

You're the Captain of your own Ship! Magick is generally perceived as a group function, but like the journey of *The Fool* in the Tarot deck, the esoteric path is ultimately personal and solitary.

On the solitary path, you are the one in charge, you are the one responsible, and you are the lone actor on the stage of life even though it is the same path and the same stage we all eventually traverse. You don't have a teacher to lean on, you are not apprenticed to a 'master,' and your only True Guide is your own Higher Self—*your own Holy Guardian Angel!*

Of course you have resources—books, courses, lectures and non-line information—to draw upon that were previously unavailable to sincere students. There was a time when only the teacher/student relationship was the reliable way to go, but that is no longer true.

There are hazards you will encounter, and you alone will meet and defeat the challenges to your success. Even with the help and guidance of others, you alone must crown yourself, just as Napoleon crowned himself emperor of the French empire.

Suggested Reading:

Andrews, Ted: *How to Meet and Work with Spirit Guides,* 2006, Llewellyn

Blunsdon, Norman: *A Popular Dictionary of Spiritualism,* 1963, Citadel

Buckland, Raymond: *Buckland's Book of Sprit Communication,* 2004, Llewellyn

Dillard, Sherrie: *You are a Medium—Discover Your Natural Abilities to Communicate with the Other Side,* 2013, Llewellyn

Eynden, Rose Vanden: *So You Want to be a Medium—A Down-to-Earth Guide,* 2006, Llewellyn

Klimo, Jon (with Foreword by Tart, Charles T.): *Channeling—Investigations on Receiving Information from Paranormal Sources,* 1987, Tarcher

Lally, Teresa: *Table Tipping for Beginners—A Time-Honored Way to Talk to Spirits,* 2012, Llewellyn

McCoy, Edain: *How to Do Automatic Writing,* 2002, Llewellyn

Owens, Elizabeth: *How to Communicate with Spirits,* 2001, Llewellyn

Robinette, Kristy: *Messenger Between Worlds –True Stories from a Psychic Medium,* 2013, Llewellyn

Webster, Richard: *Praying with Angels—With a Dictionary of Angels,* 2007, Llewellyn

Webster, Richard: *Spirit Guides & Angel Guardians, Contact Your Invisible Helpers,* 2002, Llewellyn

INDEX

This Index is more extensive and detailed than are most. Our reason for this is the belief that our readers will find value in returning to previous discussions and expositions of certain words and concepts, and then even a initial "casual" mention will later add to further studies on the same subject.

Dravidian, 240, 304

Drawing Down the Moon, 148, 223, 358

Dream Power, x

Dream Walking, 447

Dreams, v, xi, xiii, xxv, 2, 6, 77, 95-97, 101, 103, 144, 149, 151, 160, 161, 167, 185, 234, 361, 461, 476, 532, 540, 565-568, 593, 615, 618, 650, 687

Dreams as Spiritual Gateways, 96

Dreams as Spiritual Therapy, 96

Druidism, 203, 292, 660

Druidry, 221, 292, 370

Drumming, xxviii, 135, 138, 146, 149, 287, 557, 560, 561, 601, 603, 668

Drury, Neville, 645

D/s, 137, 138, 150, 164, 166

Druze, xxxiii, 220, 255, 256

Duality, xxi, 53, 54, 57, 307, 351, 361, 558, 559, 601, 602

Dyer, Wayne, 324

Dynamism, 182, 321

E

Eagle, 31, 158, 160, 327, 431, 487, 489, 604

Earth (element), 483

Earth Bound Spirits, 602

Earth Changes, 238, 441

Eastern Ways, 464

Eastern World, 464

Eckankar, 220

Ecstasy, i, xxvii, 57, 61, 130, 133, 135, 136, 138, 141, 145, 148, 149, 151, 154, 173, 175, 176, 185, 189, 190, 204, 209, 217, 222, 237, 301, 312, 340, 344, 348, 349, 351, 366, 376, 390, 561, 595, 601-604, 664, 668, 692

Ecstatic Consciousness, viii, 145, 149, 210, 340, 348, 668

Ecstatic Dancing, 147, 668

Ecstatic States, xii, xxvii, xxx, 135, 136, 138, 145, 196, 205, 229, 344, 357, 359, 404, 462, 560, 561, 601, 617, 668

Ecstatic Union, xxvii, 47, 131, 181, 339, 361, 667, 678

Ectoplasm, 385, 396-399, 584, 601, 604, 641, 653, 675

Education, xiii, xxx, xxxii, xxxvii, 54, 145, 169, 171, 200, 207-209, 217, 218, 226, 229, 234-236, 251, 258-260, 262, 263, 266, 272, 274, 275, 281, 296, 310, 326, 338, 359, 364, 365, 394, 405, 418, 423, 428, 432, 436, 440, 459, 460, 518, 556, 564, 592, 596, 609, 625, 644, 648, 652

Ego, xxvii, 129, 148, 154, 342, 349, 356, 365, 443, 495, 498, 600, 610, 616, 665

Ego Inflation, 154, 443, 495, 498

Egregor, 438, 604

Egyptians, 247, 293, 463

Egyptian Magick, xxxvii, 288, 303, 317, 370, 422

Egyptian Religion, 240, 293, 311, 370

Eidolon, 604

Ein, 316

Ein Sof, 316

"Elder Brother", 296, 402

Electric Blue, 449, 480

"Electrical and Magnetic", 152

"Electron and Positron", 152

Elementals, xx, xxxvi, 21, 23, 28, 41, 43, 282, 419, 598, 604, 644, 673, 704

Elemental Spirits, 131, 605, 681

Elephant, 161, 643, 700

Emanationism, 321

Ralph Waldo Emerson, 215, 324, 346, 351

Emotional Body, 45, 567

End of the OLD World, 392, 693

'End of the world as we know it, the', 389, 605

Endless Growth, 77, 507, 510, 523

Energy Structures, 122

Energy Waves, 549, 550

Enlightenment, i, xxiii, xxv, xxvi, xxxiv, xxxix, xli, 4, 48, 50, 65, 66, 68, 73, 81, 82, 85, 91, 94, 95, 98, 99, 101, 102, 105-107, 112-114, 125, 263, 274, 278, 291, 292,

F

M

T

GET MORE AT LLEWELLYN.COM

Visit us online to browse hundreds of our books and decks, plus sign up to receive our e-newsletters and exclusive online offers.

- Free tarot readings • Spell-a-Day • Moon phases
- Recipes, spells, and tips • Blogs • Encyclopedia
- Author interviews, articles, and upcoming events

GET SOCIAL WITH LLEWELLYN

Find us on  @LlewellynBooks
www.Facebook.com/LlewellynBooks

GET BOOKS AT LLEWELLYN

LLEWELLYN ORDERING INFORMATION

 Order online: Visit our website at www.llewellyn.com to select your books and place an order on our secure server.

Order by phone:
- Call toll free within the US at 1-877-NEW-WRLD (1-877-639-9753)
- We accept VISA, MasterCard, American Express, and Discover.

Order by mail:
Send the full price of your order (MN residents add 6.875% sales tax) in US funds plus postage and handling to: Llewellyn Worldwide, 2143 Wooddale Drive, Woodbury, MN 55125-2989

POSTAGE AND HANDLING
STANDARD (US):(Please allow 12 business days)
$30.00 and under, add $6.00.
$30.01 and over, FREE SHIPPING.

CANADA:
We cannot ship to Canada. Please shop your local bookstore or Amazon Canada.

INTERNATIONAL:
Customers pay the actual shipping cost to the final destination, which includes tracking information.

Visit us online for more shipping options. Prices subject to change.

FREE CATALOG!

To order, call
1-877-
NEW-WRLD
ext. 8236
or visit our
website